FOURTH EDITION

Strategies for Teaching Students with Learning and Behavior Problems

Candace S. Bos
University of Arizona

Sharon Vaughn
University of Texas–Austin

Allyn and Bacon

Boston London Toronto Sydney Tokyo Singapore

To Bob and Jim and Jon

Series Editor: *Ray Short*
Series Editorial Assistant: *Karin Huang*
Marketing Manager: *Kathy Hunter*
Production Administrator: *Rob Lawson*
Editorial-Production Service: *Omegatype Typography, Inc.*
Text Designer: *Denise Hoffman*
Composition Buyer: *Linda Cox*
Manufacturing Buyer: *Megan Cochran*
Cover Administrator: *Linda Knowles*
Cover Designer: *Susan Paradise*

Library of Congress Cataloging-in-Publication Data

Bos, Candace S.
    Strategies for teaching students with learning and behavior
problems / Candace S. Bos, Sharon Vaughn. — 4th ed.
        p.   cm.
    Includes bibliographical references (p.   ) and index.
    ISBN 0-205-27228-2
    1. Learning disabled children—Education—United States.
2. Problem children—Education—United States.   3. Remedial
teaching—United States.   I. Vaughn, Sharon.   II. Title.
LC4705.B67   1998
371.92'6—dc21   97-10906
                                                 CIP

Printed in the United States of America

10 9 8 7 6 5 4 3 2   RRDV   04 03 02 01 00 99 98

Photo credits: Will Hart, pp. xx, 114, 228, 276, 330, and 444; Will Faller, pp. 28, 70, 174, 374, and 414; Brian Smith, p. 486.

Appendix 5.1: "Book Selection Aids" adapted from *Children's Literature in the Elementary School,* Fifth Edition by Charlotte S. Huck, Susan Hepler, and Janet Hickman, Copyright © 1993 by Holt, Rinehart and Winston, Inc. Reprinted by permission of the McGraw-Hill Companies.

Brief Contents

Contents

CHAPTER 2

Approaches to Learning and Teaching   28

CHAPTER 3

Oral Language   70

CHAPTER 4

Reading: Word Identification   114

CHAPTER 5

Reading: Fluency and Comprehension   174

CHAPTER 9

Socialization and Classroom Management   374

CHAPTER 11

Consultant, Collaborator, and Coteacher   444

Preface

While traveling by car on a typical Arizona scorcher between Phoenix and Tucson following a state Association for Children and Adults with Learning Disabilities meeting, we were discussing the content and assignments to the methods courses we teach at our respective universities. The topic inevitably drifted to what we would like to do better. Since both of us are responsible for preparing teachers and potential teachers to work effectively with students who have learning and behavior problems, we spend a considerable amount of time considering the content of our classes. We concluded that we would like the class and the textbook for the class to provide adequate background in procedures for teaching skill and content areas such as reading, math, oral and written expression, and social and study skills. We also would like our students to understand which methods are most effective with what types of students and why.

Like many good ideas, this book is the result of that initial lengthy discussion, focusing on the ideal content of a book designed to prepare teachers to meet the needs of elementary and secondary students with learning and behavior problems. What followed was many more lengthy discussions aimed at preparing a book that would provide learning strategies and techniques as well as the foundation for using these strategies and techniques.

AUDIENCE AND PURPOSE

We have written this book for graduate and undergraduate students who are developing expertise in teaching students with learning and behavior prob-

lems. This book is also intended for professionals in the field, including special and regular education teachers, school psychologists, language specialists, and school administrators who are interested in learning more about working successfully with students who have learning and behavior problems.

The purpose of this book is to provide:

1. Information about general approaches to learning and teaching so the foundation for the methods and procedures for teaching all learners can be better understood.
2. Descriptions of methods and procedures that include sufficient detail so that teachers and other professionals can read about them and know how to use them.
3. Information regarding classroom management, consultation, and working with parents and professionals so that beginning teachers can develop a plan of action for the school year and experienced teachers can refine these skills.

ORGANIZATIONAL OVERVIEW

First we deal with foundational concepts. Chapter One describes the characteristics of the target population, a range of alternative learning environments, the teaching-learning process, and strategies for evaluating and monitoring progress, including individual educational programs. Chapter Two presents approaches to learning and teaching: operant learning and applied behavior analysis, cognitive behavior modification, sociocultural theory of cognitive development, and information processing and schema theories. These learning models provide the basis for the methods and strategies presented later in the book.

We then focus on learning and teaching in specific skill and content areas. The emphasis in Chapters Three through Ten is on methods and procedures for effectively teaching skills, strategies, and content to students with learning and behavior problems. Information is presented not only on how to teach but also on why and when to use different instructional strategies and techniques.

Because of the extensive problems experienced in the area of literacy by special learners, Chapters Three through Six deal specifically with oral language, reading, and writing. These chapters are organized to provide background in the content areas and detailed descriptions of strategies for teaching specific skills and processes. Due to the increasing focus on study skills and content area learning (e.g., social studies, science, career/vocational education) at the upper-elementary and secondary levels, Chapter Seven deals with teaching content area subjects and teaching study skills, including time and notebook management, memorization and test-taking skills, listening and notetaking skills, and textbook usage skills. Chapter Eight deals with mathematics, covering such areas as measurement, time, verbal math problem solving, and computational skill development. Chapter Nine focuses on teaching social skills and classroom management as well as information related to the social and affective development of students, including anorexia nervosa, suicide, and drug-related problems. Chapter Ten discusses the use of educational technology as a means of shaping and facilitating instruction.

Next, we focus on managing the classroom, communicating with parents, and collaborating and coteaching with general education teachers and other professionals. Chapter Eleven discusses such issues as arranging the instructional environment and scheduling. Strategies for effective mainstreaming and collaborating with regular classroom teachers are also discussed, since the majority of these students spend most of their school day in general education classes. Chapter Twelve focuses on effective communication and making and maintaining professional relationships with general classroom teachers, special education teachers, and other specialists such as school psychologists, language and occupational therapists, and school administrators. Parents, the most effective agents for change, and their special needs are also presented.

In revising this book we have listened to the suggestions of students and professors who have used it, and we have updated the text based on new intervention research and practice. The most significant changes are in the chapters on oral language, reading, written expression, and socialization as well as the information on educational technology in Chapter Ten and collaboration and coteaching in Chapter Eleven.

To reflect the increasing diversity in our schools, we have expanded the section on planning instruction for children with cultural and language diversity in Chapter Three and in Apply the Concepts in Chapters Four through Nine. In the reading chapters (Chapters Four and Five) we have added a section on metalinguistics and early literacy and expanded the sections on phonic analysis and teaching phonological awareness. We have further elaborated the sections on Reading Recovery and literature-based reading programs, including a listing of teacher resource books and bibliographies of children's literature. We have expanded our discussion on reciprocal teaching and added information on using interactive discussions. In Chapter Six we have expanded the section on teaching spelling. Throughout the chapters on language, reading, and written expression as well as Chapter Seven on content learning and study skills, we have highlighted the relationships among reading, writing, and oral language and used interactive curriculum to teach skills, strategies, and content. In Chapter Seven we have expanded the section on making adaptations to include strategies for adapting textbooks, class and homework assignments, and tests.

In Chapter Nine we have integrated the teaching of social skills with classroom management. Chapter Ten has been rewritten and provides not only basic information about computers and integrating technology into the classroom, but information about software programs and assistive technology that are particularly helpful for students with learning and behavior problems. In Chapter Eleven we have emphasized collaboration with general education teachers and strategies for coteaching. In Chapter Twelve we continue to emphasize communication with parents, paraprofessionals, and other professionals including general education teachers.

For you, the reader, we continue to provide cues, including Key Topics for Mastery and an outline at the beginning of each chapter. We have also included Think and Apply questions and a summary at the end of each chapter. Instructional Activities and chapter appendices focusing on specific academic areas have also been integrated into some chapters. We hope you find these features beneficial for your learning.

ACKNOWLEDGMENTS

Many people deserve a great deal more acknowledgment than their names appearing here will provide. We wish to acknowledge and thank the teachers whom we have written about in this book. The time we have spent in their classrooms—observing, discussing, and teaching—has afforded us the ability to write a book that is grounded in classroom experiences and practices. These teachers include Juan Caberra, Judy Cohen, Joan Downing, Mary Lou Duffy, Joyce Duryea, Jane Eddy, Louise Fournia, Joan Gervasi, Sally Gotch, Linda Jones, Sharon Kutok, Tom Lebasseur, Lorri Perrodin, Tiffany Royal, Marynell Schlegel, Mary Thalgott, and Nina Zaragoza.

We wish to acknowledge those individuals who reviewed the manuscripts of previous editions for Allyn and Bacon: Anthony DeFeo, University of Arizona; Linda Patriarcha, Michigan State University; Elizabeth Whitten, University of Illinois—Champaign; and Cynthia Wilson, University of Miami. Special thanks go to Carol Sue Englert, Michigan State University, and to Corrine Roth Smith, Syracuse University, for their expert comments. We especially wish to acknowledge Judy Englehard, Radford University; Susan Munson, Duquesne University; Sharon Raimondi, Buffalo State College; Katherine Sacca, Buffalo State College, and Sandra Squires, University of Nebraska, for their reviews of the fourth edition for Allyn and Bacon.

We also want to thank the students in our methods classes who field-tested the book and provided us with valuable ideas. Our appreciation and thanks go to Mary Alibrandi, Kwang Sun Blair, Kathy Haagenson, Pauline Havens, Carolyn Lee and Kathy Madsen for their assistance in reviewing and synthesizing the literature. A very special thanks to Lorri Perrodin, Deborah Rhein, Rhia Roberts, Jane Sinagub, and Sandra Stroud, whose suggestions, editing, and revisions are included throughout the book. To our secretaries, Patricia Foreman, Brenda Jacobson, Mary Kord, Tara Newell, and Sandy Richards, we are most appreciative.

Special thanks also to our husbands, Bob and Jim, who wondered if we would ever come out from behind our word processors.

Most important of all, we would like to thank the teacher whose observations, research, and thinking has done more to guide our development and the field of special education than any other, Samuel A. Kirk.

Last, we want to thank each other. Many people start off coauthoring a book as friends—we still are. For this, we are grateful.

Chapter 1

The Teaching–Learning Process

OUTLINE

KEY TOPICS FOR MASTERY

— *How to identify students with learning and behavior problems*
— *How to determine the severity of a student's learning and/or behavior problem*
— *How to distinguish between these concepts—"least-restrictive environment" and "mainstreaming"*
— *The teaching-learning process—the model for understanding and helping students with special needs upon which these authors' philosophy is based*
— *The importance of knowing your student—his/her knowledge, attitudes, academic levels, and learning strategies—in determining how to help him/her*
— *The importance of a teacher's self-knowledge; our beliefs and attitudes determine how we teach and profoundly affect how our students learn*
— *The instructional cycle—an effective model for developing, implementing, and evaluating a plan for instruction*
— *The IEP—Individualized Educational Program—a procedure, mandated by law, for setting annual goals and planning instruction for students receiving specific education services*
— *How to effectively evaluate student progress*

 BRIGHT IDEA

Turn to page 27 and read Think and Apply.

This book is about children and adolescents who have difficulty learning and interacting appropriately in school. If you saw these children in school you would not be able to identify them by how they look. You would, however, be able to identify them by what they do. What are these students like? Teachers describe them this way:

Servio has a very poor self-concept. He is extremely sensitive and gets upset at the least little thing. For example, yesterday he noticed that his red crayon was broken and he started to cry. When I told him he could have another red crayon, he still continued to cry, saying that he wanted this red crayon fixed. He often says he can't do things, that he doesn't care, and that he is bad. When he has problems at home he says he's going to be bad. He often says that he was punished at home for being

bad and he's going to be bad today at school. He used to throw things at school but he doesn't do that anymore. He doesn't have any friends in the class and most of the other students don't want him around them.

Dana has a great deal of difficulty with her work. She appears to have trouble remembering. Well, not always. Sometimes she remembers how to read a word; other days she looks at the same word and it's like she has to scan all of the information in her head to try to locate the name of the word. I know she is trying, but it is very frustrating because her progress is so slow. She is also very easily distracted. Even when the aide is working with her alone she will look up and stop working at the littlest things. Something like the air conditioning going on and off will distract her from her work. I know she is bright enough but she seems to have serious problems learning.

Tina is more work for me than the rest of my class put together. She has both academic problems and behavior problems. For example, after I have explained an assignment to the class, Tina always asks me several questions about the assignment. It's like I have to do everything twice, once for the class and then again for Tina. She has a terrible time with reading. She reads so slowly and she often reads the wrong word. For example, she will say carrot *for* circus *and* monster *for* mister. *She often doesn't know what she's read after she's finished reading it. Also, she can never sit still. She is always moving around the room, sharpening her pencil, getting a book, looking out the window. It is hard for her to do the same thing for more than a few minutes. She's always "bugging" the other students. She's not really a bad kid, it's just that she is always doing something she's not supposed to be doing, and she takes a lot of my time.*

The purpose of this book is to acquaint you with the teaching skills and strategies necessary to understand and teach students like Servio, Dana, and Tina. This chapter provides background information on students with learning and behavior problems and an overview of the teaching-learning process.

WHAT ARE THE CHARACTERISTICS OF STUDENTS WITH LEARNING AND BEHAVIOR PROBLEMS?

Most professionals are able to recognize with little difficulty those students with learning and behavior problems. They are students who call attention to themselves in the classroom because they have difficulty learning and interacting appropriately. Students with learning and/or behavior problems manifest one or more of the following behaviors:

— *Poor academic performance.* Students often display significant problems in one or more academic areas such as spelling, reading, and mathematics.

— *Attention problems.* Many students seem to have difficulty working for extended periods of time on a task. They may have trouble focusing on the teacher's directions. These students are often described by teachers as being easily distracted.

— *Hyperactivity.* Some students are overactive and have a difficult time staying in their seats and completing assigned tasks. They move from task to task, often from location to location in the classroom. They can be working on an assignment and the least little noise will distract them.

— *Memory.* Many students have a hard time remembering what they were taught. Often their difficulty remembering is associated with symbols such as letters and numbers. These students may remember something one day but not the next.

— *Poor language abilities.* Many students have language difficulties that are manifested in a number of ways. As toddlers, these students may have taken longer in learning to talk. Often these language problems can be corrected through speech therapy. Students may have difficulty with vocabulary, understanding the concept, using language to adequately express themselves, or producing correct sounds.

— *Aggressive behavior.* Some students are physically or verbally assaultive. They may hit, kick, get into fights, and/or verbally threaten or insult others. These children are easily upset and cope with being upset by acting out.

— *Withdrawn behavior.* Some students seldom interact with others. Unlike shy students, who may have one or two friends, these students are real loners who avoid involvement with others.

— *Bizarre behavior.* Some students display very unusual patterns of behavior. They may stare for long periods of time at objects they hold in the light, they may sit and rock, or they may display aggressive behaviors at times and withdrawn behaviors at other times.

Students with learning and/or behavior problems often exhibit more than one of these behaviors. Yet, some students exhibit these behaviors and are not identified as having learning and behavior problems. There are other factors teachers consider when determining how serious a learning and behavior problem is.

WHAT FACTORS SHOULD BE CONSIDERED WHEN DETERMINING HOW SERIOUS A LEARNING AND BEHAVIOR PROBLEM IS?

Approximately 15 to 25 percent of all students have some type of learning or behavior problem. There are several factors to consider when you are determining how serious the problem is.

1. *Persistence of the problem.* Sometimes a student has a learning or behavior problem for a short period of time, perhaps while there is some type of crisis in the family, and then it disappears. These behaviors and feeling states are not considered problems if they occur occasionally. Other students display persistent learning and behavior problems throughout their schooling experience. These persistent learning and behavior problems have more serious consequences for the student.

2. *Severity of the problem.* Is the student's learning or behavior problem mild, moderate, or severe? Is the student performing slightly below or significantly below what would be expected of him or her? Is the behavior slightly different or substantially different from the student's peers?

3. *Speed of progress.* Does the student appear to be making steady progress in the classroom despite the learning and behavior problem? We do not expect all students to learn at the same rate. In fact, in an average fourth-grade classroom the range of performance varies from second-grade level to seventh-grade level.

4. *Motivation.* Is the student interested in learning? Does the student persist at tasks and attempt to learn? Does the student initiate and complete tasks without continual praise and encouragement?

5. *Parental response.* How do the parents feel about their child's academic and/or behavioral progress? How do they think it compares with the child's progress in the past? Are they concerned about how their child's abilities compare with other children the same age? How have siblings performed in school?

6. *Other teachers' responses.* How did the student perform in previous classes? What do previous or other teachers say about learning style, academic abilities, and behavior?

7. *Relationship with the teacher.* What type of relationship does the student have with his or her present teacher? Sometimes there is a poor interpersonal match between the student and the teacher that may interfere with the student's academic performance and/or behavior.

8. *Instructional modifications and style.* What attempts has the present teacher made to modify the student's academic and/or behavioral program? Does the student seem responsive to attempts at intervention? If the student is not performing well in a traditional reading program, has the teacher tried other instructional approaches to reading? Has the student had opportunities to work with different students in the class? If the problem is behavior, what type of behavior change programs have been implemented? Are any successful?

What kind of match is there between the student and the classroom setting? Some children function best in a highly structured classroom where the rules, expectations, and assignments are very clearly stated. Other children function better in a learning environment where there is more flexibility.

9. *Adequate instruction.* Has the student had adequate exposure to the material and time to learn? Some students have little experience with school learning situations before coming to school. Other students have multiple experiences, including preschool programs that teach letters and letter sounds. Students who have less exposure to school learning situations, or whose parents provide few schoollike learning experiences, may need more time and exposure to the learning environment before gains are made. Determine what prerequisite skills are missing and how they can be acquired.

10. *Behavior-age discrepancy.* Does the student display problems that are unusual or deviant for the student's age? For example, whining and withdrawing to another room is demonstrated by many preschoolers, but few children over grade 2.

11. *Other factors.* Are there other factors that may be contributing to the student's learning and/or behavior problems? For example, how closely do the student's background experiences, culture, and language match those of the teacher and other students in the class?

Are there any health-related factors that may be interfering with the student's learning or behavior?

Have the student's vision and hearing been adequately assessed to determine whether they may be affecting the student's learning or behavior?

Considering these factors should help you identify how serious the problem is.

WHAT LEARNING AND EDUCATIONAL ENVIRONMENTS ARE AVAILABLE FOR STUDENTS WITH LEARNING AND BEHAVIOR PROBLEMS?

Most students with learning and behavior problems receive their educational program in the regular classroom. Students whose learning and behavior problems are so severe that they warrant special assistance may be involved in a range of support services. These support services include reading or math support, counseling, individualized instruction with a teaching assistant, and special education.

PL 94–142, reauthorized as the Individuals with Disabilities Education Act (IDEA), assures that a continuum of placements is available for students. This continuum is conceptualized from the least to the most restrictive. Figure 1.1 presents a model of the continuum of alternative educational placements. *Restrictive,* in an educational sense, refers to the extent to which the student is educated with nondisabled peers. A more restrictive setting is one in which the student spends no part of his or her educational program with nondisabled peers. In a less restrictive setting, the student may spend part of his or her educational day with nondisabled peers. PL 94–142 mandates that all students should be educated in the least-restrictive educational system possible.

MAINSTREAMING SPECIAL EDUCATION STUDENTS

When a special education student is *mainstreamed,* his or her placement is changed from a self-contained special education classroom to that of a regular classroom. The student may be mainstreamed for all or part of the school day.

The decision to mainstream a special education student is made by an Individual Educational Planning (IEP) and placement committee. This committee is typically made up of one or both of the child's parents, the special education teacher, relevant professionals such as the school psychologist, and the administrator who supervises the special education program in which the student participates. At the recommendation of the special education teacher and the professionals who evaluate the student's progress, the committee collectively decides whether the student's social and educational needs would best be met in the regular classroom.

Most students with emotional and learning disabilities spend at least some of their school day in regular classrooms with their nondisabled peers. Although the concept of mainstreaming was not specifically mandated in the Individuals With Disabilities Education Act (IDEA), the related concept, *least-restrictive environment* (LRE), was embraced by the law. With the emphasis on moving even more students with special needs into full-time placement in the regular classroom with the special education

■ FIGURE 1.1   *Model of the Continuum of Education Program Alternatives*

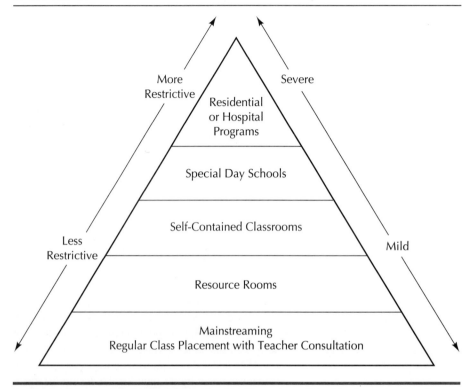

More
Restrictive

Severe

Residential
or Hospital
Programs

Special Day Schools

Self-Contained Classrooms

Less
Restrictive

Mild

Resource Rooms

Mainstreaming
Regular Class Placement with Teacher Consultation

Source: J. W. Lerner, *Learning Disabilities: Theories, Diagnosis, and Teaching Strategies.* 4th ed.,
p. 136 (Boston: Houghton Mifflin, 1985).

teacher serving as a consultant/collaborator to the classroom teacher, the emphasis on mainstreaming and consultation/collaborative models has grown (e.g., January 1988 issue of *Journal of Learning Disabilities,* Fall 1988 issue of *Learning Disabilities Focus,* April 1990 issue of *Exceptional Children,* and November/December issue of *Remedial and Special Education*). This new emphasis on mainstreaming special education students is sometimes referred to as the Regular Education Initiative.

There are several reasons why mainstreaming is important for students with learning and behavior problems. First, the research has not clearly demonstrated either the academic or social benefits of placing students in segregated special education classrooms in comparison to regular classrooms. Second, students are likely to be viewed as more socially and academically acceptable when they re-

main in the regular classroom. Third, court decisions have encouraged placement of students with learning disabilities in the regular classroom to the extent possible (Gottlieb, Alter, and Gottlieb, 1983; Hallahan, Keller, McKinney, Lloyd, and Bryan, 1988; McKinney and Hocutt, 1988; Prillaman, 1981; Schultz and Turnbull, 1984).

The Realities of Mainstreaming

A series of research studies conducted in a large Southeastern school district suggests that mainstreaming is not working as well as was intended by the law, or as was envisioned by the families of special education students and by the schools that serve them (McIntosh et al., 1993; Schumm and Vaughn, 1991; Schumm and Vaughn, 1992; Schumm et al., 1995; Vaughn and Schumm, 1994).

These studies suggest that the problem is many-faceted. First, collaboration between the special education and regular education teachers is insufficient to ensure that the Mainstreamed Special Education (MSE) student receives appropriate services. Second, classroom teachers do not specifically plan for individual MSE students; the heterogeneous makeup of the student population in most classrooms makes specific planning for individual MSE students an unrealistic expectation. Third, many mainstreamed students are inactive or passive learners who often resist any special help or accommodations offered by their teachers; they really do not want to take a more active role in their learning, and they do not want their deficiencies to become obvious to their peers.

Communication Gap between Special and Regular Education Teachers

Lawmakers intended for special education students who are mainstreamed to receive accommodations for their learning and/or emotional needs within the regular classroom. The special education teacher, as consultant/collaborator to the regular classroom teacher, is to help the regular education teacher become familiar with the mainstreamed student's IEP, then to help that teacher plan and, in some cases, deliver appropriate instruction. The regular classroom teacher has responsibility for planning and delivering the instruction or intervention the student needs.

Most secondary level (middle and high school) classroom teachers who participated in these research studies stated that they had not used IEPs or psychological reports to guide their planning for mainstreamed special education students. They had, however, gathered information from the parents and former teachers of the MSE students. Some teachers said they had very little contact with the special education teacher who monitored their MSE students and that they were not aware the student had an IEP. A few teachers had no contact with a special education teacher and were unaware that they had an MSE student in their class. In such cases, there was clearly a lack of communication between the special education teacher responsible for monitoring the progress of the MSE students and the regular classroom teacher.

MAINSTREAMING AND INCLUSION

The least restrictive environment (LRE) is required by law; however, LRE does not mean that every student must be mainstreamed. LRE refers to the level of services that is most appropriate for the student while providing the most integration with non-disabled students. Sometimes, placement in a self-contained classroom for students with disabilities is the LRE. Mainstreaming, the placement of students with disabilities from part-time to full-time in general education classes, is not required by law but can provide one way for achieving the LRE. Mainstreaming includes accommodations and support as part of a shared responsibility on the part of all educators in the school toward providing an appropriate education for the student with disabilities. Mainstreaming is a means for providing students with disabilities educational services in the general education classroom to the extent it is appropriate to meet their needs.

What is inclusion and how does it differ from mainstreaming? Inclusion refers to the full-time integration of students with disabilities in general education classrooms and often in their neighborhood schools. Inclusion and mainstreaming are often used interchangeably; however, there are differences. Advocates of full-inclusion support the notion that all students with disabilities, regardless of their special needs, should be placed full-time in general education settings all of the time (Stainback and Stainback, 1992.) Mainstreaming allows the opportunity for students with special needs to receive part of their services from a special educator in a setting other than the regular classroom. Inclusion advocates provide no options for pull-out services, because students with disabilities would not then be educated entirely in the same setting as students without disabilities.

At issue is the extent to which a continuum of services is provided. Advocates of full-inclusion are concerned that by maintaining a continuum of services we provide too easy an option for students with disabilities to be placed outside the general education classroom. Debate continues over the extent to which full-inclusion should be required for all students with disabilities (Fuchs and Fuchs, 1994). Of particular concern for students with learning disabilities is the extent to which their educational and social needs can be adequately met in the general education classroom (Vaughn and Schumm, 1995). Parents and advocates for individuals with learning disabilities are aware that before passage of IDEA there were few supports for their children/students and that the general education classroom did not adequately meet their needs. They are concerned that full-inclusion may be a return to the conditions that existed prior to IDEA.

There are many areas of agreement. All advocates want students with disabilities to be educated in general education classrooms to the extent possible. The issues relate to the type and placement of support services and the extent to which students with disabilities make adequate progress in general education settings without pull-out support. Figure 1.2 provides a description of the issues related to inclusion.

DEVELOPING AN INDIVIDUALIZED EDUCATION PROGRAM

For students who have been identified as requiring special education services (including students with learning or emotional disabilities), procedures for set-

■ **FIGURE 1.2** *Arguments for Full-Inclusion and Mainstreaming the Continuum of Services*

Arguments for Full-Inclusion

- Students with disabilities should be educated in general education classes all of the time.
- Students with disabilities should not be pulled out of the general education classroom to receive specialized education.
- Benefits of placing students with disabilities in specialized classes, either for their academic or social growth, have not been demonstrated.
- Comprehensive, professional development that prepares teachers to meet the educational and social needs of all students is required.
- All students with disabilities have the right to education in the most normalized setting, the general education classroom.

Arguments for Maintaining the Continuum of Services

- Students with disabilities should be educated in general education classes to the extent it meets their educational and behavioral needs.
- Some students with disabilities need to have their educational needs met outside of the general education classroom for part or all of the school day. A continuum of services to meet the needs of students with disabilities is required.
- Benefits and pitfalls of full-inclusion models for all students with disabilities have not been empirically documented.
- General education teachers are inadequately prepared to meet the specialized needs of all students with disabilities.
- Inclusion is a philosophy, not a place; students have the right to receive the appropriate educational services to meet their learning needs in the site that is most suitable to do so.

Source: S. Vaughn, C. Bos, and J. S. Schumm, *Teaching Mainstreamed, Diverse, and At-Risk Students in the General Education Classroom* (Boston: Allyn and Bacon, 1997), p. 30. Reprinted with permission of the publisher.

ting goals and planning instruction have been designated by law. IDEA requires that an individualized education program (IEP) be developed for each student with special educational needs. The multidisciplinary team develops and implements the IEP. The multidisciplinary team provides two major functions: (a) to determine whether a student has a disability and meets the eligibility criteria for special education, and (b) to develop the IEP which provides the foundation for establishing the student's specialized program.

Who are the members of the multidisciplinary team? Members include a representative of the local education agency, the student's parents or guardians and, when appropriate, the student, the student's teachers (special education and general education) and professionals who represent other services needed by the student, e.g., speech and language therapist, social worker, occupational therapist.

What should be included in the IEP? According to law, the IEP must include (Strickland and Turnbull, 1990):

1. The student's current level of performance in the areas of concern (e.g., reading, written expression, social skills, study skills)
2. Annual and short-term objectives related to their program
3. The specific education services to be provided and the extent to which the student will participate in the general education classroom
4. The projected date for initiation of the program and anticipated duration of such services
5. A description of the schedule and evaluation procedures for determining whether objectives are being met
6. Related services such as transportation, counseling, speech/language therapy, etc.
7. At least by the age of 16, a transition plan and transition services
8. Percentage of time in general education
9. Special instructional media and materials
10. Justification for the type of educational placement provided
11. A list of the committee members present
12. Signatures of appropriate persons, including parents and teachers

In addition to the areas mentioned above, other relevant factors such as student motivation, prior knowledge, previous learning experiences, the student's strategies for learning, and the teacher's attitudes and teaching style are generally taken into consideration when developing an individualized education program. The IEP must be reviewed at least on an annual basis.

Figure 1.3 presents a sample IEP form completed for Dereck, one of the students in Ms. Shiller's class. Ms. Shiller works with junior-high students with emotional disabilities in a self-contained setting. Dereck not only has serious emotional and behavior problems, he is also several years below grade level and his expected achievement level in reading, written expression, and math. Dereck has difficulty using oral language in that he does not vary his language style to match the context and the person to whom he is speaking. Consequently, his IEP has goals and objectives written not only for behavior and social skills but also for reading, written expression, math, and language use. A major goal for Dereck is to learn successfully in the regular classroom. Therefore, one annual goal is to attend regular classes for art, home economics or shop, math, and science by the end of the year. At this point, his social skills and behavior preclude him from attending any regular classes.

A major part of the IEP includes the annual goals and short-term objectives. The goals of an IEP usually cover the entire school year; short-term objectives usually cover a six- to nine-week period. Completion of a related set of the short-term objectives should lead to the accomplishment of the annual goal as demonstrated by the objectives and goals developed for Dereck in the area of math. The written statements of annual goals or objectives should contain enough information so that they can be evaluated to determine if they have been met. This includes:

1. A description of the behavior the student will demonstrate once the objective or goal is accomplished
2. A description of the conditions under which the behavior will occur
3. The level of performance necessary to accomplish the objective or goal (Mager, 1975)

Student's Name __Blake__ __Dereck__ __NA__
             Last   First   MI

Student's Address __1948 Ford Street 85719__ _____
                              (Zip)   Telephone Number

Reason for Conference:
___ Staffing ___ Review ✓ IEP
___ IEP was interpreted in _____ by _____

Language _____

Matric. __5/10/79__
Birthday __5/10/79__
Ethnic Code __NA__
Date __9/21/91__
Grade __7th__
✓ Original
___ Addendum

INDIVIDUALIZED EDUCATIONAL PLAN

Interpreter's Name _____

The handicapping condition is __Emotionally Handicapped__ Initiation Date __Sept. 3, 1991__ Duration Date __12 months__

The delivery system shall be   Resource ✓   Self-Contained ✓   Other _____ School __Wilcox Middle School__

The child shall participate in Special Education services approximately __4__ hour(s) per (day) week, the balance of time will be spent in regular education.
                                                                                  (circle one)

Related Service	Recommended Yes	No	Date	Init.		Related Service	Recommended Yes	No	Date	Init.
Speech Assessment		✓				Medical Svs.		✓		
Speech/Lang. Therapy		✓				Interpreter		✓		
Occupational Therapy		✓				Transportation	✓			9/3/88
Physical Therapy		✓				Other				
Counseling	✓		9/3/88							

The child's current level of education performance (functioning levels in Intellectual Ability, Academic Achievement, Performance, Psychological Processes and Behavior) including strengths and weaknesses. Include name and levels of tests.

Woodcock-Johnson-R   Grade Equiv
  Reading   5.6
  Math   3.4
  Written Lang 3.2
  Knowledge   7.8
IQ FS-WISC-R 108

Behavior - conduct disorder
       - loses temper
       hits others

The following service(s) of __Self-contained services with counseling__

The recommendation is to ___ Add
                         ___ Delete
                         _X_ Continue

Will work in class for
two-week periods without
losing temper or being
inappropriately disruptive
  Math 5.0 written Lang 7.0
  Reading 7.0

Those involved in the decision are as follows:

(Anyone who disagrees with placement recommendations should write "disagree" after his/her signature.)

__Mrs. Jane Catwell__ __9/2/91__
Building Adm./Designee   Date

__Mrs. Nancy Schiller__ __9/2/91__
Special Education Teacher   Date

__Dereck Blake__ _____
Special Education Adm./Designee   Date

__Mrs. Susan Blake__ __9/2/91__
Parent/Guardian   Date

_____ _____
Classroom Teacher   Date

_____ _____
Name/Position   Date

Evaluator/Reviewer   Date

_____ _____
Name/Position   Date

_____ _____
Name/Position   Date

The nature and content of the program has been explained to me. I also understand that: (1) all Special Education placements are on a temporary basis; (2) there will be a semester review by the staff; (3) a review of the placement and records relating to the placement can be made at any time; (4) a Special Education placement will not be made without my written consent; (5) I may obtain an independent evaluation; (6) all Special Education placements are subject to due process procedure; and (7) I may withhold my consent by refusing to sign this placement statement or withdraw my consent to the placement at any time. I approve of placement and I understand my rights.

(✓) I received prior written notice of the staffing.

__Mrs. Susan Blake__ __9/2/91__
Signature of Parent or Guardian   Date

( ) I waive prior written notice of the staffing.

( ) For parent not attending: Notified by: _____   Notified by: _____
                                Date given to parent
                                ( ) Conference ( ) Phone ( ) Other _____   Date _____

10

LONG TERM GOAL:	PROGRAM OR RELATED SERVICE _____ E.H. self contained
	PERSON(S) RESPONSIBLE _____ Ms. Schiller
Attain a grade equivalent of 5.0 in math.	DURATION OF SERVICE (DAY/WEEK/YEAR)
	FREQUENCY _____ 4 hours _____ PER _____ day
	Min./Hrs./Days DAY/WEEK/MONTH
	✓ _____ ORIGINAL _____ ADDENDUM _____ _____ OTHER

SHORT TERM OBJECTIVES	EVALUATION CRITERIA	METHOD OF EVALUATION	START DATE	DATE(S) OBJECTIVE EVALUATED	COMMENTS TM = TOTALLY MET PM = PARTIALLY MET UM = UNMET NA = NOT ATTEMPTED
The student will:					
learn multiplication facts to automatic level with 95% accuracy		Teacher-made test	9/3/91		
learn division facts to automatic level with 95% accuracy		same			
learn to add and subtract fractions with 90% accuracy		same	10/1/91		
learn to complete 2-step story problems using +, −, ×, ÷ with whole #s to 90% accuracy		same	9/15/91		
learn to measure in $\frac{1}{8}$ inch increments with 90% accuracy					

MATERIALS USED OR ADDITIONAL COMMENTS:

use computer-drill and practice software for learning facts

teach strategy for solving story problems

use manipulative for fractions

During the IEP meeting, Ms. Shiller shared the goals and objectives with Dereck and his mother. Ms. Blake, Dereck's mom, suggested two additional goals for Dereck, which Ms. Shiller incorporated into the IEP.

Parent Involvement

The people who formulated IDEA felt much like Ms. Shiller in their conviction that parents need to be actively involved in their child's education. The IEP serves as a safeguard not only for students but for parents, families, and the education team. All reasonable attempts to assure the participation of parents in the IEP should be taken. This includes:

1. Schedule the meetings at times that are convenient for parents by checking with them in advance to determine a suitable date, time, and location.

2. Notify parents well in advance of the meeting. The purpose, time and location of the meeting and the persons who will be in attendance should be included in the notice. Parents should be involved in the decision about whether the student will attend.

3. If neither parent chooses to attend after reasonable efforts to accommodate their schedules have been attempted, the school should use other methods to involve parents, including telephone calls or home visits.

4. If meeting is held without a parent in attendance, the school must document its attempts to involve the parent.

5. Parent involvement in the development of the IEP should be documented, and parents should receive a copy of the IEP.

Remember, often too much emphasis is placed on compliance rather than on genuine communication (Harry, Allen, and McLaughlin, 1995). Consider the following (Dettmer et al., 1993):

— Educators and parents are working as a team for a common goal, the student's success.
— Pay attention to when and why defensive behavior arises. Put your feelings aside and help others, including the parents, build positive relationships. If the team is unable to act positively, postpone interactions until the defensiveness can be handled.
— Remember that the values of parents are not what is being addressed, only the needs and interests of parents and their child. Consider what the problem is, not who the person is.
— Do not waste time wishing that the people would be different. Accept people as they are. Respect parents' rights to have their own values and opinions.
— Tell yourself that most parents are doing the best that they can under the circumstances of their life. People do not decide to be poor parents.

Chapter Twelve describes strategies you can use for actively involving parents in their child's education, including planning and implementing programs.

Student Involvement

By law, students only need to attend the IEP meetings if appropriate. In practice many students with learning and emotional disabilities do not attend these meetings, even when the students are in secondary-level settings. Yet involving students in this decision-making process helps them develop a commitment to learning and a sense of responsibility and control over the decisions made regarding their learning.

Why do many students not attend the conference? In interviewing junior high students with learning disabilities and their parents, two major reasons are evident (Van Reusen and Bos, 1990). First, frequently parents are not aware that students can attend. Second, even when students are invited to attend, they choose not to because they feel that they do not know what to say or do, and they are afraid that the major topic of discussion will be "how bad they are doing."

To alleviate these two concerns, Van Reusen and his colleagues developed a self-advocacy strategy (I PLAN) that is designed to inform students and prepare them to participate in educational planning or transition planning conferences (Van Reusen, Bos,

Deshler, and Schumaker, 1994). Teachers can teach students this strategy in about five to six hours over a one- to two-week period. We have found that junior high and high school students with learning disabilities who learn this strategy provide more information during IEP conferences than students who are only told about the IEP conference but not taught the strategy (Bos and Van Reusen, 1986; Van Reusen and Bos, 1990). Apply the Concept 1.1 describes this strategy and how to teach it.

HOW DO TEACHERS TEACH STUDENTS WITH LEARNING AND BEHAVIOR PROBLEMS?

Instruction for students like Servio, Dana, and Tina needs to be carefully orchestrated to take into account the interactive nature of the *teaching-learning process*. The teaching-learning process is a model of teaching and learning that takes into account the complexity of the learning environment or context, the beliefs and characteristics of the learner and teacher, and the instructional cycle the teacher orchestrates to facilitate learning. It is based on notions of *individual programming*. Although students may be instructed in groups, the teacher studies and plans for each student's needs, realizing that students have both common and unique needs. The teaching-learning process is represented in Figure 1.4. It is the foundation upon which the rest of this book rests in that it presents a reflective, problem-solving approach to teaching students with learning and behavior problems. Let us look first at the key players in this process—the learner and the teacher.

The Learner

The learner brings to school beliefs and attitudes about learning and the world in which he or she lives, a variety of skills and knowledge on which to build, and strategies to assist in the learning process. In a way, we are speaking of the *characteristics of the learner*. As teachers, we often seem most concerned about the *skill level* of students. Our assessment

process focuses on determining at what level the student is functioning and what skills the student can and cannot perform. However, *knowledge, attitudes,* and *strategic learning* can also provide us with a wealth of information concerning the learner and may prove to be the critical features when determining how to facilitate learning.

The following example illustrates the importance of the student's knowledge. Read the passage once. Your purpose for reading is so you can tell someone else what it was about when you have finished.

If the balloons popped, the sound would not be able to carry since everything would be too far away from the correct floor. A closed window would also prevent the sound from carrying since most buildings tend to be well insulated. Since the whole operation depends on a steady flow of electricity, a break in the middle of the wire would also cause problems. Of course the additional problem is that a string could break on the instrument. Then there could be no accompaniment to the message. It is clear that the best situation would involve less distance. Then there would be fewer potential problems. With face to face contact, the least number of things could go wrong.

Bransford and Johnson (1972) presented this passage to a group of students and asked them to rate the passage for comprehensibility and then to recall the passage from memory. Most students in the group rated the passage as incomprehensible and their recalls were short and disorganized. However, the same passage becomes comprehensible if you are supplied with the necessary background knowledge, in this case, the picture presented in Figure 1.5. Students who looked at this picture before reading rated the passage much higher for comprehensibility and they recalled twice as many ideas from the passage.

If the learner has little knowledge of the topic being studied, then you, the teacher, can assist the student by providing activities that build background knowledge and help the student link this new knowledge to current knowledge.

APPLY THE CONCEPT 1.1

I PLAN: AN EDUCATIONAL PLANNING STRATEGY

Purpose: To provide students with the skills and knowledge to participate effectively in an educational planning or transition planning conference.

Target Audience: The strategy can be taught to students in upper elementary, secondary, or postsecondary settings who will be participating in an educational planning or transition planning conference. This could include an IEP conference as well as other educational planning conferences.

Type of Instruction: Small group to large group instruction, usually three to ten students.

Time: Five to six hours of instruction.

Description of Strategy: The strategy the students learn consists of five steps. They complete the first step prior to the conference and use the remaining steps during the conference. The steps are:

Step 1:   Inventory your
              learning strengths
              learning weaknesses
              goals and interests
              choices for learning
Step 2:   Provide your inventory information
Step 3:   Listen and respond
Step 4:   Ask questions
Step 5:   Name your goals

To help the students remember the steps in the strategy, the acronym *I PLAN* can be made from the first letter in each step.

The teacher and students participate in activities that assist the students in creating an Inventory Sheet. This sheet lists their learning strengths, learning weaknesses to improve, learning and career goals and interests, and ways they learn best (e.g., size of group, type of activity, type of test).

The students are also taught to use *SHARE* behaviors to help with effective communication during the conference. They are:

Sit up straight
Have a pleasant tone of voice
Activate your thinking
    Tell yourself to pay attention
    Tell yourself to participate
    Tell yourself to compare ideas
Relax
    Don't look uptight
    Tell yourself to stay calm
Engage in eye communication

Teaching the Strategy: The strategy is taught by using the acquisition and generalization steps used to teach motivation strategies. Motivation strategies are techniques and procedures that involve the learner in the learning process, and they are used to increase the students' commitment to learn. They represent processes that learners can acquire and use to increase their interest and efforts in learning and to gain greater control over their own learning progress (Van Reusen, Bos, Deshler, and Schumaker, 1987). The strategies are based on research in motivation and are adapted from the learning strategies model (Deshler, Ellis, and Lenz, 1996).

The teacher uses seven steps to teach the strategy:

Step 1:   Orient and Obtain Commitment
Step 2:   Describe
Step 3:   Model and Prepare
Step 4:   Verbal Rehearsal
Step 5:   Group Practice and Feedback
Step 6:   Individual Practice and Feedback
Step 7:   Generalization

During the first step, the teacher and students discuss how involvement in education planning conferences will empower students by giving them more control over what they are learning and their plans for the future. The importance and purpose of these conferences are discussed and the teacher obtains the students' commitment to learn the *I PLAN* strategy.

During the second step, *Describe,* the strategy is described to the students and the students begin to memorize the steps in the strategy and the *SHARE* behaviors.

During the third step, *Model and Prepare,* the students work with the teacher to prepare their Inventory Sheets. Through modeling and discussion, they systematically develop lists of learning strengths and weaknesses in the areas of reading, math, writing, study skills, social skills, and vocational skills. For transition planning conferences the students develop inventories that also focus on independent living skills, career and employment skills, and community involvement. Based on these same areas and their current classes, they also identify weaknesses to improve. They also inventory their learning and career goals and interests and their preference for learning. In addition to preparing the Inventory Sheet, the teacher models the rest of the steps in the strategy *(PLAN)* and the *SHARE* behaviors.

During the fourth step, *Verbal Rehearsal,* students learn the steps in the *I PLAN* strategy and the *SHARE* behavior to an automatic level.

During the fifth step, *Group Practice and Feedback,* students review the steps in the strategy and practice using the strategy by providing feedback to each other during a simulated planning conference.

During the sixth step, *Individual Practice and Feedback,* students practice the strategy with the teacher during a simulated conference.

During the seventh step, *Generalization,* students use the steps in the strategy during the scheduled educational planning or transition planning conference. Once the strategy has been taught, it can be reviewed for each additional educational planning conference scheduled and the Inventory Sheet can be updated or redeveloped.

A teaching manual has been developed that explicitly describes how to teach the *I PLAN* strategy (Van Reusen, Bos, Deshler, and Schumaker, 1994).

■ **FIGURE 1.4**   *The Teaching-Learning Process*

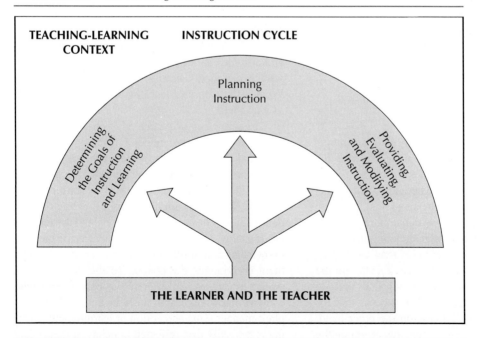

■ **FIGURE 1.5**   *Content for the Balloon Passage*

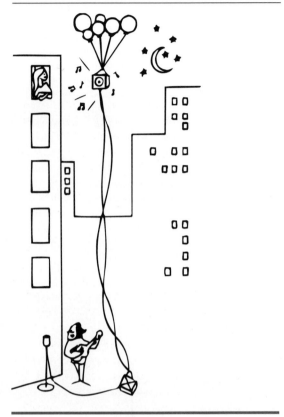

Source: From J. D. Bransford and M. D. Johnson, Contextual prerequisites for understanding: Some investigations of comprehension and recall. *Journal of Verbal Learning and Verbal Behavior, 11*(1972):719. Copyright 1972 Academic Press. Reprinted by permission.

Skills and knowledge not only play an important role in learning, but they also influence the learner's *attitudes* about learning and the world. Randy and Tamara illustrate this point. In fifth grade, Randy was determined to learn how to read, although at the time he was struggling with beginning reading books. He worked all year on his reading and at the end of the year he had grown in his reading skill by about one grade level. Still, he carried with him the attitude that reading was important and that he should continue to struggle with a process that for him was quite difficult. Tamara, on the other hand, was a sixth grader who was reading at about the third-grade level. For her, learning to read was a much easier process, yet she finished the year making only marginal gains. Why? She believed that reading simply was not necessary for her life and that her future goal, being a mother, just didn't require her to be a good reader. These students' attitudes influenced their rate of learning.

A student's *strategies for learning* also affect the teaching-learning process. When you are told to read a chapter in a textbook and study for a test, what strategies do you employ? Do you preview the chapter before reading? Do you ask questions as you read to check your comprehension? Do you underline or take notes? Do you review your notes before the test, rehearsing the important points? These are all strategies that make you a more effective student.

The Teacher

The second player in the teaching-learning process is you, the teacher. Just like the student, you bring to the learning situation your teaching knowledge and skills, your beliefs and attitudes about teaching, learning, and the world, and your strategies for teaching. One purpose of this chapter is to heighten your awareness of your beliefs and attitudes about teaching.

As you read this section, reflect on your beliefs and attitudes about teaching, learning, and students who experience learning and behavior problems. What is the nature of learning and what is your role as a teacher?

Learning can be perceived as changes in behavior that result in a student demonstrating new knowledge and skills. The role of the teacher is that of an educational technician who engineers or arranges the environment so that the probability of learning is increased. This is accomplished by providing the student with the cues to trigger learning and the rewards for learning. The student is the receiver of the new knowledge and skills, whereas the teacher imparts them or arranges the context so that they are imparted by others. An effective teacher is one who conveys knowledge and skills in a systematic, explicit manner. This perception of learning and teaching is probably best reflected in behavior theory and cognitive behavior modification, both of which are discussed in the next chapter. It is also reflected in instructional strategies and materials that are based on systematic ordering and teaching of skills. You will find that some of the strategies and materials presented in the content chapters reflect this perspective on learning and teaching.

Learning can also be perceived as a dynamic process in which the student plays an active role, constantly interacting with the environment and people around him or her. Not only do the student's notions, ideas, and skills change in the learning process but so does the environment in which the learning takes place. Thus, learning is not merely the accumulation of knowledge and skills but it is the active construction and transformation of ideas based on observations and experiences. This perception of learning is represented in information processing and schema theories, which are presented in Chapter Two. The teacher, serving as a facilitator for learning, creates an environment in which the students can take risks and develop flexible learning and thinking strategies as they acquire skills and knowledge. You will also find this perspective represented in the content chapters, chapters Three through Ten.

Just as the *characteristics of the learner* affect the teaching-learning process, so will your *beliefs and attitudes* as a teacher. And since the teaching-learning process is dynamic and interactive in nature, your beliefs and attitudes will change, depending on the needs of the learner. For example, Ms. Kranowski, a special education teacher who works with students who have learning and behavior problems, has eleven students, fourth through sixth grade, in her self-contained class. Each day after lunch they practice writing. Ms. Kranowski uses a process approach to teaching writing in which students select their own topics and write about them, sometimes taking several weeks to complete a piece. Students usually write multiple drafts, sharing their work with other students and the teacher.

At first, the learners in Ms. Kranowski's class needed to develop a process for writing. They needed to develop purposes for their writing other than to please the teacher or to complete the worksheets. As the students became more confident of their drafts,

they needed to learn such skills as how to organize a descriptive paragraph and a story, and how to use dialogue and quotation marks. Although Ms. Kranowski continues with this process approach to writing, she now also spends some time teaching skills to small groups. She uses systematic skill lessons whereby she models a skill, then has the students practice it in their own writing and in published and teacher-made materials. Whereas the first approach to teaching represents an interactive model of teaching and learning, during skill lessons Ms. Kranowski serves as the conveyor of knowledge by explicitly teaching systematic skill sequences. Ms. Kranowski's instruction shifts to reflect the needs of the students in her class.

How does Ms. Kranowski explain her simultaneous use of these different approaches to the teaching-learning process?

Well, when I first began using a process approach to teaching writing, I found that the students really learned to like writing. For me, that was a big accomplishment, since most of these kids had previously hated writing. But I also found that because these students have so many learning problems and take so much practice to learn a new skill, they just weren't getting enough opportunities to practice intensely a new writing skill when they were first trying to learn it. Consequently, they never learned the skills very well. Now, two days a week we take about twenty minutes for a skill lesson. I select the skill based on the needs of the students as a group. Right now we are working on dialogue and quotation marks. I introduce the skill and show how I use it in my writing. Then several of the students demonstrate how they can use it in their writing. We use an overhead projector, and they project their writing on the screen. We talk about how to add quotation marks, and they add them right then. For the next several weeks when they are writing their pieces, I encourage them to use dialogue, and we make an effort to compliment each other when the quotation marks are right. If the students need additional practice, I provide them with stories where they have to add quotation marks to the writing. We also take turns reading stories and books that have lots of dialogue and the students identify the dialogue and tell where the quotes go. I realize that this is really mixing two philosophies of teaching and learning, but for me it's the best way to get the job done.

The Instructional Cycle

Within the teaching-learning process, the *instructional cycle* helps to shape and sequence teaching and learning (refer to Figure 1.2 again). Ms. Kranowski uses this cycle in her teaching as she sets instructional goals, plans instruction, and provides, evaluates, and modifies instruction based on evaluation. She uses this cycle in a flexible way, taking into account the *characteristics of the learner,* her *teaching beliefs and attitudes,* and the *context* in which the teaching and learning are happening. Sometimes she changes her instructional goals based on input from the students or on feedback regarding rate of learning. Sometimes she modifies her plans and the way in which she instructs to reach her instructional goals more effectively. When Ms. Kranowski added skill lessons to the writing curriculum, she changed her plans, which resulted in changes in instruction. Let's look to see what we might want to consider when developing and implementing each part of the instructional cycle.

Determining the Goals of Instruction and Learning

Setting goals for instruction helps you know where you are going. Several questions you may want to ask when you are setting goals for instruction and learning are:

— Have I used the information I have about the characteristics of the learner?
— Have I taken into account my beliefs and attitudes?
— Have I involved the students in setting the goals?

— Have I set goals that are realistic yet challenging to both the learner and myself?
— How do these goals fit with the larger teaching-learning context (e.g., goals of the school, curriculum, long-range career goals of the student)?

When Ms. Kranowski set her instructional goals for writing she decided that she had two major objectives: (1) to have the students enjoy writing and feel good about themselves as authors, and (2) to have the students develop writing skills that would help them in school and later in life. She wanted very much to involve the students in setting goals, believing that if they set shared goals then the students would have a greater commitment to reaching those goals. She began the year by telling the students about "the way that writing works" in the classroom. She shared the importance of supporting each other, for she wanted students to set a goal of working together. As they worked together, shared their writing, and got to know each other better, Ms. Kranowski would sit down with each one of them and help them select skills for improvement. By analyzing the students' written products, observing the students as they wrote, talking with the students about their writing, and using her knowledge about the scope and sequence of writing skills, she felt comfortable working with students in selecting goals. In this way, Ms. Kranowski's instructional goals were interwoven with the students' learning goals.

Providing, Evaluating, and Modifying Instruction

Even though you approach instruction with a plan of action, it is important to remember that your plan will need to be modified and changed. Effective instruction is obtained when the instructional procedures and content match the overall teaching-learning process. Since the teaching-learning process is dynamic and flexible, the instructional process must also be dynamic and flexible.

Ms. Kranowski started with a plan of action, but found that her plan wasn't allowing the students to develop the writing skills they needed. She determined this through evaluation. She watched and listened to the students and analyzed their written products over time. She administered a criterion-referenced test to measure skills in capitalization, punctuation, spelling, and grammar. All these evaluative measures led her to the same conclusion—her students' writing skills were not improving at a rate she considered adequate.

In determining how to modify her instruction, Ms. Kranowski thought about the ideas presented in Figure 1.6. She felt she had adequately addressed the first four questions. Student motivation, attention, encouragement, and modeling had been good. She did not feel as comfortable about her answers to the next three questions: prior knowledge, manner of presentation, and practice. Sometimes she thought she wasn't focused enough on one or two writing skills. She tended to present too much and not allow for enough practice and feedback. Ms. Kranowski decided her modifications had to alleviate the problems with presentation, practice, and feedback. Her solution was the skill lessons that focused on teaching specific writing skills twice a week. For Ms. Kranowski and her students, this solution was successful. Her students began acquiring and maintaining the targeted writing skills. Now she is asking questions and planning for generalization and application.

■ **FIGURE 1.6** *Questions for Evaluating the Instructional Process*

- *Student motivation* Am I creating a context in which learning is valued?
- *Student attention* Am I creating an environment in which students can and are encouraged to attend to the learning task?
- *Encouragement* Am I creating a setting in which students are encouraged to take risks and be challenged by learning?
- *Modeling* Are the students given the opportunity to watch, listen, and talk to others so that they can see how the knowledge or skill is learned?
- *Activating prior knowledge* Am I getting the students to think about what they already know about a skill or topic, and are they given the opportunity to build upon that information in an organized fashion?
- *Rate, amount, and manner of presentation* Are the new skills and knowledge being presented at a rate and amount that allows the students time to learn, and in a manner that gives them enough information yet does not overload them?
- *Practice* Are the students given ample opportunity to practice?
- *Feedback* Are the students given feedback on their work so they know how and what they are learning?
- *Acquisition* Are the students given the opportunity to learn skills and knowledge until they feel comfortable with them and to the point they do or know something almost automatically?
- *Maintenance* Are the students given the opportunity to continue to use their skills and knowledge so that they can serve as tools for further learning?
- *Generalization* Are the students generalizing the skills and knowledge to other tasks, settings, and situations? Are the students, other teachers, or parents seeing the learning?
- *Application* Are the students given the opportunity to apply their skills and knowledge in new and novel situations, thereby adapting their skills to meet the new learning experiences?

EVALUATING STUDENT PROGRESS

According to the instructional cycle (Figure 1.4), once learning and instructional goals have been established and instruction has been planned, then instruction is implemented. However, instruction is more effective and efficient if, at the same time the instruction is being implemented, it is also being evaluated and—from the evaluation—modified.

As teachers, we evaluate student progress in our heads all the time. Think for a minute about the last time you listened to a student read aloud or watched a student complete a math word problem. Did you listen to the student's reading fluency, noticing whether or not he or she read with expression and meaning? Did you take note of the type of word identification errors the student made and the skills and strategies the student used when he or she tried to figure out an unknown word? Did you watch as the student read the word problem, analyzed the problem, and set up the computational problem? Did you notice what steps the student used to compute the answer, and if he or she checked the answer? Did you check the correctness of the answer? If you answered these questions affirmatively, then you were evaluating the student and his or her progress.

Evaluating students and making instructional decisions based on those evaluations are important for effective instruction, whether we evaluate "in our heads" or "on paper." Some general guidelines for evaluating student progress are:

1. Observe the process as well as the product. A correct product does not necessarily indicate that the student understands the process.
2. Have the student talk about what he or she is doing. Sometimes you may have difficulty understanding the process a student is using to complete a task. Asking the student to explain what he or she is doing and thinking can assist in evaluation.
3. Observe not only if the student can complete the task, but how comfortable or proficient the student is in completing it.
4. Evaluate not only for learning, but for maintenance, generalization, and application of the skill or knowledge.

As we evaluate, it is crucial to keep a written record of student progress. The written record provides a means for objectively reflecting on the data to determine if progress is evident (e.g., Deno, 1985; Fuchs and Deno, 1991; Fuchs, Deno, and Mirkin, 1984; Isaacson, 1988; Utley, Zigmond, and Strain, 1987). This written record also provides a means for communicating with others regarding student progress. Sharing progress with parents, principals, other teachers—and, most importantly, the student—provides a sense of accomplishment and satisfaction for all involved. Having students monitor their own progress can increase their motivation toward learning and give them a sense of pride in learning. Self-monitoring procedures have been used with students who have learning and behavior problems (e.g., Frith and Armstrong, 1986; Hallahan, Lloyd, Kosiewicz, Kauffman, and Graves, 1979; Jackson and Boag, 1981; Swanson, 1985).

Types of Evaluation Measures

Although a teacher or student can use many methods to evaluate progress, generally he or she will use one or more of three basic types: progress graphs and charts, performance records, and process records. The first type is frequently used for measuring daily progress on individual skills or knowledge. Performance records are usually used for measuring progress across time (e.g., grading period, semester, and year). Curriculum-based measurement (Fuchs and Deno, 1991) is an example of a performance record that is closely tied to the curriculum being taught. Process records focus not only on the progress evident in the products but also document progress in the learning process. Portfolios, learning logs, and dialogue journals can be used for this purpose.

Progress Graphs and Charts
Progress graphs and charts are generally used to measure progress on one behavior or skill. Graphs

seem particularly suited for self-monitoring because the results are displayed in such a manner that they are easy to interpret (see Figures 1.7 and 1.8). To use a progress graph, the behavior, skill, or knowledge must be quantifiable, either by time or by occurrence. For example, Ms. Shiller, the junior high teacher for a self-contained classroom of emotionally handicapped students, uses progress graphs for the following activities:

1. Silent reading rate
2. Speed in completing math facts

■ **FIGURE 1.7**   *Timing Chart Using a Line Graph*

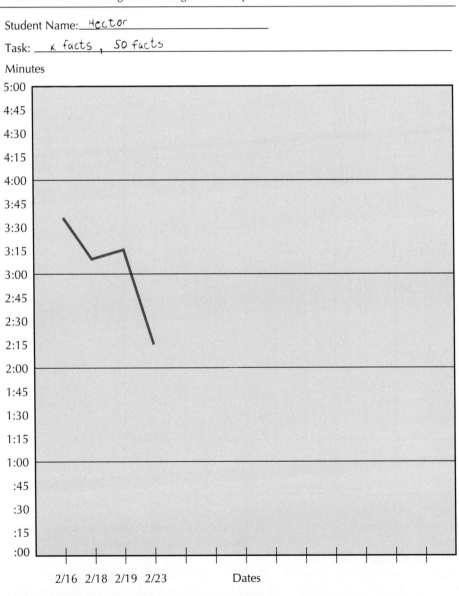

Student Name: Hector

Task: x facts, 50 facts

■ **FIGURE 1.8**   *Timing Chart Using a Bar Graph*

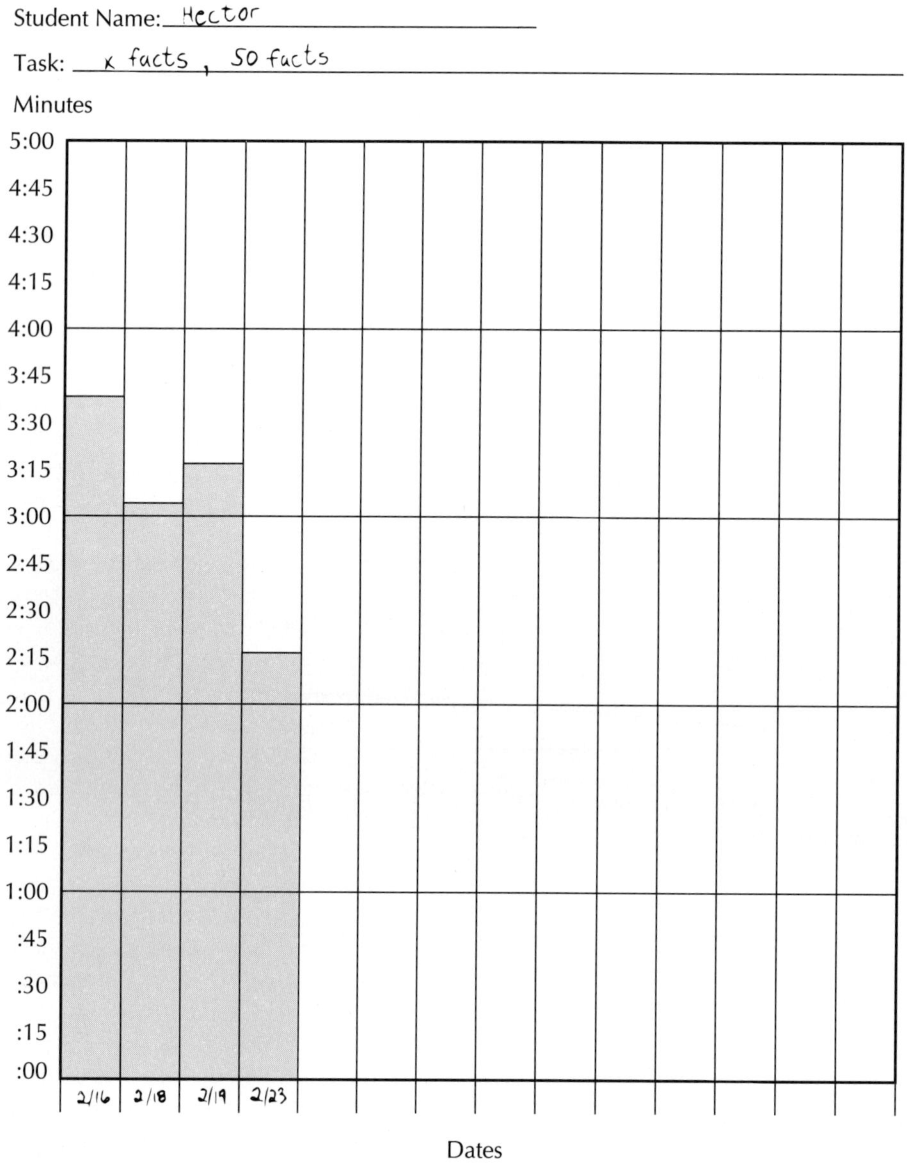

Student Name: Hector

Task: x facts, 50 facts

Minutes

Dates

3. Percent of questions answered correctly for the social studies assignment
4. Number of times student disrupted other students during the morning independent learning activity

5. Student and teacher rating of written pieces based on interest and readability

With a progress graph the measurement unit is marked on the vertical axis. For example, *time* would be marked on the vertical axis for graphing silent reading rate, and *speed* for graphing math facts completed. *Percent* would be marked on the vertical axis for graphing the percent of social studies questions answered correctly. On the horizontal axis, the occurrence unit is marked (e.g., date, teaching session, social studies assignment number). It is relatively easy to plot progress data on either a line graph, as depicted in Figure 1.7 or a bar graph (Figure 1.8).

Progress charts are usually used in the same manner as progress graphs, to measure progress on one skill or behavior. The difference between a progress chart and graph is that with a chart you report the score but do not present it in a relational manner (see Figure 1.9). Although progress charts are generally more efficient in the use of space, they do not provide the clear visual representation of the student performance; therefore, student progress or lack of it is not so automatically apparent. Consequently, graphing is generally recommended over charting for student self-monitoring.

Performance Records

Performance records are often used to record student progress across a set of skills or knowledge and for a significant length of time. An IEP is a performance record in that annual goals and short-term objectives are written, and evaluation of the goals and objectives is recorded on the IEP (see Figure 1.3). Many school districts have developed skill and knowledge competencies or objectives that students need to attain at various grade levels. These are often arranged on an individual student performance record so that as a student becomes proficient in a listed competency, it can be noted (see Figure 1.10). Many commercial reading, math, writing, and other content area programs publish performance records so student progress can be recorded. One caution in using such performance records is that, although most of them measure proficiency, they do not measure maintenance, generalization, or application. Consequently, a teacher may receive a performance record on a student and find that the student cannot perform some of the skills listed as mastered.

In addition to collecting permanent products, the teacher and/or the students may want to keep progress journals. Usually this journal accompanies the performance record or progress graphs and charts and provides the student or teacher a space where each can write comments concerning progress. Ms. Shiller found that progress journals were particularly helpful for documenting progress regarding students' behavior. She used this in combination with graphs to evaluate several students' progress. She found that her dated journal entries provided insights into how she might modify the instructional context and the instruction.

Curriculum-based measurement (CBM) is one system of performance records that highlights the close tie between curriculum and student performance, using frequent samplings from the curriculum materials to assess the student's academic performance (e.g., Fuchs and Deno, 1991; Tindal and Marston, 1990). CBM has been used successfully in mainstreamed and special-education classrooms with students who have learning and behavior problems to increase reading fluency, reading comprehension, spelling, and arithmetic computation (e.g., Deno, 1985; Fuchs et al., 1984; Fuchs, Fuchs, and Hamlett, 1989; Fuchs, Fuchs, Hamlett, and Allinder, 1991). For example, reading fluency in a third-grade class can be measured each week by having each student read 100-word passages from the reading curriculum and by graphing fluency rates across time. This type of measurement provides ongoing data for making instructional decisions. Mercer and Mercer (1993) suggest that you can assess changes in student performance over time by considering: (a) level of performance as affected by instructional change; (b) rate of learning (as reflected by changes in the slope of the trend line) compared to the goal or aim rate; and (c) variability in the consistency of the performance.

Process Records: Portfolios, Learning Logs, and Dialogue Journals

Portfolios, dialogue journals, and learning logs not only highlight product performance across time but also document progress in the learning process. In a

■ **FIGURE 1.9** *Progress Chart for Sight Words*

Name: Lisa

	3/12	3/14	3/15	3/18
sometimes	+ + +	+ + +	+ + +	+ + +
everyone	– – o	– o +	o + +	+ + +
when	– – –	o o +	– o +	o + +
themselves	– o +	o + +	o + +	+ + +
mystery	– o o	o o +	+ o +	+ o +
hurry	o o +	+ + +	+ + +	+ + +
their	– o –	o + o	+ o +	+ + +
friend	+ o +	+ + +	+ + +	+ + +
mountain	– o o	o o +	+ + o	+ + +
trail	– + –	– o –	– + +	+ o +
route	– – o	o + o	o + o	o o +

+ Correct and Automatic

o Correct but Not Automatic

– Incorrect

portfolio, samples are collected across the semester or year (e.g., Paulson, Paulson, and Meyer, 1991; Tierney, Carter, and Desai, 1991). Not only are the final products collected, but also rough drafts, planning or brainstorming sheets, and practice sheets. For example, a student's writing portfolio might contain five stories and essays as well as the brainstorm sheets, research notes, rough drafts, revisions and edited drafts associated with each piece of writing. Whereas reading samples (including oral reading

■ **FIGURE 1.10** *Competency-Based Performance Record*

Student: Karen

Competency Area and Skill	Mastery
Early Reading	
Identifies letters of alphabet	10/87
Names letters of alphabet	12/87
Holds book, turns pages one at a time	9/87
Looks first at left page, then at right	9/87
Distinguishes print from pictures	9/87
Scans left to right, top to bottom	9/87
Reads along listening to a familiar book	9/87
Rhymes words	11/87
Identifies words in a familiar book	10/87
Beginning Reading	
Reads simple stories (preprimer/primer)	3/88
Identifies consonant sounds	2/88
Identifies short vowel sounds	2/88
Identifies long vowel sounds	4/88
Identifies simple sight words in isolation	2/88
Recognizes that "s" makes words plural etc.	4/88

and discussions) can be collected on audiotape, written products can be collected for writing and math. Photographs of projects in subject areas as well as the associated written work can be collected for content area work such as social studies and science. You may want to set up a portfolio for each student in the class. Have students help select which pieces to place in the portfolio and then review the portfolios with them to identify areas of progress and assist in targeting other areas on which to work.

In addition to collecting portfolios, you may want to use learning logs or dialogue journals (e.g., Atwell, 1987; Harste, Shorte, and Burke, 1988) to share thoughts about projects on which the students are working. Learning logs allow the students to reflect on their learning and the processes they have used in learning. Learning logs provide not only another source of information and evaluation, but in the context of reading and writing Harste and his colleagues note, "When learners reflect, they come to value the strategies they are developing through engaging in reading and writing and through observing the demonstrations of other readers and writers around them" (p. 286). Because learning logs focus on communicating ideas or problems with how and what the students are learning, the focus is not on correct spelling or grammar. The entry of Jose (see Figure 1.11), a fifth grade student with written-expression difficulties, reflects what he is learning as a reader and author after reading the chapter entitled "Harassing Miss Harris" in the book, *The Great Gilly Hopkins* (Paterson, 1978).

Dialogue journals also provide a means of evaluation and allow the students the opportunity to carry on a written conversation with the teacher. Ms. Shiller regularly uses a dialogue journal to communicate with Tamara, a sixth-grade student with conduct disorders, about the literature Tamara is reading. Tamara's journal entry about the same chapter in *The Great Gilly Hopkins* reflects how she uses the journal to communicate both her learning processes and her sense of identification with Gilly (see Figure 1.10).

One of the major obstacles in evaluating student progress is planning and organizing an evaluation system. Early in the school year:

1. Determine what you want to evaluate.
2. Determine how you will evaluate it (e.g., progress graphs, charts, permanent product records, portfolios).
3. Determine if and when you will use student self-monitoring (e.g., learning logs and dialogue journals).
4. Develop the forms you need for evaluation.
5. Set up the system so that it is easy to collect, file, and retrieve progress data.

Coordinate your evaluation system with the school system, and then collect and use the data to make instructional decisions.

■ **FIGURE 1.11** *Learning Log Entry for Jose and Dialogue Journal Entry for Tamara on "Harassing Miss Harris" from* The Great Gilly Hopkins *(not corrected for spelling)*

Jose

I like this chapter of the book. Even thow it was hard to read, I liked it. I think that is becuase the auther lets you know just how terribl Gilly feels in her new school. I think that letting you know feelings makes writing more interesting.

Tamara

I just read the chapter on Harassing Miss Harris. I liked it a lot because sometimes I feel like Gilly. I feel so mad that I just want to get mad and not do the work. I really like the way the author lets you know just how Gilly feels. I guess that is why I liked it so much. You know Gilly's feelings.

INVITATION FOR LEARNING

As you read this book, we encourage you to reflect on how the information presented can be interwoven into your beliefs and thoughts about the teaching-learning process. We also encourage you to use the reflective, problem-solving orientation to teaching that Ms. Kranowski did in her classroom. A reflective, problem-solving model of teaching and learning is critical for success with students who have learning and behavior problems.

THINK AND APPLY

- What are some of the characteristics of students with learning and behavior problems?
- What factors should be considered when you are determining how serious a learning or behavior problem is?
- What is the teaching-learning process and how can you apply it to students with learning and behavior problems?
- How do the individualized educational program (IEP) and student and teacher involvement relate to the instructional cycle?
- What measures can be used to evaluate student progress?

Chapter 2

Approaches to Learning and Teaching

OUTLINE

KEY TOPICS FOR MASTERY

— *The principles of operant learning theory and the key concepts of reinforcement, shaping, modeling, Premack principle, contingencies, extinction, punishment, and time-out and their implications for teaching*

— *Strategies for increasing and decreasing behaviors and their implications for teaching*

— *The levels of mastery or learning including entry, acquisition, proficiency, maintenance, generalization, and application*

— *The principles of cognitive behavior modification including the key features of strategy steps, modeling, self-regulation, verbalization, and reflective thinking*

— *The application of cognitive behavior modification through instructional programs such as the Learning Strategies Curriculum*

— *The principles of a sociocultural theory of cognitive development including the key features of zone of proximal development, scaffolded instruction, modeling, thinking aloud, interactive dialogues, and the social nature of learning*

— *Information processing theory including the processes of attention, perception, memory, and executive functioning*

— *The interactive nature of these information processes, the important role that context and motivation play in learning, and their implications for teaching*

 BRIGHT IDEA

Turn to page 69 and read Think and Apply.

Models and theories for learning can assist us in understanding and explaining how students learn. They also guide us in modifying our teaching and the learning context to promote effective and efficient learning. This chapter overviews four theories or approaches to learning and teaching: operant learning and applied behavior analysis, cognitive behavior modification, sociocultural theory of learning, and information processing and schema theory. The models are sequenced in the chapter from less to more cognitively oriented. Many of the general principles presented in this chapter will be applied to specific content areas in the subsequent chapters. As you read this chapter, we encourage you to think about students who you know are not succeeding in school and who have learning and behavior problems. How are their learning patterns and habits explained by the various approaches to learning described in this chapter? What general teaching principles do the different approaches suggest to help such students?

OPERANT LEARNING AND APPLIED BEHAVIOR ANALYSIS

Operant learning theorists, teachers, and other professionals who employ applied behavior analysis believe that behavior is learned and, for this reason, it can be unlearned or the student can be taught new behaviors. Operant learning and applied behavior analysis focus on identifying observable behaviors and manipulating the antecedents and consequences of these behaviors to change behavior. Operant learning theory, for the most part, is not concerned with what you think or tell yourself during the learning process.

In this section on operant learning and applied behavior analysis, we will discuss how to manipulate antecedents and use consequences to increase behaviors we want to see continued, and how to eliminate undesirable behaviors. We also discuss how to teach to different levels of learning.

Manipulating Antecedents

An antecedent is an environmental event or stimulus that precedes a behavior and influences the probability that it will recur in the future. Antecedents influence desirable and undesirable behaviors. It is relatively easy for teachers to manipulate antecedents to change student behaviors. Teachers can analyze the environment and identify factors that contribute to desirable and undesirable behaviors. By identifying and changing these factors, teachers can increase student learning and minimize or eliminate antecedents that interfere. In observing antecedent behaviors the teacher usually considers several types, as delineated in the following sections.

Instructional Content
The teacher can consider a number of ways to manipulate instructional variables to control behavior, such as: making activities more interesting, incorporating student preferences, reducing task difficulties or length, providing choices, and developing functional or age-appropriate activities. By modifying the educational programs, teachers can prevent students' inappropriate or undesirable behavior, and establish a pleasant classroom environment. For example, Blair (1996) found that incorporating the students' activity preferences into circle time and academic activities in a preschool/kindergarten essentially eliminated the undesirable behavior of young students with significant behavior problems.

Classroom Schedule
A well designed schedule allows everyone to predict what will occur during the school day and assist with the allocation of instructional time. For students with learning and behavior problems, teachers need to get students involved in planning the daily schedule. It is important to avoid revising a schedule because this can be disruptive, undermining students' ability to predict what will happen during the day.

Classroom Rules
Carefully selected rules, when properly developed and stated, can contribute to a positive classroom atmosphere. They help students understand what will and will not be accepted in the classroom. It is important to select a limited number of rules to make it easier for students to remember them. Seek student input on the rules to increase their commitment to following them. State rules positively to help students identify the acceptable behavior and post the rules so students can refer to them.

Room Arrangement
Noise and crowding in the classroom sometimes increase the levels of undesirable behaviors. Arranging the furniture of the classroom to partition some areas can reduce the noise level, and limiting the number of students in one area can reduce crowding.

Peer Interactions
The classroom and the school are important social communities and peer interactions play an important role in determining the levels of desirable and undesirable behaviors. Pairing students who have good social skills with students who have more difficulty in prosocial skills, encouraging interaction between students with and without disabilities, and teaching prosocial skills are necessary for decreasing inappropriate behaviors and increasing appropriate behaviors.

Increasing Desirable Behaviors Through Consequences

During the past few weeks, Ms. Glenn has focused on teaching Marjorie, Sheila, and Jose subtraction with regrouping. During this time she demonstrated many of the principles by using "ten packs" of sticks. The students recently practiced applying the principles on the chalkboard. Ms. Glenn then asked the students to practice the skills independently by completing a math paper with twelve subtraction-with-regrouping problems. She watched them complete the first problem correctly. She then needed to teach another group, yet she wanted to be sure that these three students would continue the desirable behavior of working on their math while she was working with her other group.

According to operant learning principles, behavior is controlled by the consequences that follow it. Ms. Glenn needed to decide what consequences would follow "math performing behavior" in order to maintain or increase its occurrence. She told Marjorie, Sheila, and Jose, "If you complete this math sheet with 80 percent or better accuracy, I will let you have five minutes of free time in the Fun Corner." Free time in the Fun Corner was very reinforcing to all three students, and they accurately completed the math sheet while she worked with other students.

There are several principles to apply when attempting to maintain or increase behavior:

1. The behavior must already be in the student's repertoire. In the preceding example, Ms. Glenn's students knew how to perform the math task. If you want to maintain or increase social or academic behaviors, you must first be sure the student knows how to perform the target behaviors.

2. A consequence must follow the precise behavior you want to change or be linked to it through language. For example, "Because you completed all of your math assignments this week, I'll let you select a movie to watch on the VCR."

3. A reinforcer is whatever follows a behavior and maintains or increases the rate of the behavior.

4. To be most powerful, reinforcement should occur immediately following the behavior.

Thus, to increase behavior we can manipulate the consequence that follows the behavior. Consequences that increase behavior, such as reinforcement and the Premack Principle, will be discussed next.

Reinforcement

Reinforcement is the most significant means of increasing desirable behavior. There are two types of reinforcement, positive and negative; both increase responding. How do they differ? The major difference between positive and negative reinforcement is that *positive reinforcement* is the presentation of a stimulus to increase responding, whereas *negative reinforcement* is the removal of a stimulus to increase responding.

Positive reinforcement increases responding by following the target behavior with activities, objects, food, and social rewards, which include such things as ice cream, toys, clothes, and privileges such as helping the teacher or having an extra recess.

The effectiveness of a reinforcement program depends on the selection of reinforcers that are actually reinforcing. The use of a reinforcer preference checklist is recommended when identifying a reinforcer. Activities and events that a student selected when given a wide choice are more likely to be strongly reinforcing. To prevent students from being satiated with the reinforcer, reinforcement menus are recommended. Instead of providing one reinforcer over time, giving a choice of reinforcers increases their value and prevents the satiation.

When using reinforcers it is important to start with more *intrinsic reinforcers* such as using activities that are reinforcing to the student (e.g., listening to records, coloring) and move to more *tangible reinforcers* such as tokens and food only as necessary. For example, Christian (1983) suggests a seven-level hierarchy of reinforcers, ranging from food and hugs to internal self-reinforcement ("I did a good job"). This hierarchy is presented in Table 2.1.

The practice of negative reinforcement is often misused because the term *negative* is misinterpreted to mean harmful or bad and, therefore, the implication is that positive reinforcement is good and negative reinforcement is bad. Negative reinforcement means taking away something unpleasant contingent on the performance of a specific behavior. If a teacher scowls at a student until the student works, removing the scowl is negative reinforcement. The learning that takes place through negative reinforcement is avoidance learning. A common use in

■ **TABLE 2.1** *Practical Reinforcement Hierarchy for Classroom Behavior Modification*

Consequence Level	Examples
Positive physical contact	Hugs, pats, proximity
Food	Milk, raisins, crackers, gum
Toys	Balloon, marbles, kite, clay
School implements	Eraser, ruler, notepad, pencil
Privilege	Free time, errands, computers, eat lunch with teacher
Praise	Positive comments, grades, certificate
Internal self-reinforcement	"I did well." "My work is complete."

(Left margin arrows: Concrete, Tangible ↕ Abstract, Intrinsic)

Source: Adapted from B. T. Christian (1983). A practical reinforcement hierarchy for classroom behavior modification. *Psychology in the Schools, 20,* 83–84. Used with permission.

schools is the completion of work assignments to avoid staying after school. Students often use negative reinforcement with adults. An example is a child who throws a temper tantrum until he or she gets what he or she wants.

Secondary Reinforcers

A *secondary reinforcer* is a previously neutral behavior that is paired with a reinforcer and therefore takes on reinforcing properties of its own. Thus if the teacher always calls a student up to the teacher's desk prior to rewarding him or her, then being called to the teacher's desk becomes reinforcing—a secondary reinforcer.

Sincere praise and attention are the most frequently used secondary reinforcers. Teachers are often quite skillful at using such subtle but effective secondary reinforcers as a hand on the shoulder, a pat on the head, a smile, or a wink. Many teachers position themselves carefully in the room to be near students whose behavior they want to reinforce with their attention. Figure 2.1 provides options for letting students know you value their good work and behavior.

Token reinforcement systems are frequently used by special education teachers. A *token system* is an economy in which a symbol (e.g., points, chips, or stars) is given contingent on designated behaviors. Tokens are symbols in that they usually have little inherent value themselves but can be exchanged for valuable things or privileges. Token systems can be very simple (e.g., receiving stars for completing writing assignments, with each star worth three minutes of extra recess). Figure 2.2 presents several cards that could be used with younger students to record points. Token economies can also be very complicated and may even involve a level system with rewards and privileges varying according to the level the student is on. Students are assigned to levels contingent on their behavior. Being raised or lowered to a different level occurs as points are accumulated. Points are awarded and deducted for a full range of behaviors. More complicated token systems are typically used to manage aggressive behaviors displayed by severely disturbed students.

Shaping

If reinforcement maintains or increases the rate of behavior already occurring, what does the teacher do if the behavior is occurring at a very low rate or not at all?

For example, Mr. Kladder's goal is to shape Rhonda's behavior so that she is performing multiplication facts quickly and automatically. During the initial teaching phase Mr. Kladder rewards her for computing 3 × 5 by adding five threes. After Rhonda demonstrates she can perform this behavior with high accuracy, Mr. Kladder no longer reinforces her for adding the numbers but only for skip counting 5, 10, 15, and then writing the answer. After Rhonda is successfully able to skip count she is reinforced for computing the answer in her head and writing it down. Now Mr. Kladder begins to give Rhonda timed tests in which she is reinforced only for beating her best time. Mr. Kladder is *shaping* Rhonda's behavior by reinforcing responses that more and more closely approximate the target response.

■ **FIGURE 2.1** *33 Ways to Say "Very Good"*

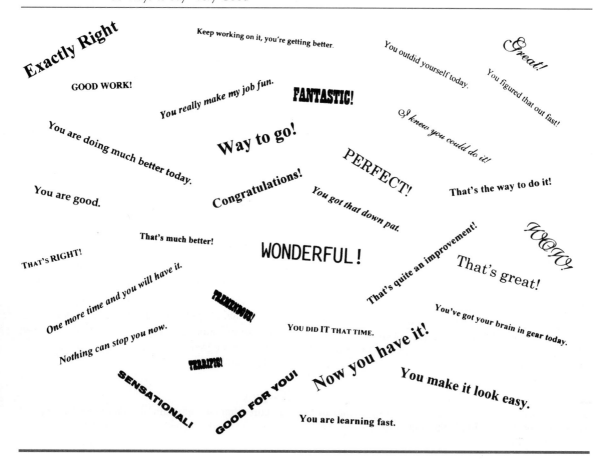

Premack Principle

If one activity occurs more frequently than another, the more frequently occurring activity can be used as a reinforcer to increase the rate of the less frequently occurring activity (Premack, 1959). For example, Adam more frequently participates in outdoor play than in writing stories. His teacher can make outdoor play contingent on completing the writing assignment. The advantage of the Premack Principle is that a teacher can use events that are already occurring in the classroom. One possibility is to inventory the student and rank behaviors from most liked to least liked, for example, (1) reading, (2) math, (3) spelling. Thus reading could be contingent on completing spelling. A more appropriate list for most students

with learning and behavior problems might include five minutes of free time contingent on completing spelling. Reinforcing activities such as talking quietly with friends or listening to music can be used to increase the rate of less desirable activities such as completing a book report.

Group Contingencies

Group contingencies can be used to increase desirable behavior or decrease undesirable behavior. When using *group contingencies,* a group of students, or an individual student, is either reinforced or loses reinforcement, contingent on the behavior of the entire group or a target student in the group. For example, the teacher could establish a twenty-minute

■ **FIGURE 2.2**   *Forms for Recording Points Earned in a Token Economy*

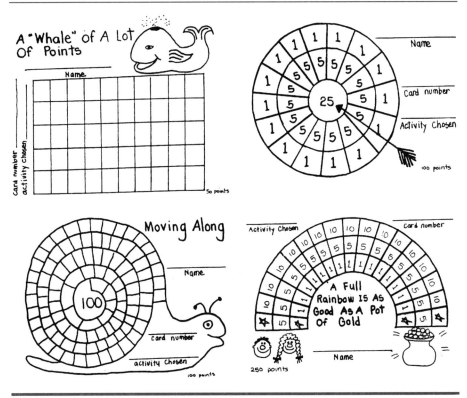

Source: Reprinted with permission from P. Kaplan, J. Kohfeldt, and K. Sturla (1974). *It's Positively Fun: Techniques for Managing the Learning Environment* (p. 19). Denver: Love.

block of free time at the end of the school day. Every time the noise level of the classroom exceeds the teacher's limits she subtracts one minute from the allocated free time. In addition to changing group behavior, group contingencies can be used to change the behavior of one student in the class. For instance, Carla is a twelve-year-old child who has been mainstreamed into a sixth-grade class. During Carla's first couple of weeks in the class she continually got into fights with her classmates during recess. The teacher told the class that she would extend their recess by ten minutes if Carla did not get into any fights during recess. The class included Carla in their group play and fighting was eliminated. However, there are dangers in group contingencies being dependent on the behavior of an individual. It is possible the indi-

vidual will use his or her position to manipulate the behavior of others in the class. It is also possible that the individual will view himself or herself negatively because of this position.

Contingency Contracting

Contingency contracting is an agreement between two or more persons that specifies their behaviors and consequences. A common example of a contingency contract is the agreement between parent and child regarding an allowance. The child agrees to perform certain behaviors in return for a specified amount of money each week. The contingency contract should specify who is doing what, when, under what conditions, and for what consequences (see Figure 2.3).

■ **FIGURE 2.3** *Sample Contingency Contract Form*

I've Got An Offer You Can't Refuse

If_____

_____ by ____

Then _____

_____

_____

_____date_____ _____student_____ _____witness_____ _____Teacher_____

Source Reprinted with permission from P. Kaplan, J. Kohfeldt, and K. Sturla (1974). *It's Positively Fun: Techniques for Managing the Learning Environment* (p. 13). Denver: Love.

Decreasing Undesirable Behaviors Through Consequences

Unfortunately, students manifest behaviors that interfere with their learning or the learning of others. Techniques for decreasing these undesirable behaviors include: extinction, differential reinforcement, punishment, and time-out.

Extinction

Extinction is the removal of reinforcement following the behavior. For example, a teacher wants to extinguish a student's behavior of shouting out and determines that telling the student to raise his hand is reinforcing the shouting out. To extinguish shouting out, the teacher removes the reinforcer ("Raise your hand") and ignores the student's shouting out.

Extinction can be an effective means of decreasing undesirable behaviors, but it is often slow and can be impractical for many behaviors that occur within the classroom because the reinforcers for the undesirable behavior are often difficult for the teacher to control. For example, let's return to the student who continually shouted out in class. In this situation the student was being reinforced not only by the classroom teacher's attention ("Raise your

hand") but also by other students who looked and attended to him when he shouted out. A teacher attempting to reduce this behavior through extinction would have to eliminate both the teacher's reinforcement and the reinforcement of others in the class. To compound the difficulty, slip-ups by the teacher or students would intermittently reinforce the behavior and maintain it for a long time.

Another characteristic of extinction is its effect on the rate at which the target behavior continues to occur. During extinction the target behavior will increase in rate or intensity before decreasing. Thus a teacher attempting to eliminate tantrums through extinction will observe the tantrums occurring more frequently, lasting longer, and perhaps even being louder and more intense than before extinction. As long as the teacher continues to withhold reinforcement, usually attention, the rate and intensity will decrease and tantrums can be eliminated. For this reason it is extremely important to chart behavior when using extinction. To document behavior change, take *baseline data,* a record of the frequency and/or duration of the behavior before implementing the intervention, and continue to take data after intervention is implemented.

Although extinction can be an effective means of decreasing undesirable behaviors, it requires patience and the ability to control all of the reinforcers. Ignoring, the most frequently applied form of extinction in the classroom, is an important skill for teachers to learn. A summary of points to remember about using ignoring as a means of decreasing undesirable behavior follows:

1. Ignoring can be effective when the behavior is being reinforced by the teacher's attention.
2. If the teacher attempts to eliminate a behavior through ignoring, the behavior must be ignored every time it occurs.
3. Ignoring will not be effective if the behavior is being maintained by other reinforcers, such as the attention of classmates.

Differential Reinforcement

Differential reinforcement involves strengthening one set of responses in contrast to another. It is an effective procedure for developing a positive behavior management plan. The main advantage of differential reinforcement is that positive consequences are used to reduce the strength of undesirable behavior. Therefore, negative side effects associated with punishment procedures are avoided. There are several forms of differential reinforcement. The definitions and examples are as follows:

Differential Reinforcement of Incompatible Behaviors (DRI) and Alternative Behaviors (DRA)
Differential reinforcement of incompatible behaviors involves identifying desirable behaviors. Reinforcement is then provided contingent on the occurrences of the targeted desirable behaviors. For example, while ignoring the out-of-seat behavior of a student, the teacher targets and reinforces the desirable behavior that is incompatible, in this case, in-seat behavior. Therefore, when Scott is sitting in his seat the teacher is quick to catch his appropriate behavior and reinforce. In addition, the teacher would intermittently reinforce Scott for being in his seat. In the case of DRI, the new response (incompatible behavior) is selected because it represents an incompatible alternative to the disruptive behavior; the two behaviors cannot occur simultaneously. The alternative behavior selected in DRA is not necessarily incompatible with the disruptive response, and the alternative response can occur at the same time as the undesirable behavior. The goal of using DRA is to strengthen a range of appropriate behaviors that teachers will attend to naturally, thereby reinforcing a broad repertoire of appropriate behavior. Careful planning should ensure that the reinforcers selected are sufficiently attractive and delivered with sufficient frequency to motivate student performance while removing reinforcers from the undesirable behavior. Both DRI and DRA ensure that new behaviors are fostered at the same time that undesirable behaviors are being diminished.

Differential Reinforcement of Other Behaviors (DRO)   Differential reinforcement of other behaviors (DRO) is the reinforcement of the nonoccurrence of target behavior during a specified time period; reinforcers are delivered following time intervals in which the target behavior did not occur. For example, a teacher may allow the student free time at the end of each 30-minute scheduled period in which no target behavior occurred. Therefore, determining the length of the reinforcement period prior to using DRO is important. Brief intervals of one to ten minutes may be selected for high rate behaviors, and intervals up to a day in length may be used for low rate behaviors. DRO may be most effective when used in combination with a DRA procedure by reinforcing occurrences of alternative behavior as well as providing reinforcement for intervals in which a zero rate of the target behavior occurred. When combined with other methods, DRO can be one of the most powerful procedures (Sulzer-Azaroff and Mayer, 1991).

Regardless of the type of differential reinforcement, reinforcing behavior through consequences requires you, the teacher, to do four things:

1. Identify the behavior you want to change (interfering behavior).
2. Identify the incompatible behavior.
3. Stop reinforcing the interfering behavior.
4. Reinforce the desirable behavior in the target child or others who are displaying it.

Response Cost
Response cost is a procedure in which a specified amount of a reinforcer is removed following each occurrence of the target behavior. Withdrawal of favored activities and tangible reinforcers are common response strategies for young children. For example, a student is not allowed to play during free choice session because of his or her aggression toward peers. One of the most common response cost strategies for older students is the use of withdrawal of tokens following a target behavior. For example, students may earn 20 points for completing each assignment throughout the day. Points can be exchanged for primary reinforcers at the end of the day. Engaging in a target behavior may result in a response cost of 30 points. Response cost is an aversive procedure which should be used carefully. It can inadvertently be used to punish positive behaviors. For example, teachers may be tempted to ask students to complete additional work if assignments are completed prior to the end of the class period. Additional

work requirements may act as a response cost for early assignment completion.

Punishment

Punishment, the opposite of reinforcement, is following a behavior with a consequence that decreases the strength of the behavior or reduces the likelihood the behavior will continue to occur. Unfortunately, punishment does not assure the desired behavior will occur. For example, a student who is punished for talking in class may stop talking, but may not attend to his or her studies for the remainder of the day.

There are many significant arguments against the use of punishment:

1. Punishment is ineffective in the long run.
2. Punishment often causes undesirable emotional side effects such as fear, aggression, and resentment.
3. Punishment provides little information to the person as to what to do, teaching the individual only what not to do.
4. The person who administers the punishment is often associated with it and also becomes aversive.
5. Punishment frequently does not generalize across settings, thus it needs to be readministered.
6. Fear of punishment often leads to escape behavior.

If there are so many arguments for not using punishment, why is it so frequently used as a means for changing behavior? There are many explanations, including lack of familiarity with the consequences of punishment and the inability to effectively use a more positive approach. Also, punishment is often reinforcing to the punisher, reducing the occurrence of the undesirable behavior, therefore reinforcing its use.

Punishment should be used only when behaviors are harmful to the child or others. In this case, the student should be told ahead of time what the consequence (punishment) for exhibiting the behavior will be. When the undesirable behavior occurs, the punishment should be delivered quickly and as soon as the inappropriate behavior is initiated. Punishment should be applied consistently every time the designated behavior occurs. If you choose to use punishment you should identify several other behaviors you would like to see maintained and give extensive reinforcement for their occurrence.

Time-Out

Time-out occurs when the student is removed from the opportunity to receive any reinforcement. Time-out is when the teacher asks a student to sit in the hall during the remainder of a lesson, when a young child is asked to leave the group, or when a student is asked to sit in a quiet chair until he or she is ready to join the group.

Unfortunately, time-out is frequently used inappropriately. The underlying principle behind the successful use of time-out is that the environment the student is leaving must be reinforcing and the time-out environment must be without reinforcement. This may not be as easy to achieve as you might think. For example, when Elizabeth was talking and interfering with others during the science lesson, her teacher thought she would "decrease" Elizabeth's behavior by sending her to time-out, which was a chair in the back of the room away from the group. The teacher became discouraged when Elizabeth's inappropriate behavior during science class increased in subsequent lessons rather than decreased. A likely explanation for the ineffectiveness of time-out in this situation is that Elizabeth did not enjoy science class and she found sitting in a chair in the back of the room looking at books reinforcing. The efficacy of time-out is strongly influenced by environmental factors. If the environment the student is leaving is unrewarding, then time-out is not an effective means of changing the student's behavior.

Teachers who use secluded time-out areas or contingent restraint (holding the student down plus withdrawal, exclusion, and seclusion) should be aware of the legal implications of such intervention, and should obtain the necessary authorization from within the school setting and from parents or guardians. A position paper on the use of behavior reduction strategies has been issued by the Council for Children with Behavior Disorders, Council for Exceptional Children (CCBD, 1990) and new policies developed for physical intervention by the Council for Exceptional Children (1995). Recom-

APPLY THE CONCEPT 2.1

PROCEDURES FOR IMPLEMENTING TIME-OUT

Time-out, like punishment, should be used as a last resort. Teachers should discuss this intervention with school administrators and parents before implementing it.

1. The student should be told in advance which behaviors will result in time-out.
2. The amount of time the student will be in time-out should be specified ahead of time.
3. The amount of time the student is in time-out should be brief (between one to five minutes).
4. The student should be told once to go to time-out. If the student does not comply, the teacher should unemotionally place the student in time-out.
5. Time-out must occur every time the undesirable behavior occurs.
6. Contingencies should be set in advance for the student who fails to comply with time-out rules.
7. Do not leave the time-out area unmonitored.
8. When time-out is over, the student should return to the group.
9. Reinforce positive behaviors that occur after time-out.

---

mended procedures for successfully implementing time-out are listed in Apply the Concept 2.1.

Peer Confrontation System

Peers as well as the teacher can serve as behavior controllers for students. In a procedure referred to as the peer confrontation system (Salend, Jantzen, and Giek, 1992), the teacher and students identify behavior problems in the group. The teacher informs the students in the group to respond to students that are having a behavioral problem in the following way:

- Teacher says, "Mark seems to be having some difficulty. Who can tell Mark what the problem is?"
- Selecting a student from the group, the teacher says, "Can you tell Mark what the problem is?"
- The teacher follows with, "What does Mark need to do to solve the problem?"

In the Salend et al. (1992) study, 12 of the 13 students indicated that they would like to continue using the peer confrontation system.

Stages of Learning

One way the principles of operant learning can be applied is through *stages of learning*. The stages of learning (see Figure 2.4) are the levels a student moves through in acquiring proficiency in learning (Rivera and Smith 1996). For example, the first stage of learning, *entry*, is the level of performance the student is presently exhibiting. During the second stage, *acquisition*, the components of the target behavior are sequenced into teachable elements. Each teachable element is taught to mastery through a high rate of reinforcement, shaping, and consistent use of cues. When the behavior is occurring at a high level of accuracy, the focus of the learning is on *proficiency*. During this stage the teacher's goal is to increase the student's accuracy and fluency in performing the behavior. At the next stage, *maintenance*, the goal is for the behavior to be maintained at the target level of accuracy and proficiency with intermittent reinforcement and a reduction in teacher assistance and cues. The next stage is *generalization*, in which the target behavior transfers across settings, persons, and materials. Stokes and Baer (1977) suggest that generalization may be a separate skill that needs to be taught. Apply the Concept 2.2 provides further information on how to teach for generalization. At the final stage, *application*, the learner is required to extend and utilize the learning in new situations. Application is a difficult skill for special learners, and the teacher's role is to demonstrate and provide a range of opportunities for applying the newly acquired skill.

In summary, the principles of operant learning and applied behavior analysis are applicable within

■ **FIGURE 2.4**   *Stages of Learning*

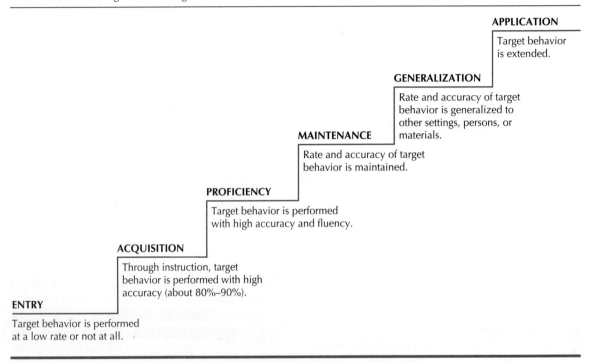

APPLICATION
Target behavior
is extended.

GENERALIZATION
Rate and accuracy of target
behavior is generalized to
other settings, persons, or
materials.

MAINTENANCE
Rate and accuracy of target
behavior is maintained.

PROFICIENCY
Target behavior is performed
with high accuracy and fluency.

ACQUISITION
Through instruction, target
behavior is performed with high
accuracy (about 80%–90%).

ENTRY
Target behavior is performed
at a low rate or not at all.

Source: Adapted from D. P. Rivera, and D. D. Smith (1997). *Teaching Students with Learning and Behavior Problems* (3rd ed.). Boston: Allyn and Bacon.

the classroom for both instructional and classroom management purposes. In a classroom based on operant learning theory, the teacher has behavioral objectives that specify the behavior the students need to perform to be judged successful. If the target response does not occur naturally, then it is important for the teacher to develop a method of shaping the behavior. The behaviors are sequenced from the simple to the more difficult. A full range of reinforcers is used, such as verbal praise, smiles from the teacher, gold stars, tokens, free time, and other specialized reinforcers that are effective with students. Students are dealt with individually, with target behaviors reflecting the needs of the student. Behaviors are initially taught through continuous reinforcement; after acquisition of these behaviors, they are maintained through intermittent reinforcement. Teachers reduce inappropriate behavior by ignoring it and reinforcing incompatible behavior. Teachers avoid the use of punishment. Behaviors are discussed in observable terms and learning is measured by the acquisition of new behaviors.

COGNITIVE BEHAVIOR MODIFICATION

Cognitive behavior modification integrates notions from operant, social, and cognitive learning theories, and assumes that cognitive behavior (thinking processes), like observable behaviors, can be changed. This model of teaching and learning incorporates many of the principles of operant learning, but it adds some additional techniques that seem relevant when the goal of instruction is to change the way one thinks. Let's look at how Mrs. Neal uses cognitive behavior modification to help Marlow and his classmates better understand their science textbooks.

APPLY THE CONCEPT 2.2

GENERALIZATION STRATEGIES

Change Reinforcement

Description/Methods

Vary amount, power, and type of reinforcers.

- Fade amount of reinforcement.

- Decrease power of reinforcer from tangible reinforcers to verbal praise.

- Increase power of reinforcer when changing to mainstreamed setting.
- Use same reinforcers in different settings.

Examples

- Reduce frequency of reinforcement from completion of each assignment to completion of day's assignment
- Limit use of stars/stickers and add more specific statements, e.g., "Hey, you did a really good job in your math book today."
- Give points in regular classroom although not needed in resource room.
- Encourage all teachers working with student to use the same reinforcement program.

Change Cues

Description/Methods

Vary instructions systematically.

- Use alternate/parallel directions.

- Change directions.

- Use photograph.

- Use picture to represent object.

- Use line drawing or symbol representation.
- Use varying print forms.

Examples

- Use variations of cue, e.g., "Find the . . ."; "Give me the . . ."; "Point to the. . . ."
- Change length and vocabulary of directions to better represent the directions given in the regular classroom, e.g., "Open your book to page 42 and do the problems in set A."
- Move from real objects to miniature objects.
- Use actual photograph of object or situation.
- Move from object/photograph to picture of object or situation.
- Use drawings from workbooks to represent objects or situations.
- Vary lower and upper case letters; vary print by using manuscript, boldface, primary type.
- Move from manuscript to cursive.

Change Materials

Description/Methods

Vary materials within task.

- Change medium.

- Change media.

Examples

- Use unlined paper, lined paper; change size of lines; change color of paper.
- Use various writing instruments such as markers, pencil, pen, typewriter.
- Use materials such as films, microcomputers, filmstrips to present skills/concepts.
- Provide opportunity for student to phase into mainstream.

(continued)

APPLY THE CONCEPT 2.2   *Continued*

Change Response Set

Description/Methods

Vary mode of responding.

- Change how student is to respond.

- Change time allowed for responding.

Examples

- Ask child to write answers rather than always responding orally.
- Teach student to respond to a variety of question types such as multiple choice, true/false, short answer.
- Decrease time allowed to complete math facts.

Change Some Dimension(s) of the Stimulus

Description/Methods

Vary the stimulus systematically.

- Use single stimulus and change size, color, shape.
- Add to number of distractors.

- Use concrete (real) object.
- Use toy or miniature representation.

Examples

- Teach colors by changing the size, shape, and shade of "orange" objects.
- Teach sight words by increasing number of words from which child is to choose.
- Introduce rhyming words by using real objects.
- Use miniature objects when real objects are impractical.

Change Setting(s)

Description/Methods

Vary instructional work space.

- Move from structured to less structured work arrangements.

Examples

- Move one-to-one teaching to different areas within classroom.
- Provide opportunity for independent work.
- Move from one-to-one instruction to small-group format.
- Provide opportunity for student to interact in large group.

Change Teachers

Description/Methods

Vary instructors.

- Assign child to work with different teacher.

Examples

- Select tasks so that child has opportunities to work with instructional aide, peer tutor, volunteer, regular classroom teacher, and parents.

Source: From S. Vaughn, C. S. Bos, and K. A. Lund, *Teaching Exceptional Children,* Spring, 1986, pp. 177–178. Copyright 1986 by The Council for Exceptional Children. Reprinted with permission.

Marlow, a seventh grader in a class for students with behavior disorders, and several of his classmates consistently have difficulty comprehending the important ideas from their textbooks, particularly in science. Even though they can identify most of the words in the text, they only remember a few details from what they read. Mrs. Neal wants to teach Marlow and his classmates how to understand and remember the major points. She decided that if she wants to teach the students this cognitive behavior, she will have to give them a consistent set of steps to use in completing the process, much in the same way we use a consistent set of steps to tie shoes. She also knows that for the students to learn what to do, they need to observe someone else. But how can she do this?

Mrs. Neal uses cognitive behavior modification. First, she selects the steps she wants to teach Marlow and the other students to use when they read their science text. Next, she and the students discuss the strategies the students currently use and their effectiveness. They also discuss the importance of improving this skill and the payoff for improvement. Mrs. Neal then tells the students about the steps she uses when she reads. To model these steps, she reads and explains what she is thinking. Then she talks them through the steps as the students try them. Finally, Mrs. Neal gives the students lots of opportunities to practice the steps when reading their textbooks, encouraging them at first to say the steps aloud as they work through them. She provides feedback on how they are doing and she also teaches them how to evaluate their own performance.

Using these systematic techniques, Mrs. Neal finds that in several weeks Marlow and his classmates are improving in their ability to remember the important information from their science text. In addition, they are beginning not to rely so much on the strategy she taught them. It is almost as if they are using it automatically, without having to consciously remember to use it. Mrs. Neal feels that she has taught her students a good strategy for thinking about what they are reading and that has changed their cognitive behavior (thinking processes). To promote generalization, Mrs. Neal discusses with Marlow and his classmates other opportunities they have for using the strategy. The students begin keeping a list on the board of all occasions when the strategy can be used. They also begin using the strategy on these different occasions (e.g., reading the newspaper during current events, reading other textbooks, editing each others' stories and essays) and discussing how useful the strategy was in helping them.

Mrs. Neal used *cognitive behavior modification* (CBM). This approach includes an analysis of the task as well as an analysis of the thinking processes involved in performing the task. It also includes a training regimen that utilizes modeling, self-instructional techniques, and evaluation of performance (Meichenbaum, 1977, 1983).

Several key learning and teaching principles are associated with CBM. One principle of CBM is *cognitive modeling* or "thinking aloud." When Mrs. Neal explained what she was thinking as she read, she was using cognitive modeling. Another principle is *guided instruction*. Mrs. Neal used this principle when she guided the students through the reading task by telling them the steps in the process as they read. *Self-instruction* is another principle. When learners use language to guide their performance, they are using self-instruction. For instance, if you talk or think through the steps in solving a complex algebra problem while completing it, you are using self-instruction.

Self-evaluation and self-regulation are two more principles of CBM. *Self-evaluation* refers to making judgments concerning the quality or quantity of performance. Mrs. Neal had Marlow and his classmates judge the quality of their performance by having them pause at the end of each section of the science text and comment on how they were doing. *Self-regulation* refers to the learner monitoring his or her own thinking strategies through language mediation. Self-regulation also occurs when the learner corrects or uses fix-up strategies when he or she detects a problem. For example, Mrs. Neal taught Marlow and his classmates to say to themselves what the main idea was when they finished reading each paragraph or section of the text. If the students could not give the main idea, then she demonstrated and encouraged them to use a fix-up strategy. In this case, she showed them how to go back and reread the first sentence in the paragraph to see if that helped them to remember the main idea. If this did not work, she demonstrated how to review the paragraph quickly.

Origins of Cognitive Behavior Modification

Cognitive behavior modification has origins in several theories of learning (Harris, 1982, 1985). From operant learning come the principles of behavior modification. Behavior modification techniques such as task-analyzing the skill to be learned, providing cues to the learner, and using reinforcement and corrective feedback have been incorporated into many CBM training programs.

Social learning theory (Bandura, 1977) has also influenced CBM. A major assumption of social learning theory is the notion that affective, cognitive, and behavior variables interact in the learning process. For example, the extent to which Eva understands the cognitive concepts of place value will affect how well she performs the behavior of computing three-digit subtraction problems with regrouping. Motivation and other affective variables also interact. Eva will probably perform the subtraction more accurately and carefully if she is determining whether there is enough money in her bank to buy a new record than if she is doing the twenty-fifth problem on a page of assigned subtraction problems.

The notion that we learn through watching others is another assumption that comes from social learning theory (Bandura, 1977). In social learning theory the importance of modeling is emphasized in relation to social behaviors (e.g., aggressive and cooperative behaviors). In CBM, modeling has been expanded to include cognitive modeling. When Mrs. Neal "talked aloud" what she was thinking as she read, she was using cognitive modeling.

Cognitive theory and cognitive training have also had a strong influence on CBM. Cognitive behavior modification explicitly teaches problem solving and knowledge construction, and relies heavily on principles of self-regulation and self-evaluation (Harris and Pressley, 1991; Lenz, Ellis, and Scanlon, 1996; Pressley, Brown, El-Dinary, and Afflerbauch, 1995).

Common Features of CBM Interventions

Cognitive behavior modification interventions or training regimens have been used to develop a range of academic and social skills. Lloyd (1980) identified five common features found in most CBM techniques: strategy steps, modeling, self-regulation, verbalization, and reflective thinking.

Strategy Steps

A series of steps is usually identified for the student to work through when solving a problem or completing a task. These steps are based on a task analysis of the cognitive and observable behaviors needed to complete the task. Before Mrs. Neal began teaching, she determined the steps in the reading strategy she wanted to teach Marlow and his classmates.

Graham and Harris and their colleagues have developed a series of writing strategies to assist students in writing stories and other pieces (Graham and Harris, 1989b, 1993; MacArthur, Graham, Schwartz, Schafer, 1995; MacArthur, Schwartz, and Graham, 1991; MacArthur, Schwartz, Graham, Molloy, and Harris, 1996). Each strategy has steps that the students learn to assist them with specific aspects of writing. For example, to help students write a story Graham and Harris (1989a) used the following strategy steps:

1. Look at the picture (picture prompts were used).
2. Let your mind be free.
3. Write down the story part reminder (W-W-W; What = 2; How = 2). The questions for the story part reminder were:
   - Who is the main character? Who else is in the story?
   - When does the story take place?
   - Where does the story take place?
   - What does the main character want to do?
   - What happens when he or she tries to do it?
   - How does the story end?
   - How does the main character feel?
4. Write down the story part ideas for each part.
5. Write your own story; use good parts and make sense.

Modeling

In CBM, modeling is used as a primary means of instruction. Research in social learning theory as well as in CBM supports the notion that modeling is a very effective teaching technique. With CBM, students are asked not only to watch observable behaviors as the instructor performs the task, but also to listen to the instructor's self-talk. In this way the instructor is modeling both observable behaviors and the unobservable thinking processes associated with those behaviors. Being able to model unobservable thinking processes is an important component for teaching such cognitive skills as verbal math problem solving, finding the main idea in a paragraph, editing written work, and solving social problems. In most instances the person modeling is the teacher or a peer, but video and puppets have also been used. Vaughn, Ridley, and Bullock (1984) used puppets as models for teaching interpersonal social skills to young, aggressive children. The puppets were used to demonstrate appropriate social behaviors and strategies for solving interpersonal problems.

Self-Regulation

Self-regulation refers to the learner monitoring his or her thinking and actions through language mediation. When Meichenbaum (1977) developed his CBM training for improving the self-control of hyperactive children, he used Vygotsky's notions about how language affects socialization and learning processes. Luria (1961) and Vygotsky (1978) suggest that children become socialized using verbal self-regulation. Children first use language to mediate their actions by overtly engaging in self-instruction and self-monitoring. Later, this language mediation becomes covert.

Using self-regulation, students act as their own teachers. Students are expected to take active roles in the learning process and to be responsible for their own learning (Harris and Pressley, 1991; Pressley et al., 1995). Although they work under the guidance of a teacher, students are expected to monitor their learning, change or modify strategies when difficulties arise, evaluate their performance, and in some cases provide self-reinforcement.

Peers have also been used to promote student regulation and monitoring. For example, MacArthur, Graham, and their colleagues (MacArthur, Schwartz, and Graham, 1991a) used a reciprocal student editing strategy to increase students' knowledge about writing and revising and to increase their revising activity. The strategy was taught by special education teachers who were using a process approach to teaching writing (see Chapter Six) and word processing. The steps in the Student Editor Strategy were:

1. LISTEN and read along as the author reads.
2. TELL what it was about and what you like best.
3. READ and make NOTES about:
   CLEAR? Is there anything that is difficult to understand?
   DETAILS? Where could more information be added?
4. DISCUSS your suggestions with the author.
5. The author makes revisions on the computer. (MacArthur et al., 1991, p. 234)

The procedure was reciprocal in that steps one and two were completed for both students. Then the two students worked independently to complete step three and again met together for step four to discuss each paper and the suggested revisions. For step five each author worked at the computer to make the revisions that he or she thought were useful.

For students with behavior disorders, particularly those with conduct disorders, aggression replacement theory (Goldstein and Glick, 1987) uses self-regulation as an effective procedure for assisting students in controlling their anger. Through aggression replacement theory students learn to identify anger-producing situations (triggers) and to recognize their responses to these situations (cues). They then learn a number of techniques designed to assist them in relaxing and cognitively handling the situation. In reviewing self-regulation outcome research conducted with students with behavior disorders, Nelson, Smith, Young, and Dodd (1991) found numerous studies indicating that self-regulation procedures can be extremely effective in enhancing both the academic and social behavior of these students.

Verbalization

Verbalization is typically a component of self-instruction and self-monitoring with overt verbalization being faded to covert verbalization. Many CBM programs rely on a "talk aloud" or "think aloud" technique (e.g., Deshler and Shumaker, 1988; Harris and Graham, 1992; Montague and Bos, 1986b). After listening to the teacher think aloud as he or she performs the targeted processes and task, students are encouraged to talk aloud as they initially learn the strategy. For example, Ramon might say the following as he completes a two-digit subtraction problem without regrouping, "Start at the one's place and take the bottom number away from the top. Write the answer in the one's place. Now go to the ten's place. Do the same thing." Usually these overt verbalizations only occur during the initial stages of learning. As the strategy becomes more automatic, students are encouraged to "think to themselves" instead of "aloud."

In addition to verbalization concerning the learning processes, students are also encouraged to make self-statements about their performance. For example, "That part is done. Now go to the next part." or "I'm getting much faster at this." or "I need to think about all my choices before I decide."

Meichenbaum (1977) has suggested several ways to encourage students to use self-talk:

1. The teacher can model self-talk and self-statements as he or she performs the task.

2. The teacher can begin with tasks at which the students are already somewhat proficient. Later, as the students are comfortable with self-talk, the teacher can switch to the targeted tasks.

3. Students can develop and use cue cards to help them remember the steps they are to talk through. For example, Camp, Blom, Herbert, and Van Doorninck (1977) used the pictures in Figure 2.5 as cue cards when teaching self-control to twelve aggressive second-grade boys. The cue cards were used as reminders to self-verbalize as the boys applied these questions first to cognitive and then to interpersonal tasks.

Reflective Thinking

Reflective thinking requires students to take the time to think about what they are doing. Teaching students who have learning and behavior problems to "stop and think" is an important skill to include in instruction. Many of these students are impulsive in their actions, seeming to act without thinking (Blackman and Goldman, 1982; Kauffman, 1985; Keogh and Donlon, 1972). These students have limited and ineffective strategies for approaching academic tasks or social situations. They approach these tasks and situations in a disorganized, haphazard way, and often without

■ **FIGURE 2.5** *Cue Cards Used for Teaching Self-Control*

1 What is my problem?

2 How can I do it?

3 Am I using my plan?

4 How did I do?

Source: Reprinted with permission from B. W. Camp and M. A. S. Bash (1985). *Think Aloud: Increasing Social and Cognitive Skills—A Problem-Solving Program for Children. Classroom Program: Grades 1–2* (pp. 48–51). Champaign, IL: Research Press.

thinking about the consequence of the actions (Torgesen, 1982; Torgesen and Licht, 1983; Wallace and Kauffman, 1986). In using CBM training programs, teachers assist students in using reflective thinking.

Let's look at how Wong, Wong, Perry, and Sawatsky (1986) encouraged reflective thinking when they taught seventh-grade students to use self-questioning when summarizing social studies texts. After teaching the students how to identify the main idea of paragraphs and how to summarize paragraphs, Wong and colleagues taught the students a summarization strategy. The questions the students asked themselves were:

1. In this paragraph, is there anything I don't understand?
2. In this paragraph, what's the most important sentence (main-idea sentence)? Let me underline it.
3. Let me summarize the paragraph. To summarize, I rewrite the main-idea sentence, and add important details.
4. Now, does my summary statement link up with the subheading?
5. When I have written summary statements for a whole subsection:
   a. Let me review my summary statements for the whole subsection. (A subsection is one with several paragraphs under the same subheading.)
   b. Do my summary statements link up with one another?
6. At the end of an assigned reading section: Can I see all the themes here? If yes, let me predict the teacher's test question on this section. If no, let me go back to step 4 (Wong et al., 1986, pp. 25–26).

Teaching Implications of CBM

Cognitive behavior modification is designed to actively involve students in learning. Meichenbaum (1977, 1983) characterizes the student as a collaborator in learning. General guidelines to consider when using CBM include:

1. Analyze the target behavior carefully.
2. Determine if and what strategies the student is already using.
3. Select strategy steps that are as similar as possible to the strategy steps used by good problem solvers.
4. Work with the student in developing the strategy steps.
5. Teach the prerequisite skills.
6. Teach the strategy steps using modeling, self-instruction, and self-regulation.
7. Give explicit feedback.
8. Teach strategy generalization.
9. Help the students maintain the strategy.

Guidelines for assessing the effects of training (see Table 2.2) have also been suggested (Rooney and Hallahan, 1985).

A substantial and growing body of research supports the use of cognitive behavior modification for developing academic, cognitive, and social skills in students with learning and behavior problems (Deshler, Ellis, and Lenz, 1996; Lenz et al., 1996; MacArthur et al., 1995; Pressley et al., 1995; Montague and Bos, 1986b; Rooney and Hallahan, 1988; Rottman and Cross, 1990, Wong, 1996). As discussed in Apply the Concept 2.3, researchers at the Kansas University Center for Research on Learning have developed a teaching model as well as a number of task-specific strategies that employ the principles of CBM.

SOCIOCULTURAL THEORY OF COGNITIVE DEVELOPMENT

The sociocultural theory of cognitive development (Vygotsky, 1978) is similar to cognitive behavior modification in that it highlights the importance of modeling and the use of language to facilitate learning. However, the theory assumes that learning is socially constructed, and as a social activity is highly influenced by the funds of knowledge that learners bring to the situation. Knowledge is meaningfully constructed in these social activities (Englert, Rozendal, and Mariage, 1994; Moll, 1990).

Vygotsky was a Russian psychologist who conducted his most important work during the 1920s and 1930s. However, due to the popularity of behavioral theories, Piaget's theory, and information processing theory, his work did not attract great interest until the last 20 years (Byrnes, 1996). The whole language approach to literacy (as discussed in Chapter 4 and 5) embraces this theory. The *Cognitive Strategy Instruction in Writing* (CSIW) (Englert, Raphael, Anderson, Anthony, and Stevens, 1991), the *Early Literacy Project* (ELP) (Englert, Garmon, Mariage, Rozendal, Tarrant, and Urba, 1995), and the *Optimal Learning Environment* (OLÉ) (Ruiz, Garcia, and Figueroa, 1996) are three examples that we highlight in this section because they focus directly on students with disabilities or young children who are at risk for developing academic learning disabilities. Although Vygotsky's theory of cognitive development embraces many concepts, we have highlighted three that are

■ **TABLE 2.2**   *Guidelines for Assessing Strategy Effectiveness*

Behavior	*Assessment Questions*
Independence	Can the student use the strategy without cues or assistance?
	Can the student match the appropriate strategy to the task?
	Can the student adapt the strategy if necessary?
Spontaneity	Does the student use the strategy without being asked or cued to do so?
Flexibility	Can the student modify and adapt the strategy to match the situation?
	Can the student pick out the cues in the situation to guide strategy use?
Generalization	Does the student use the strategy appropriately in various situations?
	Does the student use the strategy across different class periods?
Maintenance	Does the student continue to use the strategy after direct instruction of the strategy has stopped?
Reflective Thinking	Does the student stop and think about how to do a task before beginning?
	Does the student think about which strategy to use before beginning?
	Does the student reflect on his or her performance and adjust the strategy if necessary?
Improved Performance	Has the student's performance on the targeted task improved?
	Is there improvement in the student's productivity, accuracy, and task completion?
Improved Self-Concept	Does the student see himself or herself as an active participant in learning?
	Does the student see himself or herself in control of his or her learning?
	Does the student regard himself or herself as more successful?

APPLY THE CONCEPT 2.3

APPLICATION OF COGNITIVE BEHAVIOR MODIFICATION:
THE LEARNING STRATEGIES CURRICULUM

Can the principles of cognitive behavior modification be applied to academic tasks in such a way that adolescents with learning disabilities can be successful in performing the skills required for secondary school settings? This is one of the major questions that was addressed by Don Deshler, Gordon Alley, Jean Schumaker, and their colleagues at the Kansas University Center for Research on Learning. The Strategies Intervention Model (Deshler, et al., 1996; Deshler and Schumaker, 1986; Ellis, Deshler, Lenz, Schumaker, and Clark, 1991; Tralli, Colombo, Deshler, and Schumaker, 1996) is one of the most comprehensive examples of an intervention model based on cognitive behavior modification.

The goal of the Strategies Intervention model is "to teach learning disabled adolescents strategies that will facilitate their acquisition, organization, storage, and retrieval of information, thus allowing them to cope with the demands of social interaction" (Alley and Deshler, 1979, p. 8). Learning strategies are techniques, principles, or routines that enable students to learn to solve problems and complete tasks independently. Strategies include how a person thinks and acts when planning, executing, and evaluating performance on a task and its outcomes. Broadly, a learning strategy (a) includes a general approach to solving a set of problems; (b) promotes goal-directed behavior, (c) teaches selection of appropriate procedures; (d) guides implementation of a procedure; (e) shows how to monitor progress; (f) can be controlled; and (g) provides and focuses on cues to take action (Institute for Research in Learning Disabilities, 1990a, pp. 15, 21). Learning strategies instruction focuses on how to learn and how to use what has been learned.

The Learning Strategies Curriculum contains three strands of academic, task-specific strategies. The Acquisition Strand enables students to gain information from written materials and includes such strategies as the Word Identification Strategy (Lenz, Schumaker, Deshler, and Beals, 1984) and the Paraphrasing Strategy (Schumaker, Denton, and Deshler,

1984). The Storage Strand consists of strategies to assist students in organizing, storing, and retrieving information. The First-Letter Mnemonic Strategy (Nagel, Schumaker, and Deshler, 1986) is an example of a storage strategy. The Expression and Demonstration of Competence Strand contains strategies that enable students to complete assignments, express themselves, and take tests. The Test Taking Strategy (Hughes, Schumaker, Deshler, and Mercer, 1988), the Paragraph Writing Strategy (Schumaker and Lyerla, 1991), and the Error Monitoring Strategy (Schumaker, Nolan, and Deshler, 1985) are examples of strategies that assist students in taking tests, writing cohesive paragraphs, and editing written work.

Each strategy uses a teaching model that incorporates principles of cognitive behavior modification. The stages in the model are:

Acquisition

Stage 1 **Pretest and Make Commitments**

Obtain measure(s) of current functioning

Make students aware of inefficient/ineffective habits

Obtain students' commitments to learn

Stage 2 **Describe the Strategy**

Insure that students have rationales for strategy use

Insure that students know characteristics of situations for when and where to use the strategy

Describe results that can be expected

Supervise goal setting

Describe and explain the strategy steps

Present the remembering system

Stage 3 **Model the Strategy**

Demonstrate the entire strategy "Thinking Aloud"

Involve the students in a demonstration

(continued)

APPLY THE CONCEPT 2.3   *Continued*

Stage 4   Elaboration and Verbal Rehearsal

Assist students to verbally rehearse the strategy steps and what each step means

Require students to memorize the strategy

Stage 5   Controlled Practice and Feedback

Supervise practice in "easy" materials

Provide positive and corrective feedback

Move from guided practice to independent practice

Require mastery

Stage 6   Advanced Practice and Feedback

Supervise practice in materials from regular coursework

Provide positive and corrective feedback

Fade prompts and cues for strategy use and evaluation

Move from guided practice to independent practice

Require mastery

Stage 7   Confirm Acquisition and Make Generalization Commitments

Obtain measure(s) of progress

Make students aware of progress

Obtain the students' commitment to generalize

Phase I   Orientation

Discuss situations, settings, and materials in which the strategy can be used

Evaluate appropriateness of strategy in various settings and materials

Identify helpful aspects of the strategy and adjustments

Make students aware of cues for using the strategy

Phase II   Activation

Program the students' use of the strategy in a variety of situations

Provide feedback

Reinforce progress and success

Phase III   Adaptation

Identify cognitive processes

Discuss how the strategy can be modified to meet differing demands

Assist students in applying the modifications

Phase IV   Maintenance

Set goals related to long-term use

Conduct periodic reviews

Identify self-reinforcers and self-rewards

Provide feedback

(Deshler and Schumaker, 1986; Ellis, Deshler, Lanz, Schumaker, and Clark 1991; Institute for Research in Learning Disabilities, 1990b)

This teaching model relies heavily on modeling, self-instruction, and self-regulation. It encourages students to assume an active and collaborative role in learning. The teaching model has been validated with a number of specific learning strategies, for example, a strategy for learning information from textbooks (MULTIPASS) (Schumaker, Deshler, Alley, Warner, and Denton, 1982), a strategy for listening to lectures and taking notes (LINKS) (Schumaker, Deshler, Alley, and Warner, 1983), a strategy for remembering information (FIRST) (Nagel, Schumaker, and Deshler, 1986), and a strategy for paraphrasing text (RAP) (Schumaker, Denton, and Deshler, 1984). Several of the specific learning strategies are presented in the chapters on reading, written expression, and content areas learning and study skills.

Note: The University of Kansas University Center for Research on Learning requires that persons planning to implement the Learning Strategies Model obtain training available through the Center for Research on Learning, University of Kansas, Lawrence, KA 66045.

particularly important in using this theory for teaching students who may have special needs or are from diverse cultural and linguistic backgrounds. These overarching concepts include the use of resources, the social nature of learning (including the use of interactive dialogue), and the use of scaffolded instruction.

Use of Resources

One key concept associated with this theory is that the teacher needs to consider and utilize the resources that the students bring to learning (Diaz, Moll, and Mehan, 1986). These include such aspects as culture and language as well as background knowledge the learners can apply to the problem being solved or the knowledge being constructed. For example, in assisting Mexican-American elementary students to develop literacy, Moll and Greenberg (1990) began by first exploring the *funds of knowledge* that could be gained from the community and the Hispanic and southwestern cultures. They also examined how literacy functioned as a part of community and home life. They brought this information into the schools and used it to build a literacy program. In this way, culturally diverse students were given the opportunity to use sources of knowledge that are not often highlighted in traditional school curriculums.

Social Nature of Learning and Interactive Dialogue

Another important theoretical concept is the premise that learning occurs during social interactions; that is, learning is a social event in which language plays an important role. Using this concept, teachers and students discuss what they are learning and how they are going about learning. Such interactive dialogue or instructional conversations between teachers and learners provides language models and tools for guiding one's inner talk about learning (Moll, 1990; Englert et al., 1995; Bos and Reyes, 1996). Initially, a more expert person may model the self-talk and vocabulary related to the cognitive processes. However, this gives way to a collaborative or interactive dialogue in which the learner assumes increasing responsibility.

This type of teaching allows for the instruction of cognitive and metacognitive strategies within purposeful, meaningful discussions and also provides a means for selecting, organizing, and relating the content matter being discussed. For example, in reciprocal teaching (Palincsar and Brown, 1984), a technique designed to foster comprehension and comprehension monitoring, the teacher and students take turns leading dialogues which focus on their knowledge of the information they are studying and on the processes they are using for understanding and for checking their understanding (see Chapter Five).

Englert, Raphael, Anderson, and their colleagues have designed an instructional writing program based on a sociocultural theory of cognitive development entitled *Cognitive Strategy Instruction in Writing* (CSIW). The program (see Chapter Six) fosters interactive dialogue among teachers and students about the writing process and problem-solving strategies (Englert, Raphael, Anderson, Anthony, and Stevens 1991; Englert, Raphael, and Anderson 1992). In the program, think sheets help the teacher and students see, discuss, and think about the questions, text structures, and problem-solving strategies that good writers use when planning, drafting, editing, redrafting and final drafting a written piece. In this program, interactive dialogue plays a critical role in successful instruction. For example, Ms. Patrick and her students discuss editing a piece of her writing on how to plant bulbs. Ms. Patrick's goal is to demonstrate and guide students in how to reread their texts for meaning and organization from the perspective of a reader, and examine their texts to see if they accomplished their goals related to purpose and text structure (Englert, 1992). During this discussion, Ms. Patrick has put her writing on the overhead for students to comment on and edit.

T: Okay, as I read my paper . . . listen for several things. Listen for key words. [Check for] clear steps. Ask, "Does it make sense?" *She reads her own story.*

Jim: It has five key words. First, next, then, then, next. *Two students reread her paper aloud and another goes up spontaneously and circles her key words on the overhead. As students begin to circle her key words, she responds.*

T: Go ahead and circle my key words, that's just a draft; I'll be revising it anyway. *The students count five key words.*

T: Was it clear?

Ss: Yes.

T: What was clear about it?

Meg: You said how to put it in the pot and then how to do it . . . [You said] put soil in the pot.

T: Was anything unclear?

Roy: If you added more, it would be awful. I think it was perfect.

T: Even my writing isn't perfect all the time. I never said what kind of soil to put in there. And when I said pour half the soil in the pot, I wonder if they know to buy a bag.

Roy: You need to say, "First, you need to tell them to go to the store and buy pot, soil, and bulbs." They are going to say, "Where do I get this stuff?"

T: You are right . . . I think I'll write in the margins. (Englert, 1992, p. 159)

In this example, Ms. Patrick guides the students to demonstrate and discuss editing strategies. She creates a context where students come to understand and negotiate the meaning of text and to share their understandings about writing. She thinks aloud, e.g., "I think I'll write [notes] in the margin," and then demonstrates on her draft.

Scaffolded Instruction

Another concept of the sociocultural theory of learning relates to the role of the teacher or the expert, who encourages learners by providing temporary and adjustable support as they develop new skills, strategies, and knowledge. The instruction is referred to as *scaffolded instruction* (Tharp and Gallimore, 1988). The metaphor of a scaffold captures the idea of an adjustable and temporary support that can be removed when no longer necessary. Vygotsky (1978) describes learning as occurring in the *zone of proximal development* or "the distance between the actual developmental level as described by independent problem solving and the level of potential development as determined through problem solving under adult guidance or in collaboration with more capable

peers" (p. 86). Important to promoting development within the students' zones of proximal development is the teacher's ability to relinquish control of the strategies to the students. In the example of Ms. Patrick, Englert (1992) discusses how Ms. Patrick relinquishes control of her paper by letting the students circle the key words. Englert (1992) notes that this "transfer of control was prompted in earlier lessons when Ms. Patrick instructed her students to take the overhead marker and mark up texts" (p. 163). In fact, research on the CSIW program in fourth- and fifth-grade general education classrooms with students who have learning disabilities demonstrated that teachers who were most effective in promoting the student gains and transfer in writing (a) modeled the writing strategies, (b) involved students in classroom dialogues about writing, (c) promoted strategy flexibility, and (d) relinquished control of strategies to students (Anderson, Raphael, Englert, and Stevens, 1991).

In the *Early Literacy Project* (ELP) (Englert et al., 1994; 1995), the literacy curriculum is structured to include activities that provide opportunities for scaffolded instruction and the teaching of strategies. Figure 2.6 provides an overview of these activities and the principles of the ELP. Important to promoting development within the students' zones of proximal development is the teacher's ability to relinquish control of the strategies to the students. To illustrate the dialogue that works within the zone of proximal development, Englert and her colleagues (1994) describe the interactive dialogues among the teacher and students, including students at risk for learning disabilities, during the Morning News. "In this lesson, the class constructed a morning news about the information from their thematic unit on dinosaurs. Each student took responsibility for drafting a section of the story, and the class reread and edited the various sections. The teacher (T) used this opportunity to model specific writing and editing conventions and to highlight the multiple sources and classroom resources that can be employed in the literacy process.

T: Lauren, you wrote this part. Would you like to read this part for us?

L: I need help with it.

■ **FIGURE 2.6** *Early Literacy Project Principles and Activities*

Choral and Partner Reading/Writing

Description
Choral reading & taped story reading
Partner reading & partner writing
Purpose: To provide opportunities for students to fluently read & write connected texts; to provide opportunities for students to use literacy language and knowledge; to develop reading/writing vocabulary and enjoyment of reading

Thematic Unit

Description
Teacher and students brainstorm, organize, write drafts, read texts or interview people to get additional information about a topic or theme from multiple sources, and use reading/writing strategies flexibly to develop and communicate their knowledge
Oral/written literacy connections are made apparent
Purpose: Model learning processes; introduce literacy language, genre and strategies; model reading/writing processes and connections; provide interrelated and meaningful contexts for acquisition and application of literacy knowledge; conventionalize and develop shared knowledge about the purpose, meaning and self-regulation of literacy acts

Silent Reading

Description
Independent reading
Reading to an adult
Listening to new story at listening center
Purpose: Work on fluency for author's chair; provide experience with varied genres

Morning News

Description
Students dictate personal experience stories
Teacher acts as a scribe in recording ideas and as a coach in modeling, guiding, and prompting literacy strategies
Purpose: To model and conventionalize writing and self-monitoring strategies; demonstrate writing conventions; provide additional reading and comprehension experiences; promote sense of community; empower students; provide meaningful and purposeful contexts for literacy strategies

Principles of the Early Literacy Project

Using Meaningful Activities
Teaching to Self-Regulate
Apprenticing Students in the Dialogue
Empowering Students in the Community

Literature/Story Response

Description
Students read stories and respond to them in various ways (e.g., sequence stories, illustrate story events, map story events or story structure, summarize story, etc.)
Students make a personal affective response to stories
Students work with partners or small groups to develop response
Purpose: To promote students' application of literacy strategies; present varied genres to students; promote students' ownership of the discourse about texts; futher students' enjoyment of texts; make text structure visible to students

Sharing Chair

Description
Read books, poems, personal writing
Students control discourse and support each other
Students ask questions; answer questions, and act as informants to peers and teacher
Purpose: Promote reading/writing connection; empower students as members of the community; allow students to make public their literacy knowledge and performance; develop shared knowledge

Author's Center

Description
Process Writing Approach (students plan, organize, draft, edit texts)
Students partner-write and work collaboratively to brainstorm ideas, gather additional information, write drafts, share drafts, receive questions, and write final draft
Students use literacy strategies modeled in thematic units
Purpose: To develop a sense of community; develop shared knowledge; provide opportunities for students to rehearse literacy strategies; empower students in appropriating and transforming strategies

Source: Reprinted with permission from C. S. Englert, M. S. Roszendal, and M. Mariage (1994). Fostering the search for understanding: A teacher's strategies for leading cognitive development in "zones of proximal development." *Learning Disability Quarterly, 17,* p. 191.

T: Okay, would you like to pick somebody to read that part with you? *Lauren picks a student to help her pronounce unfamiliar words that she can't read.*

T: Does anyone have a question for Lauren about cavemen? *When no one responds, the teacher proceeds to illustrate.* Where did you get the idea about cavemen? When we were talking [referring to the time when she interacted with Lauren as she wrote this section], did we say that dinosaurs ate cavemen?

Ss: No.

T: You know what Lauren told me as she wrote that idea? She got it out of her imagination. But this paper is kind of telling true things, so I'm wondering if we should leave it in or take it out. SH, what do you think?

SH: There was cavemen. See that book right there? *Points to book.*

T: You can get it. I guess what I'm wondering is if we know for sure if they [dinosaurs] ate cavemen?

A: I saw it in a movie.

T: Was it a real movie or a cartoon movie?

Ss: *Ss talk about movie and book.*

T: Alright. Do we want to leave that [part] in?

Ss: U-huh!

B: Didn't dinosaurs eat other dinosaurs?

T: We have to ask Meg because she was the writer. *B turns to Meg and repeats comment. Meg agrees that B's idea can go in the story. Then the teacher turns to ask the opinion of the class.* What do you think about adding that idea [to our story], boys and girls? 'Dinosaurs eat other dinosaurs.' I want you to put thumb up if you think that is a good idea. *Surveys students.* So I'm going to put a caret here and I'm going to say, 'Dinosaurs eat other dinosaurs.' (Englert et al., 1994, p. 198)

This dialogue illustrates the way the teacher uses interactive dialogue and classroom resources to support scaffolded instruction. "For example, she encouraged Lauren to select a peer to help her read and asked students to turn to each other in making final decisions about the text. She also acknowledged the

contribution of movies, texts, and students' own imagination in the writing process" (Englert et al., 1994, p. 198).

Instructional Implications

There are many instructional implications from the sociocultural theory of cognitive development. Four that seem particularly important are:

1. Instruction is designed to facilitate scaffolding and cooperative knowledge sharing among students and teachers within a context of mutual respect and critical acceptance of others' knowledge and experiences.
2. Learning and teaching should be a meaningful, socially embedded activity.
3. Instruction should provide opportunities for mediated learning, with the teacher or expert guiding instruction within the students' zones of proximal development.
4. Students' sociocultural backgrounds should provide the basis upon which learning is built.

This last implication is highlighted in the *Optimal Learning Environment* (OLÉ) (Ruiz, Garcia, and Figueroa, 1996). It was designed for students with disabilities who are from culturally and linguistically diverse backgrounds. Apply the Concept 2.4 describes this curriculum.

Research suggests that this approach is particularly effective for students with disabilities who are from culturally and linguistically diverse backgrounds (e.g., Ruiz and Figueroa, 1995; Ruiz, Figueroa, and Boothroyd, 1995). Many of the strategies incorporated into the curriculum are further described in Chapters 4 through 6.

INFORMATION PROCESSING AND SCHEMA THEORIES

Whereas the operant learning and applied behavior analysis model focuses on observable behaviors, and views learning as the establishing of functional relationships between a student's behavior and the stimuli

APPLY THE CONCEPT 2.4

OPTIMAL LEARNING ENVIRONMENT (OLÉ)

Optimal Learning Environment (OLÉ) is built on Vygotsky's sociocultural theory (1978) and Krashen's (1985) concept of *comprehensible input*. These suggest that for culturally and linguistically diverse students who may or may not have learning disabilities, it is important for teachers to provide learning environments that enable students to go beyond their actual levels of performance with deliberate "scaffolding." Krashen's concept of *comprehensible input* (e.g., visual cues, regalia, total physical response) acts as a scaffold for students who are learning English as a second language.

The *Optimal Learning Environment* is a flexible literature-based general language arts curriculum that integrates reading, listening, speaking, and writing. Using OLÉ, teachers create a learning situation that is highly contextualized under optimal conditions where teachers employ instructional strategies conducive to language and literacy development. These twelve optimal learning conditions are:

- Student choice
- Student-centered
- Whole-part-whole approach
- Active student participation
- Focus on ideas before mechanics
- Authentic purposes for learning
- Immersion in language and print
- Teacher and peer demonstrations
- Approximation
- Immediate response
- Classrooms as learning communities
- High expectations

The optimal conditions are based on the work of Cambourne and Turnbull (1987) and classroom research with culturally and linguistically diverse students in general or special educational environments (e.g., Echevarria and McDough, 1996; Ruiz & Figueroa, 1995).

The OLÉ curriculum integrates the teaching and use of nine strategies or activities that are often used in constructivist- or process-oriented classrooms. They include:

- Interactive journals
- ABC wall chart or class book
- Shared reading with predictable texts
- Pocket chart reading with predictable texts
- Patterned writing with predictable texts
- DEAR (Drop Everything and Read) time
- Literature study
- Creating texts from wordless books
- Writers' workshop

Each strategy is a collaborative undertaking. Students as well as teachers write in *interactive journals* on a daily basis, independently choosing topics. These journals function as a record of their writing development, and students receive a response each time they write. Emergent readers and writers "read" their entries to the teacher so that the teacher can respond with a vocalized written question for students to answer.

ABC wall charts or *class books* ensure that students are learning the letters that will enable them to decode with better accuracy. Creating their own pictures and key words for each letter gives students the opportunity to relate the letters to their own knowledge and thus remember them more easily. Posting these personal letter representations in place of a conventional letter chart gives students ownership of the alphabet and boosts their self concept.

In *shared reading,* students read alone or in a small group with an expert who assists them in unlocking the alphabetic code. Fluency, automaticity, and strategic reading are the goals of shared reading, especially when predictable texts are used. Reading the text using various methods (i.e., echo reading, choral reading, Reader's Theatre, see Chapter 5) allows for automaticity and opportunities for readers to develop strategies such as predicting a word's meaning from the context or detecting the mood of the story.

After students have read a predictable book or poem many times over, they are ready to learn to decode the words out of context. *Pocket chart reading* supports students in developing this skill. With words written on sentence strips or tag board cards,

(continued)

APPLY THE CONCEPT 2.4 *Continued*

students work with the text without depending on pictures to decode.

To develop writing skills, predictable texts are used to assist in *patterned writing.* New books can be created by taking students directly through the writing process in a safe environment that is teacher-assisted. Patterned writing involves taking a piece of the predictable text and allowing students to complete the sentence or phrase with their own words.

During the 10 to 15 minutes of *DEAR (Drop Everything and Read) time,* students and teachers alike act as avid readers, either alone or sharing a favorite story with a friend. Students are encouraged to discuss a text if necessary and discuss story elements, illustrations, or interesting vocabulary words.

Literature studies are a natural progression from shared reading and DEAR time. In small groups, students are encouraged to construct meanings, interpret text, and respond to literature in many other ways. Teachers act as facilitators during these literature discussions.

Creating texts for wordless books, and *writers' workshop,* go side by side in providing teachers opportunities to demonstrate and scaffold the writing process. Figure 2.7 demonstrates how one student used the different stages of the writing process.

Authentic assessment is an integral part of OLÉ. It includes portfolio assessment by means of collecting student work samples for the different strategies. Checklists provide a means of assessing development for each strategy (see Figure 2.8).

---

in the environment, cognitive learning theory focuses on what happens in the mind, and views learning as changes in the learner's cognitive structure.

Information processing theory, one of several cognitive theories, attempts to describe how sensory input is perceived, transformed, reduced, elaborated, stored, retrieved, and used (Atkinson and Shiffrin, 1968; Neisser, 1976; Swanson, 1996). Psychologists and educators studying information processing attempt to understand how thinking processes operate to allow humans to complete such complex cognitive tasks as summarizing a chapter in a textbook, solving complex math problems, writing a mystery novel, and comparing and contrasting theories of learning.

A simplified model depicting the sequence of stages in which information is processed or learned is presented in Figure 2.9. Although the figure implies that each activity is relatively separate, these processes are highly interactive with a gradual increase in the amount of integrative and higher order processing used. This processing system is controlled by *executive functioning* or *metacognition,* which assists the learner in coordinating, monitoring, and determining which strategies the learner should employ for effective learning (Brown, 1980; Neisser, 1976; Swanson, 1996).

We can use this model to explain how Greg, a high-school student with learning disabilities, might acquire and remember some new information about "seizure" as it relates to the Fourth Amendment of the United States Constitution. Mr. Gomez is explaining the concepts of "search and seizure" to Greg and the rest of the students in government class. He writes the word *seizure* on the board and says, "Seizure is when the police take your possessions away from you because those possessions are illegal. Sometimes the police need a search warrant to seize your possessions and sometimes they do not. As you read this chapter see if you can determine the rules for when the police need a search warrant."

According to the model presented in Figure 2.9, the first step in learning and remembering the information on the concept of "seizure" is to receive the information through the senses. Mr. Gomez exposed Greg to both visual and auditory information by writing the word on the board and by talking about it.

Next, the information is transported to the sensory store. Here, both the visual representation of "seizure" and the auditory information is stored. At this point Greg has neither attended to the information nor connected meaning to it.

■ **FIGURE 2.7** *Student Example of the Stages of the Writers' Workshop*

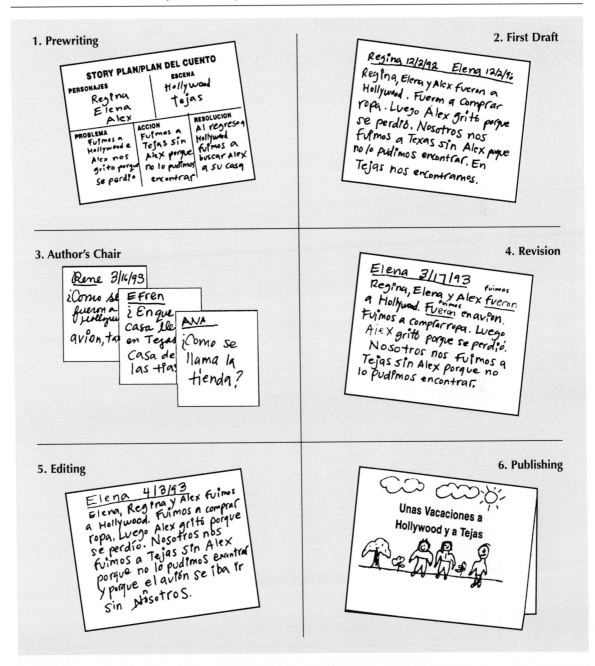

Source: Reprinted with permission from N. T. Ruiz, E. Garcia, and R. A. Figueroa (1996). *The OLÉ curriculum guide: Creating optimal learning environments for students from diverse backgrounds in special and general education* (p. 57). Sacramento, CA: Specialized Program Branch, California Department of Education.

■ **FIGURE 2.8**   *Authentic Reading Assessment for Emergent Readers*

Olé

TEACHER EVALUATION FORM

Year:

AUTHENTIC READING ASSESSMENT

Appropriate for emergent readers   (Refer to the following page for the Spanish translation of this form.)

Student:	Grade:
Title of Book:	Known Text _____ Unknown Text _____

KEY—LEVEL OF DEVELOPMENT
NE = No evidence; **B** = Beginning; **D** = Developing; **C** = Controls

	Level of Development	Comments
CONCEPTS ABOUT PRINT		
1. Knows function of print		
2. Points to beginning and end of text		
3. Finds title and author		
4. Finds a letter, word, capital letter, small letter		
5. Uses book language in reading pictures or retelling		
6. Tracks left to right, return sweep, top to bottom		
7. Can voice-print match		
8. Knows function of "." "?" "!" ","		
STRATEGIES		
1. Uses picture cues		
2. Makes predictions		
3. Relies on memory		
4. Uses rhyming		
5. Uses story context or background experiences		
6. Uses letter sounds		
7. Uses grammar		
8. Uses social resources		
9. Uses a variety of strategies to read predictable text		
10. Uses a variety of strategies to read nonpredictable text		
11. Monitors comprehension through self-correction		
COMPREHENSION		
1. Orally produces text for wordless books		
2 Orally produces text appropriate to pictures		
3. Retells story with details		
4. Demonstrates comprehension through dramatization		
5. Demonstrates comprehension through personal connection with books		
6. Compares text with other texts		
7. Uses appropriate intonation		
OVERALL IMPRESSION		
1. Confidence and degree of independence		
2. Involvement in the text		

Source: Reprinted with permission from N.T. Ruiz, E. Garcia, and R.A. Figueroa (1996). *The OLÉ curriculum guide: Creating optimal learning environments for students from diverse backgrounds in special and general education* (p. 80). Sacramento, CA: Specialized Program Branch, California Department of Education.

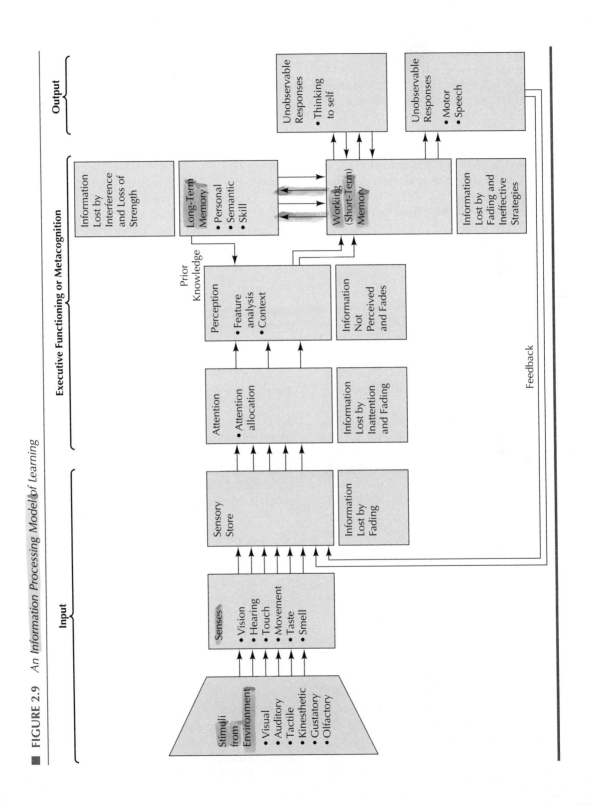

Now Greg can attend to the information, but since he cannot attend to all sensory information, he must screen out some in order to attend to specific parts. If Greg is attending to the hum of the air conditioner or thinking about a Friday night date rather than purposefully listening to the teacher, the information Mr. Gomez shared with Greg cannot be learned because Greg has not selectively attended to it.

Next, Greg can recognize or perceive the information by detecting the salient features in the information and using the context and his prior knowledge to assist in perception. For example, Greg can use salient visual features in the word *seizure,* his sight word recognition for the word (prior knowledge), and Mr. Gomez's discussion of seizure (context) to perceive the word written on the board as *seizure* rather than the word *leisure* or *search.*

Once the information is perceived, it can be held for a short period of time in working or short-term memory. However, if Greg wants to learn the information, he can either transfer and store the information in long-term memory or utilize a strategy to keep the information active in short-term memory. Unless some effort is made to remember the information, it will fade in about fifteen seconds. We can use a variety of memory strategies to keep information active. We can rehearse it (repeat it aloud and to ourselves), chunk it (group it together to make fewer pieces of information to remember), elaborate on it (expand on it by using information we already know), and so on. Greg rehearses the word and its definition by saying it several times to himself.

Greg is aware that the information related to "seizure" needs to be remembered for a long time or at least until the test next week. Therefore, the information must be meaningfully stored in long-term memory to become part of his cognitive structure. This way, he should be able to retrieve the information next week for the test. One efficient means of storing new information is to relate the new information to old information. Greg retrieves from his memory a story about a senior who tried to raise marijuana in his backyard. The police found it, arrested him, and seized the marijuana. When he hears or reads the word *seizure,* he can think of the senior having the marijuana seized. Greg also retrieves

from his memory that search and seizure are discussed in the Fourth Amendment. Greg can relate the new information to old information almost as if he were filing it in an organized filing system.

When the exam is given next week, and Mr. Gomez asks for the definition of seizure, Greg should be able to retrieve the information from long-term memory into working memory and then write the definition because he filed it in a meaningful way.

Throughout the process, learning is orchestrated by executive functioning or metacognition. For example, when Greg decided to rehearse the word and its definition rather than write them down, he was using his executive functioning to coordinate the learning process.

Although we process information in a logical sequence (see Figure 2.9), we generally process information very quickly and don't think consciously about what we are doing. We do not necessarily say to ourselves, "Now I need to rehearse this so I won't forget it," or "I have to relate this information to what I already know so that I can remember it." Information processing is also very interactive. Feedback is possible both from observable responses we make and unobservable thinking responses. These interactions are depicted by the bi-directional arrows in Figure 2.9. Let's explore information processing further by looking at each component and at the overall coordinating processes of executive functioning and metacognition.

Sensing

Sensing involves the use of one or more of our senses to obtain information. It refers to our system's capacity to use the sensory processes to obtain information, not our system's ability to attend or discriminate. Stimuli from the environment are received through all our senses. However, much of the information we learn in school-related tasks is received through visual and auditory senses.

Sensory Store
The *sensory store* holds all incoming information for approximately a second, just long enough for us to attend to and perceive it (Loftus and Loftus, 1976). Although we have the ability to retain large amounts

of information in the sensory store, the information quickly fades unless we actively attend to and perceive it (Sperling, 1960).

Attention

Most of us use the term *attention* to refer to a wide range of behaviors. We speak of attending to details when we are concerned about the quality of a job, we ask people if they are attending to us when we want them to hear what we are about to say, and we measure students on the amount of time they attend to tasks. *Selective attention* is the capacity to focus awareness on selected incoming stimuli. As depicted in Figure 2.9, we attend only to some of the information, depending on the task demands.

The importance of selective attention can be demonstrated in relation to the reading process. You have probably experienced reading a text by going through the mechanical motions (identifying the words) only to realize suddenly that you are not attending and cannot remember what you were reading. Instead, your mind has drifted to thoughts about a friend's problems, the music playing in the background, or how good the apple pie baking in the oven smells. An effective learner must selectively attend to the relevant stimuli.

Attention can only be allocated to a few cognitive processes at a time. However, the more proficient you are at a process, the less attention it will require. Well-practiced processes require little attention and are said to be *automatic,* whereas processes requiring considerable attention have been referred to as *deliberate* or purposive (Hasselbring, Goin, and Bransford, 1987; Swanson, 1996). LaBerge and Samuels (1974; Samuels, 1987) have applied these principles to the reading process. Poor readers, including many students with learning and behavior problems, must allocate so much of their attention to identifying the words in the text that little is left to allocate toward comprehension. Good readers, however, have word recognition at an "automatic" level, and therefore have more attentional capacity to allocate to understanding what they read.

Not only do students with learning disabilities have to allocate more attention to some tasks than nondisabled students, they also have difficulty selectively attending to the relevant stimuli and attending for sustained periods of time (Hynd, Obrzut, and Bowen, 1987; Richards, Samuels, Turnure, and Ysseldyke, 1990; Swanson, 1996). Because information will quickly fade from the sensory store, lessons, particularly for students with learning and behavior problems, should be planned to initially spark the attention of students and direct their attention toward the relevant information (Lerner, 1997).

Perception

Once we allocate our attention to incoming stimuli, the next step in processing is to recognize or perceive the information. *Perception* can be defined as "the process of 'recognizing' a raw, physical pattern in sensory store as representing something meaningful" (Loftus and Loftus, 1976, p. 23). Students who have perceptual disabilities usually have trouble interpreting and obtaining meaning from the stimuli in the environment.

One explanation of how perception works entails the perceiver using feature analysis and the context in which the stimulus is presented to give the stimulus meaning. In *feature analysis,* the perceiver uses the critical features to recognize the stimuli. For example, the critical feature between *n* and *u* and *p* and *b* is orientation. We process more slowly and are prone to confuse letters that have minimal feature differences such as *C* and *G* or *b* and *d* (Kinney, Marsetta, and Showman, 1966). Similar findings have been shown with speech sounds (phonemes). Feature analysis is used across a variety of contexts. For instance, a listener might use the salient clue "Once upon a time" to recognize that she is listening to a story.

The perceiver also uses the *context* in which the stimulus is presented to assist in perception. Read the two words presented in Figure 2.10. Did you have any difficulty reading *THE CAT?* Now look closely at the *H* and the *A.* They are the exact same visual image. The context provided by the words facilitates the appropriate interpretation (Neisser, 1967). Context also plays an important role in perceiving auditory stimuli. Our store of background information, as

■ **FIGURE 2.10** *Effect of Context on Letter Recognition*

THE CHT

represented in long-term memory (see Figure 2.9), interacts with the incoming stimuli to assist us in the perception process.

Perception involves the simultaneous use of both feature analysis and use of context and prior knowledge. Feature analysis has been referred to as *bottom-up processing* "because information flows from little perceptual pieces (features), which serve as the foundation of perception, to larger units built from them (e.g., letters, words, pictures)" (Anderson, 1980, p. 43). If we processed every feature of every letter when reading a page, it is estimated that we would be making an average of 100 feature analyses per second. But because we can also use context and prior knowledge to assist in perception, we do not need to detect every feature, every letter, or even every word (Smith, 1978; Goodman, 1996). When context or prior knowledge guide perception, we refer to the processing as *top-down processing,* since high-level general knowledge determines the interpretation of low-level perceptual units (Anderson, 1995). It is the interaction of bottom-up and top-down processing that makes for efficient perceptual processing (Chase and Tallal, 1991; Rumelhart, 1980).

Working Memory

Once information is perceived it can move into working or short-term memory. *Working memory* can be thought of as activated memory since it represents the information that is easily accessible. Working memory has a limited capacity in that we have the ability to store only a small amount of information in working memory at any one time (i.e., seven bits of information plus or minus two bits) (Miller, 1956).

Working memory can be contrasted with long-term memory. Long-term memory represents the information stored outside the attentional spotlight

(Rumelhart, 1977). Working memory is similar to the material on a computer screen in that it will be lost when the power is turned off unless the information has been saved (Lerner, 1997). An example can clarify the difference between short-term and long-term memory.

Study the following numbers so that you can remember them: 9-6-5-8-2-4-1-7. Now cover the numbers, wait for at least fifteen seconds, and then write them. After you attended and perceived the numbers, you probably studied them to keep them active in your working memory and then you wrote them. To keep the numbers active you may have rehearsed the numbers, closed your eyes and tried to visualize them, or used some other memory strategy.

Now write the phone numbers of your two best friends. This information is stored in long-term memory. You had to search your long-term memory for your two best friends. You probably used their names in searching, although you could have used their appearances or an idiosyncratic characteristic. Then you retrieved their phone numbers and transferred them to working memory. Once the information was in working memory you were ready to use the information, so you wrote their phone numbers.

Now, without looking back, write the numbers you were asked to remember earlier. You will probably have difficulty with this task. Since information fades from working memory if you do not work with it, and since you filled your working memory with the phone numbers of your two best friends, you probably cannot write the original numbers. If you had stored the original numbers in long-term memory, you might be able to retrieve them, but the task did not require you to do this. Consequently, they are lost forever.

A number of concepts were demonstrated by this example:

1. Working or short-term memory is activated memory.

2. Working memory has a limited capacity. We can keep a limited amount of information in working memory (i.e., seven pieces of information plus or minus two pieces). These pieces can be of various sizes or comprehensiveness. For example, they may be seven single digits, seven phone numbers, seven sentences, or seven major concepts.

3. The more we cluster or group information into larger related concepts, the more information we can keep in working memory.

4. If we do not actively work with the information in working memory, it will fade rapidly (in about fifteen seconds).

5. We can use various strategies to keep information active in working memory. For example, we can rehearse the information, elaborate on it, create visual images of it, and so on.

6. Information in working memory is easily replaced by new incoming information (e.g., recalling your friends' phone numbers).

7. Information not transferred to long-term memory cannot be retrieved.

8. Information that is stored in long-term memory is sometimes retrievable. How the information is organized in long-term memory affects how easily it can be retrieved.

9. Information from long-term memory is transferred to working memory. Then you can use that information (e.g., writing the phone numbers of your best friends).

Some students with learning and behavior problems have difficulties with tasks requiring them to listen to or look at numbers, pictures, letters, words, or sentences, hold them in working memory, and then recall them (e.g., Brainerd and Reyna, 1991; Howe, Brainerd, and Kingma, 1985; Swanson, 1991; 1996; Torgesen, Rashotte, Greenstein, Houck, and Portes, 1987).

Students with significant reading disabilities have smaller working memory spans than average readers (Swanson and Trahan, 1992). Furthermore, tasks such as reading require integrative hemisphere processing and these students perform differently, not necessarily due to structural differences, but due to dynamic processing differences (Obrzut, 1995).

Long-Term Memory and Schemas

We have already discussed the role that long-term memory plays in learning. Using Figure 2.9 as a reference, we see that *long-term memory* aids us in perceiving incoming stimuli. It provides the context that allows us to use top-down processing when perceiving information (e.g., to perceive the stimuli *THE CAT* even though the visual images of the *H* and the *A* are the same). It helps us fill in the words or speech sounds of a conversation that we do not fully hear because we are at a noisy party. Information is retrieved from long-term memory and transferred to working memory before it can be used to make responses.

If long-term memory plays such an important part in the information processing system, how is it organized? If it has to hold all the information we know, including our store of knowledge about the world, procedural information on how to do numerous skills such as tie shoes and play basketball, and information about our goals and values, how does long-term memory keep all this information straight? Cognitive psychologists do not know just how this vast array of information is organized, but they do have some logical hunches.

According to one theory, schema theory, our knowledge is organized into schemas. *Schemas* can be defined as organized structures of stereotypic knowledge (Schank and Abelson, 1977). They are higher-order cognitive structures that assist in understanding and recalling events and information.

It is hypothesized that we have innumerable schemas or scripts for events and procedures and it is our schemas that allow us to make inferences about the events that happen around us (Rumelhart, 1980; Spiro, 1980).

Read the following short passage about an event John experienced.

John had been waiting all week for Friday evening. He skipped lunch just to get ready for the occasion. At 6:30 P.M. he got in his car and drove to the restaurant. He planned to meet several friends. When he arrived, he got out of his car and waited outside for his friends.

At this point you are probably using a general schema for restaurants. You could answer such questions as "Is John going to eat dinner?" "Will John eat dinner with his friends?" However, you have not been given enough information to utilize a more specific restaurant schema. Now read on to see how your schema is sharpened.

> After a few minutes, John's friends arrived. They entered the restaurant and walked up to the counter. John placed his order first. After everyone ordered, they carried the trays of food to a booth.

How has your schema changed? You should be using a more specific schema, one for fast-food restaurants. Now you can probably answer more specific questions such as "What kind of food did John and his friends probably eat?" "Did John leave a tip?" Utilizing schemas (e.g., our prior knowledge about stereotypic events) allows us to make inferences, thereby filling in the gaps and giving meaning to incoming information. Schemas serve a crucial role in providing an account of how old or prior knowledge interacts with new or incoming information (Anderson, 1977; Rumelhart, 1980; 1985).

The early work in schema theory is usually credited to Bartlett (1932) who, in his book *Remembering,* argued that memory is not simply recalling what one remembers almost in a templatelike fashion, but it is *reconstructive.* In other words, in comprehending and recalling information, our prior knowledge interacts with incoming information, and to some extent it changes the information to fit with our prior knowledge. To verify his premise about schemas, Bartlett had English subjects read and then recall a folktale from another culture immediately after they read it and again at later times.

If you want to join in Bartlett's experiment, read the folktale in Apply the Concept 2.5 and then in several hours, write what you remember about the tale.

Bartlett's subjects showed clear distortions in their memory of the story. These inaccuracies appear to be systematic in that the individuals distorted the folktale to fit with their own cultural stereotypes. Many of the people omitted proper names, unfamiliar details, and hard-to-interpret aspects of the tale.

They made the tale shorter, more coherent, and more consistent with their cultural expectations.

Within and across schemas, concepts or ideas are organized so as to promote understanding and retrieval. Information can be stored in semantic networks composed of concepts and relationships between concepts (Kintsch, 1974; Rumelhart, 1980). Figure 2.11 presents a representation of the concept of *bird.* (Your network for *bird* is probably more extensive than the one presented in this figure.) The closer together the concepts are in the network, the better they serve as cues for each other's recall (Swanson and Cooney, 1996). For example, *wings* should serve as a better recall cue for *bird* than should *two.* A concept does not exist in isolation in semantic memory but is related to other concepts at higher, lower, or the same levels. In the case of *birds,* it could be filed along with *reptiles* and *mammals,* under the superordinate concept of *animals.*

Schemas and semantic networks allow us to organize our knowledge in such a way that we can retrieve information and effectively add new information to long-term memory. They also assist us in determining the relationships among ideas.

Memory that deals with concepts and semantic networks like the ones just described is referred to as *semantic memory.* In contrast, visual and other sensory images of events in one's life are referred to as *episodic memory.* Students with memory difficulties may have good episodic memory, but more difficulty storing and accessing semantic memory. Hence, while they can remember the event, they may struggle to remember the concepts.

Executive Functioning or Metacognition

The specific processes in the information processing system (i.e., attention, perception, working memory, and long-term memory) are controlled or coordinated by what has been referred to as *executive functioning* (see Figure 2.9). In the same way that a business executive has many departments that he or she has to coordinate and many decisions to make regarding how best to use those various departments, the learner has to coordinate his or her various learning processes

APPLY THE CONCEPT 2.5

ACTIVATING SCHEMA

Read the following folktale:

"War of the Ghosts"

One night two young men from Egulac went down to the river to hunt seals, and while they were there it became foggy and calm. Then they heard war-cries, and they thought: "Maybe this is a war-party." They escaped to the shore, and hid behind a log. Now canoes came up, and they heard the noise of paddles, and saw one canoe, and they said: "What do you think? We wish to take you along. We are going up the river to make war on the people."

One of the young men said: "I have not arrows."

"Arrows are in the canoe," they said.

"I will not go along. I might be killed. My relatives do not know where I have gone. But you," he said, turning to the other, "may go with them."

So one of the young men went, but the other returned home.

And the warriors went on up the river to a town on the side of Kalama. The people came down to the water, and they began to fight, and many were killed. But presently the young man heard one of the warriors say: "Quick, let us go home. That Indian has been hit."

Now he thought: "Oh, they are ghosts." He did not feel sick, but they said he had been shot.

So the canoes went back to Egulac, and the young man went ashore to his house, and made a fire. And he told everybody: "Behold, I accompanied the ghosts, and we went to fight. Many of our fellows were killed, and many of those who attacked us were killed. They said I was hit, and I did not feel sick."

He told it all, and then he became quiet. When the sun rose he fell down. Something black came out of his mouth. His face became contorted. The people jumped up and cried.

He was dead.

In an hour or so, write what you remember about this folktale and then compare it to the original passage. Does your retelling differ from the passage? If so, how does it differ? Does your retelling reflect your culture better than the culture depicted in the passage?

Source: R. C. Bartlett, *Remembering* (Cambridge, England: Cambridge University Press, 1932). Reprinted with the permission of Cambridge University Press.

---

and strategies and make decisions regarding learning. For example, as learners, we must decide (1) which stimuli to attend to (e.g., the book we are reading and/or the smell of the apple pie baking); (2) whether to rely more on feature analysis or context and prior knowledge when perceiving information; (3) what memory strategies are most effective for keeping the information active in working memory; and (4) what is an effective and efficient way to store the information so we can retrieve it later. Making decisions allows us to control the learning process.

This executive functioning has also been referred to as metacognition (Brown, 1980; Flavell, 1976). *Metacognition* is generally considered to have two components (Brown, 1980):

1. An awareness of what skills, strategies, and resources are needed to perform a cognitive task
2. The ability to use self-regulatory strategies to monitor the thinking processes and to undertake fix-up strategies when processing is not going smoothly

In many ways, metacognition and executive functioning are similar to the concepts of self-evaluation and self-regulation presented in the section on cognitive behavior modification.

Metacognition and executive functioning require the learner to monitor the effectiveness of his or her learning and, based on feedback, regulate learning by activating task-appropriate strategies.

■ **FIGURE 2.11**   *A Semantic Network for the Concept of "Bird"*

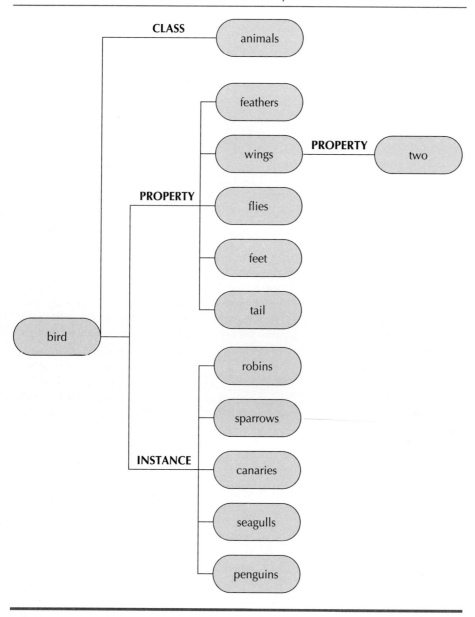

Read the short essay in Apply the Concept 2.6 and see how you use your metacognition.

Students with learning and behavior problems certainly have potential for difficulties with executive functioning or metacognition. For example, the essay you read in Apply the Concept 2.6 was also read by groups of seventh graders, some of whom had reading disabilities and others who were average achievers. They were asked to read the essay to see if it made sense. Although most of the average-

APPLY THE CONCEPT 2.6

COMPREHENSION MONITORING

Read the following short essay:

> There are some things that almost all ants have in common. For example, they are all very strong and can carry objects many times their own weight. Sometimes they go very, very far from their nest to find food. They go so far away that they cannot remember how to go home. So, to help them find their way home, ants have a special way of leaving an invisible trail. Everywhere they go, they put out an invisible chemical from their bodies. This chemical has a special odor. Another thing about ants is they do not have noses to smell with. Ants never get lost (Bos and Filip, 1984, p. 230).

As you read the first part of this essay, you probably read along smoothly and quickly, comprehending the information and confirming that in fact what you are reading makes sense. However, when you read the last couple of lines of the essay, you probably slowed your reading rate, possibly went back and reread, and/or stopped and thought about what you were reading. If these are the types of cognitive strategies in which you engaged, then you were using your executive functioning or meta-cognition to monitor your information processing system.

achieving students recognized the inconsistency, most of the students with learning disabilities reported that there was nothing wrong with the essay (Bos and Filip, 1984). Wong suggests that, because most students with reading disabilities have difficulty with decoding, many of their cognitive resources are allocated to this task, leaving limited resources for comprehension. Others have found similar metacognitive deficits for these students on reading, writing, and math tasks (Cherkes-Julkowski, 1985; Montague and Bos, 1986b; Torgesen, 1985; Swanson, 1996; Swanson and Trahan, 1992; Welch, 1992; Wong, Wong, and Blankinsop, 1989).

Teaching Implications of Information Processing and Schema Theories

Information processing and schema theories have definite educational implications for students with learning and behavior problems. As you read the content chapters in this book, think about how information processing theory helped to shape the instructional techniques. When teaching, think about how you can modify your teaching and the learning environment to facilitate directing a student's attention to the relevant stimuli and his or her perception of the incoming information. For example, teachers

who frequently made suggestions about students using metamemory strategies and gave cues for their use found that the students showed better maintenance and more deliberate use of the strategies than students whose teachers rarely made such suggestions (Lucangeli, Galderisi, and Cornoldi, 1995). What strategies can you teach students so that information can stay active in working memory, and how can you present information to facilitate its storage and organization of long-term memory? How can you teach students to use executive functioning to coordinate the various learning and memory strategies?

Several general implications are:

1. *Provide cues to students so they might be guided to the relevant task(s) or salient features of the task.* For instance, when giving a lecture, provide cues to assist the students in attending to the key points by giving an overview of the lecture, writing important concepts on the board, provide the students with a written outline of the lecture, or teaching the students how to listen and look for behaviors that signal important information (e.g., raised voice, repetition).

2. *Have students study the critical feature differences between stimuli when trying to perceive differences.* For example, highlight the "stick" part of the letters *b* and *d;* provide instances and noninstances when discussing a concept.

3. *Have the students use the context to aid in perception.* Students are not likely to substitute *bog* for *dog* if they are reading a story or sentence about a dog.

4. *Facilitate the activation of schemas and provide labeled experiences.* In this way students can develop adequate schemas and modify their current schemas for better understanding of the concepts being presented in both skill and content area subjects.

5. *Teach students to use specific memory strategies.* These could include association, visualization, chunking, and rehearsal.

6. *Use organization techniques to assist students in organizing their long-term memories* using such content enhancements as semantic maps, relationship charts, and concept diagrams.

7. *Teach students how to be flexible thinkers and to solve problems, thereby encouraging them to use executive functioning.*

SUMMARY

This chapter presents approaches to learning and teaching for guiding the teaching-learning process. The models provide principles that influence the way you, as a teacher, observe, record, interact, and evaluate the teaching-learning process with students.

The first model, operant learning theory and applied behavior analysis, focuses on observed behavior and the antecedents and consequences that control the behavior. In this model the teacher is able to modify the antecedents, by adjusting such variables as the class climate and schedule. The teacher can also increase or maintain desirable behaviors through positive and negative reinforcement, secondary reinforcers, the Premack Principle, shaping, and group contingencies. Through operant learning the teacher is also able to decrease undesirable behaviors by using extinction, differential reinforcement, punishment, and time-out. Teachers can use the principles from operant learning to enhance students' progress through the stages of learning. These include entry, acquisition, proficiency, maintenance, generalization, and application. The teaching-learning process in the operant learning model is highly teacher-directed.

The second model, cognitive behavior modification, utilizes principles from both operant learning theories and cognitive-oriented theories. Key features of cognitive behavior modification interventions are that they include strategy steps, modeling, self-regulation, verbalization, and reflective thinking. Through cognitive behavior modification the student and the teacher have a more interactive role in the teaching-learning process.

The third model, a sociocultural theory of learning, emphasizes the social nature of learning and encourages interactive discussions between students and teachers. In these discussions the teacher is encouraged to use the students' funds of knowledge and to provide the needed support for the student to acquire new strategies, skills, and knowledge.

The fourth model, information processing and schema theories, is a pair of cognitive theories that attempt to explain how information is received, transformed, retrieved, and expressed. Key features of information processing are sensing, sensory store, attention, perception, memory, and executive functioning or metacognition. The information processing model focuses on an interactive role between the teacher and the student, with the concentration on activating prior background knowledge in the student, relating new learning to information the learner already has learned, and maintaining the student as an active learner who thinks about how he or she thinks, studies, and learns.

Throughout the remaining chapters you will see many examples of the principles for teaching and learning that were presented in this chapter. These examples will assist you in understanding how the different approaches to learning and teaching can be applied when interacting with students. In a sense, this chapter provides the theoretical underpinnings for the strategies presented in the subsequent chapters. As you read the subsequent chapters, think about how theory guides the instructional practices and how it will guide your teaching as you work with students experiencing learning and behavior problems.

THINK AND APPLY

— Within the operant learning model, what procedures can be used to increase desirable behavior? Decrease undesirable behavior?

— What are the stages of learning and how can they be applied using the operant learning model?

— What are the common characteristics of most cognitive behavior modification interventions?

— Using principles associated with cognitive behavior modification, design a strategy that one could use to solve subtraction problems with regrouping.

— What implications does a sociocultural perspective have on teaching and learning?

— Why does a sociocultural theory provide particularly relevant support and scaffolds for students who are culturally and linguistically diverse?

— How does long-term memory relate to working memory and perception?

— Using implications from information processing and schema theories, what could you do to assist a student who is having difficulties remembering the information needed to pass an objective social studies test?

Chapter 3

Oral Language

OUTLINE

KEY TOPICS FOR MASTERY

- *The concept that language is a vehicle or tool for communication and that it includes oral and written language as well as sign and gestures*
- *The differences and interrelationships between language comprehension (receptive language) and production (expressive language)*
- *The components of language including content (semantics), form (phonology, morphology, and syntax), and use (pragmatics) and the interrelationships among these components*
- *The development of oral language during the school-age years and the difficulties that students with learning, language, and behavior problems experience with oral language during the school-age years*
- *The twelve general principles for teaching oral language and examples of how to teach each principle*
- *Strategies for teaching content including word-finding ability and using more elaborative language; strategies for teaching form; and strategies for teaching use*
- *The integral relationship between language and culture and strategies for enhancing language development by using the students' cultural backgrounds*
- *The acquisition of basic interpersonal communicative skills and cognitive/academic language proficiency in second-language and dialect learners and its implications for teaching language to students with learning and behavior problems*

 BRIGHT IDEA

> *Turn to page 110 and read Think and Apply.*

Jerry is a handsome second grader who is good at sports. He seems bright until you hear him talk. Whether he is having a conversation with you or trying to read, he has difficulty thinking of the right words. Yesterday he was trying to describe the work that he and his dad had done on his go-cart. He could not think of the words *screwdriver, hammer, sand, wheels, axle, steering wheel,* and *engine.* Sometimes he attempted to describe what he was trying to say; for example, when he could not think of *screwdriver,* he said, "It's the thing you use to put in things that are kind of like nails." Sometimes he can only think of a word that is similar to the word he is trying to say; for example, "I was using the hitter to hit some

nails." Jerry also has trouble remembering words when he reads. He does not remember simple sight words and consequently has to resort to attempting to sound out the words. Often the words he cannot remember are not phonetic (e.g., *come, are, was, very*), so his strategy is only somewhat useful. Jerry is currently in a second grade classroom but he receives speech and language therapy for his language problems and services from the special education teacher for his reading difficulties.

Carmen is in eighth grade. If you just listen to Carmen, you would not necessarily recognize that she has a language problem. Her vocabulary is adequate for a student her age, and she uses fairly sophisticated sentences. But Carmen's language frequently seems to get her in trouble. Carmen is growing up in a tough neighborhood, and she is bused across town. She has difficulty switching her language style to match this new context. She continues to use her "street language," resulting in the interpretation that she is both arrogant and disrespectful to teachers. Carmen also has other problems using language effectively. She has difficulty determining when the listener is not understanding what she is trying to explain. Instead of reexplaining her point, she continues with her description or explanation. When the listener asks her to clarify a point, Carmen implies the listener is stupid. She also fails to take turns easily during conversations. She either monopolizes the conversation or expects the other person to do all the talking while she gives little feedback to let the other person know that she is listening. Consequently, Carmen is perceived as a student with behavior problems, although there is no indication of any serious emotional problems. She sees her counselor once a week and has a special education English class. In the last several months, the speech/language pathologist has been consulting with the special education teacher and counselor concerning Carmen. They are working with Carmen to help her use language more effectively and to vary it across contexts. It will be interesting to see if this will help to eliminate some of the social and behavior problems Carmen is currently experiencing.

Teddy is a language-delayed child. He started talking at age three and a half, and now, as a third grader, his language seems more like that of a first grader. He began receiving speech and language therapy at age four. Although he is currently placed in a self-contained class for students with learning disabilities, he receives speech and language therapy for thirty minutes, four days a week. Teddy is delayed in all aspects of language. His vocabulary is limited, he uses simple sentence patterns, and he uses language primarily to obtain information and attention and to inform others of his needs. He rarely initiates a conversation, but he will carry on a conversation if the other person takes the lead. Mrs. Borman, his self-contained special education teacher, is working closely with the speech/language patholo-

gist to help ensure that Teddy is receiving the structured language programming he needs throughout the school day. One of Mrs. Borman's roles in this programming is to provide Teddy with many opportunities to practice and receive feedback on the skills he is learning in speech/language therapy.

As special education teachers, we will undoubtedly work with students like Jerry, Carmen, and Teddy. To assist these students in developing effective language and communication skills, we need to understand the *content of language instruction* and *strategies for teaching language.*

CONTENT OF LANGUAGE INSTRUCTION

Language is a vehicle for communicating our ideas, beliefs, and needs. It is "a code whereby ideas about the world are represented through a conventional system of arbitrary signals for communication" (Bloom and Lahey, 1978, p. 4). Language allows us to share our knowledge with others and, as discussed in Chapter Two, organize the knowledge in our long-term memory so that we can retrieve it and use it to communicate.

The major purpose for language is communication. Both in school and in our society language is a powerful resource. We use language to:

— Maintain contact with others
— Gain information
— Give information
— Persuade
— Accomplish goals
— Monitor our own behavior when we talk to ourselves

Language functions as an integral part of the communication process because it allows us to represent ideas by using a conventional code.

A person's ability to understand what is being communicated is referred to as *comprehension* or *receptive language,* whereas a person's ability to convey the intended message is referred to as *production* or *expressive language.* A basic assumption for the communication process to be effective is that both the speaker and the listener use the same code and know the same rules of language. You have probably had the experience of trying to explain a need to someone who speaks a different language. You probably found yourself using many more gestures than usual. This is because although your listener could not understand your verbal communication code, he or she could understand your nonverbal code (gestures).

Some students with learning and behavior problems experience developmental delays in *comprehension* or receptive language. They frequently ask for information to be repeated or clarified. In school these students have difficulties with:

— Following directions
— Understanding the meaning of concepts (particularly temporal and spatial concepts and technical or abstract concepts)
— Seeing relationships among concepts
— Understanding humor and figurative language
— Understanding multiple meanings
— Understanding less common and irregular verb tenses
— Understanding compound and complex sentences
— Realizing they are not understanding what is being said

Students with learning and behavior problems also have delays in *production* or expressive language. Sometimes these students choose not to communicate as frequently as other students. Students with delays in expressive language have difficulty:

— Using correct grammar
— Using compound and complex sentences
— Thinking of the right word to convey the concept (*word finding*)
— Discussing abstract, temporal, or spatial concepts
— Changing the communication style to fit various social contexts
— Providing enough information to the listener (e.g., starting a conversation with, "He took it to

the fair," when *he* and *it* have not been previously identified)
— Maintaining the topic during a conversation
— Repairing communication breakdowns

Although some students with learning and behavior problems have difficulty with both receptive and expressive language, other students experience difficulty primarily with expressive language. Students who have only expressive language difficulties generally understand much more than they are able to communicate.

Relationship of Oral and Written Communication

We use language when we read and write and when we communicate orally. In written communication, the writer is similar to the speaker in that the person is responsible for sending the message. The reader is similar to the listener, whose job it is to interpret or construct the message. The relationship of speaking and listening to writing and reading is presented in Figure 3.1. Since both oral and written communication are language based, if a student is having difficulty in oral communication (e.g., understanding figurative language), he or she will also have difficulty in written communication. For example, research consistently tells us that vocabulary knowledge is one of the best predictors of reading achievement (Wiig and Secord, 1994). However, there are important differences between oral and written communication (Bunce, 1993). For example, in oral language there is a dynamic shifting between roles of the speaker and listener. A speaker can obtain immediate feedback from a listener. Consequently, the speaker can adjust the way in which the message is expressed (e.g., lower the vocabulary level, reexplain, or restate) more easily than the author. This chapter presents methods for teaching students who have difficulty with oral communication; the next three chapters describe ways for teaching students who have difficulty with written communication (reading and writing). Some of the instructional ideas will be similar because of the underlying language base of both oral and written communication. In some instances

■ **FIGURE 3.1**   *Modes of Communication*

A Model of the Communication Process

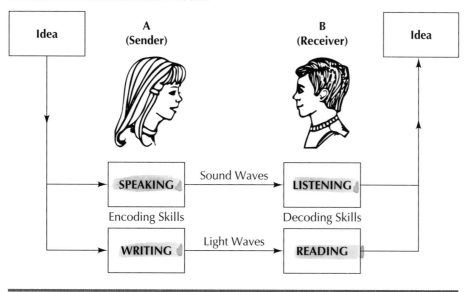

Source: Janet Lerner, *Learning Disabilities: Theories, Diagnosis, and Teaching Strategies,* 4th ed.
(Boston: Houghton Mifflin, 1985), p. 320. Adapted by permission.

an instructional strategy that is suggested as a reading comprehension strategy can also be used as a listening or writing strategy (e.g., teaching students to ask themselves the questions of Who, What, When, Where, Why, and How as they read, write, or listen). We encourage you to keep in mind the close relationship of oral and written communication as you read the next four chapters.

Components of Language

The content of language instruction for students with learning and behavior problems focuses on teaching the language code, the rules of the code, and how to use the code to communicate. To help us understand language so that we can more effectively plan the content of language instruction, we will consider several components of language.

Content

Content, also called *semantics,* refers to the ideas or concepts we are communicating. Elsa can communi-cate her desire for two chocolate chip cookies in numerous ways. For example, she can say, "I want two chocolate chip cookies," or "Me want choc-chip cookies" (while pointing to the cookie jar and then holding up two fingers). In both cases, the content or ideas are the same.

When we teach content, we are teaching concepts and helping students learn the labels (vocabulary) for those concepts. When a young child asks such questions as "What's that?" or "What are you doing?" we often respond by giving the label for the object (e.g., spoon, blanket, shirt) or the action (i.e., stirring, making the bed, ironing). In this way we are teaching the labels for the ideas or concepts.

We are also teaching content when we help students see the relationships among the ideas or concepts. The diagram or semantic network of the concept of "bird," as depicted in Figure 2.13, is one way to demonstrate how ideas are related. In this case, we used a network that represented the concept of "bird" in terms of its class, properties, and examples. Much of education, whether teaching about

fruits and vegetables in primary grades or the characteristics of capitalism and communism in high
school, centers on teaching about ideas, the relationships among the ideas, and the vocabulary that labels
the ideas (Anders and Bos, 1986; Bunce, 1993; Lenz
and Bulgren, 1995; Reyes and Bos, 1997).

Form

Form refers to the structure and sound of language.
In the example of Elsa wanting two chocolate chip
cookies, two different forms were presented for the
underlying meaning of the message. Form is usually
further divided into phonology, morphology, and
syntax.

Phonology.   *Phones* are the actual sounds produced
by speakers. *Phonemes* are the smallest linguistic
units of sound that can signal a meaning difference.
In the English language there are approximately
forty-five phonemes or speech sounds that are classified as either vowels or consonants. Learning the
speech sounds and their relationships to the written
letters can help students identify unknown words
when they read (Bradley and Bryant, 1985; Mc-
Guinness, McGuinness, and Donohue, 1995; Wagner,
Torgensen, and Rashotte, 1994). *Phonology* refers to
the rules for combining and patterning phonemes
within the language. Phonology also includes the
control of vocal features (timing, frequency, duration) that influence the meaning we express when
talking. Without changing any words, we can vary
the underlying meaning of a sentence simply by the
way we change our voice (e.g., intonation, pitch, and
stress). For example, try saying, "I like *that?*" and "I
like that." Depending on the intonation, stress, and
pitch, the first statement can mean "I don't like that"
and the second one can mean "I do like that."

Morphology.   While phonology focuses on sounds,
morphology focuses on the rule system that governs
the structure of words and word forms. While
phonemes are the smallest sound units, *morphemes*
are the smallest unit of language that convey meaning. There are two different kinds of morphemes:
root words or words that can stand alone (e.g., cat,
run, pretty, small, inside), and affixes (prefixes, suffixes, and inflectional endings) that are added to
words that change the meaning of the words (e.g.,
cat*s*, *re*run, small*est*, *trans*forma*tion*).

Helping elementary and secondary students
learn the various affixes and their meanings can assist them in decoding words, determining the meaning of words, and spelling. For example, students
who do not recognize or know the meaning of the
word *predetermination* can break it into the root
word *determine* (to decide), the prefix *pre* (before),
and the suffix *tion* (denoting action in a noun). Then
the students can decode or spell the word and generate the meaning of *predetermination* as a decision
made in advance.

Developmentally, inflectional endings are the
easiest to learn, followed by suffixes, and then prefixes (Owens, 1995; Rubin, 1988). While inflectional
endings can be taught through conversational milieu,
suffix and prefixes usually require more formal instruction in both oral and written form (Moats,
1995). The most frequently used prefixes in American English are *un–, in–, dis–,* and *non–*. Table 3.1
presents some common prefixes, suffixes, and inflectional endings with their meanings and several
examples. As you can see from the table, definitions
of prefixes and suffixes are sometimes vague. Although only one or two definitions are provided,
some affixes have four or more definitions (Gunning,
1996). Teaching this information (or a simplified list
for elementary-aged students) can assist students in
understanding and learning new vocabulary. To give
students a sense of the meanings, provide experiences with several examples.

Syntax.   *Syntax* refers to the order of words in sentences and the rules for determining the order. Just as
phonemes combine to form words, words combine to
form phrases and sentences. In the same way that
rules determine how phonemes can be combined,
rules also determine how words can be combined.
The basic syntactical structure for English is subject
+ verb + object (e.g., Mike eats cereal).

The rules for combining words vary across languages. For example, in English, adjectives almost
always precede the noun they modify (e.g., a deli-

■ **TABLE 3.1**   *Common Inflectional Endings, Prefixes, and Suffixes*

Common Forms	Meanings	Examples
	Inflectional Endings	
–ed	notes past tense on verbs	helped, studied
–ing	notes present progressive on verbs	helping, studying
–s	notes third person singular on verbs	he helps, she studies
–s	notes plurals on nouns	cats, houses
–'s	notes possessive	Jon's, cat's
–er	notes comparative (between two)	larger, younger
–est	notes superlative (among more than two)	largest, youngest
	Prefixes	
ante–	before, front	antecedent, anterior
anti–	against	antifreeze, antitoxin
bi–	two	bicycle, bisect
co–	with, together	coworker, cooperate
de–	down, remove, reduce do the opposite	decent, dethrone, devalue, deactivate
dis–	opposite	distrust, distaste
en–	to cover, to cause to be	encompass, enslave
ex–	former, from	expatriate, explain
hyper–	above, more, excessive	hyperactive, hyperventilate
hypo–	below, less	hypoactive, hypodermic
im–	not, in, into	impatient, implant
in–	not, in, into	incomplete, inclusion
inter–	between, together	interact, intervene
ir–	not, into	irreversible
mis–	wrong	miscalculate
non–	not	nonstop
out–	beyond, exceeds	outlast, outside
pre–	before, in front of	preface, precaution
pro–	before, in front of, in favor of	proceed, proactive
re–	again, backward motion	repeat, rewind
semi–	half	semifinalist
sub–	under, less than	subordinate, subtitle
super–	above, superior	superordinate
trans–	across, beyond	transportation
un–	not	unlucky, unclear
	Suffixes	
–able	capable of, tendency to	dependable
–age	result of action or place	breakage, orphanage
–al	pertaining to	personal
–ance	changing an action to a state	hindrance
–ation	changing an action to a state	determination
–ant	one who (occupation)	accountant, attendant
–en	noting action from an adjective	harden, loosen

(continued)

TABLE 3.1   *Continued*

Common Forms	*Meanings*	*Examples*
	Suffixes	
–ence	changing an action to a state	dependence, reference
–er	notes occupation or type of person	lawyer, writer, foreigner
–ful	full of	bountiful, joyful
–fy	to make	magnify, identify
–ible	capable of, tendency to	credible, collectible
–ish	belonging to, characteristic of	Finnish, greenish
–ist	one who (occupation)	artist, biologist
–ive	changes action to characteristic or tendency	creative, active
–less	unable to, without	harmless, thoughtless
–ly	denotes adverbs	loudly, friendly
–ment	result of an action (noun)	entertainment, excitement
–ness	quality, state of being	happiness, deafness
–or	notes occupation or type of person	actor, doctor
–ous	full of, having	victorious, harmonious
–some	quality or state	handsome, bothersome
–tion	changing an action to a state	confusion,
–ward	turning to	homeward, wayward
–y	characterized by, inclined to	dirty, sleepy

cious apple), whereas in Spanish, adjectives generally follow the noun they modify (e.g., *una manzana deliciosa*—an apple delicious).

Language Use

Language use or pragmatics grows significantly during the school-age years (Owens, 1995; Reed, 1994). *Pragmatics* refers to the purposes or functions of communication or how we use language to communicate (Roberts and Crais, 1989). During the school years students become quite adept in using communication for a variety of functions. During later school years students use language proficiently in figurative language, sarcasm, jokes, and multiple meanings (Schultz, 1974). Students also learn to vary their communication style or *register* based on the listener's characteristics and knowledge concerning the topic. By the age of thirteen, students can switch from peer register to adult register depending on the person with whom they are talking, and from formal register to an informal register depending on the setting and circumstances (McKinley and Larson, 1991;

Owens, 1995). Pragmatics for students in middle school is an important aspect of functioning within the classroom, because pragmatic skills are critical to academic progress and in building peer relationships (Brice and Montgomery, 1996).

The way a speaker uses language will also be influenced by the knowledge the speaker thinks the listener has about the topic being discussed. If you are describing how to hang a picture on a wall, your language is quite different if the listener is familiar with a plastic anchor and screw. The manner in which a topic is introduced, maintained, and changes, as well as how we reference topics, is governed by pragmatic rules. Students learning English as a second language and bilingual students with communication disorders may need explicit instruction in pragmatics.

Formalist views of language have assumed that language is a composite of various rule systems consisting of semantics, phonology, morphology, syntax, and pragmatics. However, more recent views of language and language intervention have highlighted language as a social tool; and as such, pragmatics is viewed as the overall organizing aspect of language (Owens, 1995; Prutting 1982). This model (see Figure 3.2) has direct implications for language intervention both in terms of targets for intervention and methods of intervention. An approach in which pragmatics is the overall organizing aspect calls for an interactive, conversational approach to teaching and one that mirrors the environment in which the language is to be used (Owens, 1995). This has been referred to as a *functional* or *holistic approach* to language intervention (Muma, 1986).

School-Age Language Development and Difficulties

Knowing how language develops during the school-age years and what difficulties students with learning and behavior problems demonstrate during these years will further help us make decisions concerning the content and focus of language instruction.

Much of the research in language development has focused on the preschool child. Between the ages of zero to five, most children become amazingly facile with their language and communication (Brown, 1973; deVilliers and deVilliers, 1978; Owens, 1995). Due to the quantity and quality of development that occurs during this period, the preschool child has been the center of focus for most language researchers. However, during the last twenty years there has been a growing interest in the language development that takes place during the school years (Nippold, 1993; Wallach and Miller, 1988; Wiig and Secord, 1994) and in the difficulties that students encounter with language in school settings (Bashir and Scavuzzo, 1992; Bunce, 1993; Damico and Simon, 1993; Wiig, 1992). Bashir and Scavuzzo (1992) summarized the longitudinal research that has studied school-aged children who have language disorders in the preschool years and noted: (1) these children show changes in the type and severity of their language problems during the school-age years; (2) the acquisition of language forms is the same as for non-disordered children but occurs more slowly; (3) language problems persist for many of these children throughout childhood and adolescence; and (4) additional language problems

■ **FIGURE 3.2**   *Components of Language from a Functionalist Perspective*

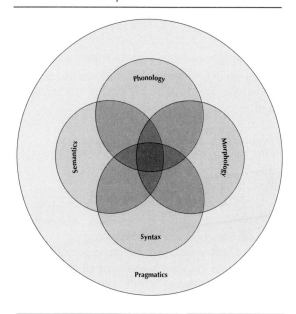

may develop in middle school when children are required to understand or produce more complex language, develop and understand narratives and expository text structures, and use language for higher-order thinking skills such as persuasion and interpretation.

Although not enough research is available to support a comprehensive scope and sequence for school-age language development, there is enough information to assist us in planning the content of language instruction.

Knowing about school-age language development is particularly important for teachers of students who have learning and behavior problems. There is growing evidence to suggest that these students have mild to moderate language problems (Gerber, 1993; Nelson, 1993; Rubin, Patterson, and Kantor, 1991; Sanger, Maag, and Shapera, 1994; Wallach, 1984; Wiig and Semel, 1984; Wiig and Wilson, 1994). The largest subgroup of students with learning disabilities are those who experience language difficulties (Simon, 1985; Wiig and Secord, 1994).

Let's examine the development of content, form, and use at the school-age level and the difficulties that students with learning and behavior problems demonstrate.

Content

During the school-age period, children increase the size of their vocabularies and their ability to understand and talk about abstract concepts.

Vocabulary Growth. During the school years, one of the areas in which students demonstrate the greatest amount of growth is vocabulary. When students enter school their estimated speaking vocabulary is about 2,500 words (Owens, 1995). In comparison, when technical words are discounted, average adult speakers converse in everyday conversation using about 10,000 words, and an estimated 60,000 to 80,000 words are known and used by the average high-school graduate (Carroll, 1964). School provides students with the opportunities to listen, read, and learn, thus increasing their vocabularies. Even math, which is often considered less language-based than social studies and science, contains a significant number of concepts and words to learn (e.g., subtract, estimate, rational number, trapezoid).

There is also an increase in the breadth and specificity of meanings. For example, the word *bird* to a preschooler may refer to animals that fly. However, most children later learn a whole set of specific vocabulary that defines different types of birds and their characteristics. The semantic network that was depicted in Figure 2.11 (page 66) grows more and more complex and more interrelated as a student's knowledge of birds increases.

During school-age years, students' ability to understand and organize abstract concepts increases significantly (Anglin, 1970; Wiig and Secord, 1994). This results in the ability to group words by such abstract features as animate or inanimate, spatial (location) or temporal (time) relationships, and so on. For example, in learning about fossils, students learn to simultaneously classify different types of fossils (e.g., trilobites, crinoids, brachiopods) according to plant/animal, extinct/not extinct, and location (e.g., sea, lake, or land).

Multiple meanings of many common words are acquired during the school-age years (Menyuk, 1971; Wiig and Secord, 1994). For example, *bank* has several meanings and can function as both a noun and verb:

Lou sat on the *bank* fishing.
You can *bank* on him to be there.
Put your money in the *bank* for now.

Students with learning and behavior problems generally have vocabularies that are more limited, and their word meanings are generally more concrete and less flexible (Gerber, 1993; Wiig and Secord, 1994). For example, in teaching a group of seventh-grade students with learning disabilities about fossils, we found the students sometimes had difficulty considering three different characteristics of fossils simultaneously (Bos and Anders, 1990a). Questions such as "Which fossils are extinct sea animals?" required them to juggle too much information. In comparison, the students could easily answer questions in which they had to deal with only one characteristic at a time, for example, "Which fossils live in the sea?" "Which fossils are animals?" and "Which fossils are extinct?"

These students also have greater difficulty understanding that words can have multiple meanings and knowing which meaning to apply. In the question, "Was the *fare* that you paid for your taxi ride to the *fair* a *fair* price?" students are required to have and use several different meanings for the word *fair.*

Figurative Language. Students also develop greater understanding and ability to use figurative language. *Figurative language* represents abstract concepts and usually requires an inferential rather than literal interpretation. Figurative language allows students to use language in truly creative ways (Owens, 1995). The primary types of figurative language include:

— *Idioms* (It is raining cats and dogs.)
— *Metaphors* (She had her eagle-eye watching for him.)
— *Similes* (He ran like a frightened rabbit.)
— *Proverbs* (The early bird catches the worm.)

Students with language disorders and other disabilities, and students who are from other cultures or who have English as their second language, tend to have difficulty with figurative language. Yet figurative language, particularly idioms, is used frequently in the classroom. Classroom research has shown that teachers use idioms in approximately 11 percent of their utterances, while third- to eighth-grade reading programs contain idioms in approximately 6.7 percent of their sentences (Lazar, Warr-Leeper, Nicholson, and Johnson, 1989). Table 3.2 presents some common American English idioms. For students with

language disorders and for second language learners, discussing and using these idioms and adding to the list can assist them in improving their understanding and use of the English language.

Word Retrieval. Some students with learning and behavior problems also experience difficulties with *word retrieval* or *word finding* (German, 1987, 1992; McGregor and Leonard, 1989). A word retrieval problem is like having the word on the tip of your tongue but not being able to think of it. The following dialogue presents a conversation between two

---

■ **TABLE 3.2** *Common American English Idioms*

Animals
a bull in a china shop
as stubborn as a mule
going to the dogs
playing possum
a fly in the ointment
clinging like a leech
grinning like a Cheshire cat

Body Parts
on the tip of my tongue
raised eyebrows
turn the other cheek
put your best foot forward
turn heads

Clothing
dressed to kill
hot under the collar
wear the pants in the family
fit like a glove
strait laced

Colors
grey area
once in a blue moon
tickled pink
has a yellow streak

red-letter day
true blue

Games and Sports
ace up my sleeve
cards are stacked against me
got lost in the shuffle
keep your head above water
paddle your own canoe
ballpark figure
get to first base
keep the ball rolling
on the rebound

Foods
eat crow
humble pie
that takes the cake
a finger in every pie
in a jam

Plants
heard it through the grapevine
resting on his laurels
shrinking violet
no bed of roses
shaking like a leaf
withered on the vine

Tools and Work
bury the hatchet
has an axe to grind
hit the nail on the head
jockey for position
throw a monkey wrench into it
doctor the books
has a screw loose
hit the roof
nursing his wounds
sober as a judge

Vehicles
fix your wagon
like ships passing in the night
on the wagon
don't rock the boat
missed the boat
take a back seat

Weather
calm before the storm
haven't the foggiest
steal her thunder
come rain or shine
right as rain
throw caution to the wind

Reprinted with permission from R. E. Owens, Jr. (1995). *Language Disorders: A Functional Approach to Assessment and Intervention* (2nd ed., p. 347). Boston: Allyn and Bacon. Compiled from Boatner, Gates, and Makkai (1975); Clark (1990); Gibbs (1987); Gulland and Hinds-Howell (1986); Kirkpatrick and Schwarz (1982); Palmatier and Ray (1989).

third-grade students—one with normal language and the other with word retrieval problems.

Setting: Third-grade classroom
  Topic: Discussion about how to make an Easter basket

Susan: Are you going to make, uh, make, uh . . . one of these things (pointing to the Easter basket on the bookshelf)?
  Cori: Oh, you mean an Easter basket?
Susan: Yeah, an Easter basket.
  Cori: Sure, I'd like to but I'm not sure how to do it. Can you help me?
Susan: Yeah, first you'll need some, uh, some, uh, the things you cut with, you know. . . .
  Cori: Scissors.
Susan: Yeah, and some paper and the thing you use to stick things together with.
  Cori: Tape?
Susan: No, uh, uh, sticky stuff.
  Cori: Oh, well let's get the stuff we need.
Susan: Let's go to, uh, uh, the shelf, uh, where you get, you know, the stuff to cut up.
  Cori: Yeah, the paper, and let's also get the glue.

It is obvious from the conversation that both students were frustrated by the communication process. Susan's language is filled with indefinite words ("thing") ("stuff"), circumlocutions ("The things you cut with"), and fillers ("Let's go to, uh, the shelf, um, where you get, you know, the stuff to cut up"). At first, students like Susan may seem very talkative because of their overuse of descriptions, circumlocutions, and fillers (Swafford and Reed, 1986); however, after listening for a while, their language seems empty of information.

Word retrieval or word finding problems can result from two possible sources (Kail and Leonard, 1986). One source is with the storage, in that the student's understanding is not elaborate. In other words, the semantic network is not well developed and the meaning is shallow (German, 1992). For example, when a student's semantic network for the concept *bird* (see Figure 2.11, page 66) is well developed it will be easier to retrieve the word than if the semantic network is limited and the word has been learned

in isolation. Therefore, in assisting students it will be important to help them develop more elaborated understandings of concepts. A second source of word finding problems is with the retrieval or search and recovery of the word. In this case, teaching and providing cues (it's what you ride; bread and _____ ; it's a type of bird) can assist in retrieval (Nippold, 1992; Wiig and Semel, 1984). Students with learning and behavior problems may have difficulty with word storage problems, word retrieval problems, or both (German, 1992).

Form

During the school-age years, students continue to grow in the ability to use more complex sentence structures (Nippold, 1993; Scott and Stokes, 1995). Although by age five most students understand and generate basic sentences, first graders produce sentences that are neither completely grammatical (*He'll might go to jail*) nor reflect the syntactical complexities of the English language. Table 3.3 presents the sequence for selected syntactical structures (Carrow, 1973). Some of the most difficult structures require the use of complex sentences and cohesive devices such as causals (*because*), conditionals (*if*), and enabling relationships (*so that*).

Another later-developing sentence structure involves passive construction (*The boy is chased by the dog*), which is usually not established until ages five to seven (Chomsky, 1969; Owens, 1995). What makes older students' language different from younger students in terms of form is the new arrangements and increasingly complex combinations of basic forms (Scott and Stokes, 1995).

As sentence complexity increases, so does the average length of sentences. Yet it is important to know that mature language still has some grammatical errors, false starts, hesitations, and revisions. Table 3.4 demonstrates the growth in the number of words per sentence or communication unit. As evident in Table 3.4, spoken sentence length matches chronological age (i.e., an eight-year-old student's sentences are, on the average, eight words long) until the age of approximately nine years, when the growth curve begins to slow. By high school, adolescents' conversational utterances average ten to

■ **TABLE 3.3** *Developmental Sequence for Comprehension of Sentence Types*

Syntactic Structure	Sentence	Age of Comprehension		
		By 75%		By 90%
Simple imperative	Go!	4–6*	to	6–0 years
Negative imperative	Don't cross!	5–6	to	7–0+ years
Active declarative				
Regular noun and present progressive	The girl is jumping.	3–0	to	3–0 years
Irregular noun and present progressive	The sheep is eating.	6–6	to	7–0 years
Past tense	The man painted the house.	5–6	to	7–0+ years
Past participle	The lion has eaten.	6–0	to	7–0+ years
Future	He will hit the ball.	7–0	to	7–0+ years
Reversible	The car bumps the train.	6–6	to	7–0+ years
Perfective	The man has been cutting trees.	7–0+	to	7–0+ years
Interrogative				
Who . . .	Who is by the table?	3–0	to	3–0 years
What . . .	What do we eat?	3–6	to	5–0 years
When . . .	When do you sleep?	3–6	to	5–6 years
Negation				
Explicit	The girl isn't running.	5–6	to	7–0+ years
Inherent	These two are different.	6–6	to	7–0+ years
Reversible passive	The boy is chased by the dog.	5–6	to	6–0 years
Conjunction				
If . . .	If you're the teacher, point to the dog; if not, point to the bear.	7–0+	to	7–0+ years
. . . then	Look at the third picture; then point to the baby of his animal.	7–0+	to	7–0+ years
neither . . . nor	Find the one that is neither the ball nor the table.	7–0+	to	7–0+ years

*4–6 = 4 years, 6 months

twelve words (Scott and Stokes, 1995). Average sentence length, however, is consistently shorter in conversational discourse than in narrative discourse (Leadholm and Miller, 1992).

Children also continue to increase in their ability to use inflectional endings, suffixes, prefixes, and irregular verbs. Table 3.5 presents the order of and age ranges for the acquisition of selected features. Students

■ **TABLE 3.4** *Average Number of Words per Communication Unit (mean)*

Grade	High Group	Random Group	Low Group
1	7.91	6.88	5.91
2	8.10	7.56	6.65
3	8.38	7.62	7.08
4	9.28	9.00	7.55
5	9.59	8.82	7.90
6	10.32	9.82	8.57
7	11.14	9.75	9.01
8	11.59	10.71	9.52
9	11.73	10.96	9.26
10	12.34	10.68	9.41
11	13.00	11.17	10.18
12	12.84	11.70	10.65

Source: W. Loban. *Language Development: Kindergarten through Grade Twelve,* Res. Report #18 (Urbana, Ill.: National Council of Teachers of English, 1976), p. 27. Reprinted by permission of the publisher.

with language problems are slower to develop advanced syntactic structures, and these delays are most evident in the elementary grades (Owens, 1995).

Use

The area of most important linguistic growth during the school-age years is language use or pragmatics (Nippold, 1993; Owens, 1995). During the school years the child becomes quite adept in using communication for a variety of functions. During later school years students become proficient in using language in sarcasm, jokes, and double meanings (Schultz, 1974). Throughout the schooling years students become more empathetic toward the listener and able to understand a variety of perspectives. Older children can vary their communication style or *register* in that they are much more aware of and take into account the listener's knowledge concerning a topic and the communication context (Eckert, 1990; Krauss and Glucksberg, 1967).

■ **TABLE 3.5** *Development of Word Formation Rules and Irregular Verbs*

Word Formation Rules and Irregular Verbs	Age Range (in Years–Months)
Regular noun plurals (balls, chairs)	3–6 to 7–0+
Present progressive tense (running)	3–0 to 3–6
Present progressive tense (going)	3–6 to 5–6
Adjective forms	
Comparative (smaller, taller)	4–0 to 5–0
Superlative (shortest, tallest)	3–0 to 3–6
Noun derivation	
–er (hitter, painter, farmer)	3–6 to 6–6
–man (fisherman)	5–6 to 6–0
–ist (artist, bicyclist)	6–6 to 7–0+
Adverbial derivation (easily, gently)	7–0+
Irregular verbs	
went	4–6 to 5–0
broke, fell, took, came, made, sat, threw	5–0 to 6–0
bit, cut, drive, fed, ran, wrote, read, rode	6–0 to 7–0
drank, drew, hid, rang, slept, swam	7–0 to 8–0
caught, hung, left, built, sent, shook	8–0 to 9–0

Source: Adapted from E. Carrow, (1973), *Test of Auditory Comprehension of Language.* Austin, TX. Urban Research Group; K. Shipley, M. Maddox, and J. Driver (1991). "Children's development of irregular past tense verb forms." *Language, Speech, and Hearing Services in Schools, 22,* 115–112; E. H. Wiig and E. Semel (1984). *Language Assessment and Intervention for the Learning Disabled* (2nd ed.). Columbus, OH: Merrill.

According to White (1975), young school-age children use language to:

— Gain and hold adult attention in a socially acceptable manner.
— Use others, when appropriate, as resources for assistance or information.
— Express affection or hostility and anger appropriately.
— Direct and follow peers.
— Compete with peers in storytelling and boasts.
— Express pride in himself or herself and in personal accomplishments.
— Role play.

By adolescence, students reflect communicative competence (Fujiki, Brinton, and Todd, 1995; Owens, 1995; Wiig and Semel, 1984) in that they can:

— Express positive and negative feelings and reactions to others.
— Present, understand, and respond to information in spoken messages related to persons, objects, events, or processes that are not immediately visible.
— Take the role of another person.
— Understand and present complex messages.
— Adapt messages to the needs of others.
— Based on prior experience, approach verbal interactions with expectations of what to say and how to say it.
— Select different forms for their messages based on the age, status, and reactions of the listeners.
— Use sarcasm and double meanings.
— Make deliberate use of metaphors.

Some students with learning and behavior disorders also experience difficulties with language *use* or pragmatics. The following dialogue demonstrates how Brice, an adolescent with behavior disorders and subsequent learning problems, has difficulty using language effectively in a conversation with a peer. He tends to switch topics (lack of topic maintenance), does not provide enough context for his listener, does not provide adequate referents for his

pronouns, and does not respond to his listener's requests for clarification.

Setting: Computer Lab
Topic: Brice is explaining to Reid how to play a computer game

Brice: Did you get in trouble for last night?
Reid: What do you mean for last night?
Brice: You know, for what you did.
Reid: I'm not sure what you are talking about.
Brice: Want to learn how to play Chopperlifter?
Reid: Yeah, I guess, but what about last night?
Brice: Well, one thing you do is put it in the slot and turn on the computer.
Reid: What thing? Do you mean the disk?
Brice: Sure I do. Now watch. (Brice boots the disk and selects Chopperlifter from a game menu.) You got to take it and go pick up the men.
Reid: You mean the helicopter?
Brice: Yeah, aren't you listening?
Reid: Yeah, but you're not telling me enough about the game.
Brice: Yes I am. You're just like my brother, you don't listen.
Reid: I'm not going to put up with this. I'll see you around.

Although not reflected in his language sample, Brice also has difficulty varying his language for different audiences. Like other students with pragmatic language problems (Nelson, 1993; Sanger, Maag, and Shapera, 1994), he sometimes sounds disrespectful to adults because he does not vary his language to suit different speakers or speaking environments. Finally, Brice and other students with pragmatic language difficulties tend to misinterpret emotions or meanings indicated by nonverbal communication, including facial expressions and body language, more frequently than their normal peers (Fujiki, et al., 1996; Giddan, Bade, Rickenberg, and Ryley, 1995; McDonough, 1989).

However, it is important to remember that content, form, and use are related. Sometimes students who appear to have difficulties with language use have these difficulties because of limited content and form. For these students, it would be important to focus instruction in the areas of content and form and see if language use automatically improves.

Conclusion

Even though students enter school with many language skills already mastered, there are still many skills that develop during the school years. Students' vocabulary grows significantly in breadth, size, and abstractness. They learn to use and control more difficult sentence structures such as compound, complex, and passive sentences, and they learn how to use figurative language, prefixes, suffixes, and inflectional endings. Students' uses for language expand and their ability to communicate increases as they become more aware of the listener and his or her needs in the communication process. In short, language development in the areas of content, form, and use increases measurably during the school-age years. Whereas this process happens almost automatically for most students because of the opportunities that school and expanding environments afford for learning language, students with learning and behavior problems are often delayed in this development and require more explicit instruction. We will now focus on the procedures for language instruction.

PROCEDURES FOR LANGUAGE INSTRUCTION

In educating students with learning and behavior problems, we have traditionally focused on teaching academic skills and have placed less emphasis on the development of oral language skills. However, it is clear that language continues to develop during the school-age years and that students with learning and behavior problems evidence difficulties in oral language that affect oral as well as written communication. Let's look at some general principles and procedures for teaching oral language skills to these students.

General Procedures for Teaching Oral Language

Opportunities for teaching oral language abound in the school setting. When we teach students new concepts and vocabulary in content area subjects we are teaching oral language. When students learn how to give oral reports or retell a story, how to introduce themselves, or how to use irregular verbs, they are learning language. A list of general procedures or guidelines for teaching language to students with learning and behavior problems is presented in Figure 3.3 and discussed in this section. The principles can serve as guidelines for teaching. You will also find that the speech/language pathologist is a good source for additional guidelines, techniques, and teaching ideas.

Teach language in purposeful contexts. Whether you are teaching a student to use causal relationships (form), to categorize fossils (content), or how to use the telephone to request information (use), it is important to teach language in context. It is difficult to imagine teaching someone how to use a ham-

■ **FIGURE 3.3** *General Principles for Teaching Language*

- Teach language in purposeful contexts.
- In most cases, follow the sequence of normal language development.
- Teach comprehension and production.
- Use conversations to promote language development.
- Adjust pacing, chunk information, and check for understanding to promote comprehension.
- Increase wait time to promote production.
- Use effective teaching strategies when presenting a new concept or skill.
- Use self-talk and parallel talk to describe what you and others are doing or thinking.
- Use modeling to demonstrate language.
- Use expansion and elaboration.
- Use structured language programs to provide intensive practice and feedback.
- Use language as an intrinsic motivator.
- Systematically plan and instruct for generalization.

mer, drill, or saw unless we had nails, boards, and probably the goal of making a simple wood project in mind. The same should apply when teaching students to use language. Rote practice of sentence structures or rehearsal of word definitions will teach the student little about how to use language.

To foster teaching language in context, plan activities that highlight the language skill you are teaching. For example, Mr. Cardoni used the contexts of following a recipe for chocolate-chip cookies and of building bird feeders to teach the vocabulary related to fractions (e.g., half, one-quarter, two-thirds, part, whole, fraction). During the activities the students measured and compared the different fractional parts (e.g., determining what fraction one teaspoon is of one tablespoon). This allowed Mr. Cardoni and his students to talk about the concepts of fractions in a situation where they played an important role in the project and to demonstrate with concrete examples the differences between fractions.

In most cases, follow the sequence of normal language development. Determining the content of instruction is a major part of the teaching-learning process, whether it be in language, academics, content areas, or social areas. Although the developmental sequence of language skills for students with learning and behavior problems is not well-documented, there is some evidence to suggest that these students develop language knowledge and skills in the same sequence as students who are normal-achieving, but at a slower rate (Reed, 1994; Wiig and Semel, 1984). They may also have more difficulty in one component of language: content, form, or use. For example, Susan, the third grader with word-finding problems (see page 82) has difficulty primarily in the area of content. On the other hand, Brice (see page 85) appears to have adequate content and form in his language, but has difficulty with use. Therefore, in planning a language program, begin by determining what knowledge and skills the student has already acquired in the areas of content, form, and use, and then target the subsequent areas in the development process. For instance, if a student is already using past tense (*The boy ate the cake*), then you might next focus on past participle (*The boy has eaten the cake*) (see Table 3.3). A speech/

language pathologist should be an excellent resource for helping to determine what to teach next.

Teach comprehension and production. Be sure to give the students opportunities to develop both their understanding (comprehension) and their ability to express (production) the new knowledge or skill you are teaching. For example, when teaching students to comprehend the past participle, you will want to label examples of events that have already happened (e.g., *Juan has sharpened his pencil. Kim has finished her math assignment.*). When providing intensive practice and feedback, you could show the students picture-sequence cards (see Figure 3.4) and have the students identify the picture that demonstrates that something "has happened." To teach production, have the students explain what has happened by using the past participle form. For example, you could ask students, "What *have* you just done?" When teaching the concepts and vocabulary associated with a new unit or piece of literature, provide students with opportunities not only to listen to explanations but to discuss their knowledge of the concepts. Using the pause procedure (Di Vesta and Smith, 1979; Ruhl, Hughes, and Gajar, 1990) provides such opportunities. The teacher pauses at logical breaks in the lecture or discussion and lets students discuss what they are learning with a partner or in a small group.

■ **FIGURE 3.4** *Sequence Cards to Help Students Comprehend and Produce Tenses*

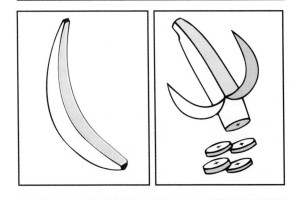

APPLY THE CONCEPT 3.1

PROMOTING LANGUAGE THROUGH CONVERSATIONS

- Talk about things in which the child is interested.
- Follow the child's lead. Reply to the child's initiations and comments. Share his/her excitement.
- Don't ask too many questions. If you must, use questions such as *how did/do . . . , why did/do . . . ,* and *what happened . . .* that result in longer explanatory answers.
- Encourage the child to ask questions. Respond openly and honestly. If you don't want to answer a question, say so and explain why. (*I don't think I want to answer that question; it's very personal.*)
- Use a pleasant tone of voice. You need not be a comedian, but you can be light and humorous. Children love it when adults are a little silly.

- Don't be judgmental or make fun of a child's language. If you are overly critical of the child's language or try to catch and correct all errors, he/she will stop talking to you.
- Allow enough time for the child to respond.
- Treat the child with courtesy by not interrupting when he/she is talking.
- Include the child in family and classroom discussions. Encourage participation and listen to his/her ideas.
- Be accepting of the child and of the child's language. Hugs and acceptance can go a long way.
- Provide opportunities for the child to use language and to have that language work for him or her to accomplish his or her goals.

Source: From R. E. Owens, Jr. (1995). *Language Disorders: A Functional Approach to Assessment and Intervention* (2nd ed., p. 416). Boston: Allyn and Bacon. Reprinted with permission.

Use conversations to promote language development. Students with language problems need opportunities to engage in conversations. Observational research has shown that teachers, in general, are not as responsive to students with language problems as they are to average- and high-achieving students (Pecyna-Rhyner, Lehr, and Pudlas, 1990). Plan opportunities for students to engage in conversations with you and other students as they work, think, and play. Using discussion groups rather than a question/answer format for reviewing a book or current event is an example of how conversations can be integrated into the classroom. During conversations, let the students direct the topics of the conversations. These conversations need not be long, and in secondary settings can be accomplished as students enter the room. Apply the Concept 3.1 provides more ideas that you can use and share with parents about how to promote language through the use of conversations.

Adjust pacing, chunk information, and check for understanding to promote comprehension. Students

with learning and behavior problems, and second language learners, often have difficulty comprehending what is being said during class, particularly in content area classes. To promote language comprehension, adjust your pacing so these students have time to process the language input. The flow of instruction need not suffer, but when you are discussing new or difficult concepts or ideas, slow the pace and highlight the key ideas by writing them on the board or overhead projector and/or repeating them. When teaching, it is not unusual for teachers to identify several students that they use to gauge the pacing of their instruction and to determine when to move on. In this group be sure to include the students with language and learning problems.

It is also helpful if the amount of information that is provided in each segment is reduced. Consequently, information can be chunked or segmented into smaller amounts. For example, when Mr. Fong observed his students in Mr. Hunt's fifth grade science class, he noticed that his students usually listened to Mr. Hunt present the first five of fifteen vocabulary words for a new chapter and they recorded about three of the words in their science notebooks. After Mr. Fong shared this information with Mr. Hunt, Mr. Hunt decided that he would chunk the vocabulary into groups of three to five and introduce each group only when they were needed rather than all of them at the beginning of a new chapter.

Checking for understanding is also important for facilitating language comprehension. Having students repeat directions or tell another student what was just discussed are ways to check for understanding other than asking questions.

Increase wait time to promote production. When Sharon Kutok, a speech/language pathologist, talks about the most important principles for teachers to use when teaching students with language and learning problems, the first one she mentions is wait time. Some students need time to understand what has just been said and to construct a response. These students may have particular difficulty with form (e.g., syntax) and need the extra time to think about the form they should use in constructing their response. For students with difficulty in the area of content, they may have difficulty with word retrieval or word finding (German, 1992).

Use effective teaching strategies when presenting a new concept or skill. Critical to new content or concepts is the use of effective teaching strategies. Student's knowledge of concepts grow exponentially during the school age years as discussed in the section on vocabulary development. Your use of effective teaching strategies will assist students with language difficulties gain the concepts and content that are necessary for success in content area classes. Based on the teaching-learning process, there are a number of effective teaching strategies that should be incorporated into language instruction. Figure 3.5 lists key strategies you should use with teaching language.

Use self-talk and parallel talk to describe what you and others are doing or thinking. Using self-talk and parallel talk demonstrates how language is connected to activities. Self-talk describes what you are doing or thinking, while parallel talk describes what the student(s) are doing or thinking. Ms. DeLong, a special education teacher who is co-teaching in a

■ **FIGURE 3.5** *Effective Teaching Strategies for Presenting a New Concept or Skill*

When teaching new language concepts or patterns, keep the following strategies in mind:

- Gear the activities to the students' interests and cognitive level.
- Get the students' attention before engaging in communication activities.
- Bombard the student with the concept or skill frequently throughout the day in a functional manner.
- When speaking, place stress on the target concept or language pattern.
- Pause between phrases or sentences so that the student has time to process the new concept or language pattern.
- Decrease the rate of presentation when first introducing the concept or language pattern.
- When introducing a new concept or language pattern, use familiar, concrete vocabulary and simple sentence patterns (Bloom, Miller, and Hood, 1975; Reed, 1994).
- If possible, present the new concept or language pattern by using more than one input mode (e.g., auditory, visual, kinesthetic). Gestures and facial expressions that are paired with a specific language pattern often assist students in understanding the form. For example, giving a look of puzzlement or wonder when asking a question can serve as a cue to the students.
- Pair written symbols with oral language. For instance, demonstrating morphological endings such as *s* (plurals) and *ed* (past tense) can be done in writing. The students can then be cued to listen for what they see.

first grade classroom, uses parallel and self-talk when she joins the students at the different learning centers. She explains, "When I join a center, I try to sit down and join in the activities rather than asking students questions. I describe what I am doing and what other students in the group are doing. For example, I might say, 'José is making a clay animal. It's blue and right now he is putting a ferocious snarl on the animal's face. I wonder what kind of animal it is? I think I'll ask José.' In this way, the students get to hear how words can describe what someone is doing and thinking, and it focuses the attention on José and the on-going activities."

Use modeling to demonstrate language. Modeling plays an important role in learning language. Whether for learning a new sentence structure, new vocabulary, or a new function or use for language, modeling is a powerful tool. For example, Ms. Simon and her eighth-grade students in Resource English class were working on improving discussion skills during literature discussion groups. Ms. Simon was concerned about the number of students who did not clarify what they were saying when it was obvious that other students were not understanding.

To teach clarification skills, Ms. Simons initiated a discussion about clarifying ideas and then modelled how not clarifying ideas and not asking for clarification leads to confusion. She exaggerated the examples, and the students seemed to enjoy this. Next, Ms. Simons modelled clarification skills as she participated with the students in their literature discussions. As individual students used effective clarifying skills, she commented on this, so that peers were also serving as models.

Use expansion and elaboration. Language expansion is a technique used to facilitate the development of more complex language form and content. By repeating what students say in a slightly more complex manner, the teacher demonstrates how their thoughts can be more fully expressed. For example, Ms. Lee, an elementary special education resource teacher, is working to get Rob to use adverbs to describe his actions and to connect his ideas. As he finished several math problems, Rob reported, "I got the first one easy. The second one was hard." Ms. Lee replied, "Oh, you got the first one *easily, but* the second one was hard." You do not want to imply that you are correcting the student, but simply showing him or her a more complex way of expressing the thought. Also, you should expand only one or two elements at once or the expansion will be too complex for the student to profit from it.

Language elaboration is used to build on the content of the student's language and provide additional information on the topic. For example, Chris, a fourth-grade student with language disabilities, was

explaining that snakes have smooth skin. Peggy Anderson elaborated on Chris's idea by commenting, "Snakes have smooth skin and so do lizards. Are there other animals in the desert that have smooth skin?"

Use structured language programs to provide intensive practice and feedback. Teaching in context is critical for learning and generalization. However, sometimes by teaching in context we do not provide the students with adequate opportunities to practice a new skill. Students who have learning problems need the practice and feedback provided in many language programs and activities to gain mastery of the skill. For example, *DISTAR Language* (Engelmann and Osborn, 1987) and *Figurative Language: A Comprehensive Program* (Gorman-Gard, 1992) provide intensive practice in different language content and forms. However, these programs should not serve as the students' entire language program. Although they provide practice and feedback, they generally do not teach the skill within the relevant contexts that are needed for purposeful learning and generalization.

Use language as an intrinsic motivator. Because language is such an enabling tool, it carries a great deal of intrinsic reinforcement for most children. Rather than using praise ("I like the way you said that" or "Good talking"), we can capitalize on the naturally reinforcing nature of language. For example, during a cooking activity Mr. Warren asks the students, "How can we figure out how much two-thirds of a cup plus three-fourths of a cup of flour is?" After Lydia explained, Mr. Warren comments, "Now we know how to figure that out. Shall we give it a try?" Later, the teacher asks how to sift flour. After Rona explained, he says, "I've got it. Do you think we can sift it just the way Rona explained to us?" Rather than commenting on how "good" their language was and disrupting the flow of communication, Mr. Warren complimented Lydia and Rona by letting them know how useful the information was. When a student's purposes and intents are fulfilled because of the language he or she uses, those language behaviors are naturally reinforced. The student learns that appropriate language use is a powerful tool in controlling the environment (Owens, 1995; Reed, 1994).

Systematically plan and instruct for generalization. As is the case when teaching other skills, language instruction must incorporate into the instructional sequence a variety of contexts, settings, and persons with which the student interacts if he or she is to generalize the language skills.

Because language is a tool that is used across so many contexts, it is relatively easy to incorporate generalization into language instruction. Mrs. McDonald, the self-contained special education teacher, and Ms. Cortez, the speech/language pathologist, are working with Julie, a second-grade child with learning disabilities, on sequencing events and using sequence markers (e.g., first, second, next, last). When Julie goes to language classes, Mrs. McDonald sends a note that lists, in order, the activities Julie participated in thus far during the day. When Julie returns from language class, Ms. Cortez sends back a note that lists her language activities. Each teacher then converses with Julie about what she did in the other teacher's class, emphasizing sequence and sequence markers. Other activities also build generalization for Julie. Whenever either teacher or Julie's mom reads Julie a story, Julie retells the story and is asked sequence questions. During the weekly cooking activity, Julie and the other students tell the steps in making the food for the day, and these steps are written on large chart paper with numbers listed beside them. Julie also arranges picture sequence cards and is then asked to describe them. In this way Julie is receiving numerous opportunities to generalize this language skill to a variety of contexts, persons, and settings.

Teaching Content

We teach language content throughout the day. For example, one of the major goals in teaching a new unit in social studies and science is for the students to understand and use the new vocabulary. What are some of the basic vocabulary categories that we may want to teach? Table 3.6 lists some general categories of words and word relationships. Let us look at some strategies for teaching content or vocabulary, whether it be the more general vocabulary listed in Table 3.6, or the specific vocabulary found in content area instruction.

Emphasize the distinguishing and critical features of the concepts being taught. When teaching new concepts, emphasize the features that are important to the meaning. For example, when teaching the concepts of "mountains" and "hills" the distinguishing or critical features to emphasize are "size" and "height." In comparison, the "texture of the land" is not important since it is not a feature that usually helps us distinguish between hills and mountains.

Concepts should be introduced in a number of different ways. When teaching the concept of "precipitation," for instance, present pictures of different types of precipitation (e.g., snow, rain, sleet, hail, and mist). Have the students tell about a time when they remember each type of precipitation. Discuss what is happening to the water in the atmosphere when it is precipitating and discuss what the weather is like when precipitation is present.

Present examples and nonexamples of the concept. For example, when learning about cactus, have the students generate two lists of plants, one that represents examples of cacti and one that represents nonexamples. Then talk about and list the features that make the cacti different from the nonexamples.

Categorize new concepts so that students understand how the concept relates to other concepts. If the concept of "melancholy" is being taught, the students should learn that this is an example of a feeling or emotion. Other feelings are "gladness," "relief," and "hurt." Characteristics of people who are melancholy are "not happy," "quiet," "not talkative," and "somber." These ideas can be positioned in a visual diagram, such as a *semantic map,* which shows how the different concepts relate to one another (see Figure 3.6).

Present new vocabulary in simple sentences or phrases. It is harder to learn a new concept or idea if the teacher is using difficult language to explain what it means. The rule of thumb is to use simple sentences or phrases to introduce new concepts (i.e., four- to seven-word sentences and two- to four-word phrases.)

■ **TABLE 3.6** *Categories of Words and Word Relationships*

Categories	*School-Related Examples*
Existence/Nouns	science, math, reading, vowels, consonants, sentences, paragraphs
Actions/Verbs	verbs often used in instruction—draw, write, circle, underline, discuss, compare, critique, defend
Attributes/Adjectives	words that describe such attributes as size, shape, texture, weight, position (high/low, first/last), color, age, speed, affect, attractiveness
Attributes/Adverbs	words that describe actions, such as easily, hurriedly, busily, willingly
Prepositions	locative (in, on, under, beside, in front of, ahead of, behind), directional (off, out of, away from, toward, around, through), temporal (before, after, between), for, from, at, of, to, with, without

Personal pronouns	*Subjective*	*Objective*	*Possessive*
	I	me	my, mine
	you	you	your
	she, he, it	her, him, it	her, his, its
	we	us	our
	they	them	their

Demonstrative pronouns	this, that, these, those
Indefinite and negative pronouns	a/an, someone, somebody, something, somewhere, anyone, anybody, anything, anywhere, no one, nobody, nothing, nowhere, the
Antonyms	full/empty, boiling/freezing, easy/hard, soft/hard
Synonyms	pants/slacks/trousers/britches laugh/giggle/chuckle happy/glad/pleased/elated/tickled pink
Homonyms	sail/sale, bear/bare
Multiple-meaning words	run fast, run in your stocking, go for a run, in the long run
Comparative relationships	taller than, shorter than
Spatial relationships	*see* Prepositions
Temporal-sequential relationships	words connoting measurement, time (days of the week, minutes, seasons), temporal prepositions (first, last, next, then)
Conditional relationships	if . . . then
Causal relationships	because, therefore, since
Conjunctive relationships	and
Disjunctive relationships	either . . . or
Contrastive relationships	but, although
Enabling relationships	in order that, so that
Figurative language	*Idioms:* catch a plane; hit the road *Metaphors:* her eagle-eye *Similes:* her eyes twinkled like stars; busy as a beaver *Proverbs:* The early bird catches the worm

■ **FIGURE 3.6** *A Semantic Map of the Concept of "Melancholy"*

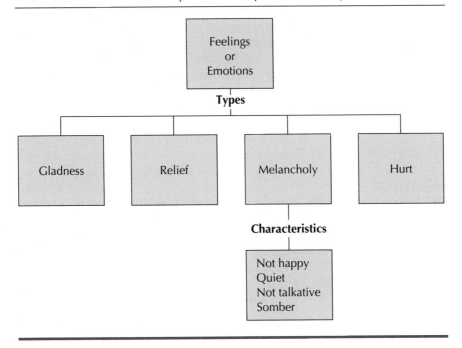

Use games and other activities to reinforce newly introduced concepts. For example, Twenty Questions is a good game to use to get students to think about the characteristics of a concept and the categories in which the concept falls. This game is played by having one person think of an idea or concept (e.g., parakeet) and having the rest of the students ask questions that can be answered with "yes" or "no" in order to guess the concept (e.g., Is it a plant? Is it smaller than a person?). The object of the game is to guess the concept before twenty questions have been asked.

Oral or written *cloze* passages as shown in Figure 3.7 can be used to highlight a particular set of concepts being taught.

Name That Category is a game that can be played similarly to Name That Tune, except the object of the game is to earn points by naming the category when examples of a category are given. The sooner the category is named, the more points the player(s) receives.

Idioms, metaphors, similes, and proverbs can be used when playing Charades, with the students acting out the literal meanings of the phrases (e.g., catch a plane, blow your stack).

Additional ideas for teaching new concepts and the relationships among those concepts, particularly as they relate to teaching content area subjects (i.e., science, social studies, vocational areas), are discussed in Chapter Seven. A number of language materials and programs are available for teaching concepts to school-age students. Chapter Appendix 3.1 (pp. 111–113) presents the names and short descriptions for several of these programs and materials.

Increasing Word-Finding Ability

Another difficulty that some students with learning and behavior problems encounter is word finding. These students know the word but are unable to recall it automatically. Most frequently, these words are nouns. Several techniques can be used to assist students in increasing their ability to recall words,

■ **FIGURE 3.7** *Sample Cloze Emphasizing Prepositions*

Cloze passages can be used either as an oral or written activity or combined with the oral activity reinforcing the written.

> More than anything else, Robert wanted _____ climb _____ the top _____ the mountain. Every day _____ his way home _____ school he looked up _____ the mountain. It was so high that the few trees _____ the top looked very small. He had heard that it would take a day _____ climb _____ the summit, and a day to get back _____ the mountain. One evening when he was looking _____ his window, he saw a campfire burning _____ the top of the mountain. He knew _____ only he practiced hiking, he could make it.
>
> Well, this spring he would start practicing. He and his friend, Jim, could join the Young Hikers' Club and _____ early summer they would be ready _____ the climb. Robert could hardly wait _____ spring _____ come.

thereby increasing the accuracy and fluency of their expressive language (Casby, 1992; Clark and Klecan-Aker, 1992; Gerber, 1993; German, 1992; McGregor and Leonard, 1989).

Teach students to classify and categorize words. Teaching students to classify and categorize words should improve their long-term memory and thus help them recall and retrieve specific words. When learning new concepts, students should be encouraged to name the category and then rapidly name the vocabulary in the category. Pictures, written words, and graphic representations such as a semantic map (see Figure 3.6) may help with this activity.

Teach students to use visual imagery. Getting students to "see" in their minds the objects they are trying to retrieve can sometimes help them think of the word. To help students develop these mental images, encourage them to picture new words in their minds. For example, when students are trying to learn the parts of a flower, have them picture a flower in their minds, with the labels for the parts written on the different parts. Have them talk about the kind of flower they pictured, discussing the parts as they describe the flower.

Teach students to use word association clues to help in retrieving words. Activities in which students learn and practice word associations (e.g., bread and _____ ; red, white, and _____) can facilitate word retrieval. These activities may be as broad as asking students to name as many things as they can think of in a given amount of time. But generally the teacher will want to focus the associations. Figure 3.8 presents a variety of association tasks that are more focused. In using these focused activities, keep the pace rapid and the total time for the activity short (two to five minutes). If students have established strong word associations, then when they cannot think of the correct word, providing an associative clue may assist them in retrieving the correct word.

Teach students to use synonyms and antonyms. When students cannot recall the precise word they want, an alternate word can be used. Students may be taught to state that the desired word "is the opposite of _____" or "is almost like _____." For example, when struggling to find the word "joyful," a student can be encouraged to say, "It's when you're really happy," or "It's the opposite of feeling sad."

Use phonic, semantic, or multiple choice cues to assist students in recalling words. Providing students with cues can assist them in retrieving words. For example, you might cue, "It starts with a /k/" (phonic cue), It's not a peach, it's a _____ " (semantic cue), or "It's either a banana, a cat, or a bowl" (multiple choice cue).

Increasing Elaboration in Language
Some students with learning and behavior problems use language that is not very elaborated. When asked to retell stories or events, or to give descriptions, these students provide only the most basic information.

To teach language elaboration, Wiig and Semel (1984) suggest that the teacher use a sequence of three steps for, first, an object or pictured object; then for an event or pictured event; and finally for an

■ **FIGURE 3.8** *Associative Tasks for Improving Word Retrieval and Developing Vocabulary*

Free Association Tasks

Name as many things as you can in a specified amount of time (usually one to three minutes).

Controlled Association Tasks

Name as many foods, animals, things you take hiking, kinds of fish, etc., as you can think of in a specified amount of time (usually one to three minutes).

Antonym Association Tasks

Listen to each word and tell me the word that means the exact opposite.

girl
man
hot
inside
happy

Synonym Association Tasks

Listen to each word and tell me the word that means about the same thing.

small
giggle
mad
rapid

Categorization Tasks

Listen to these words and tell me what they are.

dog, cat, fish, alligator
bread, fruit, vegetables, chicken
robin, sparrow, eagle

Temporal Relationship Tasks

Listen to each word and tell me what you think of.

winter   (ice skating, skiing, sledding)
evening   (watching TV, supper, homework)
Christmas   (gifts, Santa Claus, carols)

Agent-Action Relationship Tasks

Listen to the names of these animals and objects. Each of them goes with a special action. Tell me what special thing each one of these does.

plane   (flies)
lion   (roars)
doorbell   (rings)

Action-Object Relationship Tasks

Listen to these actions. Each one goes with special objects. Tell me what the objects are.

fly   (planes, helicopters, kites)
run   (animals, insects)
button   (shirts, jackets)

Source: Reprinted with the permission of Macmillan College Publishing Company from *Language Assessment & Intervention for the Learning Disabled,* Second Edition by Elisabeth Hemmersam Wiig and Eleanor Semel. Copyright © 1984 by Macmillan College Publishing Company, Inc.

event sequence or pictured event sequence. Their three steps for an object or pictured object are:

1. *Model elaboration by introducing familiar objects or pictured objects and by demonstrating verbal descriptions of their attributes and functions.* In this step you are describing the object, noting its attributes and functions. In some instances you may want to contrast it to similar or related objects. For example, describe a cactus and compare it to a rosebush.

2. *Have students elaborate in response to direct questions.* After modeling, ask the students direct questions about the object that require the student to focus on its attributes and functions. For example: What kind of stem does a cactus have? Why does it have such a chunky stem?

3. *Have students spontaneously describe the object or pictured object.* Ask the student to describe the object, using such cues as: Tell me about the cactus. What else can you tell me about it? Are there any other things about it that are important? In what way is a cactus like a rosebush?

The sequence for teaching events and event sequences would be the same.

Teaching Form

Form refers to the structure of language. Tables 3.3 and 3.5 present syntactical and morphological forms that are relevant when teaching school-age students with language and learning problems. Some procedures and activities for teaching these language forms are:

Teach new sentence structures or prefixes, suffixes, and inflectional endings according to developmental sequences or the order of difficulty. Tables 3.3 and 3.5, as well as language programs and activities designed to teach form (see Chapter Appendix 3.1), can assist you in deciding the order in which to teach the various sentence and morphological forms.

When teaching a new structure or form, use familiar, concrete examples and vocabulary. For example, Mrs. Ogle wants to have her students work on passive sentences. She begins by having her students act out simple events (e.g., Julio tagged Maria during a relay race). Then she asks the students to tell her a sentence about the event. She writes it on the board (*Julio tagged Maria*). Next she shows the students how she can say what had happened in a different way (*Maria was tagged by Julio*). Then the students act out other events and give passive sentences. In this way, Mrs. Ogle starts with concrete experiences and uses familiar, simple vocabulary to teach the new sentence structure.

Use simple sentences when teaching a new sentence or morphological form. When Mrs. Ogle initially taught her students passive sentences, she used very simple sentences. She could have said, "Julio chased Maria while playing tag," but this sentence would have been much more difficult for the students to put in the passive form.

Once the students have learned the new form have the students extend it to situations that need more elaborated and complex sentences and less familiar vocabulary. For example, when teaching the

morphological ending *er,* move from familiar vocabulary such as *teacher, reader,* and *writer,* to less familiar vocabulary such as *painter, plumber, framer,* and *landscaper* in the context of house construction, and to the exceptions in this area, such as *mason* and *electrician.*

Use actual objects and events or pictures of them when initially teaching a new structure or form. Also, pair oral communication with written communication. Mrs. Ogle uses the event of playing tag in order to teach passive sentences. She also pairs the oral sentences with the written sentences by writing them on the board. Word and sentence boundaries are clarified by written language, and pictures or actual experiences can assist the students in focusing on the target language pattern. Figure 3.9 demonstrates how pictures and written words demonstrate possessives.

New sentence or word forms should be introduced in a variety of ways. For example, when teaching comparative and superlative forms of adjectives during a measuring activity, Ms. Kamulu has the students determine who has the "long/longer/longest" pencils, pens, scissors, shoelaces, hair, and so on. Numerous comparisons can be made by using items found in a classroom, and the various comparisons may be depicted on a chart such as the one shown in Table 3.7. Students can then use the examples and the

■ **FIGURE 3.9** *Visual Representation Depicting Possessive Marker*

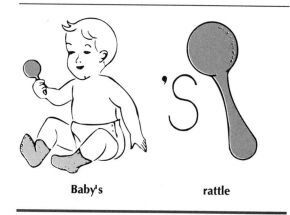

Baby's   rattle

■ **TABLE 3.7** *Comparison Chart*

Item	Long	Longer	Longest
red pencils	Susan	Kim	Danny
blue pencils	Susan	Cori	Ken
yellow pencils	Kim	Danny	Ken
white shoelaces	Kim	Danny	Ken
black shoelaces	Cori	Susan	Kim
brown hair	Cori	Kim	Susan
blond hair	Danny	Ken	Steve

chart to discuss the comparisons and to practice the targeted language skills.

Teaching Use

Instruction in language use is often one of the most important areas for students with learning and behavior problems. One way to organize pragmatic language instruction is based on five ways in which language is used (Wells, 1973). These include ritualizing, informing, controlling, feeling, and imagining. Table 3.8 presents the five areas with a list of pragmatic skills related to each area. These skills are drawn from *Let's Talk for Children* (Wiig and Bray, 1983), a language program designed to assist preschool and early elementary-level children to acquire, use, maintain, and generalize communication functions, and *Let's Talk: Developing Prosocial Communication Skills* (Wiig, 1982a), a language program designed for preadolescents, adolescents, and young adults.

Other pragmatic skills that can be taught include:

— Vary language to match the person to whom one is talking (e.g., speak differently to a young child, a peer, and an adult).
— Vary language to match the context in which the language is occurring (e.g., school, playground).
— Maintain a topic during a conversation.
— Take turns during a conversation.

— Recognize when the listener is not understanding and take clarifying actions to assist the listener.
— Be a considerate speaker and listener (i.e., attend to the cognitive, affective, and language needs of the other person).

Several guidelines can be used when teaching the various skills associated with language use.

Use role playing to simulate different situations in which the targeted pragmatic skills are required. Ms. Peterson uses role playing in her class so students will have some idea what it will feel like when they are put in a situation that requires them to communicate in a certain way or for a specific purpose. Last week the students had to ask each other for directions to their houses during "pretend" telephone conversations. This week students are practicing how to ask questions during a simulated science lecture.

Use pictures or simulations to represent feelings. Some students have difficulty discriminating different nonverbal and verbal communication that accompanies various feelings. By using pantomime or pictures, students can determine what feelings are being expressed and can discuss the cues that helped them determine the feelings. Encourage students to attend to other students' feelings by using such statements as, "You look like you're feeling. . . ." or "I bet you feel really. . . ." or "I can't tell how you're feeling."

Use conversations as a framework for teaching functional language. Conversations about topics familiar to the students or about common experiences can serve as ideal situations for building students' pragmatic skills (Hoskins, 1990). The teacher can serve as a facilitator by assisting the students in using the following conversational skills (Hoskins, 1987):

— Introducing a topic
— Maintaining a topic
— Introducing a topic in an elaborated form
— Extending a topic
— Changing a topic
— Requesting clarification
— Responding to requests for clarification

■ **TABLE 3.8**   *Intervention Areas in the Functional Use of Language*

Area Examples

Ritualizing
    Greeting and farewells
    Introductions
    Requests to repeat and requests to clarify
    Initiating and responding to telephone calls

Informing
    Asking for and telling name, address, and telephone number
    Asking for and telling about size, color, amounts, tastes and flavors, sounds, and textures
    Asking for and telling about the actions of people and animals
    Asking for and telling about the action and functions of objects
    Asking for and telling about the location of objects
    Asking for and giving directions
    Asking for and telling about the time of events
    Asking for and telling about conditions and states
    Asking for and telling about reasons and causes
    Asking for and telling about preferences
    Asking for and telling about abilities
    Asking for and telling about information on using a telephone

Controlling
    Asking for and telling about wants and needs
    Asking for and offering favors, help, or assistance
    Giving and responding to warnings
    Suggesting and responding to suggestions
    Asking for and giving permission
    Asking for and telling about intentions
    Promising and responding to promises
    Negotiating and responding to negotiations for an exchange
    Reminding and responding to reminders
    Asking and responding to requests to discontinue or change actions
    Making and responding to a complaint
    Asking for and telling about terms

Feeling
    Expressing and responding to affection
    Expressing and responding to expressions of appreciation
    Expressing and responding to expressions of approval, support, congratulations, or compliments
    Asking for and telling about feeling states and conditions
    Asking for, telling about, and responding to attitudes and reactions
    Apologizing and responding to apologies
    Expressing and responding to agreements and disagreements

Imagining
    Understanding and telling a story
    Understanding and telling a fantasy
    Understanding and telling a joke
    Using speculation

PLANNING INSTRUCTION FOR STUDENTS WHO ARE CULTURALLY AND LINGUISTICALLY DIVERSE (CLD)

As a teacher, you will have students from many different cultures and students who are in the process of acquiring English as a second language or second dialect. You may or may not be familiar with the culture and language of these students. Still, it will be important for these students to feel comfortable in your class and to learn.

Francisco is a good example of such a student. he immigrated from Costa Rica to New Mexico at the age of four with his parents and siblings. Moving from a rural community in Costa Rica, his parents spoke only Spanish when they arrived. Francisco and his family now live in a Spanish-speaking community within an urban setting. While he has some exposure to English and his father is taking a night course to learn English, Francisco entered school at age five with Spanish as his first language and only limited knowledge of his second language, English. This same scenario is true of children who immigrate from many countries including Central and South American countries, Asian and Pacific Island countries, and Eastern European countries. The U.S. Department of Education estimates that of the 40 million students in public and private schools, over 2 million have limited proficiency in English (Diaz-Rico and Weed, 1995).

The implications of this are that a growing number of students who enter school in the United States are learning English as a second language while in school. As a special education teacher, your knowledge of second language acquisition and general instructional guidelines can help make school a success for students like Francisco. Students must know that their home language and culture are viewed as assets rather than obstacles to learning (Altwerger and Ivener, 1994).

To promote learning, you should incorporate their first language and culture into the curriculum, demonstrate that you value their culture and language, have high expectations for these students, and make accommodations so that they can learn suc-

cessfully. Research on the characteristics of effective teachers of students with cultural and linguistic diversities (Garcia, 1991; Ladson-Billings, 1995; Tikunoff, 1983) indicates that effective teachers:

- Have high expectations of their students and believe that all students are capable of academic success.
- See themselves as members of the community and see teaching as a way to give back to the community.
- Display a sense of confidence in their ability to be successful with students who are culturally and linguistically diverse.
- Communicate directions clearly, pace lessons appropriately, involve the students in decisions, monitor students' progress, and provide feedback.

Second Language Aquisition

When students are acquiring a second language, an important variable is the degree of acquisition or proficiency in the first language. Cummins (1991) in a review of research concluded that the better developed the students' first language proficiency and conceptual foundation, the more likely they were to develop similarly high levels of proficiency and conceptual ability in the second language. He has referred to this as the *common underlying proficiency* and has used the analogy of an iceberg (see Figure 3.10) to explain the relationship between first and second language acquisition, and why proficiency in the first language compliments proficiency in the second language (Cummins, 1981).

As can be seen from Figure 3.10, both languages have separate surface features, represented by two different icebergs. However, less visible below the surface is the underlying proficiency that is common to both languages. For example, Table 3.9 compares the phonological, morphological, and syntactical features in Spanish and English, and Table 3.10 highlights some of the grammatical contrasts in Black Vernacular English and Standard American English. Regardless of the language a person is using, the thoughts that accompany the talking, reading, writing, and listening come from the same

■ **FIGURE 3.10** *Iceberg Analogy of Language Proficiency*

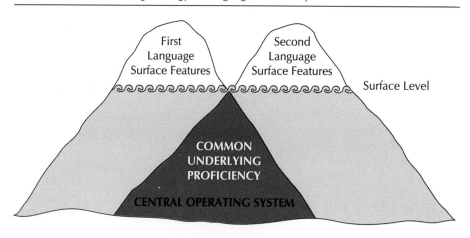

Source: Adapted from J. Cummins (1981). *Bilingualism and Minority Language Children.* Ontario: Ontario Institute for Studies in Education.

■ **TABLE 3.9** *Comparison of Spanish and English Languages*

Phonological

Fewer vowel sounds: no short *a* (hat), short *i* (fish), short *u* (up), short double *o* (took), or schwa (sofa)

Fewer consonant sounds: no /j/ (jump), /v/ (vase), /z/ (zipper), /sh/ (shoe), /ŋ/ (sing), /hw/ (when), /zh/ (beige)

Some possible confusions:
/b/ pronounced /p/: *cab* becomes *cap*
/j/ pronounced /y/: *jet* becomes *yet*
/ŋ/ pronounced as /n/: *thing* becomes *thin*
/ch/ pronounced as /sh/: *chin* becomes *shin*
/v/ pronounced as /b/: *vote* becomes *boat*
/y/ pronounced as /j/: *yes* becomes *jes*
/sk/, /sp/, /st/ pronounced as /esk/, /esp/,
  /est/: *speak* becomes *espeak*
/a/ pronounced as /e/: *bat* becomes *bet*
/i/ pronounced as /ē/: *hit* becomes *heat*
/ē/ pronounced as /i/: *heal* becomes *hill*
/u/ pronounced as /o/: *hut* becomes *hot*
/o͞o/ pronounced as /o͞o/: *look* becomes *Luke*

Morphological

de (of) used to show posses-sion: *Joe's pen* becomes *the pen of Joe*

mas (more) used to show comparison: *faster* becomes *more fast*

Syntactical

use of *no* for *not:* He no do his homework.

no *s* for plural: my two friend

no auxiliary verbs: She no play soccer.

adjectives after nouns: the car blue

agreement of adjectives: the elephants bigs

no inversion of question: Anna is here?

articles with professional titles: I went to the Dr. Rodriguez.

Source: Adapted from C. A. O'Brien (1973). *Teaching the Language-Different Child to Read.* Columbus, OH: Merrill.

■ **TABLE 3.10**   *Grammatical Contrasts between Black Vernacular English and Standard American English*

BVE Grammatical Structure	SAE Grammatical Structure
Possessive –'s	
Nonobligatory word where word position expresses possession.	Obligatory regardless of position.
Get *mother* coat.	Get *mother's* coat
It be mother's.	It's mother's.
Plural –s	
Nonobligatory with numerical quantifier.	Obligatory regardless of numerical quantifier.
He got ten *dollar.*	He has ten *dollars.*
Look at the cats.	Look at the cats.
Regular past –ed	
Nonobligatory; reduced as consonant cluster.	Obligatory.
Yesterday, I *walk* to school.	Yesterday, I *walked* to school.
Irregular past	
Case by case, some verbs inflected, other not.	All irregular verbs inflected.
I *see* him last week.	I *saw* him last week.
Regular present tense third person singular –s	
Nonobligatory.	Obligatory.
She *eat* too much.	She *eats* too much.
Irregular present tense third person singular –s	
Nonobligatory.	Obligatory.
He *do* my job.	He *does* my job.
Indefinite an	
Use of indefinite *a.*	Use of indefinite *an.*
He ride in *a* airplane.	He rode in *an* airplane.
Pronouns	
Pronominal apposition: pronoun immediately follows noun.	Pronoun used elsewhere in sentence or in other sentence; not in apposition.
Momma *she* mad. She . . .	Momma is mad. *She* . . .
Future tense	
More frequent use of *be going to* (gonna).	More frequent use of *will.*
I *be going to* dance tonight.	I *will* dance tonight.
I *gonna* dance tonight.	I *am going to* dance tonight.
Omit *will* preceding *be.*	Obligatory use of *will.*
I *be* home later.	I *will* (I'll) *be* home later.
Negation	
Triple negative.	Absence of triple negative.
Nobody don't never like me.	*No* one ever likes me.
Modals	
Double modals for such forms as *might, could,* and *should.*	Single modal use.
I *might could* go.	I *might be able to* go.

(continued)

TABLE 3.10   *Continued*

Questions

Same form for direct and indirect.
   What *it is*?
   Do you know what *it is*?
	Different forms for direct and indirect.
	   What *is it*?
	   Do you know what *it is*?

Relative pronouns

Nonobligatory in most cases.
   He the one stole it.
   It the one you like.
	Nonobligatory with *that* only.
	   He's the one *who* stole it.
	   It's the one (that) you like.

Conditional if

Use of *do* for conditional *if*.
   I ask *did* she go.
	Use of *if*.
	   I asked *if* she went.

Perfect construction

Been used for action in the distant past.
   He *been* gone.
	Been not used.
	   He left a long time ago.

Copula

Nonobligatory when contractible.
   He sick.
	Obligatory in contractible and noncontractible forms.
	   He's sick.

Habitual or general state

Marked with uninflected *be*.
   She *be* workin'.
	Nonuse of *be;* verb inflected.
	   She's working now.

Source: From R. E. Owens, Jr. (1995). *Language Disorders: A Functional Approach to Assessment and Intervention,* 2nd ed. Boston: Allyn and Bacon, pp. A-8, A-9. Reprinted with permission.

language core. One implication of this analogy is that individuals who are *balanced bilinguals* have an advantage over monolingual individuals in that they have greater cognitive flexibility and a greater understanding of language (Galambos and Goldin-Meadow, 1990; Skutnabb-Kangas, 1981).

Important to the learning process is the developmental nature of the second language. Cummins (1984) suggested that, in general, students acquire competency with the *basic interpersonal communication skills* (BICS) prior to competency with *cognitive academic language proficiency* (CALP). The BICS refer to the conversational competencies that we develop with a second language. They are the greetings and the "small talk" between peers that do not require much cognitive effort or social problem solving. The CALP, on the other hand, refers to the more cognitively demanding language skills that are required for new learning that is characteristic of school settings. In general, BICS develop in a second

language prior to CALP. Cummins (1981) suggested that it takes from one to two years to develop BICS, while it takes five to seven years to develop CALP.

While these generalizations are influenced by situational factors, linguistic input, and the learner characteristics, they do have implications for teaching. You might assume that students who can converse easily in their second language are ready to learn new concepts, strategies, and skills in that language, but this is not necessarily the case. For example, when Jong Hoon entered Ms. Miles's third-grade class, she immediately noticed that he conversed easily with the other students in the class and with her. Jong Hoon immigrated from Vietnam two years ago and began learning English through the school's ESL program. His parents are also taking English in a night course and feel that learning English is important for their economic and personal success in America. Still, Vietnamese is the language spoken primarily in the home.

As Ms. Miles became familiar with Jong Hoon she realized that while his conversational skills made him a comfortable member of the classroom community, he was not proficient in academic tasks such as reading and writing in English. She also found that in social studies and science, it was important for her to provide lots of context for teaching new concepts. When Ms. Miles referred Jong Hoon for possible special education services because of his difficulty with academics, she was not aware of typical patterns of second language acquisition difficulties. But in problem solving discussions with the bilingual speech/language pathologist and ESL teacher, she learned that different timelines for developing academic knowledge and skills are to be expected and not confused with learning disabilities (Duran, 1989; Langdon, 1992; Hamayan and Damico, 1991; Willig and Ortiz, 1991).

Strategies for Teaching Culturally and Linguistically Diverse Learners

When planning for second language learners who may or may not also have learning and behavior problems, it is important to incorporate the first language and culture to the extent possible. For example, in preparing for a thematic unit on California, Ms. Miles worked with the ESL teacher and incorporated an extended segment on farming communities in the unit because Jong Hoon and other students came from Asian and Mexican farming communities. For Jong Hoon and the other students she checked out books and magazines from the school and public libraries about farming and rural life in China, Vietnam, and Mexico. The students also had the opportunity to visit not only a California market, but also Asian and Mexican food markets. They compared the foods from the three markets and learned how the foods were grown. For Jong Hoon and the other students who came from other cultures and who were in the process of acquiring English as a second language, providing the link to their cultures helped to give them a context in which the students could build both their language and cognitive skills. This is an example of the *context embedded communication and instruction* that Cummins (1981) and others (Chamot and O'Malley, 1994) recommend to facilitate second language learning.

Other teaching strategies and accommodations include:

— Simplify your language.
— Repeat important phrases and emphasize key vocabulary.
— Demonstrate concepts; use manipulatives.
— Make use of all senses.
— Adapt the materials, don't "water down" the content.
— Increase wait time.
— Respond to the *message,* not to the correctness of the pronunciation or grammar.
— Don't force reluctant students to speak.
— Pair or groups native speakers together.
— Learn as much as you can about the language and culture of your students.
— Build on the students' prior knowledge.
— Bring the students' home language and culture into the classroom and curriculum. (Bos and Reyes, 1996; Sullivan, 1992; Towell and Wink, 1993).

Many educators suggest that students should be encouraged to continue to develop proficiency in their first language even if it is not formally supported through bilingual education (e.g., Cummins, 1989; Baker, 1993). To promote this, teachers can:

— Encourage students to use the first language around the school.
— Provide opportunities for students from the same language group to communicate with one another in their first language where possible (e.g., in cooperative learning groups on at least some occasions).
— Recruit people who can tutor students in the first language.
— Provide books written in the various languages in both the classrooms and school library.
— Incorporate greetings and information in the various languages in newsletters and other official school communications (Cummins, 1989).

As a special education teacher, you will undoubtedly work with students who are culturally and linguistically diverse. Making accommodations and using strategies that promote second language acquisition while fostering an understanding of the students' first languages and cultures will assist your students in becoming successful learners.

METALINGUISTICS

When students use metalinguistics, they think about, analyze, and reflect on language as an object in much the same way one describes a table or friend (Wallach and Miller, 1988). *Metalinguistics* refers to the awareness that learners develop about language, and it requires that the learner shift attention from the meaning of language to its form, thereby seeing language as an entity separate from its function (Reed, 1994).

Young children learn to use language without really understanding how it operates and functions. They use the linguistic rules that govern language, but if you asked them to tell you about or explain the rules, they would have great difficulty. As children mature, however, they become more sophisticated language learners. For example, when preschool children begin telling you that "care" and "bear" rhyme, that "little" and "lucky" start with the same sound, or they can clap the number of words in a sentence, they are using metalinguistics. Starting about age two children begin to develop metalinguistic knowledge and skills. Wallach and Miller (1988) have arranged information on the development of metalinguistic skills to correspond in rough approximations to Piaget's stages of cognitive development (see Table 3.11). It is evident from this table that during the second stage, children develop metalinguistic knowledge and skills that are important for the development of early literacy. These are discussed in more detail in the next chapter on word identification.

Teaching students with learning and behavior problems to understand how language operates is important for their success as language users. For example, understanding that words can have multiple meanings, that figurative language does not use literal meanings, and that you can manipulate language style or register to fit the audience and context allows

students to become highly sophisticated users of language. Labeling and explaining such language concepts is critical to the development of metalinguistic knowledge and skills. Examples of language concepts that can be taught include:

— Word boundaries and syllables
— Figurative language and multiple meanings
— The structure of stories (e.g., setting, problem, episodes with attempts to solve the problem and outcomes from the attempts, final resolution, and ending)
— How to manipulate speech style to fit the audience and context

As you read the next three chapters on teaching reading and written expression, think about how written language and print support the development of metalinguistic knowledge and skills.

INSTRUCTIONAL ACTIVITIES

This section provides instructional activities that are related to oral language. Some of the activities teach new skills; others are best suited for practice and reinforcement of already acquired skills. For each activity, the objective, materials, and teaching procedures are described.

■ Find the Way

Objective: To provide students with practice in giving and interpreting directions.

Grades: All grades

Materials: (1) Maps of different areas. For example, use a map of the school for younger students, and use a map of the local area, the state, or the area you are studying in social studies for older students. The map should be labeled. (2) Put the names of places on the map and on small cards so the cards can be drawn during the game.

Teaching Procedures: One student is designated as "It." This student is given a map and draws a card

■ **TABLE 3.11**   *Stages of Children's Metalinguistic Development*

Stage One (Ages 1½ to 2)
- Distinguishes print from nonprint
- Knows how to interact with books: right side up, page turning from left to right
- Recognizes some printed symbols, e.g., TV character's name, brand names, signs

Stage Two (Ages 2 to 5½ or 6)
- Ascertains word boundaries in spoken sentences
- Ascertains word boundaries in printed sequences
- Engages in word substitution play
- Plays with the sounds of language
- Begins to talk about language parts and about talking (speech acts)
- Corrects own speech/language to help the listener understand the message (spontaneously or in response to listener request)
- Self-monitors own speech and makes changes to more closely approximate the adult model; phonological first; lexical and semantic speech style last
- Believes that a word is an integral part of the object to which it refers (word realism)
- Able to separate words into syllables
- Unable to consider that one word could have two different meanings

Stage Three (Ages 6 to 10)
- Begins to take listener perspective and use language form to match
- Understands verbal humor involving linguistic ambiguity, e.g., riddles
- Able to resolve ambiguity: lexical first, as in homophones; deep structures next, as in ambiguous phrases ("Will you join me in a bowl of soup?"); phonological or morphemic next (Q: "What do you have if you put three ducks in a box?" A: "A box of quackers.")
- Able to understand that words can have two meanings, one literal and the other nonconventional or idiomatic, e.g., adjectives used to describe personality characteristics such as *hard, sweet, bitter*
- Able to resequence language elements, as in pig Latin
- Able to segment syllables into phonemes
- Finds it difficult to appreciate figurative forms other than idioms

Stage Four (Ages 10+)
- Able to extend language meaning into hypothetical realms, e.g., to understand figurative language such as metaphors, similes, parodies, analogies, etc.
- Able to manipulate various speech styles to fit a variety of contexts and listeners

Source: From G. P. Wallach and L. Miller (1988). *Language Intervention and Academic Success.* San Diego: College Hill, p. 33. Reprinted with permission.

that gives the name of the place he or she is to find. The student draws the route on his or her map. The other students are given the same map, but they do not know the destination or the route. Without showing the map to the other students, the student who is "It" must describe, by using words only, how to get to the destination. The other students are allowed to ask three questions to help clarify the directions.

To modify this exercise into a game format, each student can receive a point for each time he or she is successful in directing the other students to the location. After a student has finished, discuss how he or she was effective in giving directions and make recommendations to improve his or her language abilities.

Adaptations: A similar format can be used with one student directing the other students on a treasure hunt.

■ Many Meanings

Objective: To give students practice using homonyms and multiple meaning words.

Grades: Intermediate and secondary

Materials: (1) Any generic gameboard with a die or spinner and pieces to serve as players. (2) A variety of meaning cards and homonyms or words that have multiple meanings (e.g., *heal-heel, meet-meat*) written on one side.

Teaching Procedures: Have the students set up the game and clarify the rules. For each turn a student rolls the die or spins the spinner. The student then picks a card and uses each homonym in a separate sentence to show the difference between the meanings of the words or the multiple meanings. If the student's sentences reflect correct meanings, he or she moves the marker the number of spaces shown on the die or spinner. If the student is unable to make a sentence, other students may help him or her, but the student cannot move the marker. The student to reach the finish line first wins.

Adaptations: Have the students work in teams or have the students give definitions of the words rather than using them in sentences.

■ Surprise Pouches

Objective: To give students practice in describing objects.

Grades: Primary

Materials: (1) Cloth pouch with a drawstring. (2) Small objects that will fit in the pouch.

Teaching Procedures: Place a small object in the pouch and have one student in the group feel the object without looking in the pouch. The student cannot give the name of the object, but must describe it. The student describes what he or she feels while the rest of the students in the group try to guess what is in the pouch. When the student feeling the object thinks the other students have guessed correctly, he or she takes the object out to see if the students are right. Have the students discuss how the descriptive words helped them guess the object. For example, "Smooth and round made me think it was a ball."

Put a new object in the pouch and have another student describe the object. Each student should get several turns at describing the objects.

■ I Spy

By: Deborah Rhein

Objective: To provide students opportunities to develop descriptive vocabulary.

Grades: Elementary

Materials: Objects in classroom, playground, or any surrounding environment.

Teaching Procedure: Locate an object in the environment. Provide the students with clues that describe the object using the stem "I spy . . ." For example, "I spy something that has green, narrow leaves." "I spy something that has rough bark." After each clue the students try to guess what you are spying. The first person to identify the object becomes the next person to select an object.

Adaptations: For some students you may need to assist in picking an object and giving "I spy" clues.

■ The Add-On Game

Objective: To provide students practice in remembering and recalling lists of ideas.

Grades: Primary

Materials: Starter phrases that allow students to develop a list. For example:

> I am going on a trip to Disneyland and in my suitcase I will pack . . .
> I am going to a restaurant and I am going to eat . . .
> I went to Old McDonald's farm and saw . . .

Teaching Procedures: The students and teacher sit in a circle. A student begins the game by saying, "I am going on a trip to Disneyland and in my suitcase I will pack. . . ." This student names one article appropriate to take on the trip. The next person in the circle then repeats the sentence, listing the first item and adds another item. The next person repeats both items and adds a third, and so on. This game can be played in two ways. To play competitively, the person is eliminated from the game when he or she cannot list all the items. The last person to be "out" wins the game. To play cooperatively, the object of the game is for the group to beat the number of items remembered in previous games. In order to keep all students in the game, each student may be allowed two assists from a friend during the game (students are not "out" when incorrect). If a student has already used the two assists, then the number of items the group has correctly remembered is determined and compared to see if the group beat previous scores.

Adaptations: This can be adapted to current events or holidays (e.g., gifts for Christmas or treats you got for Halloween).

■ Round Robin Stories

By Deborah Rhein

Objective: To provide students opportunities to develop story grammar.

Grades: Elementary

Materials: None required although a picture of a scene or setting may help the students start the story.

Procedures: To get the students ready to start Round Robin Stories tell them that they are going to be telling a story as a group and that each student is to build onto the story. Using a picture (if available and needed), tell what the story is going to be about. For example, "This story is about a group of friends who want to earn money to buy something." Then begin telling the story and include the students as characters in the story. After several sentences, start a sentence and have one student in the group finish the sentence. Based on their ending, start another sentence and have another student finish it. As students become accustomed to this story telling process, students should be able to build directly on each other's sentences without your starting each sentence.

Adaptations: Use the same procedure but use wordless picture books to guide students in telling the story.

■ Barrier Game

Objective: To provide pairs of students practice in describing how to make something and to provide practice in listening to directions.

Grades: Elementary

Materials: (1) Colored blocks for building objects or crayons for drawing objects. (2) Some type of barrier to block the view between the two students or the student and the teacher.

Teaching Procedures: Divide class into pairs and explain the directions to the students. Have the students sit so that the barrier is between them. One student draws a simple picture or builds a simple block design. During or after the building or drawing, he or she describes to the other student how to make the design. The other student attempts to duplicate the work, and can ask questions to get help. When the other student has finished, remove the barrier and have the students compare their work.

Adaptations: After the students become successful at the activity, the number of questions that can be asked can be limited.

■ Category Sort

Objective: To provide students practice in sorting objects or word cards by categories.

Grades: Primary

Materials: (1) Objects or word cards that can be sorted by one or more categories (e.g., colored bears, colored blocks, colored buttons, colored marbles, types of animals, types of food). (2) Word cards that represent categories. (3) Sorting boxes (i.e., small boxes into which the students can sort).

Teaching Procedure: Put a category word card next to each box. Demonstrate how to name each object or word card and then put all the like objects or cards in the same box. Once the student has sorted the objects or cards, he or she names each category and the objects or cards in each category. The student then talks about what is alike about all the objects or cards in one category.

■ Create a Comic

Objective: To provide students practice in using dialogue and telling stories.

Grades: Intermediate and junior high

Materials: (1) Familiar comic strips or sequences in comic books. Blank out the words in the balloons.

Teaching Procedures: Present the comic strip to the students and discuss with them what they know about the comic strip characters, what is happening, and what could be written in each of the balloons. Have the students write in the different balloons. Take turns reading the comic strip with different students reading what different characters say. The different comic strips can be put into a comic book that can be shared with other students.

Adaptations: After students are comfortable with this activity they can illustrate and dictate their own comic strips.

■ My Collage

Objective: To provide students with the opportunity to discuss their characteristics and to increase self-awareness.

Grades: Intermediate and junior high

Materials: (1) A variety of magazines, including teen-oriented magazines. (2) Poster board, scissors, and glue for making the collage. Cut the poster board into squares.

Teaching Procedures: Introduce the activity by having the students talk about and write down words that describe themselves. Pass out the magazines and have students find pictures, words, phrases, and sentences that describe themselves. Once the students each have about twenty pictures, words, phrases, or sentences that describe themselves, have them construct their collages.

The students then share their collages with the class and discuss why they chose different pictures, words, or phrases. Next, they write a description of themselves, again using the collage as a guide. Encourage the students to use descriptive language.

■ Play the Part

Objective: To provide students practice in using language during simulations of typical interactions.

Grades: Intermediate and secondary

Materials: Simulation cards. Each card should describe the situation, the characters, and the goal of the language interaction. Several examples are given below.

Situation 1
Two friends meet a third person who is an old friend and known to only one of them. **Characters:** new friend, old friend, person making the introductions. **Goal:** introduce new friend to old friend and get a conversation started between the three of you.

Situation 2
One person approaches another asking how to find a store about ten blocks away. **Characters:** stranger, person giving directions. **Goal:** give directions that will allow the stranger to find the store.

Situation 3
Two friends are in a store. One tells the other that he or she intends to steal a small item from the store. **Characters:** friend, person persuading. **Goal:** convince the friend not to shoplift.

Teaching Procedures: Explain that each person is to assume the described role and participate as if this were a real situation.

Have the students assume the various characters and discuss what they are going to say in their roles. The students then carry out the role play. Have the students discuss how effective each person was in using his or her language to accomplish the goal.

■ **Does It Make Sense?**

Objective: To provide students practice in determining if sentences are syntactically and semantically correct and in modifying sentences to make them correct.

Grades: All grades

Materials: (1) Generic gameboard, spinner, or die and playing pieces. (2) Does It Make Sense Cards with sentences written on them, some of which are syntactically and semantically correct and some of which are not correct. Complexity of sentences will depend on the language development level of the students participating in the activity. For example:

> Semantically and syntactically correct:
> *Tamara and Jesse were walking along the road when they saw a limousine pass by.*
> Semantically incorrect (nonsensical or illogical):
> *Tamara and Jesse were walking along the road when they saw a limousine walk by.*
> Syntactically incorrect (grammar not correct):
> *Tamara and Jesse were walking along the road when they see a limousine passed by.*
> Semantically and syntactically incorrect:
> *Tamara and Jesse were walking along the road when they see a limousine walk by.*

Teaching Procedures: Have students set up the game and clarify the rules. For each turn a student rolls the die or spins the spinner. The student then picks a card and reads or listens to someone read the sentence. He or she then decides if the sentence "makes sense" and if not, changes the sentence so that it makes sense. If the student is correct in determining if the sentence makes sense, and is accurate in correcting an incorrect sentence, he or she moves the marker the number of spaces shown on the die or spinner. If the student is not correct, other students may help him or her, but the marker may not be moved. The student to reach the finish line first is the winner.

■ **Listen Carefully!**

Objective: To provide students practice in monitoring their comprehension as they listen and to question the integrity of the text.

Grades: Primary and intermediate

Materials: (1) Stories or expository pieces that have been modified so that they have inconsistencies in the meaning, sequence, vocabulary use, or grammar. For example:

> Beavers are brown, furry animals with long necks. They weight about forty to fifty pounds. They live in ponds on the desert. Sometimes they have to build their own pond. They do this by cutting down trees using their strong teeth. They put the trees on a dam they build, then they drag the trees to the pond. Finally, they pack mud and leaves in the dam so that it will hold back the water in the stream to form a pond.

(2) Stories or expository pieces that you have not modified.

Teaching Procedures: Explain to the students that you are going to read a story and that you would like them to judge how well they think the piece is written. Read the story as they listen, then ask the students if everything made sense. In the discussion, assist the students in identifying the text inconsistencies and telling why certain parts did not make sense. At the end of the discussion have the students rate how well they think the piece is written.

Adaptations: Students could read rather than listen to the pieces before they discuss them.

SUMMARY

Language is a vehicle for communicating our ideas, beliefs, and needs. We use language to gain and give information, accomplish goals, support interpersonal relationships, and monitor our own behavior and thinking. Although most children enter school with many language skills already mastered, language continues to develop throughout the school years. Students realize significant growths in vocabulary, the ability to represent abstract concepts in language, and the ability to use figurative language, sarcasm, and humor. They communicate easily, using complex sentences and other more advanced sentence and word forms. They increase in the ability to use language to accomplish goals. They also learn how language operates and are able to talk about the characteristics of language (metalinguistics).

Some students with learning and behavior problems experience considerable difficulty in the development of language skills during the school-age years. Some of these students may have problems primarily focused in one of the three components of language (content, form, and use), but because of the interactive nature of these components such students generally have difficulty in all three areas.

In planning instruction for students with language difficulties, we should take into consideration what language skills the students have already developed, what skills developmentally come next, and whether the child is from a culturally or linguistically diverse background. In this way we can target skills that will build directly on the students' current skills. When implementing instruction, we should present new skills in context, using intensive practice to reinforce the skills being taught. This means that we have to plan activities in which the language will be a functional and useful tool for communication.

Given the complexity of language at the school-age level and the need to teach language in context, providing language instruction for students with learning and behavior problems is a challenge. As you work on this challenge we encourage you to work with a speech/language pathologist. You should find this specialist willing to participate in collaborative language programs for students. Such efforts will help to make your instruction consistent and integrative. Finally, we encourage you to accept the challenge of teaching language. Providing students with the language skills to be effective communicators in school and other life settings may be one of the most important tasks we undertake as special education teachers.

THINK AND APPLY

— What are the major components of oral language? Listen to a conversation between two students and think about how the components function.
— What three general teaching strategies can you easily employ when building oral language skills? Converse with a child and use these strategies.
— Name at least five different functions for which we use language. Observe students as they play and note the different ways they use language.
— Using several of the principles recommended for teaching content, plan how to teach students to categorize ideas about a topic.
— What is word-finding difficulty? Describe several strategies you could use to help a student who has word-finding difficulty.
— When planning instruction for students whose first language is not English, what considerations should you keep in mind?

APPENDIX 3.1

Selected Programs for Teaching Language[1]

Programs for Global Language Development

Conceptbuilding: Developing Meaning Through Narratives and Discussion (1992) by Peg Reichardt. Eau Claire, WI: Thinking Publications.

> Basic concepts are practiced in a practical application of storytelling, verbal mediation, and drawing. Activities include temporal, spatial, quantity, and quality concepts. Designed for students from K–5.

HELP 3 (1988), *HELP 4* (1989) *HELP 5* (1991) by Andrea M. Lazzari and Patricia M. Peters. East Moline, IL: LinguiSystems, Inc.

> Each book targets a different set of linguistic concepts. HELP 3 is aimed at increasing ability to integrate conceptual thinking skills with language concepts. Activities include practice on linguistic concepts, paraphrasing activities, thinking and problem-solving tasks, and pragmatic skills. HELP 4 targets language in daily life. Exercises include tasks in defining and describing activities, linguistic concepts, and use of humor and riddles. HELP 5 has exercises for processing information, comparing and contrasting words, understanding math language, and activities using words to express opinions and feelings. Contains IEP goals. The *HELP 3 & 4 Language Pictures* (1989) and the *HELP 3 & 4 Language Game* (1990) can be used in conjunction with the sourcebooks or alone to teach the same concepts in the books of the same number.

Language Lessons in the Classroom (1993) by Susan Diamond. Phoenix, AZ: ECL Publications.

> Aimed at providing activities for the classroom consultant, this can also be used by regular educators to develop language skills. Intended for students for grades K–5. This sourcebook includes over 140 language lessons.

The Magic of Stories: Literature-Based Language Intervention (1995) by Carol J. Strong and Kelly Hoggan North. Eau Claire, WI: Thinking Publications.

> This program utilizes children's literature and twenty-two strategies to help students understand and retell stories. The strategies include discussion webs, episode webs, extensions, flow charts, journals questioning, semantic-word maps, story generation, story-grammar, cue charts, story maps, and think alouds. There are ten stories for early grades (K–2), ten for middle grades (3–4) and ten for upper grades (5–7).

Peabody Language Development Kits (Rev. Ed. 1981) by L. M. Dunn, J. O. Smith, K. B. Horton, D. D. Smith. Circle Pines, MN: American Guidance Service.

> This program consists of two kits, one for kindergarten and one for first grade. Each kit consists of lesson manuals, picture cards grouped by categories, puppets to demonstrate concepts, posters depicting scenes and stories, sound books of sound and song activities, and colored chips for manipulation activities such as counting, sequencing, and grouping.

SCAMPER Strategies: FUNdamental Activities for Narrative Development (1995) by Carol A. Estereicher. Eau Claire, WI: Thinking Publications.

> SCAMPER is an acronym for substitute, combine, adapt, modify, put to other uses, eliminate, and rearrange, which is the strategy students will learn as they develop oral and written narrative skills. This helps students learn story grammar and work with "wh-questions." It is designed to be used for grades 2–9 and can also be used as a classroom-based collaboration tool.

300+ Developmental Language Strategies for Clinic & Classroom (1993) by Charlann S. Simon. Tempe, AZ: Commi-Cog.

> Once a part of the *Communicative Competence* program, this sourcebook offers strategies for building general oral language and pragmatic skills. It includes a section for addressing language-learning in the classroom as well as for ESL students. Many of the activities are reproducible. For students aged preschool to grade 8.

[1]Compiled by Deborah Rhein, M.S. CCC/SLP.

(continued)

APPENDIX 3.1 *Continued*

Programs for Auditory Processing

HELP for Auditory Processing (1994) by Andrea M. Lazzari and Patricia M. Peters. East Moline, IL: LinguiSystems, Inc.

This sourcebook includes exercises for processing information in word classes, following directions, identifying relevant details, making inferences, asking and answering questions, sequencing information, and listening to sounds in words. It includes IEP goals and is designed for ages 6 to adult. Additional exercises by the same authors can be found in *HELP 1* (1987). This first of the HELP series focuses on auditory skills. Skills addressed are auditory discrimination, question comprehension, auditory association, and auditory memory. Program includes IEP goals, extension activities, and answer keys. This can be used in conjunction with *HELP 1 & 2 Language Pictures* (1988) and *HELP 1 & 2 Language Games* (1990) to cover the same skills. Designed for ages 6 to adult.

Listening in Room 14 (1994) by Melanie McDonald and Ann Shaw-King. East Moline, IL: LinguiSystems, Inc.

Aimed at helping students increase classroom listening skills, the exercises involve instruction on focusing on sounds, localizing sounds, discriminating sounds, words and sentences, following directions, and listening comprehension. There are three workbooks, covering grades PreK–K, 1–3 and 4–6. This program can be administered in large groups as well as individually.

The Listening Kit (1992) by Susan Rose Simms, Mark Barrett, Rosemary Huisingh, Linda Zachman, Carolyn Blagdon, and Jane Orman. East Moline, IL: LinguiSystems, Inc.

A multisensory listening program that combines listening, thinking, and language, this program includes several components. It teaches the need to attend through tasks involving following directions, answering questions, and sequencing. Critical thinking is targeted by tasks requiring students to express opinions, draw conclusions, and ask questions. Reasoning is taught through

tasks involving inferencing, predicting, and problem solving. Set includes a practice book, a game board, cards, pawns, a game book, three audio tapes, and an accompanying tape book. Intended for students age 5 to 12.

Question the Direction (1988) by Robert A. Mancuso. East Moline, IL: LinguiSystems, Inc.

Program designed to help students recognize when they don't understand directions. It provides practice with directions that are vague, unfamiliar, distorted, lengthy, unknown, and unreasonable. Students are expected to develop both auditory and questioning skills. Designed for students age 6 to 11.

Programs for Grammar

HELP for Grammar (1995) by Andrea M. Lazzari. East Moline, IL: LinguiSystems, Inc.

In-depth grammar practice of cumulative grammatical exercises. Activities include applications for nouns, pronouns, adverbs, and adjectives, and contextual usages. For ages 8 to adult, it includes answer key and IEP goals. *HELP 2* (1987) and *HELP 1 & 2 Language Pictures* (1988) and *HELP 1 & 2 Language Game* (1990) by the same authors, are also designed to help teach grammar.

Gramopoly (1996) by Raelene Hudson. East Moline, IL: LinguiSystems, Inc.

A grammar-training program presented in a Monopoly™ style game board. Students practice nouns, pronouns, adverbs, interjections, verbs, adjectives, conjunctions plus prepositional phrases, articles, and helping verbs. Designed for players ages 10–15.

Teaching Morphology Developmentally (Revised) (1989) by Kenneth G. Shipley and Carolyn J. Banis. Tucson, AZ: Communication Skill Builders.

This program is designed for students age 2.5 to 10. Activities for teaching bound morphemes include present progressive, plurals, possessives, past tenses, third person singulars, and superlatives. Includes 552 stimulus cards, a manual, and a reproducible worksheet manual.

Programs for Pragmatic Remediation

Pragmatic Language Intervention by Lynn S. Bliss. (1993). Eau Claire, WI: Thinking Publications.

This program, aimed at students between preschool and grade 8, teaches specific communication skills, and when and where to use them. In a dialogue format, a specific linguistic structure or pragmatic rule is targeted. This includes fifty reproducible illustrations.

Ready-to-Use Social Skills Lessons and Activities for Grades 1–3 (1995) edited by Ruth Weltmann Begun. West Nyack, NY: Center for Applied Research.

Develop positive social communication with these systematic reproducible lessons. Students obtain instruction in social uses of communication.

Room 14 (1993) by Carolyn Wilson. East Moline, IL: LinguiSystems, Inc.

Uses stories, comprehension activities and organized lessons to teach social skills. Skills targeted include how to make and keep friends, fitting in at school, handling feelings, self-control, and responsibility. Program includes instructor's manual, activity book, and picture book, and is intended for students age 6–10.

Programs for Vocabulary Development and Word Retrieval

HELP for Word Finding (1995) by Andrea M. Lazzari and Patricia Peters. East Moline, IL: LinguiSystems, Inc.

Exercises to enhance word-finding strategies and increase vocabulary. Includes exercises for automatic associations, thematic groupings, definitions, answering questions, parts of speech, and use of contextual cues. Intended for ages 6 to adult, the program includes an answer key and IEP goals. *HELP 1* (1987), *HELP 1 & 2 Language Pictures* (1988), and *HELP 1 & 2 Language Game,* by the same authors, also address word-finding and vocabulary development.

Language Quicktionary (1990) by Debbie Richardson, Sandra Hoerchler and Janelle Platte Hollis. East Moline, IL: LinguiSystems, Inc.

Played like Pictionary™ , where students draw names and guess words given contextual cues. Cues include synonyms, analogies, attributes, antonyms, definitions, and rhyming. Intended for students age 8–14.

The WORD Kit–Elementary (1988) by Rosemary Huisingh, Linda Bowers, Mark Barrett, Carolyn LoGiudice, and Jane Orman. East Moline, IL: LinguiSystems, Inc.

The authors have combined speaking, listening, thinking, and writing to teach associations between words, synonyms, antonyms, definitions, absurdities, and multiple definitions. This program, intended for elementary ages, includes a manual with over 200 activities, 300 illustrated pictures, and a game to allow students to use vocabulary in context.

The Word Finding Intervention Program (1994) by Diane J. German. Tucson, AZ: Communication Skill Builders.

This program is aimed at students with an adequate receptive vocabulary who have difficulty accessing those words for communication. This intervention program utilizes a three-part system of remediation, compensatory modifications, and self-advocacy instruction. It includes IEP objectives, reproducible forms, and vocabulary lists for grades 1–3 and 4–6. Intended for students age 6 to adult.

Chapter 4

Reading: Word Identification

OUTLINE

KEY TOPICS FOR MASTERY

— *The interrelationships among oral language, reading, and writing and the need to integrate activities across oral language and literacy*

— *The concept that reading is a constructive, strategic, and interactive process that requires the reader to search actively for meaning*

— *The concept that readers use a variety of cuing systems to identify words when reading including semantic, syntactic, and grapho-phonic cues*

— *Learning to read is a socially mediated activity, and teaching strategies that guide students to understand and effectively use the cognitive process involved in reading are most desirable*

— *Whole-language instruction uses principles of a sociocultural theory of cognitive development and builds on the integral relationships between language and literacy*

— *The concepts of metalinguistics and metacognition and their influence on reading and learning to read*

— *The strategies that good readers use to identify words when reading*

— *Strategies for teaching word identification and decoding to students learning to read including meaning-emphasis strategies and code-emphasis strategies*

— *Techniques for building sight words so that they are recognized immediately*

— *A strategy for teaching a word-identification strategy to older students who have difficulty decoding words when reading*

 BRIGHT IDEA

Turn to page 166 and read Think and Apply.

In the elementary school day, more time is spent teaching reading than any other subject. As students move into upper elementary, middle, and high school, reading becomes a major avenue through which information is provided. Listen to teachers as they discuss curricular issues. The reading process and how to accommodate students who are struggling with the reading process are frequently central issues in the discussions. It is not surprising that more students are referred for special education services because of problems in reading than for difficulties in any other academic area.

In this chapter we will look at the reading process, its relationship to oral language, metalin-

guistics, metacognition, and writing. We will also present some selected approaches for teaching students how to use word identification strategies for identifying and learning unknown words and techniques for building sight vocabulary. In the next chapter we will discuss instructional strategies for assisting students to become fluent readers and active comprehenders as they read.

Although we have divided our discussion of reading and writing instruction into three chapters (Chapters Four through Six), we stress the importance of the relationships between reading and writing. Critical to successful instruction for students with learning and behavior problems are opportunities for them to write about what they are reading and learning and to write stories similar in structure to the ones they are reading, to read each other's writing and discuss the role of the author, and to talk about the processes and strategies involved in reading and writing. As you read the next three chapters, think about how reading and writing are related and can be taught in such a way that one complements and supports the other. Also think about how the strategies and instructional ideas that were discussed in the previous chapter on oral language are related to reading and writing and could be incorporated into your teaching.

THE READING PROCESS

"Reading can be compared to the performance of a symphony orchestra," according to Anderson, Hiebert, Scott, and Wilkinson (1985, p. 7). These authors explain that, like a symphony's performance, reading is a holistic act. Even though reading is sometimes characterized by specific skills, such as discriminating letters, identifying words, and understanding specific vocabulary, performing the subskills one at a time does not constitute reading. Reading can take place only as an integrated performance. Like a good

performance, excellence comes with participating in the activity over long periods of time. Interest in the activity is increased when it is shared as a social event and discussed with other participants. Like a musical score, there may be more than one interpretation of the text. Just as the interpretation depends on the musicians and the conductor, meaning is dependent on the background of the reader, the purpose for reading, and the context in which reading occurs. Reading, therefore, is meaning-based, entails the active construction of meaning, and requires the reader to be strategic and to interact with the text. Reading, like other language-learning activities, is mediated by others. Let's look at these five concepts (see Figure 4.1) in greater detail.

1. *Reading is an active search for meaning.* "Reading is not walking on the words; it's grasping the soul of them" (Freire, 1985, pp. 18–19). Since reading entails constructing meaning, it requires the reasoning and thinking processes sometimes called *comprehension.*

2. *Reading is a process of constructing meaning from text.* Remember what happened in Chapter Two when you, like Bartlett's subjects, read and recalled "War of the Ghosts"? You took the information presented in the folktale and constructed the meaning. That meaning was affected not only by the information presented by the author but also by your

■ **FIGURE 4.1** *The Reading Process*

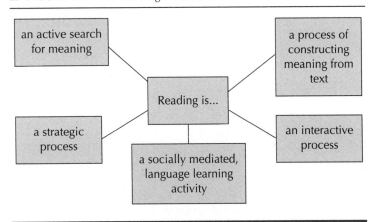

background knowledge. In fact, you might want to take a few minutes to write again what you remember about the legend and then compare it to the text and to what you wrote the last time. You will probably find that as your specific memory of the "War of the Ghosts" becomes less clear, you have to construct more and more of the legend, and that this last construction more closely resembles your schema for legends and your cultural beliefs. When a reader reads, the author does not simply convey ideas to the reader but stimulates the reader to construct meaning from his or her experiences (Horn, 1937). This construction of meaning does not occur necessarily in a straightforward manner. Instead, the reader gradually constructs meaning or makes hypotheses, tests them, and then confirms, modifies, or rejects the hypotheses (Goodman, 1984; 1996).

3. *Reading is a strategic process.* When we say that reading is strategic, we mean that reading requires the reader to use a variety of thinking strategies to construct meaning from the text. Some of those strategies are related to *comprehending* and are based on your purposes for reading. If you are reading an article from a popular magazine in a waiting room, you use comprehension strategies different from those you use when reading a textbook for a test. When something is unclear, you have other strategies upon which you can rely. You can go back and reread the information, or you can continue on to see if further clarification is provided. Knowing about these strategies and knowing in which situations to apply different strategies is called *metacognition.* As discussed in the section on information processing in Chapter Two, it is these metacognitive processes that make us effective and efficient thinkers or readers.

Not only does reading entail strategies for comprehending, it also entails the attentional, perceptual, and memory processes necessary to identify or recognize words in the text. Remember in Chapter Two how you had no difficulty reading "THE CAT" even though the "H" and the "A" were exactly the same? You used selective attention, feature analysis, context, and your background knowledge from long-term memory to help you interpret these words. This process of recognizing words, sometimes referred to as *word identification* or *decoding,* involves understanding and utilizing a variety of strategies to translate printed words into meaning.

4. *Reading is an interactive process.* When we read we interact with the ideas presented by the author of the text. Reading is a predictive process in which the reader is constantly establishing and evaluating hypotheses about what the author is saying. Goodman (1967, 1984) has referred to this as a psycholinguistic guessing game, since the reader utilizes his or her knowledge about the topic and about language to predict the author's meaning for the text.

Several types of knowledge (Rumelhart, 1985) or cue systems (Goodman, 1984; 1993) are available for the mature reader to use as he or she interacts with the author's ideas and to guide the reading process.

Grapho-phonic knowledge represents a particular combination of cues that readers and writers use. These include the sound system (phonology), the graphic system (orthography), and the relationships between phonology and orthography (Goodman, 1993). This set of complex relationships is also referred to as *phonics* (Eldredge, 1995; Goodman, 1993) or the *alphabetic principle* (Clark and Uhry, 1995; Moats, 1995).

When we teach these relationships, we often refer to this as *phonics instruction,* which entails learning the relationship between written letters (graphemes) and their speech sounds (phonemes). This system is relatively complex because in the English language these relationships do not necessarily have a one-to-one correspondence. For example, the letter *a* sounds different when you say the words *all, at,* and *ate.* In comparison, the sound–symbol relationships for vowel sounds in Spanish are much less varied. Instructional strategies that teach students these relationships (as presented in this chapter) improve word identification skills, thereby providing students with one type of knowledge to use when decoding unknown words.

A second type of knowledge, *syntactic knowledge,* refers to the reader's understanding of the grammar and syntax of the language. In English, the syntactic rules that apply to oral language (as discussed in Chapter 3) also apply, for the most part, to our written language. However, our written language generally reflects a more *formal* grammar than our oral language. Teaching students syntactic patterns as presented in the previous chapter can assist students in understanding what they read.

Semantic knowledge refers to the reader's understanding of concepts and the relationships among those concepts. If you are reading a technical medical journal you will probably have difficulty interacting with the text and constructing meaning because you do not have enough knowledge of the topic being discussed. In the same vein, when children are asked to read about a topic in which they have little background knowledge, they also may have difficulty constructing the meaning. Therefore, prereading activities that provide opportunities for the students to relate their background knowledge or gain more background knowledge (as discussed in the next chapter and Chapter 7) can facilitate comprehension and reading.

An effective reader flexibly uses all three types of knowledge to confirm his or her hypotheses about the meaning of the text.

5. *Reading as a language learning activity is socially mediated.* Literacy develops in a social setting because of the "human need to communicate and interact with significant others in the environment" (Goodman, 1980, p. 3). Learning to read, like learning to listen, speak, and write, is socially mediated (Vygotsky, 1978). When children and teachers talk about what they are reading, they share what they already know about the topic and integrate their knowledge with that of the text, thus constructing meanings that are relevant to them. When children and teacher talk about reading, they are sharing the strategies they use to construct meaning from the semantic, syntactic, and grapho-phonic cues.

These five characteristics of reading have special implications for students who are learning to read English as a second language. Apply the Concept 4.1 discusses one such child, Alfonso, who also has learning problems.

Integrating Language Instruction: Literacy and Whole Language

As discussed in Chapter Three, listening, speaking, reading, and writing are highly related activities and are reciprocal in nature. Today many teachers recognize these reciprocal relationships and use approaches which integrally tie instruction in reading to writing and incorporate strong oral language components. For example, newly published literature-based reading series (see Chapter Five) closely tie the teaching of reading to process-oriented approaches to teaching writing (see Chapter Six).

A number of literacy educators have stressed the importance of integrating reading and writing with oral language (e.g., Cambourne, 1988, 1995; Goodman, 1996; Harste, 1990; Weaver, 1990). One of the best examples of this orientation is represented in whole language (Goodman, 1986, 1992). Whole language emphasizes the need for curriculum integrated around problem solving using authentic literature and trade books. Whole language is based on the following ideas:

1. Language is for making meanings, for accomplishing purposes.
2. Written language is language—thus what is true for language in general is true for written language.
3. The cuing systems of language are always simultaneously present and interacting in any instance of language use.
4. Language use always occurs in a situation.
5. Situations are critical to making of meaning. (Altwerger, Edelsky, and Flores, 1987, p. 145)

In a whole language classroom, the curriculum is organized around themes and units that integrate oral language, reading, and writing and oftentimes include the integration of social studies, science, and math. Whole-language teaching integrates reading and writing and is not overly constrained by attempts to sequence a hierarchy of reading and writing experiences or by teaching skills in isolation. Learning to read is not learning to recognize words, it is learning to make sense of texts (Goodman and Goodman, 1982, p. 127). In whole language, no sep-

APPLY THE CONCEPT 4.1

DEVELOPING INSTRUCTIONAL PLANS FOR READERS
ACQUIRING ENGLISH AS A SECOND LANGUAGE

Alonso is a fourth-grade student with learning difficulties whose first language is Spanish. He has received Spanish reading and language arts instruction from kindergarten through the third grade at the same elementary school. Alonso has been receiving special education resource services since the second grade. He is reading and performing below grade level in Spanish. While Alonso is proficient in English Basic Interpersonal Communication Skills (BICS) (Cummins, 1984), he has difficulty completing academic tasks in his second language. (See Chapter Three for a dsicussion of BICS and CALP.) Now that Alonso is in the fourth grade, he is expected to learn to read English as well as Spanish.

In learning to read English, there may be persistent breakdowns in his English reading (Gibbons, 1993). He may not be familiar with the graphophonic relationships and may not recognize which words carry the most important information, his background knowledge may be limited or culturally mismatched, he may not be able to tell if a prediction makes sense, and lastly, Alonso may not recognize his miscues or know how to correct them. Good teaching tells us not to become discouraged, but rather to search out research-based methods that have worked with students like Alonso.

Unfortunately, research confirms the above scenario and tells us that Latino students read significantly below average as a group (Williams, Reese, Campbell, Mazzeo, and Phillips, 1995). Language differences and the time that it takes to acquire English as a second language have adverse effects on second language learners' reading development and proficiency (Cummins, 1994). In addition to these

"givens," teaching Alonso to read English may prove to be more challenging because of his apparent difficulties in learning. As teachers we must be aware of all of these variables when designing a successful plan for teaching students like Alonso.

A number of researchers in the field of bilingual education contend that elementary students who are able to read in their first language become more proficient in English as their second language, than those who are unable to read in their first language (García, Pearson, and Jiménez, 1994). Alonso's ability to read Spanish then, will have a positive effect on his English reading aptitude. In Alonso's English instruction, emphasis should be placed on English Cognitive-Academic Language Proficiency (CALP) to build on academic concepts previously developed in Spanish (Cummins, 1984). Transferring this learning from his native language to English will form a strong foundation of shared concepts on which additional English learning such as vocabulary, syntax, and semantics can take place.

Alonso will also learn English faster if there is a significant amount of comprehensible input provided, which is to say that the level of English instruction is one that he can readily understand (Cummins, 1994). Highly contextualized learning situations including the use of pictures, objects, field trips, guest speakers, and role play situations will further Alonso's English learning experiences.

Applying well-researched methods for teaching English reading with bilingual students is the best way to empower students like Alonso to experience success in their acquisition of English.

arate phonics instruction is taught. Rather, using a sociocultural theory of cognitive development (Vygotsky, 1978) (see Chapter Two), teachers guide students in learning about appropriate conventions of language as they engage in authentic language and literacy activities (Cousin, Prentice, Aragon,

Leonard, Rose, and Weekley, 1991; Eldredge, 1995). Teachers also consider both the content taught and the manner in which it is taught in terms of students' culture, history, and community (Edelsky, Altwerger, and Flores, 1991; Westby, 1992). In reading and writing workshops, students, regardless of their levels of development, are encouraged to take risks and to try out their hypotheses about literacy (e.g., Allen, Michalove, Shockley, and West, 1991; Atwell, 1991; Short and Burke, 1991).

Whole language supports the idea that students who are challenged with reading and writing may need more support (i.e., scaffolded instruction) and additional time to accomplish the tasks, rather than a specific skills approach (Goodman, 1996; Rhodes and Dudley-Marling, 1996; Stires, 1991). Whole language also supports the idea that "Children who have trouble in reading and writing do have strengths— making sense of language is natural for people" (Goodman, 1986, p. 56). Goodman discusses the importance of "revaluing" programs for students; such programs have two overarching objectives: (1) to support students in revaluing themselves as language learners and to get them to believe that they are capable of becoming fully literate; and (2) to support students in revaluing reading and writing as functional, meaningful language processes rather than sequences of skills to be memorized and practiced.

Instructional Implications

What does this philosophy and theory of language learning say to those of us who work with students who have difficulty learning to read and using reading to learn in other content areas? First, we need to assist students in developing a concept of reading that focuses on meaning or comprehension rather than word identification. For more information on this, see *Whole Language and Literature-Based Reading Programs* in Chapter Five. Second, our instruction should provide students with the opportunity to develop semantic, syntactic, and grapho-phonic knowledge. Third, by using the teaching procedures presented in Chapter Two (modeling, thinking aloud, scaffolded instruction, interactive discussions), we can assist students in developing and learning how to use their semantic, syntactic, and grapho-phonic knowledge and to construct meaning from text. This can help them actively search for meaning, construct meaning, and use strategic and interactive processes. Fourth, integrating oral and written language using authentic, meaningful learning experiences can provide students

with a context for learning that is meaningful, motivational, and successful.

The questions we can ask as we make teaching decisions regarding reading are related to the general instructional questions we asked in Chapter One.

— Based on observations and discussions with the student: what is the student's concept of reading and literacy?
— What attitudes does the student have toward reading and literacy, and how does the student perceive himself or herself as a reader, writer, and learner?
— What purposes do reading and literacy serve for the student?
— What processes and strategies related to reading and literacy does the student currently have and use?
— What prior knowledge concerning the topics of the text does the student bring to the literacy experience?
— What is the student's literacy level and how does this compare to his or her cognitive abilities?
— How does the student use language and literacy?
— How has and how are language and literacy processes being taught?
— How are reading, writing, and oral language integrated in the classroom?
— How does teaching style match the student's learning characteristics?

Using these questions as a framework, let's apply these concepts to some students and see how this information guides our teaching (see Apply the Concept 4.2).

Metalinguistics and Early Literacy

In many ways the development of metalinguistics and emergent and early literacy go hand in hand (Clay, 1991; Kamhi and Catts, 1989). In Chapter Three we learned that metalinguistics is an awareness that learners develop about language as an entity in itself. Table 3.11 (see p. 105) presented stages of

APPLY THE CONCEPT 4.2

DEVELOPING INSTRUCTIONAL PLANS FOR STUDENTS WITH READING DIFFICULTIES

Shawn talks about reading as "saying the words right." When you listen to Shawn read aloud, he seems to call out the words, paying little attention to meaning. Even his intonation reflects his definition of reading. He doesn't read with expression, nor does he pay attention to punctuation. What he does when he mispronounces a word tells us about the type of knowledge that he relies on to identify words. His errors usually sound or look similar to the words, but they don't necessarily make sense nor are they always the correct part of speech. For example, when reading a passage about living in China, Shawn sometimes said *horse* for *house, mate* for *mat,* and *bool* for *bowl.* He rarely went back to reread. When he was encouraged to reread a sentence, he usually read it the same way. When he was asked to try to figure out a word in a sentence, he attempted to give each letter a sound and then said the sounds quickly. These attempts sometimes resulted in nonsense words and rarely the correct word.

Even though Shawn has adequate language skills and cognitive abilities, sometimes he cannot even give the gist of what he has read. He tends to remember a few of the isolated facts. Shawn is in third grade and he reads comfortably in books at the first- to beginning second-grade level. It is this low achievement in reading, despite adequate language and cognitive skills, that caused Shawn's regular third-grade teacher to refer Shawn for special education services.

Shawn says he likes to read, but he rarely selects reading as a free-time activity. He does not make regular trips to the library, nor does reading appear to play an important role in his home. His major way of gaining information is through television.

The reading emphasis in Shawn's first- and second-grade classes was on word identification, particularly phonics.

What should be our plan of action for Shawn? First, we need to help him gain a different understanding of what reading is about and how to use his semantic and syntactic knowledge when reading. Helping Shawn learn to ask himself questions

about the meaning as he reads or teaching him to summarize what he has read (techniques described in the next chapter) could assist him in changing his ideas about reading. We may also want to use pre-reading activities to assist Shawn in setting purposes for reading, and to encourage him to predict as he reads (techniques presented in the next chapter). At the same time, we may want to model how to use the meaning (semantic or context clues) to assist in identifying unknown words (described in this chapter). We also want to provide opportunities for him to read for pleasure, listen to others read, and read along with others. Taped books and shared reading may assist us in this endeavor. After Shawn has modified his definition of reading and is using semantic and syntactic knowledge more effectively, we may find it necessary to build his knowledge of phonics and other word level strategies such as structural analysis and syllabication.

On the other hand, when you listen to Leila read her sixth-grade social studies text, it appears that her definition of reading is right on target. She reads quickly and with expression, and she rarely hesitates. But rather than just listening, follow along as she reads. You will find that she is miscalling 30 to 40 percent of the words, resulting in major changes in the meaning. Sometimes by the end of a paragraph, you think she is not attending to the text at all. When you ask Leila about her definition of reading, she tells you that reading is "getting the main point." But Leila also lets you know that when she does not recognize a word she will "just make something up that sounds good." She confides, "This way people don't know I don't read very well." Leila also reports that she doesn't "particularly like to read because it is hard for me to remember the words." However, if someone reads to her, she can "get what the author is trying to say." When asked how she figures out words she can't remember, she says "I think of a word that makes sense."

There are lots of positive aspects of Leila's reading (e.g., her ideas about reading, her use of semantic knowledge). She has an adequate definition of reading and relies (to a point of overrelying) on her semantic and syntactic knowledge when she reads. In working with Leila it seems important that, for a while, she read text in which she can use her semantic and syntactic knowledge more effectively. She needs to feel successful and change her perception about her reading ability. As a resource teacher in an elementary school, we could facilitate this by having her read text that is more predictable, for which she has more background knowledge, and for which she can recognize more of the words. Library books of interest in the areas of social studies and science, with an estimated readability of about third to fourth grade might be one suggestion. At the same time, we want to help Leila develop her grapho-phonic knowledge. Ideas and programs presented in the "Code-Emphasis Strategies for Teaching Word Identification" section of this chapter might prove helpful. Finally, Leila reports, "I just can't remember the words." In working with Leila, if we find that she does seem to struggle with re-

membering words even after she has had the opportunity to read them many times in text, then we may want to use techniques for building sight words (described in this chapter).

As Leila becomes more confident of her reading and as her repertoire of reading skills increase, we will want Leila to move back to reading the sixth-grade social studies and science texts. This transition should be just as systematic as our initial instruction with Leila. If we expect her to *generalize* her confidence and ski]ls to the sixth-grade texts and classroom, then we want to plan systematically for her success.

Both Shawn and Leila are experiencing difficulties in reading. What we learn by studying their reading strategies and beliefs, their knowledge and skills, and the context and format for teaching lets us know that these two students need different instructional plans.

metalinguistic development in relation to Piaget's stages of cognitive development. Many of the developmental milestones that are listed relate to children's understanding of how written language works and the relationship between oral and written language. For example, in a literate environment, children as young as two years old can distinguish print from nonprint, and their scribbles they consider "pictures" from their scribbles that are "writing." During the preschool years they also develop a sense of what is a word (word boundaries) both in print and orally. In addition, they learn to separate words into syllables and to play with the sounds of language. It is not unusual to observe children in a preschool commenting when words rhyme, or making up rhymes ("Billy is silly"). They can clap and count the number of syllables in a word. Making rhymes and playing with words is one of the best predictors that children are learning to control language (Cunningham and Allington, 1994).

As emergent readers encounter print in their environment, they ask questions and learn about how language is represented in its written form. They engage in the following:

— Pretend to read favorite print (i.e., books, poems, songs, chants . . .)
— Read what they have drawn or written, even when no one else can
— Point to just one word, the first word in a sentence, one letter, the first letter in the word, the longest word, etc.
— Recognize some concrete words (i.e., their names, friend's names, words in the environment such as McDonalds)
— Recognize and generate rhyming words
— Name many letters and tell you words that begin with the common initial sound

(Cunningham and Elster, 1994; Allington, 1994; Sulzby and Teale, 1991)

One aspect of metalinguistics that seems particularly relevant to early literacy development and decoding is phonological awareness. *Phonological awareness* and *phonological processing* are the knowledge of and ability to effectively apply sound/symbol relationships (Kamhi and Catts, 1991). For example, Mary, a beginning reader, was asked to give the first letter in the word *dog* when her teacher said the word. In terms of metalinguistic skills, Mary must understand that *dog* is a word, that words are divided into sounds, and that giving the first letter in the word means giving the letter name for the first sound in the word *dog*. Scott, a first grader, was asked by his teacher to tell if the words *dog/bog* and *pat/pan* are the same or different. When Scott could not successfully complete this task, the teacher assumed that Scott had auditory discrimination problems (i.e., could not perceive the differences between speech sounds). To successfully complete this task, Scott not only must perceive the differences between speech sounds as they are presented in words, but metalinguistically Scott must know the concepts of "same" and "different" as they apply to words, and to understand that as little as one different sound makes the words different. When Scott's teacher taught him the meaning of "same" and "different" as they apply to discriminating words such as *dog* and *bog,* his difficulty in telling if two words were the same or different was resolved. In this case, Scott lacked the necessary metalinguistic skills to allow him to manipulate his language.

This phonological awareness and the ability to apply it to words are some of the best predictors of later success in reading (Adams and Brunk, 1995; Ehri and Robbins, 1992; Lyon, 1996; Spear-Swerling and Sternberg, 1996; Swank and Catts, 1994). In teaching phonological awareness to emergent and early readers, activities can be centered around these six metalinguistic skills:

— Rhyming (identifying similarities and differences in word endings)
— Alliteration and initial sound substitution (identifying similiarities and differences in word beginnings and substituting one initial sound for another)
— Segmentation (dividing words into syllables or phonemes)
— Blending (combining syllables or sounds to form words)
— Closure (providing the missing sounds to make a word)

— Sequencing of sounds and position of sounds in words (e.g., initial, middle, ending)

How do students who struggle with learning to read deal with these metalinguistic skills? There is substantial evidence to suggest that these students are delayed in phonological awareness (Foorman, Francis, and Fletcher, in press; Hodgson, 1992; Liberman and Shankweiler, 1987; Lyon, 1995; Mann, 1991; Spector, 1995; Stanovich, 1986; Tangel and Blachman, 1995; Torgesen, in press). This research suggests that it is important that we teach these metalinguistic skills to students who encounter difficulties in learning how to read. How do we as teachers provide for the opportunities to learn these metalinguistic skills? The Report of the Commission on Reading, *Becoming a Nation of Readers* (Anderson et al., 1985), indicates that these skills develop by providing students with opportunities to talk and learn about written language. This includes:

— Reading aloud with students and showing them how oral language relates to written language
— Providing students opportunities to write and experiment with written language through their writing
— Providing instruction in phonics within meaningful contexts

Metacognition and Reading

As discussed in Chapter Two, *metacognition* refers to the knowledge we have about our thinking processes or strategies, and our ability to regulate these processes or strategies to ensure successful learning. For example, metacognition in reading is deciding whether associating the word with a picture, or rehearsing the word, or both associating and rehearsing the word will be most helpful in remembering the word. Metacognition involves actively checking comprehension when reading and, if understanding is not adequate, instigating strategies to alleviate the problem. These strategies include rereading, slowing down, and holding the inconsistency in memory while reading further for clarification.

APPLY THE CONCEPT 4.3

TEACHING METACOGNITION

After Wong and Wilson (1984) showed that students with learning disabilities were less sensitive to passage organization than students without learning disabilities, they taught the metacognitive skill of organizing a passage to twenty-four students with learning disabilities who could not successfully complete this task. The researchers taught the students a five-step strategy:

1. Sort the sentences into groups (paragraphs).
2. Check the sentences. Is any sentence in the wrong group (paragraph)?

3. Put the sentences in the right order in each group (paragraph).
4. Think: What does each group of sentences say about the topic?
5. Get ready to tell the story.

Results of the post-test indicate that these students with learning disabilities readily learned how to organize sentences around the topic and subtopics of a passage. More importantly, the acquisition of this metacognitive skill increased their retention of the passage.

Students who have reading difficulties tend to have difficulty with metacognitive skills, including efficient memory processing for words (Ashbaker and Swanson, 1996; Bauer 1987; Mann 1991) and comprehension monitoring (Billingsley and Wildman, 1990; Bos and Filip, 1984; Palincsar and Brown, 1987; Wong, 1979, 1987). Research in the area of memory processing indicates that these students do not effectively use elaborative encoding strategies, such as rehearsal, categorization, and association, when trying to remember words or word lists. Studies with good and poor readers suggest that the poor readers do not automatically monitor their comprehension or engage in strategic behavior to restore meaning when there is a comprehension breakdown.

Like metalinguistic skills, metacognitive skills seem amenable to instruction. Using the teaching and learning principles of cognitive behavior modification and cognitive instruction described in Chapter Two, metacognitive skills in the area of reading have been successfully taught (Bos, 1988; Ellis, 1996; Palincsar and Brown, 1984, 1986; Pressley, Brown, El-Dinary, and Afflerbach, 1995; Wong and Wilson, 1984). Wong and Wilson applied the concept to teaching passage organization (see Apply the Concept 4.3).

STRATEGIES FOR IDENTIFYING WORDS

What do you do when you are reading and come to a word you cannot identify? Your response varies according to your purposes for reading and the type of text you are reading. When you are reading a Russian novel and you come to a name you cannot read, perhaps you skip it, use a nickname or initials, or use your knowledge of dividing words into syllables (*syllabication*) and phonics (*phonic analysis*) to pronounce it. When you are reading a science textbook and come to the name of a chemical process that you will need to discuss in class, you will probably use the grapho-phonic cuing system in terms of your knowledge of syllables, phonics, *structural analysis* (analyzing words according to root words, prefixes, and suffixes), and, if necessary, the dictionary to figure out the word. When you are reading the description of a character and come to an adjective you do not recognize, you will probably rely heavily on your *semantic and syntactic knowledge* to aid in identifying the word. In other words, you can draw upon a variety of cues and strategies to recognize an unfamiliar word. The language cuing systems can be discussed in relation to seven strategies used to identify words: visual configuration, picture clues, semantic clues, syntactic clues, structural analysis, phonic analysis, and syllabication (Ives, Bursuk, and Ives, 1979). In addition to these, a person may choose to check another source such as asking someone or looking up the word in the dictionary. Remember, readers use these strategies in concert with one another to identify or recognize words necessary to promote comprehension.

1. *Visual configuration* refers to using graphic or distinctive visual features to recognize a word or a group of words such as a phrase or whole clause. When using this skill we are attending to visual information and using our graphic knowledge to help us identify the word. We often use visual configuration to recognize words automatically. We can also use visual configuration at a less automatic level. For example, we might think to ourselves, "Does this look similar to another word?" "This is a long word." "This word has tall letters at the beginning and the end." Generally the types of visual configuration clues we use to identify a word are word length; word shape; presence of double letters and repetition of letters; use of capitals, hyphens, apostrophes, and periods; and the graphic characteristics of individual letters.

2. *Picture clues* refer to using pictures, graphs, diagrams, maps, and other types of pictured representations that surround the text to aid in word recognition. If a child is reading about an airplane and the sentence reads, "The pilots sat in the cockpit," a picture of pilots in a cockpit may help the reader identify the word *cockpit.* Picture clues can sometimes be helpful and sometimes distracting, particularly if the pictures do not fit well with the text. Some students with reading difficulties tend to overrely on picture clues.

3. *Semantic clues* refer to using the words in the text and the meaning of the text to help identify the word. When we ask a reader "What word makes sense?" we are asking the individual to use semantic clues and his or her semantic knowledge. Semantic clues also help readers determine which meaning of a word to apply. For example, context helps in deter-

mining the meaning of "lead" in the following sentences: "Put the dog on a *lead.*" "Susan had the *lead* in the school play."

4. *Syntactic clues* refer to using grammatical information to aid in identifying a word. In the sentence, "John walked down the _____," the reader knows that the word in the blank must be a noun. The individual is applying syntactic knowledge or knowledge of grammar and word order.

It is next to impossible not to use semantic and syntactic clues simultaneously. *Context clues* refer to the combination of semantic and syntactic clues. For example: "The safe was made of *lead.*" "John *led* his friend down the path." Using context clues requires the reader to rely on linguistic information that is at the sentence and text (discourse) level. The next three techniques require the reader to rely on linguistic information at the word level.

5. *Structural analysis* refers to using the meaningful subunits of a word (i.e., root words, prefixes, suffixes, and inflectional endings) as identification clues. For example, the word *reeducation* can be broken into the meaningful parts of *re,* meaning to do again, *educate,* meaning the process of teaching knowledge or skills, and *tion,* which changes the root word from a verb to a noun. Chapter 3 (pp. 77) discusses the development of prefixes, suffixes, and inflectional endings. Table 3.1 provides a list of prefixes and suffixes along with examples of their use and their common meaning. Teaching students prefixes, suffixes, and their meaning can aid not only in the identification of a word, but also in understanding its meaning.

6. *Phonic analysis* or *phonics* refers to using the sound of letters (phonemes) as word identification clues. For students to use these clues successfully, they must know the sound/symbol relationships. Depending on the dialect, English has about forty-two sounds, with a number of them spelled in more than one way. As a result, students learn more than a hundred spellings (Gunning, 1996). These sounds are divided into consonants (C) and vowels (V). Table 4.1 presents the twenty-five consonant sounds, with their typical spellings and representative words that use these sounds. The sounds are not listed in alpha-

■ **TABLE 4.1** *Consonant Sounds, Typical Spellings, and Manner of Articulation*

Consonant Sounds	Typical Spellings	Initial	Middle, Final	Manner of Articulation
/p/	p	pot, pick	stop	voiceless stop @ lips
/b/	b	bat, barn	cab, robe	voiced stop @ lips
/t/	t, –ed	time, tap	pot, messed	voiceless stop @ tongue behind teeth
/d/	d, –ed	deer, dinner	bad, ride, cried	voiced stop @ tongue behind teeth
/k/	c, k, ck, qu	kiss, can, quick	back, critique	voiceless stop @ back of mouth
/g/	g	gate, girl	rag	voiced stop @ back of mouth
/f/	f, ph	first, fit	graph, off, rough	voiceless fricative @ lip/teeth
/v/	v	very, vase	love	voiced fricative @ lip/teeth
/th/	th	the, this	mother	voiced fricative @ tongue between teeth
/th/	th	think, thin	both	voiceless fricative @ tongue between teeth
/s/	s, c	sap, cent, psychology	less, piece	voiceless fricative @ tongue behind teeth
/z/	z, –es, –s, x	zip, xerox	has, dogs, messes, lazy	voiced fricative @ tongue behind teeth
/sh/	sh	ship, sure, chef	push, mission, ration	voiceless fricative @ roof of mouth
/zh/	z, s		azure, measure, beige	voiced fricative @ roof of mouth
/ch/	ch, tch	chip, chase	much, hatch	voiceless affricate @ roof of mouth
/j/	j, g	jump, gist	judge, soldier	voiced affricate @ roof of mouth
/y/	y	you, use	feud	voiced glide @ roof of mouth
/wh/	wh	where, whale		voiceless glide @ back of mouth
/w/	w	we, witch	sewer	voiced glide @ back of mouth
/h/	h	happy, who		voiceless glide @ throat
/l/	l	lady, lion	mail, babble	liquid @ tongue behind teeth
/r/	r	ride, write		liquid @ tongue behind teeth
/m/	m	me, mom	him, autumn, comb	nasal @ nose
/n/	n, kn, gn, pn, mn	now, know, gnat, pneumonia, mnemonics	pan, sign	nasal @ nose
/ng/	ng		sing, English	nasal @ nose

Source: Adapted from V. Fromkin, and R. Rodman (1993). *Introduction to Language.* New York: Holt, Rinehart, and from L. C. Moats, (1995). *Spelling: Development, Disability and Instruction.* Baltimore: York Press.

betical order, but grouped according to the manner in which they are articulated (formed in the mouth). From this we can see how the sounds are related according to the manner in which they are produced. For example, there are eight sound pairs (e.g., /p/ and /b/, /t/ and /d/, /ch/ and /j/) in which the only difference between the two sounds is whether or not the sounds are produced with a resonance in the throat. This can be felt with the hand on the larynx or the hands placed over the ears (Moats, 1995). For students experiencing significant difficulty in learning to read and make sound/symbol associations, having them check to see if they can "feel the sound" can help them to decode a word or spell it when writing (Clark and Uhry, 1995). Information on the manner of articulation also includes information about how the air stream is affected (i.e., stop, fricative, affricate, glide, and liquid), and if the sound is nasal (i.e., /m/, /n/, and /ng/). This information is helpful when you are using a student's miscues and invented spellings to diagnose the source of difficulty. Students who know at least some phonics are likely to substitute similar *sounds*. For example, it is more likely that students would substitute *n* or *m* for *ng* than other sounds, because they are nasals. Similarly, while the substitution of *d* for *b* may be a reversal more related to visual processing, the substitution of *p* for *b* could be related to the student's not accounting for voicing.

In general, there must be a vowel in every English syllable, and consonants are formed around the vowel. Figure 4.2 presents the vowel sounds in English, moving from a closed mouth position to an open mouth position. Using this information, we can look at miscues or spelling errors and predict that if a student is using sounds to determine the letters, he or she would be more likely to substitute /e/ for /a/ than /e/ for /u/. It is also obvious why students often confuse /ir/, /er/, and /ur/ in spelling, since these three spellings represent the same sound. *Schwa* is the vowel sound often found in unaccented syllables (e.g., suppose, familiar, sofa, mission) and is the most frequently occurring vowel sound. Native speakers of Asian languages and Spanish tend to have difficulty with /ē/. When working with these children, you may want to start with the /ō/ words (Gunning, 1996).

The English language also makes use of consonant digraphs and consonant clusters. A *consonant digraph* is two consonants that represent one sound (*ph* for *f*). A *consonant cluster* or *consonant blend* is composed of two or more letters that represent the sounds of the letters clustered together. Table 4.2 provides a listing of the consonant digraphs and clusters. When students misread a cluster—reading *fog* for *frog*—ask questions that lead them to see that

they need to process two initial sounds rather than just one (Gunning, 1996).

- "What letter does the word *fog* begin with? What **two** letters does *this* word (pointing to *frog*) begin with?"
- "Listen to the word *frog*. What sound do *f* and *r* make when you say them together?"
- (Write *fog* and *frog* and have the students compare for similarities and differences in the written form. Then have them listen to the words and make comparisons.)

Native speakers of Spanish may have difficulty perceiving /b/, /v/, /k/, /z/, /sh/, /th/, and /ch/. You may need to spend additional time developing students' perception of these sounds. See Table 3.11 for additional comparisons between Spanish and English.

One frequent strategy young readers use when decoding short one-syllable words (e.g., CV, CVC, CVC + silent e) is to pronounce the beginning consonant and then the whole word (*buh-bat*) (Gunning, 1995). This suggests that students divide words into their *onset* (initial consonant or consonant cluster) and *rime* or spelling pattern (e.g., -V, -VC, -VC + silent e). Table 4.3 provides a list of high frequency rimes or spelling pattern words.

7. *Syllabication* refers to using the sounds of words to divide them into pronunciation units. A *syllable* is a unit of pronunciation, and it may include one or more sounds. Because syllabication is strictly an oral language phenomenon, it does not have a written language parallel. Consequently, its application as a word identification technique is somewhat limited. Nevertheless, dividing a word into segments or syllables is often an aid to applying phonic analysis in multisyllabic words.

For teaching syllabication, the following generalizations are suggested and are presented in their frequency of occurrence and approximate order of difficulty (Gunning, 1988).

- *Easy affixes:* Most inflectional endings, prefixes, and suffixes form separate syllables: *haunt-ed, play-ing, re-build, help-ful*). One exception is *-s*.

■ **FIGURE 4.2**   *Vowel Spellings by Mouth Position*

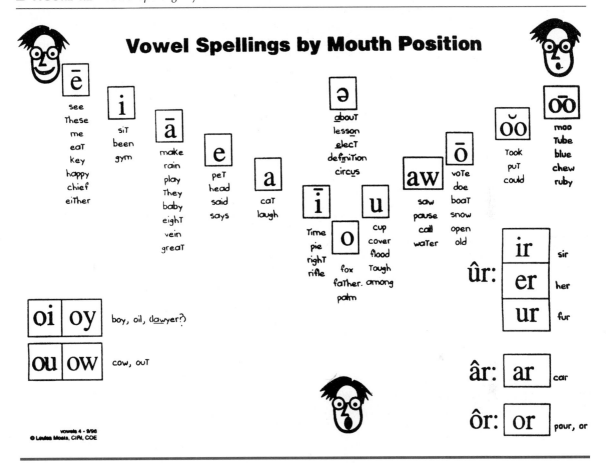

Source: Reprinted by permission of the author from L. C. Moats, (in press). *Speech to Print: Language Study for Teachers of Reading and Writing.* Baltimore: Paul H. Brookes Publishing Co.

— *Compound words:* Compound words form separate syllables: (*sun-set, some-one*).

— *Two consonants between two vowels:* When two consonants come between two vowels, as in *con-cept* and *lum-ber,* divide the word between the two consonants (VC-CV).

— *One consonant between two vowels:* When a single consonant comes between the two vowels, divide the word after the first vowel, as in *ba-con* and *ma-jor* (V-CV). The syllable to the right is often an *open syllable* and has a long vowel sound.

— *Final -le:* When the letters *le* are at the end of a word, they usually combine with a preceding consonant to create a separate syllable: *cra-dle* and *ma-ple.*

Chapter Appendix 4.1 presents a suggested scope and sequence for word identification by reading level. We can use such information to determine what to teach. Scope and sequences for word identification skills can also be found in the teachers' edition of many reading series.

■ **TABLE 4.2** *Common Consonant Digraphs and Clusters*

Common Consonant Digraphs

Correspondence	Examples
ch = /ch/	chair, church
ck = /k/	tack, pick
gh = /f/	rough, tough
kn = /n/	knot, knob
ng = /ŋ/	thing, sing
ph = /f/	phone, photograph
sc = /s/	scissors, scientist
sh = /sh/	shoe, shop
(s)si = /sh/	mission
th = /th/	there, them
th = /th/	thumb, thunder
ti = /sh/	station, action
wh = /w/	wheel, where
wr = =/r/	wrench, wrestle

Common Initial Consonant Clusters

With l	Example Words
bl	blanket, black
cl	clock, clothes
fl	flag, fly
gl	glove, glue
pl	plum, place
sl	slide, show

With r	Example Words
br	broom, bread
cr	crow, crash
dr	dress, drink
fr	frog, from
gr	green, ground
pr	prince, prepare

With s	Example Words
sc	score, scale
sch	school, schedule
scr	scream, scrub
sk	sky, skin
sl	sled, sleep
sm	smoke, smile
sn	snake, sneakers
sp	spider, spot
st	star, stop
str	street, stream
sw	sweater, swim

Common Final Consonant Clusters

With n	Example Words
nce	prince, chance
nch	lunch, bunch
nd	hand, wind
nk	tank, wink
nt	tent, sent

Other	Example Words
ct	fact, effect
mp	jump, camp
sp	wasp, grasp
st	nest, best

With l	Example Words
ld	field, old
lf	wolf, self
lk	milk, silk
lm	film
lp	help
lt	salt, belt
lve	twelve, solve

Source: Adapted from T. G. Gunning, *Creating Reading Instruction for All Children* (Boston: Allyn and Bacon, 1996)

TEACHING WORD IDENTIFICATION

Bradley is one of the third graders who struggles the most with reading. When he reads orally from first-grade level materials, the teacher pronounces about 30 percent of the words for him. He reads slowly and when he comes to a word he cannot identify, he applies inconsistent strategies. Sometimes Bradley seems to use the context (semantic cues) to assist him, and other times he appears to make wild guesses. Sometimes he attempts to sound out the letters, but usually he is not successful beyond the first two letters. Even when he does make correct sound-symbol associations, he does not successfully blend the sounds together. Even though Bradley struggles in decoding the individual words, he appears to understand what he has read because he successfully retells it and answers questions about the story. Bradley has average intelligence, understands what he hears, and communicates effectively with his

■ **TABLE 4.3**   *High Frequency Rimes and Syllables*

Vowel Sounds	Rimes and Syllables
Short Vowels	
a	–ab, –ack, –ad, –ag, –am, –amp, –an, –and, –ap, –ash, –ask, –ast, –at
e	–eb, –eck, –ed, –eg, –ell, –em, –en, –end, –ent, –est, –et
i	–ick, –id, –ig, –ill, –im, –in, –ip, –ish, –it
o	–ob, –ock, –od, –og, –op, –ot
u	–ub, –uck, –uff, –ug, –um, –ump, –un, –ung, –unk, –ut
Long Vowels	
a (CVC+e)	–ace, –ade, –ake, –ale, –ame, –ane, –ape, –ate, –ave
a (CVVC)	–aid, –ail, –ain
a (CVV)	–ay
e (CV)	–e
e (CVVC)	–eak, –eal, –eam, –ean, –eat, –eed, –eep, –eet
i (CV)	–y
i (CVC+e)	–ice, –ide, –ike, –ile, –ime, –ine, –ipe, –ite, –ive
o (CVC+e)	–oke, –ole, –one, –ope
o (CVVC)	–oad, –oat, –oast
u (CVVC)	–uit
R = Controlled Vowels	
/air/	–air, –are, –ear
/ar/	–ar, –ark, –art
/ir/	–ear, –eer
/or/	–ore, –orn
Other Vowels	
/aw/	–all, –aw, –ought
/oi/	–oil, –oy
/oo/	–ook, –oom, –oon
/oo/	–ew, –oot
/ow/	–out, –ound, –ouse, –ow, –own

peers and teachers. His math skills are at a third-grade level.

Teaching students like Bradley to read fluently and to automatically recognize the words necessary to promote comprehension requires the teacher to observe the students closely when reading and to as-

sist them in developing and using the various word identification strategies flexibly.

When beginning to work with a student who has difficulty in learning and remembering words (acquiring a sight word vocabulary) and who has limited word identification or decoding strategies, it is helpful not only to determine the student's current strategies, but also to determine what approaches he or she has previously tried, how consistently, for how long, and with what success. Taking into consideration the student's current reading strategies and metalinguistic and metacognitive skills as well as the previous instructional history, you can better select strategies or approaches that encourage the student to become a flexible, competent reader.

The rest of this chapter focuses on teaching strategies and approaches that promote the development and use of word identification strategies. The first section presents strategies and approaches to word identification and early reading that emphasize teaching decoding strategies within the context of meaningful stories and books. The second section presents code-emphasis strategies and approaches to teaching word identification and early reading, stressing systematic introduction of phonic and structural analysis. The third section presents several activities that provide students with repeated opportunities to practice identifying words in isolation and to use associative clues to assist in word recognition. The fourth section presents a strategy for word identification that has proven particularly successful with older students who are having difficulty identifying multisyllabic words.

Meaning–Emphasis Approaches

Meaning–emphasis strategies for teaching word identification use visual configuration and context clues (pictures, semantic and syntactic cues) and, if taught, phonic and structural analysis, within the context of meaningful stories and books. This section presents four related approaches that have been used with students who experience difficulties in developing fluent word recognition and effective word identification strategies. Apply the Concept 4.4 provides information on ways to teach phonic analysis in context.

APPLY THE CONCEPT 4.4

USING AN ANALYTIC OR ANALOGY METHOD TO TEACH PHONIC ANALYSIS

The analytic or analogy method for teaching phonics relies on the students' abilities to see the similarities among the words they can already identify and to induce from those words the sound-symbol relationships between oral and written language. This method of teaching phonics requires that the students already have a pool of sight words and some decoding skills (Ehri and Robbins, 1992).

The steps in the analytic method for teaching phonics as adapted from Karlin (1980) are as follows:

1. *Select a sound-symbol relationship to teach, using the children's needs and the developmental sequence presented in Chapter Appendix 4.1 as a guide.* Write a list of words on the chalkboard that have the target sound-symbol relationship. Tell the children to look at the words as you read them aloud. For example:

   pat
   pill
   purse
   pottery

   Emphasize the beginning sound as you read each word. Through discussion, help the students make the following generalizations:

   a. The words all start with the same letter.
   b. The words all sound alike at the beginning.

   Tell the students to underline the letter that is the same in the words.

   Next, have the students listen to other words that begin the same as the words in the list. (These words should be in the student's listening vocabulary.) For example, *poison, pillow, pin, pollution, pot,* and *pepper.* Ask the students to think of new words that start with the selected phonic element.

   Finally, have the students listen to new words, only some of which begin with the target sound. Ask the students to judge which words begin with the target sound.

2. *Sound substitution.* In this step students are asked to apply their new generalization about

the sound-symbol relationship to help identify unknown words. To do this, write a sight word on the chalkboard; below it write a similar word with the target sound. For example:

   day
   pay

Ask the students what is similar about the two words. Now refer the students to the list of words on the chalkboard that begin with *p.* Model as you think aloud how to take away the *d* in *day* and write a *p* in its place. Cue the students, "Remember how words that start with a *p* sound? So now *day* is changed to _____."

Repeat this procedure with other words, each time getting the students to note the likenesses and differences and to substitute letters or sounds to identify the unknown word.

3. *Contextual application.* This step requires the students to apply their new rule when reading in context. The new words that were learned in step 2 are put in sentences, and the students are asked to read the sentences. If the students cannot remember the new words, they are asked to think of a word that makes sense and begins with the sound that *p* makes. Finally, this activity is completed with reading other sentences that contain new words that start with *p.*

Initially you may want to control the position of the sound-symbol relationship within the word, for example, by introducing a consonant sound first in the initial position, then final position, and then medial position.

Using this method has the advantages of teaching students to use phonic analysis skills in conjunction with other word identification skills, and of directly teaching students that words are composed of sounds. However, studies suggest that beginning readers need some decoding skills to be sufficiently analytic to read words by analogy (Ehri and Robbin, 1992).

Modified Language Experience Approach

This approach to teaching early reading facilitates the transfer from oral language to written language by capitalizing on the child's linguistic, cognitive, social, and cultural knowledge and abilities (Stauffer, 1970). Language experience approaches are congruent with principles based on Vygotsky's theory of cognitive development, and on learning frameworks such as whole language and process writing (Veatch, 1991). These approaches encourage students to rely on the use of their own language, repeated reading, visual configuration, and context clues to identify words. Language experience approaches are often considered language arts approaches, since they integrate oral language, writing, and reading (Allen, 1976; Tierney and Shanahan, 1991). Several methods for teaching language experience approaches have been developed: Allen's Language Experience Approach in Communication (Allen, 1976; Allen and Allen, 1966–68; 1982); Ashton-Warner's Organic Reading (Ashton-Warner, 1958, 1963, 1972) and Stauffer's Language-Experience Approach (Stauffer, 1970). The modified language experience approach we describe is designed for students who have limited experience or success with reading and little or no sight vocabularies. The objectives are:

1. To teach the concept that text is talk written down
2. To teach the metalinguistic skills of sentence and word segmentation
3. To teach left-to-right progression
4. To teach use of semantic and syntactic clues
5. To teach recognition of words both within the context of the experience story and in isolation

The approach is built on the idea that oral and written language are interdependent and that oral language can serve as the base for the development of written language.

— PROCEDURES: The procedures for this modified language experience approach are similar to those suggested by Stauffer (1970). However, more structure and practice have been incorporated into this modification to provide for the needs of students who experience difficulties in learning to read. It is designed to be used individually or with small groups of two to five students. At the heart of this approach is the language experience story, a story written by the students about events, persons, or things of their choice (see Figure 4.3).

First day: For the *first day* of instruction, guidelines for developing a language experience story are:

1. *Provide or select an experience.* Provide or have the students select an experience of interest to them. Sometimes a picture can help stimulate ideas, but be sure the students have experiences related to the picture. Remember—you are relying on the students' memory of the experience and their memory for the language used to describe the experience.

2. *Explain the procedure to the students.* Explain that the students are going to be dictating a story about the selected experience. This story will then become their reading text or book.

3. *Discuss the experience.* Discuss the experience with students so that they can begin to think about

■ **FIGURE 4.3** *Dictated Language Experience Story*

Woody Woodpecker was driving a jet to outer space and saw some aliens. And he got on his jet and went to Jupiter and saw some people from outer space and they were driving jets, too.

what they want to put in the dictated story. Students with learning and behavior problems sometimes have difficulty organizing their thoughts. The discussion can serve as time for the students to plan what they want to say. To facilitate the planning process you may want to write notes.

4. *Write the dictated story.* Have the students tell the story while you write it. Students should watch as you write or type it. If you are working with several students you may want to write the story on large chart paper. Have each of the students contribute to the story. If you are working with an individual, sit next to the student so that he or she can see what you write. Encourage the students to use natural voices. The language experience story presented in Figure 4.3 was dictated by Sam, a third grader reading at the primer level.

5. *Read the story to the students.* Ask the students to listen to the story to see if they want to make any changes. Make changes accordingly.

6. *Have students read the story.* First have the students read the story together with you (choral reading) until they seem comfortable with the story. When you are choral reading point to the words so that the students focus on the text as they read. Next have the students read individually and pronounce words they cannot identify. In some cases a student may give you a lengthy story, yet his or her memory for text is limited. When this occurs, you may work on the story in parts, beginning with only the first several sentences or first paragraph.

7. *Encourage the students to read the story to others.* This is often a very intrinsically reinforcing activity.

8. *Type the story.* If not already typed, type the story and make one copy for each student. Also make a second copy for each student to keep and use for record keeping.

Second day: For the *second day* of instruction, guidelines for reading the story are:

1. *Practice reading the story.* Have the students practice reading the story using choral reading, individual reading, and reading to one another. When the students are reading individually and they come to a word they do not recognize, encourage them to look at the word and think of what word would make sense. Having the students read to the end of the sentence can also help them to think of a word that makes sense. If students cannot recall the word, pronounce it.

2. *Focus on individual words and sentences.* Have the students match, locate, and read individual sentences and words in the story. Discuss what markers are used to denote sentences and words. Finally, have the students read the story to themselves and underline the words they think they know.

3. *Check on known words.* Have each student read the story orally. Record the words the student knows on your copy of the story.

4. *Type the words from the story on word cards.* Type the words each student knows from the story on word cards.

Third day: Guidelines for the *third day* are:

1. *Practice reading the story.* Repeat the type of activities described in step 1 of the second day.

2. *Focus on individual sentences and words.* Repeat the type of activities described in step 2 of the second day.

3. *Check on known words.* With the word cards in the *same order* as the words in the text, have each student read the word cards, recording the words the student knows.

Fourth day: Guidelines for the *fourth day* are:

1. *Practice reading the story.* Repeat the type of activities described in step 1 of the second day.

2. *Focus on sentences and words.* Repeat the type of activities described in step 2 of the second day.

3. *Check on known words.* With the cards in *random order,* have each student read the words, recording the words each student knows.

Fifth day: Guidelines for the *fifth day* are:

1. *Check on known words.* Repeat step 3 from the fourth day, using only the words the student knows from the previous day.

2. *Enter known words in word bank.* Each student should make word cards (3 × 5 index cards or scraps of poster board work well) for the words that he or she can identify in step 1. These words should be filed by the student in his or her word bank (index card box). Words the student cannot identify should not be included.

3. *Read, illustrate, and publish the story.* Have the students read the story and decide if they want to illustrate it and/or put it into a language experience book. Books can be developed for individual students or one book can be made for the group. Students can then share these books with each other, with other interested persons, and place them in the library.

Once the students have completed at least one story and have developed fifteen to twenty words in their word banks, they can begin to use the banks for a variety of activities, such as generating new sentences, locating words with similar parts (i.e., inflectional endings, beginning sounds, shapes), and categorizing words by use (e.g., action words, naming words, describing words).

As the number of sight words continues to increase, students can write their own stories, using the words from the word bank to assist them. More suggestions for developing activities based on the word bank are given in Figure 4.4.

— COMMENTS: The modified language experience approach provides a method for teaching children initial skills in reading, including the recognition of sight words. The approach utilizes the students' memory and oral language skills as well as visual configuration and context clues. Once the initial sight vocabulary has been built to between 30 and 100 words, students should be encouraged to read other books and stories. This approach emphasizes recognition of single words (i.e., pointing to words during reading, identification and use of single words on word cards) and may not encourage reading for meaning (Tierney, Readence, and Dishner, 1995). It would be important to provide students with access to literature through listening to give them opportunities for constructing meaning.

This approach lends itself to the use of computer technology, particularly with the use of word processing and desktop publishing software that incorporates voice and graphics such as Children's Writing and Publishing Center (Learning Company) and *Kidwriter II* (Davidson and Associates) or language experience–based software programs such as *Writing to Read* (Martin and Friedburg, 1986). For example, Stratton, Grindler, and Postell (1992) integrated word processing and photography into a language experience with middle school students.

Activities are incorporated into the approach to encourage the development of the metalinguistic skills of sentence and word segmentation. However, this approach does not present a systematic method for teaching phonic and structural analysis. For students who have difficulty with these skills, a more structured method of teaching phonic and structural analysis may be needed after they have developed an initial sight vocabulary. This approach may not provide some students with enough drill and practice to develop a sight vocabulary. In those cases, it will be necessary to supplement this approach with activities presented in the section on techniques for building sight words. For a research review of language experience approaches to teaching beginning reading, see Stahl and Miller (1989).

Patterned Language Approach

One of the major problems for students who have difficulty learning to read is that they get little practice reading. Many of the books these children attempt to read, contain too many words they do not recognize. Therefore, they do not get the opportunity to let the flow of the language assist them in identifying unknown words or to experience the success of fluent reading.

Predictable books, especially those that repeat language patterns, foster reading fluency (Rhodes and Dudley-Marling, 1996) and provide opportunities for students to build on the language patterns and pictures to promote word recognition. Predictable books are those that follow a set pattern, making it easy for the child to predict the words and meaning. *Brown Bear, Brown Bear, What Do You See?* (Martin, 1983) is a well known example. In the

■ **FIGURE 4.4**   *Suggested Activities for Word Bank Cards*

1. Alphabetize words in word banks.

2. Match the word with the same word as it occurs in newspapers, magazines, etc.

3. Make a poster of the words known.

4. Complete sentences using word banks. Provide students with a stem or incomplete sentences and have students fill slot with as many different words as possible. Example:

   He ran to the _____. The _____ and _____ ran into the park.

5. Find or categorize words in word banks:

naming words	science words
action words	color words
descriptive words	animal words
words with more than one meaning	names of people
words with the same meaning	interesting words
opposites	funny words
people words	exciting words

6. Locate words beginning the same, ending the same, or meaning the same.

7. Locate words with various endings.

8. Match sentences in stories with words from word bank.

9. Make punctuation cards. Locate and match punctuation in stories.

10. Construct sentences, questions, and commands from words in word banks.

We	went	to	the	farm	.
Where	are	we	going	?	
Go	to	the	farm	!	

11. Have students describe someone or something, using words from the word banks separately or organized into sentences. Have other students guess the person or thing.

12. Have students select a word from their word bank and use it in as many different sentences as possible.

13. Have students play dominoes with each other's words. (Ending and beginning letters must match.)

pot	Tom	mother

14. Use word bank cards for matching-card games, such as grab and bingo.

15. Organize words into a story. Students might need to borrow words for this use and may wish to illustrate or make a permanent record of it.

16. Delete words from a story. Have students use words from their word banks to complete the story.

17. Scramble the sentences in the story and have students rearrange them in an appropriate order.

18. Scramble the words in a student's sentence and have students unscramble them.

19. Create advertisements with word cards.

20. Establish class word banks for different classroom centers, such as science words, number words, weather words, house words, family words.

Source: Adapted from R. J. Tierney, J. E. Readence, and E. K. Dishner, *Reading Strategies and Practices: Guide for Improving Instruction* (Boston: Allyn and Bacon, 1980), pp. 285–287.

book *It Didn't Frighten Me!* (Goss and Harste, 1985), the pattern is repetitive throughout the book with the only change being the color and type of animal (e.g., orange alligator, silver tiger, pink di-nosaur). Some predictable books are cumulative, such as *I Went Walking* (Williams, 1990); each time the text says, "I went walking. What did you see?" an animal is added.

In the last ten years, there has been tremendous growth in the number of early reading books that use simple predictable language patterns and rhyme, paired with well-matched picture clues in the illustrations. (See Chapter Appendix 4.2 for a list of predictable books.) In addition, a number of education companies publish series of easy, predictable books (e.g., Rigby Education, Scholastic, The Wright Group, Troll Books).

The patterned language approach (Bridge and Burton, 1982; Bridge, Winograd, and Haley, 1983; Heald-Taylor, 1987; Martin and Brogan, 1971; Martin, 1990; Rhodes, 1979, 1981; Trachtenburg and Ferruggia, 1989) uses highly predictable reading materials and provides many opportunities for the teacher and students to read together (choral reading). It is based on assumptions that repetition of predictable language and choral reading will assist the students in learning to make the connections between oral language and the printed word (Smith, 1988; Goodman, 1996).

━ **PROCEDURES:** The procedures for the patterned language approach rely heavily on the students making predictions and on using predictable reading materials to increase the likelihood that the predictions will be logical. Bridge, Winograd, and Haley (1983) suggest the following steps when using the patterned language approach with low-skill first-grade readers:

1. Read the book aloud to the students. Reread the book, inviting the students to join in when they can predict what will come next. Have the students take turns choral reading the book.
2. Put the text of the book on a large paper without the book's picture cues. Read and choral read the story from the chart. Give the students sentence strips with sentences from the story. Have them match the strips to the chart and then read the sentences.
3. Give the students individual word cards from the story, in order. Have the children place each card under the matching word in the chart.
4. Read and choral read the story from the chart. Place the individual word cards from sections of the story in random order at the bottom of the chart. Have the students match the word cards to the words in the story.

The sentence- and word-matching procedures are used so that the students will attend to the grapho-phonic clues as well as the semantic and syntactic clues. An important aspect of instruction is having the students discuss the patterns and compare the language patterns (Lynch, 1986). Also, using patterned language and predictable books provides easy entry into writing: Students can expand the books by furnishing more examples of the patterns presented, or they can develop and write their own books.

━ **COMMENTS:** Bridge, Winograd, and Haley (1983) coupled this approach with a language experience approach (Cunningham, 1979) then compared it to the standard procedures in a basal reader. When they compared the reading of the low-skill first-grade readers in the study, they found that students who used the patterned language approach learned significantly more words. While this approach is similar to Holdaway's procedures for using a Shared Book Approach (Holdaway, 1979) and Van Allen's Language Experience Approach (Allen and Allen 1966–68) for reading, it offers more specific procedures, routines, and predictable texts which are helpful for students having difficulty learning to read (Tancock, 1994).

Reading Recovery

Reading Recovery is a preventative program designed for children who are having difficulty learning to read during their first year of reading instruction. The program was developed and researched by Marie Clay (1985, 1991a, 1993b), a leading educator and psychologist in New Zealand, and disseminated widely in the United States (DeFord, Lyons, and Pinnell, 1991). The program is short-term, usually lasting from twelve to fifteen weeks, and uses one-on-one instruction for thirty minutes each day to provide children strategies for reading. Supplemental to the reading and writing instruction that occurs in the classroom, the program ties reading and writing activities. Children are taught how to use a variety of word identification and comprehension strategies and how to orchestrate the strategies while attending to the meaning of the text (Clay 1993b; DeFord, Lyons, and Pinnell, 1991).

The materials include many simple books, particularly predictable and patterned language books, that progress in difficulty from books usually built on one sentence pattern organized around a theme familiar to most children (Level 1), to books that roughly correspond to typical books and stories used at the end of first grade (Level 20) (Peterson, 1991). While there is no formula for determining the level of a book or selecting an individual book for a student, the following criteria are used (Peterson, 1991):

— Familiarity of the topic/text, given the students' own experiences and knowledge
— Degree to which illustrations match the print to provide support to the reader
— Familiarity of and repetition of language patterns and vocabulary
— Familiarity of story sequence, narrative style, and episodic structure

Table 4.4 describes the general features of the book levels, and Chapter Appendix 4.3 provides a list of books by Reading Recovery level. "The key to selecting appropriate materials is learning how to think about the relationship between various features of texts and the experiences of individual readers" (Peterson, 1991, p. 128).

— **PROCEDURES:** Reading Recovery provides extra help for individual children during the early period of literacy development and is designed for the lowest achieving readers in a first-grade classroom. Children having difficulty are individually assessed by a Reading Recovery teacher using the *Observation Survey* (Clay, 1993a) to determine which children are having the most difficulty with literacy development. This survey affords the teacher the

opportunity to closely observe the child completing a variety of literacy activities including letter identification, word recognition of a simple word list, reading a simple book, writing a story or words the child knows, and writing a dictated sentence. In addition, children participate in the evaluative activity, *Concepts about Print* (Clay, 1982), which includes left-to-right and top-to-bottom directionality, word segmentation, sound segmentation, punctuation, and capitalization (Clay, 1993a, 1993b).

When a child begins the program, the child and teacher spend the first two weeks of instruction *roaming around the known* (Clay, 1993b). The teacher does not systematically teach but rather explores reading and writing with the child. Together they enjoy books, write collaborativly, and get to know each other. Generally, the teacher selects tasks that are easy for the child, using them to increase his or her knowledge of the child and to build a sense of trust.

After the first two weeks, the teacher begins using a consistent lesson framework to assist the child in discovering the patterns and strategies associated with literacy. (See Figure 4.5.)

1. *Rereading familiar books.* The teacher and child begin the thirty-minute lessons by rereading books that are familiar to the child. After a book has been introduced and read by the child, it is placed in the child's reading box. During this part of the lesson both the child and teacher select familiar books to read. Some of the books may be selected by the teacher because they provide opportunities for teaching and reviewing certain strategies (Pinnell, Fried, and Estice, 1990). Other books may be selected by the child. Rereading allows the child to participate in fluent reading in much the same way that using language experience stories written by the child allows for the reading of familiar text. During this time the teacher observes closely to see if the child is using such strategies as rereading sentences when miscalled words change the meaning of the text.

2. *Rereading the previous lesson's new book and taking a running record.* During this part of the les-

■ **TABLE 4.4**   *Sources of Predictability Used in Determining the Level of Books*

Levels	Sources	Levels	Sources
1–4	• Commonly used oral language patterns and vocabulary used repeatedly. • Illustrations support text because they clearly portray the text without much clutter or extraneous detail. • Each book presents a complete message or story likely to be familiar to the students. • Language reflects syntax and organization of young children's speech and sentences are comparably short. • Print appears in the same position on each page.	*9–12 cont.*	• Illustrations provide moderate support. • Oral and written language structures are both used. • Sentence length increases and can be almost double to books in Levels 5–8.
5–8	• The book contains memorable, repetitive language patterns and vocabulary, but two to three patterns are used. • Some syntax is more typical of written than oral language. • Illustrations provide moderate support to text. • At about Level 8, sentences become less descriptive of concrete objects and actions.	*13–15*	• Books in levels 13 to 15 have varied sentence patterns. • There is a greater variety of words and more specialized vocabulary. • Illustrations provide support for overall meaning of the story but cannot be used to interpret the precise message of the printed text. • Written language structures are used, with oral language structures in dialogue. • Stories have elaborated episodes and events.
9–12	• Stories are expanded with sequences of episodes that are completed across several pages. • Three or more sentence patterns or varied sentence patterns are repeated (often in the form of refrains). • Some unfamiliar or idiomatic expressions and vocabulary are used.	*16–20*	• Vocabulary is varied and rich with no effort to repeat words solely to serve as signposts for readers. • Written language forms are common. • Illustrations create and portray atmosphere of study but do not necessarily support content of text. • Books have full pages of print and episodes are often longer than entire books at the lower levels. • Characters are fictional personalities and episodes develop around fanciful, imaginative events.

Source: Adapted from B. Peterson, "Selecting books for beginning readers," In D. E. DeFord, C. A. Lyons, and G. S. Pinnell (eds.), *Bridges to Literacy: Learning from Reading Recovery* (Portsmouth, N.H.: Heinemann, 1991), pp. 119–138.

son, the teacher takes the role of observer and recorder to determine how the child is using word identification, comprehension, and monitoring strategies when reading the book that was introduced and read once the previous day. This reading is to be independent, although the teacher may provide a word when the child is completely stopped. "The child is not expected to read this book with complete

■ **FIGURE 4.5**   *Reading Recovery Lesson Framework*

Reading familiar stories

- Child rereads several of the stories that he or she has already read that are in his or her familiar book box
  - Provides child opportunities to engage in fluent reading, use reading behaviors independently
  - Provides teacher opportunities to observe how child is using reading behaviors independently

Rereading the previous lesson's new book and taking a running record

- Child reads previous lesson's book without teacher support while teacher records
  - Provides teacher opportunity to observe child's reading behaviors and make adjustments in lesson

Working with letters

- Child learns letters using magnetic and other letters and writes words (if letters are not known)

Writing a message or storage

- Child composes a sentence or simple story with teacher support
- Child reconstructs sentence from cut-up sentence strip
  - Provides child the opportunity to make connections between reading and writing and to develop phonological awareness

Reading a new book

- Teacher introduces and child reads a new book
  - Provides child opportunity to learn and use reading strategies in new text

---

accuracy, but it should not be so difficult that the child has to struggle. An accuracy check [on word recognition] confirms the teacher's selection of the right level of difficulty. If the child is reading at about 90 percent to 95 percent accuracy, the text is probably in the appropriate range (Pinnell, Fried, and Estice, 1990, p. 284).

3. *Working with letters.* If a child does not recognize and write the upper- and lowercase letters, the teacher works with the child, generally using plastic or magnetic letters. Clay (1993b) suggests that when a child knows more than 10 letters, an alphabet book can be made with the upper- and lowercase letters and a key picture the child associates with the letter. Leaving blank pages for the letters the child does not know gives the child some idea of the size of the task as well as a sense of accomplishment as the letters are learned and entered in the book.

4. *Writing a message or story.* The child composes a brief message or story usually one to two sentences in length. This is done with assistance from the teacher, using a writing book in which the binding is turned horizontally so the top page can be used as a practice area and the bottom page used to write the message (see Figure 4.6). Sometimes related messages are written over several lessons, thus composing a story. The message is written word by word with the child or teacher saying the words slowly. When appropriate, the child is encouraged to predict the letters that represent the sounds. The teacher may also draw empty boxes on the practice page to represent each letter in a word. The child then listens to predict the letters; written or magnetic letters may be used. In this supported situation, the child discovers sound/symbol relationships and participates in structural and phonic analyses. The child then reads the message. The teacher then writes the message on a sentence strip and cuts the strip so the child can reassemble it and compare it to the sample in the writing book.

5. *Reading a new book.* At each lesson the teacher introduces a new book to the child, who then reads it. The goal of instruction is to introduce a book so that the children can read the new text with a high degree of successful processing. Clay (1991b) suggests that the teacher create a scaffold within which the children can complete a first reading of the story. Clay's suggestions use principles of scaffolded instruction (see Chapter Two) in that the teacher guides the child to bring to mind his/her own background knowledge, and the teacher introduces some aspects of the new knowledge so that the child can experience success.

■ **FIGURE 4.6** *Child's Writing in a Writing Book with Use of Boxing*

Clay (1991b) explains that "it is a process of drawing the children into the activity before passing control to the children and pushing them gently towards problem-solving the whole first reading of the story for themselves" (p. 265). The teacher and child look through the book and talk about it. They look at the pictures, make predictions, talk about their knowledge and experiences related to the story, introduce the characters, draw attention to the important ideas or new vocabulary, and "give opportunities for the child to hear the new words which he [or she] will have to guess from the pictures and language context" (Clay, 1985, p. 68).

Clay suggests (1991b) that the teacher might initiate any of the following depending upon the children:

— Invite the children to respond to the new book using illustrations and linking the book to other familiar stories.
— Draw from the children's experiences and in doing so uncover potential confusions, which can be clarified.
— Provide a framework for anticipating what will occur by sketching the plot or sequence of events up to the climax.
— Anticipate the literacy language or features that may not be familiar to the children and talk about the language or features in this introduction.
— Repeatedly use a difficult sentence pattern found in the story and have the children repeat it.

After introducing the book, the teacher then assists the child in reading it. The teacher supports the child by encouraging the use of various strategies for word identification and comprehension, models and reinforces the use of strategies, and discusses and enjoys the book with the child.

According to Clay (1991a), these powerful "in the head" strategies include:

— Searching for and using meaning, language structure, and visual information
— Self-monitoring (checking on their own reading using meaning, syntax, and visual information)

— Cross-checking one source of information against another
— Self-correcting through predicting, monitoring, and searching for additional information (Clay, 1991c)

For example, when a child comes to a word that he or she cannot identify, the teacher might encourage using the pictures to assist. Or, depending upon the word (e.g., *bunny*) and the child's skills, the teacher might use magnetic letters to make a known word that looks similar (e.g., *funny*) and then substitute letters so the child can compare the two words by seeing and saying the differences. The teacher might also have the child reread the sentence and think about what word would make sense.

Critical to success is a teacher who is watching and listening to the child and then varying the instruction to assist the child in developing strategies for reading. The teacher also relies heavily on modeling and talking about the reading strategies as they are applied by the teacher and child. The children are also encouraged to talk about their strategies. For example, a common query by the teacher is, "How did you know that?"

Children continue in the program until they have developed the kind of independent reading system that good readers use. This is usually twelve to fifteen weeks after beginning the program. Clay comments, "There is no fixed set of strategies nor any required levels of text nor any test score that must be attained to warrant discontinuing. It is essential that the child has a system of strategies which work in such a way that the child learns from his [or her] own attempts to read (Clay, 1985, p. 82). Figure 4.7 presents some of the strategies that a child ready to discontinue the program will use as well as ideas for teaching the strategies.

— **COMMENTS:** The effectiveness of this preventative program has been investigated, first in New Zealand (Clay, 1985, 1991a) and more recently in the United States and other countries (Center, Wheldall, Freeman, Outhred, and McNaught, 1995; Iversen and Tunmer, 1993; Pinnell, Lyons, DeFord, Bryk, and Seltzer, 1994; Pinnell, DeFord, Lyons, and Bryk,

■ **FIGURE 4.7** *When to Discontinue Reading Recovery: Strategies and Teaching Tips*

Directional Movement

Child's Strategy

Child has control over left-to-right and top-to-bottom progression and will be aware of his or her tendency to lose control and will check his or her own behavior.

Teaching Tips

• Point to the starting position on the page or line.
• Assist the child in using hand movements that match voice to text.

One-to-One Matching

Child's Strategy

Child uses a controlled one-to-one matching of spoken to written words for checking purposes.

Teaching Tips

• Point with your finger to match the child's voice and do not move on when he or she makes an error that you feel he or she could self-correct.
• Say: *"Read with your finger?"*
  "Did that match?"
  "Were there enough words?"

Self-Monitoring

Child's Strategy

Child checks on himself or herself, noticing miscues and checking for meaning.

Teaching Tips

• Cue to child to reread and point to each word. Say: *"Use a pointer and make them match."*
• Direct the child's attention to the meaning. Say: *"Look at the picture to see what is happening."*
• When the child self-corrects, say *"I like the way you did that, you found the hard part."*
• When child gives signs of uncertainty even though he or she takes no action, say (as appropriate):
  "Was that OK?"
  "Why did you stop?"
  "What did you notice?"

Use of Multiple Cue Sources

Child's Strategy

Child uses the different cues in concert (syntactic, semantic, and graphophonic cues).

Teaching Tips

• Use the following questions in flexible ways:
  "Does that sound right?"
  "Does that make sense?"
  "Does it look right?"
  "What would you expect to see?"
  "Can we say it that way?"
• When a child uses multiple cue sources and self-corrects, say:
  "I like the way you found out what was wrong all by yourself."

(continued)

FIGURE 4.7   *Continued*

Cross-Checking

Child's Strategy

Child monitors his or her own reading and notices discrepancies in his or her own responses by comparing one kind of cue with another cue.

Teaching Tips

- Point out discrepancies between the two cue sources. Say: *"It could be _____ by the way it looks, but does it make sense?"*

- Talk with the child about the cues he or she is using:

  "What lets you know that the word was _____?"

  "What other cues did you use to help you know the word?"

Source: Adapted from M. M. Clay (1985). *The Early Detection of Reading Difficulties* (3rd ed.). Portsmouth, N.H.: Heinemann.

1995; Shanahan and Barr, 1995; Spiegel, 1995). Studies evaluating the use of Reading Recovery have been encouraging. For example, several years after the end of the program a group of ethnically mixed New Zealand children, who were originally selected in first grade as being the lowest 20 percent of their class in reading and writing, were achieving at a level commensurate with that of a randomly selected group of children who served as controls (Clay, 1985). In subsequent studies, the results have also been encouraging, but long-term effects, change in classroom instruction, and the cost of preparing teachers and implementing the programs in schools have been of some concern (Center et al., 1995).

Fernald (VAKT) Method

The Fernald method (Fernald, 1943, 1988) uses a multisensory or visual-auditory-kinesthetic-tactile (VAKT) approach to teach students to read and write words. This method was used by Grace Fernald and her associates in the clinic school at the University of California at Los Angeles in the 1920s. It is designed for students who have severe difficulties learning and remembering words when reading, who have a limited sight vocabulary, and for whom other methods have not been successful. It is usually taught on an individual basis.

■ **PROCEDURES:** The Fernald method consists of four stages through which students progress as they learn to identify unknown words more effectively. The first stage, which is the most laborious, requires a multisensory approach and utilizes a language experience format. By the final stage, the students are reading books and are able to identify unknown words from the context and their similarity to words or word parts already learned. At this stage, the students are no longer tracing or writing a word to learn it.

Stage One: Guidelines for Stage One are as follows:

1. *Solicit the student's commitment to learn.* Tell the student that you are going to be showing him or her a technique for learning to read unknown words that has been successful with many students who have not learned in other ways. Inform the student that this method will take concentration and effort on his or her part, but it should be successful.

2. *Select a word to learn.* Have the student select a word (regardless of length) that he or she cannot read but would like to learn to read. Discuss the meaning of the word and listen for the number of syllables.

3. *Write the word.* Sitting beside the student, have him or her watch and listen while you:

a. Say the word.

b. Using a broad-tipped marker on a piece of unlined paper approximately 4" × 11", write the word in blackboard-size script, or in print if cursive writing is not used by the student. Say the word as you write it.

c. Say the word again as you smoothly move your finger underneath the word.

See Figure 4.8 for a model.

4. *Model tracing the word.* Model how the student is to trace the word so that he or she might learn it. Do not explain the process but simply say to the student, "Watch what I do and listen to what I say."

a. Say the word.

b. Trace the word using one or two fingers. The fingers should touch the paper in order to receive the tactile stimulation. As you trace the word, say the word. When discussing this process, Fernald (1943) stresses that the student must say each part of the word as he or she traces it. This is necessary to establish the connection between the sound of the word and its form, so that the student will eventually recognize the word from the visual stimulus alone. It is important that this vocalization of the word be natural; that is, it should be a repetition of the word as it actually sounds—not a stilted, distorted sounding-out of letters or syllables in such a way that the word is lost in the process. The sound for each letter is never given separately nor over-emphasized. In a longer word, like *important,* the student says *im* while tracing the first syllable, *por* while tracing the second syllable, and *tant* as he or she traces the last syllable.

c. Say the word again while moving the tracing finger(s) underneath the word in a sweeping motion.

Model this process several times and then have the student practice the process. If the student does not complete the process correctly, stop the student when he or she makes an error and cue, "Not quite. Watch me do it again." Continue this procedure until the student is completing the three-stage process correctly.

■ **FIGURE 4.8**   *Sample Words Using Fernald Technique*

5. *Trace until learned.* Have the student continue tracing the word until the student thinks he or she can write the word from memory.

6. *Write from memory.* When the student feels he or she is ready, remove the model and have the student write the word from memory, saying the word as he or she writes. Fernald (1943) stresses that the student should always write the word without looking at the copy. She comments:

> When the child copies the word, looking back and forth from the word he is writing to the copy, he breaks the word up into small and meaningless units. The flow of the hand in writing the word is interrupted and the eye movements are back and forth from the word to the copy instead of those which the eye would make in adjusting to the word as it is being written. This writing of the word without the copy is important at all stages of learning to write and spell. The copying of words is a most serious block to learning to write them correctly and to recognize them after they have been written (pp. 37–39).

It is also important that the student write the word as a unit. If the student makes an error in writing the word or hesitates unduly between letters, stop the student immediately, cross out the word, and have him or her again practice tracing the large model. The word is never erased and rewritten. Fernald states, "The reason for this procedure is that the various movements of erasing, correcting single letters or syllables, and so forth, break the word up into a meaningless total which does not represent a word" (p. 39). It also can interfere with the student's motor memory for the word. The student should write the word from memory correctly at least three consecutive times.

7. *File the word.* After the word has been written three times correctly, the student should place it in his or her word bank.

8. *Type the word.* Within an interval of twenty-four hours, each word learned using this process should be typed and read by the student. This helps establish the link between the written and typed word.

The number of words learned per session using this VAKT process depends on the number of tracings a student needs to learn a new word. This number varies greatly among students. We have worked with students who need less than five tracings to learn a new word, whereas other students required over fifty tracings when first beginning this approach.

Fernald (1943) reports, "As soon as a child has discovered that he can learn to write words, we let him start 'story writing'" (p. 33). As the student writes a story and comes to a word he or she cannot spell, the tracing process is repeated. These stories should be typed within twenty-four hours so that the student may read the newly learned words in typed form within the context of the story.

Fernald suggests no arbitrary limit be set for the length of the tracing period (Stage One). The student stops tracing when he or she is able to learn without it. This is usually a gradual process, with the student sometimes feeling the need to trace a word and sometimes thinking the word does not need to be traced.

Stage Two: When the student no longer needs to trace words to learn them, he or she moves to Stage Two. In this stage, the teacher writes the requested word in cursive (or manuscript) for the student. The student then simply looks at the word, saying it while looking at it, and then writes it without looking at the copy, saying each part of the word as he or she writes it from memory. As with Stage One, words to be learned are obtained from words the student requests while writing stories. The word bank continues to function as a resource for the student, but a smaller

word box can be used since the teacher is writing the words in ordinary script size.

Stage Three: The student progresses to the third stage when he or she is able to learn directly from the printed word without having it written. In this stage the student looks at the unknown printed word, and the teacher pronounces the word. The student then says the word while looking at it and then writes it from memory. Fernald reports that during this stage, students still read poorly but are able to recognize quite difficult words almost without exception after once writing them.

During this stage the student is encouraged to read as much as and whatever he or she wants. Unknown words are pronounced, and when the passage is finished, the unknown words are learned by using the technique described in the preceding paragraph.

Stage Four: The student is able to recognize new words from their similarity to words or parts of words he or she has already learned. At first, a student may need to pronounce the word and write it on a scrap of paper to assist in remembering it, but later this becomes unnecessary. The student continues to read books of interest to him or her. When reading scientific or other difficult material, the student is encouraged to scan the paragraph and lightly underline each word he or she does not know. These words are then discussed for recognition and meaning prior to reading.

— **COMMENTS:** Empirical evidence lends support to this approach for teaching word identification to students with severe reading disabilities (Berres and Eyer, 1970; Coterell, 1972; Fernald, 1943; Kress and Johnson, 1970; Thorpe and Borden, 1985). Although this approach tends to be successful with such readers, the first several stages are very time-consuming for both the teacher and the student. Consequently, it should be used only if other approaches have not been successful.

Code–Emphasis Approaches

Some students with reading difficulties are successful in developing a basic sight vocabulary and strategies for identifying words using the approaches discussed in the previous section. Some students, however, may profit from teaching strategies and approaches that systematically emphasize phonic and structural analysis for assisting students in "cracking the code." Grossen and Carnine (1992) suggest the following principles of behavior theory and metalinguistic skills:

1. Introduce letter-sound correspondence in isolation.
2. Teach students to blend sounds to read words.
3. Provide immediate feedback on oral reading errors.
4. Provide extensive practice.

This method of teaching letter sounds and blending is referred to as the *synthetic method* for teaching phonics because individual sounds are learned and then "synthesized" into words. This method contrasts the *analytic method* for teaching phonics where the student "analyzes" words to learn letter/sound relationships and does not say sounds in isolation (see Apply the Concept 4.4)

Typically, the reading materials associated with these approaches are controlled for the phonic and structural patterns they use. Apply the Concept 4.5 describes how word structure techniques are used with individual students.

Let's look first at several programs and approaches for teaching phonic and structural analysis using the four principles outlined by Grossen and Carnine. These programs and approaches include linguistic approaches, *Making Words, Reading Mastery* and *Corrective Reading, Phonic Remedial Reading Lessons,* and the Gillingham-Stillman Method.

Linguistic Approach

The linguistic approach uses highly controlled text and word families (also called rimes, phonograms, or spelling patterns) (e.g., *-at: sat, fat, rat, bat, cat*) to teach initial reading. This approach was introduced by linguists Bloomfield and Barnhart (1961) and Fries (1963) in the early 1960s, and it gained popularity as an approach to teaching beginning reading

in the late sixties and early seventies. This approach is based on several assumptions delineated in *Let's Read* (Bloomfield and Barnhart, 1961):

1. Language is primarily speech. Instruction in reading should be based on the oral language acquired by the child in the first five years of his or her life.
2. English has an alphabetic writing system whose code is easily broken. The child's immediate task when he or she starts to read is to master that code.
3. Language is systematic. It employs contrasting patterns that consistently represent differences in meaning . . . taking advantage of the patterns and contrasts.

The linguistic approach is based on the alphabetic principle and language principles discussed in the section on phonic analysis (pp. 126) and on the metalinguistic and phonological awareness skills of rhyming, alliteration, segmentation, blending, closure, and sequencing of sounds. When using word families in conjunction with consonant substitution or onset rime, the teacher capitalizes on the principle of minimal contrast and the student's knowledge of letter/sound relationships.

— **PROCEDURES:** The procedures for using this approach are outlined in linguistic reading materials (see Figure 4.9). In using this approach the words are often introduced before the students read. Words are introduced by using a word family format, with the students taking turns reading the words (e.g., *an: fan, can, ran, tan, pan*). When students cannot identify a word in the list, they are encouraged to look at another known word in the list and make the sound substitution or to think of the family and then add the beginning sound. Sight words are kept to a minimum and are introduced as whole words. When reading, students are cued to look for the family when they come to words they cannot identify. Families are introduced systematically, generally with short-vowel sound families (e.g., *-at, -an, -ot, -et, -en, -and, -ap, -it*) presented before long-vowel sound families (e.g., *-ade, -ake, -oat*).

Linguistic readers provide extensive exposure and practice for each word family or phonogram,

APPLY THE CONCEPT 4.5

USING CODE-EMPHASIS TECHNIQUES TO TEACH INITIAL READING

Cassandra first began to feel successful about her reading in the second half of second grade. Cassandra did not attend either preschool or kindergarten and had limited reading experiences when she entered first grade. During first grade Cassandra worked in a basal reading series along with the other students in her class. Her teacher augmented this series with language experience stories and read to the students quite frequently. The reading series focused on learning basic sight vocabulary and then later introducing sound-symbol relationships. In first grade Cassandra never could learn more than ten words that she regularly remembered. She did learn some sound-symbol relationships but she did not use them to help her figure out unknown words. At the beginning of second grade Cassandra began receiving help from a resource teacher, Ms. Kaufman. Ms. Kaufman wanted Cassandra to feel good about reading and began by using a combination of the modified language experience approach and patterned language approach. Even though Cassandra learned to identify more words, she seemed to forget the words quickly and she rarely transferred them to different texts. Ms. Kaufman lamented, "Sometimes I felt like all my teaching was to no avail. When I was sure Cassandra knew a story one day, the next day she looked at me like she had never seen it before." Despite this difficulty in remembering printed words, Cassandra had adequate oral language skills and enjoyed listening to and discussing stories.

Right after the winter holiday, Ms. Kaufman decided it was time to make a change in Cassandra's reading program. She was going to systematically teach Cassandra a few sound-symbol relationships and then teach her how to blend these sounds together to make words. Cassandra could then practice using controlled text that contained words with the sound-symbol relationships she already knew. Ms. Kaufman realized that this approach portrayed reading as "reading the words or cracking the code" rather than "reading for meaning." However, Cassandra was having so much difficulty with natural and predictable text, she

decided to try this systematic phonic approach using controlled text.

To help Cassandra continue to develop her "reading for meaning" skills, Ms. Kaufman read to Cassandra or had Cassandra listen to taped books at least twice a week. Then they discussed the reading.

Cassandra made progress as a result of this approach, which focused on the structure of the words rather than on the words as wholes. When she came to a word she did not know she could sound it out. Eventually she recognized the words without sounding them out, and through systematic instruction in phonics she learned how to apply and use more and more sound-symbol relationships. Ms. Kaufman felt that two factors accounted for Cassandra's success with this approach to beginning reading. First, it was very systematic and provided for a lot of practice and repetition. Second, it gave Cassandra a strategy for figuring out words that did not rely so heavily on her memory skills.

Ms. Kaufman used an approach to teaching initial reading that started with the smallest units (sound-symbol relationships) and then taught the student to combine these units together to form words. Words were then combined to form sentences, sentences combined to form paragraphs, and so on.

Sergio is a third grader who reads books with an estimated readability of high first grade. Ms. Kaufman has been working with Sergio for the last year. She has used lots of predictable books, augmented by the sight word association procedure and the cloze procedure to initially teach Sergio to read. Sergio is making good progress and is now reading less predictable reading materials. He is using context and picture clues quite effectively, but Sergio needs more strategies for identifying unknown words. Therefore, Ms. Kaufman wants to teach Sergio how to use phonic and structural analysis.

Ms. Kaufman began to teach Sergio phonic and structural analysis skills using an analytic method. This method teaches these word analysis skills through inductive reasoning. Using this method, Ms. Kaufman began to point out the phonic and structural similarities among Sergio's sight words, encouraging him to generate the phonic and structural analysis rules. However, Sergio had difficulty generating these rules.

Now Ms. Kaufman is using a *synthetic method* for teaching phonic and structural analysis skills. This method uses deductive reasoning. In other words, Ms. Kaufman first teaches Sergio specific sound-symbol relationships. Then she teaches Sergio how to apply these rules to identify unknown words by sounding out the word and then blending the sounds together until Sergio recognizes the word. This is the same method of teaching phonics that Ms. Kaufman used with Cassandra.

The analytic and synthetic methods for teaching phonic and structural analysis skills capitalize on a student's ability to utilize such metalinguistic skills as rime, segmentation, and blending. If a student does not have these skills, then instruction in these metalinguistic skills should be built into the reading program.

■ **FIGURE 4.9**   *Selected Linguistic Reading Programs*

Learn to Read Program (U.S.A.: Walker Publishing Co., 1983)

Let's Read (Detroit: Wayne State University Press, 1965)

The Linguistic Readers (New York: Benziger, 1971)

Merrill Linguistic Readers (Columbus, Ohio: Merrill, 1986)

Miami Linguistic Readers (Lexington, Mass.: D. C. Heath, 1970)

Steck-Vaughn Phonic Readers (Austin, Texas: Steck-Vaughn Co., 1991)

Sullivan Associates Programmed Reading (New York: Sullivan Press, Webster Division, McGraw-Hill, 1968)

Pattern language and predictable books that provide text with word family patterns can also be used.

■ **FIGURE 4.10**   *Sample Linguistic Reading Story*

Nat and the Rat

Nat is a cat.

She is a fat cat.

She likes to sit on her mat.

Dad likes to pat Nat.

One day Nat sat on Dad's lap for a pat.

Nat saw a rat.

She jumped off Dad's lap and ran after the rat.

That made Nat tired.

So Nat sat on her mat.

using highly controlled vocabulary (see Figure 4.10). The vocabulary in the beginning readers usually consists of a few word families and a few sight vocabulary words. Matrices can be developed that depict the single-syllable words that can be generated when given a specific vowel sound (see Table 4.5). Word families can then be developed by grouping together all the words in a column. Table 4.3 (p. 131 provides a chart showing the variety of word families or rimes that can be taught.

— COMMENTS: The linguistic approach has demonstrated its usefulness with students who are having difficulty developing sight vocabulary and learning phonic generalizations. Because of its highly controlled vocabulary, students are frequently able to experience success. Two cautions should be mentioned, however. First, this approach concentrates on giving the students the skills to "crack the code." Due to this emphasis and such highly controlled text, little stress can be placed on comprehension or the use of context

■ **TABLE 4.5** *Short "a" Word Family Matrix*

	b	c	d	g	l	m	n	p	s	t
b			bad	bag			ban			bat
c	cab		cad			cam	can	cap		cat
d	dab		dad			dam	Dan			
f	Fab		fad				fan			fat
g	gab			gag	gal			gap	gas	
h			had	hag	Hal	ham			has	hat
j	jab			jag		jam		jap		
k										
l			lad	lag				lap	lass	
m		Mac	mad	Mag		Mam	man	map		mat
n	nab			nag			Nan	nap		nat
p			pad		pal	Pam	pan		pass	pat
r				rag		ram	ran	rap		rat
s			sad	sag	Sal	Sam		sap		sat
t	tab		Tad	tag		Tam	tan	tap		
v							van			vat
w				wag						
y										

clues. To demonstrate this point, reread the text given in Figure 4.10 and then try to generate eight comprehension questions, making sure that several are inferential. Second, some words introduced in a family may represent unfamiliar or abstract concepts. For example, when learning the *og* family, a student may be asked to read about "the fog in the bog."

Making Words

Making Words (Cunningham and Hall, 1994a) and *Making Big Words* (Cunningham and Hall, 1994b) is a systematic method in which students use letters to build words. Using a specific set of letters (e.g., a, c, h, r, s, t), students make approximately fifteen words beginning with two-letter words (e.g. at) and progressing to three-, four-, and five-letter words (e.g. tar, cart, star, cash) until the final word is made (i.e., scratch). *Making Words* allows the students to manipulate laminated letters to build their words and learn about phonological awareness, letter-sound relationships, and spelling patterns. The lesson is based on the research that has demonstrated the strong relationship between spelling and phonological aware-

ness, knowledge of sound-letter relationships, and ability to identify words in reading (Adams, 1990; Henderson, 1990; Spear-Swerling and Sternberg, 1996; Zutell and Rasinski, 1989). The lessons highlight word family/phonogram/spelling pattern instruction and teach high-frequency patterns such as those listed in Table 4.3 (e.g., at, ack, eat, ice, ight, ock, ot, ug, unk).

▬ **PROCEDURES:** Each lesson consists of two steps: Making Words (about fifteen minutes) and Word Sorting (about ten minutes). Schumm and Vaughn (1995) added a third step, Making Words Quickly (about three minutes) to help students develop fluency in writing the words. To use Making Words, each student needs a set of laminated letters with upper case on one side and lower case on the other side. The teacher will need large letter cards and a sentence strip chart to hold the cards and words that are constructed. Prior to class, the letters the student will need during the lesson (the letters for the final word the students will construct, for example *scratch*) are put in plastic bags and given to each student. The three steps progress as follows:

- *Making Words*

  After the students have identified their letters, the teacher writes the numeral on the board for the number of letters the students are to put in their words. Next, the teacher cues the students to make different two-letter words. For example, with the word *scratch* the teacher might ask the students to construct the word *at*. When working with a class of students, after each word is constructed the teacher selects one student who was correct to use the set of large letters and the chart to spell the word for the other students to check their work. Then, the teacher might ask the students to add *c* to the word *at* to make *cat,* or to make the word *art* and then rearrange the letters to make the word *tar.* The teacher continues to guide students through the lesson by directing them to make words with their letters. The last word includes all the letters a student has been given for the lesson.

- *Word Sorting*

  The teacher puts up on the sentence strip chart all the words the students have constructed. The teacher then asks the students how some of the words are alike, and students sort the words by spelling patterns. For example, the teacher would take the word *car* and have the students find the other words that begin with *c*—*cars, cash, cart;* or take the word *art* and have the students find the other *art* words—*cart, chart.* Other students hypothesize why the words are alike, which assists the students in seeing the spelling patterns.

- *Making Words Quickly*

  Students write as many words as they can using the day's letters, writing the words in a Making Words Log. Students first write the letters from the lesson, and when the teacher says "Go," they write words for two minutes.

— COMMENTS: Both special education and general education teachers have found this practice an effective and efficient way to organize for teaching phonological awareness and word identification, and students report that they enjoy the activity and manipulating the letters (Cunningham, 1991; Schumm and Vaughn, 1995). Because each lesson progresses from making easy words to making a big word that uses all the letters, the lessons provide practice for a range of learners (Cunningham and Cunningham, 1992).

Reading Mastery and Corrective Reading

Reading Mastery: Distar (Direct Instructional System for Teaching Arithmetic and Reading), (Engelmann and Bruner, 1988), *Reading Mastery Rainbow Edition* (Engelmann and Bruner, 1995), and *Corrective Reading* (Engelmann, Becker, Hanner, and Johnson, 1988; 1989) are highly structured reading programs that utilize a direct instruction model for teaching (Carnine, Silbert and Kameenui, 1997) and a synthetic method for teaching phonic and structural analysis. These programs stress the synthetic method by directly teaching individual sound-symbol relationships and teaching the students to build these elements into words. The programs include components in decoding and comprehension. Whereas *Reading Mastery* is designed for elementary-level students, *Corrective Reading* is designed for students in grades four through twelve who have not mastered decoding and comprehension skills. Both programs are designed to be taught in small to medium-sized groups.

— PROCEDURES: *Reading Mastery* and *Corrective Reading* are built on the following principles:

1. Explicitly teach rules.
2. Provide extensive practice with the rules.
3. Provide practice in a variety of contexts, including words both in isolation and in text.
4. Provide corrective feedback.
5. Require active and frequent participation on the part of the learner.
6. Teach skills in a cumulative manner.
7. Provide a reinforcement system, including a point system within the program.
8. Provide a monitoring system.

When the students and the teacher are learning individual words, the students are cued, "Do it with me. Sound it out. Get ready." The teacher points to each letter while the students say each sound without pausing in between sounds (e.g., *mmmmmmeeeeee*). When the students can sound the word successfully they are then cued, "Say it fast. What is the word?" The teacher points to the word and the students respond with the word (e.g., *me*).

In both programs the teacher is given specific procedures to follow, including scripted lessons. These scripted lessons specify what the teacher is to say and do, including tone of voice and hand movements. Part of Lesson 4 from *Corrective Reading, Decoding—Level A*, is presented in Figure 4.11. Lessons are designed to last from 30 to 50 minutes with time provided for direct teaching, group reading, individual reading practice, and monitoring of progress. *Corrective Reading* teaches skills in word identification including word-attack basics, decoding strategies, and skill application and skills in comprehension including thinking basics, comprehension skills, and concept applications. The program provides daily feedback and has a built-in reinforcement system.

— **COMMENTS:** Research suggests that these programs are effective in improving reading skills of students with reading difficulties and students from disadvantaged backgrounds (Becker, 1977; Carnine, Silbert, and Kaneenui, 1997; Gersten, Becker, Heiny, and White, 1984; Gersten, Carnine, and Woodward, 1987; Kameenui et al., in press; Polloway, Epstein, Polloway, Patton, and Ball, 1986). These results may be related to the fact that both *Reading Mastery* and *Corrective Reading* are well-designed for systematic skill development and monitoring of that development. Much of the teaching of phonic analysis skills is conducted in an explicit manner, which may also be advantageous for a student with learning and behavior problems. Several cautions, however, should be noted. First, there is a strong emphasis on phonic and structural-analysis skills, the use of passages that have a "low probability" for the use of context clues, and the absence of illustrations and picture clues. Use of literature and trade books should provide stu-

dents with additional opportunities to build meaning-based strategies. Second, these programs rely heavily on oral presentation by the teacher and oral responses and reading by the students. Third, the programs are difficult to modify to meet individual needs, since detailed scope and sequences of skill development are not provided, but only detailed scripted lessons.

Phonic Remedial Reading Lessons

The *Phonic Remedial Reading Lessons* (Kirk, Kirk, and Minskoff, 1985) were originally developed in the 1930s to teach phonic analysis skills to students who had mild mental retardation. The lessons follow principles of systematic programmed instruction in that they utilize such principles as minimal change, one response to one symbol, progress from easy to hard, frequent review and overlearning, corrective feedback, verbal mediation, and multisensory learning. The lessons are designed as an intensive phonics program to be used individually or in groups of no more than two to three students. They are not recommended as a general technique for teaching beginning reading, but rather as a technique for students who have not yet learned an efficient method of identifying unknown words (Kirk, Kirk, and Minskoff, 1985).

— **PROCEDURES:** The program begins by developing the readiness level for the lessons. These readiness skills include auditory discrimination and auditory sound blending. Figure 4.12 presents a simple procedure for teaching sound blending. Developing readiness also includes learning the sound-symbol associations for the short *a* sound and eleven consonants.

Once these skills have been learned, the first lesson is introduced (see Figure 4.13). For each lesson, students sound out each word in each line, one letter at a time, and then give the complete word. Each lesson is organized into four parts and is based on the principle of minimal change. In the first part, only the initial consonant changes in each sequence; in the second part, only the final consonant changes; in the third part, both the initial and final consonants change; and in the fourth part, the space between letters in a word is normal.

Lesson 4

Decoding—Level A

Core skills are being introduced in this lesson. The following skills are being learned and practiced.

- Pronouncing orally presented words so that all the sounds are audible
- Identifying the middle sound in words such as **seed** that are presented orally
- Identifying the eight sounds that have been introduced (exercise 3)
- Reading word parts and two-sound words (exercise 4)
- Reading three-sound words (exercise 5)
- Rhyming, in which specified sounds precede specified endings (exercise 6)
- The worksheet includes the following activities.
- Writing sounds dictated by the teacher
- Sounding out word parts and words
- Matching sounds
- Matching and copying sounds
- Scanning a display of letters for a specific letter that appears repeatedly in the display
- Individual checkout on reading worksheet words

Remember, you can earn 4 points if everybody in the group responds on signal, follows along when somebody else is reading, and tries hard.

EXERCISE 1   Pronunciations
Task A
1. **Listen. He was mad.**
   Pause. **Mad. Say it.** Signal. *Mad.*
2. **Next word. Listen. They wrestled on a mat.**
   Pause. **Mat. Say it.** Signal. *Mat.*
3. **Next word: ram. Say it.** Signal. *Ram.*
4. Repeat step 3 for **sat, reem, seem.**
5. Repeat all the words until firm.

Task B   Sit, rim, fin
1. **I'll say words that have sound ĭĭĭ. What sound?**
   Signal. *ĭĭĭ.* **Yes, ĭĭĭ.**
2. Repeat step 1 until firm.
3. **Listen: sit, rim, fin.**
   Your turn: sit. Say it. Signal. *Sit.*
   Yes, sit.
4. **Next word: rim. Say it.** Signal. *Rim.*
   Yes, rim.

5. **Next word: fin. Say it.** Signal. *Fin.*
   Yes, fin.
6. Repeat steps 3–5 until firm.
7. **What's the middle sound in the word rrriiimmm?** Signal. *ĭĭĭ.* **Yes, ĭĭĭ.**
8. Repeat step 7 until firm.

EXERCISE 2   Say the sounds
1. **Listen: sssēēē.** Clap for each sound.
2. **Say the sounds in sssēēē. Get ready.**
   Clap for each sound. *sssēēē.* Repeat until the students say the sounds without pausing.
3. **Say it fast.** Signal. *See.*
4. **What word?** Signal. *See.* **Yes, see.**
5. Repeat steps 1–4 for **sad, mad, mat, me, seed, in, if, sat, rat, ran.**

i d e

d r t

s a m

EXERCISE 3   Sound introduction.
1. Point to **i. One sound this letter makes is ĭĭĭ. What sound?** Touch. *ĭĭĭ.*
2. Point to **d. This letter makes the sound d. What sound?** Touch. *d.*
3. **Say each sound when I touch it.**
4. Point to **i. What sound?** Touch under **i.** *ĭĭĭ*
5. Repeat step 4 for **d, ē, d, r, t, s, ā, m.**
   To correct:
   a. Say the sound loudly as soon as you hear an error.
   b. Point to the sound. **This sound is _____. What sound?** Touch.
   c. Repeat the series of letters until all the students can correctly identify all the sounds in order.

Individual test
I'll call on different students to say all the sounds. If everybody I call on can say all the sounds without making a mistake, we'll go on to the next exercise.
Call on two or three students. Touch under each sound. Each student says all the sounds.

Source: From *Corrective Reading: Series Guide* by Siegfried Engelmann, Wesley C. Becker, Susan Hanner, and Gary Johnson. Copyright © Science Research Associates, Inc. 1978. Reprinted with permission of the publisher, Macmillan/McGraw-Hill School Publishing Company.

■ **FIGURE 4.12**   *Procedure for Teaching Sound Blending*

To train a child in sound blending, use the following procedure.

Teacher: "Say shoe."
 Child: "Shoe."
Teacher: "Now,, what am I saying? **/sh-sh-sh/ oo-oo-oo/**." (Say it with prolonged sounds, but no break between the sounds.) If the child responds correctly, say: "Good. Now what am I saying?" (Give a little break between the sounds.) "**/Sh/oe/.**" Then say (with the child), "Shoe. Now what am I saying?" (Give a quarter-second break between the sounds.) "**/Sh/oe/.**"
 Child: "Shoe."
Teacher: "Shoe. Good. What am I saying now?" (with a half-second break between the sounds) "**/Sh/oe/.**"
 Child: "Shoe."
Teacher: "Now what am I saying?" (give a one-second break between the sounds) "**/Sh/oe/.**"

At each step, if the child does not respond with "shoe," repeat the previous step and then again stretch out the sounds, confirming or prompting at each step. Proceed by increasing the duration until the child can say "shoe" in response to the sounds with approximately one second between them.

Repeat this experience with the word "me."

The main task for the teacher is to give a word with two sounds, increasing the duration of time between them until the child gets the idea of putting the sounds together. Then the child is presented with three-sound words such as /f/a/t/, and then with four-sound words such as /s/a/n/d/. It is important to recognize that the number of sounds in a word may not correspond to the number of letters in a word. For example, the word "shoe" has four letters, but only two sounds. The teacher must be careful to present the sounds correctly and use the correct timing.

Source: S. A. Kirk, W. D. Kirk, and E. H. Minskoff, *Phonic Remedial Reading Lessons* (Novato, Calif.: Academic Therapy Publications, 1985), pp. 12–13. Reprinted by permission.

In addition to these drill lessons, high-frequency sight words are introduced and highly controlled stories are interspersed throughout the program. Frequent review lessons are also provided.

— COMMENTS: This program provides for a systematic and intensive approach to teaching phonic analysis skills to beginning readers. However, the approach places little emphasis on comprehension and reading for meaning and incorporates limited practice in connected text. The authors suggest using other books to provide students with the opportunity to try both their word-identification and comprehension skills in other reading materials.

Gillingham-Stillman Method

The Gillingham-Stillman method (Gillingham and Stillman, 1973) can be classified as a synthetic method of teaching word identification that incorporates a multisensory (VAK: visual-auditory-kinesthetic) approach. Like the Fernald technique, it is designed for children who are unable to learn to read using more wholistic approaches, specifically those with learning disabilities and dyslexia. This method involves repeated associations between how a letter or word looks, how it sounds, and how the speech mechanism or hand feels when producing it. It is designed for third- through sixth-grade students of average or above average ability and normal sensory acuity. With some adaptations it can be modified to work with both older and younger students.

— PROCEDURES: This method is designed to teach students how to identify words by teaching phonic generalizations and how to apply these generalizations in reading and spelling. It is to be used as the exclusive method for teaching reading, spelling, and penmanship for a minimum of a two-year period. Initially students who use this method should read only materials that are designed to conform with

■ **FIGURE 4.13**   *First Lesson from Phonic Remedial Reading Lessons*

a

a t	s a t	m a t	h a t	f a t
a m	h a m	S a m	P a m	t a m
s a d	m a d	h a d	l a d	d a d
w a g	s a g	t a g	l a g	h a g

s a t	s a p	S a m	s a d
m a p	m a m	m a d	m a t
h a g	h a m	h a t	h a d
c a t	c a p	c a d	c a m

s a t	a m	s a d	p a t	m a d
h a d	m a t	t a g	f a t	h a m
l a g	h a m	w a g	h a t	s a p
s a d	t a p	c a p	d a d	a t

map	hag	cat	sat	ham	tap
sap	map	hat	sad	tag	am
Pam	mat	had	tap	hat	dad
fat	mad	at	wag	cap	sag

Source: S. A. Kirk, W. D. Kirk, and E. H. Minskoff, *Phonic Remedial Reading Lessons* (Novato, Calif.; Academic Therapy Publication, 1985), p. 22. Reprinted by permission.

the method. Other written information such as content area textbooks should be read to the students.

The method is introduced by discussing the importance of reading and writing, how some children have difficulty learning to read and spell using whole-word methods, and how this method has helped other students. Thereafter, a sequence of lessons is completed, beginning with learning the names of the letters and the letter sounds, learning words through blending sounds, and reading sentences and stories.

Teaching Letters and Sounds: The teaching of letter names and letter sounds employs associations be-

tween visual, auditory, and kinesthetic inputs. Each new sound-symbol relationship or phonogram is taught by having the students make three associations.

1. *Association I (Reading).* The students are taught to associate the written letter with the letter name and then with the letter sound. The teacher shows the students the letter name. The students repeat the name. The letter sound is learned using the same procedure.

2. *Association II (Oral Spelling).* The students are taught to associate the oral sound with the name of the letter. To do this the teacher says the sound and asks the students to give its corresponding letter.

3. *Association III (Written Spelling).* The students learn to write the letter through the teacher modeling, tracing, copying, and writing the letter from memory. The students then associate the letter sound with the written letter by the teacher directing them to write the letter that has the _____ sound.

When teaching these associations:

1. Cursive writing is preferred and suggested over manuscript.

2. Letters are always introduced by a key word.

3. Vowels and consonants are differentiated by different colored drill cards (i.e., white for consonants, salmon for vowels).

4. The first letters introduced (i.e., *a, b, f, h, i, j, k, m, p,* and *t*) represent clear sounds and nonreversible letter forms.

5. Drill cards are used to introduce each letter and to provide practice in sound and letter identification.

6. The writing procedure is applied to learning all new letters. The procedure for writing is:

    a. The teacher makes the letter.

    b. The students trace the letter.

    c. The students copy it.

    d. The students write it from memory.

Teaching Words: After the first ten letters and sounds have been learned using the Associations, students begin blending them together into words. Words that can be made from the ten letters are written on yellow word cards and kept in student word boxes (jewel cases). Students are taught to read and spell words.

To teach blending and reading, the letter Drill Cards that form a word (e.g., *b - a - t*) are laid out on the table or put in a pocket chart. The students are asked to give the sounds of the letters in succession, repeating the series of sounds again and again with increasing speed and smoothness until they are saying the word. This procedure is used to learn new words. Drill and timed drill activities are used to give the students practice reading the words.

To teach spelling, the analysis of words into their component sound should begin a few days after blending is started. To teach this method of spelling

the teacher pronounces a word the students can read, first quickly and then slowly. The teacher then asks the students, "What sound did you hear first?" and then asks, "What letter says /b/?" The students then find the *b* card. When all cards have been found, the students write the word. Gillingham and Stillman (1973) stress the importance of using this procedure for spelling. After the teacher pronounces /bat/:

Child repeats /b/	Child names letters b-a-t	Child writes, naming each letter while forming it b-a-t	Child reads /bat/

This procedure is referred to as Simultaneous Oral Spelling, or SOS. Gillingham and Stillman comment that after a few days of practice in blending and SOS, it should be an almost invariable routine to have the students check their own errors. When a word is read wrong, the student should be asked to spell what he or she has just said, and match it against the original word. When a word is misspelled orally the teacher may write the offered spelling and say, "Read this (e.g., *bit*)." The student would respond, "Bit." The teacher would say, "Correct, but I dictated the word /bat/."

As the students continue to learn and practice new words, they also continue to learn new sound-symbol associations or phonograms. As new phonograms are introduced, more and more words are practiced and added to the word boxes. An example of a daily lesson that lasts from forty-five to sixty minutes might be:

Practice Association I with learned phonograms
Practice Association II with learned phonograms
Practice Association III with learned phonograms
Drill words for reading
Drill words for spelling and writing

Sentences and Stories: When the students can read and write three-lettered phonetic words, sentence and story reading is begun. This begins with reading simple, highly structured stories, called "Little Stories." These stories are first practiced silently until the students think they can read them perfectly. They can ask the teacher for assistance. The teacher pronounces nonphonetic words and cues the student to sound out phonetically regular words. Then the students read the sentence or story orally. The story is to be read perfectly with proper inflection. Later, the stories are dictated to the student. An example of a story is:

Sam hit Ann.
Then Ann hit Sam.
Sam ran and Ann ran.
Ann had a tan mitten.
This is Ann's tan mitten.
Ann lost it.
Sam got the mitten.
Sam sent the mitten to Ann.

— **COMMENTS:** The Gillingham-Stillman method incorporates multisensory techniques into a synthetic approach for teaching phonics and phonological awareness. This method explicitly teaches the structure of language and the alphabetic principle. A number of programs have utilized these principles including:

— *Multi-Sensory Approach to Language Arts for Specific Language Disability Children* (Volumes: 1–3) (Slingerland, 1971; 1976; 1981)
— *Wilson Reading System* (3rd ed.) (Wilson, 1996)
— *Recipe for Reading* (Traub and Bloom, 1978)
— *Glass Analysis* (Glass and Glass, 1976)
— *Lindamood Auditory Discrimination in Depth* (Lindamood, 1975)
— *Writing Road to Reading* (Spalding and Spalding, 1990)

Although the Gillingham-Stillman method does provide a systematic means of teaching phonics, several cautions are relevant. First, the method requires students to learn both letter names and letter sounds. Letter sounds are used when reading but letter names are repeated when the students are spelling words. Learning two associations and when to use letter names and when to use letter sounds may be confusing. Second, the reading material has been criticized by some as being uninteresting and so highly structured that transference to "natural" text is sometimes difficult, hence students are given a distorted view of the reading process. Third, this method requires a substantial commitment on the part of the teacher and the students: a minimum of two years with five sessions per week is suggested.

Techniques for Building Sight Words

Some children who experience difficulties with developing automatic recognition of printed words need additional opportunities to practice recognizing and remembering the words they are learning. This is especially problematic when students have difficulty with high-frequency words—words such as *the, you, and,* and *was.* Because these words occur often, it is inefficient for students to have to slowly decode the words each time they see them in print. It is important for students to develop automaticity with high-frequency words—that is, to recognize them on sight (LaBerge and Samuels, 1974). In selecting words to teach, choose words from word lists such as the Instant (Sight) Words presented in Figure 4.14 that the students do not recognize on sight. Or when listening to students read, keep a running record of words that students continue to have difficulty learning to recognize by sight.

This section presents several activities that teachers and students can use to assist students in remembering words. In addition, a number of games and computer programs can be used. These activities are not approaches to reading and should not be used in isolation but as supplemental activities used in conjunction with the meaning-emphasis and code-emphasis strategies and approaches discussed in the previous two sections.

Sight Word Association Procedure

The sight word association procedure (Bradley, 1975) uses corrective feedback and drill and practice to assist students in associating spoken words with written form. The sight word association procedure (SWAP) is best used as a supplemental activity for the acquisition of sight vocabulary. By using visual configuration to identify words, it teaches sight vocabulary to an automatic level. The procedure is

■ **FIGURE 4.14** *The Instant (Sight) Words*

The First 100 Words (approximately first grade)				The Second 100 Words (approximately second grade)			
Group 1a	*Group 1b*	*Group 1c*	*Group 1d*	*Group 2a*	*Group 2b*	*Group 2c*	*Group 2d*
the	he	go	who	saw	big	may	ran
a	I	see	an	home	where	let	five
is	they	then	there	soon	am	use	read
you	one	us	she	stand	ball	these	over
to	good	no	new	box	morning	right	such
and	me	him	said	upon	live	present	way
we	about	by	did	first	four	tell	too
that	had	was	boy	came	last	next	shall
in	if	come	three	girl	color	please	own
not	some	get	down	house	away	leave	most
for	up	or	work	find	red	hand	sure
at	her	two	put	because	friend	more	thing
with	do	man	were	made	pretty	why	only
it	when	little	before	could	eat	better	near
on	so	has	just	book	want	under	than
can	my	them	long	look	year	while	open
will	very	how	here	mother	white	should	kind
are	all	like	other	run	got	never	must
of	would	our	old	school	play	each	high
this	any	what	take	people	found	best	far
your	been	know	cat	night	left	another	both
as	out	make	again	into	men	seem	end
but	there	which	give	say	bring	tree	also
be	from	much	after	think	wish	name	until
have	day	his	many	back	black	dear	call

Source: Edward Fry. Reprinted with permission.

appropriate to use with students who are beginning to learn to identify words across various contexts or texts, or with students who require more practice of new sight vocabulary than the amount provided in the current reading program. It is designed to be used individually or with small groups.

— **PROCEDURES:** Begin by selecting words from the text that the students consistently miscall or do not identify at an automatic level. Write each word on a word card. The procedure for teaching these words (usually five to ten words at a time) is:

1. Discuss the words with the students to assure that they understand the meanings of the words as the words are being used in the text.

2. Present the words to the students one word at a time. Each word is exposed for five seconds, with the teacher saying the word twice.

3. Shuffle the cards and ask the students to identify the word on each card. Provide corrective feedback by verifying the correctly identified words, giving the correct word for any word miscalled, and saying the word if the students do not respond in five seconds.

4. Present all the words again, using the same format given in step 2.

5. Have the students identify each word, using the same format given in step 3. Repeat this step at least two more times or until the students can automatically recognize all the words.

If students continue to have difficulty recognizing a word after the seventh exposure to the word, switch from a recall task to a recognition task. To do this, place several word cards on the table and have the learners point to each word as you say it. If the students still continue to have difficulty learning the words, use a different technique to teach the words, such as picture association techniques, sentence/word association techniques, or a cloze procedure. A record sheet for keeping track of individual student responses is presented in Figure 4.15.

After teaching the words on the initial day, the words should be reviewed for several days to determine if the words are being retained.

— **COMMENTS:** This procedure provides a technique for systematically practicing sight words. It utilizes principles of corrective feedback and mass and distributed practice to teach individual sight words. However, there are several important cautions regarding sight word association. First, this is only a supplemental technique and it needs to be used in conjunction with an approach to reading that stresses reading text and utilizing other word identification strategies. Second, students should understand the meanings of the words being taught. Third, in addition to the isolated word practice provided by this technique, students should be given ample opportunity to read these words in context.

Picture Association Technique
When identifying a word, using a picture to aid in identifying the word can sometimes be beneficial, particularly if the picture is well matched to the text.

■ **FIGURE 4.15**   *Sight Word Association Procedure (SWAP) Record Sheet*

| | | | | | | | | | ✓ Correct |
| | | | | | | | | | 0 Incorrect |

Words	Initial Teaching					Retention			Comments
	1	2	3	4	5	1	2	3	

It allows the readers to associate the word with a visual image. It is on this premise that picture association techniques use pictures to help students associate a spoken word with its written form. Like SWAP, the picture association technique is designed to assist students in learning sight words. It is meant to be used in conjunction with a reading approach that stresses reading words in text. When reading text, students should be encouraged not only to think of their picture association, but also of a "word that makes sense."

— **PROCEDURES:** Select words that the students are having difficulty identifying when reading. At first, choose words that are easily imaged such as nouns, verbs, and adjectives. Write each word on a card (usually four to seven words are taught at the same time). On a separate card, draw a simple picture or find a picture and attach it to the card. In some cases, the students may want to draw their own pictures. Use the following procedure to teach the picture-word association:

1. Place each picture in front of the student, labeling each one as you present it. Have the students practice repeating the names of the pictures.

2. Place next to each picture the word it represents, again saying the name of the word (see Figure 4.16). Have the students practice saying the names of the words.

3. Tell the students to match the words to the pictures and to say the name of the word while matching it. Repeat this process until the students easily match the pictures and words.

4. Place the words in front of the students and have them identify the words as you say them. If they cannot identify the correct word, have them think of the picture to aid in their recognition. If they still cannot point to the word, show them the picture that goes with the word.

5. Have the students recall the words by showing the word cards one at a time. Again, if the student cannot recall a word, have them think of the picture. If they still cannot think of the word, tell them to look at the picture that goes with the word.

■ **FIGURE 4.16** *Picture Word Association Cards*

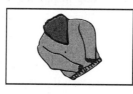

sweater

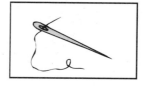

needle

sewing

6. Continue this procedure until the students can identify all the words at an automatic level. The same record sheet as the one used for SWAP (Figure 4.15) can be used for this procedure.

7. Have the students review the words on subsequent days and, most importantly, give the students plenty of opportunities to read the words in context. When a student is reading and cannot identify a word, encourage him or her to think of the picture and to think of a word that makes sense.

— **COMMENTS:** This picture association technique assists students in forming visual images that may facilitate their identification of words. As with the sight word association procedure, this procedure should be used only as a supplemental procedure. The students should be given ample opportunities to read the words in text and they should understand the meanings of the words they are learning.

Picture associations have been used in beginning reading programs such as the Peabody Rebus Reading Program (Woodcock, Clark, and Davies, 1969) and word processing programs such as Kid Writer Deluxe (Davidson). Students learn to read these symbols and then transfer their skills to traditional print by making picture/word association.

Sentence/Word Association Technique

The sentence/word association technique encourages students to associate an unknown word with a familiar spoken word, phrase, or sentence to aid in recognizing the word when reading. This technique, which is designed to be used individually or in small groups, relies on the students' abilities to associate old information with new information.

— **PROCEDURES:** Select from four to seven words that the students are consistently having difficulty recognizing. Discuss the words with the students and ask them to find the words in the text and read them in a sentence. Tell the students to decide on a key word, phrase, or sentence that will help them remember the word. For example, for the word *was* a sentence might be "Today he is, yesterday he _____."
For the word *there* the sentence might be "Are you _____?" Put the words to be taught on word cards and put the associated word, phrase, or sentence on separate cards. Teach the associations between the key word, phrase, or sentence and the unknown word, using the same procedures described for the picture association technique. The key in teaching is to have the students associate the new unknown word with a familiar clue. After teaching, when a student is reading and comes to one of the new words and cannot recognize it, have the student think of the associated clue. If the student cannot think of the associated clue orally, tell him or her.

— **COMMENTS:** We have used this technique with students who have reading disabilities and frequently cannot remember or confuse such words as *was, were, there, they, that, them, this, these, those, when, what, where,* and *who.* After using sentence/word association, these students will see the unknown word, remember their associated key clue, say it aloud, and then remember the word. As soon as the associated clue is no longer needed, the students seem to quit using it. As with the previous two techniques, this is only a supplemental procedure. Students should be given ample opportunities to practice their newly learned sight words in context.

Word Wall

The Word Wall (Cunningham, 1995) is an activity used to teach and reinforce sight word acquisition. The Word Wall is a large, permanent bulletin board to which five words are added each week in alphabetical order. When a new word is added, the teacher and students talk about its meaning, use the word in sentences, and determine whether its spelling follows a regular or irregular pattern. The words remain on the wall through the school year. Students can use these words to help them spell words they are writing, and eventually learn to read and spell the words through repeated practice. Cunningham (1995) suggests that some students might need portable Word Walls, especially if they move from classroom to resource room. A portable word wall is a file folder with one area for each letter of the alphabet. Each week the five new word wall words are added to the wall and the students' folders.

Teaching a Word Identification Strategy

What would you say if a junior high student asked you, "What do you do when you are reading and come to a word you don't recognize?" You might say that at first you decide if you need to identify the word. If the decision is yes, then you use the appearance of the word and the context to try to figure it out. If that doesn't work, you look for any prefixes, suffixes, or endings, and separate them from the root word. Then you try to say each part and figure it out. If that doesn't work, you try to break the word into syllables and then sound it out. If that still doesn't work, you look it up in the dictionary. What you have reported to the student is a strategy for applying the word identification skills you already have.

Based on the Strategies Intervention Model (see Chapter Two), Lenz and his colleagues (Lenz, Schumaker, Deshler, and Beals, 1984) developed and researched the effectiveness of teaching a word identification strategy to students with learning disabilities. Using the strategy with twelve junior high students with learning disabilities, they found that after instruction the students made fewer word recognition errors than before instruction (Lenz and Hughes, 1990). However, the increases in word recognition did not automatically result in gains in reading comprehension for all students.

The acquisition and generalization steps from the Strategies Intervention Model are used to teach this word identification strategy. The teaching procedure for this strategy entails pretesting the skill, obtaining a commitment from the students, and then describing and modeling the strategy. Then the students rehearse the steps in the strategy, practice and master the strategy in instructional level materials, and eventually practice and master the strategy in grade-appropriate material. Finally, the strategy is post-tested, and the students work to generalize the strategy to a variety of reading situations.

The steps the students use to identify the unknown words are:

Discover the word's context.

Isolate the prefix. To isolate the prefix of a difficult word, students must look at the beginning of the word to see if the initial letters of the word match any of the prefixes they know. If they do recognize a prefix, they should isolate it. For example, *ex/claim.* If students do not recognize a prefix, they should proceed to step 3.

Separate the suffix. To separate the suffix, students must look at the end of the word to see if the last letters match any of the suffixes they know. If they do recognize a suffix, they should separate it; if not, they should go to the next step.

Say the stem. The stem is what is left after the students isolate the prefix and separate the suffix. If they can immediately say the stem, that means they can say the prefix, stem, and suffix together, which means saying the whole word. Once the students can say the whole word, they should read the entire sentence again and make sure they understand what it means. Reading can then be continued. If students cannot say the stem, they should proceed to step 5.

Examine the stem. When examining the stem, students need to dissect it into easy-to-pronounce parts. To do this, they will need to apply the Rules of Twos and Threes (see Figure 4.17). Once they have examined the stem and can pronounce the whole word, students should go back and reread the whole sentence to check their understanding. If they still cannot figure out the word after examining the stem, they need to go to step 6.

Check with someone.

Try the dictionary. If students cannot find someone to ask or if the person doesn't know, then they should try the dictionary. This step can also be used if students have dissected a word and they do not know what it means.

The mnemonic for the steps in this strategy is DISSECT, from the first letter in each step. Specifics for teaching the word identification strategy, including scripted lessons, cue cards for learning and generalizing the strategy, and worksheets for practice, are presented in the instructor's guide, *The Word Identification Strategy* (Lenz et al., 1984).

This strategy provides an example of how metacognitive skills can be taught to students. However, it is important to remember that such a strategy requires that the students already have developed basic word identification strategies (i.e., context clues, phonic analysis, structural analysis and syllabication).

■ **FIGURE 4.17** *Word Identification Strategy Rules for Examining the Stem of a Word*

RULES OF TWOS AND THREES

Rule 1

If a stem or part of the stem begins with:

- A vowel, divide off the first two letters.
- A consonant, divide off the first three letters.

Rule 2

If you can't make sense of the stem after using Rule 1, take off the first letter of the stem and use Rule 1 again.

Rule 3

When two different vowels are together, try making both of the vowel sounds (diet).

If this does not work, try pronouncing them together using only one of the vowel sounds (believe).

Source: B. K. Lenz, J. B. Schumaker, D. D. Deshler, and V. L. Beals, *Learning Strategies Curriculum: The Word Identification Strategy* (Lawrence: The University of Kansas, 1984), p. 71. Copyright 1984 by University of Kansas. Reprinted by permission and with the recommendation that training be obtained from the Institute for Research in Learning Disabilities, University of Kansas, Lawrence, Kansas 66045.

INSTRUCTIONAL ACTIVITIES

This section provides instructional activities that are related to word identification. Some of the activities teach new skills; others are best suited for practice and reinforcement of already acquired skills. For each activity, the objective, materials, and teaching procedures are described.

■ Grocery Store

Objective: To increase the students' awareness of print in the environment and to provide practice in matching words.

Grades: Primary

Materials: (1) An area that is set up as a grocery store. (2) Commonly used packaged and canned goods with labels left on (e.g., Jello, toothpaste, corn flakes, chicken noodle soup). Remove the contents of packaged goods and reclose the box. (3) Cards with names of items written on them. (4) Baskets and/or bags children can use when shopping.

Teaching Procedures: This center can be used in a variety of ways. Word cards can be placed by each food item. When the student is shopping and selects a food item, he or she also picks up the card, reads it, and matches it to the label on the box. When the child goes through checkout, he or she can read each card and hand the cashier the item that goes with it. Or the teacher and child can decide which items the child wants to buy. The teacher gives those word cards to the child, and he or she shops for those items by matching the cards to the items on the shelves.

Children can serve as stock persons by reshelving the items the other children have purchased. When a stock person reshelves an item, he or she can find the card that matches the item and then place the card next to the item.

■ My Sound Book

Objective: To provide the students practice in finding pictures that start with a specific consonant or vowel sound.

Grades: Primary

Materials: (1) Three-ring binder or folder into which "Sound Pages" can be inserted. (2) Magazines, old books, or workbooks that can be cut up. (3) Stickers, scissors, and glue.

Teaching Procedures: Explain to the students that each of them will be making a book where they can collect and keep pictures and stickers that start with various sounds. Select one sound that the students are learning and have the students write the letter representing the sound on the top of the page. Then have them look through magazines, old books, and workbooks to find pictures starting with the sound. Once they have selected the pictures, have them say the names to you so that you both can determine if the pictures represent the designated sound. Then have the students glue the pictures on the sound pages, leaving room to add other pictures they find while looking for pictures representing other sounds. Have the student put the sound page in the notebook and share his or her pictures with other students. Continue until the book is complete. As students collect stickers, you may want to encourage them to put them in the sound book.

■ Vowel Match

Objective: To provide the students practice in decoding words that have various vowels sounds.

Grades: Primary and intermediate

Materials: (1) One file folder that is divided into two playing areas that consist of ten boxes for each player. In each box, paste a picture that illustrates a vowel sound. (2) From thirty to forty playing cards with pictures illustrating vowel sounds.

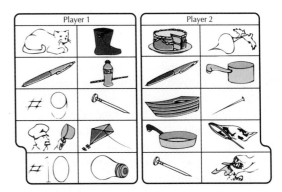

Teaching Procedures: Explain the game to the students. Shuffle and place cards face down near the players. Each student draws a card and checks to see if the vowel sound illustrated on the card matches one of the pictures on his or her side of the game folder. If it does, the player places the card over the picture on the game folder. If the picture does not match, the card is discarded. The player to cover all the boxes first wins the game.

Adaptations: This game is easily adapted to teaching rhyming words and other sounds such as consonant digraphs or blends.

■ Sight Word Bingo

Objective: To provide the students practice in recognizing words.

Grades: Primary and intermediate

Materials: (1) Poster board cut into 10 × 8 inch pieces to use for Bingo cards. (2) List of new words students have encountered in their reading. Such lists can be found in the back of basal readers or in books of lists such as *The New Reading Teacher's Book of Lists* (Fry, Fountoukidis, and Polk, 1985). To make the Bingo cards randomly select words from the list and write them on the card as illustrated. (3) Colored markers.

Word Bingo			
happen	should	night	enough
below	never	complete	thought
grow	where	while	building
every	through	include	were
country	even	important	between

Teaching Procedures: One student (or the teacher) is designated as the caller. Each of the remaining students gets a Bingo card. The caller randomly selects a word from the list and says the word. The students place a colored marker on the square in which the word is written. The first person to cover all the squares in a horizontal, vertical, or diagonal row calls, "Bingo." The caller and the student then verify the words. If verified, that student wins.

Adaptations: Bingo is a generic game that can be adapted to provide practice for a variety of skills. For example:

> *Consonant Bingo:* Put pictures of objects that start with initial consonants, blends, or digraphs on the Bingo cards. The caller says the letter(s) and the students mark the picture(s) that has the same consonant, blend, or digraph. This can also be adapted for final consonants.
> *Prefix Bingo:* Write prefixes on the Bingo cards. The caller says a word with a prefix or gives the definition of a prefix, and the students mark the prefix on their cards.
> *Math Fact Bingo:* Write the answers to math facts on the Bingo cards. The caller says a math fact and the students mark the answer.

■ Rotten Egg

Objective: To provide students practice in recognizing words.

Grades: Primary

Materials: (1) 30 index cards (3 × 5 inch) consisting of 15 pairs of words. Write or type the words across each end of the card so that the students can see the words as they hold the cards like playing cards. (2) One Rotten Egg card.

Teaching Procedures: Explain that the game is played like Old Maid. The dealer deals all the cards face down to the players. The players pick up the cards and match any pairs that they may have in their hands. Starting to the left of the dealer, player #1 lays down any matching pairs in his or her hand and names them. Once this student has put down any matching pairs, he or she then picks a card from the cards of another player. If it matches a card in player #1's hand, he or she names the pair and lays it down on the table. If the child cannot pronounce the word, the teacher or another student helps. The student must keep the pair of cards in his or her hand until the next turn. If the chosen card does not match one in player #1's hand, he or she keeps it. Play then proceeds to player #2 on the left and continues in the same manner until all word pairs are matched. The person left with the Rotten Egg card is the loser.

Adaptations: This game may also be played with a Happy Face card instead of a Rotten Egg card. The person ending up with the Happy Face card wins.

The game can also be adapted to other skills. For example, card pairs can be made that require the students to match initial or final sounds in words (e.g., *cat* and *cost; elephant* and *tent*), prefixes or suffixes (e.g., *repeat* and *rewind; painter* and *carpenter*), or synonyms or antonyms (e.g., *happy* and *glad; hot* and *cold*).

■ Silly Stories

Objective: To give the students practice in using context to decode words.

Grades: Primary and intermediate

Materials: Short stories written at the students' instructional reading levels with the adjectives and adverbs left out and replaced by blanks. For example:

The _____ farmer had a hat, an
_____, _____ hat. Oh, how he
liked that _____, _____ hat! But
one day a _____, _____ wind took
the _____ hat right off his head. The
farmer ran _____, _____ chasing
the hat, but he just could not catch it. . . .

Teaching Procedures: First discuss what kinds of words are left out of the story. Give each student a copy of the story and have the students read the story and decide on words that make sense. Have them read their versions of the stories to the group and discuss how different words can go in the same blank

and still make sense. Finally, as a group, create a silly story by filling in words that don't make sense.

Adaptations: Vary the parts of speech that are deleted.

■ Compound Concentration

Objective: To give the students practice in identifying compound words and to illustrate how words may be combined to form compound words.

Grades: Intermediate and secondary

Materials: 36 index cards (3 × 5 inch) on which the two parts of 18 compound words have been written. Make sure that each part can only be joined with one other part.

Teaching Procedure: Explain the game. Have the students shuffle the cards and place the cards face down in six rows with six cards each. Each player takes a turn at turning over two cards. The student then decides whether the two words make a compound word. If the words do not make a compound word, then the cards are again turned face down and the next player takes a turn. If the words make a compound word, then the player gets those two cards and turns over two more cards. The student continues playing until two cards are turned over that do not make a compound word. The game is over when all the cards are matched. The winner is the player with the most cards.

Adaptations: Concentration can be adapted for many skills. Students can match synonyms, antonyms, prefixes, suffixes, initial or final consonants, categories, and math facts.

SUMMARY

Reading is a strategic thinking process in which readers use their prior knowledge to interact with the text to construct meaning. A number of factors may be related to students' difficulty in becoming effective readers, including poor teaching and limited opportunities to read and write, delays in oral language or language differences, and inefficient cognitive, metacognitive, and/or metalinguistic processing.

Many students with learning and behavior problems experience difficulties in learning to read, particularly in learning and applying word identification strategies. There are a variety of reasons why they have difficulties identifying unknown words and learning to read. Some children have not been provided with methods and materials that build on the natural pattern and flow of language. For these students, approaches such as whole language, modified language experience approach, patterned language books, or Reading Recovery may assist them in learning to read. These instructional approaches, which are meaning-oriented, emphasize the use of semantic, syntactic, and visual configuration clues.

In contrast, other students may profit from code-emphasis strategies that emphasize phonic and structural analysis (e.g., sounds, syllables, structural units). Many of these programs, such as linguistic reading programs, *Corrective Reading, Phonic Remedial Reading Drills,* and Making Words explicitly teach word parts and incorporate them into highly controlled reading materials. Students who have not succeeded in using meaning-oriented approaches may need these highly structured programs for success.

Students with severe reading problems may profit from approaches that incorporate the kinesthetic and tactile input modes into their programs. Whereas the Fernald (VAKT) approach incorporates these modes into a meaning-emphasis approach to initial teaching, the Gillingham-Stillman method incorporates these modes into a code-emphasis approach.

Other students may not have received the necessary opportunities to practice identifying words and therefore do not recognize them at an automatic level. For these students, the addition of supplementary activities such as games, computer programs, the sight word association procedure, or the picture association or sentence/word association procedures, may provide the additional practice.

Some older students have the necessary basic word identification skills but fail to apply them in a systematic manner. Teaching students a consistent method for identifying words can be quite helpful.

As teachers, we need to determine the most effective and efficient ways for students with learning and behavior problems to develop and utilize word identification strategies. By taking into account the characteristics of the learners and their past and current reading program, we can make "educated guesses" concerning which approaches might be the most advantageous. As teachers, it is important to know a variety of teaching strategies and approaches so that we might meet the differing needs of these students.

THINK AND APPLY

- What are the characteristics of the reading process and how are oral language and written expression related to reading?
- What are the types of cues and knowledge that a reader uses to identify words? Listen to a primary-grade student reading a book. Listen and watch for the types of cues and knowledge the child uses.
- Compare and contrast meaning-emphasis and code-emphasis approaches or strategies for teaching word recognition. Look at reading materials representative of each orientation to help you make your comparisons.
- What are the similarities and differences between the Fernald method and the Gillingham-Stillman method?
- When would a student most likely profit from learning the word identification strategy DISSECT?
- Describe how using a language experience story for reading could be used to build oral language.

APPENDIX 4.1

Scope and Sequence for Word Identification

Pre-primer

Grapheme-phoneme associations for consonants: *b, c /k/, d, f, g /g/, h, j, l, m, n, p, r, s, t, w*
Substitution: substituting initial and final consonants in known words
Context clues: using context and consonants to recognize unknown words
Morphemic analysis: inflectional endings *s* (plural marker—*dogs*) and *ed (called)*

Primer

Grapheme-phoneme associations:
    consonants: *k, v, y, z*
    consonant digraphs: *ch, sh, th*
    consonant blends: *pl, st, tr*
    short vowels: *a, e, i, o, u*
    spelling patterns: *er, or, ur, ar, ow, et, an, ight, at, ay, all*
Substitution: using grapheme-phoneme associations and parts of known words to recognize unknown words
Context cues: using semantic and syntactic cues to monitor responses to unknown printed words
Morphemic analysis
    inflectional endings: *s* (3rd person singular verbs—*eats*), *d (liked), es (boxes), 's (possessive—Ann's), er*
      (comparative—*faster*)
    suffix: *er* (as agent—*farmer*)

First Reader

Grapheme-phoneme associations:
    consonant: *x*
    consonant digraphs:[1] *wh, kn /n/, wr /r/, ck /k/*
    consonant blends: *br, cr, dr, fr, gr, bl, cl, fl, sl, sc, tw, ld, nd*
    short vowels: *y*
    long vowels: *a, e, i, o, u, y*
    vowel digraphs: *ay, ea /ĕ/ & /e/, ee, oa, ow /ō/*
    vowel diphthongs: *oi, oy, ow /ou/*
    spelling patterns: *alk, eigh, ind, old, ook*
    generalization: In the initial position, *y* represents a consonant sound; in other positions, a vowel sound.
Morphemic analysis:
    inflectional endings: *ing, (walking), est (fastest)*
    compound words: compounds comprised of 2 known words
    contractions: *not = n't (doesn't), will/shall = 'll (I'll)*[2]
Structural analysis:
    separating monosyllables into parts
    counting the number of vowel sounds in a word as a clue to the number of syllables
Synthesis: blending sounds into syllables; syllables into words

Second Reader

Grapheme-phoneme associations:
    consonants: *c /s/, g /j/*
    generalization: When *c* and *g* are followed by *e, i,* or *y* they usually represent their soft sounds
    consonant digraphs: *ph /f/, tch /ch/, gn /n/, mb /m/, dge /j/*

(continued)

APPENDIX 4.1 *Continued*

consonant blends: *gl, pr, qu /kw/, sk, sm, sn, sp, sw, scr, sch, str, squ, thr, lk, nk*
vowel digraphs: *ai, oo /ōō/ & /oo/, ey, ew, ei, ie, ue*
vowel diphthongs: *ou, au, aw*
schwa: /ə/ as represented by an initial vowel *(ago)*
r-controlled vowels: *ar, er, ir, or, ur, oor (door, poor), ear (year, earn, bear, heart), our (hour, four)*
spelling pattern: *ough (through, though, thought, rough)*
generalizations:

    1) When *c* and *g* are followed by *e, i,* or *y* they usually represent soft sounds
    2) A single vowel letter at the end of an accented syllable usually represents its long sound
    3) A single vowel letter followed by a consonant other than *r* usually represents its short sound in an accented syllable
    4) A single vowel letter followed by a single consonant, other than *v,* and a final *e* usually represents its long sound and the *e* is silent

Morphemic analysis:
inflectional endings: *s' (boys'), en (beaten)*
prefix: *un*
suffixes: *ful, fully, ish, less, ly, ness, self, y*
contraction: *have = 've (I've)*[2]
generalizations:

    1) Divide between the words that form a compound; other divisions may occur in either or both parts
    2) Divide between the root word and an affix; other divisions may occur in either the root or affix recognizing words with spelling changes made by adding suffixes when: the final *e* has been dropped (*hide— hiding*), *y* has changed to *i (baby—babies),* and a final consonant has been doubled *(sit—sitting)*

Syllabication generalizations:

    1) Usually divide between consonants that are not a digraph or blend
    2) A single consonant between 2 single vowels may go with either syllable
    3) Final *e* and the preceding consonant usually form the final syllable

Accenting: hearing and marking-accented syllables

Third Reader

Grapheme-phoneme associations:
consonant blends: *spl, spr, ng, nt*
generalization: A single vowel letter or vowel combination *(dangerous)* represents a schwa sound in many unaccented syllables

Morphemic analysis:
prefixes: *dis, ex, im, in, post, pre, re, sub, super, trans*
suffixes: *or* (as agent—*actor*), *ous, tion, sion, ment, ty, ic, al, able*
contractions: *are = 're (they're),*[2] *would/had = 'd (I'd)*[3]

Structural analysis: syllabicating words of more than 2 syllables
Accenting generalizations:

    1) Usually the first syllable in a 2-syllable word is accented
    2) Usually affixes are not accented

[1]Silent consonants are included under consonant digraphs.

[2]More words with this contraction are likely to be encountered at higher reader levels.

[3]Most contractions of *would/should ('d)* and *is/has ('s)* are likely to be encountered above the third-reader level.

Source: From *How to Increase Reading Ability: A Guide to Developmental and Remedial Methods,* 9th ed. by A. J. Harris and E. R. Sipay. Copyright © 1990 by Longman Publishing Group.

APPENDIX 4.2 ▬▬▬▬▬▬▬▬▬▬

Predictable and Patterned Language Books

Finger Rhymes and Nursery Songs
(books that encourage and develop oral language production and responses and invite students to engage in readinglike behaviors)

Adams, Pam. *This Old Man.* New York: Grossett and Dunlap, 1974.

Aliki. *Go Tell Aunt Rhody.* New York: Macmillan, 1974.

Aliki. *Hush Little Baby.* Englewood Cliffs, NJ: Prentice-Hall, 1968.

Battaglia, Aurelius. *Old Mother Hubbard.* Racine, WI: Golden Press, 1972.

Bayley, Nicola. *The Nicola Bayley Book of Nursery Rhymes.* Knopf, 1975.

Brown, Marc. *Finger Rhymes.* Dutton, 1980.

Brown, Marc. *Hand Rhymes.* Dutton, 1985.

Declacre, Lulu, ed. *Arroz Con Leche: Popular Songs and Rhymes from Latin America.* Scholastic, 1989.

Demi, *Dragons, and Kites and Dragonflies: A Collection of Chinese Nursery Rhymes.* Harcourt, 1986.

Glazer, Tom. *The Mother Goose Songbook.* Illustrated by David McPhail. Doubleday, 1990.

*Griego, Margot C., et al. *Tortillas Para Mama and Other Nursery Rhymes/Spanish and English.* Illustrated by Barbara Cooney. Henry Holt, 1981.

Hawkins, Colin, and Jacqui Hawkins. *Old Mother Hubbard.* Putnam, 1985.

_____. *I Know an Old Lady Who Swallowed a Fly.* Putnam, 1987.

Higgins, Doin. *Papa's Going to Buy Me a Mocking Bird.* New York: Seabury Press, 1968.

Hill, Eric. *Nursery Rhyme Peek-a-Book.* Price, Stern, Sloan, 1982.

Jones, Carol. *Old MacDonald Had a Farm.* Houghton Mifflin, 1989.

_____. *This Old Man.* Houghton Mifflin, 1990.

Keats, Ezra Jack. *Over in the Meadown.* New York: Scholastic Press, 1974.

Langstaff, John. *Oh, A-Hunting We Will Go.* New York: Antheneum, 1974.

Lobel, Arnold. *The Random House Book of Mother Goose.* Random House, 1986.

O'Neill, Mary. *Hailstones and Halibut Bones.* Garden City: Doubleday, 1961.

Oxenbury, Helen. *Helen Oxenbury's Nursery Rhyme Book.* Morrow, 1986.

Peek, Merle, adapted and illustrated. *Mary Wore Her Red Dress and Henry Wore His Green Sneakers.* Clarion, 1985.

_____. *Roll Over! A Counting Song.* Clarion, 1981.

Petersham, Maud, and Miska Petersham. *The Rooster Crows: A Book of American Rhymes and Jingles.* New York: Scholastic Press, 1971. .

Prelutsky, Jack. *Read-Aloud Rhymes for the Very Young.* New York: Knopf, 1986.

Quackenbush, Robert. *She'll Be Coming Around the Mountain.* Philadelphia: Lippincott, 1973.

Quackenbush, Robert. *Skip To My Lou.* Philadelphia: Lippincott, 1973.

Raffi. *Down By the Bay: Songs to Read,* illustrated by Nadine Bernard Westcott. Crown, 1987.

_____. *Five Little Ducks,* illustrated by Jose Aruego and Ariane Dewey. Crown, 1989.

Spier, Peter. *The Fox Went Out on a Chilly Night.* Garden City: Doubleday, 1961.

Sutherland, Zena. *The Orchard Book of Nursery Rhymes.* Illustrated by Faith Jacques. Orchard, 1990.

Watson, Clyde. *Father Ox's Pennyrhymes.* New York: Scholastic Press, 1971.

Westcott, Nadine Bernard. *Peanut Butter and Jelly: A Play Rhyme.* Dutton, 1987.

_____. *Skip to My Lou.* Joy Street/Little, Brown, 1989.

Westcott, Nadine Bernard. *I Know an Old Lady Who Swallowed a Fly.* Boston: Little, Brown, 1980.

Wyndham, Robert. *Chinese Mother Goose Rhymes.* Illustrated by Ed Young. Philomel, 1968.

Zemach, Margot. *Hush, Little Baby.* New York: E. P. Dutton, 1976.

Cumulative Tales

(books that build sequentially on a connected idea)

Duff, Maggie. *Rum Pum Pum.* New York: Macmillan, 1978.

Emberly, Barbara. *Drummer Hoff.* Englewood Cliffs, NJ: Prentice-Hall, 1967.

Galdone, Paul. *Cat Goes Fiddle-i-Fee.* New York: Clarion,

(continued)

APPENDIX 4.2 *Continued*

Galdone, Paul. *Henny Penny.* New York: Scholastic Press, 1968.

Galdone, Paul. *The Gingerbread Boy.* Boston: Houghton Mifflin, 1975.

Hawkins, Colin, and Jacqui Hawkins, *I Know an Old Lady Who Swallowed a Fly.*

Hayes, Sarah. *This Is the Bear,* illustrated by Helen Craig. Lippincott, 1986.

Hutchins, Pat. *The Doorbell Rang.* Greenwillow, 1986.

Kent, Jack. *The Fat Cat.* New York: Scholastic Press, 1971.

McGovern, Ann. *Too Much Noise.* New York: Scholastic Press, 1967.

Nodset, Joan. *Who Took the Farmer's Hat?* New York: Scholastic Press, 1963.

Peepe, Rodney. *The House that Jack Built.* New York: Delacorte, 1970.

Robart, Rose. *The Cake That Mack Ate,* illustrated by Maryann Kovalski. Joy Street/Little, Brown, 1986.

Rosen, Michael. *We're Going on a Bear Hunt.* Illustrated by Helen Oxenbury. Macmillan, 1989.

Tolstoy, Alexei. *The Great Big Enormous Turnip.* New York: Franklin Watts, 1968.

Vipoint, Elfrida. *The Elephant and the Bad Baby,* illustrated by Raymond Briggs. Coward McCann, 1969.

Wahl, Jan. *Drakestail.* New York: Greenwillow, 1978.

Williams, Linda. *The Little Old Lady Who Was Not Afraid of Anything.* Illustrated by Megan Lloyd. Harper & Row, 1986.

Wood, Audrey. *The Napping House.* Harcourt, 1984.

Sequential Phrases and Patterns

(books that denote a numerical hierarchy or a time sequence)

Carle, Eric. *The Very Hungry Caterpillar.* Cleveland, OH: Collins, World, 1969.

Carle, Eric. *The Grouchy Ladybug.* New York: Crowell, 1977.

_____. *The Very Busy Spider.* Philomel, 1984.

_____. *The Very Quiet Cricket.* Philomel, 1990.

dePaola, Tomie. *Pancakes for Breakfast.* New York: Harcourt Brace Jovanovich, 1976.

Galdone, Paul. *The Three Bears.* New York: Scholastic Press, 1972.

Galdone, Paul. *The Three Billy Goats Gruff.* New York: Seabury Press, 1973.

Hutchins, Pat. *Titch.* New York: Collier Books, 1971.

Kraus, Robert, *Where Are You Going, Little Mouse?,* illustrated by Jose Aruego and Ariane Dewey. Greenwillow, 1986.

Kraus, Ruth. *The Carrot Seed.* New York: Harper & Row, 1945.

Sendak, Maurice. *Chicken Soup With Rice.* New York: Scholastic Press, 1962.

Schulevitz, Uri. *One Monday Morning.* New York: Scribner's, 1967.

Ward, Cindy. *Cookie's Week.* New York: Scholastic, 1988.

Wolff, Ashley. *A Year of Beasts.* Dutton, 1986.

Wolff, Ashley. *A Year of Birds.* Putnam, 1984.

Repetitive Language and Story Patterns

(books with repetitive words, sentences, or phrases invite the reader to learn to read naturally by responding through chanting, choral reading, or chiming in during the repetitive refrains or familiar parts)

Bennett, Jill. *Teeny Tiny.* Illustrated by Tomie de Paola. Putnam, 1986.

Barton, Byron. *Buzz, Buzz, Buzz.* New York: Scholastic Press, 1973.

Brown, Marcia. *The Three Billy Goats Gruff.* New York: William R. Scott, 1961.

Brown, Margaret Wise. *Four Fur Feet.* New York: William R. Scott, 1961.

Brown, Ruth. *A Dark Dark Tale.* Dial, 1981.

Burton, Marilee Robin. *Tail Toes Eyes Ears Nose.* Harper & Row, 1989.

Campbell, Rod. *Dear Zoo.* Four Winds, 1983.

Carle, Eric. *Do You Want to Be My Friend?* New York: Thomas Y. Crowell, 1971.

Carle, Eric. *Have You Seen My Cat?* Picture Book, 1987.

Galdone, Paul. *The Little Red Hen.* New York: Scholastic Press, 1973.

Galdone, Paul. *The Three Little Pigs.* New York: Seabury Press, 1970.

Ginsberg, Mirra. *The Chick and the Duckling.* New York: Macmillan, 1972.

Ginsberg, Mirra. *Good Morning Chick.* Illustrated by Byron Barton. Greenwillow, 1980.

Guarino, Deborah. *Is Your Mama a Llama?,* illustrated by Steven Kellogg. Scholastic, 1989.

Hill, Eric. *Where's Spot?* Putnam, 1980.

Kraus, Robert. *Whose Mouse Are You?* New York: Collier Books, 1970.

Lillegrad, Dee. *Sitting in my Box.* Dutton, 1989.

Martin, Bill, Jr. *Brown Bear, Brown Bear, What Do You See?* New York: Holt, Rinehart & Winston, 1967.

Shaw, Nancy. *Sheep in a Jeep.* Illustrated by Margot Shaw. Houghton Mifflin, 1986.

Tafuri, Nancy. *Have You Seen My Duckling?* Greenwillow, 1984.

Thomas, Patricia. Illustrated by Mordicai Gerstein. *There Are Rocks in My Socks! Said the Ox to the Fox.* New York: Lothrop, 1979.

Van Laan, Nancy. *The Big Fat Worm.* Illustrated by Jon Agee. Dutton, 1989.

Williams, Sue. *I Went Walking.* Harcourt, 1990.

Zemach, Margot. *The Teeny Tiny Woman.* New York: Scholastic Press, 1965.

Predictable Plots

(books that provide readers with easy text, which encourages predictability and extends meaning)

Brown, Margaret Wise. *Goodnight Moon.* New York: Harper & Row, 1947.

Burningham, John. *Mr. Grumpy's Outing.* New York: Scholastic Press, 1970.

Flack, Marjorie. *Ask Mr. Bear.* New York: Macmillan, 1952.

Hutchins, Pat. *Good-Night, Owl!* New York: Macmillan, 1972.

Hutchins, Pat. *Happy Birthday, Sam.* Puffin/Penguin, 1981.

Hutchins, Pat. *Rosie's Walk.* New York: Macmillan, 1968.

_____. *You'll Soon Grow Into Them, Titch.* Greenwillow, 1983.

Kesselman, Wendy. *There's a Train Going by My Window.* Garden City: Doubleday, 1982.

Rice, Eve. *Benny Bakes a Cake.* Greenwillow, 1981.

_____. *Sam Who Never Forgets.* Greenwillow, 1977.

Sendak, Maurice. *Where the Wild Things Are.* New York: Harper & Row, 1964.

West, Colin. *"Pardon," Said the Giraffe.* New York: Harper & Row, 1986.

Wildsmith, Brian. *The Cat Sat on the Mat.* Oxford, 1983.

Adapted from R. J. Tierney, J. E. Readence, and E. K. Dishner, (1995). *Reading Strategies and Practices: A Compendium* (4th ed., pp. 123–126). Boston: Allyn and Bacon.

APPENDIX 4.3 ━━━━━━━━━━━━━━━━━━━━━━━━━━━━━━━━

Sample Books for Use with Reading Recovery

	Author or Series	*Book*	*Publisher*
Level 1	Brian Wildsmith	Cat on the Mat	Oxford
	Sunshine	Huggles Can Juggle	Wright Group
	Bruce McMillan	Growing Colors	Lothrop, Lee, & Shepard
	Picture Puffin	Weather	Puffin
Level 2	Joy Cowley	Huggles Goes Away	Wright Group
	Rigby	Ants Love Picnics Too	Rigby
	Eric Carle	Have You Seen My Cat?	Picture Books Studio
Level 3	Manipulative Series	Little, Big, Bigger	Bowmar
	Sue Williams	I Went Walking	HBJ
	Dominie	Me	Dominie Press Inc.
Level 4	Bill Martin	Brown Bear, Brown Bear	Holt, Reinhart, and Winston
	Rigby	I Spy	Rigby
	Brian Wildsmith	My Dream	Oxford
Level 5	William Stobbs	One, Two, Buckle My Shoe	Bodely
	L. Wood	Frog and the Fly	Oxford
	Sunshine	Monkey Bridge	Wright Group
Level 6	Barbro Lindgren	Sam's Teddy Bear	Morrow
	Barbro Lindgren	Sam's Ball	Morrow
	Rookie Reader	Too Many Balloons	Children's Press
	Merle Peek	Mary Wore Her Red Dress	Clarion
Level 7	Charles Shaw	It Looked Like Spilt Milk	Harper & Row
	Magic Circle	From My Windows	Ginn
	Rookie Reader	Just Like Me	Children's Press
	Rigby	The Boogly	Rigby
Level 8	Eric Hill	Where's Spot?	Putnam
	Start To Read	Benny's Baby Brother	School Zone
	Ready to Read	The Wind	Richard Owen
	Story Box Read Togethers	Smarty Pants	Wright Group
Level 9	Pat Hutchins	Rosie's Walk	Macmillan
	Critterland Adventures	Huzzard Buzzard	Children's Press
	Sunshine Science	Are You a Ladybug?	Wright Group
	Tadpoles	Tricking Tracey	Rigby
Level 10	Cindy Wheeler	Marmalade's Nap	Knopf
	Sunshine Social Studies	Tree	Wright Group
	Sunshine Science	Underwater Journey	Wright Group
	Rigby	The Wedding	Rigby

Level 11	Picture Puffin	I'm the King of the Castle	Penguin
	Rigby	I Saw a Dinosaur	Rigby
	Breakthrough	Signs	Longman
	Robert Kraus	Whose Mouse Are You?	Macmillan
Level 12	John Burningham	The Cupboard	Crowell
	Ready to Read	I'm the King of the Mountain	Richard Owen
	Read-Alongs	Jessie's Flower	Rigby
	Sunshine	Red Socks and Yellow Socks	Wright Group
	Byron Barton	Buzz Buzz Buzz	Penguin
Level 13	Alexei Tolstoy	The Great Big Enormous Turnip	Macmillan
	Sunshine	Cloud	Wright Group
	Start to Read	Jack, Mace and the Big Race	School Zone
	Critterland Adventures	Rapid Robert Roadrunner	Children's Press
Level 14	Pam Adams	There Was an Old Lady . . .	Scholastic
	Dominie	Choose Me!	Dominie Press Inc.
	Reading Unlimited	Happy Faces	Scott, Foresman, & Co.
Level 15	Audrey Wood	The Napping House	HBJ
	Rookie Reader	Messy Bessy	Children's Press
	Sunshine	A Hundred Hugs	Wright Group
	Suzy Klein	Don't Touch!	Penguin
Level 16	Mercer Mayer	There's A Nightmare In My . . .	Dial
	I Can Read Book	Albert the Albatross	Heinemann
	Sunshine	The Poor Sore Paw	Wright Group
	Dominie	Big or Little	Dominie Press Inc.
Level 17	Pat Hutchins	The Doorbell Rang	Greenwillow
	Paul Galdone	The Little Red Hen	Scholastic
	Rigby	No Dinner for Sally	Rigby
	Reading Unlimited	Loose Laces	Scott, Foresman, & Co.
Level 18	Eric Carle	The Very Hungry Catapillar	Penguin
	Maurice Sendak	Where the Wild Things Are	Harper & Row
	Rigby	Brave Ben	Rigby
Level 19	Arnold Lobel	Frog and Toad Are Friends	Harper & Row
	B. Byars	Go and Hush the Baby	Viking
	Read by Reading	The King's Cat	Scholastic
	Reading Unlimited	Mystery Seeds	Scott, Foresman, & Co.
Level 20	Maurice Sendak	Chicken Soup with Rice	Scholastic
	Jellybeans	Long Grass of Tumbledown Road	Wright Group
	Reading Unlimited	Lizards and Salamanders	Scott, Foresman, & Co.

Source: Adapted from G. S. Pinnell, D. E. DeFord, and C. A. Lyons (1988), *Reading Recovery: Early Intervention for At-Risk First-Graders.* Arlington, Va.: Educational Research Service; and from M. Clay and B. Watson (1987), *Reading Recovery Book List,* Auckland, New Zealand: University of Auckland.

Chapter 5

Reading: Fluency and Comprehension

OUTLINE

KEY TOPICS FOR MASTERY

— *Reasons why students may have difficulty with fluency*
— *Strategies for reading aloud, repeated reading, and choral repeated reading and its benefits*
— *Reasons that students may have difficulty comprehending what they read*
— *A framework for reading comprehension including the relationship among the reader, text, and author and the categories of textually explicit, textually implicit, and scriptually implicit question-answer relationships*
— *Guidelines for promoting reading comprehension including activities for before, during, and after reading*
— *Strategies for activating background knowledge including brainstorming, PreReading Plan, Text Preview, K-W-L, and story schema activation*
— *Strategies for promoting questioning including reciprocal questioning, question-answer relationships strategy, and self-questioning strategies*
— *Strategies for promoting paraphrasing, retelling and summarization including the paraphrasing strategy, the summarization strategy, and story mapping and retelling strategies*
— *Comprehensive approaches for teaching reading and reading comprehension including the directed reading activity, the directed reading-thinking activity, reciprocal teaching and collaborative strategic reading, and whole language and literature-based reading programs*

 BRIGHT IDEA

Turn to page 223 and read Think and Apply.

Reading provides a window for learning in schools and in later life. Research indicates that a key to becoming a good reader is to have opportunities to read. As teachers our goal is to provide students with a wide choice of literature and other reading materials, with opportunities to read and discuss what is being read and with instruction in strategies that allow students to comprehend actively and think critically about what they are reading. Whereas the last chapter focused on strategies for word identification and decoding, this chapter presents strategies oriented toward fluency and comprehension.

TEACHING FLUENCY

Although Jeff can recognize most of the words in his second-grade reader, he continues to sound out the words rather than rely on the visual configuration of the word, context clues, and his memory. Consequently, his reading, whether oral or silent, is very slow. He expends so much effort on identifying the words that he frequently misses the main points of the passage.

Diane, a fourth grader, had great difficulty learning to read. After several years of failure, she finally learned to identify words readily by using a linguistic approach. However, Diane's rate of reading is slow and she is experiencing some difficulties in comprehension. When asked to define reading, she places emphasis on "reading the word correctly" rather than on understanding what she reads. Though Jeff and Diane have developed a system for identifying words, they are having difficulties reading fluently (quickly and easily). Research indicates that students with significant reading disabilities have difficulty developing fluency and continue to be slow readers into adolescence and adulthood (Shaywitz and Shaywitz, 1996, Stanovitch, 1986; Torgesen, in press). For these students, their ability to listen to text and understand the information usually exceeds their ability to gain understanding from reading (Mosberg and Johns, 1994). Fluency instruction may be one means of improving their ability to recognize words automatically and to allocate more effort toward constructing meaning from what they are reading.

Fluency instruction is designed to increase both word recognition and rate of reading. According to the theory of automaticity (LaBerge and Samuels, 1974; Samuels, 1987), fluent readers automatically process information at the visual and phonological levels, and are therefore able to focus most of their attention on the meaning codes in the text and integrate this information with their background knowledge. Researchers have found that fluency is a good predictor of comprehension (Rasinki, 1990).

Let's look at several strategies for helping students develop fluency in their reading and ideas for making difficult books accessible and easy books acceptable.

Reading and Reading Aloud

Students develop reading fluency through reading and through listening and watching others read aloud. For example, Anderson, Wilson, and Fielding (1988) found that one of the better predictors of reading achievement was the amount of time fifth-grade children spent reading books out of school. Within the last decade, a growing emphasis has been placed on the importance of reading aloud to children as a means for developing not only an enjoyment of literature and books, but also as an avenue for learning to read and building fluency (Kimmel and Segal, 1988; Reutzel, Hollingsworth, and Eldredge, 1994; Shany and Biemiller, 1995; Trelease, 1995).

Reading aloud promotes the development of reading and fluency in a number of ways. First, it allows the teacher to model fluent reading. When reading aloud to a group of students just learning to read, the use of big books can be helpful because it allows the teacher to make more visible the literacy act and creates interest in the story. If the teacher or parent or volunteer is reading aloud to one child, then sitting next to the child or having the child sit on the teacher's lap (depending on the age of the child) makes it easy for the child to interact with the print, the pictures, and the teacher. When reading aloud, read with expression and have the characters take on different voices.

Second, reading aloud allows the students to listen to and discuss books that may be difficult for them to read. Many students with learning and behavior problems have listening comprehension that is several years more advanced than their reading comprehension. Reading a book aloud affords the students the opportunity to talk about literature that is at a more advanced level.

Third, reading aloud provides background knowledge for the students reading the book themselves. Once children have listened to a book, they are more likely to select it as a book they want to read. In a study of kindergartners, Martinez and Teale (1988) found that children chose very familiar books (read repeatedly by the teacher) to read during freetime three times more frequently than unfamiliar books (unread). Since students have already listened to and talked about the book, they will have a wealth of knowledge about the book to assist them in reading.

Fourth, reading aloud can be orchestrated so that older, less adept readers can read books to young children and serve as cross-age tutors. This provides the opportunity for the older students to read aloud and to serve as the role model of a "good reader," an opportunity not often available in the regular or resource classroom.

Jim Trelease, author of *The New Read-Aloud Handbook* (1995), suggests that reading aloud

— Provides a positive reading role model
— Furnishes new information
— Demonstrates the pleasures of reading
— Develops vocabulary
— Provides examples of good sentences and good story grammar
— Enables students to be exposed to a book they might not otherwise be exposed to
— Provides opportunity for discussions concerning the content of the book

Repeated Reading

Have you noticed how young children thoroughly enjoy having the same story read to them many, many times? As you sit with them and read a familiar book, they automatically begin to read along with you. At first, they join in on some of the words and phrases. Eventually, they are reading with you for most of the book. With repeated reading of a story, the children are becoming so familiar with the text that their memory becomes a great aid to them. Repeated reading is based on the notion that as students repeatedly read text, they become fluent and confident in their reading (Samuels, 1979). And because they are exposed to the same story several times, they have the opportunity to practice identifying unknown words while relying on their memory of the language flow to assist them.

— **PROCEDURES:** Repeated reading consists of rereading short, meaningful passages several times until a satisfactory level of fluency is reached. The procedure is then repeated with a new passage. The general format for this reading procedure is to have the student repeatedly read passages that range from 50 to 200 words in length, until they reach a more fluent reading rate (e.g., 85 words per minute) and with an adequate word recognition level (e.g., 90 percent word-recognition accuracy). When a student reads under the direct supervision of a teacher, the words a student does not recognize are pronounced by the teacher. To foster comprehension, discussion of the book follows reading.

Carbo (1978) and Chomsky (1976) have used tape-recorded books for this procedure. Using taped books, the students listen to the stories and follow along with the written text. They listen to and read the same story until they can "read the book by themselves." The teacher then listens to students individually read the story and discusses the story with the students. Guidelines for tape-recording books, keeping records of students' reading, and using computers are presented in Apply the Concept 5.1.

— **COMMENTS:** Students reading below grade level who have used repeated reading have consistently demonstrated gains in both fluency and reading comprehension (Carbo, 1978; Chomsky, 1976; Herman, 1985; O'Shea, Sindelar, and O'Shea, 1987; Rashotte and Torgesen, 1985; Rasinski, 1990; Shany and Biemiller, 1995; Weinstein and Cooke, 1992). Using tape-recorded stories, Carbo (1987) found that rereading small segments of text may be helpful. When Shany and Biemiller (1995) compared (a) teacher assistance during repeated reading with (b) students listening to taped readings on a speed-controlled recorder, they found that reading rates and reading comprehension increased in both cases. Students who used a tape recorder, however, read twice the amount and had higher listening comprehension scores.

Given this information, we suggest that combining the patterned language approach (discussed in Chapter Four) with repeated reading could be a powerful strategy for building fluency in students with limited reading skills.

Choral Repeated Reading

Choral repeated reading is a strategy that combines ideas and procedures from repeated reading and choral reading. It was developed by one of the authors (Bos, 1982), because of her concern that fluency-building strategies for less-adept readers tend to ignore the teaching of either word identification skills or comprehension (e.g., neurological impress). We have used the approach with students who have

APPLY THE CONCEPT 5.1

USING TAPED BOOKS AND COMPUTERS FOR REPEATED READING

Selecting Books

Select books that are of interest to the students, or have the students select the books. You can also record books and stories that the students write. Patterned language books are a good source for students just learning to read (see Chapter Appendix 4.2). *The New Read-Aloud Handbook* by Jim Trelease (1995) is another good source for books.

Tape Recording the Books

Record with Pauses: Student Can Reread

Read the book and decide where to break the text for repeated reading. Mark these spots in the text. For younger students you may want to use a picture of a stop sign.

Get ready to record by gathering the book, a good quality tape and tape recorder with a counter, and a signal (e.g., bell, beeper, rattle) to signal the places to stop.

Record the book, using a natural rate of reading and expression. When you come to a spot where you are supposed to stop, signal the stop. Wait at least five seconds before you continue. When you continue say the page number first and then continue.

Write the counter number next to the signal in the book so students will know how far to rewind if they want to go back and reread with the tape.

No Pauses: The Student Can Read Along

Use the same procedure but signal only the turning of pages. Or, purchase prerecorded taped books. You can ask parent volunteers to record the books; Kirk (1986) suggests forming student committees to select, practice, and record the books.

Storing the Taped Books

Store the books on a shelf. Glue or tape a library pocket on the back of the book and place the tape in the pocket. In the inside cover place a Reading Record Sheet, where the students record their name and the date they first read the book. In this way you and the students know who has read a book. These students can then get together to discuss the book.

Keeping Student Records

Have each student make a reading folder. Staple forms inside the folder on which the student can record the name of the book, the author, the date, how he or she read the book, and with whom he or she discussed the book. In this way, both the teacher and the student have a record of the student's reading.

Computer-Based Reading Practice

Computer software provides another avenue for children to repeatedly read books using the computer. For example, *Living Book Series* (Discus Books) and *Wiggleworks* (Scholastic) both provide opportunities for students to listen to books being read, to read along with the computer, and, in the case of *Wiggleworks,* to record their own reading of the book. Reading software provides flexibility; the text can be read in sentences or phrases, or the students can highlight individual words and have them pronounced. Many of these programs easily switch languages (most commonly between English and Spanish), and have built-in record keeping systems so teachers know the number of times students read the books and the type of assistance they use.

Research suggests that computer reading programs help students with learning disabilities to build word recognition and reading comprehension (Leong, 1995; Lundberg, 1995; Torgesen and Barker, 1995).

Name of Book	Author	Dates	Read with				Discussed with	
			Self	*Tape*	*Student*	*Teacher*	*Student*	*Teacher*

significant reading difficulties in word identification and reading rate.

— PROCEDURES: Choral repeated reading is designed for students who are able to comprehend material read to them but, due to difficulties in word identification and reading rate, are unable to read material commensurate with their listening comprehension level. Students should have a sight vocabulary of at least twenty-five words. We suggest the following procedure:

1. Explain the technique to the student.

2. With the student, select a book of interest that is one to two levels above his or her current instructional reading level and that has frequent repetition of words. At times, we have used books from the patterned language book list shown in Chapter Appendix 4.2. Have the student read a short passage from the book to check word recognition. It should range from 75 to 85 percent. If it is much lower, a different book should be selected.

3. Establish a purpose for reading by introducing the book and making predictions. Read the book with the student, using the following three-step process:

   a. *Teacher reads:* Start at the beginning of the book and read a piece of text to the student, ranging from several sentences to a paragraph. (The length of each section should be short enough that the student can rely on his or her short-term memory as an aid for reading.) Read at a normal rate and move your finger smoothly along underneath the words as the student watches, making sure that your reading matches your movement from word to word.

   b. *Teacher and student read:* Read the same section together aloud with the student. Continue to point to the words. The two of you may read the section once or several times, rereading until the student feels comfortable reading the section independently.

   c. *Student reads:* Have the student read the section independently. Pronounce any un-

known words and note words the student consistently has difficulty recognizing.

4. After reading each section, discuss how it related to your predictions and what you have learned. New predictions and purposes for reading can be set.

5. Repeat the three-step process throughout the book. The length of each section usually increases as the book is read, and the number of times you and the student read together usually decreases. For some students the first step is discontinued.

6. Write on word cards the words the student consistently has difficulty identifying automatically. Use a variety of activities to give him or her more experience with these words. For example, discuss the word meanings or locate the words in the text and reread the sentences. Use the supplemental whole-word activities discussed in Chapter Four such as the sight word association procedure, the sentence/word association procedure, or the cloze procedure. You can also have the student use some of the word identification instructional activities described in Chapter Four.

7. Have the student keep records of his or her progress (see Figure 5.1). Using bar or other types of graphs can be particularly reinforcing for students as they gain fluency, because the increases are so clearly depicted. Word recognition and reading rate can be checked easily by having the student read 100 words of the book he or she is currently reading. Have the student record his or her results on the graph or chart. Check progress at least every third day when initially using the procedure.

In this method, reading sessions usually last fifteen to twenty minutes, with most of the time focusing on oral reading. As the student becomes more confident in reading ability, use repeated readings with tape-recorded books or stories as independent reading activities. Spelling words can be selected from words in the books and words can be organized to teach phonic and structural analysis skills (see Chapter Four).

— COMMENTS: We have used this procedure with a number of students who have severe word identification and/or fluency problems. Because choral

■ **FIGURE 5.1** *Forms for Recording Reading Fluency*

Name _____

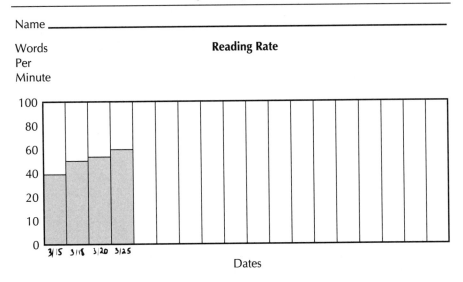

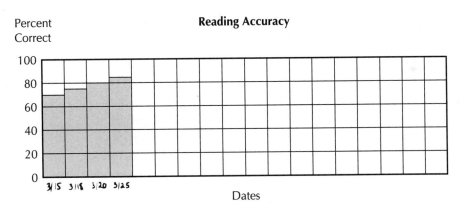

Name:_____

Text:_____

Ratings:
  3 Excellent
  2 Fair
  1 Needs Improvement

	1st Reading	2nd Reading	3rd Reading
Dates	_____	_____	_____
Word pronunciation	_____	_____	_____
Phrasing	_____	_____	_____
Rhythm	_____	_____	_____
Intonation	_____	_____	_____
Expressiveness	_____	_____	_____

Comments:

repeated reading allows the teacher and student to attend to word identification skills and comprehension as well as fluency, it is a more comprehensive reading procedure than either neurological impress or repeated readings. Using the three-step process also allows the student to read more difficult books. We have found this particularly rewarding for older nonreaders in that it quickly gives them success in reading books. Others have noted that choral reading is valuable not only for increasing fluency but also for teaching students to read (Walley, 1993) and for helping students learn English as a second language (McCauley and McCauley, 1992).

Making Easy Books Acceptable and Difficult Books Accessible

One key to becoming a fluent reader is to read. Yet students with learning and behavior problems who have difficulty reading are generally not provided as any opportunities to read books in school and do not select reading books as a leisure time activity (Anderson, Wilson, and Fielding, 1988; Spear-Swerling and Sternberg, 1996). Stanovitch (1986) has referred to this as the "Matthew effect" in that students who read well read more and improve their reading abilities, while those who read poorly read less, increasingly falling further behind in developing proficiency. Two reasons why these students may choose not to read are because they perceive easy books as unacceptable and embarrassing, and when they try to read books that they perceive as interesting, they are too difficult. Fielding and Roller (1992) discuss several strategies that teachers can use to make easy books more acceptable or legitimate, including:

- *Model your own use and enjoyment of easy books.* In adult life, most pleasure reading is easy reading.
- *Alter the purposes for easy reading.* Have students read easy books for the purpose of reading to younger students or children in preschool.
- *Have students make tape recordings of their reading.* Students will oftentimes choose easier

books and reread them several times so that they "sound good" on the tape recording.
- *Broaden the definition of acceptable reading.* Poems, songs, raps, jump-rope chants, and cheers oftentimes are easier because of the predictable language and repetition such as Joanna Cole's (1989) collection of popular jump-rope chants in *Anna Banana* and Joanna Cole and Stephanie Calmenson's (1990) collection of children's street rhymes in *Miss Mary Mack.*
- *Make simple nonfiction books available.* Books that contain new information about a topic of student interest are often not perceived by the student as easy or boring.

Chapter Appendix 5.1, Book Selection Aids for Children's Literature, contains a section on booklists for various levels of readers, including reluctant readers, that can serve as a resource.

Fielding and Roller (1992) also discuss several strategies for making difficult books more accessible to older readers with disabilities. These strategies include:

- Allowing students to spend some independent reading time reading difficult books, particularly if they work in groups
- Reading aloud to the students
- Partner reading, in which less able and more able readers are paired
- Preceding difficult books with easier books about the same topic or genre (e.g., comets, solar system, scary books, fairy tales, mystery books), thereby familiarizing the child with the vocabulary and text structure in books that are easier

Cautions Regarding Fluency Techniques

It is suggested that when teaching fluency, techniques for improving word identification skills and comprehension should be taught. As presented in the repeated choral reading technique, word recognition and word extension activities can be developed naturally from the text. For example, the same activities that are recommended for the word cards generated from language experience stories (see Figure 4.3) can be used with word cards generated from these fluency techniques. Although improving fluency can provide students with more attention to allocate toward comprehension, not all students will automatically acquire the skills associated with effective comprehension. For some students, methods of teaching comprehension may be required.

TEACHING COMPREHENSION

Comprehension is the ultimate goal of the reading process. It is constructing meaning by integrating the information provided by the author with the reader's background knowledge. It is a process by which the reader interacts with the text to construct meaning. There are many reasons why students may have difficulty comprehending what they read.

As a fourth grader reading at second-grade level, Amanda would probably better comprehend what she reads if she did not have to allocate so much attention to word identification. On the other hand, Scott is a word caller. He thinks reading is "reading the words correctly." Even though he is able to read fluently, he does not attend to the meaning of the passage. He frequently has difficulty recalling both the gist and details of a story. Carrie is diagnosed as having language disabilities, with difficulties in syntax and semantics. These low oral-language skills affect her comprehension of what she reads.

Sam can remember what he reads but does not relate it to what he already knows about the topic (schema). Therefore, he has particular difficulty answering questions that require him to use his background knowledge. Ron, on the other hand, relies too heavily on his background knowledge. This is adversely affecting his reading comprehension.

Kim fails to monitor her comprehension as she reads. She often reports that everything makes sense. Yet when her teacher asks questions it becomes obvious that Kim has achieved limited comprehension.

All these students are struggling with reading comprehension although their problems are very different. For students such as Amanda, word identification difficulties get in the way of comprehension. Focusing on building word identification skills is

probably appropriate for her. However, comprehension skills should not be ignored. This may mean building listening comprehension at her current grade level as well as working on reading comprehension at her current reading level. For Amanda, it is making sure that reading is perceived as understanding and interacting with the text to construct meaning, and not just reading the words correctly. Although word identification skill development will be important, it needs to be coupled with comprehension.

For Scott, the major portion of reading instruction should focus on comprehension. The teacher needs to assist Scott in changing his definition of the reading process. Helping Scott set comprehension-oriented purposes for reading and teaching him how to ask questions as he reads should assist him in changing his definition of reading.

Carrie's difficulties relate to a language problem that affects her reading comprehension as well as her receptive language. For students such as Carrie, instruction in reading comprehension often parallels instruction in receptive language. Both reading and listening comprehension can be improved simultaneously. For example, when Carrie either listens to or reads a story she needs to learn to ask and answer such questions as, "Who is the story about?" "Where did it happen?" "What was the problem in the story?" "What happened to solve the problem?" "How did the story end?"

Some students fail to relate what they are reading to what they already know about the topic. This is the case with Sam. Other students have limited background knowledge to bring to the reading process. Research in schema theory has shown that the knowledge one brings to the reading task affects comprehension, particularly inferential comprehension (Anderson, Reynolds, Schallert, and Goetz, 1977; Carr and Thompson, 1996; Hansen and Pearson, 1983; McKeown, Beck, Sinatra, and Loxterman, 1992). Teaching strategies that encourage students to activate their knowledge, or activities that provide opportunities for students to enrich their backgrounds prior to reading, can facilitate comprehension.

Although some students do not rely enough on background knowledge, other students may rely too much on background knowledge, as is the case with Ron. Often these are the same students who tend to overrely on context clues when identifying unknown words. When these students begin reading informational and technical texts that require accurate recall of information, comprehension problems become more evident. Comprehension strategies that encourage self-questioning can encourage such students to pay closer attention to the information presented in the text.

Kim, like many other students with learning disabilities, has difficulty with the metacognitive skill of comprehension monitoring (Bos and Filip, 1984; Ellis, 1996; Palincsar and Brown, 1987; Wong, 1987, 1996; Zabrucky and Ratner, 1992). Strategies that teach students to ask questions about their comprehension and that require them to paraphrase and summarize what they read should help them develop metacognitive skills.

Increasing emphasis is being placed on reading comprehension and techniques for improving reading comprehension (e.g., Pearson and Camperell, 1994; Pressley, Brown, El-Dinary, and Afflerbach, 1995). First, we will look at a framework for reading comprehension to better understand the scope of comprehension. Then we will focus on instructional strategies for improving reading comprehension. Finally, we will discuss approaches used for teaching reading and reading comprehension.

A Framework for Reading Comprehension

One way of guiding reading comprehension instruction is to determine the different reasoning and information processing skills that are required by readers in order to construct meaning from what they read. Read the passage in Apply the Concept 5.2.

Now answer each of the following questions and think about the processes that were needed for you to arrive at an answer.

1. What did Pat do first to get help?
2. Where did you find the information to answer the question?

The answer, of course, is in the text. If information is found in the text, then we say that the information is *textually explicit* or *literal* (i.e., taken

directly from the text) or we are *reading the lines* (Dale, 1966).

3. What time of day was it in the story?
4. Where did you find that information?

You may have automatically answered question 3 as "early in the morning" or "in the morning" without looking back at the text. If you did this, now go back and read to see if that information is in the text. It is not. Instead, you will find in the first paragraph that "Pat watched the sun come up over the mountains." You may have automatically integrated that information with your background knowledge to conclude, "It was in the morning." When information is not in the text but requires you to integrate your background knowledge with text information to generate the answer, then we say the information is *implicit* or *inferential* (e.g., not stated directly in the text). Can we be more specific about this kind of implicit information? Pearson and Johnson (1978) refer to this kind of relationship between the question and the answer as *scriptually implicit*. It requires you to use your schema or *script* about "morning" to generate the answer. Dale (1966) has referred to this as *reading beyond the lines*.

5. Was Pat successful in using the CB radio?
6. Where did you find that information?

It was in the text, but not nearly so clearly as in the case of the first question. In this case you had to read several sentences and piece the information together. The information was *implicit* in that it was not directly stated in the text, but it did not require you to use your background knowledge in the same way that question 4 did. Pearson and Johnson (1978) refer to this kind of implicit information as *textually implicit*. The relationship between the question and the answer required you to get the information from the text, but the relationship is not clearly (*explicitly*) stated. You had to use your knowledge about language and how ideas related to answer the question. Dale (1966) has referred to this relationship as *reading between the lines*.

Therefore, when teaching reading comprehension, we can divide comprehension into types of rea-

APPLY THE CONCEPT 5.2

THE DRIVE TO BIG LAKE

Pat and her father were driving to Big Lake in the Blue Mountains. They were going to Big Lake to go fishing. As they drove Pat watched her father talk on the C.B. radio and watched the sun come up over the mountains.

When Pat and her father were near Big Lake it became very foggy. Pat's father drove slowly but did not see a sharp bend in the road. The car ran off the road and into a ditch. Pat was OK, but she knew that she needed to get help for her father.

She climbed out of the car and went to the road. She thought maybe a car would come by, but none did.

She walked down the road. She was looking for a house. As she walked, she yelled for help.

Then she remembered the C.B. radio that was in the car. She ran back to the car. She had never used the C.B., but she tried to call for help on it. A fisherman at Big Lake was listening to his C.B. Pat told him where she and her father were. Fifteen minutes later help came.

By this time Pat's father had opened his eyes and was OK. The police helped Pat and her father get the car out of the ditch and back on the road. Everyone was proud of Pat.

Source: C. S. Bos, *Inferential Operations in the Reading Comprehension of Educable Mentally Retarded and Average Students.* Doctoral dissertation, University of Arizona, Tucson, 1979, p. 164.

soning according to how readers have to activate their background knowledge to construct the meaning. These three arbitrary categories are:

— *Textually explicit:* Information is derived directly from the text with minimal input from the readers' background knowledge.
— *Textually implicit:* Information is derived from the text but readers are required to use their background knowledge to put together the ideas presented in the text.
— *Scriptually implicit:* Information is not stated in the text. Readers have to activate and use their background knowledge to obtain the information.

We can also categorize comprehension by the type of information or relationship it represents. For example, the first question, "What did Pat do first to get help?" requires the reader to focus on the sequence of the events in the story. Therefore, it requires a sequencing or temporal relationship. The question "Why was everyone proud of Pat?" requires a causal relationship. Barrett (1976) has identified a number of types of information or relationships that

can be represented in text (e.g., details, main ideas, sequence, cause and effect) as part of his taxonomy of reading. We can combine types of information with processes required (i.e., textually explicit, textually implicit, and scriptually implicit) to form a matrix for reading comprehension (Figure 5.2).

This matrix can be used in planning comprehension instruction, such as planning activities that will encourage students to engage in all the different facets of comprehension (cells in the matrix). For example, to work on sequencing of ideas, students could retell a story by having each student in the group tell one episode from the story; copy a story onto sentence strips and discuss how to arrange the sentences in a logical order; read an explanation of how to do something and write a list of the steps in order; ask each other sequence questions about a description of how to make something; and write a description of how to make something and then have the other students in the group read the description and make the object. Whereas all of these activities focus on sequencing, both explicit and implicit comprehension are required to complete the various activities.

A matrix rather than a taxonomy is used to depict the various aspects of comprehension because

■ **FIGURE 5.2**   *Matrix for Reading Comprehension*

Type of Reasoning Based on Background Knowledge

Type of Information or Relationship	*Textually Explicit*	*Textually Implicit*	*Scriptally Implicit*
Detail	X	X	X
Main idea/Summary	X	X	X
Sequence	X	X	X
Comparative relationship	X	X	X
Cause/Effect relationship	X	X	X
Conditional relationship	X	X	X
Vocabulary definition	X	X	X
Vocabulary application	X	X	X
Figurative language definition	X	X	X
Figurative language application	X	X	X
Conclusion	X	X	X
Application		X	X
Analysis		X	X
Synthesis		X	X
Evaluation			X

comprehension should not necessarily be thought of as a set of hierarchical skills. The comprehension process entails ongoing transactions between the text, the reader, and the author (Goodman, 1996; Rosenblatt, 1978).

When reflecting on text, we read to reflect on the quality of the information or content presented and on the quality or the manner in which the piece is written (literary style). Barrett (1976) has referred to the first area of reading comprehension as *evaluation* and the second area as *appreciation*. Others have referred to the evaluation of the information as *critical reading* and to the appreciation and evaluation of literary style as *aesthetic reading* (Rosenblatt, 1978).

Both critical reading and aesthetic reading require readers to reflect and make comments and judgments about what they have read and believe. For example, after Mrs. Gomez's intermediate-level special education class finished reading about Pat and her father (Apply the Concept 5.2), Mrs. Gomez encouraged the students to comment on the quality of the piece by starting the discussion. She commented, "I liked the story, but I thought the author could have told us more information about how Pat got help." Figure 5.3 lists sample areas of critical and aesthetic reading and sample comments teachers might use to encourage critical and aesthetic reading.

Guidelines for Promoting Comprehension

In the past, instruction in reading comprehension has consisted of the teacher asking students questions and monitoring their responses. Teachers generally provided minimal substantive information concerning what reading comprehension is, why it would be useful, or how to do it (Anderson, Brubaker, Alleman-Brooks, and Duffy, 1986; Durkin, 1978–79).

■ **FIGURE 5.3**   *Critical and Aesthetic Reading*

Critical Reading

Critical reading: the reader reflects upon and makes judgments about the content or information in the piece.

Sample Areas of Reflection or Judgment	*Sample Comments*
Reality or Fantasy	I don't think the author expected us to think this could really happen.
Fact or Opinion	You really get the idea they are pushing their point of view.
Adequacy and Validity	Some of this information just isn't right.
Worth	This piece really helped me write my report. I think this article could hurt his political campaign.

Aesthetic Reading

Aesthetic reading: the reader reflects upon and makes judgments about the literary style of a piece.

Sample Areas of Reflection or Judgment	*Sample Comments*
Plot	I like the way the author always kept me interested in what was happening.
Characters	I didn't know enough about the witch to really understand why she did it.
Imagery	I could just picture myself being there.
Language	When the author said, "That was one frightened man," it sounded great.

Furthermore, teachers provided a steady diet of literal comprehension questions, a ratio of 4:1 literal to inferential, with lower reading groups getting asked even more literal questions than higher-level groups (Guszak, 1972).

As teachers of students with learning and behavior problems, we have to provide instructional strategies that will demonstrate to students how to interact with the text in such a way as to construct meaning. Asking questions after reading will not necessarily provide this instruction. Therefore, our instruction in reading comprehension should incorporate many of the aspects of cognitive behavior modification and the sociocultural theory of learning (see Chapter Two), including the modeling and "think aloud" procedures. Using scaffolded instruction, the teacher's instruction is guided as much out of the analysis of the learner's understanding as it is from the analysis of the text (Dole, Brown, and Trathen, 1996; Pearson and Fielding, 1991; Pressley et al., 1995). Based on notions from information processing and schema theories, our instruction should also assist students in activating their prior knowledge about the topic before they read so that they can apply this knowledge during reading and after they read. Our instruction should also demonstrate to students the importance of predicting and questioning as they read. In this way, comprehension is the association of new information with prior knowledge or experience (Perez and Torres-Guzman, 1992).

Comprehension instruction should encourage students to engage actively in the comprehension process through discussions. This can be prompted by the following guidelines:

1. *Before reading,* activate the students' background knowledge for the selected passage and/or provide experiences to enrich their backgrounds. Assist students in thinking about how this text may be related to other texts in terms of content, storyline, and text structure. Help them set purposes for reading by predicting and asking questions about what they are going to read.

2. *During reading,* encourage students to self-question and monitor their comprehension as they read.

3. *After reading,* use follow-up activities such as:
   a. Discussions that focus on the content of the reading as well as evaluation of the content and the writing style
   b. Discussions that encourage students to generate more questions and ideas for further reading and investigation
   c. Retellings that assist students in summarizing and organizing what they have read

Whether reading narrative or expository texts, five learning goals to strive for when teaching reading comprehension are: (a) determining importance and activating background knowledge, (b) summarizing information, (c) drawing inferences, (d) generating questions, and (e) monitoring comprehension (Dole, Duffy, Roehler, and Pearson, 1991). The next three sections highlight specific strategies associated with various goals.

Activating Prior Knowledge

What strategies can the teacher use that will help to activate relevant background knowledge (schema), prior to reading? Five such activities are discussed: brainstorming, the PreReading Plan (Langer, 1981), Text Preview (Graves, Cooke, and LaBerge, 1983) K-W-L (Ogle, 1986), and a schema activation strategy (Hansen, 1981).

Activating prior knowledge is particularly important for students with learning and behavior problems. It is also important for second language learners or students from culturally diverse backgrounds, for they bring unique real-world knowledge to learning

situations (Bos and Reyes, 1996; Jiménez, García, and Pearson, 1996). As with all learners, their prior knowledge is crucial to the successful construction of meaning. Apply the Concept 5.3 presents ideas for facilitating and teaching comprehension with these students. While the strategies in this section may be used as specific activities, they should also be integrated into reading lessons, such as the ones described in the final section of this chapter, and integrated into discussions about the literature and literacy.

Brainstorming

Brainstorming is a teaching strategy that activates the students' relevant prior knowledge, aids the teacher in determining the extent of the students' prior knowledge, and stimulates interest in the topic.

— **PROCEDURES:** Brainstorming works best with groups of students reading the same or related selections. Prior to beginning the activity, determine the major topic or concept presented in the selection(s). Next, decide what to use as a stimulus to represent that topic. It might be a single word or phrase, a picture, a poem, or a short excerpt from the reading passage. Prior to reading, conduct the brainstorming session.

1. Present the stimulus to the students.
2. Ask the students to list as many words or phrases as they can associate with the stimulus. Encourage them to think about everything they know about the topic or concept. Allow several minutes for the students to think and get ready to report their ideas. (If appropriate, have students write their ideas.)
3. Record their associations on the board. Ask for other associations and add them to the list. Do not make any judgments concerning the appropriateness of any of the associations.
4. With the students, categorize the associations. Clarify the ideas and discuss what titles to use for the categories.

You may also want to organize the ideas into a map. Strategies for organizing story maps are discussed later in this chapter, and strategies for developing content maps are discussed in Chapter Seven.

APPLY THE CONCEPT 5.3

*STRATEGIES FOR PROMOTING READING COMPREHENSION
FOR STUDENTS WHO ARE CULTURALLY DIVERSE
AND/OR SECOND LANGUAGE LEARNERS*

For students from culturally and linguistically diverse backgrounds and for second language learners, a number of strategies can be used to promote reading comprehension.

Making Input More Comprehensible

* Begin teaching new concepts by working from the students' prior knowledge and incorporating the funds of knowledge from the students' communities.
* Use demonstrations and gesture to augment oral and written communication.
* Discuss connections between the concepts being read and the students' home cultures.
* Encourage students to share the new vocabulary in the first language and incorporate the first language into instruction.
* If students share a common first language, pair more proficient second language learners with less proficient peers, and encourage students to discuss what they are reading.
* Provide opportunities for students to learn to read and to read in their first language.

* Highlight key words and phrases in text and incorporate them into semantic maps.
* Teach text structures and use visual representations of text structures.
* When asking questions or discussing new ideas or vocabulary, slow the pace.
* Repeat key ideas and write them.
* Use "think-alouds" to make comprehension strategies more explicit.

Incorporating Multicultural Literature into the Reading Program

* Select literature that reflects various cultures.
* Study authors from various cultures.
* Read literature that incorporates various dialects.
* Select genres that are typical of different cultures.
* Utilize book lists, directories, and textbooks on multicultural education as resources for multicultural literature.
* In the classroom and school libraries, have literature written in the students' first languages available to the students.

Although the brainstorming activity usually ends before reading begins, we recommend that you encourage students to continue to add to their list of associations as they read and after they read. Review the list and add any new associations.

— **COMMENTS:** Brainstorming is a quick and simple way of activating background knowledge. It usually takes five to ten minutes to complete. However, for some student and topic combinations, simple associations without further discussion may not provide enough input to activate and build the students' prior knowledge. The next procedure provides additional activities for further activating relevant schema.

PreReading Plan

The PreReading Plan (PReP) is a three-phase instructional/assessment strategy that builds on the instructional activity of brainstorming. Designed by Langer (1981), it assists students in accessing knowledge related to the major concepts presented in a reading selection.

— **PROCEDURES:** Prior to beginning the activity, provide a phrase or picture to stimulate group discussion about a key concept in the text. For example, if a science selection was about the types and characteristics of mammals, *mammals* might serve as the stimulus word. After introducing the topic, conduct the following three-phase process:

1. *Initial association with the concept.* Cue the students by saying, "Say anything that comes to mind when . . . (e.g., you hear the word *mammals*)." Have the students free associate, writing a list of their associations. Record the associations on the board, noting the student's name by each association.

2. *Reflections on initial associations.* Now ask the students, "What made you think . . . (the responses given by each of the students during Phase 1)?" This phase requires the students to bring to the conscious level their prior knowledge and how it relates to the key concept. It also allows the students to listen to each other's responses. Langer states, "Through this procedure they [students] gain the insight which permits them to evaluate the utility of these ideas in the reading experience" (1981, p. 154).

3. *Reformation of knowledge.* After each student has had an opportunity to think and tell about what triggered his or her ideas, ask the students, "Based on our discussion, have you any new ideas about . . . (e.g., mammals)?" This phase gives the students the opportunity to discuss how they have elaborated or changed their ideas based on the previous discussion. Because the students have the opportunity to listen to other students, new links between prior knowledge and the key concept are also formed.

Based on the information gathered during this three-phase procedure, Langer presents a means of assessing prior knowledge into levels to determine if further concept building will need to be completed prior to reading (see Figure 5.4). In a study with Nicholich (Langer and Nicholich, 1981), Langer found this assessment method a better predictor of reading comprehension for a particular passage than

■ **FIGURE 5.4**   *PreReading Plan: Levels of Prior Knowledge*

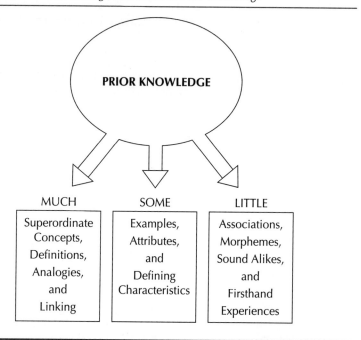

Source: J. A. Langer, "Facilitating Text Processing: The Elaboration of Prior Knowledge," in J. A. Langer and M. T. Smith-Burke, (Eds.). *Reader Meets Author/Bridging the Gap* (Newark, Del.: International Reading Association, 1982), p. 156. Reprinted by permission of Judith A. Langer and the International Reading Association.

either IQ or standardized reading scores. The three levels and their instructional implications are:

1. *Much knowledge.* Students whose free associations reflect superordinate concepts, definitions, analogies, or a linking of the key concept to other relevant concepts demonstrate *much* integration of the key concept with concepts already in accessible memory. Comprehension for these students should be adequate.

2. *Some knowledge.* Students whose free associations are primarily examples, attributes, or defining characteristics have *some* knowledge concerning the concepts being taught. Comprehension should be adequate, but some instructional activities that assist the students in making the critical links between existing and new knowledge may be necessary.

3. *Little knowledge.* Students whose free associations reflect morphemes (prefixes, suffixes, root words), rhyming words, or unelaborated or unrelated firsthand experiences demonstrate *little* knowledge of the concept. These students need concept instruction before reading commences, with the reported firsthand experiences serving as a reference point for starting instruction.

— COMMENTS: The PreReading Plan provides a direct means of activating the students' background knowledge. The authors have frequently used both brainstorming and PReP, particularly with upper elementary and secondary students with learning and behavior problems. We find that taking the extra time to conduct the PreReading Plan is worthwhile since it requires the students to bring to the conscious level why they made their associations, and it gives them the opportunity to reflect on what they have learned through the discussion. Have students add to and adjust their lists during reading and after they read.

Text Preview

Text Preview is designed to increase students' prior knowledge, provide motivation for students to read, and provide a scaffold for text comprehension (Graves, Cooke, and LaBerge, 1983). Text Preview

can be used with students from middle school to high school at varying levels of ability and with narrative or expository texts.

— PROCEDURES: The two major steps in using Text Preview are preparing the preview and then using it with the students.

1. *Preparation and construction of Text Previews.* A Text Preview is a detailed script or synopsis of a passage that is written in an organized framework that enhances student comprehension of the text by bridging it to their real-world experiences. It has three sections: (a) one that piques student interest, (b) a brief discussion of the text's theme (e.g., for stories this could include the setting, character descriptions, and essential story organization, and (c) questions or directions that guide student reading.

2. *Presentation of Text Previews.* The following steps are suggested for implementing the Text Preview and should take no longer than five to ten minutes (Graves et al., 1985).
- Tell students that a new story will be introduced to them.
- Have students listen as you read the interest-building portion of the preview.
- Present the theme and through discussion relate the theme to students' background knowledge.
- Present the questions or directions that guide student reading.
- Have students read the text.

— COMMENTS: Text Previews take a considerable amount of time to prepare. Students report, however, that previews enable them to understand text to a fuller extent. Text Previews can be especially beneficial for teachers working with students who have learning or behavior problems, and with second language learners. When using Text Previews with expository text, the teacher may want to include important points, vocabulary, and more implicit and experience-based thinking (Readence, Bean, and Baldwin, 1995). Additionally, teachers can use Text Previews as potential writing assignments. Students can be assigned to develop Text Previews for other students' guided reading. Critical thinking about the ideas presented in a text selection will ensue as students create Text Previews for one another.

K-W-L

K-W-L is a strategy designed to activate students' background knowledge and to assist students in setting purposes for reading expository text (Ogle, 1986, 1989). This strategy is based on research that highlights the importance of background knowledge in constructing meaning (e.g., Anderson, 1977; Anderson, Reynolds, Schallert, and Goetz, 1977).

— PROCEDURES: The K-W-L strategy consists of three basic steps representative of the cognitive/metacognitive steps employed by the students as they utilize the strategy:

> accessing what I Know
> determining what I Want to Learn
> recalling what I did Learn

To assist the students in using the strategy, Ogle developed a simple worksheet for the students to complete during the thinking-reading process (see Figure 5.5).

During the *Know* step the teacher and students engage in a discussion designed to assist students in thinking about what they already know about the topic of the text. For this step the teacher starts by using a *brainstorm* procedure (see section on Brainstorming). As in the PreReading Plan, students are encouraged to discuss where or how they learned the information so as to provide information concerning the source and substantiveness of their ideas. After brainstorming, the teachers and students discuss the general *categories of information* likely to be encountered when they read, and how their brainstormed ideas could help them determine the categories. "For example, the teacher might say 'I see three different pieces of information about how turtles look. Description of looks is certainly one category of information I would expect this article to include'" (Ogle, 1986, p. 566).

During the *Want to Learn* step, the teacher and students discuss what they want to learn from read-

ing the article. While most of the W step utilizes group discussion, before students begin to read, they each write down the specific questions in which they are most interested.

During the *What I Learned* step, the students write what they learned from reading. They should also check the questions that they generated in the *Want to Learn* step to see if they were addressed in the article.

— COMMENTS: K-W-L represents a strategy for assisting students in actively engaging in the reading process and for assisting teachers in teaching reading using an interactive model of reading. Informal evaluation of the strategy indicates that students recalled more information in articles when they used K-W-L and that they enjoyed using the strategy and used it independently (Ogle, 1986). Carr and Ogle (1987) added mapping and summarizing activities to K-W-L to gain the advantage of these powerful comprehension tools. Ogle (1989) added a fourth column "what we still want to learn" and referred to this adaptation as KWL Plus. This addition encourages further research and reading.

Story Schema Activation Strategy

Hansen (1981) developed a technique designed to get students to think about and apply what they already know (schemas) to stories. The technique encourages students to discuss, prior to reading, something they have done that is similar to the event in the story and to hypothesize what will happen in the story. In this way they are encouraged to activate and integrate schema-based inferences.

— PROCEDURES: Although Hansen (1981) used instructional-level basal readers, high-interest/low-vocabulary stories or literature books could be used. Prior to working with the students, preview the story and select three important events or ideas and/or three events or ideas the students might have difficulty understanding. For each idea, think of questions that require the students to think about something that happened to them that is similar to what happened in the story, and questions to help them predict what they think will happen in the story.

■ **FIGURE 5.5** *K-W-L Strategy Sheet*

K-W-L Strategy Sheet

1. K—What we know	W—What we want to find out	L—What we learned and still need to learn

2. Categories of information we expect to use
   A.   E.
   B.   F.
   C.   G.
   D.

Source: D. M. Ogle, "K-W-L: A teaching model that develops active reading of expository text," *The Reading Teacher, 39* (1986) p. 565. Reprinted with permission of the International Reading Association.

The technique consists of two structured discussion periods, one prior to reading and one after reading.

1. *Prereading discussion.* The purpose of this discussion is to get the students to activate prior knowledge and make predictions about the passage based on their prior experiences. This period begins with a discussion about the importance of comparing their own lives to situations in a text. For example:

Teacher: What is it that we have been doing before we read each story?

Focus of responses: We talk about our lives and how we might have experiences similar to the story.

Teacher: Why do we make these comparisons?

Focus of responses: These comparisons will help us understand the stories.

Teacher: Last week I asked you to think what it would be like to live in another country. Today, pretend that you are going on a trip with your Dad and he gets hurt. Have you ever been around someone else when he or she got hurt?

Gist of responses: Students relate personal experiences and explain how the experiences relate to the text.

Next introduce the three main ideas from the story. First, ask the students to relate a previous experience to the main idea. Second, have the students predict something similar that might happen in the story. For example:

Important idea:	Pat has to stay calm and get help.
Previous experience:	Tell us about a time when you had to get help.
Hypothesis question:	In our next story, Pat and her dad are going on a trip. Pat's dad gets hurt and she has to get help. How do you think Pat will get help?

The students discuss and write the answers. This prereading discussion period takes from fifteen to twenty minutes, after which the students read the story.

2. *Postreading discussions.* After reading, discuss the story and ask scripturally implicit questions. Ask the students to support their answers by either referring to the text or their prior knowledge. Discuss the questions and answers that were made prior to reading.

— **COMMENTS:** Hansen originally used this strategy with second graders. Later, Hansen and her colleagues (Hansen and Hubbard, 1984; Hansen and Pearson, 1983) used the strategy with other readers, including good and poor readers. They found the poor readers benefited substantially from the instruction, whereas the good readers did not benefit as much since they already seemed to activate appropriate schema. The poor readers not only correctly answered more scripturally implicit (inference) questions, but also more explicit questions.

Questioning Strategies

Asking questions is a major vehicle used by teachers to foster understanding and retention and check for comprehension. When questions are asked about information in text, that information is remembered better. Asking higher-level questions (see Figure 5.2) that require integration of background and text knowledge will promote deeper processing and therefore more learning (Sundbye, 1987), and simply asking "Why?" can significantly increase retention of information (Menke and Pressley, 1994).

However, simply asking questions does not ensure that students will develop questioning strategies. As already demonstrated, teacher and student questioning prior to reading helps to activate prior knowledge and to set purposes for reading. Self-questioning during reading (e.g., "Does this make sense?" "Am I understanding what I am reading?" "How does this relate to what I already know?" "What will happen next?") assist students in comprehension and monitoring comprehension (one of the metacognitive activities discussed in Chapter Two).

This section presents four techniques for teaching questioning strategies. These techniques require teachers to model comprehension questions and comprehension monitoring questions, teach students to recognize types of questions, and encourage students to self-question before, during, and after they read.

ReQuest or Reciprocal Questioning
The ReQuest procedure is a reciprocal questioning technique designed to assist students in formulating their own questions about what they read. The procedure was developed by Manzo (1969; Manzo and Manzo, 1993), who stressed the importance of students setting their own purposes for reading and asking their own questions as they read.

— **PROCEDURES:** This procedure relies heavily on modeling, which is a major premise of cognitive behavior modification and sociocultural theory of learning (Chapter Two). To use this procedure, select materials at the students' instructional to independent reading levels. You and the students read a sentence or section of the passage and then take turns asking each other questions. Your role is to model "good" questioning and to provide feedback to students about their questions. In modeling, include questions that require you to use scripturally and textually implicit information and that require critical and aesthetic reading. Also include monitoring questions (e.g. "Does this make sense?").

Manzo suggests that this procedure first be introduced on an individual basis and then used in small groups. The following explanation can be used to introduce ReQuest:

The purpose of this lesson is to improve your understanding of what you read. We will each read silently the first sentence [section]. Then we will take turns asking questions about the sentence [section] and what it means. You will ask questions first, then I will ask questions. Try to ask the kinds of questions a teacher might ask in the way a teacher might ask them.

You may ask me as many questions as you wish. When you are asking me questions, I will close my book (or pass the book to you if there is only one between us). When I ask questions, you close your book (Manzo, 1969, p. 124).

The rules are: (1) the answer "I don't know" is not allowed; (2) unclear questions are to be restated; and (3) uncertain answers are to be justified by reference to the text or other source material if necessary. In addition, you and the students may need to discuss unfamiliar vocabulary.

The procedure itself consists of the following steps:

1. *Silent reading.* You and the students read the sentence or section.

2. *Student questioning.* Close your book while the students ask questions. Model appropriate answers and reinforce appropriate questioning behavior. The students ask as many questions as possible.

3. *Teacher questioning.* The students close their books and you ask questions. The Matrix for Reading Comprehension (Figure 5.2) can be used as a guide. Don't forget to ask some critical and aesthetic questions—including questions that focus on text conventions such as plot, characters, themes, arguments, etc.

4. *Integration of the text.* After completing the procedure with the first sentence or section, repeat the process with subsequent sentences or sections. Integrate the new section with previous sections by asking questions that relate to new and old sections.

5. *Predictive questioning.* When the students have read enough to make a prediction about the rest of the passage, terminate reciprocal questioning and ask predictive questions (e.g., "What do you think

will happen?" "Why do you think so?"). If the predictions and verification are reasonable, you and the students move to the next step.

6. *Reading.* You and the students read to the end of the passage to verify your predictions. Discuss your predictions.

━ **COMMENTS:** One important aspect of this strategy is the questions that the teacher models. Manzo and Manzo (1990, 1993) suggest that teachers employ a variety of questions including:

- *Predictable questions*—the typical *who, what, when, where, why,* and *how questions*
- *Mind-opening questions*—designed to help the students understand how written and oral language are used to communicate ideas
- *Introspective questions*—metacognitive questions oriented toward self-monitoring and self-evaluation
- *Ponderable questions*—questions that stimulate discussion and for which no right or wrong answer is apparent
- *Elaborative knowledge questions*—questions that require the students to integrate their background knowledge with the information given in the text.

The ReQuest procedure assists students in developing appropriate questions. We have used several variations of these procedures. For instance, we have introduced the ReQuest procedure as a game. The students and teacher take turns asking questions and keeping score of appropriate answers. We also recommend that the text be read in longer, more natural segments rather than individual sentences. Legenza (1974) has adapted this procedure by having kindergarten children ask questions about a picture rather than a text.

One major concern regarding ReQuest is how to get this questioning attitude to generalize to other reading situations. Students may need to be cued to remember to stop while reading and ask themselves questions like the type asked during the ReQuest procedure. Or students may need to be taught a self-questioning strategy.

Question-Answer Relationships Strategy

The question-answer relationships (QARs) strategy (Raphael, 1982, 1984, 1986) is designed to assist students in labeling the type of questions being asked and to use this information to help guide them as they develop an answer. QARs was developed by Raphael and Pearson (1982) to facilitate correct responses to questions. The strategy is based on question/answer relationships developed by Pearson and Johnson (1978) (e.g., *textually explicit, textually implicit,* and *scriptually implicit*), discussed earlier in this chapter. It helps students realize they need to consider both the text and their prior knowledge when answering questions and to use strategic behavior to adjust the use of each of these sources.

■ **PROCEDURES:** QARs was originally taught by Raphael (1984), using the three categories of information suggested in the Matrix for Reading Comprehension (Figure 5.2). The three categories were renamed for use with students.

1. *Right There.* Words used to create the question and words used for the answer are in the same sentence (textually explicit).
2. *Think and Search.* The answer is in the text, but words used to create the question and those used for an appropriate answer would not be in the same sentence (textually implicit).
3. *On My Own.* The answer is not found in the text but in one's head (scriptually implicit).

Based on input from teachers, Raphael (1986) modified these categories to include two major categories (*In the Book* and *In My Head*) and then further divided these categories, as shown in Figure 5.6.

Teaching QARs consists of first having students learn to differentiate between the two major categories and then between the subcategories. The students also learn how to apply knowledge of the question-answer relationships as a strategy for improving reading comprehension. A cue card, which labels and explains the four types of question-answer relationships, is used during instruction (Figure 5.7).

Raphael suggests the following procedure for introducing QARs. The first day, introduce the students to the concept of question-answer relationships (QARs), using the two major categories. Use several short passages (from two to five sentences) to demonstrate the relationships. Provide practice by asking students to identify the type of QAR, the answer to the question, and the strategy they used for finding the answer. The progression for teaching should be from highly supportive to independent:

1. Provide the text, questions, answers, QAR label for each question, and reason for why the label was appropriate.
2. Provide the text, questions, answers, and QAR label for each question. Have the students supply the reason for the label.

■ **FIGURE 5.6**   *Relationship Among the Four Types of Question-Answer Relationships*

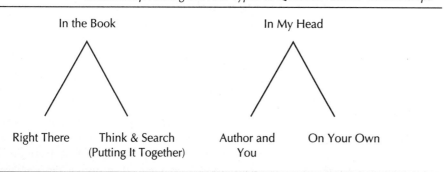

Source: Adapted from T. E. Raphael, "Teaching Question-Answer Relationships, Revisited," *The Reading Teacher, 39*(6) (1986) p. 517.

■ **FIGURE 5.7** *Illustrations Explaining Question-Answer Relationships (QARs) to Students*

In the Book QARs	**In My Head QARs**
Right There	**Author and You**
The answer is in the text, usually easy to find. The words used to make up the question and words used to answer the question are **Right There** in the same sentence.	The answer in *not* in the story. You need to think about what you already know, what the author tells you in the text, and how it fits together.

Think and Search (Putting It Together)	**On My Own**
The answer is in the story, but you need to put together different story parts to find it. Words for the question and words for the answer are not found in the same sentence. They come from different parts of the text.	The answer is not in the story. You can even answer the question without reading the story. You need to use your own experience.

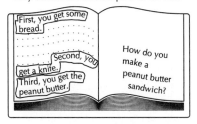

Source: T. E. Raphael, "Teaching Question-Answer Relationships, Revisited," *The Reading Teacher,* 39(6) (1986) p. 519. Reprinted with permission of the International Reading Association.

3. Provide the text, questions, and answers, and have the students supply the QAR labels and reasons for the labels.

4. Provide the text and questions, and have the students supply the answers, QAR labels, and reasons for the labels.

When the students have a clear picture of the difference between *In My Head* and *In the Book,* teach the next level of differentiation for each one of the major categories. First, work on *In the Book,* then go to *In My Head.* The key distinction between the two subcategories under *In My Head* (i.e., *Author*

and You and *On My Own*) is "whether or not the reader needs to read the text for the questions to make sense" (Raphael, 1986, p. 519). When the information must come from the reader, but in connection with the information presented by the author, then the QAR is *Author and You.* For example, in the story about Pat and her father (Apply the Concept 5.2), the question "How did the fisherman alert the police?" requires the reader to use his or her background knowledge but relate it to the information in the text. In comparison, the question "What would you have done if you were in Pat's shoes?" is an example of an *On My Own* QAR.

Once the students are effectively using the QAR strategy in short passages, gradually increase the length of the passages and the variety of reading materials. Review the strategy and model its use on the first question. Have the students then use the strategy to complete the rest of the questions.

— COMMENTS: After teaching this strategy using the original three categories, Raphael (1984) found that groups of low-, average-, and high-achieving, fourth-grade students had higher performance on a comprehension test and gave evidence that the question-answer relationships strategy transferred to reading improvement in the content areas. Whereas this strategy helped lower-achieving students to answer all three types of questions, for high-achieving students it facilitated only the answering of scripturally implicit questions. For the low-achieving students, strategy training particularly improved their performance on textually explicit and implicit questions. Simmonds (1992) taught 24 special education teachers to implement either QARS or selected traditional methods of reading comprehension instruction including the skills of answering literal questions (recall of factual information and main ideas), locating supportive details, and drawing conclusions. Using a lesson sequence similar to the one just described, they found students who participated in the QARS instruction performed better than the other students on tests of comprehension over the social studies text they read. Labeling the types of questions and then using that information to assist in answering questions appears to be an effective strategy for students and one that encourages active involvement in the comprehension process.

Self-Questioning Strategies

Self-questioning strategies are a good example of how metacognition assists students in reading. These questions typically have the student focus on activating prior knowledge and setting purposes for reading, asking questions to assist the comprehension process, checking understanding during reading, and reviewing after reading to determine understanding. For example, Alvermann and her colleagues (Alvermann et al., 1989) suggest the following self-questions to foster comprehension:

Think Ahead
• What is this section about?
• What do I already know about the topic?
• What do I want to find out?
• What is my goal?
• How should I go about reading to meet my goal?

Think While Reading
• What have I read about so far?
• Do I understand it?
• If not, what should I do?
• What is the author saying, and what did I think about it?

Think Back
• Have I learned what I wanted to learn?
• How can I use what I read?

One strategy, developed by Wong and Jones (1982), focuses primarily on asking questions related to the main idea. When investigating the reading comprehension skills of upper elementary students with learning disabilities, Wong (1979) found that in text without inserted questions, the students had poorer recall of the thematically important ideas than average readers. She hypothesized that the students do not self-question when they read. To demonstrate this point, she inserted questions in the text for a second group of students with learning disabilities and average students, and she no longer found significant differences between the recall of the two types of readers. Whereas the inserted questions resulted in significantly better recall for the students with learning disabilities, no such effect was evident with average readers, indicating that the students with learning disabilities were not as effective at self-questioning.

Based on this research, Wong and Jones (1982) developed a self-questioning technique to determine if junior-high students with learning disabilities could be taught to self-question as they read.

— PROCEDURES: First, teach the students the concept of a main idea. During this stage, teach the students how to identify the main idea(s) in paragraphs. For Wong and her colleagues, this took up to three one-hour sessions.

During the next stage, teach the students the steps in self-questioning strategy:

1. *What are you studying this passage for?* (So you can answer some questions you will be given later.)
2. *Find the main idea(s) in the paragraph and underline it (them).*
3. *Think of a question about the main idea you have underlined. Remember what a good question should be like.* ("Good questions" are those that directly focus on important textual elements. Write the question in the margin.)
4. *Learn the answer to your question.* (Write the answer in the margin.)
5. *Always look back at the previous questions and answers to see how each successive question and answer provide you with more information.*

In teaching, model the strategy and then have the students study the steps in the strategy. Next, have the students practice using this strategy on individual paragraphs and provide them with immediate corrective feedback. Have the students use a cue card to assist them in remembering the steps in the strategy. When the students are successful, switch to multiple paragraph passages and gradually fade the use of the cue card. Give feedback at the end of each passage. At the end of each lesson, discuss the students' progress and the usefulness of the self-questioning strategy.

▬ **COMMENTS:** Results from the Wong and Jones (1982) study indicate the students with learning disabilities who learned the self-questioning strategy performed significantly higher on comprehension tests than students who were not taught the strategy.

Another self-questioning strategy was developed at the Kansas University Center for Research on Learning (Clark et al., 1984; Nolan, Alley, and Clark, 1980). It was used to assist secondary-level students with learning disabilities in comprehending and remembering the important information presented in content area textbooks. Students read the title of a section and then ask questions regarding *who, what, when, where, why,* and/or *how.* They then read the section to answer their question(s).

We have used the WH Questions Plus HOW to facilitate the comprehension of elementary students with learning and behavior problems. When reading expository text, students mark in the text using symbols where they find the answers to the WH questions plus HOW and then record their answers on the textframe in Figure 5.8. (If students cannot mark in the text, post-its with the different symbols can be placed in the text.) We have also used the WH Questions Plus HOW to assist students in journal writing. We have found that using this strategy helps students understand what they read and to write journal entries that are more elaborated and comprehensible.

These self-questioning strategies proved effective in increasing the students' reading comprehension. This may be related to the development of comprehension monitoring, which these techniques encourage.

Paraphrasing, Summarization, and Retelling Strategies

Giving the gist, main idea(s), or summary of a paragraph, a narrative, or an expository text is a skill that many students with learning and behavior problems have difficulty developing (Brown and Palincsar, 1982; Graves, 1986; McCormick, 1992; Wong, 1979). Several strategies have been developed and tested with students who have reading disabilities (Gajria and Salvia, 1992; Schumaker, Denton, and Deshler, 1984; Wong, Wong, Perry, and Sawatsky, 1986).

Paraphrasing Strategy
This learning strategy, developed and validated at the Kansas University Center for Research on Learning (Schumaker, Denton, and Deshler, 1984), instructs students in recalling the main ideas and specific facts of materials they read.

▬ **PROCEDURES:** To teach the strategy, you would use the Strategy Intervention Model presented in Chapter 2.

The steps in the strategy that the students learn are as follows:

1. *Read a paragraph.* Read the paragraph silently. As you read, be sure to think about what the words mean.

■ FIGURE 5.8   *Textframe for Answering WH and HOW Question*

Student Name: _____

Title: _____

Who? 	
What? 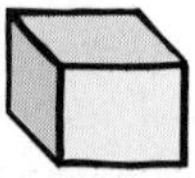	
Where? 	
When? 	
Why? 	
How? 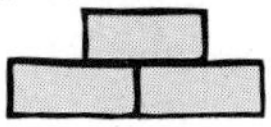	

---

2. <u>A</u>*sk yourself, "What were the main ideas and details of this paragraph?"* After reading the paragraph, ask yourself, "What were the main ideas and details?" This question helps you to think about what you just read. To help you, you may need to look quickly back over the paragraph and find the main idea and the details that are related to the main idea.

3. <u>P</u>*ut the main idea and details in your own words.* Now put the main idea and details into your own words. When you put the information into your own words, it helps you remember the information. Try to give at least two details related to the main idea.

The acronym for the steps in the strategy is RAP. (Paraphrasing is like rapping or talking to yourself.) Students are also given rules for finding the main idea. They are:

1. Look for it in the first sentence of the paragraph.
2. Look for repetitions of the same word or words in the whole paragraph (Schumaker, Denton, and Deshler, 1984, p. 59).

Figure 5.9 lists the criteria used when generating a paraphrase. Specifics for teaching the strategy, including a scripted lesson, cue cards for learning and generalizing the strategy, record and worksheets, and suggested materials for practicing the strategy, are presented in the instructors' guide, *The Paraphrasing Strategy* (Learning Strategies Curriculum) (Schumaker, Denton, and Deshler, 1984).

▬ **COMMENTS:** Students with learning disabilities who learned and used the paraphrasing strategy increased their ability to answer comprehension questions about materials written at their grade level from 48 percent to 84 percent (Schumaker, Denton, and Deshler, 1984). This strategy provides an example of how metacognitive skills can be taught to students. Although the research was conducted with high-school students, we have used the strategy with upper elementary students and found it successful.

■ **FIGURE 5.9** *Paraphrasing Strategy: Requirements for a Paraphrase*

Requirements for a Paraphrase

1. Must contain a complete thought
   - subject
   - verb
2. Must be totally accurate
3. Must have new information
4. Must make sense
5. Must contain useful information
6. Must be in your own words
7. Only one general statement per paragraph is allowed

Source: J. B. Schumaker, P. H. Denton, and D. D. Deshler, *The Paraphrasing Strategy* (Lawrence: University of Kansas, 1984), p. 60. Copyright 1984 by the University of Kansas. Reprinted by permission and with the recommendation that training be obtained from the Institute for Research in Learning Disabilities, University of Kansas, Lawrence, Kansas 66045.

When using this strategy, the students orally repeat the paraphrases into a tape recorder rather than writing them. This approach seems particularly advantageous for students with learning and behavior problems, since many of them also experience writing problems. However, once the students have mastered the skill, it may be helpful for students to write their paraphrases. These can then serve as an overview from which the students can integrate the information across the entire passage. You and the students may also want to vary the size of the unit that the students paraphrase. For example, in some books it may be more advantageous to paraphrase each section or subsection rather than each paragraph.

Summarization Strategy

Summarization also requires the student to generate the main idea and important details from a text. Based on analyses of informational or expository texts, Brown and Day (1983) generated five rules for writing summaries:

1. Delete irrelevant or trivial information.
2. Delete redundant information.
3. Select topic sentences.
4. Substitute a superordinate term or event for a list of terms or actions.
5. Invent topic sentences when none are provided by the author.

Gajria and Salvia (1992) used these same rules to teach sixth through ninth grade students with learning disabilities how to summarize expository passages. Gajria and Salvia (1992) employed many of the principles of cognitive behavior modification (see Chapter Two). The teaching principles include explicit explanation of the rules, modeling of the strategy, guided practice in controlled materials, monitoring with corrective feedback, independent practice, and teaching each rule to criterion.

▬ **PROCEDURES:** To teach the summarization strategy, use sets of short paragraphs, each set highlighting a different rule. In this way the rules can be explained, modeled, and practiced individually. Then apply the rules to informational passages. Gajria and

Salvia (1992) adapted passages from the *Timed Reading Series* (Spargo, Williston, and Browning, 1980). As the students learn the rules and their application, give them greater responsibility for practicing the rules and checking that each rule has been applied. Figure 5.10 presents a checklist students can use to judge the qualities of their summaries.

— **COMMENTS:** When Gajria and Salvia (1992) taught the summarization strategy to 15 students with learning disabilities they found that at the end of instruction (ranging from 6.5 to 11 hours), students in the trained group performed significantly better than an untrained control group of students with learning disabilities on main idea/inference questions and factual questions, better than a group of average-achieving students on main idea/inference questions, and similar to the average group on factual questions. Students who participated in the strategy instruction also generalized these skills as demonstrated by increased performance on a read-

ing test. Wong, Wong, Perry, and Sawatsky (1986) found that teaching main ideas and summarization skills with the use of a concept map (see Figure 5.11 and Chapter 7) was also effective for middle-grade students with learning problems. They used three rules adapted from Aulls (1978): (1) The main idea is the most general statement in the paragraph. It should explicitly explain the general topic. (2) Most of the other sentences should refer to it. (3) Most of the other sentences should elaborate or qualify this statement (p. 102). In using the concept map, Wong and colleagues added the procedure of covering the main idea box in the center of the map and asking the students if the other sentences made sense without the main idea. Wong et al., (1986) commented, "The use of this extra rule greatly helps students grasp that when you remove the main idea sentence, the semantic integrity of the paragraph collapses" (p. 24).

Story-Mapping and Story-Retelling Strategies

Whereas teaching students to paraphrase can assist them in determining the main idea and related details for the expository texts they read, strategies which incorporate the use of story grammar can be used when students read and recall narratives. Story-retelling strategies provide the students with a framework for retelling the key points of narrative texts. The strategies can be combined with story maps, which provide the students with a visual guide to understanding and retelling stories.

Both story-mapping and story-retelling strategies are based on the notions that narratives are composed of a fairly predictable set of components and that narratives have an overall text structure or grammar that is unique to them. In general, narrative texts can be organized into components such as the setting, the problem statement, the goals, event sequences or episodes, and the ending (Grasser, Golding, and Long, 1991; Mandler and Johnson, 1977; Stein and Glenn, 1979). The event sequences can be further broken down into initiating events, reactions, and outcomes. Using this grammar, visual displays of a story or story maps can be generated that show

■ **FIGURE 5.10** *Student Checklist for Summaries*

Student Name: _____
Date: _____
Title of Reading: _____

Read your summary and rate it for each element by checking the appropriate rating.

Yes	Somewhat	No	Elements of a Good Summary
___	___	___	Summary gives the main idea.
___	___	___	Main idea is stated first.
___	___	___	Summary states all the important ideas.
___	___	___	Summary states only the most important information.
___	___	___	Details are combined so that the summary is brief.
___	___	___	Summary is clear.

Source: Adapted from T. G. Gunning (1996). *Creating Reading Instruction for All Children,* 2nd ed. (Boston: Allyn and Bacon).

■ **FIGURE 5.11**   *Type of Concept Map Used to Teach Main Idea*

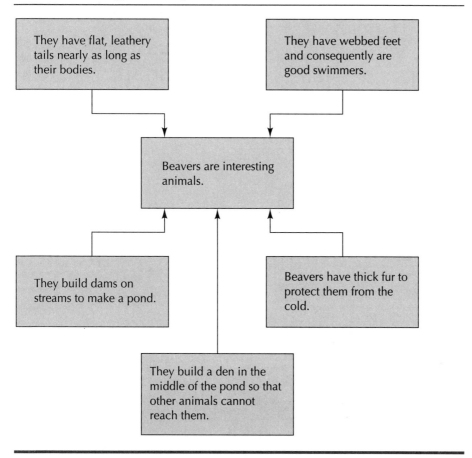

Source: Adapted from Wong, Wong, Perry, and Sawatsky (1986).

the story components and their relationship one to another. Figure 5.12 shows the visual framework for a simple story.

Educators have taught students how to use story maps and story strategies to aid in comprehending and retelling stories (Baumann and Bergeron, 1993; Bos, 1987; Emery, 1996; Idol, 1987a, 1987b; Williams, Brown, Silverstein, and deCani, 1994). For example, Idol (1987a, 1987b) used a model-lead-test paradigm (Carnine, Silbert, and Kameenui, 1997) to teach story mapping to five intermediate-grade students with learning disabilities. Bos (1987) used a story-retelling strategy to assist intermediate stu-

dents with learning and language disabilities in retelling stories.

— PROCEDURES: Idol (1987b) used the story map in Figure 5.12 to teach story mapping. She used the following procedure to teach story mapping:

1. During the *model* phase, model how to use the story map by reading the story aloud, stopping at points where information pertaining to one of the story components is presented. Ask the students to label the part and then demonstrate how to write the information onto the story map. Have the students

■ **FIGURE** 5.12 *Simple Story Map*

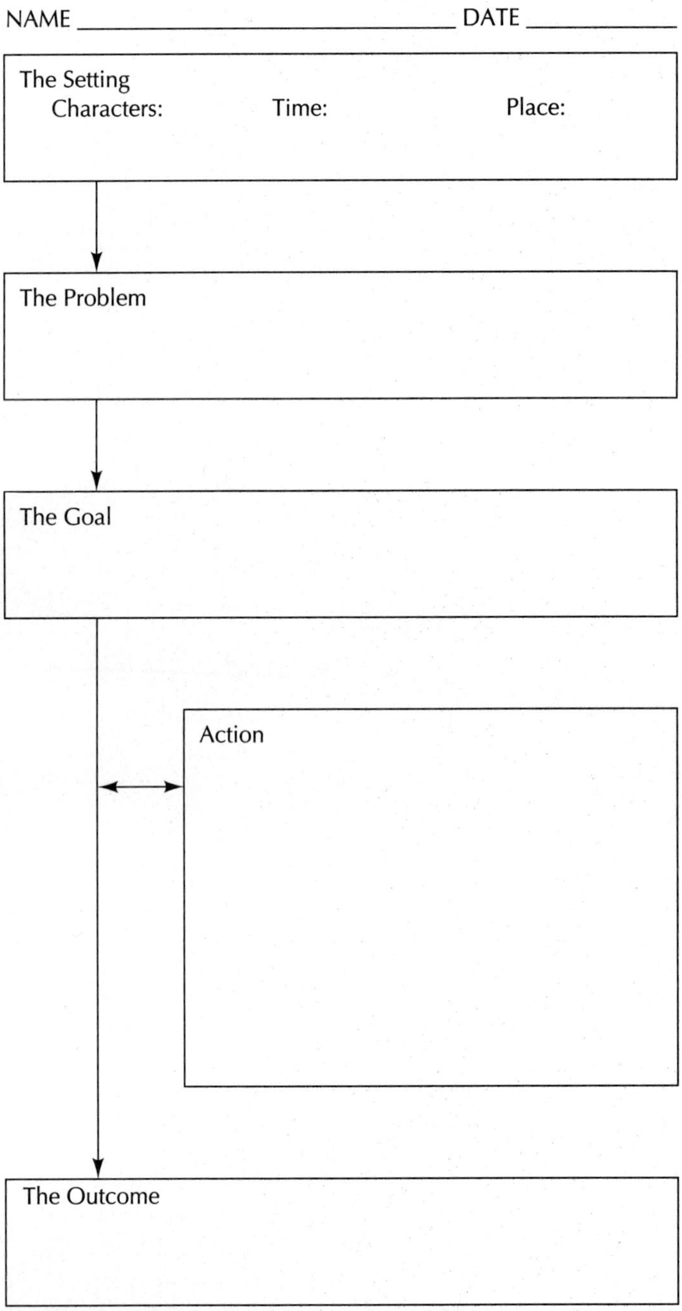

NAME _____ DATE _____

```
┌─────────────────────────────────────────────────┐
│ The Setting                                       │
│     Characters:        Time:           Place:     │
│                                                   │
└─────────────────────────────────────────────────┘
                    │
                    ▼
┌─────────────────────────────────────────────────┐
│ The Problem                                       │
│                                                   │
└─────────────────────────────────────────────────┘
                    │
                    ▼
┌─────────────────────────────────────────────────┐
│ The Goal                                          │
│                                                   │
└─────────────────────────────────────────────────┘
         │
         │        ┌────────────────────────────────┐
         │        │ Action                          │
         ◄───────►│                                 │
         │        │                                 │
         │        │                                 │
         │        └────────────────────────────────┘
         ▼
┌─────────────────────────────────────────────────┐
│ The Outcome                                       │
│                                                   │
└─────────────────────────────────────────────────┘
```

Source: From Group Story Mapping: A Comprehension Strategy for Both Skilled and Unskilled Readers. By L. Idol, 1987, *Journal of Learning Disabilities, 20,* p. 199. Copyright 1987 by PRO-ED, Inc. Reprinted by permission.

copy the information onto their own maps. If the information is implicit in the story, model how to generate the inference.

2. During the *lead* phase, have students read the story independently and complete their maps, prompting when necessary. Encourage the students to review their maps after completing the story, adding details that may have been omitted.

3. During the *test* phase, ask students to read a story, generate their map, and then answer questions such as: Who were the characters? Where did the story take place? What was the main character trying to accomplish?

One of the authors (Bos, 1987) used principles based on cognitive behavior modification to teach a story-retelling strategy. The procedures are:

1. Motivate the students to learn the strategy by demonstrating how it will help them remember what they have read.

2. Describe the components in a story and the steps used to identify and remember the different components (see Figure 5.13). Explain how this strategy will help the students "STORE" and remember the important parts of the story.

3. Model how to use the strategy by orally reading the story and labeling each component as you read.

■ **FIGURE 5.13** *Story-Retelling Strategy*

STORE the Story

Setting—Who, What, When, Where

Trouble—What is the trouble to be solved?

Order of Action—What happened to solve the trouble? (correct/logical order)

Resolution—What was the outcome (resolution) for each action?

End—What happened in the end?

Source: C. S. Bos, *Promoting Story Comprehension Using a Story Retelling Strategy.* Paper presented at the Teachers Applying Whole Language Conference, Tucson, Az., October 1987.

Then retell the story using "STORE the Story" as a cue for remembering the different parts.

4. Practice together reading stories, labeling the components, and retelling the stories. The students can retell their stories to the teacher, to each other, tape record their retellings, or answer questions about the stories.

5. Have the students independently read stories and retell them by using the "STORE the Story" strategy.

■ **COMMENTS:** Results from both studies indicate that students were able to recall substantially more relevant information after learning each strategy. They were also able to answer more explicit and implicit comprehension questions about the stories. Students were also more likely to label the parts of the story in their retellings, thereby providing the listener with a framework for listening. These same strategies have also been adapted and used to help students plan and write stories.

One aspect that is particularly challenging for students to comprehend is different characters' perspectives and internal reactions as the story progresses (Emery, 1996; Shannon, Kameenui, and Baumann, 1988). Emery (1996) suggests using story guides in which the story events are outlined in one column and different characters' perspectives are listed in subsequent columns. This assists the students in seeing how different characters react to different events in the story. Using "why" questions about the characters during discussions (e.g., "Why did the characters act that way?" "Why did the characters feel that way?") also promotes comprehension.

Comprehensive Approaches for Teaching Reading Comprehension

So far we have talked about techniques to facilitate the use of specific comprehension skills such as activating prior knowledge, assisting students in asking and answering questions, and helping students paraphrase, recall, and summarize what they have read. In this section we will look at approaches to teaching reading and reading comprehension. These approaches are broader in that they incorporate a variety of comprehension and, in some cases, word identification skills. The first approach, the Directed Reading Activity (Betts, 1946), has been the standard framework used for teaching reading in basal readers. The Directed Reading-Thinking Activity (Stauffer, 1969, 1970) is an adaptation of this approach which encourages active participation on the part of the reader. Reciprocal teaching (Palincsar and Brown, 1984), collaborative strategic reading (Klingner, Vaughn, and Schumm, 1996), and POSSE (Englert and Mariage, 1991) combines four reading comprehension strategies: *predicting, clarifying, summarizing,* and *questioning,* to present a framework for teaching reading comprehension that reflects the more recent research in schema theory and metacognition. The fourth orientation, whole language (Goodman, 1986; 1996) and literature-based approaches to reading (Cullinan, 1992; Holdaway, 1979), emphasize the use of literature as the major medium for teaching reading; they stress reading comprehension and meaning-emphasis strategies for teaching word identification.

Directed Reading Activity

The Directed Reading Activity (DRA), developed by Betts (1946), is the general framework or lesson plan used in many basal readers. The DRA is a systematic method for providing instruction in reading, including procedures for teaching word identification as well as comprehension.

➤ **PROCEDURES:** This general method for teaching reading is designed to be used with students reading at any level who are reading the same selection. Betts describes the DRA procedures:

> First, the group should be prepared, oriented, or made ready, for the reading of a story or selection. Second, the first reading should be guided silent reading. Third, word-recognition skills and comprehension should be developed during the silent reading. Fourth, the rereading—silent or oral, depending upon the needs of the pupil—should be done for purposes different from those served by the first, or silent, reading. Fifth, the follow-up on the "reading lesson" should be differentiated in terms of pupil needs. (1946, p. 492)

The following outline presents the stages usually found in a DRA (Betts, 1946).

1. Readiness
   a. Developing conceptual background
   b. Creating interest
   c. Introducing new vocabulary
   d. Establishing purposes for reading
2. Directed silent reading
   a. Constructing meaning
   b. Monitoring comprehension
3. Discussion and comprehension check
   a. Revisiting purposes for reading
   b. Clarifying concepts and vocabulary
   c. Correcting difficulties in applying word identification and comprehension strategies
   d. Evaluating student performance
4. Rereading
   a. Clarifying information
   b. Obtaining additional information
   c. Enhancing appreciation and understanding
   d. Providing opportunities for purposeful oral reading
5. Follow-up activities
   a. Extending skill development
   b. Enriching and generalizing

➤ **COMMENTS:** Although the DRA is suggested as a framework for teaching in many basal readers, modifications will probably be necessary for students who experience reading difficulties. These students may need more direct instruction of comprehension strategies than is provided in the DRA format and more prereading activities that focus on activating background knowledge. For example, the PreReading Plan or the schema activation strategy could be added to the readiness stage of the DRA to activate and build prior knowledge.

Another caution concerning the DRA is that it is teacher-dominated and, therefore, may not facilitate the development of independent reading skills. Encouraging the students to set their own purposes for reading, to self-question as they read, and to generate their own questions and follow-up activities is emphasized in the next technique, the Directed Reading-Thinking Activity.

Directed Reading-Thinking Activity (DR-TA)

The Directed Reading-Thinking Activity (DR-TA) was developed by Stauffer (1969, 1970, 1976) as a framework for teaching reading that stresses students' abilities to read reflectively and to use prediction. The purpose of the DR-TA is to provide readers with the ability to:

— Determine purposes for reading
— Extract, comprehend, and assimilate information
— Use prediction while reading
— Suspend judgments
— Make decisions based on evidence gained from reading

It is based on the notion that reading is a thinking process that requires students to relate their own experiences to the author's ideas, and thereby construct meaning from the text.

In using this approach, the construction of meaning starts by setting purposes for reading and generating hypotheses about meaning. It continues as the students acquire more information and confirm or disconfirm hypotheses and establish new hypotheses. It ends when the hypotheses have been confirmed and the purposes for reading have been met.

Stauffer (1969) describes a number of distinguishing features about group DR-TA activities:

1. Pupils of approximately the same reading level are grouped together.

2. The group size ranges from two to ten students to promote interaction and participation.

3. All students in a group read the same material at the same time. This permits each member to compare and contrast predictions, paths to answer, and evaluations with those of his or her peers.

4. Purposes for reading are declared by the *student;* students ask questions to become active readers and thinkers.

5. Answers to questions are validated. Proof is found and tested, with the group judging whether or not the offered proof is trustworthy.

6. Immediate *feedback* helps develop integrity and a regard for authenticity.

7. The teacher serves as a facilitator or moderator and asks provocative questions that require the students to interpret and make inferences from what they have read.

The DR-TA can be used with reading materials written at any level and having either narrative or expository structures. Stauffer (1969) suggests that primer and preprimer materials that have limited plots will not lend themselves to this procedure.

— **PROCEDURES:** An outline for guiding a DR-TA is presented in Figure 5.14. The processing entailed in a DR-TA is summarized as follows:

1. Pupil actions
  a. Predict (set purposes)
  b. Read (process ideas)
  c. Prove (test answers)
2. Teacher actions
  a. What do you think? (activate thought)
  b. Why do you think so? (agitate thought)
  c. Prove it! (require evidence) (Stauffer, 1969)

Adapt the following specific procedures when using a DR-TA:

1. After each student receives a copy of the material, direct the students to identify a purpose for reading by studying the title, subtitles, pictures, and so on, to develop a hypothesis about what the passage is about. Questions you might ask to stimulate hypotheses are:
  a. What do you think a story with this title might be about?
  b. What do you think might happen in this story?
Have students share these hypotheses, discussing how they arrived at them. Have students use information from their prior knowledge to substantiate their predictions.

2. Once each student has stated his or her hypothesis, encourage the students to adjust their rate of silent reading to their purpose for reading.

■ **FIGURE 5.14** *Directed Reading-Thinking Activity Outline*

I. Identifying purposes of reading
   A. Individual pupil purposes delimited by
      1. Pupil experience, intelligence and language facility
      2. Pupil interests, needs, and goals
      3. Group interests, needs, and goals
      4. Influence of the teacher
      5. Influence of the content
         a. nature and difficulty of the material
         b. title and subtitles
         c. pictures, maps, graphs, charts
         d. linguistics clues
   B. Group purposes determined by the
      1. Experiences, language facility, and intelligence of each member of the group
      2. Interests, needs, and goals of each member of the group
      3. Consensus of the group and/or of subgroups
      4. Influence of the teacher
      5. Influence of the content
II. Adjusting rate of reading to the purposes declared and to the nature and difficulty of the material. This adjustment is made to
   A. Survey: to overview a selection or text
   B. Skim: to read swiftly and lightly for single points
   C. Scan: to read carefully from point to point
   D. Read critically: to read, to reread, and to reflect so as to pass judgment
III. Observing the reading
   A. Noting abilities to adjust rate to purpose and material
   B. Recognizing comprehension needs and providing help by clarifying
      1. Purposes
      2. Concepts
      3. Need for rereading
   C. Acknowledging requests for help with word recognition needs by providing immediate help in the use of
      1. Context clues: meaning clues
      2. Phonetic clues: sound clues
      3. Structural clues: sight clues
      4. Glossary clues: meaning, sound, and sight clues
IV. Developing comprehension
   A. Checking on individual and group purposes
   B. Staying with or redefining purposes
   C. Recognizing the need for other source material
   D. Developing concepts
V. Fundamental skill training activities: discussion, further reading, additional study, writing
   A. Increasing powers of observation (directed attention)
   B. Increasing powers of reflection by
      1. Abstracting: reorganizing old ideas, conceiving new ideas, distinguishing between ideas, generalizing about ideas, and making inductions and analyses

2. Judgment: formulating propositions and asserting them
3. Reasoning: inferring and demonstrating, and systematizing knowledge deductively

C. Mastering the skills of word recognition: picture and language context analysis, phonetic and structural analysis, and dictionary usage

D. Developing vocabulary: pronunciations; word meanings; semantic dimensions; analogous words, contrasted words; word histories; new words

E. Developing adeptness in conceptualization and cognitive functioning: making and testing inferences; particulars, classes, and categories; reversibility, mobile equilibrium and conservation

F. Mastering the skills of oral reading: voice enunciation,, and expression; reading to prove a point or to present information; reading to entertain (prose and poetry); choral reading

---

Source: R. G. Stauffer, *Directing Reading Maturity as a Cognitive Process* (New York: Harper & Row, 1969), pp. 41–42.

3. Teach or remind the students of the strategy they are to use when they come to a word they cannot identify:

a. Read to the end of the sentence.

b. Use picture clues, if available.

c. Sound out the word.

d. Ask the teacher or a friend for help.

4. Select a logical segment of the passage and direct the students to read it to themselves to check on their predictions. Be responsible for ensuring that students read for meaning by observing reading performance and helping those who request help with words.

5. When the students have finished reading, have them discuss their predictions. Target questions to ask are:

a. Were you correct?

b. What do you think now?

Have students reread orally the sections of the text that confirm or contradict their hypotheses. Assist the students in determining if other source materials may be necessary to clarify meaning, and have the students discuss concepts and vocabulary that are critical to the comprehension process.

6. Repeat the procedure (hypothesis setting, silent reading to validate, oral reading to prove, and discussion) with subsequent segments of the text.

7. Once the passage is completed, use skill activities to teach "skill training" (Stauffer, 1969). This en-

tails rereading the story, reexamining selected words, phrases, pictures, and/or diagrams for the purpose of concurrently developing the students' reading-thinking abilities with the other reading-related skills (Tierney, Readence, and Dishner, 1995). These might include word attack skills and concept clarification and development.

Stauffer (1969) suggests that once the students are comfortable with the DR-TA process they should be encouraged to use an individualized DR-TA. In other words, the students should use this systematic, predictive process as they read individually. Figure 5.15 presents a sample worksheet that students might use to guide them as they complete individual DR-TAs.

— COMMENTS: The DR-TA provides the teacher with a procedure for teaching students to become active thinkers as they read. This is particularly relevant for students with learning and behavior problems since it requires the students to assume responsibility for the reading-learning process. Dixon and Nessel (1992) present strategies for DR-TA with second language learners. In comparison to the DRA, where the teacher sets the purpose for reading and preteaches vocabulary, the DR-TA encourages the students to set their own purposes and decide which vocabulary warrants further development. However, two cautions seem relevant to the DR-TA. First, it

■ **FIGURE 5.15** *Directed Reading-Thinking Activity Individual Prediction Sheet*

Name:

Passage/Book

Pages	Prediction	Outcome

Summary

requires a great deal of self-directiveness on the part of the students, particularly the individualized DR-TA. Second, it does not teach word identification skills in a systematic manner, which may be necessary for students who have difficulties with decoding.

Reciprocal Teaching, Collaborative Strategic Reading, and POSSE

Reciprocal teaching (Palincsar and Brown, 1984, 1986), collaborative strategic reading (Vaughn, Klingner, and Schumm, 1996), and POSSE (Englert and Mariage, 1991) are more comprehensive approaches to teaching reading comprehension. These approaches are built on notions associated with metacognition, schema theory, and a sociocultural theory of learning. From metacognition comes the strong emphasis on comprehension monitoring (e.g., checking to see if understanding is adequate given the purposes for reading). From schema theory, these approaches incorporate activities that encourage students to activate and use relevant background knowledge. From a sociocultural theory of learning comes scaffolded instruction in which the teacher and students take turns assuming the leader role.

These approaches build on the notion that successful comprehension and learning is based on six activities:

1. Clarifying the purpose of reading (i.e., understanding the task demands, both explicit and implicit)
2. Activating relevant background knowledge
3. Allocating attention so that concentration can be focused on the major content at the expense of trivia
4. Critical evaluation of content for internal consistency and compatibility with prior knowledge and common sense
5. Monitoring ongoing activities to see if comprehension is occurring, by engaging in such activities as periodic review and self-interrogation
6. Drawing and testing inferences of many kinds, including interpretations, predictions, and conclusions (Brown, Palincsar, and Armbruster, 1984, p. 263)

While all three approaches build on these activities, reciprocal teaching was developed first and collaborative strategic reading and POSSE further elaborate on reciprocal teaching. In the initial research on reciprocal teaching Palincsar and Brown (Palincsar, 1982; Palincsar and Brown, 1984) chose four comprehension strategies to teach seventh-grade students who had average decoding skills but had significant difficulty with comprehension. The four strategies were *summarizing* (self-review), *questioning, clarifying,* and *predicting.* They used an interactive mode of teaching that emphasized modeling, feedback, and scaffolded instruction. This was con-

ducted in the context of a dialogue between the students and teacher as they participated in the process of reading with the goal of deriving meaning from the text.

— PROCEDURES: The procedure used to teach the four strategies was *reciprocal teaching,* a technique in which the teacher and students took turns leading a dialogue that covered sections of the text. The procedure is similar to, but more extensive than, the reciprocal questioning-ReQuest procedure (Manzo, 1969), a comprehension technique discussed in the section on questioning. Palincsar and Brown (1984) described the teaching procedure as follows:

> The basic procedure was that an adult teacher, working individually with a seventh-grade poor reader, assigned a segment of the passage to be read and either indicated that it was her turn to be the teacher or assigned the student to teach the segment. The adult teacher and the student then read the assigned segment silently. After reading the text, the teacher (student or adult) for that segment asked a question that a teacher or test might ask on the segment, summarized the content, discussed and clarified any difficulties, and finally made a prediction about future content. All of these activities were embedded in as natural a dialogue as possible, with the teacher and student giving feedback to each other. (Palincsar and Brown, 1984, pp. 124–125)

Initially, the students had great difficulty assuming the role of dialogue leader. The teacher was sometimes forced to construct paraphrases and questions for the students to mimic. Gradually, however, the students became more capable. In providing feedback, the teacher used:

> *Prompting.* "What question do you think might be on a test?"
> *Instruction.* "Remember, a summary is a short version—it doesn't include details."
> *Modifying the activity.* "If you can't think of a question right now, go ahead and summarize and then see if you can think of one."
> *Praise.* "That was a clear question, because I knew what you wanted." "Excellent prediction—let's see if you're right."

Corrective feedback. "That was interesting information. It was information I would call a detail. Can you find the most important information?"

Modeling. "A question I would have asked would be. . . ."

The following reciprocal teaching dialogue (Palincsar, 1988) illustrates how a teacher working with at-risk elementary students who have listened to a passage about aquanauts used the four comprehension strategies and the reciprocal teaching techniques.

Student 1:	My question is, what does the aquanaut need when he goes under water?
Student 2:	A watch.
Student 3:	Flippers.
Student 4:	A belt.
Student 1:	Those are all good answers.
Teacher:	Nice job. I have a question too. Why does the aquanaut wear a belt, what is so special about it?
Student 3:	It's a heavy belt and keeps him from floating up to the top again.
Teacher:	Good for you.
Student 1:	For my summary now. . . . This paragraph was about what the aquanauts need to take when they go under the water.
Student 5:	And also about why they need those things.
Student 6:	That's the special things they need.
Teacher:	Another word for gear in this story might be *equipment,* the equipment that makes it easier for the aquanauts to do their job.
Student 1:	I don't think I have a prediction to make.
Teacher:	Well, in the story they tell us that there are "many strange and wonderful creatures" that the aquanauts see as they do their work. My prediction is that they will describe some of these creatures.

Palincsar (1988) suggests that to introduce reciprocal teaching, it is logical to start with a discussion regarding why text may be difficult to un-derstand, why it is important to have a strategic approach to reading and studying, and how reciprocal teaching will help students understand and monitor their understanding. The students are given an overall description emphasizing the use of interactive dialogues or discussions and of a rotating leader. To ensure a level of competency, each strategy is introduced in a functional manner (e.g., summarize a television show or movie) and opportunities provided for the students to practice using the strategy. Palincsar (1988) provides a number of suggestions regarding each comprehension strategy:

Questioning
— Encourage students to ask "teacherlike" questions.
— Fill-in-the-blank questions should be discouraged.
— If the students cannot think of a question, have the students summarize first.
— Provide prompts if needed (e.g., identify the topic, provide a question word).

Summarizing
— Encourage students to identify the "main idea" and an example of supportive information.
— Encourage students to attempt their summaries without looking at the passage.
— Remind students of the rules for generating summaries:
  Look for a topic sentence.
  Make up a topic sentence if one is not available.
  Give a name to a list of items.
  Delete what is unimportant or redundant.

Predicting
— Begin a new passage by having students predict based on the title.
— Encourage students to share information they already know about the topic.
— Refer to, and interweave the text with, their predictions and background knowledge as you read.
— Use headings to help students make predictions.
— Use other opportunities to predict, such as when the author asks questions or gives information about what will be covered next.

— Predictions should be used in an opportunistic and flexible manner.

Clarifying
— Opportunities for clarifying generally occur when:
　　Referents (e.g., *you, he, it*) are unclear.
　　Difficult or unfamiliar vocabulary is presented.
　　Text is disorganized or information incomplete.
　　Unusual, idiomatic, or metaphorical expressions are used.
— Clarifying will not always be necessary.
— It may be helpful if students are asked to point out something that might be unclear to a younger student.

— **COMMENTS:** Palincsar and Brown studied the effectiveness of reciprocal teaching by using the technique with poorly comprehending seventh-grade students who were taught individually or in groups of four to seven students (Brown, Palincsar, and Armbruster, 1984; Palincsar, 1986; Palincsar and Brown, 1984). After instructing approximately thirty minutes over a number of weeks, they found the effects of this instruction to be substantial, reliable, durable over time, and generalizable to classroom settings. Even substantial improvements in standardized reading comprehension scores were reported for the majority of students. Similarly, Klinger and Vaughn (1996) found substantial increases in reading comprehension when collaborative strategic reading was employed with second language students with learning disabilities.

By adding a cooperative learning component to reciprocal teaching and simplifying the cues for the different strategies, Vaughn, Klingner, and Schumm (1996) developed collaborative strategic reading. This approach utilizes cooperative learning in heterogeneous classrooms to help students read content-area textbooks more efficiently and effectively. A well-structured learning environment seems to be one key to the success of collaborative strategic reading. Students learn procedures and practice well-defined roles. For example, in a group of four students, each might assume one of the following roles:

— *Encourager*—lets everyone know when they're doing a good job and gets everyone to participate
— *Timer*—keeps groups on-time and on task
— *Strategy Monitor*—moves group through the stages of the strategy
— *Reader*—reads aloud sections of text, as necessary.

Collaborative strategic reading has four steps or comprehension strategies as noted in Figure 5.16.

Englert and Mariage (1991) combined reciprocal teaching and the teaching of expository text structure to develop a strategy called POSSE (Predict, Organize, Search, Summarize, and Evaluate). To facilitate the students' use of the strategy in their discussions about the text, they emphasized the following cues through the use of a cue card:

> Predict
> 　I predict that . . .
> 　I'm remembering . . .
> Organize
> 　I think one category might be . . .
> Search/Summarize
> 　I think the main idea is . . .
> 　My question about the main idea is . . .
> Evaluate
> 　I think we did (did not) predict this main idea (Compare)
> 　Are there any clarifications?
> 　I predict the next part will be about . . . (p. 128).

As the students and teachers discussed the text using the strategy, they completed a strategy sheet that highlights each step in the strategy and integrates concept maps to assist students in organizing their thoughts and searching for the structure of the text. Figure 5.17 depicts a partially completed strategy sheet for an informational text about the Bermuda Triangle. One of the keys to success with this strategy was the teachers' transfer of control for the reading, discussion, and mapping to the students in the discussion groups.

Reciprocal teaching, collaborative strategic reading, and POSSE combine many of the principles of teaching and learning discussed in Chapter Two, and it explicitly teaches students several strategies for comprehending text.

■ **FIGURE 5.16** *Steps in Collaborative Strategic Reading*

Preview

We preview before reading. Previewing has two steps:

- *Brainstorming:* Think about what you already know about the topic

- *Predicting:* Find clues in the title, subheadings, or pictures about what you will learn. Skim the text for key words that might give you hints.

Click and Clunk

We find clicks and clunks while we are reading. When we understand what we read, everything "clicks" along smoothly. But when we don't understand, "clunk," we stop. When we get a clunk, we use fix-up strategies to figure out what the clunk means:

- Reread the sentence with the clunk and the sentences before or after the clunk, looking for clues.

- Reread the sentence without the word. Think about what would make sense.

- Look for a prefix or suffix in a word.

- Break the word apart and look for smaller words.

- Use a picture.

- Ask for help.

Get the Gist

We get the gist after reading each paragraph or section of a passage. To get the gist means to summarize or restate the most important idea. Do not include the supporting details. State the gist in your own words using the cues:

- Decide who or what the paragraph is mostly about (the topic).

- Name the most important idea about the topic.

Wrap Up

We wrap up after finishing the day's reading assignment. Wrap up includes:

- Asking (teacher-like) questions about the passage.

- Review by thinking about what was important that you learned from the day's reading assignment.

Compliments and Suggestions

We think of a compliment to give the person on the right about how they did in today's activity. We share compliments and give suggestions to help do better next time.

Source: Adapted from S. Vaughn, J. K. Klingner, and J. S. Schumm (1996). *Collaborative Strategic Reading.* Miami: School Based Research, University of Miami.

■ **FIGURE 5.17** *Partially Completed POSSE Strategy Sheet*

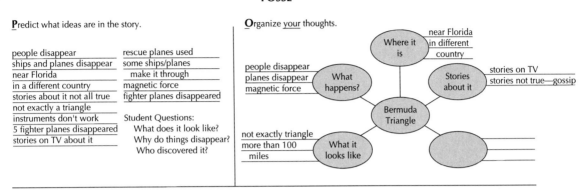

POSSE

<u>**P**</u>redict what ideas are in the story.   <u>**O**</u>rganize <u>your</u> thoughts.

people disappear	rescue planes used
ships and planes disappear	some ships/planes
near Florida	make it through
in a different country	magnetic force
stories about it not all true	fighter planes disappeared
not exactly a triangle	
instruments don't work	Student Questions:
5 fighter planes disappeared	What does it look like?
stories on TV about it	Why do things disappear?
	Who discovered it?

<u>**S**</u>earch for the structure.

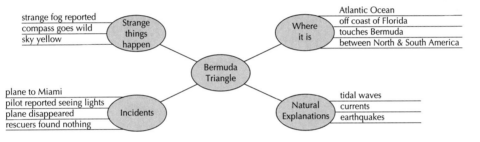

<u>**S**</u>ummarize. Summarize the Main Idea in your own words. Ask a "Teacher" Question about the Main Idea.

<u>**E**</u>valuate. Compare. Clarify. Predict.

Source: "Making Students Partners in the Comprehension Process: Organizing the Reading 'POSSE'" by C. S. Englert and T. V. Mariage, 1991; *Learning Disabilities Quarterly, 14,* p. 129. Copyright 1991 by the Council for Learning Disabilities. Reprinted by permission, Council for Learning Disabilities.

Whole Language and Literature-Based Reading Programs

As discussed in Chapter Four, a growing emphasis is being placed on literacy programs that stress whole language (integration of reading, writing, and oral language) and the use of literature and "real books" rather than traditional basal-reading materials (e.g., basal readers, workbooks, and worksheets). It is reflected in the new editions of many basal reading programs which have shifted from basal readers toward the use of big books, anthologies, literature sets, and teacher resource books.

Whole language and, to varying degrees, literature-based reading programs are derived from a psycholinguistic model of reading and a philosophy of learning and education as articulated by Goodman (1984, 1986, 1996). The philosophy is evident in the following statements:

> "a psycholinguistic approach" to reading would be the very antithesis of a set of instructional materials. . . . The child learning to read seems to need the opportunity to examine a large sample of language, to generate hypotheses about the regularity underlying it, and to test and modify these hypotheses on the

basis of feedback that is appropriate to the unspoken rules that he happens to be testing.

None of this can, to our mind, be formalized in a prescribed sequence of behaviorally stated objectives embalmed in a set of instructional materials, programmed or otherwise. The child is already programmed to learn to read. He needs written language that is both interesting and comprehensible and teachers who understand language-learning and appreciate his competence as a language-learner. (Smith and Goodman, 1971, pp. 179–180)

As Goodman and Goodman (1982) state:

In this method there are no prereading skills, no formalizing reading readiness. Instead, learning is expected to progress *from whole to part,* from general to specific, from familiar to unfamiliar, from vague to precise, from gross to fine, from highly contextualized to more abstract. Children are expected to read, first, familiar meaningful wholes—easily predictable materials that draw on concepts and experiences they already have. These may be signs, cereal boxes, or books. . . . By carefully building on what children already know, we assure their readiness. (p. 127)

— PROCEDURES: The focal points of whole language and literature-based reading programs center on: (1) involving students in lots of reading and writing; (2) creating an environment that accepts and encourages risk-taking; (3) maintaining a focus on meaning (Goodman, 1986; 1996; Weaver, 1990). A teacher using a whole language approach would draw heavily on the principles associated with a sociocultural theory of learning (see Chapter Two). As Watson and Crowley (1988) explain:

In their own unique ways all whole-language teachers facilitate certain activities and procedures:

1. They find out about students' interests, abilities, and needs. And then they go an important step further—they use that information in planning curriculum.
2. They read to students or tell them stories every day.
3. They see to it that students have an opportunity to participate in authentic writing every day.
4. They see to it that students have an opportunity to read real literature every day.
5. They initiate discussions in which students consider the processes of reading and writing.

6. They know that kids can help other kids many times and in many ways that no one else can; therefore, they take advantage of the social nature of literacy (reading and writing) in order to promote it. (p. 235)

Strategies for comprehension are taught within the context of books; teacher and students discuss not only the content but the processes used in constructing meaning from text (Goodman, Watson, and Burke, 1996).

Literature circles are often used to structure discussions about books (Short and Harste, with Burke, 1995). Literature circles facilitate literacy in that they provide opportunities for students to explore ideas about the content and craft of literacy and to think critically and deeply about what they read (Short and Burke, 1991). In literature circles, the teacher initially introduces several books for which there are multiple copies and the group decides which book to read. Students read the book or, if too long, chapters or smaller segments of the book and then meet in literature circle to discuss the book. The first day the discussion starts with a broad focus (e.g., "What was the story about?"). In the discussion the teacher listens to what the students highlight as interesting or challenging and also leads the students to talk about the outstanding characteristics of the book (e.g., character development, plot development, use of dialogue). As the discussions progress across several meetings, the teacher models and guides the students in making connections between the book they read and their personal experiences and other literature they have read or written (Bos, 1991). Apply the Concept 5.4 presents a list of sample questions that fosters discussion and understanding of literature both from the reader's and writer's perspectives. The questions focus on character development, authenticity, mood, voice, writing style and genre, text structure, comparison across literature, and tying reader to author. At the end of each discussion, the group decides what they want to discuss the next time. They prepare for the next discussion by rereading sections of the book or related literature (Bos, 1991). Students also keep notes about the discussion and their reading in Literature Logs (Atwell, 1984).

Goldenberg and his colleagues (Goldenberg, 1992; Saunders, Goldenberg, and Hamann, 1992)

APPLY THE CONCEPT 5.4

*DISCUSSION QUESTIONS TO FOSTER UNDERSTANDING
OF READING AND WRITING*

- Is the story like any other story you have heard, read, or watched? How are they alike? (comparisons across literature)
- What questions would you ask if the author were here? How might the author answer these? (tying reader to author)
- Who are the main characters of the story? What kind of people are they? How does the author let you know? (character development)
- Do the characters change during the story? How do they change? What changes them? Do the changes seem believable? (character development)
- How does the author make the story seem possible? (authenticity)
- Does the language used in the story seem real for the character? (authenticity)
- Did you notice any natural breaks in the book where it seemed like a good place to stop? (text structure)

- Think of a different ending or beginning to the story? How would the rest of the story have to change to have the different ending or beginning work? (text structure)
- Are there any signs or clues that the author gives you to help you with the break? If so, what are they? (writing style and genre)
- Does the story create a specific feeling or mood? What words does the author use to create the mood? (mood)
- Is there anything unique about this author's style? If so, what? (writing style)
- What does the author do to help you feel like you are part of the story? (writing style)
- Who is the teller or narrator of the story? How would the story change if the narrator were someone different? (voice)

Source: Adapted from G. D. Sloan (1984). *The Child as Critic* (2nd ed.). New York: Teachers College Press; and K. Vandergrift (1980). *Child and Story.* New York: Neal-Schuman.

suggest that the discussions are interactive instructional conversations. They highlight the following as elements of effective instructional conversations:

— *Fewer "known-answer" questions.* Discussion focuses on questions for which there is more than one correct answer.

— *Responsivity to student contributions.* Although the teacher has an initial plan and focus, the teacher is also responsive and helps the students explore their ideas as they are raised in the discussion.

— *Connected discourse.* The discussion is characterized not by the teacher asking questions and students answering, but by multiple, interactive turn-taking across the students and teacher.

— *Challenging, but non-threatening atmosphere.* The teacher encourages risk-taking, different ideas, and different points of view. The teacher creates a "zone of proximal development" (see Chapter Two) in which students are challenged in a positive climate. The teacher is a collaborator more than an evaluator.

— *General participation, including self-selected turns.* The teacher and students interact in a discussion fashion with the students volunteering without the teacher necessarily giving permission to talk.

In planning for an instructional conversation about a story or book, Goldenberg (1992) suggests the following:

1. Select a story or book that is appropriate for your students.
2. Read the story (or book) several times until you feel you understand it thoroughly.
3. Select a theme to focus the discussion, at least initially.
4. Identify and provide, as needed, background knowledge students must have in order to make sense of what they will be reading.
5. Decide on a starting point for the discussion to provide an initial focus.
6. Plan and think through the lesson mentally.
7. Consider some suitable follow-up activities, particularly ones that will help you gauge what students have learned from the instruction conversation (pp. 322–323).

In whole language, writing is reciprocally tied to reading so that the students have opportunities to work in the roles of both reader and author (Bos, 1991; Hansen, 1992). Process writing (see Chapter Six) and conferencing about books and written pieces allows the teacher to facilitate the students' understanding of the processes associated with language learning.

Literature for reading and topics for writing are oftentimes self-selected, giving the students the opportunity to explore topics of interest to them. Students also learn about the authors and illustrators of the books they are reading. With this approach, the librarian, annotated bibliographies of children's literature, and teacher resource books are important tools for teaching. Figure 5.18 provides a list of teacher resource books on the use of whole language and literature-based reading. Chapter Appendix 5.1 provides a list of bibliographies and books to aid in the selection of children's literature. These books are invaluable resources in putting together text sets (related books) on different topics or themes (e.g., characters with disabilities, books about famous African-Americans, themes about survival), on different types of text (e.g., fairy tales and folk lore; picture books; wordless books; biographies), by the same author or illustrator (e.g., Beverly Clearly, Katherine Patterson, Tomie de Paola, Betsy Byars), or with the same character (e.g., Ramona and Henry

Huggins series by Beverly Clearly; Amelia Bedelia series by Peggy Parish; Nate the Great series by Marjorie Sharmat). In addition, *The Reading Teacher* regularly reviews children's books and publishes the results of competitions for children's and teachers' choices for favorite books. The books are grouped by the following categories: all ages, beginning independent reading, younger readers, middle grades, and older readers.

— COMMENTS: This orientation to teaching literacy reflects a philosophy of language learning that is student-centered. For students with learning and behavior problems, such a student-centered approach should be advantageous particularly when ample opportunities are provided for teaching literacy strategies during reading and writing. Research investigating the use of literature-based reading programs and whole language with students who are experiencing reading difficulties is limited both in scope and rigor, but there is some evidence that such approaches improve students' attitude toward reading and reading achievement (Allen, Michalove, Shockley, and West, 1991; Mills, O'Keefe, and Stephens, 1992; Roser, Hoffman, and Farest, 1990; Morrow, 1992; Stires, 1991; Tunnell and Jacobs, 1989). However, caution has been raised concerning the need for more varied, explicit, and intense instruction for students with learning disabilities (Mather, 1992; Pressley and Rankin, 1994).

INSTRUCTIONAL ACTIVITIES

This section provides instructional activities that are related to reading comprehension and fluency. Some of the activities teach new skills; others are best suited for practice and reinforcement of already acquired skills. For each activity, the objective, materials, and teaching procedures are described.

■ Critiquing Oral Reading

Objective: To provide students the opportunity to critique their oral reading.

■ **FIGURE 5.18** *Selected Teacher Resource Books on Whole Language and Literature-Based Reading*

Atwell, Nancie (1991). *Side by Side: Essays on Teaching to Learn.* Portsmouth, NH: Heinemann.

Cambourne, B. (1988). *The Whole Story: Natural Learning and the Acquisition of Literacy in the Classroom.* Auckland, NZ: Ashton-Scholastic.

Edelsky, C., Altwerger, B., and Flores, B. (1991). *Whole Language: What's the Difference?* Portsmouth, NH: Heinemann.

Freeman, E. B., and Person, D. G. (1992). *Using Nonfiction Trade Books in the Elementary Classroom from Ants to Zeppelins.* Urbana, IL: National Council of Teachers of English.

Goodman, K. (1986). *What's Whole in Whole Language?* Portsmouth, NH: Heinemann.

Goodman, K. (1996). *On Reading.* Portsmouth, NH: Heinemann.

Goodman, K. S., Bird, L. B., and Goodman, Y. M. (1991). *The Whole Language Catalog.* Santa Rosa, CA: American School Publishers, Macmillan/McGraw-Hill.

Goodman, Y. M., Watson, D. J., & Burke, C. L. (1996). *Reading Strategies: Focus on Comprehension* (2nd ed.). Katonah, NY: Richard C. Owens.

Hansen, J., Newkirk, T., and Graves, D. (Eds.). (1985). *Breaking Ground: Teachers Relate Reading and Writing in the Elementary School.* Portsmouth, NH: Heinemann.

Kimmel M. M., and Segel, E. (1988). *For Reading Out Loud! A Guide to Sharing Books with Children.* New York: Dell.

Korbin, B. (1988). *Eyeopeners! How to Choose and Use Children's Books about Real People, Places, and Things.* New York: Penguin.

Moss, J. F. (1984). *Focus Units in Literature: A Handbook for Elementary School Teachers.* Urbana, IL: National Council of Teachers of English.

Norton, D. E. (1991). *Through the Eyes of a Child: An Introduction to Children's Literature* (3rd ed.). Columbus, OH: Merrill.

Oppenheim, J., Brenner, B., and Doegenhold, B. D. (1986). *Choosing Books for Kids: Choosing the Right Book for the Right Child at the Right Time.* New York: Ballantine Books.

Peetoom, A. (1993). *Shared Reading: Safe Risks with Whole Books.* Richmond Hill, Ontario, CA: Scholastic-TAB Publications.

Raines, S. C., and Canady, R. J. (1991). *More Story Stretchers: More Activities to Expand Children's Favorite Books.* Mt. Rainer, MD: Gryphon Press.

Reed, A. J. S. (1994). *Comics to Classics: A Parent's Guide to Books for Teens and Preteens.* Newark, DE: International Reading Association

Robb, L. (1996) *Reading Strategies That Work: Teaching Your Students to Become Better Readers.* New York: Scholastic.

Short, K. G., and Burke, C. (1991) *Creating Curriculum: Teachers and Students as a Community of Learners.* Portsmouth, NH: Heinemann.

Short, K. G., Harste, J. C., with Burke, C. (1995). *Creating Classrooms for Authors and Inquirers.* Portsmouth, NH: Heinemann.

Short, K. G., and Pierce, K. M. (Eds.). (1990). *Talking about Books.* Portsmouth, NH: Heinemann.

Stires, S. (Ed.). (1991). *With Promise: Redefining Reading and Writing for "Special" Students.* Portsmouth, NH: Heinemann.

Tompkins, G. E., and McGee, L. M. (1993). *Teaching Reading with Literature: Case Studies to Action Plans.* New York: Merrill/Macmillan.

Trelease, J. (1995). *The New Read-Aloud Handbook* (4th ed.). New York: Penguin.

Weaver, C. (1990). *Understanding Whole Language: From Principles to Practice.* Portsmouth, NH: Heinemann.

Wepner, S. B., and Feeley, J. T. (1993). *Moving Forward with Literature: Basals, Books, and Beyond.* New York: Merrill/Macmillan.

Grades: Primary and intermediate

Materials: (1) A book or story the student is reading. (2) A tape recorder and a labeled blank tape for each student.

Teaching Procedures: Explain that the purpose of the activity is to give the students an opportunity to listen to how they read. Let the students know that they are to listen for things they do well and things they want to work on. Model the process by practicing, recording, listening, and critiquing a passage you read. Before the students read into the tape recorder, have them practice the segment. Each student should practice and then read and record a passage of about 100 to 500 words. After the students record, they should listen to their tapes and finish writing the following statements:

When I read orally, I do a really good job of
_____ .

One thing I could do better when I read out loud is
_____ .

It is important to have students start with the things they do well.

Listen to and discuss each tape and then ask the students to critique each presentation. Have the students record their oral reading every three to six weeks so that they can compare and hear how they are improving.

Adaptations: Each student can record two passages—one that has been practiced and one that is unpracticed.

■ Readers' Theatre

Objective: To provide students practice in oral reading and to become familiar with literature.

Grades: All grades

Materials: (1) Copies of plays, folktales, or other literature that has a great deal of dialogue. The literature will vary depending on the ages and reading abilities of the students.

Teaching Procedures: Introduce the literature piece to the students and explain the various characters and the role of the narrator. After the students select parts, prepare their copy of the literature piece (script) by highlighting the part they are to read. Tell the students to work in pairs and practice reading their parts in the scripts. Finally, have the students practice reading the script in a dress rehearsal and then a final presentation. For the final presentation,

have the students read the scripts to another class and/or videotape it.

Adaptations: Students may want to develop this into a play by making costumes and memorizing their lines. Students may also want to write their own stories to read.

■ Story Jumble

Objective: To provide students practice in sequencing a story.

Grades: Primary and intermediate

Materials: Short stories written at the students' independent reading levels that have been cut into story parts (e.g., setting, episodes, endings), paragraphs, or sentences. Mount each segment of the story on an index card.

Teaching Procedures: Present the cards to the students and have them read each part and arrange them so that the story makes sense. Then have the students read the story again to check to see if it makes sense. If students disagree as to the order, have them explain why they prefer a certain order.

Adaptations: Students can work on this activity in groups of two or three students or individually.

■ Predict the Plot

Objective: To provide students practice in predicting the events and plots in stories.

Grades: Intermediate and secondary

Materials: Cartoon strips such as Peanuts, Broomhilda, or Beetle Bailey.

Teaching Procedures: Select a cartoon strip and expose one frame at a time for the students to read. Then have them predict the plot by asking such questions as:

What do you think is going to be pictured in the next frame? Why?

Of the ideas we have generated, which one do you like best? Why?

How do you think the cartoonist will end this story? Why?

Read the next frame, discussing the previous predictions and making predictions about the next frame. After the story is completed, have the students draw and write their own cartoons, using the characters presented in the strip or creating new characters. Then the students may share their cartoons with each other.

Adaptations: Mystery and adventure stories also lend themselves to this type of plot prediction. Segments of the story could be read and then predictions made. Students could also finish this activity by writing a mystery or adventure story.

■ Stake-Out

Objective: To give students the opportunity to arrange the paragraphs of articles in a logical order.

Grades: Intermediate and secondary

Materials: (1) At least two newspaper articles with at least four paragraphs written at the students' instructional to independent reading levels. Cut each article up by paragraphs, and mount each paragraph from the same story on the same color index card. (2) Write clues on another set of index cards that will help the students find the various paragraphs located in a given area (e.g., room, school).

Teaching Procedures: Place the paragraphs to the articles around the room or school. Divide the students into teams that consist of two or three members. Explain to the teams that their goal is to use the clues to find the various parts to their newspaper article, and then to arrange the article so that it makes sense. Explain that the parts to their article will all be on the same color index cards. Use either the rule that the first team that completes the task wins, or that a certain time limit is available for the stake-out and the team must complete it by that time if they are to win.

Give each team the clues and have them begin. When time is complete, have each group read the article. The class then determines if the order is correct. Have the students justify the order they selected.

■ Judge the Ad

Objective: To provide students the opportunity to think critically about advertisements.

Grades: Intermediate and secondary

Materials: Ads cut from newspapers and magazines.

Teaching Procedures: Select examples of ads that provide a fair representation of a product and ones that present a biased or unfair representation. Discuss with the students what makes the ad fair, unfair, or biased. Then have the students each select an ad for a product they know about and would like to purchase. Ask them to study the ad to determine if it is "fair." Have each student present his or her ad to the other students and build a case for why the ad is fair or unfair. Encourage the students to provide evidence for their opinions.

■ WH-Game

Objective: To provide students practice in answering who, what, when, where, why, and how questions.

Grades: All grades

Materials: (1) Generic gameboard, spinner or die, and markers. (2) WH Cards, which are small cards with "WH-Game" written on one side and one of the following words written on the other side: Who, What, When, Where, Why, How. (3) Sets of Story and Article Cards, which are copies of short stories and articles mounted on cards. There should be one copy for each player. Select topics of interest for the age level of students.

Teaching Procedures: Explain the game to the students or have them read written directions. First, the players set up the game. Next, they select a set of Story or Article Cards. All players read the story or article and place their cards face down. Then, each player takes a turn by throwing the die or spinning and selecting a WH-Card. The player must make up a question using the WH word indicated on the card and answer it correctly in order to move his or her marker the indicated number of spaces. If another player questions the validity of a player's question or answer, the players may look at the story or article

card. Otherwise, these cards should remain face down during play. After ten questions have been asked using one Story or Article card, another set is selected. The students read this card and then the game continues. The first player to arrive at the finish wins.

Adaptations: Students may also work in pairs, with one person on the team making up the question and the other person answering it.

SUMMARY

Many students with learning and behavior problems struggle with learning word identification skills. We, as special education teachers, spend a considerable amount of our instructional time focusing on these skills, assuming that fluency and comprehension will follow. What we have found is that these students also experience difficulties in reading fluently and in integrating their background knowledge with the text in order to construct meaning and comprehend the text. Consequently, we need systematically to plan and implement fluency and comprehension instruction.

Strategies for fluency instruction first focus on providing students frequent opportunities to listen to literature being read aloud and on having students read familiar books. In addition, the strategies of repeated reading and repeated choral reading are stressed because they provide students with additional instructional support when developing fluent reading patterns.

Much of what teachers refer to as instruction in reading comprehension is, in fact, better described as the assessment of students' comprehension after they have read. So as to draw attention away from teacher questioning, this chapter presents a framework for reading comprehension that is not tied to level of reading comprehension questions. Instead, it is tied to the reasoning processes required (i.e., textually explicit, textually implicit, or scriptually implicit) and the types of information or relationships represented. We can use this matrix in planning instruction in that we can implement techniques and strategies that will assure many different facets of comprehension are tapped.

In discussing methods for teaching reading comprehension, emphasis is placed on the importance of planning activities before the students read that will help them activate their background knowledge or schemas. Techniques such as brainstorming, the PreReading Plan, Text Preview, K-W-L, and a schema-activation strategy can facilitate this process. In the area of questions, emphasis is placed on helping students learn to predict and ask their own questions rather than just respond to the questions of the teacher.

Teaching students strategies for activating prior knowledge, predicting, self-questioning, and comprehension monitoring (e.g., story retelling, paraphrasing, summarizing, directed reading-thinking, reciprocal teaching) is the key to teaching comprehension. A steady diet of strategies for effective comprehension rather than a steady diet of answering literal comprehension questions should not only teach students how to understand what they read but also how to be strategic thinkers. This strategic thinking orientation toward teaching reading and reading comprehension is represented in such comprehensive approaches as directed reading-thinking activities, reciprocal teaching, collaborative strategic reading, and whole language and literature-based reading programs.

THINK AND APPLY

— Describe several reasons why a student might have difficulty with fluency or reading comprehension.

— Why is it important to read aloud to a student who is having difficulty learning to read?

— Describe the framework for reading comprehension presented in this chapter. After reading a piece of text, write several questions/answers of each of the following types: textually explicit, textually implicit, and scriptually implicit.

— Select an informational text that you plan or might plan to read with students. Describe how you would use brainstorming, PreReading Plan, Text Preview, or K-W-L to assist students in activating background knowledge.

— Describe how a "think-aloud" would be used with a paraphrasing or retelling strategy. Select a passage and a strategy (e.g., RAP, STORE) and do a think-aloud by describing what you are thinking as you carry out the steps in the strategy.

— Compare and contrast the Directed Reading Activity and the Directed Reading-Thinking Activity.

— What four comprehension and comprehension-monitoring strategies are highlighted in reciprocal teaching?

— Describe how you would set up a special-education classroom using a whole language or literature-based reading program.

APPENDIX 5.1 ▬▬▬▬▬▬▬▬▬▬

Book Selection Aids for Children's Literature

Comprehensive Lists, Directories, and Children's Literature Textbooks

Children's Books in Print. (Annual). New York: R.R. Bowker, $124.95.

A comprehensive listing of children's books currently in print. Includes titles for grades K–12. Titles are arranged alphabetically by author, title, and illustrator. Also includes children's book awards for the previous ten years.

Children's Literature in the Elementary School (5th ed.) (1993). C. S. Huck, S. Hepler, and J. Hickman. Fort Worth: Harcourt Brace Jovanovich, 840 pp. $48.

Includes overview of children's books by types, strategies for teaching, and resource lists.

The Elementary School Paperback Collection. (1985). J. T Gillespie. Chicago, IL: American Library Association, 306 pp., $17.50.

Includes 3,800 titles for preschool through sixth grade, arranged by popular interest categories, with descriptions including age level and a brief summary.

Fiction, Folklore, Fantasy and Poetry for Children 1876–1985. (1986). New York: R.R. Bowker, 2 vols., 2,563 pp., $495.

Contains 133,000 entries compiled from a variety of sources and indexed by author, title, illustrator, and awards.

Magazines for Children. (1989). D. R. Stoll (Ed.). Newark, DE: International Reading Association, 48 pp., $5.25, paper.

Lists more than 125 magazines for infants through teenagers. Includes age and subject indexes.

Magazines for Young People (2nd ed.) (1991). B. Katz and K. S. Katz. New York. R.R. Bowker, 273 pp., $49.95.

Evaluates over 1,000 magazines, journals, and newsletters for children and teachers in 60 subject areas.

Subject Guide to Children's Books in Print. (Annual). New York: R.R. Bowker. $124.95.

A companion volume to *Children's Books in Print.* Arranges all children's titles currently in print using over 6,000 subject headings. Particu-

larly useful for finding and ordering titles on specific subjects; however, titles are not annotated.

General Selection Aids

Adventuring with Books: A Booklist for Pre-K–Grade 6 (9th ed.). (1989). M. Jett-Simpson (Ed.). Urbana, IL: National Council of Teachers of English, 550 pp., $16.50, paper.

Annotates about 1,800 children's titles published from 1984 to 1988. Annotations include summary, age, and interest levels. Content are arranged by genre, broad subject, and theme. Author, title, and subject indexes.

Award-Winning Books for Children and Young Adults. (Annual). B. L. Criscoe. Metuchen, NJ: Scarecrow Press, $37.50.

Lists books that won awards during the previous year. Includes description of the awards, criteria used for selection, plot synopses of winners, grade levels, and genres.

Best Books for Children: Preschool Through Grade 6 (4th ed.). (1990). J. T. Gillespie and C. J. Naden. New York, R.R. Bowker, 950 pp., $44.95.

An annotated listing of 11,299 books that are selected to satisfy recreational, curricular needs, and interests of elementary school children.

Books are arranged by broad age groups that are divided by types of books. Contains author, title, subject, and illustrator indexes.

Bibliography of Books for Children. (1989). H. Shelton (Ed.). Wheaton, MD: Association for Childhood Education International, 112 pp., $11.00.

Lists the best books reviewed by the Association for Childhood Education over the previous two years. Books are evaluated for readability and absences of sexism and racism. Entries are annotated and grouped by age levels. Indexed and cross-referenced.

The Horn Book Guide to Children's and Young Adult Books. (Semiannual). Boston: Horn Book.

Provides short reviews of children's and young adults books published in the United States during the prior publishing season with references to longer reviews in *Horn Book Magazine.*

Books are given a numerical evaluation from one to six.

New York Times Parents' Guide to the Best Books for Children. (1988). E. R. Lipson. New York: Times Books/Random House, 421 pp., $12.95.

Indexes books by age appropriateness, listening level, author, title, illustrator, and subject. Books are arranged in broad categories such as wordless books, picture storybooks, and so on.

Tried and True: 500 Nonfiction Books Children Want to Read. (1992). W. Moss and J. Moss. New York: R.R. Bowker, 300 pp., $34.95.

Lists popular titles arranged by grade level, then by books to be read for pleasure and books to be read for research.

Your Reading: A Booklist for Junior High and Middle School Students. (1988). J. E. Davis and H. K. Davis (Eds.). Urbana, IL: National Council of Teachers of English, 494 pp., $13.95.

An annotated list of over 2,000 books for grades 5–9 arranged in broad subject categories. Includes author and title indexes.

Booklists for Various Levels of Readers

The Best: High/Low Books for Reluctant Readers. (1990). M. L. Pilla. Littleton, CO: Libraries Unlimited, 100 pp., $12.50, paper.

Includes books of high literary quality for reluctant readers in grades 3–12. Has brief annotations, reading and interest levels, and popular subject headings.

Beyond Picture Books: A Guide to First Readers. (1990). B. Barstow and J. Riggle. New York, R.R. Bowker, 354 pp., $39.95.

Annotates 1,600 first readers for ages 4 to 7, with a plot summary, brief evaluation, and bibliographic information. Indexes by title, illustrator, readability, series, and subject.

Books for Children to Read Alone: A Guide for Parents and Librarians. (1988). G. Wilson and J. Moss. New York: R.R. Bowker, 184 pp., $39.95.

Lists books in which concepts and language structures are accessible to beginning readers in the first through third grades. Includes subject index.

Choices: A Core Collection for Young Reluctant Readers (Vol. 2). (1990). J. Cummins and B. Cummins (Eds.). Evanston, IL: John Gordon Burke, Publishers, 544 pp., $45.00.

Annotates 275 books for second through sixth graders reading below grade level, published between 1983 and 1988, with plot summary, interest level, and reading level. Contains author and subject indexes.

Easy Reading: Books Series and Periodicals for Less Able Readers (2nd ed.). (1989). R. Ryder et al. Newark, DE: International Reading Association, 96 pp., $8.75.

An annotated list reviews 44 book series and 15 periodicals for readers grades 4–12 who have difficulty with materials generally written for their age level.

Booklists and Indexes for Particular Subjects

Picture Books and Concept Books

A to Zoo: Subject Access to Children's Picture Books (3rd ed.). (1989). C. W. Lima. New York: R.R. Bowker, 939 pp., $44.95.

Provides subject access to over 8,000 picture books through 600 subject headings with cross references and full bibliographic citations. Most titles are useful for children from preschool through second grade. Includes author, illustrator, and title lists.

Picture Books for Children (3rd ed.). (1990). P. J. Cianciolo. Chicago, IL: American Library Association.

An annotated listing of picture books divided into major subject areas such as "Me and My Family" or "The Imaginative World." Annotations include descriptions of media, age levels, and brief synopses of plot. Material is largely new to this edition, so older editions remain useful.

Wordless/Almost Wordless Picture Books: A Guide. (1991). V. H. Richey and K. Tuten-Pucket. Littleton, CO: Libraries Unlimited. 125 pp., $17.50.

Lists books with a brief annotation. Includes thematic and subject indexes.

Folklore and Storytelling and Reading Aloud

Books Kids Will Sit Still For: The Complete Read-Aloud Guide (2nd ed.). (1990). J. Freeman. New York: R.R. Bowker, 660, pp., $34.95.

Lists over 2,000 titles recommended for reading aloud including plot summaries, extension ideas, and related titles.

(continued)

APPENDIX 5.1   *Continued*

Stories: A List of Stories to Tell and Read Aloud (7th ed.). (1987). N. B. Iarusso (Ed.). New York: New York Public Library Publication Office, 120 pp., $6.00.

> Suggests proven stories to tell and read aloud to children. Includes poetry. Entries are briefly annotated.

Storytelling Folklore Sourcebook (1991). N. J. Livo and S. A. Rietz. Littleton, CO: Libraries Unlimited, 400 pp., $34.00.

> A sourcebook of folk tales, legends, songs, poetry, and aphorisms.

Historical Fiction, History, and Biography

American History for Children and Young Adults: An Annotated Bibliographic Index. (1990). V. Van Meter. Littleton, CO: Libraries Unlimited, 324 pp., $32.50.

> Books reviewed between 1980 and 1988 arranged by time periods, subdivided by subject. Indexed by grade level.

Index to Collective Biographies for Young Readers (4th ed.). (1988). K. Breen (Ed.). New York: R.R. Bowker, 494 pp., $44.95.

> Indexes biographies in collections by individuals' names and by subject. Biographies are suitable for elementary school through junior high school.

World History for Children and Young Adults. (1991). V. Van Meter. Littleton, CO: Libraries Unlimited, 425 pp., $29.50.

> Lists and annotates books about work history by time period and subject. Includes fiction and nonfiction.

Cultural and Sexual Identity

American Indian Reference Books for Children and Young Adults. (1990). B. J. Kuipers. Littleton, CO: Libraries Unlimited, 200 pp., $32.50.

> Lists over 200 nonfiction sources of materials on Native Americans for grades 3–12. Includes strengths and weaknesses of each book as well as curriculum uses. A section of the book deals with general selection criteria to use for these subjects.

Basic Collection of Children's Books in Spanish. (1986). I. Schon. Metuchen, NJ: Scarecrow, 230 pp., $17.50.

> Over 500 titles for grades Pre-K through 6 arranged in Dewey order, with access through author, title, and subject indexes.

Bilingual Books in Spanish and English for Children. (1985). D. C. Dale. Littleton, CO: Libraries Unlimited, 163 pp., $23.50.

> Annotated entries provide evaluation of 254 bilingual books for preschool and elementary school children published and distributed in the United States.

The Black Experience in Children's Books. (1989). B. Rollock (selector). New York: New York Public Library Publications Office, 112 pp., $5.00.

> An annotated list that presents titles about the African-American experience in the United States as well as in other areas of the world. Criteria for selection and inclusion in the list are determined.

Books in Spanish for Children and Young Adults: An Annotated Guide (Series III). (1985). I. Schon. Metuchen, NJ: Scarecrow, 108 pp., $16.50.

> Contains listing of books for preschool through high-school students that have been published since 1982. Books represent diverse Hispanic cultures including Mexico, Central and South America, and Spain.

Our Family, Our Friends, Our World: An Annotated Guide to Significant Multicultural Books for Children and Teenagers. (1992). L. Miller-Lachman. New York. R.R. Bowker, 400 pp., $39.95.

> Annotated lists of fiction and nonfiction about ethnic and cultural minority groups in the United States and Canada and about cultures in various parts of the world.

Other Social Issues

Books to Help Children Cope with Separation and Loss (Vol. 3). (1988). J. E. Bernstein and M. K. Rudman (comp.). New York: R.R. Bowker, 532 pp., $44.95.

> Includes several chapters on bibliotherapy plus annotated lists of titles in such categories as death, divorce, adoption, and foster children, and loss of mental or physical functions. About 600 books are arranged by topic with an annotation evaluation and recommendations for use with children. Age level from 3 to 16; interest

and reading levels are included in each annotation.

Portraying the Disabled: A Guide to Juvenile Fiction. (1991). D. Robertson. New York: R.R. Bowker, 500 pp., $39.95.

Updates *Notes from a Different Drummer* and *More Notes from a Different Drummer,* books which provide annotated lists of titles that portray the disabled. Includes titles that promote better understanding and acceptance of the disabled.

Portraying the Disabled: A Guide to Juvenile Non-Fiction. (1991). J. B. Friedberg, J. B. Mullins, and A. W. Sukiennik. New York: R.R. Bowker, 363 pp., $34.95.

Updates *Accept Me as I Am* listing over 350 titles about the disabled. Includes introductory essays about the portrayal of disabilities in literature for children.

Information about Authors and Illustrators

Behind the Covers: Interviews with Authors and Illustrators of Books for Children and Young Adults. (1985). J. Roginski. Littleton, CO: Libraries Unlimited, 249 pp., $23.50.

Interviews 22 authors and illustrators about their work.

Bookpeople: A First Album and *Bookpeople: A Second Album.* (1990). S. L. McElmeel. Littleton, CO: Libraries Unlimited, 175 pp., $17.00, paper and 200 pp., $18.00, paper.

A First Album introduced 41 authors and illustrators of picture books. *A Second Album* introduced authors of intermediate books (grades 3–9). Brief biographies with highlights of life and career and select bibliographies.

Books by African-American Authors and Illustrators for Children and Young Adults. (1991). H. E. Williams. Chicago, IL: American Library Association, 270 pp., $39.00.

Presents a comprehensive listing of works by African-Americans. Clear, concise annotations are given in three sections divided by reading/interest level: Pre-K–4, 5–8, 9+. Also includes profiles and critical discussion of 53 African-American authors and illustrators.

Something About the Author. (61 volumes, added to periodically). A. Commarie. Detroit, MI: Gale Research, $70.00/volume.

Clear and sizable essays on contemporary authors and illustrators. Updating allows more recent authors to be included. Contain photographs as well as reproductions from works of the illustrators. Suitable for middle-grade children to use for gathering biographical information.

Source: Adapted from Charlotte S. Huck, Susan Hepler, and Janet Hickman, *Children's Literature in the Elementary School,* 5th ed. Copyright © 1993 by Holt, Rinehart and Winston, Inc. Used with permission.

Chapter 6

Written Expression

OUTLINE

KEY TOPICS FOR MASTERY

— The **writing process approach** to written language instruction—its elements, implementation, and benefits to students

— The many positive outcomes that occur when students with learning and behavior problems are given **choices** about writing topics, **encouragement** and support in their writing, and sufficient **time** for that writing

— The **writing conference**—its importance in helping a student improve a piece of writing

— The principles for establishing a **writing community** within the classroom

— Why **error analysis** must be the first step in developing an effective spelling program

— Principles and strategies for teaching spelling skills to students with learning disabilities, including empirically based instructional practices

— Special considerations to be made in deciding appropriate handwriting instruction for students with learning disabilities

 BRIGHT IDEA

Turn to page 275 and read Think and Apply.

A high school teacher of students with learning disabilities reports, "The adolescents in my program do not want to write. They do not even want to answer questions in writing. Writing a theme for a class is torture."

Most young children love to scribble. They enjoy writing and drawing on paper, sidewalks, chalkboards, and, unfortunately, even on walls. On the first day of school when first graders are asked if they know how to write, most of them say yes. What happens to the interest and joy in writing from age three to age thirteen?

Many researchers in the field feel that students do not spend enough time on writing as a craft and are given too little choice about what they write. Writing has many negative associations for students because it is often used as a form of punishment and when their writing is returned to them it is filled with corrections. This chapter is about what happens in writing when students are given choices in topics, and time and

encouragement to write. The chapter presents background and instructional procedures for using the writing process approach to instruction. Getting started in writing, the writing process, and establishing a writing community are discussed. In addition, this chapter presents approaches to teaching spelling and handwriting to students who have learning difficulties, and provides a table showing the pros and cons of teaching cursive versus manuscript or both.

TEACHING THE WRITING PROCESS

Several years ago Marynell Schlegel, a resource room teacher who works with students who have learning and emotional disabilities, decided she disliked teaching writing almost as much as the students hated learning it. An interview with these students on

APPLY THE CONCEPT 6.1

KNOWLEDGE OF WRITING STRATEGIES

Students identified as learning disabled differ from low-achieving and high-achieving students in their knowledge of strategies related to writing. They are less aware of steps in the writing process and ideas and procedures for organizing their written text. Students with learning disabilities are also more dependent on external cues such as how much to write, teacher feedback, and mechanical presentation of the paper. They demonstrate significant difficulties planning, writing, and revising text (Englert, Raphael, Fear, and Anderson, 1988).

the characteristics of good writing revealed that they perceived good writing as spelling words correctly, writing "correct" sentences, and having good handwriting—the very skills these students often have the most difficulty developing. None of the children included a purpose for writing in their description of good writing. Writing was not perceived by them as a means of conveying a message, which is considered by experts to be the most important element in writing (Murray, 1984, 1985).

During the summer Ms. Schlegel decided to read about writing and to change her writing instruction. She decided to implement the writing process approach to written expression (Graves, 1983; MacArthur, Graham, Schwartz, and Schafer, 1995).

The Writing Process for Students with Learning and Behavior Problems

After spending the summer preparing for the changes in her instructional approach to writing, Ms. Schlegel decided she was ready to begin. She arranged for students with writing problems to come to the resource room for four fifty-minute periods a week. During this time they were to write. Writing included selecting topics of their choice and, within each written piece, focusing first on the message and only later on the mechanics of writing. Skills such as organizing ideas and editing for capitalization, punctuation, and spelling would be taught based on the students' individual needs and within the context of their written pieces rather than through the familiar

drill and practice activities. Ms. Schlegel initiated the program with many reservations. She was concerned that this writer-centered format for teaching writing would require her to have a built-in scope and sequence for the development of written expression. She had taught reading and math for a number of years and had developed a scope and sequence of the skills required at each grade level, but written expression was much less developed in her mind and in the various teachers' guides she consulted. Marynell knew that one way to develop a better understanding of what to teach and how to teach it was to observe students as they learn to become writers. Getting ready to implement the writing process approach to instruction involves considerations in several areas, including setting, scheduling and preparing materials, teaching skills, and the teacher's role as a writer.

Setting

To ensure a successful writing program for her students who had already experienced failure in writing, Marynell decided that one of the most important components would be the environment. According to Graves (1983), the setting should create a working atmosphere similar to a studio, which promotes independence and in which students can easily interact. Figure 6.1 depicts how Marynell arranged her room to create such an atmosphere. Materials and supplies for writing, and the students' individual writing folders were stored in specific locations in the room. Students knew where materials could be found, so they did not have to rely on the teacher to get them started at the beginning of the writing

■ **FIGURE 6.1**   *Setting the Stage*

1. Create a working atmosphere that is similar to a studio.
2. Create an atmosphere where students can interact easily.
3. Create an atmosphere which encourages independence.

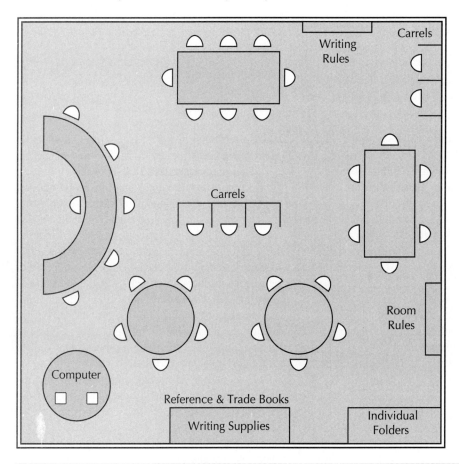

period. The room was arranged so students could work together or individually. The room arrangement facilitated conferencing between small groups of students, teacher and student, and student and student.

Scheduling and Preparing Materials

Marynell set up individual writing folders. In the daily writing folders, illustrated in Figure 6.2, students kept all their unfinished writing, a list of possible writing topics, a list of all writing pieces they had completed, a list of writing skills they had mastered, a list of skills and topics in which they had expertise, and dates when conferences with the teacher were held. A list of the words an individual student was learning to spell, along with a procedure for learning the words and measuring mastery, was also included in the folder (see Figure 6.3). In addition to this current writing folder, students had access to their permanent writing folder, which included all of the writing they had completed.

■ **FIGURE 6.2** *Individual Writing Folder*

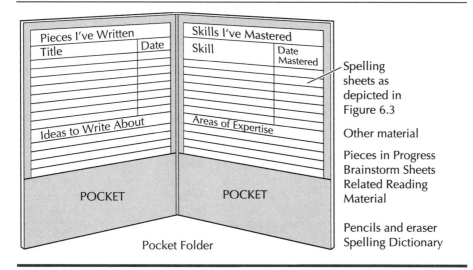

Spelling sheets as depicted in Figure 6.3

Other material

Pieces in Progress
Brainstorm Sheets
Related Reading
Material

Pencils and eraser
Spelling Dictionary

■ **FIGURE 6.3** *Sample Spelling Form for the Individual Spelling Folder*

Student: _____

Words I'm Learning to Spell

Date	Word	Written on Card	Practiced Using Strategy	Learned for Test	Learned in Writing	Date Mastered
3/12	1. mystery	✓	✓	✓		
	2. chasing	✓	✓	✓		
	3. haunted	✓	✓	✓		
	4. wouldn't	✓	✓			
	5. elsewhere	✓	✓	✓		
	6. whatever	✓	✓	✓		
	7. their	✓	✓	✓		
	8. there	✓	✓	✓		
	9.					
	10.					

In setting up the writing program Marynell also made a substantial time commitment. Her previous written language instruction had focused on short periods of time several days a week—just enough time for the student to complete a skill activity or a piece of writing on an assigned topic. Her research convinced her that students need an extended period of time on a daily basis if they are to develop as writers. So, coordinating with the regular classroom teachers, Marynell scheduled fifty minutes per day, four days per week, for writing.

She scheduled approximately eight to ten students to come to the resource room during the writing period. These students were experiencing difficulties in written expression.

Teaching Skills

Students with learning disabilities display a wide range of abilities in writing (Berninger, Abbott, Witaker, Sylvester, and Nolen, 1995). They are also very different in terms of the writing skills they need to acquire and the ways in which they respond to instruction (Berninger et al., 1995). Variables such as motivation and attitude must be considered as well as writing skills when designing effective writing skills programs for students with learning problems.

Therefore, the skills that Marynell taught during each writing period varied in response to the students' needs. Most of the time was devoted to individual writing and conferences with classmates and the teacher. Time for sharing ideas and drafts was often scheduled near the end of the period.

Marynell conducted short (five to fifteen minutes) skill lessons with individuals or small groups of students. The topics and groupings for these lessons were based on the students' needs. Skill lessons were decided based on observations of student writing, requests for help, and data collected from conferences. Students were selected to participate in the skill lessons contingent on their abilities and needs. The same topic with different activities was usually covered for four lessons to help provide sufficient practice. To help promote generalization, Ms. Schlegel and students would use conferences to discuss how the skill was working in the writing process.

Ms. Zaragoza is an elementary teacher who used the writing process with all of her students. Ms. Zaragoza felt that the writing process approach was successful with all learners in her classroom because she organized short skill lessons, five to ten minutes each day, for small groups of youngsters, and individual skill lessons for students who had specific difficulties. When Ms. Zaragoza noticed that several students were having difficulty with a particular skill (e.g. quotation marks), or she felt that several students were ready to learn a more advanced writing procedure (e.g., the difference between first and third person when writing), she would organize a skill group. She taught approximately one skill group a day and advertised the skill group by writing the name of it on the board as well as the time it would occur. She would write the names of the students who she felt would benefit from the skill group on the board but would also allow other students to "sign up" for the skill group. A skill group would last for one day or several depending upon the difficulty of the skill. Ms. Zaragoza also taught daily skill lessons to individual students. These skill lessons sometimes were responses to the "teachable moment"—for example, a student might ask how to develop an ending for a story—and other times the individual skill lessons were planned and scheduled. Ms. Zaragoza's viewpoint was that "practice in writing is essential to enhancing writing skills, but practice alone is insufficient. Skill groups are an essential way to keep students moving and learning as writers."

Teachers as Writers

Writing with the students was also an important part of Ms. Schlegel's writing program. She planned her schedule so that she was writing when the students entered the room at the beginning of the period. She found that this set the tone and facilitated getting the students to start writing. Ms. Gervasi, a teacher of emotionally disturbed adolescents, thinks that a teacher's writing is the most important ingredient to success with the students. Ms. Gervasi frequently writes with her students and shares her writing with them. Because she writes, she feels she can better understand their writing difficulties and can speak with them author to author.

Setting the tone for writing requires the teacher to write, to share his or her writing, to be genuinely interested in what the students say in their writing, to listen carefully, and to confer and provide feedback. According to Graves (1983), the tone for writing is set by what the teacher does.

Using the Writing Process in General Education Classrooms

Ms. Zaragoza conducts workshops for teachers on the use of writing process. During these workshops she is frequently asked whether youngsters who are at risk for learning problems or identified as learning disabled can successfully use this approach. She conducted three year-long case studies with students who were identified as gifted, low-achieving, and learning disabled in which she examined their progress in writing and writing related skills (e.g., capitalization, spelling, punctuation) (Zaragoza and Vaughn, 1992). For the first two months the student with learning disabilities was very hesitant about writing. He asked for constant teacher assistance and would not write unless a teacher worked closely with him. He wrote slowly and neatly even on first drafts. His first piece of writing was untitled and incomplete. He was insecure about working with other students and never volunteered to share his writing. His piece, entitled *Disneyworld,* demonstrated an understanding that you can write down what you really think. He included his own dog in a Disneyworld theme ("Goofy is a dog I like to play with but Goofy is not better than my dog."). The other students loved this story, and asked him to read it over and over again. Subsequently, he volunteered frequently to share his writing in front of the class. He had a flair for good endings and became the class expert on developing endings. For example, in *The Spooky Halloween,* he ended with "Halloween is nothing to play with." *Freddy Is In My Room* ended with "Give it up." The ending that was most appreciated by all was from *Part 4.* This story was about a child who, because he did not get a Christmas present, wanted to die. He went to the graveyard and started to lie down, but then said, "Holy macaroni not this dead." These case studies revealed that students across achievement groups benefit from participating in writing process. These students demonstrated gains on standardized writing measures as well as increased confidence and skills in their daily writing. Their teacher was most satisfied with their increased active learning style in the classroom.

Elements of the Writing Process

The elements of the writing process include prewriting, composing, revising, editing, and publishing. Authors do not pass through these elements as stages in the order they are listed. In fact, many authors circle back through previous elements and jump ahead to later ones while they are writing their drafts. For example, Steven realized after he read his draft to his friend Jacob that he needed to have more information about what submarines look like on the inside. He returned to the prewriting stage and checked out several books on submarines so he could complete his story.

Some elements of the writing process are not used at all. For example, Sheryl decided she was going to write about her first date with Jerry, and she used little of what we describe as prewriting as she began her writing. Mark discussed an idea for writing with his teacher and then, after writing a draft and reading it to a friend, decided he was unhappy with the topic and left it. These elements are not stages that a writer passes through but merely processes that are often used in writing.

In prewriting, a writer collects information about a topic through observing, remembering, interviewing, and reading. In composing, the author attempts to get ideas on paper in the form of a draft. This process tells the author what he or she knows and does not know. During revising, points are explored further, ideas are elaborated, and further connections are made. When the author is satisfied with the content, he or she edits the piece, reviewing it line by line to determine that each word is necessary. Punctuation, spelling, and other mechanical processes are checked. The final element is publication. If the piece is a good one for the author, it is published. Obviously, not all pieces are published.

Stires (1983) and Zaragoza and Vaughn (1992), who have used the writing process approach with students with learning disabilities, concluded that students with disabilities differ from other students in the degree to which components of the writing process are difficult for them. Many students with learning disabilities experience significant problems in editing and writing final copies because they have difficulty with mechanical skills such as spelling, punctuation, and handwriting. These students often produce well-developed stories but they are hard to read because of the mechanical errors. Other students with learning disabilities have difficulty organizing their first drafts and need to rethink sequencing and order during their revisions.

Englert and her colleagues (Englert, Raphael, Anderson, Anthony, and Stevens, 1991) taught youngsters the acronym "POWER" to assist them in using the sub-processes of the writing process.

P̲   Plan
O̲   Organize
W̲   Write
E̲   Edit/Editor
R̲   Revise

Prewriting: Getting Started

The first hurdle in starting the writing process approach with your students is topic selection.

Selecting Topics. "The most important thing children can learn is what they know and how they know it" (Graves, 1985, p. 39). This is the essence of topic choice. Once students can identify what they know and talk about it, they have completed the first step in topic selection.

Give each student and yourself a piece of paper. Say to them, "You know lots of things about yourself, about your family, and about your friends. You have hobbies and activities that you like to do. You have stories about things that have happened to you and/or to others you know. You have lots of things to share with others. I want you to make a list of things you would like to share with others through writing. Do not put them in any specific order—just write them as you think of them. You will not have to write on all of these topics. The purpose of this exercise is to think of as many topics as you can. I will give you

about ten minutes. Begin." Model the process for the students by writing as many topics as you can think of during the assigned time. When time is up, tell the students to pick a partner and share their topics with him or her. They may add any new topics they think of at this time. When they finish sharing their topics with their partner, share your list with the entire group and comment on topics you are looking forward to writing about as well as the topics you feel you may never write about. Ask for volunteer students to read their topic lists to the entire group. Now ask the students to select the three topics they are most interested in writing about and to write them at the top of their lists and then place their topic lists in their writing folders. Explain that these lists can be consulted later for possible topics. Also, if the students think of new topics they want to write about, they may add them to their lists. Finally, ask the students to select a topic and begin writing.

Topic selection is decided by the student. It is not decided by the teacher through story starters, picture cues, or other stimuli. Every student knows things and has stories to tell. We need to have confidence in them and give them an opportunity to discover what they know.

Problems in Topic Selection. There are two common problems in topic selection: difficulty in finding a topic and persistence in writing about the same topic.

Maintaining a supply of writing topics is difficult for some students and rarely a problem for others. When students tell you stories, ask them if the story generates a topic they want to write about. When students are reading or you are reading to them, ask if the reading has given them ideas for their own writing. If they were going to write the ending of this story, how would they do it? If they were going to continue this story, what would happen? If they were going to add characters to the story, what type of characters would they add? Would they change the setting?

You can also facilitate topic selection by presenting a range of writing styles including stories, factual descriptions, mysteries, and observations. Students often begin writing by telling personal experiences. Through your writing and the writing of other authors, the students can be introduced to a wide range of categories that can provide alternative topics. One teacher sent student reporters to other classrooms to interview students about what topics they thought would be interesting to write about.

Marynell's resource room contained a list of suggestions for what the students should do when they are stuck about a topic for writing (see Figure 6.4). A good example of how a friend can help was observed in Marynell's classroom.

Ruth Ann, a student in Marynell's classroom, was stuck for a topic. "What can I write about?" she asked as Marynell observed during writing period.

"Check on the poster, check in your folder, or ask a friend," Marynell suggested.

Ruth Ann got up and went over to another table where Cary was working on the first draft of a piece about a talking dishwasher. "Can you help me?" Ruth Ann asked. "I don't know what to write about."

■ **FIGURE 6.4** *Up in the Air for a Topic?*

- Check your folder and reread your idea list.
- Ask a friend to help you brainstorm ideas.
- Listen to others' ideas.
- Write about what you know: your experiences.
- Write a make-believe story.
- Write about a special interest or hobby.
- Write about how to do something.
- Think about how you got your last idea.

"Let me find my idea sheet so I can help you out," replied Cary. "And go get a piece of paper while I finish this." The rest of the interview between Cary and Ruth Ann is described in Apply the Concept 6.2.

In addition to difficulty in thinking of a topic, students often repeat the same topic. Many children with learning and behavior problems find security in repeating the same topic or theme in their writing. They like the control they have over the language, spelling, and content. Look carefully at their work and determine whether or not the stories are changing through vocabulary development, concept development, story development, or character development. It could be that the student is learning a great deal about writing even though the story content is changing very little. Continue to confer and ask questions about the student's writing. If you feel the student is not moving forward, then suggest a change in topic.

Another problem that may concern some teachers is when one student selects a topic and other students copy the idea. For example, Scott wrote a story about a talking dictionary that was stolen and how Scott endangered his life to recover the dictionary. The idea had special meaning for him since he generally misspelled about 50 percent of the words he used in his writing. Once the story was shared with his classmates, over half of the other children wrote about talking objects, including dishwashers, brooms, and shoes. These stories written by other students (repeating Scott's theme) served as a vehicle for several students to write better developed stories than they had written previously, and for one rather good storyteller, Cary, to expand the story format into a traditional murder mystery for her next story. Of course, when she shared her story, many students followed by copying the theme.

Brainstorming. Many students with learning and behavior problems begin writing without much planning about what they are going to write. They find that when they read their drafts aloud, others have difficulty understanding the story or following the sequence. Sometimes we need to teach students prewriting skills so the writing and rewriting stages are easier.

APPLY THE CONCEPT 6.2

A FRIEND HELPS WITH TOPIC SELECTION

Ruth Ann returned with a piece of blank paper, which she handed to Cary. Cary wrote Ruth Ann's name on the paper and underlined it. Then she conducted a rather sophisticated interview.

"Think of three ideas. Want to write about your first day of school?"

"I can't remember. That was five years ago," answered Ruth Ann.

"How about the first day in the learning lab?" continued Cary.

"I don't remember that either. It was over a year ago."

Looking at her idea sheet, Cary commented, "I'm writing about a talking dishwasher. Do you want to write about that?"

"Not really," replied Ruth Ann.

"Where do you go on vacations?" asked Cary.

"To Iowa, but I've already written about that."

"Well, have you ever been to a circus?" Cary pursued.

"No."

"How about a zoo?"

"The Los Angeles zoo," Ruth Ann answered.

"Do you want to write about that?" asked Cary.

"Yeah," remarked Ruth Ann, "that's a good idea."

Cary wrote the number 1 on the paper she had labeled with Ruth Ann's name, and wrote, "las

angels zoo" beside it. She remarked, "I don't know how to spell Los Angeles."

"Don't worry," Ruth Ann commented. "I can find that out when I start writing about it."

"OK, let's think up another idea. Have you ever ridden a horse?" asked Cary as she continued the interview.

"No," replied Ruth Ann.

"Do you have any pets?" asked Cary.

"Yea, I have a cat named Pierre."

"Do you want to write about him?" continued Cary.

"Yes, I could do that," replied Ruth Ann enthusiastically.

Cary wrote the number 2 on the paper and beside it wrote, "writing about your cat."

The interview continued, with Cary explaining that it is helpful to think up three ideas so that you have some choice when you decide what to write about. After more questioning, Ruth Ann decided it would be okay to write about a talking shoe, so Cary wrote down Ruth Ann's third idea. Then Cary helped Ruth Ann decide that she was first going to write about her cat. Cary wrote this idea at the bottom of the page and starred it to note that Ruth Ann had selected this topic. Cary ended the interview with the request, "Put this paper in your writing folder so that the next time you have to select a topic we'll already have two ideas thought up."

Students with learning disabilities are limited in text organization skills because they have difficulty categorizing ideas related to a specific topic, providing advanced organizers for the topic, and relating and extending ideas about the topic (Englert and Raphael, 1988).

In teaching the thinking that goes into a piece, teachers need to model their thinking as they move from topic selection to writing a first draft. Some teachers have found it helpful to teach this thinking process by writing their ideas in an organized structure (Bos, 1991; Thompkins and Friend, 1986). In

Ms. Schlegel's classroom this was referred to as brainstorm sheets; however, they have also been called structured organizers (Pehrsson and Robinson, 1985), semantic maps (Pearson and Johnson, 1978), and story frames or maps (Fowler and Davis, 1985). Although these visual organization devices have been used as aids to reading comprehension, they also serve to facilitate the writing process (Pehrsson and Robinson, 1985). Ms. Turk, a resource teacher who works with Ms. Schlegel, used a "think-aloud" technique to model how to use the brainstorm sheet presented in Apply the Concept 6.3. She drew a large

APPLY THE CONCEPT 6.3

SAMPLE BRAINSTORM SHEET

Name: Mrs. Turk

Date: 2/17

Working Title: Horseback Ride

Setting:

Where: Mt. Graham

start at trash dump

When: When I was ten years old

Who: Dad and I, also mom and brother

Dad and I were riding on trail.

Trail got bad.

Action: Dad's horse stumbled on rock.

Dad fell off + hurt his arm.

Finally he got on horse. I helped.

Rode to top of mt.

Mom met us. So did brother.

Went to hospital.

Ending: Dad was OK.

brainstorm sheet on the board and then introduced the brainstorming technique to the students.

Ms. Turk began, "I want to write a story about a time when I was really scared. So I decided to write about the time when I was about ten years old and my dad and I went for a horseback ride. He got hurt and I wasn't sure we'd get back to the car. There is so much to remember about this story that I am going to jot down a few ideas so that when I begin to write my story, I can remember them all and put them in order. To help me organize my ideas, I'm going to use a brainstorm sheet."

At this point, Ms. Turk explained the brainstorm sheet and the parts of a story. Through class discussion, the students identified a story they had written recently and each part in their story.

Ms. Turk continued modeling, using the brainstorm sheet. "I am going to call my story the 'Horseback Ride' for now. I may want to change the name later since it's easier for me to think of a title after I write the story. Well, it happened when we were on a trip to Mount Graham. So I'm going to write 'Mt. Graham' by 'Where.' I'm not sure how to spell Mt. Graham, but it doesn't matter that I spell it correctly now. I can find out later. Also, since the brainstorm sheet is for me, I don't have to write sentences—just ideas that will help me remember when I'm writing my first draft of the story." Ms. Turk continued to think aloud as she completed the sheet.

Ms. Turk demonstrated that the students did not have to fill in the brainstorm sheet in a linear fashion. Sometimes it is easier to fill out the ending first. She also demonstrated how, after she listed all the ideas under the action section, she could go back and number them in the order that made the most sense.

In subsequent lessons Ms. Turk demonstrated how to write a story from the brainstorm sheet. She also worked individually with students to write brainstorm sheets and to use them in their writing.

During the year several different brainstorm sheets were used in Ms. Turk's classroom. Figure 6.5 shows a brainstorm sheet that was developed for expository writing (writing that describes the facts or information about a subject area; often associated with social studies and science). However, the students also used this brainstorm sheet for stories. They wrote the title in the center circle, and information related to the setting, problem, action, and ending in the four other circles and their accompanying lines. Students also developed their own brainstorming sheets. For example, Cary combined topic

■ FIGURE 6.5 *Brainstorm Sheet*

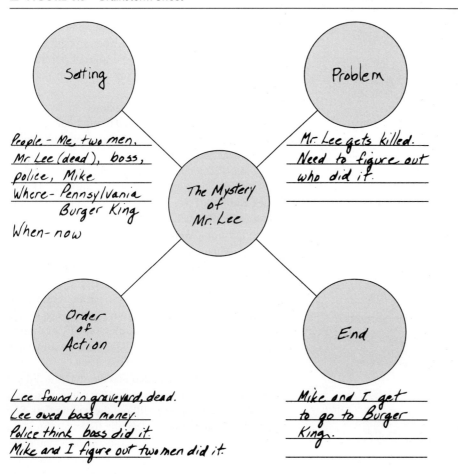

selection and brainstorming together and developed the brainstorm sheet presented in Figure 6.6. Her rationale was, "You really need to pretty well think through a piece before you decide if you want to write about it."

Teaching students to think about what they are going to say before they write is generally a helpful technique. However, completing a visual representation prior to writing may not facilitate writing for all students (see Apply the Concept 6.4).

Composing

Many students with learning and behavior problems begin the writing process here. They think of a topic and, without much planning, begin to write. They write ideas as they think of them and each idea they write serves as a stimulus for the next idea (Graham, Harris, and MacArthur, 1995). Thus, the goal is to guide students to be more reflective as they write (Graham, Harris, and MacArthur, 1995).

Some authors suggest using cue cards to assist students in writing better developed stories. A cue card used by Montague and Leavell (1994) asks students to consider these elements when composing: Where and when; character (have them think and feel just like real people); problem and plan; and story ending. Englert and her colleagues (Englert et al., 1991) developed think sheets to assist students in

■ **FIGURE 6.6** *Cary's Brainstorm Sheet*

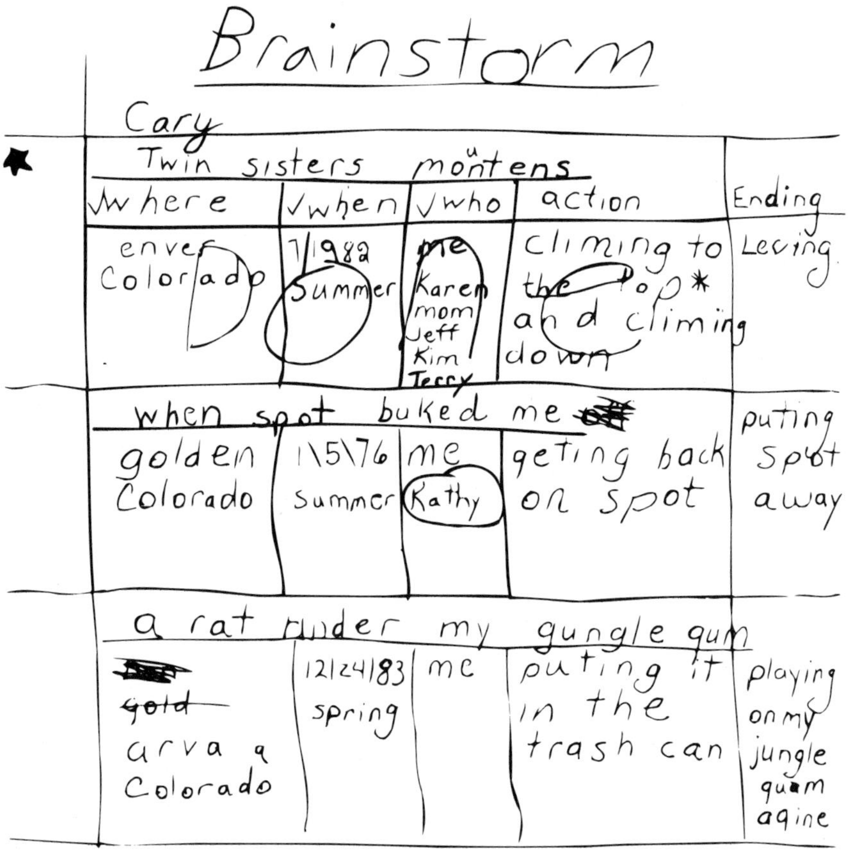

Brainstorm

Cary

★ Twin sisters mo̎ntens

Where	when	who	action	Ending
enver Colorado	7/1982 Summer	me Karen mom Jeff Kim ~~Terry~~	climing to the top * and climing down	Leving

when spot buked me

| golden Colorado | 1\5\76 Summer | me Kathy | geting back on spot | puting Spot away |

a rat nnder my gungle qum

| ~~gold~~ arva a Colorado | 12\24\83 spring | me | puting it in the trash can | playing on my jungle quam agine |

planning and then organizing their ideas prior to writing. Figure 6.7 presents the plan think sheet, and Figure 6.8 presents the organizing think sheet for the text structure associated with explanations.

Once children begin composing, sharing their work with others plays an important role. Children need time to read and discuss their pieces with individual students, small groups of students, and the teacher. The author's chair (Graves and Hansen, 1983) is a formal opportunity to share writing. Leila, a behaviorally disturbed fifth grader, signed up for "author's chair" early during the week. She thought her story about a dog who could fly was pretty good and she looked forward to reading it to the entire class. During "author's chair," she sat in a special chair in a circle, which included all students and the teacher. She enjoyed the attention from the group while she prepared to read. During her reading she could tell the story was going over well because the students were laughing and listening carefully. After the reading she asked them if they had any comments or questions. She called on several students who commented on sections of the story they liked and other students who asked questions. Mike wanted to know more about what the wings on the dog looked like. Rhonda wondered why the story ended the way it did. Leila answered the questions with the ownership of a professional author and made some decisions about parts she would change and how she would add more description about what the dog

APPLY THE CONCEPT 6.4

THE BIG PICTURE

"The most difficult thing for me to teach my students," said Ms. Zaragoza, "is to think about the ideas in their writing, not about whether or not they can spell the words correctly. My students thought good writing and good spelling were the same thing."

A common problem with poor writers is that they are overly concerned with the surface structure of their writing—the spelling, grammar, and punctuation. Many students with learning problems do not focus on thinking about their story. Their stories are often poorly organized and their ideas are disconnected and/or missing. These same students can *tell* you about the story, but have a hard time getting all of the ideas about the story in writing.

Following is the description of a procedure developed by Kucer (1986) to help poor writers focus on the "big picture" of writing:

1. Give students notecards and allow them to write possible topics on the cards (one topic per card). Students then share ideas about topics and make additions on their topic cards.
2. Students select a writing topic about which they would like to write.
3. Major ideas related to the writing topic are written on notecards. The major ideas may come from the student's knowledge and experience, or, if the writing is in a content area, the student may need to seek the assistance of class notes, books, and magazines. Major ideas are written as key concepts or thoughts rather than complete sentences.
4. Students share their major ideas about the topics with each other. They make any additions or comments about the ideas they feel will be helpful in writing about the topics.
5. Once major ideas are selected, they are organized in a meaningful sequence.
6. With their cards as a guide, students write their pieces.

---

looked like. Sharing, as Leila did in the "author's chair," motivates her to keep writing and will help her with rewriting.

Teachers often need to set rules about students' behavior when a classmate is sharing their work in the "author's chair." These rules may include: raise your hand, ask a question or make a positive comment, give feedback when asked. Apply the Concept 6.5 discusses using the writing process approach in a heterogeneous classroom.

Revising

Revising is a difficult task for all authors, especially beginning writers. Getting the entire message down on paper the first time is difficult enough; making changes so the piece is its best and can be understood by others is a most formidable task. Many authors need to go back to prewriting and obtain more information, or they spend time conferring with others to find out what parts of the piece are going over well

and what parts need additional work. It is also at this stage that some authors abandon the piece. They feel it can never be really good, and so they start again with a new idea.

Most students with learning and behavior problems have difficulty revising. They approach revision as a "housekeeping" task, making few or no substantive changes (MacArthur, Graham, and Schwartz, 1991). Many would like to move straight to publication, with little or no revision. Teachers often find it is best to allow students initially to move to publication without much revision, and then, through conferencing and reading the work of others, encourage students to see the benefits of revision. Ms. Gervasi, a middle school teacher, suggests modeling and patience. From her experience in using the writing-process approach with students, she finds they will eventually revise their pieces, but it usually takes time.

At first, their writing is more like a journal—a chance to write about how they feel and what is hap-

■ **FIGURE 6.7** *Plan Think Sheet*

PLAN

Name _____   Date _____

TOPIC: _____

WHO: Who am I writing for?
_____
_____

WHY: Why am I writing this?
_____
_____

WHAT: What do I know? (Brainstorm)
1. _____
2. _____
3. _____
4. _____
5. _____
6. _____
7. _____
8. _____

HOW: How can I group my ideas?

[   ]   [   ]
_____   _____
_____   _____

[   ]   [   ]
_____   _____
_____   _____

How will I organize my ideas?
___ Comparison/Contrast   ___ Problem/Solution
___ Explanation   ___ Other

Source: Cognitive Strategy Instruction in Writing Project, by C. S. Englert, T. E. Raphael, and L. M. Anderson, 1989, East Lansing, MI: Institute for Research on Teaching. Reprinted by permission.

pening in their relationships. It is an intimate exchange between them and the teacher, and eventually between them and selected students, and finally between them and a larger audience. This progression does not happen quickly, nor in this order. For some students, it takes the entire school year. Ms. Gervasi helps students with revising by demonstrating how she rewrites pieces. She even brings in

■ FIGURE 6.8   *Organization Think Sheet for Explanation of Text Structure*

Explanation Organization Form

What is
being
explained?

Materials/things you need?

Setting?

What are
the steps?

First,

Next,

Third,

Then,

Last.

Source: Cognitive Strategy Instruction in Writing Project, by C. S. Englert, T. E. Raphael, and L. M. Anderson, 1989, East Lansing, MI: Institute for Research on Teaching. Reprinted by permission.

letters she is writing to ex-students and discusses the revision process she uses. Ms. Gervasi writes a lot of poetry and shares her poetry with her students. Figure 6.9 shows a drawing and a poem written by an adolescent in response to a poem written by his teacher.

It is important during revising to focus on the message and content rather than mechanics. Telling

APPLY THE CONCEPT 6.5

CAN THE WRITING PROCESS APPROACH MEET THE NEEDS OF ALL STUDENTS IN A HETEROGENEOUS CLASSROOM?

A study that demonstrated the practicality and effectiveness of the writing process approach for meeting the diverse writing skill needs of students in a heterogeneous classroom was conducted by Zaragoza and Vaughn (1992). For six months they studied three second graders in a regular classroom setting as the writing process approach was implemented with their class.

One of the three youngsters in this study was a girl previously identified as low-achieving. The second youngster was a boy who had been diagnosed as having a learning disability in the areas of reading and written language and who had problems with distractibility and behavior as well. The third youngster was a gifted child from India; she had lived in the United States from the age of three and was highly verbal, cooperative, and self-motivated.

When the writing process approach was initiated, the writing skills of the low-achiever and those of the student with learning disabilities were so underdeveloped that it was difficult to read anything that either of them wrote. In addition, they had difficulty thinking about what they might write and were reluctant to put any words on paper. The gifted learner spelled imperfectly, but she enjoyed writing and had no difficulty expressing her thought in writing.

Progress was initially slow for both the low-achiever and the student with learning disabilities. However, as they witnessed their peers busily discussing and writing their ideas, and as their teacher worked with them to develop their own ideas for writing, they grew increasingly comfortable and confident in expressing those ideas in writing. Realizing that errors in spelling, punctuation, capitalization, and language did not matter in the initial stages of their writing encouraged the children to take risks. Mistakes could wait to be corrected during the final stages of the writing process.

All three children made gains in written expression, spelling, punctuation, usage (grammar), proofing (identifying errors), and dictation (writing correctly from dictation). In addition, a writing-attitude scale administered at the conclusion of the study showed that all three students developed positive attitudes toward writing. Their positive attitudes were further demonstrated by the fact that all three children continued to write during the summer following the six-month period of study.

Source: Adapted from N. Zaragoza and S. Vaughn (1992). The effects of process writing instruction on three second-grade students with different achievement needs. *Learning Disabilities Research and Practice, 7,* 184–193.

students to add at least three things to make your piece better, significantly improves writing (Graham, MacArthur, and Schwartz, 1995).

Hansen (1985) discusses the importance of not focusing on spelling until the student is finished with composing: "If writers think they should spell correctly on early drafts, they interfere with the main goal of their own writing: produce an interesting message (p. 185)." Hansen continues, "Further, if they think the spelling in every piece of writing must be corrected, they interfere with their own progress because the time they spend fixing the spelling on a deadend piece of writing would be better spent on a piece of writing that may turn out to be significant" (p. 185). Thus, whereas correcting mechanical errors such as spelling and punctuation may occur during the composing and revising process, it is not focused on until the next stage—editing.

Editing

In addition to editing their own work, students serve as editors for the work of their peers. This can work

■ **FIGURE 6.9**   *Sample Poem Written by Student*

Shyness

My Shyness is like the color white
It is wanting to tell a girl how you feel
Shyness is girls who look up with a smile
Shyness is wishing I could disappear
From a crowd

several ways. One way is to have students edit their own work first and then to ask a friend to edit it. Another possibility is to establish a class editor. The responsibility of the class editor is to read the material and search for mechanical errors. The role of the class editor could rotate so that every student has an opportunity to serve in that capacity.

Whereas revision focuses mainly on content, editing focuses mainly on mechanics. After the student and teacher are happy with the content, it is time to make corrections for spelling, capitalizing, punctuation, and language. Students are expected to circle words they are unsure how to spell, put boxes in places where they are unsure of the punctuation, and underline the sentences where they feel the language may not be correct. Students are not expected to correct all errors but are expected to correct known er-

rors. Figure 6.10 provides a poster that can be used in a classroom to remind students of the editing rules. Figure 6.11 depicts a form that can be included inside the students' folders to remind them of editing skills they know how to use.

Although many spelling, punctuation, and language modifications are made during writing and re-

■ **FIGURE 6.10**   *Editing Rules*

(Circle) misspelled words.

Put a box around punctuation.

Underline writing that doesn't sound so good.

Add a ∧ to insert a word or phrase.

Add a ①∧ with a number to insert a sentence.

■ **FIGURE 6.11**   *Editing Skills I Know*

Spelling

1. done
2. was
3. from
4. come
5. girl
6. because
7. what
8. where
9. children
10. playground

Punctuation

1. Put a period at the end of a sentence.
2. Put a question mark at the end of an asking sentence.

Capitalization

1. Capitalize the first letter of a sentence.
2. Capitalize the first letter of a person's name.
3. Capitalize the name of a town.

vising, when students edit they focus solely on mechanical errors. Often they need to read the text for each type of error. First, they read the text, looking for spelling difficulties; next, they read the text, looking for punctuation and capitalization difficulties; and finally, they read the text, looking for language problems such as noun-verb agreement. Young students may not know what noun-verb agreement is, so they should simply look for sentences that do not "sound right" when they read them aloud.

Publishing

Not all writing is published; often only one in five or six pieces is published. What does it mean to have a piece published? A piece is prepared in some way that it can be read and shared by others. Often this is in the form of books that have cardboard binding decorated with contact paper or scraps of wallpaper. Sometimes these books include a picture of the author, a description of the author, and a list of books published by the author.

Young children who are writing shorter pieces may be publishing every two weeks, whereas older students who spend more time composing and revising would publish less frequently. Why publish? Publishing is a way of confirming a student's hard work and sharing the piece with others. Writing requires an audience, and periodically we need to share what we write. It is important for *all* students to publish—not just the best authors. Publishing is a way of involving others in school and home with the students' writings.

Aspects of the Writing Process

The Writing Conference

Conferring, which occurs throughout the writing process, is the heart of the writing procedure. The student comes to the writing conference prepared to read his or her piece, to describe problem areas, and to be asked questions. When students confer with the teacher, they know they will be listened to and responded to. The teacher's nonverbal and verbal interactions communicate to them that he or she wants to listen and help.

Students also know that they will be asked challenging questions about their work. Questions are not asked in a rapid-fire sequence with little time for the student to formulate answers. Instead, questions should be carefully selected and enough time should be allowed for the student to respond. Conferences need to focus on specific areas and should not cover all parts of the writing. During the conference with the author of "My best football game" (see Apply the Concept 6.6), the teacher realized there were many problems with the piece of writing. She was aware of grammatical, spelling, and punctuation errors. She was also aware the story rambled, did not provide sufficient details, and lacked the voice of the author. However, she was ecstatic that this fourteen-year-old student had produced a piece of writing that he was excited about. Apply the Concept 6.7 presents the conference the teacher had with the student.

Some key points about conferring with students are:

1. Follow the lead of the child during the conference. Do not attempt to get the writer to write about a topic because it is of interest to you or to write the story the way you would write it.
2. Listen and accept what the child says. When you talk more than the writer during conferences you are being too directive.
3. Ask questions the student can answer.
4. Ask questions that teach. (Apply the Concept 6.8 illustrates a conference in which the teacher asks questions that teach.)
5. Conferences should be frequent and brief. Although conferences can range from thirty seconds to ten minutes, most of them last only two to three minutes.

During conferences we listen to what students have written and we tell them what we hear. We and other students make comments and suggestions based on what we have learned from writing. As Nancy Atwell (1985) suggests, we can only offer—writers may reject our advice.

APPLY THE CONCEPT 6.6

SAMPLE STUDENT WRITING

"My best football game"

Football is my favrite game I like to play it even when I was little I played for a good team the bandits and one game we played against Macarther school and it started off with us 0 and them 7 and then the game was tied 7 to 7 and then it was time for me to sit on the bench and the score was 7-14 we was winning soon they told me to go back into the game it was getting close to the end and we wanted to win they said it was my turn to run a play and so I ran fast down the feild after the ball was Mike and I look back and see the ball coming right at me and I thoght I was going to miss it but I kept looking at it and after I watched it I reached up and pulled the ball down and I kept on running and we won the game 7 to 21.

Establishing a Writing Community

Writing requires trust. For students to write well within their classroom, an environment of mutual trust and respect is essential. The writer must also be able to depend on the predictability of the classroom structure. Establishing a writing community requires the following:

1. *Write every day for at least thirty minutes.* Students need time to think, write, discuss, rewrite, confer, revise, talk, read, and write some more. Good writing takes time.
2. *Encourage students to develop areas of expertise.* At first, students will write broadly about what they know. However, with encouragement, they can become class experts in a particular area, subject, or writing form. It will take them time and inducement before they discover their own writing "turf."
3. *Keep students' writing in folders.* Folders should include all writing as documentation of what each student knows and has accomplished. This means students' work stays with them during the year. Work can be referred to for illustration of gains made, to indicate skills learned, and to demonstrate range of topic. Selected pieces from the year should be with the student for the next year.
4. *The teacher writes.* Teachers write outside of the classroom and with the students in the classroom. Using an overhead or easel, teachers may share with the students how they compose. Just

APPLY THE CONCEPT 6.7

CONFERENCING WITH THE AUTHOR OF "MY BEST FOOTBALL GAME"

Teacher: "Mark, this football game was a special one for you. I bet you have a lot of feelings about this game. What are some of your feelings about this game?"

Mark: "I felt good."

Teacher: "Did you feel good like when you remember your homework or was it stronger than that?"

Mark: "It was stronger. I felt great. Like I was a hero or something."

Teacher: "Like a hero?"

Mark: "Yeah, like in the movies I really saved the game. Well, I guess not really saved the game because we were already winning. But it was, like, cause I made the last touchdown it really said something."

Teacher: "What do you think it said?"

Mark: "It said, hey, watch out cause I'm good. Also, that we won and I scored the final points. It was great."

Teacher: "What could you do so the reader of your piece would know all of the things you just told me?"

Mark: "I guess I could include more about how I felt and all."

Teacher: "How could you do that? Where would it go?"

The teacher decided it was too early to focus on mechanical errors such as spelling and punctuation. Besides being discouraging to Mark, focusing too early on mechanical errors sidetracks the writer from the story. After the author's story is complete, then working on mechanical errors can begin.

---

as students share their writing with each other, the teacher shares his or her writing with the students.

5. *Share writing.* Conclude the writing time with an opportunity for students to read their writing to others and to exchange comments and questions.

6. *Read to the students.* Share and discuss books, poems, and other readings. There is a strong connection between reading and writing.

7. *Expand the writing community outside of the classroom.* Place published books by students in your class in the library for use by other students and allow students to share their writing with other classes. Encourage authors from other classrooms to visit and read their writings.

8. *Develop children's capacity to evaluate their own work.* Students need to develop their own goals and document their progress toward them. By conferring with the teacher, they will learn methods for evaluating their own work.

9. *Slow the pace.* Graves (1985) says, "Teachers need to slow down so kids can hurry up." Teachers need to be patient when they ask questions, allowing the students time to answer.

10. *Considerations for culturally and linguistically diverse students.* Students from diverse cultures whose first language is other than English often have specific needs in writing. With a few minor adjustments, teachers can create classroom communities that promote their success and learning. See Apply the Concept 6.9 for suggestions.

The writing process approach to instruction with children who have special needs requires time—time to set up the classroom, follow the progress of students, confer with students, and teach skills. More importantly, it requires time each day for the students to write. (See Apply the Concept 6.10.) Suzanne, a teacher of emotionally disturbed adolescents who has used the writing process approach for the first time this year, comments, "Yes, it takes a great deal of time but it is worth it. The students want to write. They

APPLY THE CONCEPT 6.8

CONFERENCING: FOLLOWING THE LEAD OF THE STUDENT

During conferences, the teacher listens to what students say, follows the lead of the students, and asks questions that teach.

Teacher: "How's it going, Karin?"

Karin: "Not very good. I don't know what to write about."

Teacher: "You are having trouble with a topic?"

Karin: "I was going to write about how I want to go and live with my real mom again but I don't know what to say. All I do is write that I want to live with my real mom and then the story is over."

Teacher: "It's hard to think of what else might go in the story?"

Karin: "Well, yeah. I guess I could tell why, but I don't know why, I just want to."

Teacher: "Would it be any easier to get started if you told the story as though it were about someone else?"

Karin: "Like I could tell about a kid who wanted to go and live with her real mom. Then I could tell it like a story."

Teacher: "What are some of the things you might write if you told the story this way?"

have even started their own school newsletter. Best of all, they are seeing the connection between reading and writing. I feel it is worth the time."

Using Computers to Facilitate Writing

The use of word processors, spelling checks, and speech synthesizers to facilitate writing effectiveness for students with learning disabilities has been well documented (MacArthur, 1988; Morocco, Dalton, and Tivnan, 1992; Morocco and Neuman, 1986). Of particular importance is the way these tools can be used to assist students whose writing or motor skills interfere with their ability to develop independent writing skills. The computer can also provide public visibility of the writing by displaying it on the monitor. This provides easy discussion between students and teachers and allows for immediate and facile editing (Zorfass, Corley, and Remz, 1994). When a computer-based speech recognition program was provided to college students with learning disabilities, the students performed significantly better on tasks of written expression than those without the speech recognition program, and as well as

those who were provided an assistant (Higgins and Raskind, 1995).

Computers facilitate writing for students with learning problems because they:

— make revising and editing easier
— increase the amount and quality of revision completed
— provide spell checking features
— produce neat printed copies that enhance readability
— allow for easy error correction (MacArthur, Graham, Schwartz, and Schafer, 1995)

TEACHING SPELLING

Most students with learning and behavior disorders need specific instruction in the mechanics of writing, such as spelling and handwriting.

Manuel hates spelling and finds it the most frustrating part of writing. He is an eighth-grade student who is adjusting to the transition from a self-

APPLY THE CONCEPT 6.9

CONSIDERATIONS FOR CULTURALLY AND LINGUISTICALLY DIVERSE STUDENTS

Creating a learning community in the classroom that provides opportunities for all students to succeed is essential to promoting effective written expression. A few guidelines follow:

- Have high expectations for all students. Teachers demonstrate respect and provide opportunities when they treat each student as an able writer and provide the support necessary to assure their success.
- Allow students to write about topics they know and have experienced. Students with diverse backgrounds and experiences should be viewed as possessing a rich source of material for writing. Students benefit when they are encouraged to tap into their backgrounds and experiences and to share them with others.
- Allow students to teach all of us about their backgrounds and experiences through their writing. Students' writing can be viewed as an opportunity for them to better inform us about themselves, their families and communities and their interpretations of them. Students will want to write when they perceive that their writing has a purpose and is instructive to others.

- Encourage parent or family involvement in writing. Parents and/or family members often have a rich bank of stories and experiences that they are willing to share with the class if encouraged to do so. These experiences and stories can provide background for students' writing or can be used to prompt stories and ideas.
- Create a classroom setting that is culturally compatible. The social organization of the classroom can facilitate or impair the written expression of students from diverse cultures. Whole class instructional formats with high expectations for students to volunteer to answer questions may not be compatible with their cultural backgrounds. Read and ask questions about the cultures of the students in your classroom so you can establish a writing lab that is responsive to their learning styles.
- Use materials, stories, and books that are culturally relevant. Read stories about a range of cultures to students. Encourage students to exchange stories that are culturally familiar. Provide examples of cultures that are similar and different from the ones represented in your classroom.

contained classroom for emotionally disturbed students to a resource room in a junior high setting. He has been involved in the writing process approach for the past two years and has learned to use writing to express his feelings, convey information, and create stories. Manuel is proud of the way his writing has improved and he often shares his stories with others. But he has difficulty with spelling. Manuel has learned to use inventive spelling (spelling words the way they sound or the way he thinks they are spelled) to aid in getting his ideas on paper, but he has difficulty editing because he is unable to detect or correct most of his spelling errors. Manuel, like many stu-

dents with learning and behavior disorders, needs specialized instruction in spelling in order to be a successful writer.

Spelling is an important tool in our society. Many people measure one's intelligence or education by the ability to spell. Spelling is particularly difficult in the English language because there is not a one-to-one correspondence between spoken words and written words. We learn to spell many words by remembering the unique combination or order of letters that produce the correct spelling of that word. Spelling facilitates the writing process by freeing the writer to concentrate on content. Although most

APPLY THE CONCEPT 6.10

TEN POINTERS FOR TEACHING WRITING TO STUDENTS WITH SPECIAL LEARNING NEEDS

1. *Allocate adequate time for writing.* Adequate time is a necessary but not sufficient criterion for improving the writing skills of special learners. Students who merely spend ten to fifteen minutes a day practicing the craft of writing are not spending adequate time to improve their skills. Students need a minimum of thirty minutes of time for writing every day.

2. *Provide a range of writing tasks.* Writing about what students know best—self-selected topic—is the first step in writing. After students' skills improve, the range of writing tasks should broaden to include problem solving, writing games, and a variety of writing tasks.

3. *Create a social climate that promotes and encourages writing.* Teachers set the tone through an accepting, encouraging manner. Conferences between students, students and teachers, and students and other persons in the school are conducted to provide constructive feedback on their writing and to provide an audience to share what is written.

4. *Integrate writing with other academic subjects.* Writing can be integrated with almost every subject that is taught. This includes using writing as a means of expression in content area subjects such as social studies and science as well as part of an instructional activity with reading and language arts.

5. *Focus on the processes central to writing.* These processes include prewriting activities, writing, and rewriting activities.

6. *During the writing phase focus on the "higher order" task of composing, and attend to the basic elements of spelling and punctuation after the writing is complete.* With some students, their mechanics of writing are so poor that they interfere with their ability to get ideas down on paper successfully. With these students, focus first on some of the basic elements so that the writing process can be facilitated.

7. *Teach explicit knowledge about characteristics of good writing.* The implicit knowledge about writing needs to be made explicit. For example, different genres and their characteristics need to be discussed and practiced.

8. *Teach skills that aid "higher level" composing.* These skills include conferencing with teachers and peers, and strategy instruction. Strategy instruction may provide guidelines for brainstorming, sentence composition, or evaluating the effectiveness of the written piece.

9. *Ask students to identify goals for improving their writing.* Students can set realistic goals regarding their progress in writing. These goals can focus on prewriting, writing, and/or rewriting. Both the students and the teacher can provide feedback as to how successful the students have been in realizing their goals.

10. *Do not use instructional practices that are not associated with improved writing for students.* Several examples of instructional practice not associated with improved writing are grammar instruction, diagramming sentences, and overemphasis on students' errors.

Source: Adapted from S. Graham and K. R. Harris (1988). Instructional recommendations for teaching writing to exceptional students, *Exceptional Children, 54*(6):506–512.

students with learning disabilities have spelling difficulties (Johnson and Myklebust, 1967), spelling is often difficult even for those without a learning disability. Most beginning writers identify spelling as the key problem they need to solve in writing (Graves, 1983). Many good readers are poor spellers, and almost all poor readers are poor spellers (Carpenter and Miller 1982; Frith, 1980).

Students who have a very difficult time learning to read perform worse than average readers on tasks of phonological awareness (see Phonology in Chapter 3) (e.g., Vellutino and Scanlon, 1987). Ehri (1989) suggests that they have phonological difficulties because they have not learned to read and spell. Thus, their lack of phonological awareness is due to this deficit in their learning and is not a *cause* of their reading and spelling difficulties.

This section will focus on teaching spelling to students who have learning difficulties. Techniques for analyzing students' spelling errors will be discussed first, followed by a discussion of principles to be applied in developing spelling programs, approaches to teaching spelling, and what the research has to say about teaching spelling.

Spelling Instruction

The first step in developing an appropriate spelling program is to determine the type and pattern of the students' spelling errors. After completing an error analysis, a spelling approach based on students' needs can be implemented.

Error Analysis
Error analysis should be done by using both dictated spelling tests and a student's written work. Random errors do not occur in the spelling of most students with learning disabilities. They are consistent in the types of misspellings to which they are prone (De-Master, Crossland, and Hasselbring, 1986).

When Manuel and his teacher, Mr. Larkin, attempted to develop Manuel's spelling program, they began by selecting samples of Manuel's written work, which included writing he created and work written from dictation. Mr. Larkin examined these pieces to determine if there was a pattern to Manuel's spelling errors. He asked himself the following questions about Manuel's spelling:

1. Is he applying mistaken rules?
2. Is he applying rules that assist him in remembering spellings?
3. Is he making careless errors on words he can spell?
4. Is he spelling words correctly in isolation but not in context?
5. Are there frequently used words that he is consistently misspelling?

After examining Manuel's work and answering these questions, Mr. Larkin discovered:

1. Manuel did not apply the "ing" rule appropriately. For example, *run* became *runing*.
2. Manuel did not use the spelling rule "*i* before *e* except after *c*." For example, he spelled *believe* as *beleive* and *piece* as *peice*.
3. He was inconsistent in spelling words. He would spell them correctly in one piece of written work but not in another.
4. He spelled several words correctly on spelling tests but not in context.
5. He misspelled many frequently used words, such as *there, was, because, somewhere, very,* and *would.*

After answering the questions, Mr. Larkin examined Manuel's work to look for the following error patterns.

1. Additions of unneeded letters (e.g., *boxxes*)
2. Omissions of letters (e.g., *som*)
3. Reflections of mispronunciations (e.g., *ruf* for *roof*)
4. Reflections of dialect (e.g., *sodar* for *soda*)
5. Reversals of whole words (e.g., *eno* for *one*)
6. Reversals of consonant order (e.g., *cobm* for *comb*)
7. Reversals of consonant or vowel directionality (e.g., *Thrusday* for *Thursday*)
8. Phonetic spellings of nonphonetic word parts (e.g., *site* for *sight*)
9. Neographisms, which are spellings that don't resemble the word (e.g., *sumfin* for *something*)
10. Combinations of error patterns

In addition to examining Manuel's work, Mr. Larkin interviewed and observed Manuel to determine what strategies he used when he was unable to spell a word and whether he used any corrective or proofreading strategies after he wrote. Mr. Larkin observed Manuel's writing and then asked him the following questions:

1. *When you finish writing a piece, what do you do?* (Mr. Larkin was attempting to determine if Manuel rereads for spelling errors.)

2. *If you are writing and do not know how to spell a word, what do you do?* (Mr. Larkin was attempting to determine what, if any, strategies Manuel used. Did he use invented spelling to facilitate the writing process and underline the word so he could check the spelling later? Did he stop and try to visualize the word or look for how it was spelled in another location? Did he continue writing and go back later to check the spelling?)

Mr. Larkin discovered that Manuel used few strategies to check or recall spelling when he was writing. In addition to teaching and rehearsing spelling rules, Manuel needed to learn and apply strategies for improving his spelling. After error analysis, intervention included discussing with Manuel the types of errors he was making, teaching him proofreading skills, teaching him techniques for remembering the correct spelling of words, and teaching him one of the spelling approaches (discussed in a later section of this chapter, Spelling Approaches). Before looking at specialized approaches to teaching spelling to students with learning and behavior disorders, we will first examine traditional approaches to spelling instruction.

Traditional Spelling Instruction

Spelling is taught in most classrooms through an integrated whole language approach or the use of spelling basal programs. Typical spelling basals included a prescribed list of weekly words to be mastered by all students. The usual procedure is that a pretest occurs on Monday, followed on Tuesday by a description of the spelling theme (e.g., long *e* words, homophones, *au* words, etc.). Wednesday and Thursday are usually assignments from the text that students work on independently. These assignments usually include dictionary activities, sentence or paragraph writing using the spelling words, writing the words a designated number of times, using the words in sentences, stories, or crossword puzzles, and so on. Friday is usually designated for the post-test in spelling. Although variations on this format occur, such as the teacher who attempts to individualize the spelling program, most classrooms follow a procedure similar to this.

How effective is this procedure for teaching spelling to students with learning disabilities? What other procedures might need to be considered to develop effective spelling strategies for students with learning problems? Spelling practices used in most classrooms are based more on tradition than they are on research (Gettinger, 1984; Gordon, Vaughn, and Schumn, 1993). For students with learning difficulties, the introduction of all the words at once, often words that are not in the students' reading vocabularies, and the lack of systematic practice and specific feedback make spelling difficult if not impossible for most. Before discussing specific strategies for teaching spelling to students with learning disabilities, the following section will discuss the role of phonics rules in teaching spelling.

Phonics Rules for Spelling

How much emphasis should be given to teaching phonics rules to improve spelling? There is probably no area of the language arts curriculum that has been more carefully reviewed, researched, and debated than spelling. At the heart of many of the debates is the efficacy of using a phonics approach to teaching spelling. Some researchers suggest that a phonics approach increases spelling ability (Baker, 1977; Gold, 1976; Thompson, 1977), whereas others argue that students learn the rules without direct instruction in phonics (Schwartz and Doehring, 1977), and still others insist that intensive phonics instruction is not necessary (Grottenthaler, 1970; Personkee and Yee, 1971; Warren, 1970). Recent evidence suggests that students who are taught spelling alongside a code-based (phonics) reading instruction improve in both spelling and word reading (O'Connor and Jenkins, 1995). At least for young children, a code-based approach to reading and spelling is likely to be both necessary and helpful.

Since there is a lack of consistency with phonics rules, primary emphasis should be given to basic spelling vocabulary with supplemented instruction in basic phonics rules (Graham and Miller, 1979). According to Graham and Miller (1979), the phonetic skills that should be taught include base words, prefixes, suffixes, consonants, consonant blends, digraphs, and vowel sound-symbol associations.

The important relationship between rhyming and spelling is illustrated in Apply the Concept 6.11.

Principles for Teaching Spelling to Students with Learning Difficulties

Several principles should be included in any spelling approach used with students who have learning problems.

Teach in Small Units. Teach three words a day rather than four or five a day (or fifteen at the beginning of the week). In a study (Bryant, Drabin, and Gettinger, 1981) in which the number of spelling words allocated each day to students with learning disabilities was controlled, higher performance and less distractibility and less variance in overall performance were obtained from the group with learning disabilities assigned three words a day, when compared with groups assigned four and five words a day.

Teach Spelling Patterns. If the spelling lists each week are based on spelling patterns (Bloodgood, 1991), students have a better chance of learning and remembering them. A sample of several word lists based on patterned spelling follow:

List 1	List 2	List 3
cat	am	aim
bat	slam	claim
rat	clam	chain

fat	tram	rain
sat	tam	train
can	Pam	gain
fan	same	regain
ran	fame	brain
man	tame	pain
tan	blame	afraid
	flame	braid
	frame	

Zutell (1993) and Graham, Harris, and Loynachan (1996) recommend the use of contrast words to assist in identifying and teaching spelling patterns. Thus, the spelling patterns that are taught in the sample word lists 1–3 would be supplemented with several words that do not fit the pattern. Students would then be encouraged to identify the pattern and sort the words that do not fit.

Provide Sufficient Practice and Feedback. Give students opportunities to practice the words each day with feedback. Many teachers provide this by having students work with spelling partners who ask them their words and provide immediate feedback. The following methods can be used for self-correction and practice. Fold a paper into five columns. Write the correctly spelled words in the first column. The student studies one word, folds the column back, and writes the word in the second column. The student then checks his or her spelling with the correctly spelled word in column one. Folding the column back, the student writes the word in the third column. The student continues writing the word until it is spelled correctly three times. The student then moves to the next word. He or she continues until the word is spelled correctly three times in a row. This procedure should not be confused with spelling assignments that require the student to write the assigned spelling words a designated number of times. These procedures are often ineffective because the student does not attend to the details of the spelling word as a whole, the student often writes the word in segments, and he or she usually copies rather than writes from memory. The student also fails to check words after each writing, sometimes resulting in words

APPLY THE CONCEPT 6.11 ▬▬▬▬▬▬▬▬▬▬▬▬▬▬▬

RELATIONSHIP BETWEEN RHYMING AND SPELLING

Rhyming and alliteration are positively and significantly related to progress in spelling (Bradley and Bryant, 1985). A possible explanation is that rhyming teaches students to identify phonological segments and it demonstrates how words can be grouped together according to common sounds. Students' participation at an early age, prior to school, in rhyming games and activities may be an important prerequisite to spelling success.

being practiced incorrectly. Adding peer tutoring can help alleviate these problems (see Apply the Concept 6.12).

Select Appropriate Words. The most important strategy for teaching spelling is that the students already should be able to read the word and know its meaning. Spelling should not focus on teaching the students to read and know the meaning of the word. Selection of spelling words should be based on the students' reading and meaning vocabularies. Ideally, high frequency words should be used (Graham and Voth, 1990).

Teach Spelling Through Direct Instruction. Incidental learning in spelling is primarily reserved for good spellers. Spelling words can be selected from the students' reading or written words or can be part of a programmed text, such as lists provided in basal readers. Direct instruction includes mastery of specific words each day, individualized instruction, and continual review.

Use Instructional Language. The language of instruction, or the dialogue between the teacher and the student, is critical to success in spelling, particularly for youngsters with learning and behavior problems. Gerber and Hall (1989) indicate that teachers' language provides a structure that calls attention to critical relationships within and between words and also isolates critical letter sequences. For example, "You wrote "nife"; however, the word *knife* starts with a silent letter. It is very unusual and you just have to re-

member that it is there. Think about the letter *K* as looking like an open jacknife and remember that the word *knife* starts with a *K*."

Maintain Previously Learned Words. Maintenance of spelling words requires previously learned words to be assigned as review words, interspersed with the learning of new spelling words. Previously learned words need to be frequently reviewed to be maintained. Gettinger, Bryant, and Fayne (1982) conducted a study with students with learning disabilities to determine the efficacy of a spelling procedure designed to practice the principles of teaching smaller units, sufficient and distributed practice, and maintenance of words learned. Experimental group students with learning disabilities were able to reach an 80 percent criterion on more of the spelling words and were able to spell 75 percent of the transfer words when compared with a control group of students with learning disabilities involved in a spelling program that did not emphasize these principles.

Teach for Transfer of Learning. After spelling words have been mastered, provide opportunities for students to see and use spelling words in context.

Motivate Students to Spell Correctly. Using games and activities, selecting meaningful words, and providing examples of the use and need for correct spelling are strategies that help motivate students and give them a positive attitude about spelling (Graham and Miller, 1979).

APPLY THE CONCEPT 6.12

PEER TUTORING AND SPELLING

Use of *peer tutors* to teach spelling can be helpful in improving spelling for the tutors and the tutees. When a peer tutoring system was used with a mainstreamed student with learning disabilities and a good speller from the classroom, the spelling performance of the student with learning disabilities improved and both students rated the peer tutoring system favorably (Mandoli, Mandoli, and McLaughlin, 1982). To increase effectiveness, peer tutors should be trained to implement the spelling approach most suitable for the target student.

Include Dictionary Training. As part of the spelling program, dictionary training should be developed, which includes alphabetizing, identifying target words, and locating the correct definition when several are provided. Some students can develop a personal spelling dictionary to assist with their writing (Scheuremann, Jacobs, McCall, and Knies, 1994).

Spelling Approaches

There are many approaches to teaching spelling. No one approach has been proven to be superior to others with all students with learning disabilities. Some students learn effectively with a multisensory approach, such as the Fernald method, and others learn best with a combination of several approaches. The following are several approaches to teaching spelling, all of which make use of the principles discussed in the previous section. Apply the Concept 6.12 describes the effects of peer tutoring as a procedure for teaching spelling.

Test-Study-Test Method. This method of learning spelling words is superior to the study-test method (Fitzsimmons and Loomer, 1978; Yee, 1969). In using the test-study-test method, students are first tested on a list of words and then instructed to study the missed words. Strategies are taught for recalling the correct spelling of these words. These strategies often include verbal mediation—saying the word while writing it or spelling it aloud to a partner. After

instruction and study, students are then retested over the words. Using this process, students then correct their own spelling test, which is an important factor in learning to spell.

Several word study techniques that can be applied when using the test-study-test method are presented in Figure 6.12.

Visualization Approach. This approach to spelling teaches students to visualize the correct spelling as a means to recall. The visualization approach uses the following procedures:

1. The teacher writes a word that the child can read but cannot spell on the board or on a piece of paper.
2. The student reads the word aloud.
3. The student reads the letters in the word.
4. The student writes the word on paper.
5. The teacher asks the student to look at the word and "take a picture of it" as if his or her eyes were a camera.
6. The teacher asks the student to close his or her eyes and spell the word aloud, visualizing the letters while spelling it.
7. The teacher asks the student to write the word and check the model for accuracy.

The Five-Step Word-Study Strategy. This strategy requires the student to learn and rehearse the following five steps and practice them with the teacher

■ **FIGURE 6.12** *Word Study Techniques*

Fitzgerald Method (Fitzgerald, 1951a)

1. Look at the word carefully.
2. Say the word.
3. With eyes closed, visualize the word.
4. Cover the word and then write it.
5. Check the spelling.
6. If the word is misspelled, repeat steps 1–5.

Horn Method 1 (E. Horn, 1919)

1. Look at the word and say it to yourself.
2. Close your eyes and visualize the word.
3. Check to see if you were right. (If not, begin at step 1).
4. Cover the word and write it.
5. Check to see if you were right. (If not, begin at step 1).
6. Repeat steps 4 and 5 two more times.

Horn Method 2 (E. Horn, 1954c)

1. Pronounce each word carefully.
2. Look carefully at each part of the word as you pronounce it.
3. Say the letters in sequence.
4. Attempt to recall how the word looks, then spell the word.
5. Check this attempt to recall.
6. Write the word.
7. Check this spelling attempt.
8. Repeat the above steps if necessary.

Visual-Vocal Method (Westerman, 1971)

1. Say word.
2. Spell word orally.
3. Say word again.
4. Spell word from memory four times correctly.

Gilstrap Method (Gilstrap, 1962)

1. Look at the word and say it softly. If it has more than one part, say it again, part by part, looking at each part as you say it.
2. Look at the letters and say each one. If the word has more than one part, say the letters part by part.
3. Write the word without looking at the book.

Fernald Method Modified

1. Make a model of the word with a crayon, grease pencil, or magic marker, saying the word as you write it.
2. Check the accuracy of the model.
3. Trace over the model with your index finger, saying the word at the same time.
4. Repeat step 3 five times.
5. Copy the word three times correctly.
6. Copy the word three times from memory correctly.

Cover-and-Write Method

1. Look at word. Say it.
2. Write word two times.
3. Cover and write one time.
4. Check work.
5. Write word two times.
6. Cover and write one time.
7. Check work.
8. Write word three times.
9. Cover and write one time.
10. Check work.

Source: S. Graham and L. Miller, "Spelling Research and Practice: A Unified Approach," *Focus on Exceptional Children, 13*(2) (1980): 11. Reprinted with permission.

and then alone. The steps are (1) say the word, (2) write and say the word, (3) check the word, (4) trace and say the word, (5) write the word from memory and check, and (6) repeat the five steps. When the student learns this technique the teacher models the procedure, then the student practices the procedure with assistance from the teacher, and finally the student demonstrates proficiency in the application of the procedure without teacher assistance. This procedure has been effectively used with elementary students with learning disabilities (Graham and Freeman, 1986).

Johnson and Myklebust Technique. Johnson and Myklebust (1967) suggest working from recognition to partial recall to total recall when teaching new spelling words. Recognition can be taught by showing the students a word and then writing the word with several unrelated words, asking the students to circle the word they previously saw. The task can gradually be made more difficult by writing distracting words that more closely resemble the target word. In teaching partial recall, the correct word can be written with missing spaces for completing the spelling under it. For example.

with

w __ th

wit __

__ ith

wi __ __

w __ __ __

__ __ __ __

Total recall requires the students to write the word after it is pronounced by another or write the word in a sentence. This approach gives repeated practice and focuses the students on the relevant details of the word. Johnson and Myklebust (1967) also suggest that when initial spelling tests are given, the teacher may need to say the word very slowly, emphasizing each syllable. As students learn to spell the words correctly, the test is given in a normal voice and rate.

Cloze Spelling Approach. This is referred to as the cloze spelling approach because the student needs systematically to supply missing letters in much the same way the students supply words in the cloze reading procedure. The cloze spelling approach uses a four-step process for teaching students to spell words.

1. *Look-study.* The student is shown the word on a card. He or she looks at the word and studies the letters and their order.

2. *Write missing vowels.* The student is shown the same word on a card with blanks where the vowels usually appear. The student writes the entire word, supplying the missing vowel(s).

3. *Write missing consonants.* The student is shown the word with blanks where the consonants usually appear. The student writes the entire word, supplying the missing consonant(s).

4. *Write the word.* The student writes the word without the model.

Fernald Method. Fernald (1943) felt that most spelling approaches were useful for the extremely visual student but not for those students who need auditory and kinesthetic input for learning. Because poor spellers are characterized as having poor visual imagery, many may need to be taught through multisensory approaches such as the Fernald method.

According to Fernald (1943), specific school techniques that tend to produce *poor* spellers include:

1. Formal spelling periods in which children move through a series of practice lessons, writing, and taking dictation with little time to think about how the word is spelled before writing it.

2. Focus on misspellings and spelling errors, because it builds a negative attitude toward spelling.

A brief description of the Fernald approach to teaching spelling includes the following procedures:

1. The teacher writes the word to be learned on the chalkboard or paper. The word can be selected from the spelling book or by the child.

2. The teacher pronounces the word clearly. The student repeats the pronunciation of the word while looking at the word. This is repeated several times.

3. The teacher allows time for the student to study the word for later recall. If the student is a kinesthetic learner, the teacher writes the word in crayon and has the student trace the letters of the word with his or her finger. Fernald found that tracing is necessary in learning to spell only when the spelling difficulty is coupled with a reading disability.

4. Remove the word and have the student write it from memory.

5. The student turns the paper over and writes the word a second time.

6. The teacher creates opportunities for the student to use the word in his or her written expression.

7. The teacher gives written, not oral, spelling drills.

In contrast with Fernald's approach, which recommends not focusing on the student's errors and suggests blocking out errors immediately, other researchers have found some support for a spelling strategy that emphasizes imitation of students' errors plus modeling (Kauffman, Hallahan, Haas, Brame, and Boren, 1978; Nulman and Gerber, 1984). Using the imitation plus modeling strategy, the teacher erases the misspelled word and imitates the child's error by writing it on the board. The teacher then writes it correctly with the student and asks the student to compare what he or she wrote with the correct spelling of the word.

Gillingham and Stillman Approach. According to Gillingham and Stillman (1973), "spelling is the translation of sounds into letter names (oral spelling) or into letter forms (written spelling)" (p. 52). Spelling is taught by using the following procedures:

1. The teacher says the word very slowly and distinctly and the student repeats the word after the teacher. This is referred to as *echo speech.*

2. The student is asked what sound is heard first. This process continues with all of the letters in the words. This is referred to as oral *spelling.*

3. The student is asked to locate the letter card with the first letter of the word on it and then write the letter. The student continues with this process until the cards for each letter are found, placed in order, and written. This is referred to as *written spelling.*

4. The student reads the word.

When writing the word, the student orally spells the word letter by letter. This establishes visual auditory-kinesthetic association.

Correctional procedures in the Gillingham and Stillman approach include:

1. The student checks his or her own written word and finds errors.
2. If a word is read incorrectly, the student should spell what he or she said and match it with the original word.
3. If a word is misspelled orally, the teacher writes what the student spelled and asks him or her to read it, or the teacher may repeat the pronunciation of the original word.

Constant Time Delay Procedure. The time delay procedure is a method designed to reduce errors in instruction. Stevens and Schuster (1987) applied the procedure this way:

1. The verbal cue, "Spell ＿＿＿＿＿＿＿＿ (target word)," is immediately followed with a printed model of the target word to be copied by the student.
2. After several trials in which there is no time delay between asking a child to spell a word and providing a model of the word, a five-second delay is introduced. This allows the child to write the word, or part of the word, if he or she knows it, but does not require him or her to wait very long if he or she is unable to correctly write the word.
3. The amount of time between the request to spell the word and the presentation of the model can be increased after several more trials.

The time delay procedure has been effective with students with learning disabilities and has several advantages as a spelling instructional method. It is a simple procedure that is easy to implement. It is fun for the student because it provides for nearly errorless instruction.

Self-Questioning Strategy for Teaching Spelling. Wong (1986) has developed the following self-questioning strategy for teaching spelling.

1. Do I know this word?
2. How many syllables do I hear in this word?

3. Write the word the way I think it is spelled.
4. Do I have the right number of syllables?
5. Underline any part of the word that I am not sure how to spell.
6. Check to see if it is correct. If it is not correct, underline the part of the word that is not correct and write it again.
7. When I have finished, tell myself I have been a good worker.

Morphographic Spelling. Developed by Dixon (1976, 1991), Morphographic Spelling provides a highly structured and sequenced approach to teaching remedial spelling to fourth graders through adulthood. This teacher-directed approach assumes that students have some spelling skills and begins with teaching small units of meaningful writing (morphographs). Students are taught to spell morphographs in isolation, then to combine them to make words.

From the Research:
Instructional Practices in Spelling

Most students with learning disabilities have problems with spelling. Yet students with learning disabilities have been the focus of relatively few research studies on spelling acquisition. Gordon, Vaughn, and Schumm (1993), in a search for empirically based instructional practices for improving the spelling skills of students with learning disabilities, reviewed fifteen studies on spelling acquisition, dated from 1978 to the present, in which students with learning disabilities were the focus of the research.

Findings from the studies can be grouped into six areas of instructional practice: (1) error imitation and modeling; (2) unit size; (3) modality; (4) computer-assisted instruction (CAI); (5) peer tutoring; and (6) study techniques.

1. *Error imitation and modeling.* Students with learning disabilities need to compare each of their incorrectly spelled words with the correct spellings. The teacher imitates the student's incorrect spelling and, beside it, writes the word correctly. The teacher then calls attention to features in the word that will help the student remember the correct spelling.

2. *Unit size.* Students with learning disabilities tend to become overloaded and to experience interference when required to study several words at once. Students with learning disabilities can learn to spell if the unit size of their assigned list is reduced to only three words per day and if effective instruction is offered for those three words.

3. *Modality.* It has long been thought that students with learning disabilities learn to spell most easily when their modality preferences are considered. An investigation of the usefulness of a spelling study by (1) writing the words, (2) arranging and tracing letter shapes or tiles, and (3) typing the words at a computer, revealed that students with learning disabilities learned equally well when studying words by any of these procedures. Of significance, however, was the fact that most of the students preferred to practice their spelling words at a computer. Because students' preferences are likely to affect their motivation to practice, teachers are wise to consider students' personal preferences.

4. *Computer-assisted instruction (CAI).* Computer-assisted instruction (CAI) has been shown to be effective in improving the spelling skills of students with learning disabilities. CAI software programs for spelling improvement often incorporate procedures that emphasize awareness of word structure and spelling strategies, and make use of time-delay, voice simulation, and sound effects. Such capabilities make the computer an instructional tool with much potential to aid and motivate students with learning disabilities in learning to spell.

5. *Peer tutoring.* While a teacher's individual help is preferable, the realities of the classroom frequently make individualized instruction difficult to offer. Structured peer tutoring can be a viable alternative. In a study conducted by Harper and colleagues (1991), peer tutoring was extended to a classwide setting and incorporated a team game format into daily peer tutoring sessions. The students with learning disabilities tutored by their peers for the game achieved 100 percent mastery of their weekly spelling words.

6. *Study techniques.* Study techniques help students with learning disabilities organize their spelling study by providing a format for that study. As they approach the study of a new word, they know exactly how to go about their study; this is in contrast to the haphazard, unproductive study used by students who follow no such strategy.

Most of the research investigating the effectiveness of spelling interventions for students with learning and behavior problems has involved the use of teaching single words from lists rather than spelling in context (Fulk and Stormont-Spurgin, 1995). Nevertheless, spelling instruction for students with learning problems is best conducted explicitly and directly rather than through indirect methods that are often part of whole-language approaches (Graham and Harris, 1994).

TEACHING HANDWRITING

Often described as the most poorly taught subject in elementary curriculum, handwriting is usually thought of as the least important. Unfortunately, handwriting difficulties provide barriers to efficient work production and influence grades received from teachers (Briggs, 1970; Markham, 1976). Many students dislike the entire writing process because they find the actual motor skill involved in handwriting so laborious.

Despite the use of word processors, typewriters, and other devices that can facilitate the writing process, handwriting is still an important skill. Taking notes in class, filling out forms, and success on the job often require legible, fluent writing.

Handwriting Problems

Students with dysgraphia have severe problems learning to write. Hamstra-Bletz and Blote (1993, p. 60) define dysgraphia as follows:

> Dysgraphia is a written-language disorder that concerns the mechanical writing skill. It manifests itself in poor writing performance in children of at least average intelligence who do not have a distinct neurological disability and/or an overt perceptual-motor handicap. . . . Furthermore, dysgraphia is regarded as a disability that can or cannot occur in the presence of other disabilities, like dyslexia or dyscalculia.

Students with dysgraphia may exhibit any or all of the following characteristics:

■ **TABLE 6.1** *Manuscript versus Cursive*

Manuscript	*Cursive*
1. It more closely resembles print and facilitates learning to read.	1. Many students want to learn to write cursive.
2. It is easier for young children to learn.	2. Many students write cursive faster.
3. Manuscript is more legible than cursive.	3. Many adults object to students using manuscript beyond the primary grades.
4. Many students write manuscript at the same rate as cursive and this rate can be significantly influenced through direct instruction.	
5. It is better for students with learning disabilities to learn one writing process well than to attempt to learn two.	

1. Poor letter formation
2. Letters that are too large, too small, or inconsistent in size
3. Incorrect use of capital and lower case letters
4. Letters that are crowded and cramped
5. Inconsistent spacing between letters
6. Incorrect alignment (letters do not rest on a base line)
7. Incorrect or inconsistent slant of cursive letters
8. Lack of fluency in writing

Fortunately, with direct instruction and specific practice many of these problems can be alleviated.

Manuscript and Cursive Writing

Traditionally, most students learn manuscript writing first and then, in about second or third grade, make the transition to cursive writing. Although this procedure seems to be effective for most students, many students with learning disabilities have difficulty with the transition from one writing form to another. Many learning-disability specialists advocate the use of instruction in only one form of handwriting, either manuscript or cursive. Some argue that manuscript is easier to learn, is more like book print, is more legible, requires less difficulty in making movement (Johnson and Myklebust, 1967), and should be the only writing form taught. Others feel cursive is faster, is continuous and connected, is more difficult to reverse letters, teaches the student to perceive whole words, and is easier to write. They feel cursive should be taught first as the only writing form. (See Table 6.1 for a summary of arguments for manuscript versus cursive.) Some critics maintain time could be better spent in teaching students to keyboard.

The greater bulk of evidence appears to be in the direction of teaching students with learning disabilities to use manuscript effectively and neatly, with the exception of learning to write their name in cursive. For most students with learning disabilities and with handwriting difficulties, manuscript should be taught in the early years and maintained throughout the educational program. Some students with learning disabilities can and want to make the transition to cursive, and benefit from its instruction. On some occasions, students who have struggled with manuscript writing feel learning cursive is "grown up" and thus respond well to the introduction of a new writing form.

Reversals

When five-year-old Abe signed his name on notes to his grandmother, he often reversed the direction of the *b* in his name. When writing other letters he would often write them backwards or upside down. His mother was very concerned because she worried that it might be an indication that Abe was dyslexic or having reading problems. Many parents are concerned when their children make reversals and often their alarmed response frightens their children. Most children, age five and younger, make reversals when writing letters and numbers. Reversals made by students before the age of six or seven are not an indication that the student has learning disabilities or is dyslexic and are rarely cause for concern.

Teachers should recognize that:

1. Reversals are common before the age of six or seven. Teachers should provide correctional procedures for school-age students who are reversing letters and numbers but should not become overly concerned.

2. A few students after the age of seven continue to reverse numbers and letters and may need direct intervention techniques.

For students who persist in reversing letters and numbers, the following direct instructional techniques may be helpful.

1. The teacher traces the letter and talks aloud about the characteristics of the letter, asking the students to model the teacher's procedure. For example, while tracing the letter *d* the teacher says, "First I make a stick starting at the top of the page and going down, and then I put a ball in front of the stick." The student is asked to follow the same procedure and to talk aloud while tracing the letter. Next, the student

is asked to do the same procedure, this time drawing the letter. Finally, the student is asked to draw the letter and say the process to himself or herself.

Tracing letters is a frequently used method of improving legibility; however, there is little research that suggests tracing is an effective method of teaching letter formation. Hirsch and Niedermeyer (1973) found that copying is a more effective technique for teaching letter formation than tracing.

2. The teacher and the student can develop a mnemonic picture device that helps the student recall the direction of the letter. For example, with a student who is reversing the direction of the letter *p,* the teacher might say, "What letter does the word *pie* begin with? That's right, *pie* begins with the letter *p.* Now watch me draw *p.*" Drawing the straight line, the teacher says, "This is my straight line before I eat pie, then after I eat pie my stomach swells in front of me. Whenever you make *p* you can think of pie and how your stomach gets big after you eat it, and that will help you make a *p* the right way." This procedure can be repeated several times, with the student drawing the letter and talking through the mnemonic device. Different mnemonic devices can be developed to correspond with the specific letter or number reversal(s) of the child.

The next section focuses on teaching handwriting, including discussions on posture, pencil grip, position of the paper, and legibility and fluency in writing. Specific instructional techniques such as the Hanover approach and Hagin's Write Right-or-Left are also discussed.

Components of Handwriting

Teaching handwriting requires the teacher to assess, model, and teach letter formation, spacing, and fluency as well as posture, pencil grip, and position of the paper. A brief description follows of these important components to an effective handwriting program.

Legibility
Legibility is the most important goal of handwriting instruction, and incorrect letter formation the most

frequent interference. The following four letters account for about 50 percent of all malformed letters at any grade level: *a, e, r,* and *t* (Newland, 1932). Spacing between letters, words, and margins, connecting lines, and closing and crossing of letters (e.g., *t, x*) also influence legibility (Kirk and Chalfant, 1984).

The following remedial procedures for teaching letter formation are suggested by Graham and Miller (1980):

1. Modeling
2. Noting critical attributes (comparing and contrasting letters)
3. Physical prompts and cues (physically moving the student's hand or using cues such as arrows or colored dots)
4. Reinforcement (providing specific reinforcement for letters or parts of letters formed correctly, and corrective feedback for letters that need work)
5. Self-verbalization (saying aloud the letter formation and then verbalizing it to self while writing)
6. Writing from memory
7. Repetition

A summary of approaches to teaching letter formation is presented in Figure 6.13.

Fluency
Nine-year-old Marta's handwriting has improved considerably during the past year. She and her teacher have identified letters that were not formed correctly and Marta has learned to write these letters so they are legible. Now that her handwriting is easier to read, the teacher realizes Marta has another handwriting problem. In the regular classroom Marta has difficulty taking notes and writing down assignments that are given orally, because she is a very slow writer. She needs to learn writing fluency, which is the ability to write quickly and with ease without undue attention to letter formation. Marta's teacher decides to teach fluency by gradually increasing expectations about the speed at which letter

■ **FIGURE 6.13**   *Letter Formation Strategies*

Fauke Approach (Fauke et al., 1973)

1. The teacher writes the letter, and the student and teacher discuss the formational act.
2. The student names the letter.
3. The student traces the letter with a finger, pencil, and magic marker.
4. The student's finger traces a letter form made of yarn.
5. The student copies the letter.
6. The student writes the letter from memory.
7. The teacher rewards the student for correctly writing the letter.

Progressive Approximation Approach (Hofmeister, 1973)

1. The student copies the letter using a pencil.
2. The teacher examines the letter and, if necessary, corrects by overmarking with a highlighter.
3. The student erases incorrect portions of the letter and traces over the teacher's highlighter marking.
4. The student repeats steps 1–3 until the letter is written correctly.

Furner Approach (Furner, 1969a, 1969b, 1970)

1. The student and teacher establish a purpose for the lesson.
2. The teacher provides the student with many guided exposures to the letter.
3. The student describes the process while writing the letter and tries to write or visualize the letter as another child describes it.

4. The teacher uses multisensory stimulation to teach the letter form.
5. The student compares his or her written response to a model.

VAKT Approach

1. The teacher writes the letter with crayon while the student observes the process.
2. The teacher and student both say the name of the letter.
3. The student traces the letter with the index finger, simultaneously saying the name of the letter. This is done successfully five times.
4. The student copies and names the letter successfully three times.
5. Without a visual aid, the student writes and names the letter correctly three times.

Niedermeyer Approach (Niedermeyer, 1973)

1. The student traces a dotted representation of the letter 12 times.
2. The student copies the letter 12 times.
3. The student writes the letter as the teacher pronounces it.

Handwriting with Write and See (Skinner & Krakower, 1968)

The student traces a letter within a tolerance model on specially prepared paper. If the student forms the letter correctly, the pen writes gray; if it is incorrect, the pen writes yellow.

Source: S. Graham and L. Miller, "Handwriting Research and Practice: A Unified Approach," *Focus on Exceptional Children, 13*(2) (1980):11. Reprinted with permission.

formation occurs. Marta selects two paragraphs and is told to write them as quickly as she can while still maintaining good letter formation. The teacher times her in this procedure. They decide to keep a graph of her progress by indicating the time it takes her each day to write the two paragraphs legibly. Marta finds the graphing of her progress very reinforcing (see Figure 6.14 and Apply the Concept 6.13). Since Marta's fluency problems were not just for copying but also for writing from dictation, her teacher implemented the same program, this time requiring Marta to time herself on oral dictations. Marta's time

■ **FIGURE 6.14** *Marta's Fluency*

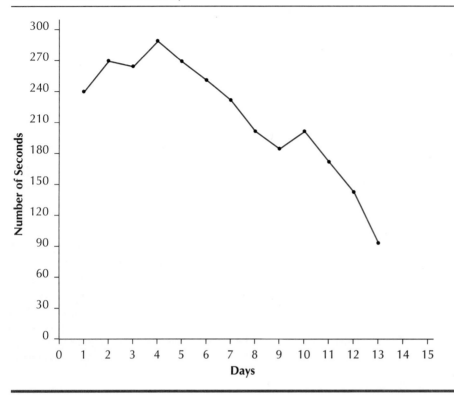

for completion of the passage decreased considerably over a three-week period.

Posture, Pencil Grip, and Position of the Paper

Many students have handwriting problems because they do not correctly perform three important components of the handwriting process.

Posture. The hips should touch the back of the chair and the feet should rest on the floor. The torso leans forward slightly, in a straight line, with both forearms resting on the desk and elbows slightly extended.

Pencil Grip. The pencil should be held lightly between the thumb and first two fingers, about one inch above the point. The first finger rests on top of the pencil. The back of the pencil points in the direction of the shoulder and rests near the large knuckle of the middle finger.

Position of the Paper. When writing manuscript, the paper should be in front of the student. For a righthander, the left hand holds the paper in place, moving it when necessary. In writing cursive, the paper is slanted counterclockwise for a righthander and clockwise for a lefthander.

APPLY THE CONCEPT 6.13

OBTAINING A FLUENCY SAMPLE

The following procedures can be used to obtain a fluency sample:

1. Have the student become familiar with the test sentence.
2. The teacher tells the student to write the test sentence a designated number of times at his or her usual rate (two-to three-minute sample).

3. After relaxing, have the student write the sentence as well and as neatly as he or she can.
4. After relaxing, have the student write the sentence as quickly and as many times as he or she can in three minutes.
5. After relaxing, the student and the teacher repeat this process with the same sentence.

Instructional Principles

The following instructional principles are suggested for any effective handwriting program.

1. Use direct instruction.
2. Provide individualized instruction.
3. Use a variety of techniques and methods, matching the students' individual needs.
4. Teach handwriting frequently, several times a week.
5. Give short handwriting lessons in the context of the students' writing assignment.
6. Handwriting skills should be overlearned in isolation, then applied in context and periodically checked.
7. Students should evaluate their own handwriting and, when appropriate, the handwriting of others.
8. The teacher's handwriting should be a model for the students to follow.
9. Teach handwriting not just as a visual or a motor task, but as both (Hagin, 1983).

Self-instructional strategies can be taught to students to improve their handwriting (Graham, 1983; Kosiewicz, Hallahan, Lloyd, and Graves, 1982). The self-instructional procedure that was used in the Graham (1983) study was based on a cognitive-behavioral model. The six-step procedure follows:

Step 1: The teacher models the writing of the target letter and describes the formation of the letter. The student then describes the formation of the letter. This step is repeated three times.

Step 2: The teacher writes the letter while describing the process. This continues until the student can recite the process for writing the letter.

Step 3: The student traces the letter, and the teacher and the student recite the process of the letter formation together.

Step 4: The teacher writes the letter, traces it, and then verbally discusses the process, including corrections (e.g., "My letter is too slanted.") then provides self-reinforcement (e.g., "Now, that looks a lot better."). The procedure continues with and without errors, until the student can model the process.

Step 5: The teacher writes the letter and the student copies it while defining the process and providing self-correction. The student needs to complete this process successfully three times before moving to step 6.

Step 6: The student writes the letter from memory.

Following are several methods devised for teaching students who have handwriting difficulties.

■ **FIGURE 6.15**   *Write Right-or-Left: Learning Motifs*

Ferry boats

Teaches smooth movements across the page.

Waves

Foundation for the letters a, c, d, g, and q

Pearls

Foundation for the letters e, i, h, j, m, n, u, y, and z

Wheels

Foundation for the letters o, v, b, w, and x

Arrows

Foundation for the letters k, l, t, r, and f

Source: Adapted from R. H. Hagin, "Write Right or Left: A Practical Approach to Handwriting," *Journal of Learning Disabilities, 16*(5) (1983):266–271.

Write Right-or-Left

Hagin (1983) suggests a process for teaching cursive that is based on manuscript and the vertical stroke learned in manuscript. In Hagin's *Write Right-or-Left* approach, the student learns cursive writing in the following manner:

1. The student learns motifs which form the foundation for later letter formation. These motifs are taught and practiced on the chalkboard. See Figure 6.15 for an illustration of the motifs and the letters that correspond with them.

2. After the motifs are learned at the chalkboard, the student learns and practices the letters associated with each of the motifs at the chalkboard.

3. At the desk, the student traces the letters while verbal cues as to letter direction and formation are given by the teacher.

4. In this step the student writes the letters without a model.

5. Through matching, the student compares the model with the product produced in step 4. Both the teacher and the student give feedback and determine whether additional practice is needed before the next step.

6. The student writes a permanent record of the letters that have been mastered.

The Hanover Method

Hanover's method (1983) of teaching cursive writing is founded on a single principle—the grouping of letters based on similar strokes into letter families. The letter families include:

e, l, h, f, b, k	This is the *e* family and is taught first.
b, o, v, w	This family has a handle to which the next letter is attached.
n, s, y	This family is grouped together to emphasize the correct formation of hump-shaped letters.
c, a, d, o, q, g	This is the *c* family.
n, m, v, y, x	This is the hump family.
f, q	This family has tails in the back.
g, p, y, z	This family has tails in the front.

Some letters are included in more than one group. According to this approach, cursive letters are learned faster and easier when they are taught in their grouped families because of the similar strokes within the groups.

Teaching Handwriting at the High School Level

Handwriting often becomes important in the junior high and high school period because of the emphasis on taking notes and submitting written assignments. Many students have found that although the content of their assignment is correct they have lost points or were given a lower grade because their handwriting was difficult to read. Teaching handwriting to older students is difficult because the immediate needs of most older students are content-related and it is often difficult for the teacher to justify instructional time for handwriting, and because most materials for handwriting instruction are developed for younger students and are insulting to high school students. The teacher needs to carefully evaluate the handwriting problems of the students to determine if handwriting instruction could be helpful in a relatively short period of time, or if the students should learn compensatory methods such as typing or word processing. The two most important criteria for evaluating handwriting at the high school level are legibility and fluency.

In selecting curriculum for older students, specific attention should be given to the students' letter formation and fluency within context. Corrective feedback, short trace and copy exercises, and content exercises that require little thinking and allow the students to concentrate on letter formation and fluency should be emphasized when teaching handwriting to older students (Ruedy, 1983).

INSTRUCTIONAL ACTIVITIES

This section provides instructional activities that are related to written expression, including spelling and handwriting. Some of the activities teach new skills; others are best suited for practice and reinforcement of already acquired skills. For each activity, the objective, materials, and teaching procedures are described.

■ Proofreading with "Scope"

Objective: To teach students a mnemonic strategy ("SCOPE") to help with proofreading their writing.

Grades: Intermediate and advanced

Materials: A student-generated writing piece that needs to be edited.

Teaching Procedures: Discuss with the students how they often get into difficulty because they are not sufficiently skilled at proofreading their papers before they submit them and therefore get low grades because their papers have many errors. Teach the students a mnemonic strategy, "SCOPE," that will assist them in proofreading their work before they submit it.

> S—*Spelling:* Is the spelling correct?
> C—*Capitalization:* Are the first words of sentences, proper names, and proper nouns capitalized?
> O—*Order of Words:* Is the syntax correct?
> P—*Punctuation:* Are there appropriate marks for punctuation where necessary?
> E—*Express Complete Thought:* Does the sentence contain a noun and a verb or is it only a phrase?

Next, demonstrate using "SCOPE" with a sample piece of writing on an overhead projector. Give the students ample practice and opportunity to apply "SCOPE" to their own work.

■ Writing an Autobiography

Objective: To provide students practice in developing written expression and to learn more about self and family.

Grades: Adapted for all levels

Materials: Writing materials.

Teaching Procedures: During the academic year, read autobiographies to the students and discuss their contents. Ask the students what information they feel they would need to write an autobiography and how they might be able to obtain that information (e.g., students may need to interview parents and grandparents).

Have the students write an autobiography, conferencing frequently with other students and teachers.

Autobiographies, with pictures, are then displayed in the classroom and school library.

The Life of JUAN GONZALES
by Juan Gonzales

My mother says she remembers
very well the day I was born.
She was at my grandmothers
She said all of a sudden she
had great pain and went
oh my God !! My mother knew
I was going

■ Writing a Teacher Evaluation

Objective: To practice critical thinking and writing skills.

Materials: Writing materials.

Teaching Procedures: Tell the students that teachers have many opportunities to evaluate them and their work. Discuss several of the criteria used to evaluate students. Then discuss what an evaluation instrument is and how it is often used. Brainstorm some of the possible criteria and content areas that an evaluation instrument designed to assess the quality of teachers should possess.

Have the students break into small groups to write an evaluation instrument. The students then share and discuss their instruments. Then, selecting the best parts from each group's evaluation, the students construct a final version of the evaluation and complete it on selected teachers.

Teacher Evaluation

Write the number next to the item that accurately reflects your opinion about your teacher.

| 1 | 2 | 3 | 4 | 5 |

never   all the
                                                                                              time

1. Corrects our homework on time. _____
2. Tells funny stories. _____
3. Gives us adequate instructions for our assignments. _____

■ Interview a Classmate

Objective: To give students practice in developing and using questions as a means for obtaining more information for the piece they are writing.

Grades: Adapted for all levels

Materials: (1) Writing materials and a writing topic. (2) A list of possible questions. (3) A tape recorder (optional).

Teaching Procedures: Using the format of a radio or television interview, demonstrate and role-play "mock" interviews with sport, movie, music, and political celebrities. Give the students opportunities to play both roles.

Discuss what types of questions allow the interviewee to give elaborate responses (e.g., open questions), and what types of questions do not allow the interviewee to give a very expanded answer (e.g., closed questions). Practice asking open questions.

Use a piece that you are writing as an example, and discuss who you might interview to obtain more information. For example, "In writing a piece about what it might be like to go to the St. Louis World's Fair in 1904, I might interview my grandfather, who was there, to obtain more information."

Ask the students to select an appropriate person to interview for their writing piece and to write possible questions. In pairs, the students refine their questions for the actual interview. The students then conduct the interviews and later discuss how information from the interview assisted them in writing their piece.

■ Who Am I?

Objective: To give students practice in writing complete sentences with correct capitalization and ending punctuation. Students will use describing words specific to themselves without describing so specifically as to "give themselves away." Students will print or write their neatest printing or manuscript so that their handwriting alone doesn't give a clue to their identity.

Grades: All levels

Materials: (1) Paper and pencil. (2) Dictionary.

Teaching Procedures: Prepare a "Who Am I?" paper and read it to the class. For example:

> I have brown hair and brown eyes. I was born in February. I have a sister and no brothers. I used to have two dogs but now I don't have any pets. I love Mexican food, football games, and snow skiing. My favorite color is red but I like to wear turquoise clothes.
> WHO AM I?

Read to the class a description of someone in the room. See if they can guess who it is. Then tell the students to write a description of themselves. Provide some examples they might want to use.

> your hair and eye color
> your age or birth month
> if you are a boy or girl
> how many brothers or sisters you have
> some of your favorites (color, sport, food, movie)
> what you like to do for fun
> your pets (but not their names)
> DO NOT TELL YOUR NAME

Remind the students to use their neatest handwriting so that their handwriting does not "give away" who they are. Then collect their descriptions and randomly distribute them so that each student has one other than his or her own. The students read the descriptions out loud and members of the class guess who is being described.

Adaptations: Students can be directed to write descriptions of political leaders, historical characters, characters from their reading, and so on.

■ Johnny Can Write!

By: Sandra Stroud

Objective: To help a beginning writer increase his writing fluency, and to provide a model for correct sentence construction.

Grades: K–8

Materials: Pencil and paper.

Teaching Procedure:

Step One: A list of story titles is shown and, if necessary, read to the students. They are each encouraged to select a topic about which they would enjoy writing. The students then write their titles at the top of their papers and write about their topic as well as they can. They are cheerfully told the spelling of any words for which they ask. An example follows.

My best Friend name is

michell IS my best Friend because He lat me paly with has games and ride has bike we play Football and boket ball to.

Step Two: As the students finish their paragraphs, they take turns reading them to their teacher or other helper. They are then asked to tell their teacher more about their topic. With input from the student, the teacher rewrites the paragraph. The student then orally reads the revised paragraph with the help of the teacher.

My Best Friend

Michael Pearson is my best friend. Michael is in the eighth grade at this school and he lives near me. I have known Michael for two years. Sometimes I go over to Michael's house and he lets me play with his games and ride his bicycle. We like to play football and basketball, and sometimes we go fishing. I'm glad that I have a good friend like Michael.

Step Three: The student copies the paragraph from the teacher's paper and then orally reads the revised paragraph with the help of the teacher.

My Best Friend

Michael pearson is my best Friend. Michael is in the eighth grade at this school and he lives near me. I have known michael For two years. Sometimes I go over to michael's house and he lets me play with his games and ride his bicycle. We like to play Football and basetball, and somdimes We go Fishing. I'm glad that I have a good Friend like Michael.

■ Expressing an Opinion

By: Sandra Stroud

Objective: To evoke students' thoughts and opinions on topics of vital interest to them, so that they will write those thoughts and opinions with enthusiasm.

Grades: Middle and high school, with a fourth-grade reading level as a minimum.

Materials: Pencil, paper, computers for word processing.

Teaching Procedure: The teacher is alert for newspaper and magazine articles that are sure to be of interest to students in the class, and makes photocopies of an article for every student. After building the students' interest in the topic of the article, the teacher requests that the students follow along, reading silently as the teacher reads aloud. The teacher takes care to read the article smoothly, with lots of expression, and at an appropriate pace for these students.

When the reading is finished, a class discussion ensues. Once the discussion has reached some intensity, the students are asked to turn to pencil and paper to write their thoughts and opinions on this topic. They are told not to worry about spelling or other errors.

The following day, the students are taken to a computer lab to type their articles at the computers.

(While keyboarding skills are not required, students should first have some knowledge of the word-processing program and operation of the computers.) The teacher will find that, as they type, most of the students will correct and greatly expand upon their compositions.

The preceding activity is beneficial to students for the following reasons:

1. *Encourages students to write.* Students who are reluctant to write are far more willing and interested in writing when asked to react to a topic of great interest to them. When assured that spelling and other kinds of mechanical errors (which can be corrected later on) will not be held against them, they express themselves using the rich and varied language of their thoughts.

2. *Builds vocabulary and word recognition.* As students listen and read silently while the teacher is reading orally, new words enter their reading vocabulary. They simultaneously see a word, hear it pronounced, and learn its meaning from its use in the context.

3. *Encourages student participation.* When the topic for reading and discussion is one that is very close to students' hearts, they are eager to read silently with their teacher. Even the most reticent student will usually wish to participate in the class discussion that follows.

SUMMARY

Students start school feeling confident they know how to write. It is not uncommon to see young children writing notes to grandparents and other significant persons, making up letters and words as they go along, assured they are able to communicate in print. Most of these same students later find expressing themselves in writing one of the most difficult tasks required of them in school. The chapter described a process approach to writing instruction and discussed how to teach spelling and hand-writing skills as aids to written expression. The assumption underlying the writing process approach presented in this chapter is that all children know something, and writing gives them the opportunity to share what they know. This approach has potential with students who have learning and behavior problems, as it focuses on writing from their own experiences and feelings, allowing them a systematic process for interacting with peers and teachers and providing consistent opportunities to write and receive feedback.

This chapter presented procedures for starting the writing process approach, including a description of materials needed, skills taught through the process approach, and the teacher as writer, modeling through writing and sharing with students. The elements of the writing process approach, which include prewriting, composing, revising, editing, and publishing were defined, and examples were presented of how they are taught and integrated into the writing process approach with students who have learning and behavior problems. Guidelines for conducting effective writing conferences, the key to successful writing, were described, and examples of students conferring with each other as well as with the teacher were provided.

In addition to describing the writing process as an approach to written expression, this chapter discussed how to teach spelling and handwriting skills to students with learning and behavior problems. Most of those students need direct instruction in spelling and handwriting, and this chapter provided specific instructional techniques that have been successful. Since effective spelling instruction begins with understanding the types of spelling errors the student makes, how to conduct an error analysis in spelling was presented. Principles for teaching spelling to students with learning difficulties were discussed and spelling approaches were presented.

The handwriting section of the chapter discussed the advantages and disadvantages of teaching manuscript and/or cursive, as well as information all teachers should know about reversals. Approaches to teaching handwriting were also presented.

THINK AND APPLY

— Think about the elements of the writing process approach to instruction. How can you integrate them in your instruction?

— What is a writing conference and how can it be used with students with learning and behavior problems?

— What are several critical aspects to establishing a writing program for students with learning and behavior problems?

— In what ways can the computer facilitate writing for students with learning problems?

— How do you conduct and apply error analysis to the spelling errors of students with learning problems?

— What are the key principles for teaching spelling to students with learning problems?

— Can you describe several methods of teaching spelling to students with learning and behavior problems?

— Can you describe several methods of teaching handwriting to students with learning and behavior problems?

— What instructional principles are suggested for an effective spelling program?

— Why is it true that 'less is more' when increasing the spelling vocabularies of students with learning disabilities?

— "Rhyming and alliteration are positively and significantly related to progress in spelling" (Bradley and Bryant, 1985). What is a possible explanation of this phenomenon?

— What instructional principles are suggested for an effective handwriting program?

Chapter 7

Content Area Learning and Study Skills

OUTLINE

KEY TOPICS FOR MASTERY

- *The role that concepts and related vocabulary play in content learning*
- *Strategies for determining which concepts and vocabulary to teach*
- *How to evaluate the considerateness of texts including readability*
- *How to adapt textbooks using study guides, highlighting, and alternative reading materials*
- *How to develop listener-friendly lectures*
- *How to make and adapt class assignments, homework, and tests*
- *How to use before, during, and after learning activities such as advance organizers, semantic feature analysis, semantic mapping, discussion webs, and concept diagrams to teach content*
- *How to teach personal development skills such as scheduling, self-regulation, notebook organization, and classroom participation*
- *How to teach students to take notes from lectures and learning from text using learning strategies such as Multipass*
- *Strategies for remembering content information such as key word mnemonics and strategies for taking tests*

 BRIGHT IDEA

Turn to page 329 and read Think and Apply.

When Ms. Cho moved from her elementary resource room job to a high school resource position, her experience and education in teaching learning strategies and writing process serves her well for part of the school day. However, in addition to the two English periods she teaches daily, she is also expected to teach sections of American history and American government to students with learning and behavior problems. Although she minored in political science and history in college, she feels as if her content knowledge is rusty in these areas and her techniques for teaching content information are limited. She has also been asked to teach a section of general science, but she has chosen to team-teach the class with a science teacher, because of her limited content knowledge and desire to integrate the students in special education into general education classes.

When Desmond entered Bailey Middle School, he had been receiving help in a special education resource room since second grade. During that time, Mrs. Jackson, the resource room teacher, had been working with Desmond on word identification and basic comprehension skills as well as spelling and writing compositions. In elementary school, Desmond went to the resource room for forty-five minutes every afternoon. He consistently missed either social studies or science in the general education classroom while he was receiving special assistance in the resource room.

Desmond made many changes when he transitioned to middle school. While he attends resource English and reading, he also has social studies, science, and home economics classes in general education classes. All of these classes require him to listen to lectures in class and take notes, read chapters with technical vocabulary and answer the questions at the end of each section, take timed tests, write reports, and keep track of assignments and turn them in on time. By the end of the first nine weeks, Desmond is receiving failing slips in all three classes. He is frustrated by his classes and is becoming disruptive.

Doreen worked hard in high school and, despite her reading and writing disabilities, graduated with a high enough grade point average to enter college. However, as a freshman in a large university, she is finding herself overwhelmed by the demands of her classes. She is barely passing freshman English and classical literature and is even struggling in her math and science courses—areas that were her strengths in high school. Doreen can't seem to get organized. She has difficulty estimating how long it will take her to complete an assignment, and she is unable to keep up with the reading assignments in literature class. Doreen is a bright student with good potential to succeed as an architect or engineer, but she may never get through the basic liberal arts courses required for her degree.

Both Desmond and Doreen need strategies to assist them in being more effective learners. They need study skills in managing their time, organizing their notebooks, taking notes, studying for tests, taking tests, reading textbooks, learning new vocabulary, and writing reports and essays. Desmond and Doreen have mastered many of the basics of reading and writing, but they are having difficulty applying them in content area classes.

Ms. Cho, Desmond, and Doreen are experiencing difficulties functioning in the secondary and postsecondary school environments. In these environments the task demands for teachers and students change dramatically. The special education teacher often coteaches, teaches content subjects, or needs to provide content area teachers with learning and teaching strategies to facilitate learning content area information. The students are asked to apply learning strategies and study skills as well as skills in listening, reading, writing, and math, in order to learn content area subjects such as biology, American history, art history, welding, computer programming, and home economics (Putnam, Deshler, and Schumaker, 1993; Tralli, Colombo, Deshler, and Schumaker, 1996).

Link (1980) surveyed 133 secondary and upper elementary teachers and administrators and asked them to rank twenty-four academic skills on a 1–7 Likert scale. Putnam (1992, Putnam, Deshler, and Schumaker, 1993) interviewed 120 at the seventh- and tenth-grade levels about the use of tests. The top ten skills identified by Link are presented in Figure 7.1. These skills reflect study skills rather than basic skills in reading and writing. The importance of study skills is clear when one considers that Putnam found almost 50 percent of grades are determined by tests. Students with learning and behavior problems often need instruction in study and test taking skills.

This chapter focuses on strategies for teaching content area subjects, making adaptations, and teaching learning strategies and study skills. The chapter is divided into three sections. First, we will look at teaching strategies to assist low-achieving students learning content area information. These strategies are useful to special education teachers whether they are directly teaching the content or collaborating with content area teachers (Bos and Duffy, 1991; Deshler, Ellis, and Lenz, 1996; Lenz, Bulgren, and Hudson, 1990; Nolet and Tindal, 1993; Tindal and Nolet, 1996). Next, we will discuss what general education teachers and their students think about teachers making adaptations. In the same light, we will also present some general strategies for making adaptations for

■ **FIGURE 7.1** *Academic Skills Rated as Most Essential for Adequate Classroom Performance*

1. Follow oral and written directions.
2. Make logical deductions.
3. Read at grade level.
4. Recall information for tests.
5. Locate answers to questions.
6. Turn in assignments on time.
7. Ask relevant questions.
8. Clearly express ideas in writing.
9. Locate information in textbooks.
10. Participate in discussions.

Source: Adapted from D. Link, *Essential Learning Skills and the Low Achieving Student at the Secondary Level: A Rating of the Importance of 24 Academic Abilities.* Unpublished master's thesis, University of Kansas, Lawrence, Kansas, 1980.

textbooks, lectures, assignments, and tests. Finally, we will examine methods of teaching students to be more effective and efficient learners. Many of the reading comprehension and writing strategies highlighted in Chapters Five and Six are effective in promoting content area learning and effective studying and learning. In addition, the Strategies Intervention Model in the section on cognitive behavior modification presented in Chapter Two can be used to teach many of the study skills and learning strategies suggested in this chapter.

Although the focus of this chapter is on teaching and learning strategies for secondary and postsecondary level students, many of the techniques presented are appropriate for upper elementary students. Both students and teachers alike have commented that using such techniques in upper elementary grades would greatly facilitate low-achieving students in secondary settings.

TEACHING CONTENT AREA INFORMATION

If you are going to teach content, whether it be in courses of home economics, history, auto mechanics, biology, or government, then one of your major tasks is to teach the important concepts and their relationships (Bos and Anders, 1990c). The goal is to enhance the content so that the "critical features of the content are selected, organized, manipulated, and complemented in a manner that promotes effective and efficient information processing" (Lenz, et al., 1990, p. 132). Both the content enhancement (Lenz and Bulgren, 1995) and the teaching steps described in the interactive model for teaching concepts (Anders and Bos, 1984), as presented in the following pages, highlight the importance of using teaching routines. These researchers also recommend using instructional devices such as semantic maps or concept diagrams to organize and guide the learning of content information.

Concepts are general ideas that are associated with smaller but related ideas (Anders and Bos, 1984). The following concept might be used in a science course:

> Bacteria are a class of microscopic plants that help people, other animals, and plants; however, bacteria also do things that hurt people, other animals, and plants.

Several related ideas that elaborate on the concept of bacteria are:

> Bacteria are small; you use a microscope to see them; bacteria multiply; bacteria live in soil, water, organic matter, plants, or animals; bacteria can make you ill; bacteria can spoil food.

The vocabulary associated with the general concept and its related concepts is the *conceptual vocabulary*. These are the words that are necessary for understanding the general idea and are associated with it. Examples of the conceptual vocabulary for a unit on bacteria in a science text are: *bacteria, microscope, colony, multiply, reproduce,* and *decay.* These words and their meanings facilitate understanding of the general concept.

Process for Teaching Concepts

A six-step process or teaching routine (Lenz and Bulgren, 1995) can be used to teach concepts and their labels. The first step in teaching content area information is planning and deciding what concepts and related conceptual vocabulary to teach. Admittedly, some concepts and vocabulary are more important than others. Deciding what concepts and labels to teach is a crucial part of content area teaching. The six-step process is presented in Figure 7.2 and discussed in more detail in the following sections.

Step One: Selecting Concepts and Related Vocabulary

The first step in getting ready to teach content information is selecting the major concepts and related vocabulary to be taught, and generating a framework for facilitating understanding of the ideas to be learned. Selecting the major concepts and related vocabulary to be taught in a unit, a chapter, a section of a book, or a lecture is best completed prior to having the students interact with the material (Bos and Anders, 1990b). As the teacher, you need to determine

■ **FIGURE 7.2**   *A Process for Teaching Concepts*

A six-step process can be used to teach concepts and their labels:

1. Decide what concepts and related conceptual vocabulary to teach.
2. Evaluate the instructional materials to be used for "friendliness or considerateness."
3. Assess the students on their background knowledge for the concepts and related vocabulary.
4. Utilize prelearning or prereading activities to facilitate and support learning.
5. Conduct the learning or reading activity.
6. Provide postlearning activities that further reinforce and extend the concepts and information learned.

the conceptual framework for the unit so that the information might be presented in an organized fashion based on this framework.

The process a teacher uses for determining the major concepts depends on his or her expertise and knowledge in the content area, knowledge of the structure of the textbook information, and knowledge about the students' background for the content and their study/reading skills (Bulgren and Lenz, 1996; Reyes and Bos, in press). A teacher who has specialized in a given content area can probably generate concepts from personal knowledge and experiences, and use the assigned textbook as the primary resource for verifying the appropriateness of those concepts. A teacher with limited background knowledge could use a variety of resources, such as the assigned textbooks, trade books, state or local curriculum guides, media computer-based resources, and other teachers or experts in the field. Some texts—especially those written for students with reading problems—tend to include too much detail and fail to explain the overall concept or to relate the concepts (Anders and Mitchell, 1980; Armbruster and Anderson, 1988; Scanlon and Anders, 1988).

After articulating the major concepts to be learned, you next generate and organize the related vocabulary. To do this, study the assigned text and instructional materials and compile a list of relevant related words and phrases from the text. As you read,

you may realize that some important vocabulary is missing from the text; if so, add it to the list.

To organize the list of vocabulary, group words that are related together. Then create a semantic or content map to visually represent the relationships among these terms (Scanlon, Duran, Reyes, and Gallego, 1992). Figure 7.3 depicts a map developed with the conceptual vocabulary a teacher generated from a chapter in a biology text. The map highlights the critical vocabulary and the organization and relationships of the concepts (Anders and Bos, 1984; Lenz and Bulgren, 1995). The map helps to solve an all too common problem that confronts content area teachers: deciding what concepts and related vocabulary to teach in a content lesson.

Step Two: Evaluating Instructional Materials

Before teaching the concepts and related vocabulary, teachers need to evaluate the instructional materials they intend to use in teaching the unit. Within the last decade educators have become much more interested in the characteristics of instructional materials. They have concentrated on textbooks, because textbooks still continue to be the predominant medium of instruction (Alvermann and Moore, 1991; O'Brien, Stewart and Moje, 1995). In terms of curriculum, textbooks structure from 65 to 90 percent of secondary classroom instruction (Woodward and Elliott, 1990). How concepts are presented in a text will affect how easily they are comprehended by the students (Anders and Guzzetti, 1996; McKeown, Beck, Sinatra, and Loxterman, 1992). The manner in which the text is organized (e.g., use of headings and subheadings, highlighted words, marginal notes) will also affect comprehensibility of the text.

Readability
Traditionally, emphasis in evaluating content area texts was placed on the readability of the text as determined by readability formulas (e.g., Dale and Chall, 1948; Fry, 1977). Most readability formulas, including the Fry readability formula presented in Figure 7.4, are based on two factors: sentence complexity as measured by sentence length and word difficulty as indexed by word length or frequency.

■ **FIGURE 7.3**   *A Content Map of a Biology Chapter on Mollusks*

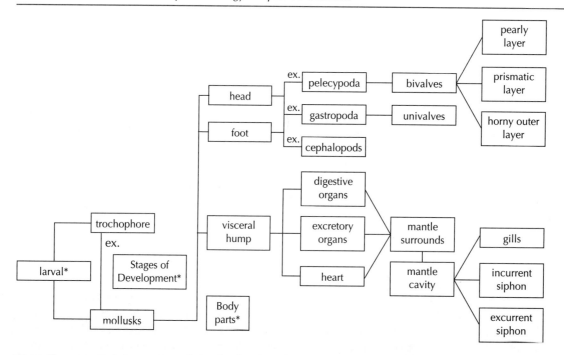

*Note: There seem to be two concepts being developed (apologies to the biologists among us):
1.   When classifying animals biologists look for relationships between animals during the various stages of development from birth to adulthood.
2.   Biologists describe the body parts of animals and the functions of each part.

Source: P. L. Anders and C. S. Bos, "In the Beginning: Vocabulary Instruction in Content Classes,"
Topics in Learning and Learning Disabilities 3(4) (1984):56. Reprinted with permission of Pro-Ed.

Readability formulas should be used cautiously and as only one aspect of evaluating a text for several reasons (Anders and Guzzetti, 1996). First, the typical standard error of measurement for readability formulas is plus or minus approximately 1.5 grade levels (Singer and Donlan, 1989). Consequently, a text whose readability formula is predicted as 7.5 can range by chance from 6.0 to 9.0. Second, readability formulas do not take into account many characteristics of *text* that are important in comprehension and learning. For example, to reduce the reading level or difficulty as measured by readability formulas, textbooks and, particularly, adapted textbooks that are designed for students with learning and behavior problems are written using short sentences. Oftentimes this means that important relational words such as *and, or, because,* and *if . . . then* have been eliminated to shorten the length of the sentences, and consequently reduce the readability level as predicted by the formula. However, it is these relational words that signal the reader to the relationships among the concepts (Davison, 1984). Consequently, although the readability according to the formula may be reduced, the text is actually more difficult to understand. Third, readability formulas neglect to consider the characteristics of the *reader* that affect comprehension, including interest, purpose, background knowledge, and perseverance.

Considerate or User-Friendly Text
What characteristics should be considered when evaluating how considerate or user-friendly a text is?

■ **FIGURE 7.4** *Fry Readability Graph. Graph for Estimating Readability—Extended*

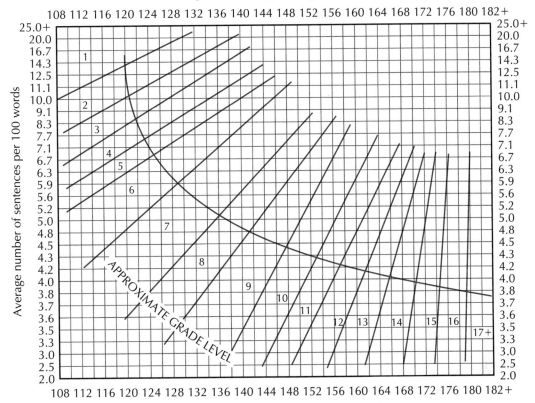

1. Randomly select three text samples of exactly 100 words, beginning with the beginning of a sentence. Count proper nouns, numerals, and initializations as words.
2. Count the number of sentences in each 100-word sample, estimating the length of the last sentence to the nearest one-tenth.
3. Count the total number of syllables in each 100-word sample. Count one syllable for each numeral or initial or symbol; for example, 1990 is one word and four syllables, LD is one word and two syllables, and "&" is one word and one syllable.
4. Average the number of sentences and number of syllables across the three samples.
5. Enter the average sentence length and average number of syllables on the graph. Put a dot where the two lines intersect. The area in which the dot is plotted will give you an approximate estimated readability.
6. If there is a great deal of variability in the syllable or sentence count across the three samples, more samples can be added.

Source: Edward Fry, "Fry's readability graph: clarifications, validity, and extension to level 17." *Journal of Reading,* 21 (1977):242–252. Reproduction permitted—no copyright.

Armbruster and Anderson (1988) have conducted a program of research to develop salient criteria for determining the considerate text. Their criteria fall into three broad categories: structure, coherence, and audience appropriateness.

1. *Structure* refers to the manner in which the text is organized and how the text signals its structure. Use of titles, headings, subheadings, introductions, and summary statements, informative and relevant pictures, charts, and graphs, highlighted key concepts, marginal notes, and signaling words (e.g., *first, second, then, therefore*) can facilitate comprehension. In evaluating the text, it is important not only to check if such structural features are used, but if they match the content. For example, sometimes headings will not relate well to the text contained under the headings. In this case, the structural features may serve more as a source of confusion than as an aide. Also, check to see if the highlighted words in the text represent the important concepts or simply the words that are difficult to decode.

Also, consider if the format and the Table of Contents assist the reader in drawing relationships between the various chapters by using such devices as sections and subsections? Do introductions to each section or chapter encourage the reader to draw connections between previous ideas and concepts already discussed and the new ideas to be presented?

2. *Coherence* refers to how well the ideas in a text "stick together" (Armbruster and Anderson, 1988). With coherent text the relationships among concepts are clear. For example, when Herman, Anderson, Pearson, and Nagy (1987) rewrote text about the circulatory system and made explicit the connections between motive and action, form and function, and cause and effect, student learning improved. Coherence is also facilitated by using different kinds of *cohesive ties*—linguistic forms that help convey meaning across phrase, clause, and sentence boundaries (Anders and Guzzetti, 1996; Halliday and Hassan, 1976). Examples of cohesive ties are *conjunctions* and *connectives, pronoun referents* (using a pronoun to refer to a previously mentioned noun), and *substitutions* (using a word to replace a previously used noun or verb phrase).

3. *Audience appropriateness* refers to how well the textbook is suited to the readers' content knowledge, reading and study skills. The text needs to provide enough explanation, attributes, examples, and analogies to provide readers with adequate information to relate to their background knowledge. Superficial mentioning of new topics for which the reader has limited background knowledge does little to build understanding. On the other hand, too many or too technical supporting details can obscure the important concepts.

Another area to consider with relation to the audience is the explicitness of main ideas. As was discussed in the chapters on reading (Chapters 4 and 5), many students with learning and behavior problems have difficulty identifying and comprehending the main ideas of a text. Therefore, text in which the main ideas are explicit and regularly placed at the beginning of paragraphs and sections should facilitate learning. However, in examining social studies textbooks designed for the second, fourth, sixth, and eighth grades, Baumann and Serra (1984) found that only 27 percent of the short passages contained explicitly stated main ideas, only 44 percent of the paragraphs contained them, and only 27 percent of the paragraphs began with them.

Part of the process of preparing to teach content knowledge is evaluating instructional materials for readability and friendliness. By considering the structure, cohesion, and audience appropriateness when evaluating text or other types of instructional materials (e.g., films, lectures, demonstrations), the teacher develops a good idea of how considerate or user-friendly the materials are. Based on this evaluation, the teacher may decide to modify, augment, or adapt the instructional materials (see the section on adapting textbooks in this chapter).

The ultimate judge of the readability and friendliness of a textbook is the reader. The **FLIP Chart strategy** helps students learn to evaluate text on their own (Schumm and Mangrum, 1991). (FLIP stands for **F**riendliness, **L**anguage, **I**nterest, **P**rior knowledge.) By filling out charts like the one shown in Figure 7.5, students learn what is comfortable for them individually as readers. After students have completed the FLIP chart you can learn (through class discussions

■ **FIGURE 7.5** *The FLIP Chart*

Title of assignment _____

Number of pages _____

General directions: Rate each of the four FLIP categories on a 1–5 scale (5 = high). Then determine your purpose for reading and appropriate reading rate, and budget your reading/study time.

F = Friendliness: How friendly is my reading assignment?

Directions: Examine your assignment to see if it includes the friendly elements listed below.

Friendly text features

Table of contents	Index	Glossary
Chapter introductions	Headings	Subheadings
Margin notes	Study questions	Chapter summary
Key terms highlighted	Graphs	Charts
Pictures	Signal words	Lists of key facts

1 ———————————2 ———————————3 ———————————4 ———————————5

No friendly text features   Some friendly text features   Many friendly text features

Friendliness rating _____

L = Language: How difficult is the language in my reading assignment?

Directions: Skim the chapter quickly to determine the number of new terms. Read 3 random
paragraphs to get a feel for the vocabulary level and number of long, complicated sentences.

1 ———————————2 ———————————3 ———————————4 ———————————5

Many new words;   Some new words: No new words;
complicated sentences   somewhat complicated sentences   clear sentences

Language rating _____

I = Interest: How interesting is my reading assignment?

Directions: Read the title, introduction, headings/subheadings, and summary. Examine the
pictures and graphics included.

1 ———————————2 ———————————3 ———————————4 ———————————5

Boring   Somewhat interesting   Very interesting

Interest rating _____

**P = Prior knowledge: Who do I already know about the material covered in my reading
assignment.**

Directions: Think about the title, introduction, headings/subheadings, and summary.

1 ———————————2 ———————————3 ———————————4 ———————————5

Mostly new information   Some new information   Mostly familiar information

Prior knowledge rating _____

Overall, this reading assignment appears to be at:
  ❏ a comfortable reading level for me
  ❏ a somewhat comfortable reading level for me
  ❏ an uncomfortable reading level for me

Source: J. S. Schumm, and C. T. Magnum (1991). FLIP: A framework for textbook thinking. *Journal of
Reading, 35,* 120–124. Copyright by the International Reading Association.

and individual conferences) what is difficult for them in terms of text friendliness, language, interest, and prior knowledge. Students with reading and learning problems especially need to learn how to talk about the textbook and any problems they have with it. Classroom discussions based on the FLIP chart strategy also help students think as a group about effective strategies for coping with text they find difficult.

Step Three: Assessing Students' Prior Knowledge

Before content area teachers assign a specific chapter to read or present a lecture on a topic, they need to assess the students' background knowledge for the concepts and related vocabulary to be covered. Research in schema theory indicates that prior knowledge plays a critical role in determining how effectively students will comprehend and retain the information and vocabulary to be presented (Lee, 1992; Stahl, Hare, Sinatra, and Gregor, 1991; Stahl, Jacobson, Davis, and Davis, 1989). One technique for assessing prior knowledge is using the PreReading Plan, with which you are familiar (see Chapter 5). This plan not only assesses students' knowledge, but also

serves to activate their knowledge, thus facilitating comprehension.

A second procedure that can be used to assess and activate students' background knowledge is semantic mapping (Johnson, Pittelman, and Heimlich, 1986; Pearson and Johnson, 1978; Scanlon, et al., 1992). Like PReP, this technique uses free association as a stimulus activity to generate a list of words and phrases related to the key concept. The teacher and students take the associations given by the students and relate them to the key concept, developing a network that notes the various relations (e.g., class, example, property or characteristics). A semantic map for the concept of "desert" was developed with a group of fifth-grade students with learning disabilities preparing to study deserts, using the associations they gave. The map, shown in Figure 7.6, indicates that the students can give examples and properties or characteristics of a desert. However, the students did not produce any superordinate class relations or a definition ("What is it?"). Additionally, the property and example relations that were generated lacked technical vocabulary despite further probing on the part of the teacher. The semantic map in Figure 7.6 serves not only as a visual representation for the students' current understanding of the

■ **FIGURE 7.6**   *Semantic Map of Fifth Grade Students' Knowledge of Deserts*

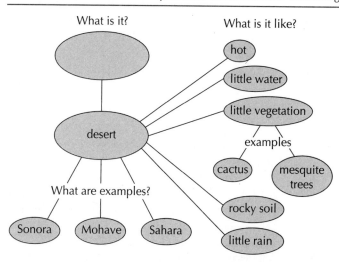

concept of deserts, but the map also functions as an initial blueprint for teaching (Bos and Anders, 1992; Reyes and Bos, in press).

Using activities such as semantic mapping and PReP not only provides the teacher with valuable information concerning the students' knowledge, it also activates their knowledge. This is particularly important for second language and culturally diverse learners who may have limited knowledge of more formalized content. In our work we have found that promoting discussions during these activities and encouraging students to relate firsthand experiences helps both the students and teacher to make connections (Reyes and Bos, 1996). For second language learners, having the student clarify concepts in their first language can also facilitate activation of background knowledge and understanding of key concepts (Bos and Reyes, 1996; Reyes, Duran, and Bos, 1989).

Based on assessment information from such procedures as PReP or semantic mapping, decisions can be made as to the need and type of further prelearning activities to provide.

Step Four: Using Prelearning Activities

Limited background knowledge signals the teacher that students need more instruction to learn the information that will be presented in the text or lecture. Teachers can present any number of prelearning activities—advance organizers, semantic feature analysis, semantic mapping, concept diagrams—that students can use before reading an assigned text or listening to a lecture. All these activities enhance the content and have been referred to as content enhancement devices (Bulgren, Schumaker, and Deshler, 1988). Teachers can also use other learning experiences such as field trips, experiments, computer simulations, and films.

Advance Organizers

The concept of advance organizers was introduced by Ausubel in the 1960s. He defined an advance organizer as information that is presented "in advance of and at a higher level of generality, inclusiveness, and abstraction than the learning task itself" (Ausubel and Robinson, 1969, p. 606).

The purpose of an advance organizer is to facilitate learning information. It is based on schema theory and the notion that some students need to have a framework provided for the material to be learned to help them assimilate the new information into their current schemas or cognitive structure. Mayer (1979) reviewed the studies that have tested the effectiveness of advance organizers on learning and drew the following conclusions:

1. Groups given advance organizers consistently perform better than control groups with none. This advantage diminishes when material is familiar, when learners have an extensive background of knowledge about the area, when learners have high IQs, and when tests fail to measure the breadth of transfer ability.

2. Advance organizers particularly aid students of lower ability and/or limited background knowledge.

3. Advance organizers are more effective when presented prior to a learning task rather than after the task.

Using this information, Lenz (1983; Lenz, Alley, and Schumaker, 1987) demonstrated that both the quality and quantity of learning for adolescents with learning disabilities could be significantly improved by using advance organizers. He found that regular content area teachers are able to implement advance organizers with minimal teacher training (forty-five minutes). The teachers who utilized the advance organizers expressed satisfaction with the students' response to the instruction as well as the improvement in the overall quality of their own instruction. However, Lenz did find that teacher use of an advance organizer alone was not enough to facilitate student learning. "Learning disabled students had to be made aware that advance organizers were being presented and then had to be trained in the types of information presented in the advance organizer and ways in which that information could be made useful" (Lenz, 1983, p. 12).

━ **PROCEDURES:** Lenz identified ten steps in using an advance organizer (see Figure 7.6). The resource teacher trained the students in the resource classroom to utilize advance organizers by giving the students a worksheet with each of the ten steps as headings. The students then practiced listening to advance organizers given by the resource teacher and completing the worksheets. Next, the students used the advance organizer worksheet in mainstreamed content area classes, with the resource teacher and students meeting afterward to discuss the success of the worksheets. They discussed how the advance organizer information can be used to organize notes and how the worksheet can be modified to assist the students to cue in on the most common organizing principles used by particular teachers.

In giving an advance organizer, the teacher provides an organizational framework for the information to be learned (see Figure 7.7, step 3). This framework might be an outline, a diagram, or picture in which the parts are labeled, or a content map, as discussed earlier. Townsend and Clarihew (1989) found that a pictorial component in a verbal advance organizer was necessary to improve the comprehension of eight-year-old students with limited background knowledge. The use of visual representations or pictures may be particularly salient for students with learning and behavior problems.

Semantic Feature Analysis

Like an advance organizer, semantic feature analysis (SFA) is a prelearning activity that serves to organize the major concepts and related vocabulary to be taught in a unit, chapter, or lecture. This activity aids students in seeing the relationships between the major concepts, the related vocabulary, and their current knowledge of the topic.

The theoretical foundation for the SFA teaching strategy is schema theory (Rumelhart, 1980), the closely related knowledge hypothesis (Anderson and Freebody, 1981), concept attainment theory (Klausmeier and Sipple, 1980), and a Vygotskian perspective of cognitive development (Vygotsky, 1978) (see Chapter Two). These theories suggest that knowledge is hierarchically organized, that relating the new concepts to students' prior knowledge will help students learn these new concepts, that teaching attributes of a concept as well as teaching examples

and nonexamples are important to concept learning, and that principles of scaffold instruction and interactive dialogues will promote learning.

■ **PROCEDURES:** The first step in preparing for the SFA activity is to develop a relationship chart. This chart is based on the notion that ideas or concepts are related to one another in terms of a hierarchy of abstractness. The most inclusive or abstract ideas are called *superordinate concepts;* the most concrete or narrow ideas are identified as *subordinate concepts.* Ideas or concepts that fall in between the superordinate and subordinate concepts are referred to as *coordinate concepts* (Frayer, Frederick, and Klausmeier, 1969). These ideas are then organized into a relationship chart, and the students and teacher discuss the relationship between the various levels of concepts and their own background knowledge. This SFA activity was originally developed for use in teaching isolated vocabulary (Johnson and Pearson, 1984). In their interactive teaching research, Bos and her colleagues have adapted this strategy to text (Anders and Bos, 1986; Bos and Anders, 1992; Reyes and Bos, in press).

When Ms. Cho used this technique in her American government class, she first read the assigned American government chapter on contracts. As she read, she listed the important concepts or vocabulary and then arranged them according to superordinate, coordinate, and subordinate concepts. She used words as well as relevant phrases.

Contracts	Counter Offer
Promise	Holding Good
Contracting Parties	Conditions
Buyer	Acceptance
Seller	Consideration
Written Contracts	Statute of Frauds
Verbal Contracts	Legal Obligation
Contractual Offer	Legal Action

Next, she organized the vocabulary into a relationship chart (see Figure 7.8). The superordinate concept "Contracts" is used as the name for the chart. The five coordinate concepts (main ideas in the text) serve as the column headings and are listed as the im-

■ **FIGURE 7.7**   *Steps in Using an Advance Organizer*

Step 1: Inform students of advance organizers
     a. Announce advance organizer
     b. State benefits of advance organizer
     c. Suggest that students take notes on the advance organizer

Step 2: Clarify action to be taken
     a. State teachers' actions
     b. State students' actions

Step 3: Identify topics of tasks
     a. Identify major topics or activities
     b. Identify subtopics or component activities

Step 4: Provide background information
     a. Relate topic to the course or previous lesson
     b. Relate topic to new information

Step 5: State the concepts to be learned
     a. State specific concepts/ideas from the lesson
     b. State general concepts/ideas broader than the lesson's content

Step 6: Clarify the concepts to be learned
     a. Clarify by examples or analogies
     b. Clarify by nonexamples
     c. Caution students of possible misunderstandings

Step 7: Motivate student to learn
     a. Point out relevance to students
     b. Be specific, short-term, personalized, and believable

Step 8: Introduce vocabulary
     a. Identify the new terms and define
     b. Repeat difficult terms and define

Step 9: Provide an organizational framework
     a. Present an outline, list, or narrative of the lesson's content

Step 10: State the general outcome desired
     a. State objectives of instruction/learning
     b. Relate outcomes to test performance

Source: Adapted from B. K. Lenz, "Promoting Active Learning Through Effective Instruction," *Pointer, 27*(2) (1983):12. Copyright 1983 by Heldref Publications.

portant or major ideas. The related vocabulary or subordinate concepts are listed down the side of the chart. Notice that Ms. Cho left blank spaces for adding important ideas and important vocabulary to the chart. In this way students during discussion would be encouraged to add relevant information from their background knowledge.

The relationship chart became Ms. Cho's instructional tool. She duplicated it and she made a transparency to project on the screen at the front of the class. She used the relationship chart as her prelearning activity to assist students in seeing relationships among the important ideas and the related vocabulary. To do this, Ms. Cho gave each student a copy of the relationship chart and, using the model relationship chart projected on the screen, she introduced the topic (superordinate concept) of the assignment. The students then discussed what they

■ **FIGURE 7.8**   *Relationship Chart: Contracts*

CONTRACTS   Name _____

Period _____

Important Ideas

Important Vocabulary	Contract	Promise	Written Contracts	Verbal Contracts	Conditions		
Legal Action							
Consideration							
Legal Obligation							
Holding Good							
Contractual Offer							
Counteroffer							
Acceptance							
Statute of Frauds							
Contracting Parties							

+ = positive relationship
– = negative relationship
0 = no relationship
? = unknown relationship

already knew about contracts. Next, she introduced each coordinate concept (important idea) by assisting the students in generating meanings. During this introduction and throughout the activity, she encouraged students to add their personal experiences or understandings of the terms. For example, when Ms. Cho presented the major idea of "contract," Joe inquired if a contract had to be written to be legal. This led to Anne's conveying a firsthand experience of her dad making a verbal contract and having the contract honored in court even though it was not written. The discussion ended with one purpose for reading being the clarification of what was needed for a verbal contract to be considered legal.

Following the discussion of the coordinate concepts, Ms. Cho introduced each subordinate concept.

Again, Ms. Cho and her students predicted what the meanings would be in relation to the topic of "contracts." For the more technical vocabulary (e.g., *contractual offer, Statute of Frauds*), sometimes Ms. Cho provided the meaning or the students decided to read to clarify the concept. After introducing each concept, she and the students discussed the relationship between each coordinate concept or phrase and each subordinate term or phrase. They used the following symbols to signify each of the relationships: a plus sign (+) represented a positive relationship, a minus sign (–) represented a negative relationship, a zero (0) signified no relationship, and a question mark (?) represented that no consensus could be reached without further information.

Ms. Cho found that student involvement during the discussion was important to the success of the SFA strategy. One key to a successful discussion was to encourage students to ask each other why they reached a certain relationship rating. This seemed to encourage students to use their prior knowledge regarding the topic, and in turn, seemed to encourage other students to activate what they already knew about the vocabulary. When trying to justify a positive and negative relationship between "holding good" and "promise," several of Ms. Cho's students discussed the relationship of moral obligation to legal obligation, using firsthand experiences and episodes from several specific TV programs as their rationales.

After completing the relationship chart, Ms. Cho guided the students in setting purposes for reading. These purposes, for the most part, focused on the chart, reading to confirm their predictions and to determine the relationships between the terms for which no agreement could be reached. After completing the reading, Ms. Cho and the students reviewed the relationship chart, using discussion. They changed any of the relationships if necessary and reached consensus on those previously unknown.

Sometimes when Ms. Cho and her students used a relationship chart, they found that some information was still unclear after reading the text. Then, they checked other sources such as experts in the field, technical and trade books, and other media. Ms. Cho also taught the students how to use the relationship chart to study for chapter tests. The students learned to ask each other questions based on the meanings of the concepts and vocabulary and on their relationships (e.g., What is a contractual offer? What are the conditions necessary to have a contract?). She even demonstrated how the chart could be used to write a report about the concepts.

■ **COMMENTS:** One of the authors and her colleagues have conducted a series of intervention studies using the SFA teaching strategy with secondary students who have learning disabilities. Whether comparing it to the more traditional activity of looking the words up in the dictionary (Bos, Anders, Filip, and Jaffe, 1985; Bos, Anders, Jaffe, and Filip, 1989) or the direct instruction of word meanings (Anders, Bos, Jaffe, and Filip, 1986; Bos, Allen, and Scanlon, 1989; Bos and Anders, 1990a, 1992), they found that when teachers and researchers used this strategy, students consistently learned more vocabulary and had better comprehension of the chapters they read. Bos and her colleagues feel that one of the most important questions asked during discussion is "Why?" (e.g., "Why is *evidence* positively related to *evidence in court*?"). Students need to justify their reasoning. By answering "Why?" questions, students think through concepts, reaching a deeper understanding and more effectively relating new information to old.

Semantic Mapping, Graphic Organizers, and Discussion Webs

Semantic mapping (Pearson and Johnson, 1978), graphic organizers (Barron, 1969), structured overviews (Barron and Earle, 1973), and discussion webs (Alvermann, 1991) are four similar ways of visually representing the concepts and important vocabulary to be taught (see Figure 7.6). These content enhancement devices can be used as prelearning activities that assist students in activating their prior knowledge and in seeing the relationships between new concepts and related vocabulary.

■ **PROCEDURES:** In using maps, organizers, overviews, or webs, the teacher can begin by putting the major concept for the lecture or text on the board and then having the students generate a list of related vocabulary from their background knowledge, as was described in the section on brainstorming (see Chapter 5). However, when presenting more technical vocabulary, the teacher could begin by writing on the board the list of important vocabulary he or she generated in reviewing the text chapter or developing the lecture. After the words have been listed, discuss the meanings of the words, using a procedure similar to the one just presented in the section on semantic feature analysis. Next, arrange and rearrange the vocabulary with the students until you have a map that shows the relationships that exist among the ideas.

For example, when presenting the following words for a chapter on "Fossils," the students and teacher first grouped the animals together.

trilobites	small horses
crinoids	winged insects
ferns	geography of the present
dinosaurs	land masses
lakes	brachiopods
bodies of water	saber-tooth tigers
animals	guide fossils

geography of the past	rivers
trees	plants
oceans	continents

Next, they grouped the plants together. In the case of guide fossils and several other types of fossils with which the students were not familiar (e.g., crinoids, trilobites), they decided to wait until they had done some reading before placing the concepts on the map. Finally, they grouped together the geography terms.

After the map is completed, instruct the students to refer to the map while reading and/or listening to the lecture. Like the relationship chart of semantic feature analysis, the semantic map can provide a framework for setting purposes for reading. The students read to confirm and clarify their understanding in relation to the map and make changes in it during discussions held as they read or after completing a chapter. The map can also serve as a blueprint for studying and for writing reports.

The discussion web (Alvermann, 1991) is particularly helpful for assisting students in seeing both sides of an issue (see Figure 7.9). Alvermann sug-

■ **FIGURE 7.9**   *Discussion Web*

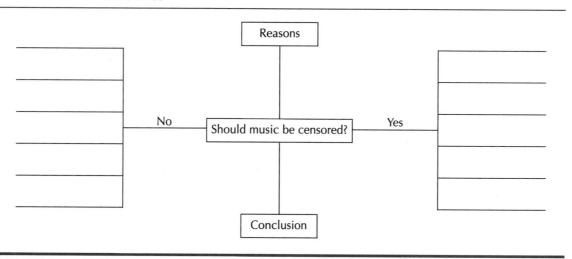

Source: Adapted from D. E. Alvermann (1991). The discussion web: A graphic aid for learning across the curriculum. *The Reading Teacher, 45*(2), 92–99. Copyright by the International Reading Association.

gests introducing the key concepts and a provocative question such as "Should music be censored?" using discussion. As the students read or listen to information, they think about reasons both positive and negative, then work in small groups to complete their webs, and then present and discuss their webs. This tool provides a structure for *critical thinking* by examining both sides of an issue carefully before making judgments.

■ **COMMENTS:** Recently, a number of researchers have investigated the use of mapping, graphic or-

ganizers, and webbing with students who are low achievers or have learning disabilities. In some cases the students generated the maps as described above (Bos, Allen, and Scanlon, 1989; Bos and Anders, 1990a; Boyle, 1996; Scanlon, Deshler, and Schumaker, 1996), while in other studies the framework for the map or organizer was already generated and the students filled in the information (Horton, Lovitt, and Bergerud, 1990; Idol, 1987a,b; Lovitt and Horton, 1994). In other studies, the map or visual spatial display (see Figure 7.10) is presented to the students in completed form, and systematic Direct Instruction

■ **FIGURE 7.10**   *Visual Spatial Display*

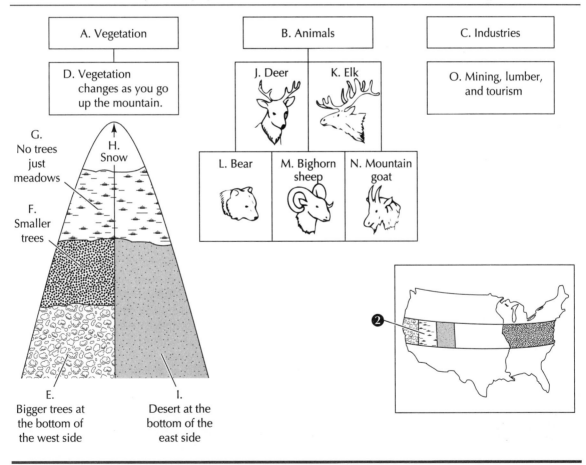

Source: From "Teaching Content Area Material to Learning Disabled Students" by C. Darch and D. Carmine, *Exceptional Children, 53,* 1986, p. 243. Copyright 1986 by The Council for Exceptional Children. Reprinted with permission.

(Carnine, 1989) is used to assist the students in learning the information contained in the display (Bergerud, Lovitt, and Horton, 1988; Darch and Carnine, 1986). Consistently the research has been encouraging in this area: the use of semantic maps or visual representations of information increases the learning performance of students with learning and behavior problems.

Concept Diagrams

Concept diagrams (Bulgren with Lenz, Deshler, and Schumaker, 1994; Bulgren, Schumaker, and Deshler, 1988) provide another means for enhancing the content presented in text or lectures. Building on the work in concept development, the diagram (see Figure 7.11) uses a concept comparison table to assist students in determining the characteristics, examples

■ **FIGURE 7.11**   *Concept Diagram*

CONCEPT DIAGRAM

Concept Name: fossils

Definitions: Fossils are remains or prints of plants or animals who lived thousands of years ago which have been preserved in the earth.

Characteristics Present in the Concept:

Always	Sometimes	Never
remains or prints	frozen in ice	still alive
plants or animals	trapped in tar	still decaying
thousands of years old	crushed by water	
preserved in the earth	in volcanic ash	

Example:

- tigers in La Brea tar pits
- Siberian mammoth
- petrified forest in Arizona
- fish skeleton in limestone layers

Nonexample:

- your pet cat
- elephant in Africa today
- tree limbs and leaves in your yard
- fish in supermarket

and nonexamples, and a content-related definition of a concept.

— **PROCEDURES:** When using a concept diagram, the first step is to prepare the diagram. First, the teacher identifies major concept(s) and related concepts of which the students need a deeper or more technical understanding. In a science chapter on fossils, Mr. Thomas felt that it was important that the students develop a more technical understanding of the concept of fossils, so this became the concept to diagram. Second, Mr. Thomas used the instructional materials and his knowledge to list important characteristics of fossils. He also thought about whether or not each characteristic is "always present," "sometimes present," or "never present." Third, he located examples and nonexamples of the concepts in the instructional materials. He found in reviewing the chapter that nonexamples were not provided, so he decided to show the students fossils and nonfossils to help them to start thinking about examples and nonexamples. Finally, Mr. Thomas constructed a definition. Lenz and Bulgren (1995) specify a concept definition as the "naming of the superordinate concept which includes the concept under consideration, a listing of the characteristics which must always be present in the concept, and a specification of the relationships among those characteristics" (p. 33).

After preparing the concept diagram, the next step is using it with the students to develop their understanding of the concept. The teaching sequence includes:

1. Give an advance organizer.
2. Elicit a list of key words or ideas related to the major concept.
3. Explain or review the symbols of the concept diagram.
4. Name and define the concept. (This may be completed after the students have discussed characteristics and examples/nonexamples if a teaching method oriented more toward discovery is being used.)
5. Discuss the characteristics always present, sometimes present, and never present.
6. Discuss examples and nonexamples of the concept.
7. Link the examples and nonexamples to the characteristics.
8. Give a post organizer.

This teaching sequence or concept teaching routine (Bulgren, Schumaker, and Deshler, 1988) should employ interactive discussions that encourage the students to fine-tune and deepen their understanding of the concept being studied.

— **COMMENTS:** When Bulgren and her colleagues (Bulgren et al., 1988) worked with content area high school teachers in whose classes students with learning disabilities were mainstreamed, they found that when the teachers used the concept diagrams and the concept teaching routine, the learning performance of both the students with learning disabilities and the other students in the class improved.

Concept diagrams are part of the content enhancement model (Bulgren and Lenz, 1996; Lenz, Bulgren, and Hudson, 1990) suggested as a complement to the learning strategies developed at the University of Kansas (see Chapter Two, Cognitive Behavior Modification).

Steps Five and Six: Reinforcing Concept Learning During and After Learning

In a typical "learning from reading" or "learning from lecturing" assignment, the teacher has three opportunities to enhance the learning of concepts and the related vocabulary: *before* the reading or listening, *during* the actual reading or lecture, and *after* the assignment has been read or heard. The previous section discussed prelearning activities that can be used to enhance content and facilitate concept learning.

Whether using an advance organizer, semantic feature analysis, semantic map, or concept diagram, these frameworks can be used to guide students as they read the text or listen to the lecture and as they react to their learning. For example, the list of major ideas obtained from the advance organizer can serve as the framework in which students can take notes when listening to a lecture. After the lecture, students can meet in small groups and share their notes to create one overview that can serve as a study guide for the test. Students can be instructed on how to develop questions based on a concept diagram or semantic map. These questions can serve as self-questions to be asked when reading and when studying for a test.

Students generally require considerable practice in using these content enhancement devices. Additionally, devices used for one content area may not be transferred to other areas automatically (Scanlon, Deshler, and Schumaker, 1996). Thus, numerous applications of each strategy may need to be taught explicitly (Billingsley and Wildman, 1990; Bulgren and Lenz, 1996; Hudson, Liqnugarls-Kraft, and Miller, 1993). Second language learners who have learning disabilities are sometimes referred to as doubly challenged when learning content information. Apply the Concept 7.1 presents ideas for promoting content learning for these students.

MAKING ADAPTATIONS

What Do Teachers and Students Think About Making Adaptations?

Special and general education teachers understand the need to make adaptations for those students in their classrooms who have special learning needs, and they express the desire to make those modifications. In actuality, however, research indicates most content area teachers seldom implement many adaptations for a number of reasons (Schumm and Vaughn, 1992; Schumm, Vaughn, and Saumell, 1992). First, adapting textbooks takes time, and teachers' time for planning and preparing for instruction is already limited. Second, textbook adaptations often slow down instruction, and teachers cannot cover as much material as they would like. Third, some teachers think that making adaptations for the few students who need them is not fair to the higher achieving students who are ready to work at a

faster pace. When asked to make specific modifications for a student with learning disabilities in her high school French class, a teacher commented, "I have a number of students in my class who would benefit from the modifications you are asking me to make for John. I'm not sure it would be fair to the other students for me to do these things for John and not offer the other students the same opportunities."

We have investigated how students feel when teachers make adaptations for individual students within the regular classroom, and the kinds of adaptations students view as acceptable and unacceptable. Some of the findings of these studies surprised us and should put to rest some of the concerns teachers have about taking the time to make adaptations (Schumm et al., 1992; Vaughn, Schumm, and Kouzekanani, 1993; Vaughn, Schumm, Niarhos, and Daugherty, 1993).

Both elementary and secondary students overwhelmingly preferred teachers who made adaptations for students who needed more help. They liked teachers who used flexible grouping for learning, who met with and assisted students with individual needs, and who varied instruction to meet those needs. However, they also preferred teachers who gave all students the same homework assignments. Elementary students didn't mind if some students were given different tests as long as the tests were the same length and took the same amount of time. Secondary students preferred teachers who gave all students the same tests and textbooks.

An especially interesting finding was that students who are high achieving not only were aware that certain students in their classrooms needed extra help, but they also preferred a teacher who made adaptations to help all the students learn. No high-achieving student in these studies expressed concern that instructional time would be taken away from him or her if the teacher took the time to give extra help to those who needed it. The following comment by one high-achieving high school student illustrates the altruism that was typical: "Even though I am smart enough to deal with any method of teaching, I realize not everyone else is. I like to see a diversified method of teaching in which the individual needs of students are met. Often students who do not perform

APPLY THE CONCEPT 7.1

TEACHING CONTENT TO SECOND LANGUAGE LEARNERS

Second language readers who may also have learning disabilities, have specific difficulties with vocabulary, syntax, and background knowledge when learning to read English. The *Cognitive Academic Language Learning Approach* (CALLA) (Chamot and O'Malley, 1994) is an interactive content-based approach to content learning that makes use of interactive teaching and metacognitive strategies that increase general reading skills in second language learners (Chamot and O'Malley, 1994). Some of these strategies include: elaboration and active use of prior knowledge, planning or setting a purpose for learning, monitoring for comprehension with questions, and self-evaluation.

Metacognition is more prevalent in the latter two strategies listed above. In monitoring comprehension with questions, teachers can teach students to make inferences or self-question for clarification, by explicitly modeling either or both techniques. Self-evaluation allows students to reflect on what they have learned, read, or discussed. Self ratings and learning logs can be used with all grade levels. The benefits of having students think about their learning can be transferred to their becoming more successful both in the content and in the use of the second language.

---

as well are overlooked as ignorant and stupid, unable to learn. But these students are the ones that must be concentrated on so that they can develop better." (Vaughn, Schumm, Niarhos, and Daugherty, 1993).

In contrast to the high-achieving students, low-achieving students were more likely to prefer a teacher who made no adaptations for students with special needs. Two possible reasons that low-achieving students felt negatively about teacher adaptations were that, (1) they were concerned about "fitting in" socially and did not wish to have their deficiencies revealed to their peers and, (2) many low-achieving students are passive learners (Torgesen, 1982; Torgesen and Licht, 1983). If they have a teacher who makes adaptations, they may be forced to take a more active role in their own learning—something that many low-achieving students are reluctant to do.

Adapting Textbooks

Despite these concerns, however, research indicates that students at all achievement levels feel that they need textbook adaptations and are not getting the adaptations they need (Schumm et al., 1992). Apply the Concept 7.2 lists textbook adaptations you might

consider, three of which are discussed here in greater depth.

Study Guides

Study guides are tools teachers can use to lead students through a reading assignment. A typical study guide is a series of questions or activities that students complete while they read a selection. As Wood, Lapp, and Flood (1992, p. 1) put it, "Study guides are designed to accompany reading, not follow it." Study guides help direct students to the key points to be learned. They also provide structure for students to reflect about what they are reading and to engage in higher-order thinking. In short, study guides can help "tutor" a student through a chapter.

Commercially prepared study guides can be purchased as supplements to some textbooks. The advantage of commercially prepared study guides is that they are already done. Real time savers! The disadvantage is that the publisher does not know your style of teaching, your emphasis, or your school district's requirements. Moreover, the publisher does not know your students. Many teachers elect to construct their own study guides.

Many types of study guides exist. Some are designed to help students activate prior knowledge,

APPLY THE CONCEPT 7.2

GUIDELINES FOR ADAPTING CONTENT AREA TEXTBOOKS

Substitute the Textbook for students who have severe word-recognition problems:

- Audiotape textbook content.
- Read textbook aloud to students.
- Pair students to master textbook content.
- Use direct experiences, films, videotapes, recorders, and computer programs as substitutes for textbook reading.
- Work with students individually or in small groups to master textbook material.

Simplify the Textbook for students whose reading level is far below that of the textbook used in class:

- Construct abridged versions of the textbook content or use the publisher's abridged version.
- Provide students with chapter outlines or summaries.
- Use a multilevel, multimaterial approach.

Highlight Key Concepts for students who have difficulty comprehending textbook material:

- Preview reading assignments with students to orient them to the topic and provide guidelines for budgeting reading and study time.
- Provide students with a purpose for reading.
- Provide an overview of an assignment before reading.
- Structure opportunities for students to activate prior knowledge before starting a reading assignment.

- Introduce key vocabulary before assigning reading.
- Develop a study guide to direct learning.
- Summarize or reduce textbook information to guide classroom discussions and independent reading.
- Color-code or highlight textbooks.
- Reduce length of assignments.
- Slow down the pace of reading assignments.
- Provide assistance in answering text-based questions.
- Demonstrate or model effective reading strategies.
- Place students in cooperative learning groups to master textbook content.
- Teach comprehension-monitoring techniques to improve ongoing understanding of text material.
- Teach students to use graphic aids to understand textbook information.

Increase Idea Retention for students who have difficulty with long-term memory.

- Structure postreading activities to increase retention of content.
- Teach reading strategies to improve retention.
- Teach students to record key concepts and terms for study purposes.
- Teach memory strategies to improve retention of text material.

Source: From J. S. Schumm and K. Strickler (1991). Guidelines for adapting content area textbooks: Keeping teachers and students content. *Intervention in School and Clinic, 27*(2), 79–84. Copyright (1991) by PRO-ED, Inc. Reprinted with permission.

others to help students understand literal or inferential information in the textbook, others to foster peer interaction and discussion, and still others to help students recognize meaning patterns in text (e.g., cause and effect, compare and contrast). Following

are some general suggestions for developing study guides (Wood et al., 1992):

— *Decide whether a guide is needed.* Is textbook information particularly dense? Are there few considerate features? Will student with special needs need support and guidance to get through the chapter and to grasp the most important ideas?

- *Analyze the chapter.* Can some parts be omitted? Are some parts easier to understand than others? What skills will your students need to read and understand this material?
- *Decide how you want to structure your study guide.* Create one that includes the suggested components.

All study guides should also include the following components (Hudson, Ormsbee, and Myles, 1994):

- Specific information about the reading assignment (page numbers, title)
- Learning objectives of the assignment
- Purpose statement for the assignment
- Introduction of key terms or vocabulary
- Activities for students to complete
- Questions for students to answer as they read

Text Highlighting

Students with comprehension problems have difficulty sifting out important information. Underlining or highlighting key points in the textbooks can help students attend to the most salient information (Wood and Wooley, 1986). In reading the textbook, highlight the information you think is most important. Then student or adult volunteers can use your book as a guide to highlight the same information in books for students with reading and learning disabilities. Keep in mind that you will also want to teach students this and other textbook study skills (see the section on teaching study skills).

Using Alternative Reading Materials

For students with very low reading skills who are able to learn by listening:

- *Audio-tape textbook chapters.* Adult and student volunteers can read the chapters on audio tape. Students can then listen to the tapes at home or in their resource classes. Apply the

Concept 7.3 provides ideas for taping content area textbooks.

- *Read text aloud to students.* Encourage students to follow along, reading silently. Pause frequently to assess student learning from the reading.
- *Pair a good reader with a poor reader.* The good reader reads the textbook material aloud and, together, the two students learn the content.

Sometimes you will find it necessary to use alternative materials that present similar content. Films, videotapes, and trade books provide good sources. Computer software programs in which the text can be read by the computer, such as encyclopedias on CD-ROM, are other resources.

Developing Listener-Friendly Lectures

Since the popularity of personal computers, people have discussed software programs in terms of their "user friendliness." In other words, is the program easy to understand? Does the program use familiar language or at least define unfamiliar terms? Does the program give you cue words to signal the important ideas and processes? If you don't understand something, does the program allow you to ask questions? Does the program have more than one way to explain a difficult concept or process? If the program has these features, then one might consider it "user friendly."

Now take a minute to go back and reread the previous paragraph but substitute the word *lecture* for the word *program* (hence the term *listener-friendly lecture*). Just as using "considerate" or "user friendly" text assists students in learning the critical information, a well-organized lecture makes the students' work easier in that it assists them in seeing relationships among concepts and in distinguishing important from supplementary information. It also helps them relate new information to old. Well-designed lectures seem particularly beneficial for second language learners and for listeners with relatively limited language skills and little prior knowledge of the content because of the reduced

APPLY THE CONCEPT 7.3

AUDIOTAPING CONTENT AREA TEXTBOOKS

Students who have low reading skills or vision impairments can listen to chapters that have been audiotaped by classmates or volunteers. Recordings for the Blind & Dyslexic (800-221-4792) is a nonprofit organization that records trade books and textbooks for individuals who are blind, have low vision, or have learning disabilities. This organization provides on-loan recorded books at all academic levels.

Audiotaped books are increasingly popular and acceptable to students. Students can listen to the tapes in a listening center in elementary classrooms, resource rooms, school libraries, or at home. Here are some suggestions for audiotaping reading assignments:

- Instead of recording an entire chapter verbatim, read the key sections and paraphrase the less important sections.
- Code the text so that readers or listeners will know whether the person on the tape is reading or paraphrasing.
- Provide a short advanced organizer on the tape to help students get ready to read and listen.

- Insert questions that readers or listeners can stop and think about.
- Remind readers or listeners to stop periodically and think about what they have read.
- Use a natural tone of voice and a comfortable rate.
- Have students experiment with taped texts to see whether they comprehend better with or without the text.

---

processing burdens (Cronbach and Snow, 1977; Tobias, 1978).

As you plan your teaching, the following guidelines can make your lectures *"listener-friendly"*:

- Use advance organizers.
- Use cue words or phrases to let students know what information is important (e.g., "It is important that you know . . .," "They key information to remember is . . .," "In summary . . .").
- Repeat important information.

- Write important information on board, transparency, and handout.
- Stress key points by varying the tone and quality of your voice.
- Number ideas or points (e.g., first, second, next, then, finally).
- Write technical words or words that are difficult to spell.
- Use a study guide that lists the major concepts, with space for students to add other information.

- Use pictures, diagrams, and semantic maps to show relationships among ideas.
- Provide examples and nonexamples of the concepts you are discussing.
- Ask questions or encourage discussion that requires students to relate the new information to ideas they already know (from their own background or your previous lectures).
- Stop frequently and have students work with partners and discuss what they have learned.
- Allow time at the end of a lecture for students to look over their notes, summarize, and ask questions.

Table 7.1 provides cues that can assist students in "seeing" the key information. By using these guidelines you will naturally incorporate indicate what information is important.

Using the Pause Procedure

One technique that has demonstrated its effectiveness for students with learning and behavior problems in enhancing the understanding and recall of information presented through lectures is the pause procedure (e.g., DiVesta and Smith 1979; Ruhl, Hughes, and Schloss, 1987; Ruhl, Hughes, and Gajar, 1990). The procedure consists of pausing during natural breaks in the lectures and having students work in partners for about two minutes to discuss what they are learning and review their notes. At the end of the two minutes, ask students whether they have any questions or concepts that

■ **TABLE 7.1** *Cues to Listen and Watch for in Lectures*

Type of Cue	Examples
Organizational Cues	Today, we will be discussing . . .
	The topic I want to cover today . . .
	There are (number) points I want you to be sure to learn . . .
	The important relationship is . . .
	The main point of this discussion is . . .
	Any statement that signals a number of position (e.g., first, last, next, then).
	To review/summarize/recap . . .
Emphasis Cues	
Verbal	You need to know/understand/remember . . .
	This is important/key/basic/critical . . .
	Let me repeat this . . .
	Let me check, now do you understand . . .
	Any statement is repeated.
	Words or terms are emphasized.
	Teacher speaks more slowly, loudly, or with more emphasis.
	Teacher stresses certain words.
	Teacher spells words.
	Teacher asks rhetorical question.
Nonverbal	Information written on overhead/board
	Information handed out in study guide
	Teacher emphasizes point using gestures.

Source: Adapted from S. K. Suritsky and C. A. Hughes (1996). Notetaking strategy instruction. In D. D. Deshler, E. S. Ellis, and B. K. Lenz, *Teaching adolescents with learning disabilities* (2nd ed.), p. 275. Denver: Love.

or clarification. Then re-

, college students with and
ies performed better than
ithout the pauses for dis-
hoice tests and on free re-
~~calls of the information~~ presented (Ruhl et al., 1990).

Adapting Class Assignments and Homework

In a survey of students with and without learning disabilities in grades 6–8, the students with learning disabilities had greater difficulty completing homework assignments because of problems with attention, motivation, and study skills (Gajria and Salend, 1995). After conducting a comprehensive review of the literature, Cooper and Nye (1994) concluded that homework assignments for students with disabilities should be brief, focused on reinforcement rather than new material, monitored carefully, and supported through parental involvement.

The most important aspect of making assignments is to give complete information. You need to let students know why the assignment is important, when it is due, what support they will have for completing the task, and steps necessary for getting the job done. Having complete information helps to motivate students. The tips in Figure 7.12 can help you provide students with a complete set of directions.

Class assignments and homework can be adapted for special learners to that they can experience success without undue attention being brought to their learning difficulties. The key to success is to make assignments appropriate in content, length, time required to complete, and skill level needed to accomplish the task. It is also important to explain the assignments, model several problems if appropriate, and check for understanding (Sawyer, Nelson, Jayanthi, Bursuck, and Epstein, 1996). Students should know how and where to get help when they get stuck.

Constructing and Adapting Tests

The best way to discover what students have learned is to construct student-friendly tests, adapt test administration and scoring as necessary, consider alternatives to testing (such as assessment portfolios), and teach test-taking skills.

Student-friendly tests are considerate to the test taker in content and format. The content has been covered in class or assigned readings, and students have been told explicitly that they are responsible for learning it. The format is clear and easy to understand.

To construct student-friendly tests, you must first decide what skills and concepts to include.

In test format, directions should be clear and unambiguous, and items should be legible and properly spaced. Students should have sufficient room to

---

■ **FIGURE 7.12** *Tips for Giving Assignments*

1. Explain the purpose of the assignment. Stress what you expect students to learn and why learning the skill or concept is important. Connect the skill or concept to real-life applications.
2. Explain in detail the procedures for completing the assignment. Ask one or two students to summarize the procedures, to check for understanding.
3. Get students started by modeling one or two problems or by providing an example.
4. Describe the equipment and materials needed to complete the assignment.
5. Anticipate trouble spots and ask students how they might tackle difficult parts in the assignment.
6. Explain when the assignment is due.
7. Explain how the assignment will be graded and how it will impact students' grades.
8. Describe appropriate ways to get help or support in completing the assignment.
9. For an in-class assignment, explain your expectations for student behavior while they complete the assignment, and what students who finish early should do.
10. Address student questions.

place their answers, and specific guidelines if answers are to be written on a separate sheet (Salend, 1994). Attention to format is important for all students, but particularly for those who have difficulty reading and taking tests and who are very anxious about test taking.

Even with student-friendly tests, students with learning and behavior problems may have difficulty reading tests, working within time constraints, or resisting distractions during a test. Poor or laborious writing may cause them to tire easily and inhibit performance on a test. Figure 7.13 suggests accommodations for test administration and scoring. As you decide which, if any, adaptations to use, consider the material to be covered by the test, the test's task requirements (e.g, reading, taking dictation), and the particular needs of special learners.

Creating Portfolios to Supplement or Replace Tests

In addition to or instead of tests, consider using portfolios as an assessment tool. **Assessment portfolios** are collections of work samples that document a student's progress in a content area. You can use portfolios to provide tangible evidence of student performance over a period of time. Portfolios can include writing samples of all stages of the writing process in all genres. Suggestions for developing assessment portfolios include:

— Develop a portfolio plan consistent with your purposes for the assignment.
— Clarify what work will go into portfolios.
— Start with only a couple of different kinds of entries and expand gradually.
— Compare notes with other teachers as you experiment with portfolios.
— Have as a long-term goal the inclusion of a variety of assessments that address content, process, and attitude goals across the curriculum.
— Make portfolios accessible in the classroom. Students and teachers should be able to add to the collection quickly and easily.
— Develop summary sheets or graphs that help to describe a body of information (e.g., "I can do" lists, lists of books read, or pieces of writing

■ **FIGURE 7.13**   *Testing Accommodations*

- Teach students test-taking skills.
- Give frequent quizzes rather than only exams.
- Give take-home tests.
- Test on less content than rest of the class.
- Change type of questions (e.g., essay to multiple choice).
- Use tests with enlarged print.
- Use black-and-white copies (versus dittos).
- Highlight key words in questions.
- Provide extra space on tests for answering.
- Simplify wording of test questions.
- Allow students to answer few questions.
- Give extra help preparing for tests.
- Give the actual test as a study guide.

- Give practice questions as a study guide.
- Give open-book and note tests.
- Give tests to small groups.
- Give extended time to finish tests.
- Read test questions to students.
- Allow use of learning aids during tests (e.g., calculators).
- Give individual help with directions during tests.
- Allow oral instead of written answers (e.g., tape recorders).
- Allow answers in outline format.
- Allow word processors.
- Give feedback to individual students during test.

Source: M. Jayanthi, M. H. Epstein, E. A. Polloway, and W. D. Bursuck (1996). Testing adaptions: A national survey of the testing practices of general education teachers. *Journal of Special Education.*

completed). Let students record these data when possible.

— Work with the student to choose a few representative samples that demonstrate the student's progress.

— Review portfolios with students periodically (at least four times during the school year). The review should be a time to celebrate progress and to set future goals.

— Encourage students to review portfolios with a classmate before reviewing with the teacher. Students should help make decisions about what to keep.

— In preparation for a parent conference, have students develop a table of contents for the portfolio (Radencich, Beers, and Schumm, 1993 pp. 119–120).

Examples of items you can include in a portfolio are as follows (Radencich et al., 1993):

Student assignments and work samples
Student interviews
Self-assessments
Audiotapes
Videotapes
Diagnostic tests
Achievement tests
Teacher-made tests
Pages from journals
Awards
Personal reading and writing records
Peer assessment
Interest and attitude inventories
Photographs
Copies of passages read fluently
Contributions from parents
Report cards
List of accomplishments
Observation checklists

Students with learning and behavior problems need a cadre of study skills and learning strategies to succeed in these classes. Let's look at some strategies for teaching those.

STUDY SKILLS AND LEARNING STRATEGIES

In addition to learning content area information, students with learning and behavior problems also need to develop study skills, learning strategies, and habits. They need to develop effective metacognitive strategies. Particularly as students move into secondary and postsecondary settings, the task demands require more emphasis on such skills as time management, self-monitoring and feedback, listening and notetaking, studying from textbooks, and test-taking skills (Brinckerhoff, Shaw, and McGuire, 1992). Surveys and observational studies conducted in secondary settings show: (1) a heavy reliance on written products as a means of evaluating performance, (2) the need to listen to lectures containing few advance organizers and limited opportunities for interactions, and (3) a limited amount of individual help and teacher feedback (Putnam, 1992; Schumaker, Wildgen, and Sherman, 1982; Schumm, Vaugh, Haager, McDowell, Rothlien, Saumell, 1995).

Study skills can be defined as those competencies associated with acquiring, recording, organizing, synthesizing, remembering, and using information and ideas (Devine, 1987). Study skills are the key to independent learning, and they help students gain and use information effectively. Lock (1981) divides study skills into three areas:

1. *Personal development skills:* personal discipline, management and organizational skills, self-monitoring and reinforcement, and positive attitude toward studying

2. *Process skills:* technical methods of studying such as notetaking, outlining, learning information from a text, and library reference skills

3. *Expression skills:* retrieval skills, test-taking skills, and using oral and/or written expression to demonstrate understanding

As would be expected, these are the skills that students with learning and behavior problems have difficulty developing. One reason for this may be that most study skills are not directly and systematically taught in the same manner in which reading and math skills are taught (Devine, 1987).

Personal Development Skills

Personal development skills include personal discipline, goal setting, management and organizational skills, self-monitoring and reinforcement, and positive attitude toward studying. Many of the personal management and organizational skills related to school focus on time management and scheduling, self-monitoring and reinforcement, and notebook organization.

Time Management and Scheduling

Jon's mom is concerned because Jon, her son with learning disabilities, falls asleep while trying to finish book reports the night before they are due. Even if she gets him up early in the morning, there is little chance Jon will have time to finish—and then there would only be a first draft. This just seems to be the way that Jon works. Even though Jon knows about the assignments for three weeks, he waits until two nights before they're due to start reading, despite her queries about homework. Granted, it takes Jon longer than the other students to select, read, and report on a book, but Ms. Brice, his teacher, had given him enough time by giving him the assignment early. He has the skills to get a B or C on the assignment if he would just start earlier.

Many parents and teachers can identify with this scenario. Jon has the skills to complete the assignment successfully, but he just lacks the personal management skills, particularly time management. *Time management* is simply organizing and monitoring time so that tasks can be scheduled and completed in an efficient and timely manner. The following ideas can be used to teach students how to schedule and manage their time.

Rationale. The first step in getting students to schedule and manage their time is to build a rationale for its importance to success in school and later life.

Bragstad and Stumpf (1982) suggest nine reasons (as presented in Figure 7.14) why time management is worth the investment.

Determining How the Time Is Spent. Before students can decide how to schedule their time they need to determine how they are currently spending it. Using a schedule, such as the one presented in Figure 7.15, have students keep track of their activities for one or two weeks. Also have them list the school assignments they have for the time period and if they have "too little," "enough," or "too much" time to complete them.

Estimating Time. Before students can accurately schedule, they need to have a good idea of how long it takes to complete various tasks. As part of the time management process, have students determine how long it takes them to complete regularly scheduled tasks such as meals, commuting, reading assignments in their various textbooks, writing a paragraph on a topic, completing a ten-problem math assignment, answering five questions over a chapter, and so on. Although there will probably be considerable variability in the time taken to complete a task, most students with learning and behavior problems underestimate the time it takes. Having students get an idea of the time required can be helpful when planning a schedule.

Scheduling. If students feel that they do not have enough time to get their tasks completed or if they do not have regular times for studying, encourage them to set up a schedule. Some suggestions that students might want to use when setting up their schedules are:

1. Plan regular study times.

2. Plan at least one-hour blocks of time in which to study.

3. Plan which assignments you are going to work on during the study time.

4. Take the first five minutes of each study activity to review what you have done already and what you have already learned, and to plan what you are

■ **FIGURE 7.14** *Why Bother with a Time Schedule?*

Each year in school, assignments seem to become longer and more difficult. If you want to be a successful student, scheduling your time will be helpful. Here are some of the advantages of scheduling time that other high school students have discovered:

1. Parents will "get off your back" when they see that you have planned your study time. As they observe you becoming responsible, they may gradually stop checking on what you are doing.

2. Writing down what you must do each day relieves your mind. Then when you study, you can focus and think more effectively.

3. You are less likely to procrastinate, that is, to put off your work, if you have a set time to begin.

4. When you set a certain amount of time to do each assignment, your concentration improves so that you work better. This saves time. You may even beat the clock as you become more efficient.

5. With a schedule, you are less likely to let a ten-minute break extend into the rest of the evening.

6. You experience a feeling of satisfaction when you are in control of your life, knowing *what* you want to do *when*. You feel better about yourself.

7. Organizing your time helps you come to class prepared; you learn more because the class presentation or activity has more meaning. As a result, your grades improve.

8. When you assume control of your time, you feel relaxed and ready to have fun when you have some free time because your work is up-to-date. You get rid of that feeling of anxiety or pressure.

9. Scheduling your use of time is the intelligent way to operate if you want to learn, to achieve, and to have more time for fun with your friends.

Source: B. J. Bragstad and S. M. Stumpf, *A Guidebook for Teaching Study Skills and Motivation* (Boston: Allyn and Bacon, 1982), p. 200. Reprinted with permission.

going to accomplish today. This helps promote long-term learning and a sense of accomplishment.

5. When studying longer than one hour, plan breaks and stick to the time allowed for the breaks.

6. Use daytime or early evening for study if possible. Most people are less efficient at night.

7. Work on your most difficult subjects when you are most alert.

8. Distribute your studying for a test rather than cram.

9. Balance your time between studying and other activities. Allow time for recreational activities.

10. Reward yourself by marking through your schedule each time you meet a scheduled commitment and by crossing off items you complete on your "to do" list.

Not only should regular times for studying be listed on the schedule, but due dates for assignments and dates for other events should be noted so that the

schedule also serves as a calendar. Students should also be encouraged to set aside some time they can use as they please, if they accomplish their tasks on schedule during the day or week. This type of self-determined reinforcer may serve as an extra motivation for some students.

▬ **MONITORING:** Setting up a schedule will do little good unless students follow and monitor their schedules. Using a weekly schedule have students fill in those activities they feel are important to monitor. Figure 7.16 presents a schedule for Jon. His study time, time spent working out, time spent on his after-school job, and TV time were the most important tasks for him to monitor, so he scheduled them in each week. He also noted when the next book report was due and he assigned time to begin reading the book on a daily basis so that the last night "impossible job" would not continue to plague him.

Jon developed a contract with himself. If he studied at least 80 percent of the time he had scheduled during the week, then he could work out at the

■ **FIGURE 7.15** *Weekly Schedule and Activity Summary*

NAME: ___Jon___

WEEK OF: ___Sept 25___

ACTIVITY SUMMARY

Activity	Number of hours per week
Sleep	51
Meals	14
Job	3
Transportation	5
Class Time	30
Talking on Phone	2
Watching TV	9
Other Recreation	19
Study	8

COMMENTS:

Had report due Thurs. for history Didn't have enough time to get it done well. Just an OK job.

	MON.	TUES.	WEDS.	THURS.	FRI.	SAT.	SUN.	
6:00 a.m.	get up & eat →							6:00 a.m.
7:00	ride bus	ride bus	rie bus	ride bus	ride bus	sleep	sleep	7:00
8:00								8:00
9:00	History English							9:00
10:00	P.E.					do yard work	go to Church	10:00
11:00	Welding	*Same every day*						11:00
12:00	Lunch					work	eat lunch	12:00
1:00 p.m.	Algebra					go to the gym	read mags	1:00 p.m.
2:00	General Science							2:00
3:00	ride bus					gym	play video games	3:00
4:00								4:00
5:00	watch TV	play video games	work on report	gym	goof off with		games	5:00
6:00	eat dinner	eat		eat	friends	eat dinner	eat	6:00
7:00	watch TV	watch TV	eat dinner	dinner	date		watch TV	7:00
8:00			go to library	watch movie on VCR			study	8:00
9:00	study		to work on report					9:00
10:00	sleep	sleep	on report	sleep				10:00
11:00			sleep		sleep		sleep	11:00
12:00						sleep		12:00
1:00 a.m.								1:00 a.m.
2:00								2:00

gym or "goof off" two extra hours on Saturday. In this way Jon is not only monitoring his schedule but setting goals and providing rewards for meeting his goals. Although Jon realizes that schedules need to be flexible, he has found that planning, even when plans change, helps him get more work accomplished in a timely manner. Apply the Concept 7.4 describes some high- and low-tech approaches to scheduling.

— **USING A "TO DO" LIST:** Using a "to do" list simply takes away the burden of remembering by writing it down. Notice how the schedule that Jon uses integrates a "to do" list with the weekly schedule (see Figure 7.16). Jon's resource teacher taught him an additional way to use his "to do" list and schedule. She showed him how to break a difficult assignment into several smaller tasks and then add each task to the "to do" list so that he is not trying to

■ **FIGURE 7.16**   *Weekly Schedule and To-Do List for Jon*

NAME: _Jon_

WEEK OF: _Oct 14_

	MON.	TUES.	WEDS.	THURS.	FRI.	SAT.	SUN.	
6:00 a.m.	get up and eat →							6:00 a.m.
7:00	ride					sleep	sleep	7:00
8:00	bus							8:00
9:00	History	Same every day				house +		9:00
10:00	English					yard	go to	10:00
11:00	PE					chores	church	11:00
12:00	Welding Lunch						eat	12:00
1:00 p.m.	Algebra					eat	read	1:00 p.m.
2:00	General					go	for fun	2:00
3:00	Science ride					to gym	goof off	3:00
4:00	bus						and eat	4:00
5:00	recreational activity			study	eat have fun	eat and have fun		5:00
6:00	eat →							6:00
7:00	study	study	study	study			study	7:00
8:00								8:00
9:00	↓	↓	↓	↓			↓	9:00
10:00	sleep →						sleep	10:00
11:00	↓				sleep →		↓	11:00

TO DO LIST						
history paper due math assign finish book	math assign	math assign book report due	math assign welding project due	science test math test	chores mow grass pull weeds fix cooler	start English paper

APPLY THE CONCEPT 7.4

TECHNOLOGY FOR STUDENT SELF-MANAGEMENT

In today's high-tech world, portable personal record keeping systems are increasingly available and affordable. Digital- or software-based applications include a range of products—for example, programmable wristwatches, hand-held word processors with small view screens, and miniaturized laptop computers. Such devices aid in scheduling time, keeping addresses and phone numbers, and accessing information resources, which can be ideal for students with planning and self-management needs. Personal record keeping software products might include the following features: notetaker, planner, calendar, schedule, spreadsheet, programmable clock, timer or stopwatch, and capability permitting the user to create a personal information database.

Many low-tech applications are available as well that have been developed specifically for student use, such as the familiar assignment notebooks and notebook organizers that students carry. Directly teaching students how to use these devices to maximum advantage increases their ability to apply personal development skills and become independent learners. Adaptations of notebook organizers for students with special needs include, for example, a time management program called "Plan Your Day," which uses a system of picture prompts, laminated cards, pocket folders, and stickers. Information about self-management products from a variety of manufacturers for students with special needs, including print, video, and software products, may be obtained from PCI Life Skills Educational Publishers in San Antonio, TX (1-800-594-4263).

---

complete the entire task in one night. She also showed him how to cross off completed tasks, something that gives him a real sense of accomplishment. Hence, the "not enough time" scenario described earlier is becoming less and less frequent. This is important for Jon since he plans to attend a community college and study electronics next year.

Self-Monitoring and Reinforcement

"By the end of the month I want to lose five pounds. If I reach my goal, I'm going to buy a new pair of jeans." How many times have you set a goal and then promised yourself some kind of reinforcement if you reach that goal? Then you probably start weighing yourself and you might even put a chart on the wall next to the scale and keep track of the number of pounds you are losing.

In the case of students with learning and behavior problems there is much research to support the notion that they have difficulty goal setting and self-monitoring, whether it be in the areas of attention and memory, reading comprehension, or personal

and management skills (Bos and Filip, 1984; Palincsar and Brown, 1987; Schunk, 1989, 1996; Tollefson, Tracy, Johnsen, Buenning, and Farmer, 1981; Torgesen and Licht, 1983; Wilson and David, 1994).

Van Reusen and Bos (1992) developed a strategy that students can use to assist them in setting goals and keeping track of their progress. The strategy uses the acronym MARKER (it gives students a *mark* to work toward and is a *marker* of their progress), and includes the following steps:

Make a list of goals, set the order, set the date.
Arrange a plan for each goal and predict your success.
Run your plan for each goal and adjust if necessary.
Keep records of your progress.
Evaluate your progress toward each goal.
Reward yourself when you reach a goal, and set a new goal.

For each goal, students use a Goal Planning Sheet (see Figure 7.17) to answer the following questions:

■ **FIGURE 7.17**   *Goal Planning and Monitoring Sheet*

Name: _____   Class: _____   Date: _____

1. Goal: _____

2. Reason(s) for working on goal: _____

3. Goal will be worked on at: _____

4. Date to reach goal (due date): _____

5. Materials needed: _____

_____

_____

_____

_____

_____

_____

_____

_____

_____

_____

6. Steps used to reach the goal: _____

_____

_____

_____

_____

7. Progress toward the goal: Record in each box the date and progress rating.

   3—Goal reached   2—Good progress made   1—Some progress made   0—No progress made

Date / Rating					
Date / Rating					
Date / Rating					

8. Reward for reaching goal: _____

Source: Adapted from A. K. Van Reusen and C. S. Bos (1992). *Use of the goal-regulation strategy to improve the goal attainment of students with learning disabilities* (Final Report). Tucson, Ariz.: University of Arizona.

— Can I describe my goal?

— What is the reason or purpose for the goal?

— Where am I going to work on and complete this goal?

— How much time do I have to complete the goal?

— What materials do I need to complete the goal?

— Can I divide the goal into steps or parts? If so, in what order should I complete each step or part?

— How am I going to keep records of my progress?

— How will I reward myself for reaching my goal?

The teacher can use the steps in the Strategies Intervention Model (see Chapter Two: Cognitive Behavior Modification) to teach the students the strategy. After learning the strategy, students usually work on one to three goals at a time, keeping progress data on each goal.

When Van Reusen and Bos (1992) used this strategy with middle and high school students with learning disabilities and behavior disorders, they found that students accomplished more goals and gained a more informed perspective of their educational and personal goals.

Similar to the goal regulation strategy of Van Reusen and Bos (1992), Lenz, Ehren, and Smiley (1991) developed a goal attainment system to assist secondary students with learning disabilities to successfully complete project assignments. Students structured their goal setting, task planning, and task monitoring using a Student Management Guide in which they evaluated the project, set goals and timelines, and then monitored their progress. This system was helpful to the students in increasing the number of projects successfully completed and the quality of the goals set.

Hughes and his colleagues (Hughes, Ruhl, Deshler, and Schumaker, 1995) have developed an assignment completion strategy for the Strategies Intervention Model that is similar. The steps in this learning strategy include:

Psych up   (Prepare your assignment monitoring form and your mind.)

Record and ask   (Record the assignment, think about it, and ask questions.)

Organize   (Break the assignment into parts, estimate and schedule the number of study sessions, and organize your materials.)

Jump to it   (Survey the assignment, set goals and a reward.)

Engage in the work   (Follow the instructions, note questions, and get help if you need it.)

Check the work   (Check for requirements and quality, store the assignment and reward yourself.)

Turn it in   (Take it to class, turn it in, record the date, and praise yourself.)

Set your course   (Record your grade, evaluate your assignment, and think about future assignments.)

Notebook Organization

Although Susan shows up on time for each of her high school classes, the only things she regularly remembers are her comb and make-up. Her notebook, pencils, assignments, and textbooks show up on an irregular basis. When she does bring her notebook, it is so disorganized that it proves to be of little assistance to her. Susan is not unlike other students with learning and behavior problems. Their difficulty in organizing materials is frequently observed by teachers and parents. Teachers of these students and other low-achieving students have found it helpful to take the time to conduct a unit on notebook organization, providing information about the type of notebook materials that facilitate both flexibility and organization.

You may want to start the year in a resource or self-contained secondary program by conducting a unit on notebook organization and time management. In fact, if you know the previous spring who your students are going to be, you may want to send home a suggested list of materials that students and parents should purchase. Figure 7.18 presents an adapted list of those materials Scheuneman and Lambourne (1981) suggest for a "guaranteed successful notebook system." A three-ring binder is

■ **FIGURE 7.18** *List of Notebook Materials*

1 large three-ring notebook
1 school supply pouch
    4 pens (2 black, 2 blue)
    2 pencils
    1 eraser for pencil and ink
    1 first aid kit
        2 bandaids
        2 aspirins
        2 quarters for phone call
    1 small hole punch
    1 small calculator
    1 small package file cards
13 dividers with tabs marked as follows:
    schedule and calendar
    1st period (name of class)
    2nd period (name of class)
    etc.
    reference information
    dictionary (if available)
    personal word list
    extra notebook paper
    extra graph paper
1 twelve-inch metric and inch ruler
1 notebook dictionary (if available)
1 notebook calendar
8 weekly schedule sheets
1 personal word list (of commonly misspelled words)
Any relevant reference information
Notebook paper
Graph paper

Source: Adapted from R. S. Scheuneman and J. Lambourne, *Study Skills for School Success* (Tucson, Ariz.: Study Skills for School Success, 1981). Used with permission.

advantageous over other types of notebooks because it allows one to add and delete materials easily and to file materials according to classes.

The weekly schedule and the "to do" list that were presented earlier in this chapter can be used in this notebook. Most students also find it helpful to have a monthly or semester calendar in the front of their notebooks to keep track of long-term projects and activities.

Under each class section, place class syllabi and assignments at the beginning of the section. Use the extra notebook paper for taking notes and then place the dated notes in chronological order under the appropriate section. Handouts from class can also be integrated into the notes or kept at the beginning or the end of the class section. Some students have found it useful to keep an assignment sheet at the beginning of each class section using the headings of Assignment, Date Due, Progress Update, Completed, and Grade. This allows a student to keep track of his or her progress and grades for the various assignments in a class.

The personal word list can be used to keep an alphabetical list of words the student uses frequently and often misspells. For some students it may be advantageous to purchase the *Bad Speller's Dictionary* (Kreviski and Linfield, 1974) or the *Misspeller's Dictionary* (1983). These dictionaries alphabetically list words by their common misspelling. After each misspelling the correct spelling is given.

Classroom Participation

Students who participate actively in class tend to be more successful academically than their quieter, less attentive peers (Ellis, 1991). Students with learning and behavior problems may benefit from specific strategies to enhance their classroom participation. The SLANT starter strategy is part of the Strategies Intervention Model (see Chapter Two: Cognitive Behavior Modification) and was designed for the purpose of increasing active participation in class. The acronym SLANT stands for

> <u>S</u>it up
> <u>L</u>ean forward
> <u>A</u>ctivate your thinking
> <u>N</u>ame key information
> <u>T</u>rack the talker

The SLANT strategy is viewed as a starter strategy because it is taught easily, learned quickly, and readily incorporated into different settings (Ellis, 1991). Examples of <u>A</u>ctivate your thinking include asking yourself questions ("What is this about?" "What do I need to remember?"); answering your questions ("This is about _____." "I need to remember _____."); and asking the teacher a question when you do not understand. Examples of Name key information include answering the teacher's questions, sharing your ideas, and additions to other's comments (Ellis, 1991). This general set of activities can be used in any learning situation to improve students' active participation.

Process Skills

Process skills include the technical methods of studying such as notetaking, outlining, learning information from text, and research and library skills.

Listening and Taking Notes

In school, students spend more time listening than reading, speaking, or writing. On the average, teachers in secondary settings spend at least half of their class time presenting information through lectures (Putnam, Deshler, and Schumaker, 1993). Furthermore, teachers rely on information presented in class discussion and lectures as the basis for a significant number of items on tests (Putnam et al., 1993). Notetaking is one of the most efficient ways to record this information. It has several important functions:

— Notetaking increases students' attention.
— Notetaking, as opposed to just listening, requires a deeper level of cognitive processing in that the student must make sense of the information and write the ideas.
— Because the information has been processed more deeply, notetaking helps the student learn and remember the information more easily.

These three statements are supported by research which demonstrates that notetaking gives students an advantage over simply listening (Anderson and Armbruster, 1986; Kiewra, 1985). Even if students do not go back and review their notes, just the act of taking them results in greater recall of information on tests. It is not surprising that secondary teachers assign high levels of importance to listening skills and notetaking (Knowlton, 1982; Link, 1980).

Students with learning and behavior problems often have difficulties with listening and notetaking. For some students with severe writing disabilities, it will be important that they have a notetaker. Students with learning disabilities may have difficulty with:

— Paying attention
— Writing fast and legibly
— Deciding what information to write
— Spelling
— Making sense of notes after the lecture

They also have limited use of abbreviations and limited use of a comprehensive notetaking system (Suritsky and Hughes, 1996). Given the importance of taking notes and the difficulty some students encounter with this skill, as a teacher you will want to teach students how to take notes, and consider using "listener-friendly lecturers" to make notetaking easier.

Teaching Students to Take Notes. Numerous formats for notetaking have been suggested (Bragstad and Stumpf, 1982; Langan, 1982; Manzo and Manzo, 1990; Palmatier, 1971, 1973; Pauk, 1974). One aspect that these systems have in common is the focus on making notetaking and reviewing an interactive learning process (Aaronson, 1975). To facilitate this interactive process, two- or three-column notetaking systems have been developed. Figure 7.19 gives an example of each. Students take class notes in the far right-hand column in both systems, using only the front side of the paper. Modified outlining is the format that is most often suggested for taking these notes. In the two-column system, students note the key concepts in the left-hand column. Devine (1987) refers to these concepts as *triggers* since they are meant to "trigger" the ideas noted in the other column. Later, in reviewing, students should be able to cover the right column and use their personal triggers to help them remember the ideas covered in the class notes. In three-column systems, the additional column generally serves as a space to write textbook notes so that they can be integrated with class notes. This is most helpful when the teacher's lectures make frequent, direct ties to the textbook.

■ **FIGURE 7.19** *Formats for Notetaking*

SAMPLE TWO-COLUMN SYSTEM

Topic: _____

Date: _____

Triggers or Key Concepts	Class Notes

SAMPLE THREE-COLUMN SYSTEM

Topic: _____

Date: _____

Triggers or Key Concepts	Class Notes	Text Notes

The following list gives several hints for helping students develop efficient notetaking skills.

— Take notes using either a two- or three-column system.
— Take notes on only one side of the paper.
— Date and label the topic of the notes.
— Generally use a modified outline format, indenting subordinate ideas and numbering ideas when possible.
— Skip lines to note changes in ideas.
— Write ideas or key phrases, not complete sentences.
— Use pictures and diagrams to relate ideas.
— Use consistent abbreviations (e.g., w/ = with, & = and).
— Underline or asterisk information the lecturer stresses as important.
— Write down information that the lecturer writes on the board or transparency.
— If you miss an idea you want to include, draw a blank _____ so that you can go back and fill it in.
— If you cannot automatically remember how to spell a word, spell it the way it sounds or the way you think it looks.
— If possible, review the previous sessions' notes right before the lecture.

— If the lecture is about an assigned reading topic, read the information before listening to the lecture.

— As soon as possible after the lecture, go over your notes, filling in the key concept column and listing any questions you still have.

— After going over your notes, try to summarize the major points presented during the lecture.

— Listen actively! In other words, think about what you already know about the topic being presented and how it relates.

— Review your notes before a test!

Direct Instruction in Notetaking. For many students with learning and behavior problems, just telling them how to take notes is insufficient. Teachers may want to develop and conduct a unit on listening and notetaking. The following is a list of teaching ideas for developing such a unit:

1. *Have students evaluate the effectiveness of their current notetaking skills and determine if they will profit from instruction.* Generally, this can be assessed in two ways. First, have the students bring to class current examples of notes and have them evaluate them for completeness, format, ease of use for review, and legibility. Second, present a simulated ten- to fifteen-minute lecture and ask the students to take notes. Give a test covering the information on the following day. Have the students again evaluate their notes and their test results.

2. *Use videotaped or audiotaped lectures when teaching students to listen effectively and to take notes.* The use of videotaped or audiotaped lectures is particularly helpful because it allows the students to replay the tape so that they can watch or listen for main ideas. For example, you may be teaching students to watch and listen for cues the lecturer gives to note the important information. After listening to a short segment of videotape, have the students list the cues and then discuss why they are important. Then replay the segment so that students can verify their list of cues and add other cues.

3. *Control the difficulty of the lectures.* When first introducing new listening or notetaking skills such as

listening for cues or using a two-column system, begin with short, well-organized lectures with ample use of advance organizers and visual aids, covering fairly simple, relatively familiar materials. As students reach proficiency, gradually increase the length of the lectures, reduce the use of organizers and visual aids, and increase the difficulty and novelty levels of the materials.

4. *Have students learn how to review their notes for tests.* Although students may learn to take more effective notes, they may fail to use them to study for tests. Teach students how to review their notes and ask themselves questions, using the "triggers" column to develop questions over the "notes" column.

5. *Have students monitor the use and effectiveness of notetaking in other classes.* To increase the probability that students will generalize the notetaking skills to other classes, have them discuss in which classes the skills would be helpful and then have them monitor and discuss their effectiveness in those classes.

6. *Have students determine the effects that notetaking has on learning.* Students need to know there is a payoff for their increased effort. Have students rate how well they feel they have taken notes over a unit or lecture and have them monitor their performance on tests over the material. This will aid them in determining if better notetaking leads to better learning.

Learning from Text

Probably the best-known technique for learning information from text is SQ3R, developed by Robinson (1946). This acronym stands for the five steps in this study skill: Survey, Question, Read, Recite, Review. The purpose of this technique is to provide students with a systematic approach to studying text. The following is a brief description of each one of the five steps in the process.

Survey:	Read through the headings quickly to learn what is to be studied.
Question:	Change each heading into a question (to have in mind what is to be learned from the reading).

Read: Read to answer the question.

Recite: At the end of each heading, either write brief notes about the highlights of the reading or engage in self-recitation.

Review: After completing the above steps on the entire selection, review the main points of the notes by self-recitation and check to see if the information is correct. (Adapted from F. P. Robinson, Effective Study [New York: Harper and Brothers], 1946.)

Although SQ3R seems well based in information processing theory, research has yet to support its effectiveness (Adams, Carnine, and Gersten, 1982; McCormick and Cooper, 1991). One of the major difficulties associated with the SQ3R method is the complexity of the process, particularly for students who are experiencing reading problems. In content area classes, these students are often attempting to read and learn information from textbooks written above their instructional reading levels.

Multipass.   Schumaker, Deshler, Alley, Warner, and Denton (1982) have developed a strategy based on SQ3R. It incorporates the learning acquisition and generalization stages from the Strategy Intervention Model (see Chapter 2: Cognitive Behavior Modification) and it is designed for students who experience problems learning information from textbooks. This strategy is referred to as *Multipass* because the students make three passes through the text while carrying out the process. Each pass through the text (i.e., Survey, Size-up, and Sort-out) entails the use of a different substrategy. Because each substrategy represents a fairly complex set of behaviors, each of the substrategies is taught as a unit, with the students reaching proficiency in the first substrategy before they learn the next substrategy. Prerequisite skills include the ability to paraphrase and a reading level of fourth grade or above. Research conducted with eight high school students with learning disabilities indicated that the students were able to master the strategy in instructional level materials and were able to use the strategy in grade-level materials without further training or practice. The students' grade on content tests improved—from barely passing to grades of C or better.

Survey.   During the Survey Pass, students become familiar with the main ideas and organization of the chapter. In completing the Survey Pass, students are directed to do the following:

1. *Title.*   Read the chapter title and think about how it fits with what you have already studied. Predict what the chapter is going to be about.

2. *Introduction.*   Read the introduction and make a statement about the main idea of the chapter. If there is no introduction, read the first paragraph, which is generally the introduction.

3. *Summary.*   Turn to the last page of the chapter, read the summary, and make a summary statement. If there is no summary, check the last paragraph to see if it is a summary. If it is not a summary, make a mental note so that you can summarize later.

4. *Organization.*   Look through the chapter to see how the chapter is organized. Use the major headings to make a written outline. Paraphrase each heading.

5. *Pictures, maps, charts.*   Look at the illustrations. Think about why they might have been included.

6. *Table of Contents.*   Find out how this chapter fits in with the other information in the book by perusing the table of contents. Decide what relationships this chapter has with the others, especially the chapters immediately preceding and following. For example, in a history book, chapters are often related because of chronological sequence. Chapters might also have a causal relationship (e.g., Chapter 6 talks about the causes of the Depression; Chapter 7 talks about its effects). Other types of frequently occurring relationships include: general/specific, compare/contrast, and related concepts.

After completing this process, close the book and think about what the chapter is going to be about and what you already know about the topic.

Using the Strategies Intervention Model, the teacher first describes and then models this survey process. The students should practice with guidance and feedback in materials at their reading instructional level until they are effective and efficient at surveying a chapter.

Size-up. During the Size-up Pass, students gain more specific information from the chapter without reading the chapter from beginning to end. Whereas the Survey Pass provides a general framework for the chapter, the Size-up Pass allows the students to look for the information that fits into that general framework using *textual cues.* In learning the Size-up Pass, students do the following:

1. *Illustrations.* Again, look over the pictures, maps, and charts and read the captions. Think about why they are included.

2. *Questions.* Read the questions, including those found at the beginning or interspersed in the chapter. If you can already answer a study question, put a check by it.

3. *Words.* Read over the vocabulary words, including any vocabulary list and words highlighted in the chapter.

4. *Headings. Read* the heading. *Ask* yourself a question that you think will be answered in the section. *Scan* for the answer. When you find the answer, *paraphrase* it orally or state something you have learned from the information under the heading. *Note* on your outline what information you have learned from the section.

Like the Survey Pass, the teacher will need to describe the Size-up process and the students should practice in instructional level material until they are proficient.

Sort-out. During this third and final pass, the students test themselves on the material in the chapter. This pass assists them in determining what they have learned and on what information they should still concentrate. In the final pass, the students read and answer each question at the end of the chapter, using the following process.

1. *Read.* Read the study question at the end of the chapter or each question provided by the teacher.

2. *Answer.* Answer the question if you can.

3. *Mark.* If you can answer a question, put a check by it; if you cannot, put a box in front of it. If you do not know the answer, scan the headings on your outline to determine in which section it most likely will be answered. When you find the likely section, look for the answer. If you find the answer, paraphrase it and check the box. If you do not find the answer, scan the headings a second time for another likely place to find the answer. Again, look for the answer and paraphrase it if you find it. If you do not find the answer after trying twice, circle the box so you know you need to come back to it later and possibly get help.

Like the other two steps, the students should practice with materials at their instructional level until they are effective and efficient at answering questions over the material presented in the chapter.

— COMMENTS: From the description of Multipass, it should be clear that when students use this strategy they do not have to read the text in its entirety. Instead, they study the text to determine the main ideas, its overall framework and related details, and to answer the study questions. In this way students can use this strategy in textbooks that are written above their instructional level. However, several cautionary notes are in order. First, remember to have the students reach proficiency on each substrategy before they begin learning the next substrategy. Second, when the difference between the students' instructional reading level and reading level of the textbook is greater than one to two years, students may have difficulty moving from instructional-level materials to grade-level materials. Teachers will generally need to provide graduated instructional materials. (For example, Hector's instructional reading level is fifth grade and he is a ninth grader. Hector will probably need to practice using the strategy in seventh-grade material as an intermediary step.) Third, do not expect students with learning and behavior problems to transfer this study strategy automatically to various content area textbooks. You will need to instruct for generalization.

Expression Skills

Expression skills include memory, retrieval, and test-taking skills, as well as other oral and/or written expression skills used to demonstrate understanding and application of knowledge.

Remembering Information

Have you ever arrived at the grocery store without your grocery list? What are the strategies that you use to help you remember what was on the list? Maybe you counted the items on the list and now you just need to see how many of the items you can jot down. Or maybe you read the list over several times almost rehearsing it; so it was easier to recall. Or you might use association by thinking of the meals that you were planning for the next few days and seeing if you can associate the needed items with the meals. Or you might visualize your kitchen and quickly think about the refrigerator and each cabinet and the items needed from each. Finally, you might categorize the items based on the sections in the grocery store (i.e., produce, cereal, bread, frozen foods). Clearly, there are many strategies for remembering information.

In many ways, remembering information for a test is not unlike remembering the items on a grocery list. Often we are asked to remember a list of things (e.g., the major exports of England, the different kinds of flour and their uses, the names of the cranial nerves). During tests we may be asked to take this information and apply it to specific situations (e.g., to support why England's economy is struggling), but we still need to remember the basic information.

Students with disabilities often have difficulty memorizing information whether it be for tests, presentations, or written work (Ashbaker and Swanson, 1996). Sometimes the students may not understand the information to be learned, but in other cases the poor performance may be due to difficulties with re-

trieval of the information (Swanson and Cooney, 1991), failure to use deliberate memory strategies (Ceci, 1985), and/or poor motivation for school tasks (Licht, 1983). Research suggests that these students also have difficulty with **metamemory** (i.e., awareness of memory strategies and the ability to use and monitor these strategies) in that they have trouble with one or more of the following:

- Knowing, selecting, and using appropriate strategies
- Estimating their own memory capacity for specific tasks
- Predicting accuracy on a memory task
- Allotting appropriate time to study
- Deciding when they have studied enough (Hughes, 1996)

Consequently, it's important to teach students memory strategies and "tricks" for remembering. Because teachers are regularly asking students to remember information (e.g., for tests, class discussions), it is relatively easy to incorporate teaching memory strategies into the content curriculum.

Furthermore, incorporating the general teaching principles presented in Apply the Concept 7.5 makes the information more memorable and encourages learning and remembering the information.

Many content area learning strategies such as semantic mapping, advance organizers, and semantic feature analysis can be thought of as teaching procedures that facilitate memory. In addition to these kinds of activities, a number of formal strategies have been deliberately designed to improve memory. These are often referred to as *mnemonics*.

Mnemonics are strategies for improving memory. The word *mnemonics* literally means "aids memory." Mnemonics aids memory and retrieval by forming associations that do not exist naturally in the content (Eggen and Kauchak, 1992). To use mnemonics, the information needs to be distilled so that the students are learning conceptual lists or frameworks. This information is then operated on using mnemonics. Mnemonic strategies can be grouped into three types: organization and association, visualization or mental imagery, and rehearsal.

APPLY THE CONCEPT 7.5

GENERAL TEACHING PRINCIPLES FOR INCREASING STUDENT'S MEMORY OF INFORMATION

- Orient student attention before presenting information, emphasize important vocabulary and concepts when they occur.
- Activate prior knowledge and help students make connections between old and new knowledge.
- Use visual aids such as graphic organizers to highlight the important information and make it more memorable.
- Control the amount of information presented; group related ideas.

- Control the rate at which the information is presented.
- Provide time to review, rehearse, and elaborate on the information.
- Teach the students how to use and apply memory strategies and devices.
- Provide time and guidance in developing associations and mnemonics such as acronyms and acrostics.
- Provide opportunities for distributed review of information, and encourage overlearning.

Organization and Association. Organizing and associating information refers to arranging the information or associating it with other information in such a way that it is easier to remember. Study the list of terms below in order to remember them:

Democracy	Mammals
Socket Wrench	Judiciary
Biology	Anatomy
Photosynthesis	Drill Press
Lathe	Blow Torch
Freedom of Speech	Constitution

Chances are that you categorized the words according to three superordinate categories, possibly labeled *tools, science concepts,* and *social studies concepts.* Now, instead of learning twelve unrelated words you are learning three sets of four related words. Research would show that the second task is considerably easier. Research and practice have also demonstrated that students experiencing learning problems do not tend to make these associations spontaneously (Howe, O'Sullivan, Brainerd, and Kingman, 1989). Therefore, one mnemonic to teach students when trying to remember lists of information is to associate or categorize related ideas.

Another type of association is the use of acrostics and acronyms. *Acrostics* are sentences created by words that begin with the first letters of a series of words.

Do you remember learning the names of the spaces on the musical staff as the word *FACE* and the names of the lines as "*Every Good Boy Does Fine*"? *Acronyms* are words created by joining the first letters of a series of words. Examples are *radar* (radio detecting and ranging), *scuba* (self-contained underwater breathing apparatus), and *laser* (light amplification by stimulated emission of radiation).

If needed, extra letters can be inserted, or the letters can be rearranged. Schumaker, Denton, and Deshler (1984) used this strategy when developing the paraphrasing strategy RAP (*R*ead, *A*sk yourself, *P*araphrase). By teaching students to construct acronyms and acrostics, sharing them in class, and then cuing students to use them when they study and take tests, you help them to learn and retrieve information.

The FIRST-letter mnemonic strategy (Nagel, Schumaker, and Deshler, 1986) is one strategy you can teach to help students construct lists of information to memorize and develop an acronym or acrostic for learning and remembering the information. The strategy includes an overall strategy (LISTS) and a substrategy for making the mnemonic device (FIRST). The steps in the overall strategy include the following:

Look for clues. (In the class notes and textbooks, look for lists of information that are important to learn. Name or give a heading to each list.)

Investigate the items. (Decide which items should be included in the list.)

Select a mnemonic device, using FIRST. (Use the FIRST substrategy, explained shortly, to construct a mnemonic.)

Transfer the information to a card. (Write the mnemonic and the list on one side of a card and the name of the list on the other side of the card.)

Self-test. (Study by looking at the heading using the mnemonic to recall the list.)

To complete the Select step, students use the FIRST strategy to design an acronym or acrostic:

Form a word. Using uppercase letters, write the first letter of each word in the list; see whether an acronym—a recognizable word or nonsense word—can be made.

Insert a letter(s). Insert letter(s) to see whether a word can be made. (Be sure to use lowercase letters so that you know they do not represent an item on the list—-BACk, for example.)

Rearrange the letters. Rearrange the letters to see whether a word can be made.

Shape a sentence. Using the first letter of each word in the list, try to construct a sentence (an acrostic).

Try combinations. Try combinations of these above steps to generate the mnemonic.

This strategy is taught using the Strategies Intervention Model presented in Chapter 2. It can be used with most content, but is particularly effective with science and social studies in which lists of information are to be learned. The strategy provides a systematic method for students to review text and class notes, construct lists, and develop acronyms and acrostics that help them remember and retrieve information.

Visualization and Keyword Method. Another strategy that is helpful in remembering information is visualization. **Visualization** is seeing in your mind or making a visual image of what you are to remember. Sometimes the visual image is simply the information that needs to be remembered. For example, it is not unusual to notice students closing their eyes when they are trying to remember how to spell a word. They may be using visualization to recall "what the word looks like."

If the information is complex, however, it may be helpful for the students to change the image that they are to remember into a picture that will trigger or cue the information to be remembered. One strategy used to do this is the **keyword method.** Using this visualization strategy, students construct a picture that represents an interactive relationship between a concept and its definition. Figure 7.20 shows a keyword picture generated for the concept of *allegro* and its definition (i.e., to move quickly). This picture is used to link the vocabulary word with the definition using a keyword(s) that sounds like the vocabulary word. In Figure 7.20 *leg* and *row* are the keywords and are used to construct a picture that triggers the definition of *allegro*.

The following steps are suggested for creating the keyword picture (King-Sears, Mercer, and Sindelar, 1992) and uses the acronym *IT FITS.*

Identify the word or term.

Tell the definition or answer information.

Find a keyword that sounds like the new word or word you need to remember.

Imagine an interaction, that is, something that the keyword and the answer information can do together. If you draw a sketch of the interaction, you may review it later for improved memory.

Think about the keyword and the interaction.

■ **FIGURE 7.20**   *Keyword Picture Generated for the Concept* Allegro

Source: From C. A. Hughes (1996). Memory and test-taking strategies. in D. D. Deshler, E. S. Ellis, and B. K. Lenz, *Teaching adolescents with learning disabilities* (2nd ed.) (p. 223). Denver: Love. Reprinted with permission.

Study your vocabulary and the information using your keyword to help you remember. Review by asking for each item? "What was my keyword for (word)? What was happening in my picture (or image)? What is the information I am supposed to remember?

Mastropieri and Scruggs (1989) suggest three rules that help a teacher decide the type of reconstructive elaboration that might work best:

Rule A: If the stimulus-response information is already concrete and meaningful to the learners, simply provide an interactive elaboration between the stimulus and response. Use of picture or mental images is particularly helpful.

Rule B: If the information is familiar but abstract, reconstruct that stimulus into something more concrete and more meaningful for the learners, and then provide an interactive illustration or image for the learners with the reconstructed stimulus and the response. This may be accomplished by concretizing abstract concepts like "justice" or "liberty" with sym-bolic representations, such as scales, or Uncle Sam as a symbolic representation of United States policy.

Rule C: If the information is unfamiliar, such as with unfamiliar names, places, and vocabulary words, reconstruct the item into something more concrete and familiar for the learner by means of the keyword method, and then depict that more concrete and familiar response in an interactive elaborative picture or image. (p. 76)

The keyword method has been shown to be most effective in increasing the recall of information by students with learning disabilities when the keyword relationships were presented to the students rather than having individual students generate them (Mastropieri and Scruggs, 1989; Scruggs and Mastropieri, 1989). Students should have ample opportunities to create the keyword associations as a class or in cooperative groups before having students work individually.

Verbal Rehearsal. Repeating the information aloud or to yourself can help facilitate memory. Verbal rehearsal is the major cognitive strategy used to enhance short-term memory (Hughes, 1996). Rehearsal, however, is most effective if there is limited interference between the time of the rehearsal and the time of recall, if the number of items to be remembered is limited, and if the information is clustered or chunked.

General Memory Strategies. Often several mnemonics are used simultaneously. For example, after you categorized the words in a list you could use acronyms within each category to help you remember the specific words, and then use rehearsal to practice, review, and test your memory. Teaching students with learning and behavior problems which strategies to use for which types of information and how to combine strategies will generally be necessary. In addition to teaching students how to use the various memory strategies, it is also important to teach students to use periodic review to minimize forgetting.

Studying and Taking Tests

Studying and taking tests are important study skills in secondary schools. Tests are the primary means that teachers use to determine if students have learned new concepts and can apply them. For example, Putnam (1992) surveyed 120 English, science, social studies, or mathematics teachers grades 7 to 12 to determine how frequently they used tests. In a nine-week grading period, students were expected to take an average of eleven tests in each content area. On the average teachers used scores on tests to determine approximately half of a grade for a course. While a great deal of effort is placed on tests to measure learning, only 25 percent of the teachers surveyed indicated that they taught strategies for taking tests. Yet research on students with disabilities and students at risk indicates that they have limited study and test taking strategies to employ (Hughes and Schumaker, 1991; Scruggs and Mastropieri, 1988). For example, the only strategy college students with learning disabilities regularly reported using when taking objective tests was skipping over difficult/unknown items. For essay questions, only half the students reported rereading the question or proofreading their response.

Studying for Tests.   Studying for a test means that students are reviewing information on a regular basis so they are not left cramming the day before the test. To help promote positive study habits Teri Martinez, a middle school resource social studies teacher, taught the following guidelines for studying:

1. *Manage your study time.* Keep up with assignments and do daily and weekly reviews. Teri planned five minutes each day at the end of her social studies class for students to review the material. On Monday, she took an extra five minutes and had the students review the previous week's work. She used individual, small group and whole-class discussion to review.

2. *Create study aids.* Create a **semantic map** or other **graphic organizer** to help students remember key information. Teri often used an on-going map during review sessions so that the students added to the map each day. Teri also taught the students how to create and use flashcards for key concepts and vocabulary. She taught the students the following procedures.

- When learning vocabulary, put the word on one side and the definition and an example on the other side.
- When learning other information, put the question on one side and the answer on the other side.
- When learning a formula, put the formula on one side and examples of how it is used on the other side.
- Review the flashcards in random order or after sorting the cards into categories or making a semantic map.
- Keep index cards in notebooks and on desks during class.
- Make a card when learning about a key concept or idea.

3. *Learn about the test.* The more information students learn about the format, type, and time allotted for the test, the more effectively they can prepare for it. Rather than telling the students about the test, Teri would start the discussion with, "Let's talk about the test, what do you want to ask me?" She used the following checklist to guide the students' questioning:

- Format of test; types of questions
- How much test is worth
- Date of test
- Time allotted for test
- Whether or not books or notes allowed
- Information covered
- Teacher recommendations for *how to study*
- Teacher recommendations for *what to study*

4. *Predict questions.* Teri also demonstrated how the students can predict the questions that will be asked. Have the students use what they know about the teacher's testing style, their class notes, their maps and other study aids to predict questions. Two days before a test, Teri had the students work in cooperative groups and write what they thought would be the most important questions on the test and then answer them.

5. *Think positive.* An important part of doing well on a test is having a positive attitude and believing that you are going to do well. Teri finds that she enjoys working with the students on having positive attitudes. Each day during their review, she asks the students about the following:

- What they learned today
- How it relates to what they already know
- What will they be working on tomorrow
- How well they have learned the information

She also has them rate how well they think they will do on the test and think about what they could do to improve their ratings. Just before a test, Teri also takes several minutes to review test-taking strategies and have the students visualize themselves being successful as they take the test.

Test-Taking Strategies. There are a number of test-taking hints that help students be more successful on tests. The following are consistently noted as important for success:

- Bring the necessary materials.
- Be on time and sit where you will not be disturbed.
- Survey the test.
- Read the directions carefully and check that you understand them. If not, ask for assistance.
- Schedule your time.
- Be sure you understand the scoring system (i.e., Is guessing penalized?).
- If you have memorized specific outlines, formulas, mnemonics, etc., write that information before you forget it.
- When answering questions, place a mark in the margin for those questions about which you are unsure and/or want to review.
- Place the question in the context of what has been discussed in class and what you have read.
- Avoid changing answers arbitrarily.
- Review your answers and proofread written responses.

Taking Objective Tests. For students with learning and behavior problems, it may be beneficial to teach specific test-taking strategies. The test-taking strategy can be used for taking objective tests (Hughes, Schumaker, Deshler, and Mercer, 1988) and uses the Strategies Intervention Model described in Chapter Two: Cognitive Behavior Modification. Research indicated that students with learning disabilities increased their performance 20 to 40 per-

centage points by learning and applying this strategy. The steps in the strategy are:

P **P**repare to succeed
    Put your name and PIRATES on the test
    Allot time and order the sections
    Say affirmations
    Start within 2 minutes

I **I**nspect the instructions
    Read instructions carefully
    Underline what to do and where to respond
    Notice special requirements

R **R**ead, remember, reduce
    Read the whole question
    Remember what you studied
    Reduce your choices

A **A**nswer or abandon
    Answer the question
    Abandon the question for the moment

T **T**urn back

E **E**stimate your answer
    Avoid absolutes
    Choose the longest or most detailed choice
    Eliminate similar choices

S **S**urvey
    Survey to ensure all questions are answered
    Switch an answer only if you're sure

Like many learning strategies, this strategy uses an acronym to help students remember the steps in the strategy (PIRATES). When using this strategy a student repeats, for each section of the test, the second, third, and fourth steps (i.e., inspect the instructions; read, remember, reduce; answer or abandon).

In addition to this strategy, there are a number of hints for taking objective tests. Apply the Concept 7.6 presents information that is helpful when answering objective questions (e.g., true-false, multiple-choice, matching, and completion).

Taking Essay Tests. Essays tests are not used as frequently as objective tests (Putnam, 1992), but

APPLY THE CONCEPT 7.6

TIPS FOR ANSWERING OBJECTIVE QUESTIONS

True-False Questions
- Remember, *everything* in a true statement must be true. One false detail makes it false.
- Look for qualifying words that tend to make statements false, such as: *all, always, everyone, everybody, never, no, none, no one, only.*
- Look for qualifying words that tend to make statements true, such as: *generally, most, often, probably, some, sometimes, usually.*
- Simplify questions that contain double negatives by crossing out both negatives and then determining whether the statement is true or false.
- Don't change an answer unless you have a good reason to. Usually your first impression is correct.

Matching Questions
- Read directions carefully. Determine whether each column contains an equal number of items and whether items can be used more than once.
- Read both columns before you start matching, to get a sense of the items.
- Focus on each item in one column and look for its match in the other column.
- If you can use items only once, cross out each item as you use it.

Multiple-Choice Questions
- Determine whether you are penalized for guessing.
- Answer the questions you know, putting a check in the margin next to items you want to return to later.

- Read all possible options, even when you are pretty sure of the right answer.
- See whether multiple options are available (e.g., c. A and B; d. All of the above).
- Minimize the risk of guessing by reading the stem with each option to see which option is most logical.
- Use a process of elimination, crossing out options you know are wrong.
- When you do not know the answer and you are not penalized for guessing, use the following signals to help you select the right option:
  - The longest option is often correct.
  - The most complete answer is often correct.
  - The first time the option "all of the above" or "none of the above" is used, it is usually correct.
  - The option in the middle, particularly if it is the longest, is often correct.
- Answers with qualifiers such as *generally, probably, sometimes,* and *usually* are frequently correct.

Completion Questions
- Determine whether more than one word can be put in one blank.
- If blanks are of different lengths, use length as a clue for the length of the answer.
- Read the question to yourself so that you can hear what is being asked.
- If more than one answer comes to mind, write them down; then reread the question with each answer to see which one fits best.
- Make sure that the answer you provide fits grammatically and logically.

Source: Selected ideas adapted from J. Langan, *Reading and Study Skills,* 2nd ed. (New York: McGraw-Hill, 1982).

when essay questions are incorporated into a test, they make up a sizable portion of the test grade (Hughes, 1996). This type of test can be particularly difficult for students with disabilities. Not only do

they have to recall the information, they have to write clearly in terms of thought, legibility, spelling, and grammar. Students with difficulties in written expression may be able to orally express the answer to the question, but their writing skills make it difficult for them to communicate that knowledge. You may want to record the student's answers on audiotape. For some students it may be advantageous to teach a strategy for answering essay questions so that the students organize the information and communicate it effectively. One strategy developed to assist students in organizing better responses to essay questions is called ANSWER (Hughes, Schumaker, and Deshler, in preparation). The steps include:

A Analyze the situation
    Read the question carefully
    Underline key words
    Gauge the time you need

N Notice requirements
    Scan for and mark the parts of the question
    Ask and say what is required
    Tell yourself you will write a quality answer

S Set up an outline
    Set up main ideas
    Assess whether they match the question
    Make changes if necessary

W Work in details
    Remember what you learned
    Add details to the main ideas using abbreviations
    Indicate order
    Decide if you are ready to write

E Engineer your answer
    Write an introductory paragraph
    Refer to your outline
    Include topic sentences
    Tell about details for each topic sentence
    Employ examples

R Review your answer
    Look to see if you answered all parts of the question
    Inspect to see if you included all main ideas and details
    Touch up your answer

In her social studies class, Teri taught the ANSWER strategy since essay questions were one format she used in her tests. She also gave to the students the list of **direction words** for essay questions (see Figure 7.21). She demonstrated how taking one concept such as *democracy* and using different direction words will change the response. In her daily reviews Teri frequently discussed one of the cue words in relation to the content covered that day. She provided examples of how to write an answer to a question using that cue word.

INSTRUCTIONAL ACTIVITIES

This section provides instructional activities that are related to content area learning and study skills. Some of the activities teach new skills; others are best suited for practice and reinforcement of already acquired skills. For each activity, the objective, materials, and teaching procedures are described.

■ Dictionary Scavenger Hunt

Objective: To provide students practice in successfully utilizing a dictionary.

Grades: Intermediate and junior high

Materials: (1) Student dictionaries. (2) Scavenger Hunt Cards with questions such as:

    Is a puffin a small pillow?
    Is a grackle a kind of noise?
    Is a poetess a man who writes poems?
    Was Ceres the same god as Demeter?
    Is a limerick a kind of drink?

Teaching Procedures: Divide the students into teams. Each team draws fifteen Scavenger Hunt Cards and places them face down in from of them. When the signal is given, each team selects one of their cards and finds the answer in the dictionary as quickly as possible. The answer is written on a

■ **FIGURE 7.21** *Direction Words for Answering Essay Questions*

Cue	Meaning	Cue	Meaning
Analyze	Break into parts and examine each part.	Interpret	Explain and share your own judgment.
Apply	Discuss how the principles would apply to a situation.	Justify	Provide reasons for your statements or conclusion.
Compare	Discuss differences and similarities.	List	Provide a numbered list of items or points.
Contract	Discuss differences and similarities, stressing the differences.	Outline	Organize your answer into main points and supporting details. If appropriate, use outline format.
Critique	Analyze and evaluate, using criteria.		
Define	Provide a clear, concise statement that explains the concept.	Prove	Provide factual evidence to support your logic or position.
Describe	Give a detailed account, listing charac- teristic, qualities, and components as appropriate.	Relate	Show the connection among ideas.
		Review	Provide a critical summary in which you summarize and present your comments.
Diagram	Provide a drawing.		
Discuss	Provide an in-depth explanation. Be analytical.	State	Explain precisely.
		Summarize	Provide a synopsis that does not in- clude your comments.
Explain	Give a logical development that dis- cusses reasons or causes.	Trace	Describe the development or progress of the idea.
Illustrate	Use examples or, when appropriate, provide a diagram or picture.		

Add your own Direction Words and definitions!!!

sheet of paper. Then the next card is drawn and the same procedure is repeated. The game continues until all the teams answer their questions. Answers and cards are exchanged and verified. The team that finishes first and gets all the answers correct wins the game.

■ Jeopardy

Objective: To provide students practice in using reference and trade books to obtain information and to generate questions.

Grades: Secondary

Materials: (1) Reference and trade books. (2) Jeo- pardy board with four categories and five answers per category. (3) Index cards to fit in the jeopardy board.

JEOPARDY

Pop Music	Presidents	Football	Southwest
20	20	20	20
40	40	40	40
60	60	60	60
80	80	80	80
100	100	100	100

Teaching Procedures: Divide the students into three teams of two to four students. Explain to them that each team is going to make a jeopardy game for the other students to play.

To make the game, each team needs to select four categories. Then have the students use reference books, trade books, and other sources to generate five questions and answers for each category that other students could possibly answer. Have them write the questions and answers on separate index cards and order the questions and answers from easy to difficult.

Each team then takes a turn directing its jeopardy game. First, the team inserts their category names and answer cards into the jeopardy board. Then they direct the game as the two other teams compete against each other. To direct the game, one student should serve as master of ceremonies, another as timekeeper, and the rest of the students as judges.

To play, each team takes a turn selecting a category and a level underneath the category. The answer is then exposed and the team members have fifteen seconds to give the question. If the question is correct, they get the number of points indicated and are allowed to make another selection. If the answer is incorrect, the other team has fifteen seconds to give an answer.

■ Study Groups

Objective: To provide students the opportunity to work in groups when studying a textbook for a test.

Grades: Secondary

Materials: (1) Content area textbook chapter or sections over which the students are going to be tested. (2) Index cards.

Teaching Procedures: Have students who are studying for tests covering the same material work in groups of two to three students. (Note: When students first do this activity the teacher will generally need to demonstrate and guide the students through the process.)

Have the students read the assigned materials together, stopping at the end of each paragraph or section to discuss the main ideas and the important

vocabulary. Each main idea and important vocabulary for each section should be written on an index card. After the students finish reading the assignment using this technique, they should take all the main idea cards and arrange them in logical groupings or in a logical order. The students then take each important vocabulary card and write a simple definition that makes sense according to the text. Then they arrange the important vocabulary next to the related main idea. Next, each student copies onto paper the arrangement that was organized for the main ideas and vocabulary (with definitions). Finally, the students should study the paper and then take turns quizzing each other on the information.

■ Get Their Opinions

Objective: To provide students the opportunity to collect, interpret, and present information about controversial topics and to increase awareness of current topics in social studies.

Grades: Intermediate and secondary

Materials: Tape recorder and blank tapes if respondents are interviewed.

Teaching Procedures: Discuss the meanings of surveys and polls and how they are conducted. Have the students study examples of surveys to determine the topics asked and the kinds of questions asked. Tell the students to select a topic about which they want to obtain other people's opinions. Then have them develop three to five questions that one could ask someone to determine their opinion. Have them write the survey and decide who they should survey.

Discuss how to conduct a survey and how not to bias a person who is answering the survey. Next, have the students conduct the survey, recording the responses in writing or on a tape recorder. Then the students need to tabulate the results of the survey, indicating what percent of persons answered the questions in the same manner. Finally, the students report the results of the survey to the rest of the class.

Adaptations: Results can also be written as an article for a school or community newspaper.

■ Smell and Taste

Objective: To provide students the opportunity to learn the relationship between the two senses of smell and taste.

Grades: Elementary

Materials: (1) Fruit, bread, crackers, and other foods that are easy to prepare in a classroom. Cut food into bite-size pieces. (2) Smell and Taste Worksheet. (3) Blindfolds.

Smell and Taste Worksheet		
Food	Taste	Smell and Taste
apple pear	apple apple	apple pear
watermelon cantaloupe honey dew	cantaloupe honey dew cantaloupe	watermelon cantaloupe honey dew
Findings:		

Teaching Procedures: Explain the instructions and pair off the students. Give each pair of students similar foods to try and a worksheet on which to record their results. Have one student in each pair hold his or her nose and close the eyes (or use a blindfold). The other student then gives the blindfolded student one type of food at a time and asks, "Is it a(n) (pear) or a(n) (apple)?" The student then records the results on the worksheet. The student who is blindfolded then releases the hold on his or her nose and the procedure is repeated. Then the students switch places and the experiment is run again.

The students then return to the general group and discuss their findings, stating the relationship between taste and smell. The findings can be written in each student's Science Idea Notebook which contains a log of the various experiments conducted and their results.

■ Learn Those Words!

Objective: To teach students a simple strategy for memorizing vocabulary words—either English words or those of a foreign language.

Grades: Fifth through high school.

Materials: Index cards used whole, or cut in half or in thirds, a pen, and papercutter or scissors.

Teaching Procedures: When there are words that must be memorized, the student writes a word on one side of an index card and its definition or translation on the reverse side.

The student studies the words and then tests himself. He forms two piles of cards as he works, a pile for those words he knows and another for those he doesn't know. He continues to study the words he doesn't know until there are no more cards in the unknown pile.

Students should always keep a set of words with them. While they are waiting in line, or waiting for class to begin, they can test themselves on their words. They make new sets of words, and continuously review the old sets. When it comes time for a big test, they're ready!

■ Homework Treasure Hunt

Objective: To provide students with a definite purpose for their homework reading assignments.

Grades: Fourth through college.

Materials: Textbooks or supplementary content area materials.

Teaching Procedures: Instead of asking your students to read pages 28–43 for homework tonight, which causes them to focus just on covering those pages as quickly as possible without really learning the material, ask them to begin reading on page 28 and to continue reading until they have answered the five questions you've written on the chalkboard or photocopied for them. They'll have to read to page 43 to answer all the questions, but they'll be reading actively and for a purpose. Tomorrow, during your presentation, you'll have students who are prepared to participate in, and learn from, your presentation!

SUMMARY

For secondary and postsecondary settings as well as the upper elementary grades, the success with which students with learning and behavior problems are mainstreamed is dependent on the teaching effectiveness of the content area teacher and the study skills of the student. This chapter focused on those topics as well as adaptations, capitalizing on the relationship between the teacher and the learner.

Utilizing teaching strategies that assist students to organize and relate information has been shown to increase their ability to learn from text and from lectures. Therefore, it behooves us to be listener-friendly lecturers and to use such instructional techniques as advance organizers, semantic feature analysis, concept diagrams, and semantic mapping.

At the same time, we can work with students to teach them effective methods of studying. This includes time management and notebook organization skills, strategies for learning from lectures and texts (e.g., Multipass), and strategies for remembering and retrieving information and for taking tests.

If we can provide students with sound content area instruction while at the same time teaching them study skills, then we have facilitated their success in secondary school settings.

THINK AND APPLY

- Why is it difficult for students with learning problems to succeed in content area classes in secondary schools?
- What is a content analysis? Select a chapter from a content area text and complete a content analysis.
- What is "considerate" text? Using the ideas in the section on "Evaluating the Considerateness of Instructional Materials," select a text and evaluate it for considerateness and appropriateness for your students.
- Explain the difference between a concept diagram, a semantic map, and a relationship chart. Select a chapter and develop each of these instructional aids for the chapter. Compare the differences and similarities.
- What should teachers keep in mind when they are adapting a textbook? Select a chapter from a text and adapt it for students with learning and behavior problems.
- What should you include in a unit on self-management? Plan the unit for a group of students with learning and behavior problems.
- What are the characteristics of listener-friendly lectures? Plan a lecture that is listener-friendly.
- Conduct a content analysis and then develop keyword mnemonics to teach the "hard to learn" technical vocabulary.

Chapter 8

Mathematics

OUTLINE

KEY TOPICS FOR MASTERY

- *Factors that influence mathematics ability in all people*
- *Characteristics of students with learning disabilities that frequently interfere with the mastery of mathematics*
- *Teaching perspectives to consider when planning mathematics instruction for students with learning disabilities and for those with emotional and/or behavior problems*
- *Teaching an understanding of the prenumber skills, numeration, and place value*
- *Teaching the basic facts—addition, subtraction, multiplication, and division*
- *Calculators—why they are a "must" for students with learning disabilities*
- *Fractions and measurements—why overlearning at the concrete stage is critical to students' mastery of these skills*
- *How to help students with learning disabilities overcome problems with traditional written story problems*
- *Cognitive and operant approaches to increasing math performance*
- *The importance of teaching students with learning and behavior problems the mathematics necessary to operate in the "real world"*
- *Curriculums and materials that focus on the needs of students with learning disabilities*

 BRIGHT IDEA

Turn to page 373 and read Think and Apply.

Esteban, a third-grade student who spends most of his day in a special classroom for behavior-disordered students, goes to the regular third-grade classroom each day for mathematics. He is in the top math group and is proud of this achievement. His special education teacher is pleased that he is fulfilling his behavior contract and has not had any serious disturbances in the first step to more involvement in the regular classroom.

Claudia, a seventh-grade student who spends part of her day in a classroom for students with learning disabilities, is not nearly so successful in math. In fact, when asked what her favorite academic time is during the day, she quickly answers, "I love to write. In fact, I think I will be an author. I have al-

ready written several books for the classroom and one was even selected for the library." When asked what she thinks of math, she looks away and says, "No way—Don't even mention it. I can't do math. We don't get along."

Claudia has had difficulty with mathematics since she was in the primary grades. Her first-grade teacher just thought she was not very interested in math, and asked her parents to obtain special tutoring help during the summer. Her parents found that the special help did little good, and when Claudia continued to have serious difficulty with math in second grade, the teacher referred her for assessment for possible learning disabilities. The assessment results suggested she had difficulty with spatial relations and using memory to recall rote math facts. She has received special help in math for the past four years, and though she seems to have made progress, her math skills are still her weakest academic area.

Some students with learning and behavior problems have difficulty with language arts (reading, writing, and spelling), some have difficulty with mathematics, and some have difficulty with both. However, despite the number of students who have math problems, the skill that has received by far the most attention from researchers, writers, and even clinicians is reading. Reading is often viewed as an essential skill for survival in our society, whereas math is often considered less important. With an increased need for students to understand problem solving for success in the workplace, the inferior status of mathematics instruction may need to change. Presently, learning-disability resource room teachers spend approximately one-third of their time teaching mathematics (Carpenter, 1985).

This chapter's purpose is to increase your understanding of how to teach mathematics to students who have difficulty learning. The chapter begins by discussing factors and characteristics that interfere with math performance and then presents teaching perspectives that provide general guidelines for teaching math. The chapter follows with teaching suggestions for prenumber skills, followed by numbers and place value, computation, fractions, and measurement. The chapter ends by discussing strategies for teaching problem solving and approaches to increasing math performance.

FACTORS INFLUENCING MATH ABILITY

Kosc (1981) identifies the following four variables as significant influences on mathematics ability:

1. *Psychological factors* such as intelligence/ cognitive ability, distractibility, and cognitive learning strategies
2. *Education factors* such as the quality and amount of instructional intervention across the range of areas of mathematics (e.g., computation, measurement, time, and problem solving
3. *Personality factors* such as persistence, self-concept, and attitudes toward mathematics
4. *Neuropsychological patterns* such as perception and neurological trauma

Considering these four factors, it is not surprising that many students with learning and behavior problems have difficulty in math. Whereas most students with learning difficulties have average or above-average intelligence, they have been identified as inactive learners and as less likely to utilize cognitive strategies. Because much of their educational intervention has focused on computation, they often have limited exposure to other elements of math, including measurement, time, and practical problem solving. They are unable to apply the computation skills to everyday math problems. Many of these students have lowered self-concepts and lack persistence, which are characteristics that may interfere with learning math skills. The fourth factor identified, unique neuropsychological patterns, certainly characterizes many students with learning and behavior problems.

The following difficulties may interfere with the mathematics performance of a student with learning disabilities (Homan, 1970):

1. *Perceptual skills.* Because students with learning disabilities often have difficulty with spatial relationships, distances, size relationships, and sequencing, these difficulties will interfere with such math skills as measurement, estimation, problem solving, and geometry. Students with weak perceptual skills will need practice in estimating size and distance and then in verifying estimates with direct measurement.

2. *Perseveration.* Some students may have difficulty mentally shifting from one task or operation to the next. This may interfere with a student's performance on problems that require multiple operations or on applied mathematics problems that often require several steps. The teacher can provide cues to illustrate the number of steps involved in each operation. After the skills for two operations have been mastered (e.g., addition and subtraction), the teacher

can provide worksheets that include both types of problems.

3. *Language.* The student may have difficulty understanding such mathematical concepts as *first, last, next, greater than, less than,* and so on. When teaching arithmetic, the teacher's instructions should be precise. Presenting unnecessary concepts and rules is interfering and confusing to the students and distracts them from concentrating on the concept being presented. The teacher should demonstrate as well as provide instruction. Concrete objects should be used to illustrate abstract concepts. Give plenty of examples and allow students to provide examples to demonstrate understanding of concepts.

4. *Reasoning.* Reasoning is often difficult because it requires a great deal of abstract thinking. Teachers should use concrete materials and real-life application whenever possible. After students understand the mathematical concept at an automatic level, introduce tasks that ask students to think through the process, explain the rationale, and apply reason.

5. *Memory.* Many students with learning and behavior problems have difficulty remembering information that was presented to them. Teachers can assist students with memory problems by reducing the amount of new information the students are required to learn, increasing the number of exposures to the new materials, and giving the students opportunities to verbalize and demonstrate the new material.

Johnson and Myklebust (1967) referred to students with dyscalculia—poor skills in numerical calculating—as demonstrating such social difficulties as disorientation, deficiencies in self-help skills, and poor organization. Rourke's (1993) research supports the finding that social deficits are associated with individuals who have good reading and poor math skills.

In a study by Badian and Ghublikian (1983), students with significantly lower math than reading skills (low math) were compared with two other groups, students with significantly higher math than reading skills and students who had similar math and reading skills. The results indicated that the low math group demonstrated lower scores overall on the following abilities:

- paying sustained attention
- working in a careful and organized manner
- accepting responsibility

These findings partially explain why students with learning and behavior problems have difficulty with mathematics. Students with learning disabilities often have difficulty applying learning strategies and are frequently characterized as having perceptual and neurological complications. Students with emotional disturbances may have greater difficulties with mathematics than other areas because it requires persistence and concentration. Students with mild mental retardation have more difficulty with mathematics than students with learning disabilities (Parmar, Cawley, and Miller, 1994).

TEACHING PERSPECTIVES

When developing math programs for students with special needs, several teaching perspectives need to be considered for all ages and programs. These teaching perspectives include:

1. *Comprehensive programming.* Mr. Noppe was not happy with his math program. He taught a varying exceptionalities classroom (a special education classroom that serves all mildly handicapped students) at an elementary school, and 90 percent of his math program consisted of teaching math computation. In discussing his math program with a co-teacher, he said, "I know I need to include more than just computation, but I'm not sure what else I should be teaching. I guess I should ask the students to apply some of their math computation. Next year, I want to concentrate on my math program and make it more comprehensive."

Students need to be taught and involved in a full range of mathematics skills, including basic facts, operations, word problems, mathematical reasoning, time, measurement, fractions, and math application. Teachers should not focus their entire mathematics remediation on math facts and the four basic operations: addition, subtraction, multiplication, and division. The National Council of Supervisors of Mathematics (1977) described ten basic skill areas that should be part of a math program: problem solving; applying mathematics to everyday situations; alertness to the reasonableness of results; estimation and approximation; appropriate computational skills; geometry; measurements; reading and interpreting tables, charts, and graphs; using mathematics to predict; and computer literacy.

2. *Individualization.* Esteban and Claudia, the two students described in the beginning of this chapter, have very different needs in math. Students with learning difficulties are different from each other in their math abilities and disabilities. Individualized programs that respond to the needs of each student are necessary. Individualization in math programming refers not just to the task but also to the way the task is learned (Carnine, 1991). Some students learn math facts through rote drill, whereas other students learn math facts by associating them with known facts. We often assume that an individualized program means the student works alone. Individualization, however, means the program is designed to meet the individual needs of the student; thus it is often beneficial for the students to work in small groups to learn new skills and rehearse and practice problems. In addition, small groups that focus on solving the same problem can include students of different abilities, particularly when the teacher creates a cooperative environment for solving the problems and allowing the students to learn from each other.

3. *Correction and feedback.* Receiving immediate feedback about performance is particularly important in math. If students are performing an operation incorrectly, they should be told which parts are correct and which parts are incorrect. Showing students patterns in their errors is an important source of feedback. Students also need to learn to check their own work and monitor their own errors. Remember, feedback includes noticing improvements as well as monitoring needed changes.

Students in Ms. Wong's math class were given a worksheet to practice their new skill of using dol-lar signs and decimal points in their subtraction problems. Ms. Wong told the students to do only the first problem. After they completed the first problem they were to check it and make any necessary changes. If they felt problem one was correct they should write a small "c" next to the answer. If they felt it was incorrect they should mark a small "i" next to the answer. They were also to indicate with a checkmark (✓) where they felt they had made a mistake. Ms. Wong moved quickly from student to student, checking their first problem. Students who had the first problem correct were given encouragement and directions for the rest of the problems. "Good for you. You got the first problem correct and you had the confidence, after checking it, to call it correct. I see you remembered to use both a decimal point and a dollar sign. After you finish the first row, including checking your problems, meet with another student to see how your answers compare. Do you know what to do if there is a discrepancy in your answers? That's right. You'll need to check each other's problem to locate the error." When Ms. Wong locates a student who incorrectly solved the problem, she says, "Talk aloud how you did this. Start from the beginning and as you think of what you're doing, say it aloud so I can follow." Ms. Wong finds that students often notice their own errors, or she will identify some faulty thinking on the part of the students that keeps them from correctly solving the problem.

4. *Alternative approaches to instruction.* If a student is not succeeding with one approach or program, make a change. Despite years of research, no single method of mathematics instruction has been proven to be significantly better than others. This includes using a range of formats such as textbooks, workbooks, math stations, manipulatives, and so on.

5. *Applied mathematics.* Concrete materials and real-life applications of math problems make math real and increase the likelihood that students will transfer skills to applied settings such as home and work. Students continue to make progress in math throughout their school years. Emphasis needs to be on problem solving rather than rote drill and practice activities (Cawley and Miller, 1989).

After Ms. Wong's students were successfully able to use dollar signs and decimals in subtraction, she gave each of them a mock checkbook, which included checks and a ledger for keeping their balance. In each of their checkbooks was written the amount $100.00. During math class for the rest of the month she gave students "money" for the checkbook when their assignments were completed and their behavior was appropriate. She asked them to write her checks when they wanted supplies (pencils, erasers, chalk) or privileges (going to the bathroom, free time, meeting briefly with a friend). Students were asked to maintain their balance in their checkbooks. Students were penalized $5.00 for each mistake the "bank" located in the checkbook ledgers at the end of the week.

6. *Generalization.* Generalization or transfer of learning needs to be taught. As most experienced teachers know, students can often perform skills in the special education room and are unable to perform them in the regular classroom. In order to facilitate the transfer of learning between settings, teachers must provide opportunities to practice skills by using a wide range of materials such as textbooks, workbooks, manipulatives, and word problems. Teachers also need to systematically reduce the amount of help they provide students in solving problems. When students are first learning a math concept or operation, teachers provide a lot of assistance to students in performing it correctly. As students become more skillful, less assistance is needed.

After Ms. Wong's students were able to apply subtraction with dollars and decimals to their checkbooks, she obtained the math textbook that was used in the regular classroom. She wrote the assignment on the board, just as it would be done in the regular classroom. Students were asked to copy the problems from the book and complete the assignment with very little teacher assistance. Ms. Wong was attempting to see how well their skills would transfer to tasks assigned in a way similar to the way they would be assigned in the regular classroom. Ms. Wong realized that before she could say the students had mastered the skill, they needed to perform the skill outside of her classroom and without her assistance.

7. *Allow students to participate in setting their own goals for mathematics.* Participation during goal selection is likely to increase the individual's commitment to the goal. Students who selected their own math goals improved their performance on math tasks over time more than did those students whose math goals were assigned to them by a teacher (Fuchs, Bahr, and Rieth, 1989). Even very young children can participate in selecting their overall math goals and keep progress charts on how well they are performing.

The National Research Council (NRC) has conducted an examination of U.S. mathematics education from kindergarten through graduate study (National Research Council, 1989). This joint activity was conducted by the Mathematical Sciences Education Board, Board on Mathematical Sciences, Committee on the Mathematical Sciences in the Year 2000, and National Research Council. The extensive report resulting from the work of these committees not only outlines problems in mathematics education but charts a course for remedying them. The suggestions that relate to students with learning and behavior problems follow:

- Do not alter curricular goals to differentiate students; change the type and speed of instruction.
- Make mathematics education student-centered, not an authoritarian model that is teacher-focused.
- Encourage students to explore, verbalize ideas, and understand that mathematics is part of their life.
- Provide daily opportunities for students to apply mathematics and to work problems that are related to their daily lives. Instill in them the importance and need for mathematics.
- Teach mathematics so that students understand when an exact answer is necessary and when an estimate is sufficient.
- Teach problem solving, computer application, and use of calculators to all students.
- Teach students to understand probability, data analysis, and statistics as they relate to daily de-

cision making, model building, operations research, and applications of computers.
- Shift from primarily performing paper-and-pencil activities to use of calculators, computers, and other applied materials.

The National Research Council (1989) reports that mathematics is "the invisible culture of our age" and emphasizes that mathematics is embedded in our lives in many ways:

Practical—mathematical knowledge can be put to immediate use. This includes figuring unit prices, comparing interest rates on loans, appreciating the effects of inflation, calculating the effects of a salary increase, and calculating risks.

Civic—mathematical concepts relate to public policy. This includes understanding taxation, inferences drawn from statistics on crime, health issues, and other related public issues, and reading charts and graphs depicting change in spending.

Professional—mathematics is a tool for success on the job. This includes all knowledge of basic and theoretical mathematics that is necessary for success in the workplace.

Recreational—mathematics can be a source of recreation and relaxation. This includes participating in games of strategy, puzzles, lotteries, and other related activities.

Cultural—mathematics is the appreciation of mathematics for its beauty and power to solve problems. Like language, art, and music, mathematics is an important part of our human culture.

As a teacher, you may want to be sure your curriculum includes all five dimensions of mathematics: practical, civic, professional, recreational, and cultural.

It is particularly important for teachers to design mathematics programs that enhance learning for all students, especially students with diverse cultural or linguistic backgrounds. See Apply the Concept 8.1 for suggestions.

PRENUMBER SKILLS

Many students come to school with few experiences that allow them to develop important prenumber skills, such as one-to-one correspondence, classification, and seriation. The following section focuses on these important prenumber skills.

One-to-One Correspondence

Matching one object with another is a core skill in any mathematics curriculum. It eventually leads the student to a better understanding of numeration and representation. Early man used one-to-one correspondence when he kept track of how many bags of grain he borrowed from a neighbor by placing a rock in a bucket to represent each one. One-to-one correspondence is used today when we set the table, one place setting for each person; go to the theater, one ticket and seat for each person; and distribute paper in the classroom, one piece for each child. Activities for teaching one-to-one correspondence include:

1. Use every opportunity to teach students the relationship between number words (e.g., *one, two, three, four*) and objects. For example, "Here are two scissors, one for you and one for Margo." "There are five students in our group and we need one chair for each student."

2. Use familiar objects such as small cars or blocks and give a designated number (e.g., three) to each student. Pointing to the objects, ask the student to place one block next to each of the objects. "You have one block here and you placed one block next to it. You have a second block here and you placed a block next to it. And you have a third block here and you placed a block next to it."

3. Give the student a set of cards with numbers the student recognizes. Ask the student to put the correct number of blocks on top of each number card. Reverse the task by giving objects to the student and asking him or her to put the correct number card next to the objects.

APPLY THE CONCEPT 8.1

CONSIDERATIONS FOR CULTURALLY AND LINGUISTICALLY DIVERSE STUDENTS: ENHANCING SKILLS IN MATHEMATICS

An essential part of implementing a successful mathematics program is to provide instructional practices and assignments that facilitate learning in mathematics for all students, particularly those from diverse cultures and language backgrounds. Here are some suggestions to consider:

1. Continually consider ways to infuse the various cultures of students in your classroom and the cultures of students not represented in your mathematics curriculum. Students will appreciate, feel accepted, and learn a great deal about other cultures when cultural diversity is infused in their daily learning routines.

2. Develop story problems that reflect events from diverse cultures. Encourage students to design story problems that are reflective of the happenings of other cultures.

3. Read books about youngsters from other cultures. Use the stories and data from these books to design story problems.

4. In designing mathematical problems, use the data from newspapers or magazines that provide information about individuals or events representing other cultures.

5. Design mathematical studies that address real problems of individuals or groups who are not from the mainstream culture. Assign these studies to individuals, students in pairs, or small groups.

6. Assure that goals are challenging for all students and provide adequate support for their participation and effort. These challenges should provide opportunities for success, with infrequent failure.

7. Model an enthusiastic and positive attitude about appreciating and learning more about the cultures and languages of other groups.

8. Link students' accomplishments to their hard work and effort. Remind students that they performed the task well because they worked hard, persisted, reread, rethought, revisualized, modeled, and so forth (Mercer and Mercer, 1993).

9. Use manipulatives to concretely explore the meaning of mathematical symbols and problems. Manipulatives enhance learning, and provide an easy means of crossing potential language barriers.

10. Use culturally relevant materials as a "springboard" for mathematics learning (D'Ambrosio, Johnson, and Hobbs, 1995). The ways in which mathematics are practiced in various cultures, mathematical games that are played, and the use of mathematics cross-culturally can be imbedded into mathematics instruction.

11. Use the languages of the students throughout the instruction. Ask students to provide the word that means the same as "_____" and then use both words when referring to the term. Encourage all of the students in the room to use and apply multiple terms that represent the languages of the students in the class. Communicate to students that you value their home language.

12. Use technology to enhance learning and understanding of mathematical principles (Woodard, 1995). Computers provide a language that should be available to all students. Encourage expertise on the computer and provide multiple opportunities to practice math skills on the computer.

Professional Resources
1. N. S. Bley and C. A. Thornton (1995). *Teaching Mathematics to Students with Learning Disabilities* (3rd ed.). Austin: PRO-ED. Each chapter provides information on a different mathematical topic (e.g., money and time, number and place value), and provides a description of the errors commonly made by students with learning disabilities. The book provides procedures for appropriate instruction across all areas of the mathematics curriculum.

2. J. F. Cawley, A. M. Fitzmaurice-Hayes, and R. A. Shaw (1988). *Mathematics for the Mildly Handicapped.* Boston: Allyn and Bacon.

This book provides a long-term, systematic approach to providing a comprehensive curriculum in mathematics for students with mild learning disabilities. Assessment, instruction, and component analysis are an integral part of the book's focus.

3. G. Cuevas and M. Driscoll (Eds.). (1993). *Reaching all Students with Mathematics*. Reston, VA: National Council of Teachers of Mathematics.

The book discusses the current trends in mathematics instruction, with special emphasis on assisting teachers to capitalize on the increasing diversity in their classrooms. The book presents procedures for improving the performance of special student populations and programs aimed at their success.

Classification

Classification is the ability to group or sort objects based on one or more common property. For example, classification can occur by size, color, shape, texture, or design. Classification is an important prenumber skill because it focuses the student on common properties of objects and requires the student to reduce large numbers of objects to smaller groups. Most students are naturally interested in sorting, ordering, and classifying. A sample of activities for teaching classification includes:

1. Ask students to sort articles into groups. Ask them which rule they used for sorting their articles.

2. Give students an empty egg carton and a box of small articles. Ask the students to sort the articles according to one property (e.g., color). Now ask them to think of another way they can sort them (e.g., size, texture).

3. Using an assortment of articles, ask students to classify several of the articles into one group. Other students then try to guess the property(ies) that qualifies the articles for the group.

4. Students can use pictures for sorting tasks. Animals, foods, plants, toys, and people can all be sorted by different properties.

5. Board games and bingo games can be played by sorting or classifying shapes, colors, or pictures.

Seriation

Seriation is similar to classification in that it depends on the recognition of common attributes of objects. With seriation, ordering depends on the degree to which the object possesses the attribute. For example, seriation can occur by length, height, color, or weight. A sample of activities for teaching seriation might include:

1. Give students some objects of varied length and ask them to put them in order from shortest to longest.
2. Ask students to stack their books from biggest to smallest.
3. Using a peg with varied sizes of rings, put the rings on the peg from largest to smallest.
4. Fill jars of the same size with varied amounts of sand or water and ask students to put them in order.

NUMERATION AND PLACE VALUE

Teachers and parents often assume that children understand numerals because they can count or name them. Understanding numerals is a very important and basic concept; many children who have trouble with computation and word problems are missing numeral concepts. For example, Michael's beginning experiences with math were positive. He had learned to read and write numerals and even to perform basic addition and subtraction facts. However, when Michael was asked to perform problems that involved addition with regrouping, he demonstrated he had very little knowledge of numerals and their meaning (as shown here), and thus quickly fell behind his peers in math.

$$
\begin{array}{ccc}
48 & 37 & 68 \\
+26 & +55 & +17 \\
\hline
614 & 812 & 715
\end{array}
$$

Understanding numeration and place value is necessary for:

1. *Progress in computation.* Like Michael, many students fail to make adequate progress in math because they lack understanding of numerals and place value.

2. *Estimation* (e.g., "number sense"). Many students with learning difficulties in math do not have a sense of how much $1.00 is, what it means to have 35 eggs, or "about" how much 24 and 35 equals. They cannot check their answers by looking at problems and determining which answers could not be correct because the answer doesn't make "sense."

3. *Reducing conceptual errors.* Students who understand the meaning of the numerals 43 and 25 would be less likely to make the following error:

$$
\begin{array}{c}
43 \\
-25 \\
\hline
22
\end{array}
$$

4. *Understanding place value.* Students who know the meaning of the numeral 28 are going to have far less difficulty understanding the value of the "2 place" and the "8 place." Students need to understand the 2 in 28 represents two tens and the 8 represents eight ones.

5. *Understanding regrouping.* Regrouping errors, such as those below, are less likely to occur if a student understands numeration.

$$
\begin{array}{ccc}
39 & 56 & 41 \\
+27 & -18 & -24 \\
\hline
516 & 42 & 23
\end{array}
$$

6. *Application of math computation to everyday problems.* Students who do not understand the real meaning of numerals have difficulty applying computation to everyday problems.

7. *Understanding zero.* Students need to understand that 0 (zero) has more meaning than just "nothing." For example, in the number 40, students need to understand the meaning of the 0 as a place holder.

Readiness for Numeration: Seventeen Concepts

Engelhardt, Ashlock, and Wiebe (1984) identified seventeen numeration readiness concepts that can be assessed through paper-and-pencil assessment and interview. A list of the behaviors that correspond with each concept, along with examples of how each concept can be assessed, follows.

Concept 1
Cardinality—The face value of each of the ten digits (0 through 9) tells how many.

1. Identify sets with like numerousness (1–9). Circle the groups with the same number of "x's."

2. Identify, write, and name the numeral that corresponds to the numerousness of a set (1–9). Circle the numeral showing how many mice there are.

How many mice are there?

3   2   6   4   9

3. Construct sets with a given numerousness (1–9). "Draw five dots."
4. Recognize sets of one to five without counting. Place from one to five objects behind a book. Say to the students, "As soon as I move this book I want you to tell me how many objects there are." Without counting, the students should tell you how many objects are in the group.
5. Represent and name the numerousness of the empty set (zero). "The box has 2 hats in it. Make 0 hats in the circle."

Concept 2
Grouping Pattern—When representing quantity, objects are grouped into sets of a specified size (base) and sets of sets.

1. Form sets of ten from a random set of objects or marks. Circle the x's to make as many groups of ten as possible.

   xxxxxxxxxxxxxx   xxxxxx   xxxxxxx

   xxxxxxxxxxxxxx   xxxxxx   xxxxxxx

2. Construct appropriate groups to show how many. Give students about 125 popsicle sticks and rubberbands. Say, "Bundle these sticks so it will be easy to tell how many there are."

Concept 3
Place Value—The position of a digit in a multidigit numeral determines its value (places are assigned values).

1. Given two multidigit numerals with the same digits but in different orders, identify the position of the digits as distinguishing the two numerals. How are 145 and 154 alike? Different?

2. Explain that the value of a digit in a multidigit number is dependent on its position. Using the number 5, place it in each column and ask, "How does the number change?" "How much is it worth?"

100s	10s	1s

Concept 4
Place Value (base 10)—A power of ten is assigned to each position or place (the place values).

1. Identify, name, and show the values for each place in a multidigit numeral. Show the number 1,829 and say, "What is the name of the 8's place?"
2. Select the place having a given value. Show the number 6,243 and say, "Circle or point to the number in the thousands place."

Concept 5
One Digit per Place—Only one digit is written in a position or place.

1. Identify and name which numerals (digits) can be assigned to a place. Say to the students, "Tell me the numbers that can be written in the tens place."
2. State that no more than one digit should be written in a place or position. Then ask, "What's wrong with these problems?"

85	27	13
+39	+35	+48
1114	512	511

3. Rewrite or restate a nonstandard multidigit numeral (or its representation) as a numeral with only one digit in each place or position. Say to the students, "Write the number for this:"

10s	1s
5	4

Concept 6

Places–Linear/Ordered—The places (and their values) in a multidigit (whole number) numeral are linearly arranged and ordered from right to left.

1. Identify the smaller-to-larger ordering of place values in a multidigit numeral. Show the number 6,666 to the students and say, "Underline the 6 that is worth the most and put an X through the 6 that is worth the least."
2. Describe how the place values are ordered. Show the number 8,888 to the students and ask, "How can you tell which 8 is worth more?"
3. State or demonstrate that the places in a multidigit numeral are linearly arranged. Say to the students, "Rewrite this problem correctly."

$$
\begin{array}{r}
7 \quad 1 \\
2 \quad 4 \\
6 \quad 3 \quad 8 \\
+ \quad\quad 0 \\
\hline
\end{array}
$$

Concept 7

Decimal Point—The decimal point in a decimal fraction indicates the location of the units (ones) and tenths places.

1. Given a decimal fraction, identify the digit in the units (ones) place. Show the number 29.04 to the students and say, "Circle the number in the ones place."
2. Given juxtaposed digits and a digit's value, identify and place the decimal point to show the appropriate multidigit numeral. Show the number 284 to the students and say, "Place the decimal in the correct place to show 4 tenths, 2 tens, and 8 ones."
3. State the meaning (function) of the decimal point.

Concept 8

Place Relation/Regrouping—Each place in a multidigit numeral has a value ten times greater than the place to its right and one-tenth the value of the place to its left (place relationships and regrouping).

1. Describe the relationships between the values of two adjacent places in a multidigit number.

Show the number 222 to the students and say, "How does the first 2 in the number compare with the second 2?"

2. Express the value of a multidigit numeral in several ways. Give the following problem to the students: 1 hundred, 8 tens, and 6 ones can also be expressed as _____ tens and _____ ones.

Concept 9

Implied Zeros—All numerals have an infinite number of juxtaposed places, each occupied by an expressed or implied digit. In places to the left of nonzero digits in numerals for whole numbers, zeros are understood; in places to the right of nonzero digits and the decimal point in decimal fractions, zeros are understood.

1. Name the digit in any given place for any multidigit numeral. Tell the students to rewrite each numeral and show a digit in each place.

	1000s	100s	10s	1s
683				
27				
79				

2. Rewrite a given numeral with as few digits as needed. Tell the students to X out the zeros that are not needed.

0301	004
1010	105

3. State a rule for writing zeros in a multidigit numeral. Ask the students, "When do we need to write zeros in a number?"

Concept 10

Face Times Place—The value of any digit in a multidigit numeral is determined by the product of its face and place values (implied multiplication).

1. Show, name, and identify the value of a specified digit within a multidigit numeral. Show the number 1468 to the students and ask, "How much is the 6 worth: 0, 6, 10, 60, or 16?"
2. Name and identify the operation used to determine the value of a digit in a multidigit numeral.

Ask the students, "In 1468 we find 6 is worth 60 when we: add, subtract, multiply, or divide?"

3. State a rule for finding the value of a specified digit in a multidigit numeral. Ask the students, "How do you know 6 is worth 60 in the number 1468?"

Concept 11
Implied Addition—The value of a multidigit numeral is determined by the sum of the values of each digit (implied addition).

1. Express any multidigit numeral as the sum of the values of each digit.

   294 = _____ ones + _____ tens + _____ hundreds

2. Express the sum of digit values as a multidigit numeral. Ask the students to write the numeral for:

   4 ones + 3 tens + 6 hundreds = _____

3. Identify the operation used to determine the value of a multidigit numeral. Ask the students, "To know the value of 287, do we add, subtract, multiply, or divide the value of each numeral?"

Concept 12
Order—Multidigit numerals are ordered:

1. Order multidigit numerals. Say to the students, "Put these numbers in the correct order from smallest to largest: 1689, 1001, 421, 1421."

2. Describe a procedure for determining which of two unequal multidigit numerals is larger. Show the numbers 984 and 849 to the students and ask, "How do you know which is larger?"

Concept 13
Verbal Names (0–9)—In English, the verbal names for the numbers zero through nine are unique.

1. Identify the oral/written names of the ten digits. Ask the students to write the name next to each digit:

   0 _____   4 _____   7 _____
   1 _____   5 _____   8 _____
   2 _____   6 _____   9 _____
   3 _____

2. State the name for the ten digits.

Concept 14
Verbal Names with Places—In English, the verbal names for multidigit numbers (except ten through twelve) are closely associated with the written numerals (i.e., combining face and place names).

1. Give a multidigit numeral, identify the verbal name for one of the digits that includes both a face and place name. Show the number 2,847 and ask the students, "How is the 8 read?"

   a. eight   c. eighty
   b. eight hundred   d. eighteen

2. Identify the digit in a multidigit numeral that is stated first when giving the verbal name. Say to the students, "Write the number that is said first when reading the number."

   44_____   6,186_____
   284_____   37_____

3. Select two-digit numerals whose naming pattern is different from most. Ask the students to circle the numbers that when read aloud are different from the others: 17, 43, 126, 11, 281.

Concept 15
Periods and Names—Beginning with the ones place, clusters of three (whole numbers) adjacent places are called periods and are named by the place value of the right-most member of the number triad (e.g., ones, thousands, millions, etc.)

1. Given a multidigit numeral, insert commas to form "periods." Ask the students to put commas in the correct places: 28146 682 7810 192642

2. Name the periods of a given multidigit numeral. Ask the students, "Which number represents the periods?"

   284,000,163 _____

   ones, tens, hundreds, thousands, millions

Concept 16
Naming in Ones Period—Numerals in the ones period are named by stating, from left to right, each

digit's name (except zero) followed by its place name (ones being omitted). (Special rules exist for naming tens.)

1. Name three-digit numerals (tens digit not 1). Tell the students to write the name for 683.
2. Name three-digit numerals (tens digit of 1). Tell the students to write the name for 718.

Concept 17

When naming a multidigit numeral, the digits in each period are read as if they were in the ones period, followed by the period name (ones period name being omitted).

1. Name multidigit numerals up to six digits. Tell the students to write the name for 284,163.
2. Name multidigit numerals over six digits. Ask the students to read the following numbers:

1,846,283   27,219,143
103,600,101   3,078,420*

Teaching Place Value

Place value is directly related to the students' understanding of numeration. Students need to be able to:

1. *Group by ones and tens.* Using manipulatives, pictures, and then the numerals, students need practice and instruction in grouping by ones and tens. Students can sort manipulatives such as buttons or sticks in groups of tens. Students can also use a table grid to record their answers.

Tens	Ones	Numerals
2	3	23
6	2	62
4	7	47

*Source: From *Helping Children Understand and Use Numerals* (pp. 89–149) by J. M. Engelhardt, R. B. Ashlock, and J. H. G. Wiebe, 1984, Boston: Allyn and Bacon. Copyright 1984 by Allyn and Bacon. Adapted by permission.

Use "tens blocks" and "single blocks" to represent numerals. For example, 24 can be represented as:

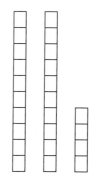

Flannel boards can also be used to group tens and ones.

2. *Naming tens.* Teach students to identify numerals by the number of tens. For example, six tens is 60, four tens is 40, eight tens is 80, and so on. Give students opportunities to count by tens and then name the number. For example, "Count by tens three times." "Ten, twenty, thirty." "Counting by tens seven times." "Ten, twenty, thirty, forty, fifty, sixty, seventy." Also give students opportunities to draw picture diagrams that represent the place values of tens and ones and to identify the number from diagrams.

3. *Place value beyond two digits.* Once students can accurately group and identify numbers at the two-digit level, introduce them to three- and four-digit numbers. It is a good idea to be certain students have overlearned the concept of two-digit place value before introducing numerals and place value greater than two digits. Many of the principles students have learned with two-digit place value will generalize to three digits and beyond. Give students plenty of opportunity to group, orally name, and sequence three- and four-digit place values.

4. *Place value with older students.* Since place value is a skill that is taught in the math developmental sequence during the primary grades, students who have not adequately learned the skill will likely have problems with computation and word problems, and yet may have little opportunity to learn place value. Many of the games and activities de-

signed to teach place value focus on young children and are less appropriate for older students. The following sources of numbers may be useful for teaching place value to older students:

a. An odometer
b. Numbers from students' science or social studies texts
c. Numbers from the population of the school (e.g., number of freshmen, sophomores, juniors, seniors, etc.)
d. Population data from the town, county, state, or country
e. The financial data page from the newspaper

COMPUTATION: ADDITION, SUBTRACTION, MULTIPLICATION, DIVISION

Most of students' time in math is spent on computation. Memorizing facts and practicing addition, subtraction, multiplication, and division problems are the major parts of many math programs. Students spend lots of time completing math sheets, workbook pages, and problems copied from a book that require the continued practice and application of math computation principles. It is probably for this reason that many students find math boring and not applicable. Computing math problems is much easier for students if they understand numeration and place value and if they are given frequent practical application of the math problems.

When students are having difficulty performing math computation, it may be because they:

1. Do not have an understanding of numeration and/or place value
2. Do not understand the operation they are performing
3. Do not know basic math facts and their application to more complicated computation

Students with attention deficit disorder often demonstrate difficulty in computation because they fail to automatize computational skills at an appro-

priate age (Ackerman, Anhalt, and Dykman, 1986). By *automatize* we mean learning computational facts so they are automatic. Students with attention deficit disorder require time for computation.

Understanding the Operation

Ask the students to demonstrate their understanding of the operation by drawing picture diagrams and illustrating with manipulatives. For example, Sylvia was able to write the correct answer to the multiplication fact $3 \times 2 = 6$. However, when asked to draw a picture to represent the problem, she drew three flowers and two flowers. She seemed totally undisturbed that the number of flowers she drew was different from the answer she wrote. When asked why she drew the number of flowers she did, Sylvia said, "I drew three flowers for the 3 and two flowers for the 2." When the teacher questioned her further, she discovered that Sylvia had no understanding of multiplication. By rote, she had memorized the answers to some of the elementary multiplication facts. The teacher used manipulatives such as chips and buttons to illustrate multiplication.

The following activities can be helpful in teaching students to understand the operation.

1. The following drawing illustrates how chips in rows can be used to illustrate multiplication. For example, ask, "How many fours make twenty?" "Fours are placed on the board _____ times."

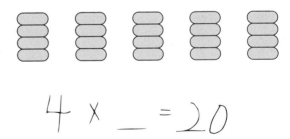

2. Have students "talk aloud" what is involved in solving a problem. Do not let them merely *read* the problem; ask them to *explain* what it means. For example, "63 – 27 means that someone had 63 pieces of gum and gave 27 pieces to a friend."

3. Have students explain the process to another student by using block manipulatives. For example, "24 + 31 is the same as adding 4 one-block pieces to 1 one-block piece and 2 ten-block pieces to 3 ten-block pieces."

4. Have students close their eyes and use noises to illustrate operations. For example, to illustrate multiplication, the teacher can tap in groups of six. "How many times did I tap a group of 6?"

tap-tap-tap-tap-tap-tap
tap-tap-tap-tap-tap-tap
tap-tap-tap-tap-tap-tap

"Yes, I tapped a group of 6 three times. Now I am going to tap a group of 6 three times again and I want you to tell me how many taps there are altogether." "Yes, when you tap a group of 6 three times there are 18 total taps." This same process can be used for addition and subtraction (Bley and Thornton, 1981).

Knowing Basic Math Facts

Two of the reasons students may have difficulty with computation have been discussed: (1) they do not understand numeration and/or place value, and (2) they do not understand the computation process. A third reason students may have difficulty with computation is they do not know the basic math facts. A common instructional misconception is that if students learn basic arithmetic facts they will no longer have difficulties with other arithmetic operations and problems. Arithmetic facts do not help the student in analyzing or understanding the application of arithmetic operations; however, they do aid in the acquisition and speed of performing arithmetic operations. Students who do not know the basic math facts are going to be considerably slower and less accurate in math computation. It is difficult for them to understand the math process because so much of their attention is focused on computing one small segment of the problem.

Using thinking strategies assists in the acquisition and retention of basic math facts (Thornton and Toohey, 1985). Without direct instruction, students with learning disabilities often do not discover and use these strategies and relationships for learning and retaining math facts (Thornton, 1978).

Some of the thinking strategies used by students who are successful at solving basic math facts (Thornton and Toohey, 1985; Thornton, Tucker, Dossey, and Bazik, 1983) can be taught to students who are having difficulties.

1. *Using doubles.* Students can learn to use doubles to solve basic math facts. If the student knows $6 + 6 = 12$, then the student can easily compute $6 + 7$. Apply the Concept 8.2 illustrates picture devices to associate with learning doubles.

2. *Counting-on.* Students do not need to resort to counting from one to solve math facts. They can learn to count on from the largest numeral in an addition fact. For example:

$$7 + 2 = \underline{\hspace{1cm}}$$

The student counts on two more from 7: "seven, eight, nine." Students can use this same principle when subtracting, only they count backwards. For example:

$$7 - 2 = \underline{\hspace{1cm}}$$

The student counts backwards two from 7: "seven, six, five." Students can be taught counting-on before operations, and then they will only need to learn to apply the principle.

3. *Using the commutative idea.* The commutative property means that adding or multiplying any two numbers always yields the same answer regardless of their order. Students can be taught that with addition and multiplication, if they know it one way they know it the other. For example:

$$3 + 5 = 8$$
$$5 + 3 = 8$$
$$2 \times 9 = 18$$
$$9 \times 2 = 18$$

4. *Thinking one more or less than a known fact.* Yvette knew several basic math facts but had trouble

APPLY THE CONCEPT 8.2

USING DOUBLES

Double	Visual Cue	Auditory Cue
2 + 2	(car picture)	The car fact (2 front tires, 2 back tires)
3 + 3	(grasshopper picture)	The grasshopper fact (3 legs on each side)
4 + 4	(spider picture)	The spider fact (4 legs on each side)
5 + 5	(hands picture)	The hands fact (10 fingers)
6 + 6	(egg carton picture)	The egg carton fact (6 in each row)
7 + 7	(crayon pack picture)	The crayon pack (7 in each row)

Source: From *Teaching Mathematics to the Learning Disabled,* Second Edition (p. 163) by N. S. Bley and C. A. Thornton, Austin, Tex.: PRO-ED. Copyright 1989 by PRO-ED, Inc. Reprinted with permission.

with the more difficult ones. When her teacher taught her how to use the math facts she knew to solve the more difficult ones, her math performance improved. For example, Yvette knew 5 + 5 = 10, but when she was presented with 5 + 6, she began counting on her fingers. Her teacher taught her to think of 5 + 6 as one more than 5 + 5, and 5 + 4 as one less than 5 + 5. Pictures such as the following can help to illustrate the principle:

5 + 5 = 10   . .   +   . .   =
             . .   .

5 + 6 =   . .   +   . .   =
           . .   . .
                        .

5 + 4 =   . .   +   . .   =
           . .   .
            .

5. *Using tens.* Students can learn that 10 + any single-digit number merely changes the 0 in the 10 to the number they are adding to it.

6. *Using nines.* There are two strategies students can apply to addition facts that involve nines. First, they can think of the 9 as a 10 and then subtract 1 from the answer. As illustrated here, the student is taught to "think" of the 9 as a 10.

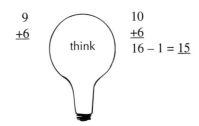

9
+6

think

10
+6
16 − 1 = 15

Second, students can think whenever there is a 9 in an addition problem the answer in the one's column is always one less than the number they are adding to the 9. For example:

9	8	9
+4	+9	+6
13	17	15

7. *Counting by twos, threes, fours, fives, and tens.* Beginning with 10, teach students to count by the number. This may be done with individual students or with a small group. It is sometimes helpful to develop a rhythm to the counting sequence:

10—20—30—40—50—60—70—80—90—100

After students can count by tens to 100, ask them to count aloud by ten from two points other than 10 and 100. For example, "Count aloud from 20 to 80." After students have learned to count by tens, they should be taught to count by fives and then by twos, threes, and fours. Being able to count by multiples helps in addition, multiplication, and division. Multiplication facts can be taught by interpreting 3×4 as counting by threes four times. Division facts, such as $8 \div 2$ can be interpreted as, "How many times do you count by twos before you reach 8?"

8. *Relationship between addition and subtraction; multiplication and division.* After students learn addition facts, they can be shown the relationship between the addition fact and subtraction. For example, if a student knows $7 + 6 = 13$, students can learn the relationships between the known addition fact and the subtraction fact, $13 - 7 =$ _____. Whenever possible, reinforce this principle as students are working, "You know $8 + 4 = 12$, so $12 - 4 =$ must be _____." Give students known addition facts and ask them to form subtraction problems. These sample relationships can be used to teach multiplication and division facts (see Figure 8.1).

If you think these strategies for assisting students in learning math facts seem logical and automatic, you are right. They are for most students. However, students with learning difficulties in math do not use these strategies automatically and it prevents them from acquiring the needed math facts for accurate and speedy computation.

When these strategies are directly taught, students' math performance improves. When Ms. Zaragoza taught math strategies to students who were having difficulty in math she used the math strategies summarized in Apply the Concept 8.3, and she used other students who were performing the math skill accurately to help her. She interviewed students who knew how to perform the skill and asked them to "talk aloud" while they solved the problems so she could learn what strategies they used. She then taught these strategies to students who were having problems.

Peer-Assisted Instructional Practices

Perhaps one of the most effective procedures for teaching math facts to students with learning and behavior problems is the use of cross-age tutors. Cross-age tutors refers to the use of older students, often students without learning or behavior problems, to serve as tutors for younger students with learning

■ **FIGURE 8.1** *Relationships between Addition and Subtraction; Multiplication and Division*

Known Addition Facts	Made-up Subtraction Facts
$5 + 5 = 10$	$10 - 5 = 5$
$3 + 2 = 5$	_____
$8 + 8 = 16$	_____
$6 + 4 = 10$	_____

Known Multiplication Facts	Made-up Division Facts
$7 \times 4 = 28$	$28 \div 4 = 7$
$8 \times 8 = 64$	_____
$5 \times 9 = 45$	_____
$5 \times 10 = 50$	_____

difficulties. Cross-age tutors are particularly effective in teaching math facts because the skills they need to be effective can be acquired quickly, in as little as two forty-five-minute periods. In a study that successfully used cross-age tutors to teach addition facts to students with learning disabilities (Beirne-Smith, 1991), tutors were trained to do the following:

— Use contingent reinforcement
— Use task and error correction procedures
— Use procedures for "counting on"
— Use procedures for rote memorization of facts
— Repeat skills and instruction till mastery

Cooperative learning groups, usually small groups of students (three to five per group), can be used to have students work together to solve problems. Maheady, Harper, and Sacca (1988) conducted a cooperative learning math instruction program for ninth and tenth grade students with mild disabilities. Students who participated in the cooperative teams performed better in mathematics and received higher grades than those who did not.

Touch Math

Touch math (Bullock, 1996, 1991; Bullock, Pierce, Strand, and Branine, 1981) is a procedure for teaching

APPLY THE CONCEPT 8.3

STRATEGIES FOR TEACHING ADDITION FACTS

Addition Facts Groups by Strategy for Recall

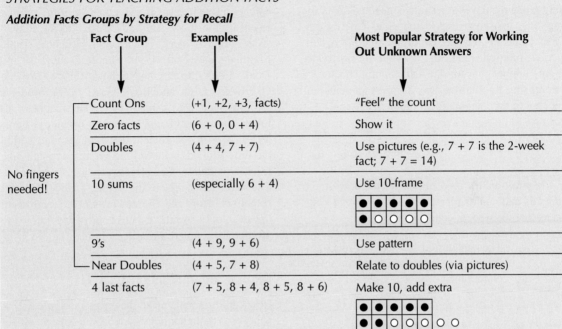

	Fact Group	Examples	Most Popular Strategy for Working Out Unknown Answers
	Count Ons	(+1, +2, +3, facts)	"Feel" the count
	Zero facts	(6 + 0, 0 + 4)	Show it
	Doubles	(4 + 4, 7 + 7)	Use pictures (e.g., 7 + 7 is the 2-week fact; 7 + 7 = 14)
No fingers needed!	10 sums	(especially 6 + 4)	Use 10-frame
	9's	(4 + 9, 9 + 6)	Use pattern
	Near Doubles	(4 + 5, 7 + 8)	Relate to doubles (via pictures)
	4 last facts	(7 + 5, 8 + 4, 8 + 5, 8 + 6)	Make 10, add extra

Note: Turn-arounds (commutatives of facts within each group) would be learned before moving to a different group of facts.

Verbal Prompts Used in the Addition Program

Fact Group	Sample Facts		Sentence Patterns (Verbal Prompts)
Count Ons	8 +2	3 +7	Start BIG and count on.
Zeroes	6 +0	0 +3	Plus zero stays the same.
Doubles	5 +5	7 +7	Think of the picture.
Near Doubles	5 +6	7 +8	Think doubles to help.
9's	4 +9	9 +6	What's the pattern?
Near Tens	7 +5	6 +8	Use 10 to help.

Source: C. A. Thornton and M. A. Toohey, "Basic Math Facts: Guidelines for Teaching and Learning," *Learning Disabilities Focus* 1(1) (1985):50, 51. Reprinted with permission of the Division for Learning Disabilities.

addition, subtraction, multiplication, and division to students with learning problems.

Many teachers comment on the effectiveness of using touch math, yet others are concerned about the long-range consequences (Fletcher and Rosenberger, 1987). Concerns include: concepts of addition, subtraction, multiplication, and division are not really taught; number concepts are lost; counting backward is confusing to children; and it leaves students unprepared to do computational problem solving.

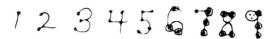

In *addition,* the student touches the dots on the numerals and counts forward. A circle around a dot means that the student counts it twice.

$$\begin{array}{r} 3 \\ + 6 \\ \hline 9 \end{array}$$
The student touches the dots and says, "One, two, three, four, five, six, seven, eight, nine."

In *subtraction,* the student learns to count backwards.

$$\begin{array}{r} 8 \\ - 3 \\ \hline 5 \end{array}$$
The student says, "Eight," and then touches the dots on the three and says, "Seven, six, five."

Multiplication is taught by skip counting.

$3 \times 4 = 12$ The student counts by threes, touching a dot on the 4 with each count, saying, "Three, six, nine, twelve."

Division is taught by skip counting.

$24 \div 6 = 4$
$////$ The student is taught to skip count by six until he or she reaches 24. The student puts a slash on the paper with each count, saying, "Six, twelve, eighteen, twenty-four."

Constant Time Delay Procedure

Constant time delay is a procedure for teaching math facts that provides for systematic assistance from the teacher through near errorless control of the prompt to ensure the successful performance of the student (Gast, Ault, Wolery, Doyle, and Belanger, 1988; Mattingly and Bott, 1990; Schuster, Stevens, and Doak, 1990; Stevens and Schuster, 1988; Wolery, Cybriwsky, Gast, and Boyle-Gast, 1991). Students are presented with a math fact. The student is allowed a specific amount of time to provide the correct answer. If the student does not respond within the time allotted, a controlling prompt, typically the teacher modeling the correct response, is provided. The student then repeats the teacher's model. Correct responses before and after the prompt are reinforced; however, only correct responses provided before the prompt are counted toward criterion.

Math Computation Errors

How could students make the errors in Figure 8.2? It appears as though all the students did was guess. Yet each of the students who computed the problems can tell you what they did to get the answer. Most errors that students make are rule governed. Although the rule they are applying may not always be obvious, they are using some rule to tell them how to compute a problem. In Figure 8.2 problem (A), Erika said, "I took 1 away from 7 to get 6, and 0 away from 5 to get 5." In problem (B), Jeff added across, adding the 3 and 1 to get 4, and 2 and 3 to get 5. In problem (C), Yolanda said, "I knew this wasn't right but it was the

■ **FIGURE 8.2**   *Math Computation Errors*

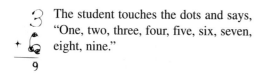

best I knew how to do. I multiplied 3 × 4 to get 12, and then 6 × 4 to get 24." In problem (D), Shawn knew that 7 plus 7 plus 7 was 21, but he was operating under the faulty rule that you always carry the smaller number, so he wrote the 2 in the ones column and carried the 1. Paulette, in problem (E), said, "I added 4 plus 1 because it was easier than adding 4 plus 3." When given several similar problems, she had no concerns about placing the number in the ones or tens column depending upon where it was easier for her to add. All of these students applied faulty rules as they performed math computations. Once the teacher discovered the faulty rules they were applying, she was able to teach them the underlying concept and the correct rule for completing computations.

Teachers can learn a great deal about students' thinking in mathematics through an oral diagnostic interview (Lankford, 1974). Such an interview will provide information about what each student is doing and why he or she is doing it that way. For the diagnostic interview to yield accurate, helpful information, the teacher must ask the student questions about math computation in a nonthreatening way. For example, "I am interested in learning what you say to yourself while you do this problem. Say aloud what you are thinking." It is often most effective to use a problem different from the one the student has performed incorrectly. The assumption behind this interview is that there is an underlying reason behind the mistakes, and understanding why a student is making errors provides valuable diagnostic information which leads directly to instruction. Roberts (1968) identified four common "failure strategies" in computation. These are summarized in Apply the Concept 8.4.

Students with learning problems are slower, but not necessarily less accurate, when it comes to doing and learning math facts (Garnett, 1992). When you teach mathematics in your classroom, consider that students with learning problems may need additional practice to learn math facts and longer time to perform mathematics computations because they often lack the "automatization" to perform math computation effectively and efficiently (Garnett and Fleischner, 1983).

Language of Math Computation

"What do you mean by 'find the difference'? Am I supposed to add or subtract? Why don't you just say it in plain English?" Many students with learning and behavior problems have difficulty with the language of computation. Yet understanding the vocabulary is important for success in the regular classroom, application to math story problems, and communication with others. Understanding the terminology of the four basic operations as well as the symbols associated with the processes is important. Students also need to understand the vocabulary that is associated with the answer derived from each of these processes. Table 8.1 illustrates the relationship between the process, symbol, answer, and problem.

After teaching the information on the chart, you can use the following activities:

1. Cover one column (e.g., the symbols) and ask the student to write the answer.
2. Place each of the symbols, answers, and problems on a separate index card and ask the student to sort them by process.
3. Play concentration with two columns. Two columns of index cards (e.g., the symbol cards and answer cards) are laid answer down and each student takes turns searching for matching pairs by selecting two cards. When the student picks up a corresponding pair, he or she keeps the pair and takes another turn.

Use of Calculators

Many students with learning and behavior problems let computation interfere with their ability to learn problem solving. They spend so much time learning to compute the problem accurately that they miss the more important aspects of mathematics such as concept development and practical application.

In 1974, the National Council of Teachers of Mathematics issued a statement that urged teachers to use calculators in mathematics instruction (NCTM, 1974). Teachers did not adequately respond to this plea, with fewer than 20 percent of elementary teachers using calculators as part of their instructional

APPLY THE CONCEPT 8.4

ERRORS IN COMPUTATION

1. *Wrong operation.* The pupil attempts to solve the problem by using the wrong process. In this example the student subtracted instead of adding.

$$\begin{array}{r} 2\,4 \\ +\ 1\,1 \\ \hline 1\ 3 \end{array}$$

2. *Computational error.* The student uses the correct operation but makes an error recalling a basic number fact.

$$\begin{array}{r} 2\,4 \\ +\ 3\,5 \\ \hline 5\ 8 \end{array}$$

3. *Defective algorithm.* The pupil attempts to use the correct operation but uses a wrong procedure for solving the problem. The error is not due to computation.

$$\begin{array}{r} 2\,4 \\ -\ 1\,7 \\ \hline 1\ 3 \end{array}$$

4. *Random response.* The student has little or no idea how to solve the problem, and writes numbers randomly.

$$\begin{array}{r} 3\,0\,4 \\ -\ 1\,9\,6 \\ \hline 3\ 9\ 6 \end{array}$$

Source: Adapted from G. H. Roberts, "The Failure Strategies of Third Grade Arithmetic Pupils," *The Arithmetic Teacher, 15* (1968) pp. 442–446.

■ **TABLE 8.1** *Relationship of Process, Symbol, Answer, and Problem*

Process	Symbol	Answer	Problem
Addition	+	Sum	6 + 4 =
Subtraction	−	Difference	5 – 3 =
Multiplication	×	Product	8 × 5 =
Division	÷	Quotient	12 ÷ 6 =

program (Suydam, 1982). Many teachers did not use calculators because they felt the use of calculators threatened the acquisition of basic skills. Mr. Coffland, a third-grade teacher, put it this way: "If I let my students use calculators to solve problems, they will not have adequate practice in basic skills. They will become too dependent on using the calculator." Research suggests that Mr. Coffland has little to fear. The results of a summary of seventy-nine studies (Hembree, 1986) on the use of calculators suggest:

1. The use of calculators does not interfere with basic mathematics skill acquisition. In fact, calculator use can increase skill acquisition.

2. Only in grade 4 does sustained calculator use interfere with skill development.

3. The use of calculators in testing situations results in much higher achievement scores, particularly when students are low in problem-solving ability.

4. Using calculators improves students' attitudes towards mathematics.

5. Calculators can be introduced at the same time that the paper and pencil practice exercises are introduced.

6. Calculators can be used by students to solve complex problems that they construct. This also provides support for improved self-concept with math skills.

In summary, as long as students are involved in basic skills instruction, the use of calculators is a positive aid to mathematics instruction. There are several ways calculators can be used with students who are having difficulty with mathematics instruction.

1. *Develop a positive attitude.* Using a calculator removes the drudgery associated with solving computations and makes problem solving fun.
2. *Increase self-concept.* Being able to compute extremely complex problems on the calculator gives students confidence in their mathematics abilities.
3. *Improve practice in problem solving.* Students are willing to tackle difficult problem-solving tasks when they have the assistance of the calculator in solving the problem. Students still have to decide what numbers are used, what operation is used, and whether additional operations are necessary. Using the calculator can free students from the burden of computation and allow more focus on thinking about the problem.
4. *Develop their own problems.* Using the calculator lets students develop their own problems. They can then exchange their problems with each other, and use their calculators to solve them.

FRACTIONS

Fractions is one of the most difficult concepts to teach. Because of the availability of calculators, teachers place less emphasis on being able to compute fractions and greater emphasis on understanding the meaning and use of fractions.

The *concept* of a fraction can be introduced before the actual fractions are even discussed. For example, Figure 8.3 shows the relationship between common fractional terminology and its represented unit.

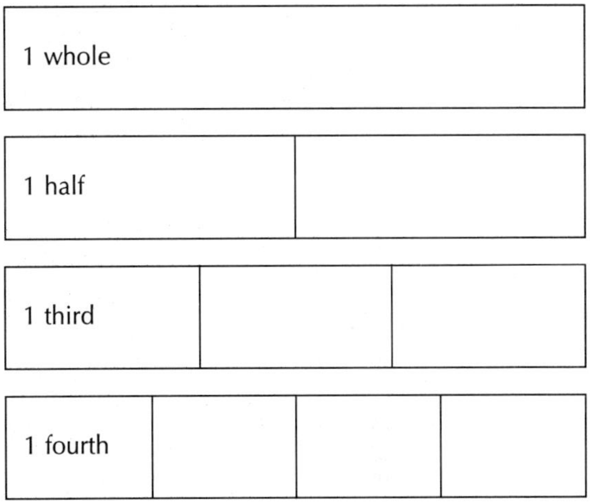

Children as young as ages three, four, and five are introduced to the concept of fractions as they help cook. "We use 1 cup of milk and 1/2 cup of flour." "You'll need to share the cookie with your brother. You each may have one-half of a cookie." Teachers

■ **FIGURE 8.3** *Unit Representation of Fractions*

often use cooking activities to enhance students' understanding of fractions.

Many manipulative aids can be used to teach fractions: colored rods, cardboard strips and squares, blocks, fractional circle wheels, cooking utensils such as measuring cups, and any unit dividers such as egg cartons and muffin pans.

Teaching fractions, as in teaching most concepts, proceeds from concrete to abstract. Apply the Concept 8.5 demonstrates the teaching sequence.

However, the use of intuitive procedures for the acquisition of knowledge in fractions is unlikely to be successful with low achievers (Kelly, Gersten, and Carnine, 1990). Success in understanding fractions is likely to occur when the following variables are presented (Kelly et al., 1990):

1. *Systematic practice in discriminating among different problem types.* Students with learning and behavior problems often confuse algorithms when computing fractions. For example, they learn to compute denominators and then use this procedure when adding, subtracting, multiplying and dividing.

2. *Separation of confusing elements and terminology.* Much of the language of learning fractions is unfamiliar and confusing to youngsters. If the

APPLY THE CONCEPT 8.5

SEQUENCE FOR TEACHING FRACTIONAL CONCEPTS

The student

1. Manipulates concrete models (e.g., manipulating fractional blocks and pegs)
2. Matches fractional models (e.g., matching halves, thirds, fourths)
3. Points to fractional model when name is stated by another (e.g., the teacher says "half" and the student selects a model of "half" from several distractors)
4. Names fractional units when selected by another (e.g., the teacher points to a fractional unit such as a "fourth" and the student names it)
5. Draws diagrams or uses manipulatives to represent fractional units (e.g., the teacher says or writes fractional units such as "whole," "half," and "third," and the student uses manipulatives or drawings to represent these units)
6. Writes fraction names when given fractional drawings (e.g., next to ▮▯ the student writes "half")
7. Uses fractions to solve problems (e.g., place $1\frac{1}{2}$ cups of sugar in a bowl)

---

language is well explained and the concepts illustrated, students are more likely to be successful in learning fractions.

3. *Use a wide range of examples to illustrate each concept.* Students have a difficult time generalizing beyond the number of examples provided by the teacher; thus, a wide range and large number of examples facilitates understanding.

MEASUREMENT

Measurement includes weight, distance, quantity, length, money, and time. Measurement can be taught almost entirely with applied problems. For example, students learn time by using the clock in the classroom or by manipulating a toy clock; they learn money by making purchases with real or toy money; and they learn measures like cup, pint, and teaspoon through following recipes. With each measurement unit taught (e.g., weight, distance, money), the students need to learn the vocabulary and concepts for that unit. Only after students understand the terminology and concepts and have had experience applying the concepts in real measurement problems should they be exposed to measurement instruction through the use of less applied procedures such as

textbooks and worksheets. Lerner (1985) refers to this as the "concrete-to-abstract progression" (p. 364). Lerner states that the teacher should plan three instructional states: (1) concrete or applied; (2) representational (e.g., toy money); and (3) abstract (e.g., workbook page with money problems). It is particularly important when teaching measurement to have overlearning occur at the concrete or applied stage. This section will focus on two forms of measurement: time and money.

Time

Even before coming to school, most children can tell time by the hour or know when the clock says it is time to go to bed or time for dinner. The following teaching sequence assists students in understanding time.

1. Teach students to sequence events. Younger students can sequence the normal routine of the school day. For instance, "First we have a group story, then reading, then we go to recess." Additional practice in sequencing events can occur with story cards, events that occur at home, field trips, and so on.

2. Ask students to identify which events take longer. Name two events (e.g., math time and lining up for recess) and ask the student to identify which event takes longer. Name several events and ask students to put them in order from the event that takes the longest to the one that is quickest to complete.

3. Incorporate calendar activities into the daily schedule. On each day discuss the special activities that will occur. For example, "Today is Monday. What special activity do we have on Monday? Yes, on Monday we go to P.E. Do we go to P.E. in the morning or in the afternoon?" When planning classroom activities, use the calendar to discuss the day and date. Mr. Kyle developed a monthly class calendar and gave a copy to each student. He frequently refers to the calendar when discussing assignments, special events, holidays, or school business.

4. Introduce students to the concept of minute, half-hour, and hour by timing activities. For example, ask students to close their eyes for one minute. Ask them how many minutes it takes them to eat lunch, or how many minutes they spend working on their math.

5. Introduce the hands of the clock only after students understand the passage of time and about how long common events take. Introduce the hour hand first, without introducing the minute hand. When students can accurately tell time by the hour, introduce the minute hand.

6. Teach students to count by fives, then introduce the minute hand by asking them to count off by five. For example, after looking at the long hand of the clock on the 3, students count by fives three times. They conclude that it is 7:15.

7. Teach students to match, recognize, and identify the time on a clock, with the time written in digit form, and with the time written out. For example:

| 1:25 |

| one twenty-five |

A scope and sequence of skills for teaching time is presented in Figure 8.4.

Money

Students with learning disabilities often have difficulty applying money concepts because they have not mastered many of the earlier concepts such as the value of coins, how coins compare (e.g., a quarter is more than two times as much as a dime), and how the value of the coins relates to what can be purchased. One parent reported that her child was frequently taken advantage of because he would trade coins of high value for coins of less value. Students with learning difficulties often do not know the price of common goods. Although they may not need to know the exact price of a loaf of bread or a television set, they should have an estimate of what these items cost.

When initially teaching students to identify money, start with real coins. After they learn to recognize real coins, switch to play money, and then to representations of money on workbook pages. The following sequence is useful when teaching money identification:

1. First teach students to match the same coins. Give students several different coins and ask them to place all of the same coins in the same group.

■ **FIGURE 8.4** *Time—Scope and Sequence of Skills*

- Tells time to the hour
- Tells time to the half hour
- Knows the days of the week
- Knows the names of the months
- Tells time to the quarter hour
- Knows the number of days in a week
- Knows the number of months in a year
- Can use a calendar to answer questions about the date, the day, and the month
- Writes time to the hour
- Writes time to the half hour
- Writes time using five-minute increments
- Can solve simple story problems using time

2. Ask students to point to the coin when you name it. Depending on the students' skill level you may want to start with two coins (e.g., a penny and a nickel) and then progress to three and four. At this point the students do not need to be able to tell the name of the coin but merely to locate it when it is named.

3. Students name the coin. At this level the students tell the name of the coin.

After students are able to identify accurately the name of the coins, the value of the coins is discussed. Coins and dollars are discussed, both in terms of their purchase power and how they relate to each other. Activities and problems that require students to use money and make change assure students that they can apply what they have learned about money. For example, students can learn to use a cash register and to balance and keep a checkbook.

A scope and sequence for teaching money is presented in Figure 8.5.

PROBLEM SOLVING

"I can read the arithmetic all right; I just can't read the writing" (Barney, 1973, p. 57). Many students with learning problems have trouble with traditional story problems in mathematics because their difficulty in reading makes understanding the math problem almost impossible. In addition, students with learning problems often have difficulty with logical reasoning, which is the basis of many story problems. It is also common that their mathematics education has focused primarily on the operation and not on understanding the why of doing it, or even a thorough understanding of the numbers involved in the operation. So, because of their difficulties with reading and logical reasoning, and perhaps because of insufficient instruction in mathematics, students with learning problems often find problem solving the most difficult part of mathematics.

Despite its difficulties, teaching problem solving may be the most important skill we teach students who have learning and behavior problems.

■ **FIGURE 8.5**   *Money—Scope and Sequence of Skills*

- Correctly identifies penny, nickel, and dime
- Knows how many cents are in a penny, nickel, and dime
- When shown combinations of pennies, nickels, and dimes, can add to the correct amount
- Can describe items that can be purchased with combinations of pennies, nickels, and dimes
- Can solve simple word math problems involving pennies, nickels, and dimes
- Correctly identifies quarter, dollar, five dollar, ten dollar, and twenty dollar
- Knows the value of combination of quarters and dollars
- Can solve verbal math problems with quarters and dollars

Whereas most other students are able to apply the operations they learn to real-life problems with little direct instruction, students with learning problems will be less able to apply these skills without instruction, rehearsal, and practice. Students with learning disabilities lack metacognitive knowledge about strategies for math problem solving. Poor math performance is not solely a function of math computation difficulties (Montague and Bos, 1990). Students who are taught strategies for problem solving are more likely to be successful than students who are taught the sequence for solving problems (Wilson and Sindelar, 1991).

Students need to know when and how to add, subtract, multiply, and divide. Knowing *when* involves understanding the operation and applying it in the appropriate situation. Knowing *how* is the accurate performance of the operation. Most students are better at *how* than at *when;* problem solving gives students practice at these skills.

Factors Affecting Successful Verbal Problem Solving

The factors that affect successful verbal problem solving or story problems (Goodstein, 1981) need to be considered by teachers when writing and selecting story problems and instructing students.

1. *Sameness analysis.* The quality of sameness in mathematical problem solving was developed by Carnine and colleagues through a series of research investigations (Engelmann, Carnine, and Steely, 1991). The idea is to connect math concepts so that students see the ways in which aspects of mathematical problem solving are the same. They identify "types" of word problems and then explicitly teach students the ways in which these word problems are alike.

2. *Cue words.* The presence or absence of cue words can significantly affect students' abilities to solve verbal word problems. The cue word *altogether* is illustrated in the following example: "Mary has 4 erasers. Joe has 7 erasers. How many erasers do they have *altogether*?" The cue word *left* is illustrated in the following example: "Jackie has 9 pieces of candy. She gave 3 pieces to Tom. How many does she have *left*?" Students need to be taught to look for cue words that will guide them in solving problems.

3. *Reasoning.* Ask students to think about the idea behind the story problem. Does it appear the person in the problem will get more or less? Why? What operation will help solve this? What numbers in the story do we have to use? Are there numbers we do not have and need to compute?

4. *Syntactic complexity.* The sentence structure within the story problem needs to be kept simple. Learner performance can be significantly impaired when the sentence contains a complex interrogative sentence structure (Larsen, Parker, and Trenholme, 1978). The sentence length and vocabulary may also affect verbal problem solving.

5. *Extraneous information.* Extraneous information in word problems causes difficulties because the majority of students attempt to use all of the information in solving the problem. For example: "Mary's mother baked 10 cookies. Mary's sister baked 8 cookies. Mary's brother baked 3 cupcakes. How many *cookies* were baked?" The information regarding Mary's brother baking three cupcakes is extraneous, yet many students will use the information in attempting to solve the problem. Extraneous information introduced into story problems is associated with decreases in accuracy and computation speed with students. Blankenship and Lovitt (1976) explain students' difficulties with extraneous information by suggesting that the difficulties are based not on reading the entire story problem but merely on knowing which numbers are needed to solve the problem. Students will construct the problem using the numbers available in the story problem, disregarding the question and the content available in the story problem. After students are successfully able to complete story problems without extraneous information, teach them to complete story problems with extraneous information.

6. *Content load.* The content load refers to the number of ideas contained within a story problem. The story problem should not be overloaded with concepts (West, 1978) and, if it is, the students need to be taught to discriminate between relevant and irrelevant concepts.

7. *Suitable content.* The story problems should contain content that is interesting and appealing to the students and relevant to the types of real problems the students have or will encounter.

Methods of Teaching Story Problem Solving

There are two important steps in preparing students for success in solving story problems: (a) provide story problems in an appropriate sequence, and (b) make students aware of the types of errors that are commonly made. Students also need to learn specific strategies that will assist them in using a successful process for mastering story problems in class and applying those principles to the mathematics of everyday life.

A step-by-step strategy for teaching sixth-grade students to solve story problems is illustrated in Apply the Concept 8.6 (Smith and Alley, 1981). Students need first to learn the strategies, practice them with support from a teacher, and then practice them independently until they can apply the principles with success. After continued success, students make

APPLY THE CONCEPT 8.6

STEPS FOR TEACHING STUDENTS TO SOLVE STORY PROBLEMS

Story Problem: Mark had $1.47 to spend. He spent
.34 on gum. How much money does he have left?

I. Read the Problem
   A. Find unknown words
   B. Find "cue words" (e.g., *left*)

II. Reread the Problem
   A. Identify what is given
      1. Is renaming needed?
      2. Are there unit changes?

B. Decide what is asked for
   1. What process is needed?
   2. What unit or category is asked for?
      (e.g., seconds, pounds, money)

III. Use Objects to Show the Problem
   A. Decide what operation to use

IV. Write the Problem

V. Work the Problem

---

adaptations in or condense the steps they use. The section on cognitive behavior modification in Chapter Two discusses how to teach students learning strategies.

Fleischner, Nuzum, and Marzola (1987, p. 216) devised the following instructional program to teach arithmetic problem solving to students with learning disabilities:

READ	What is the question?
REREAD	What is the necessary information?
THINK	Putting together = addition
	Taking apart = subtraction
	Do I need all the information?
	Is it a two-step problem?
SOLVE	Write the equation
CHECK	Recalculate
	Label
	Compare

Another strategy for solving word problems was used by Hutchinson (1993). She taught adolescent students with learning problems to solve algebra word problems by asking themselves questions and using graphs to monitor their progress. The self-questions she used included:

— Have I read and understood the sentence?
— Do I have the whole picture, a representation, for this problem?
— Have I written the representation on the worksheet?

Montague and Bos (1986a, 1986b) demonstrated the efficacy of the learning-strategy approach, described in Apply the Concept 8.7, with high-school adolescents with learning disabilities.

In summary, when teaching story problems to students with learning and behavior problems, keep the following guidelines in mind:

1. Be certain the students can perform the arithmetic computation before introducing the computation in story problems.

2. Develop a range of story problems that contain the type of problem you want the student to learn to solve.

3. Instruct with one type of problem until mastery is attained.

4. Teach the students to read through the word problem and visualize the situation. Ask them to read the story aloud and tell what it is about.

5. Ask the students to reread the story—this time to get the facts.

APPLY THE CONCEPT 8.7

TEACHING ADOLESCENTS TO SOLVE STORY PROBLEMS

The eight steps in the verbal math problem-solving strategy are described below:

1. *Read the problem aloud.* Ask the teacher to pronounce or define any word you do not know. (The teacher will pronounce and provide meanings for any words if the student asks.)

   Example: In a high school there are 2,878 male and 1,943 female students enrolled. By how many students must the enrollment increase to make the enrollment 5,000?

2. *Paraphrase the problem aloud.* State important information giving close attention to the numbers in the problem. Repeat the question part aloud. A self-questioning technique such as What is asked? or What am I looking for? is used to provide focus on the outcome.

   Example: Altogether there are a certain number of kids in high school. There are 2,878 boys and 1,943 girls. The question is by how many students must the enrollment increase to make the total enrollment 5,000. What is asked? How many more students are needed to total 5,000 in the school?

3. *Visualize.* Graphically display the information. Draw a representation of the problem.

4. *State the problem.* Complete the following statements aloud. I have . . . I want to find . . . Underline the important information in the problem.

   Example: I have the number of boys and the number of girls who go to the school now. I want to find how many more kids are needed to total 5,000.

5. *Hypothesize.* Complete the following statements aloud. If I . . . Then . . . how many steps will I use to find the answer? Write the operation signs.

   Example: If I add 2,878 boys and 1,943 girls, I'll get the number of kids now. Then I must subtract that number from 5,000 to find out how many more must enroll. First add, then subtract. + – This is a two-step problem.

6. *Estimate.* Write the estimate. My answer should be around . . . or about . . . (The skills of rounding and estimating answers should be reinforced at this step.) Underline the estimate.

   Example: 2,800 and 2,000 are 4,800. 4,800 from 5,000 is 200. My answer should be around *200*.

7. *Calculate.* Show the calculation and label the answer. Circle the answer. Use a self-questioning technique such as, Is this answer in the correct form? (Change from cent sign to dollar sign and decimal point should be reinforced when solving money problems.) Correct labels for the problems should be reinforced.

   Example:
   $$\begin{array}{r} 2{,}878 \\ +\,1{,}943 \\ \hline 4{,}821 \end{array} \qquad \begin{array}{r} 5{,}000 \\ -\,4{,}821 \\ \hline 179 \text{ students} \end{array}$$

8. *Self-check.* Refer to the problem and check every step to determine accuracy of operation(s) selected and correctness of response and solution. Check computation for accuracy. (Checking skills will be reinforced at this step.) Use the self-questioning technique by asking if the answer makes sense.

Source: From "The Effect of Cognitive Strategy Training on Verbal Math Problems Solving Performance of Learning Disabled Adolescents" by M. Montague and C. S. Bos, 1986, *Journal of Learning Disabilities, 19,* pp. 26–33. Copyright 1986 by PRO-ED, Inc. Reprinted by permission.

6. Identify the key question. In the beginning stages of problem solving, the students should write the key question so it can be referred to when the computation is complete.

7. Identify extraneous information.

8. Reread the story problem and attempt to state the situation in a mathematical sentence. The teacher plays an important role in this step by asking the students questions and guiding them in formulating the arithmetic problem.

9. Tell the students to write the arithmetic problem and compute the answer. (Some problems can be computed by the students in their heads without completing this step.)

10. Tell the students to reread the key question and be sure they have completed the problem correctly.

11. Ask the students if their answer is likely, based on their estimate.

Teaching math story problems does not have to be limited to the content area of math. Cawley (1984) discusses how story problems can be integrated with instruction in reading so that reading level does not interfere with understanding the math story problem. At the same time, story problems can enhance and support what the student is doing in reading. For example, a story about a mother duck and her babies was part of a student's reading lesson. During mathematics, the teacher makes minor changes in the story and uses it for instruction in story problems in mathematics (see Figure 8.6).

This same procedure can be used with junior high and high school students' content area textbooks. Math story problems can be taken from social studies and science tests; Cawley and Miller (1986) refer to these as knowledge-based problems. Usually these problems require specific knowledge in the content area. Cawley (1984) identifies the integration of math into other content areas as an important means of promoting generalization of math concepts.

Pictures can be used to facilitate processing information in solving mathematic word problems. For example, using Figure 8.7, the teacher could say, "The small monkeys have four bananas and the large

■ **FIGURE 8.6**   *Example of Teacher-Altered Story for Use in Story Problem Instruction*

The mother duck went to the pond with her *8* babies. They looked for their new friend. *Two* more baby ducks joined them. How many baby ducks were there?

monkeys have six bananas. How many bananas would they have if they put them all together?"

Instructional manipulatives can also be used to assist students with learning problems in solving mathematical word problems. Cuisenaire rods can be used to represent the numerical values in the problem and assist students in better understanding and solving mathematical word problems (Marsh and Cooke, 1996).

APPROACHES TO INCREASING MATH PERFORMANCE

There are three types of interventions for mathematics instruction for individuals with learning disabilities (for review, see Mastropieri, Scruggs, and Shiah, 1991). One type of intervention is cognitive, one is behavioral and the third is alternative instructional delivery systems, which includes cooperative learning, computer-assisted instruction, and interactive video disks. Mastropieri, Scruggs, and Shia reflect that a broad array of interventions are effective, including: strategy instruction, worksheets, computers, peer-assisted instruction, and direct measurement.

Cognitive Approaches

Cognitive behavior modification (CBM) can be used with instructional procedures in mathematics. Cog-

■ **FIGURE 8.7** *Pictures Help Solve Math Story Problems*

nitive behavior modification often takes the form of self-instruction, which relies on using internalized language to facilitate the problem-solving process. Based largely on the work of Meichenbaum and his associates (Meichenbaum, 1977, 1985; Meichenbaum and Goodman, 1971), CBM is receiving attention as an alternative strategy for teaching arithmetic to students with learning difficulties. Lovitt and Curtiss (1968) found that when students verbalize the answer before writing it, as opposed to just writing the answer, they make fewer computational errors. It could be that the process of verbalization focuses the students on the answer and gives them a second opportunity to check whether the answer makes sense and is correct. When verbalizations are added to the arithmetic process, either by naming the sign before proceeding (Parsons, 1972) or verbalizing the steps in the arithmetic process while solving the problem (Grimm, Bijou, and Parsons, 1973), there is a significant improvement in performance. Leon and Pepe (1983) taught a five-step self-instructional sequence to special education teachers. Students participating in arithmetic instruction from these teachers who were trained in the sequence improved greatly in both arithmetic computation and in generalizing skills acquired.

The following sequence for using self-instruction in mathematics is a modification of the approach used by Leon and Pepe (1983).

1. *Modeling.* The teacher demonstrates how to compute the problem by using overt self-instruction. This overt self-instruction, or talking aloud of the process, assists students who have learning problems in knowing what they should say to themselves and what questions they should ask to keep them focused on the process.

2. *Co-participation.* Both teacher and students compute the problem together by using overt self-instruction. This step helps the students put the procedure in their own words and yet supplies the support of the teacher while they are still learning the process.

3. *Student demonstration.* The students compute the problem alone by using overt self-instruction and the teacher monitors the students' performance. The students are more independent in this step; however, the teacher is still available to give correction and feedback.

4. *Fading overt self-instruction.* The students continue to demonstrate the computation of the problem with internal self-instruction. Often students have a check sheet of symbols or key words to cue them to the key points.

5. *Feedback.* The students complete the problem independently by using covert self-instruction and providing self-reinforcement for a job well done.

Behavioral Approaches

Behavioral techniques can be used to increase students' math performance. As you know, stimulus cues precede responses and often control or provide information to control responses. In arithmetic instruction, the teacher needs to identify the relevant cues and determine whether the students are aware of these cues and are using them appropriately. In Figure 8.8 three different problems are presented; there are many different cues a student must understand and attend to before accurately performing these problems. For example, in problem 1 of Figure 8.8 the student must know what "+" means, what the numbers represent, and what procedure to follow to perform the problem. In problem 2 the student must know what the picture represents, the difference

■ **FIGURE 8.8**   *Math Problems Enlisting Various Cues*

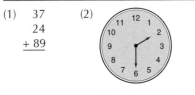

(1)   37
      24
    + 89

(2)

What time is it? _____

(3) How long is this line? _____

between the short and long hands of the clock, and what each of the numbers represents. Problem 3 requires the student's understanding of the cue *long,* and what type of tool is needed to address the problem. Math provides many stimulus cues and the teacher needs to be certain that the students recognize and understand the cues and attend to them.

Teachers can also provide cues to assist students in learning new skills. For example, the following illustrates cues a teacher provided when students were first learning long division.

÷	(divide)	6)478 8)521
×	(multiply)	
−	(subtract)	
↓	(bring down)	

Providing corrective feedback reinforces students' performances. Corrective feedback involves telling the students what they are doing well, including procedures, accuracy of responses, and work style. It also involves identifying in what area a student needs further assistance. Corrective feedback should be given frequently. Do not wait until students have completed tasks; give feedback while they are working on the task. Be precise with feedback; rather than saying, "You are doing a good job," say, "You remembered to carry. All of the answers in the first row are correct. Good job."

Task analysis is a process of specifying the behaviors needed for a particular task that can help shape student responses. The student is taught behaviors from the simple to the more complex until he or she can perform the target behavior. For example, the

teacher's goal may be for a student to complete two-place addition with carrying by solving a verbal math problem. The student's present level of performance is knowledge of math facts when adding numbers between 0 and 9. Through task analysis, the teacher identifies the many behaviors that need to be shaped before the student is performing the target behavior.

For example, the teacher identified the skills needed between knowing math facts between 0 and 9 and being able to solve a verbal math problem with two-place addition.

1. Number concepts 0–9
2. Number concepts 10–100
3. Place value
4. Simple word problems (oral) 0–9 — Answers require addition facts
5. Simple word problems (written) 0–9 — Answers require addition facts
6. Two-place addition problems
7. Word problems (oral) addition computation — Answers require two-place addition
8. Word problems (written) addition computation — Answers require two-place addition

The teacher decided that it would take approximately three months to reach the goal. She knew that her mathematics program would focus on other skills during that period (e.g., time, measurements, and graphs).

FOCUS ON REAL-WORLD MATHEMATICS

Many students with learning and behavior problems manage to graduate with only a minimum understanding of mathematics skills. Many, relieved to escape formal education in mathematics, have the unfortunate misconception that they are finished with mathematics. Unfortunately, they are sadly mistaken and they soon find that functioning as an adult requires applying mathematic concepts. Managing money, checkbooks, interest on loans, and credit cards is only the beginning. Adults must file taxes, complete employment forms for deductions, and use basic math skills in their jobs. Figure 8.9 lists the mathematics skills all students need to acquire because they are essential for survival in the real world. To function completely in society, all students should be able to demonstrate applied knowledge and understanding of these skills.

Functional Math

Halpern (1981) suggests that mathematics instruction for students with learning disabilities focus on teaching functional skills necessary for independent living. Many of the skills most important for students with learning disabilities are not contained in mathematics curricula because they do not need to be taught through direct instruction to nonlearning-disabled students. Halpern suggests students with learning disabilities learn (1) the realistic prices of products, (2) how to estimate, and (3) how to tell time and estimate time intervals. According to Halpern (1981), most arithmetic done in the real world is done orally, and yet arithmetic done in classrooms is done with pencil and paper. More attention to oral practice in the classroom is needed.

Schwartz and Budd (1981) recommend math curricula for students with mild disabilities be based on the functional math skills they need. Figure 8.10 presents an outline of content for teaching functional math.

Schwartz and Budd (1981) recommend an eight-step sequence useful for initiating teaching strategies for a functional math curriculum. This approach appears to be particularly useful with junior high and high school students.

1. *Become motivated.* Students need to feel there is a valid reason for learning to solve mathematics problems. This may include identifying how math is used at home and on the job. Students can interview their parents to determine all of the ways they use functional math. Ask former students or speakers to discuss the need for math as they join the work world.

2. *Choose the operation.* When students are able to identify the question being asked, it is much easier for them to identify the appropriate operation for resolving the question. Students must understand how the operation is performed before they use the operation in functional mathematics.

3. *Understand the problem.* Students need to understand the type of question being asked in verbal problem solving. They need to understand such terminology as *fewer, greater, more, all together, in addition to,* and *so on,* in order to be successful at functional math. Present realistic problem situations and discuss the questions being asked. Ask students to focus on key words and discuss their meaning. Assist students in identifying unnecessary information.

4. *Estimate the answer.* This step encourages students to check to determine if their selected operation is reasonable. For example, give the following problem: "How much money will John have left after he lends half of his total savings of $8.40 to his sister?" The student selects multiplication as the operation for solving the problem. The student estimates the answer and has a second opportunity to check whether the correct operation was chosen. Questions such as the following should be asked of the student: "After multiplying, will John have more money or less?" "When we lend money to people do we usually have more money or less?" "Is multiplying the correct operation?"

5. *Do the operation.* The students should be able to perform the operation, but a review of skills may be necessary.

6. *Check the answer.* The student checks to be sure the numbers were copied correctly and the problem was performed correctly. Students are encouraged to answer the question, "Is this a reasonable answer to the problem?"

7. *Understand the answer.* After determining the answer, the student should be able to interpret it. The teacher may ask additional questions that allow the student to demonstrate more fully understanding of the answer and the problem.

8. *Apply the skill.* The application of the first seven steps is discussed relative to problems generated by the students and the teacher.

■ **FIGURE 8.9** *Mathematical Concepts for the Everyday World*

More and more science and technology are permeating our society and with this, the need for more mathematics to understand the scientific and technological concepts is increasing. The new level of mathematical competencies, skills, and attitudes toward mathematics required of modern citizenry is much higher than what was expected 25 years ago. The following represent the skills and competencies considered necessary for adults to participate effectively in contemporary society:

1. Numbers and Numerals
   - Express a rational number using a decimal notation.
   - List the first ten multiples of 2 through 12.
   - Use the whole numbers (four basic operations) in problem solving.
   - Recognize the digit, its place value, and the number represented through billions.
   - Describe a given positive rational number using decimal, percent, or fractional notation.
   - Convert to Roman numerals from decimal numerals and conversely (e.g., data translation).
   - Represent very large and very small numbers using scientific notation.

2. Operations and Properties
   - Write equivalent fractions for given fractions such as 1/2, 2/3, 3/4, and 7/8.
   - Use the standard algorithms for the operations of arithmetic of positive rational numbers.
   - Solve addition, subtraction, multiplication, and division problems involving fractions.
   - Solve problems involving percent.
   - Perform arithmetic operations with measures.
   - Estimate results.
   - Judge the reasonableness of answers to computational problems.

3. Mathematical Sentences
   - Construct a mathematical sentence from a given verbal problem.
   - Solve simple equations.

4. Geometry and Measurement
   - Recognize horizontal lines, vertical lines, parallel lines, perpendicular lines, and intersecting lines.
   - Recognize different shapes.
   - Compute areas, surfaces, volumes, densities.
   - Understand similarities and congruence.
   - Use measurement devices.
5. Relations and Functions
   - Interpret information from a graphical representation.
   - Understand and apply ratio and proportion.
   - Construct scales.

6. Probability and Statistics
   - Determine mean, average, mode, median.
   - Understand simple probability.

7. Mathematical Reasoning
- Produce counter examples to test invalidity of a statement.
- Detect and describe flaws and fallacies in advertising and propaganda where statistical data and inferences are employed.
- Gather and present data to support an inference or argument.

8. General Skills
- Maintain personal bank records.
- Plan a budget and keep personal records.
- Apply simple interest formula to calculate interest.
- Estimate the real cost of an item.
- Compute taxes and investment returns.
- Appraise insurance and retirement benefits.

Source: M. C. Sharma, "Mathematics in the Real World." In J. F. Cawley (Ed.) *Developmental Teaching of Mathematics for Learning Disabled* (Austin, Tex.: PRO-ED, 1984), pp. 224–225. Reprinted with permission of PRO-ED, Inc.

■ **FIGURE 8.10**   *Content for Teaching Functional Math*

Consumer Skills
Making change
Determining cost of sale items utilizing percentages
    (e.g., "25% off")
Determining tax amounts
Doing cost comparisons
Buying on "time"
Balancing a checkbook
Determining total cost of purchases

Homemaking Skills
Measuring ingredients
Budgeting for household expenses
Calculating length of cooking and baking time when
    there are options (e.g., for a cake using two 9"
    round pans vs. two 8" round pans)
Measuring material for clothing construction
Doing cost comparisons

Health Care
Weighing oneself and others
Calculating caloric intake
Determining when to take medication

Auto Care
Calculating cost of auto parts
Measuring spark plug gaps
Determining if tire pressure is correct
Figuring gas mileage

Home Care
Determining amount of supplies (paint, rug shampoo)
    to buy
Determining time needed to do projects
Measuring rods and drapes
Finding cost of supplies
Finding cost of repairs

Vocational Needs
Calculating payroll deductions
Determining money owed
Knowing when to be at work
Doing actual math for various jobs

Source: S. E. Schwartz and D. Budd, "Mathematics for Handicapped Learners: A Functional Approach for Adolescents," *Focus on Exceptional Children 13*(7) (1981): 7–8. Reprinted with permission from Love Publishing, Denver, Colorado.

CURRICULUM AND MATERIALS

Traditional math curricula have provided problems for students with learning disabilities. These problems have been summarized by Blankenship (1984):

1. The reading vocabulary is difficult and the reading level is too high.
2. The sequencing of material presented is poor, multiple concepts are introduced, and focus skips from one concept to another.
3. There are insufficient problems covering each concept.
4. There are insufficient opportunities and problems focusing on application.
5. There is too much variance in the formatting of the pages.
6. Students often do not have the prerequisite skills that the text assumes they possess.

Teachers who attempt to use traditional curricula with students who have learning difficulties will need to control for these factors in their teaching.

Recently a number of curricula have been developed that focus on teaching math skills to students with learning difficulties.

Project Math

Project Math (Cawley, Fitzmaurice, Sedlak, and Althaus, 1976) is a well-recognized math curriculum designed specifically for students with mild disabilities. The program includes work on sets, patterns, numbers, operations, fractions, geometry, measurement, and lab activities. It is both a developmental and remedial program and it has eliminated many of the problems associated with traditional arithmetic programs. Project Math reduces the reading level, provides a direct link between assessment and instruction, teaches to mastery, and provides procedures for individualizing instruction. It appears to be a very useful program for teaching mathematics to students with learning difficulties.

DISTAR Arithmetic

The DISTAR arithmetic program (Englemann and Carnine, 1972, 1975, 1976) stresses direct instruction through a highly sequenced format that provides immediate feedback to the student. The DISTAR Arithmetic Kits come complete with a detailed teacher's guide, workbooks, teaching book, and take-homes. The teacher's guide tells the teacher exactly what to say and do—even such directions as, "Say 'Good'." The materials are designed to be fast-paced with lots of oral drill. The DISTAR Arithmetic programs have been effectively used in teaching skills to economically disadvantaged children (Abt Associates, 1976; Becker and Englemann, 1976; Stallings and Kaskowitz, 1974).

Additional Sources of Curriculum and Materials

There are many other sources of curriculum suitable for teaching mathematics to students who have learning problems.

1. The *Computational Arithmetic Program,* developed by Smith and Lovitt (1982), provides 314 worksheets to teach basic math skills from grades one through six.

2. The *Corrective Mathematics Program,* by Englemann and Carnine (1982), provides remedial basic math for students in grades three through twelve.

3. *Structural Arithmetic* by Stern (1965) involves students in kindergarten through third grade making, discovering, and learning math concepts and facts.

4. *Cuisenaire Rods,* by M. Georges Cuisenaire, to give conceptual knowledge of the basic structure of mathematics.

5. *Milliken Wordmath,* developed by Coffland and Baldwin (1985), uses computer programs to teach problem solving within the mathematics curriculum to children in fourth grade and up who are unable to

apply their computational knowledge to the solving of everyday problems.

6. *Key Math Teach and Practice* by Connolly (1985) was developed to provide diagnosis of math difficulties and remedial practice. Materials include a teacher's guide, student progress charts, and sequence charts. Activities and worksheets are also provided.

INSTRUCTIONAL ACTIVITIES

This section provides instructional activities related to mathematics. Some of the activities teach new skills; others are best suited for practice and reinforcement of already acquired skills. For each activity, the objective, materials, and teaching procedures are described.

■ Two-Digit Numbers: Focus on Reversals

Objective: To help students understand and use two-digit numbers successfully. (For use with students who write 23 for 32; 41 for 14; and so on.)

Grades: Primary

Materials: Objects that can be grouped by tens (e.g., pencils, paper, chips, sticks).

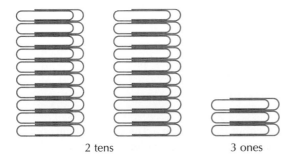

2 tens   3 ones

Teaching Procedures: Four steps are recommended: First, tell the children to group objects such as popsicle sticks or chips in tens, and then to tell the number of tens and number of ones left over. Next, the children count orally by tens and use objects to show the count (e.g., 2 tens is twenty; 6 tens is 60; and so on). When multiples of ten are established, extra ones are included (e.g., 2 tens and 3 is 23). Because of naming irregularities, teens are dealt with last.

Children then group objects by tens and write to describe the grouping. The tens-ones labels, used in early stages, are gradually eliminated. On separate sheets of paper, the students write the number that corresponds with the grouping. The children use objects (tens and ones) to help compare and sequence numbers.

■ "Two Up"

Objective: To practice multiplication facts by rehearsing counting by twos, threes, fours, etc.

Grades   Primary through intermediate

Prerequisite Behaviors: Counting by twos, threes, etc.

Materials: A set of forty-eight cards made by printing the multiples of two from 1 to 12, using a different color of pen for each set (e.g., 2, 4, . . . , 12 in red, blue, green and brown).

Teaching Procedures: Directions for playing the game are: The cards are shuffled and dealt, giving an equal number of cards to each player. The player who has the red 2 starts the game by placing the red 2 in the middle of the table. The next player must place a red 4 on top of the red 2 *or* pass. Next a red 6 is needed, and so on. Each of the players play in a similar manner. A player can only play one card each turn.

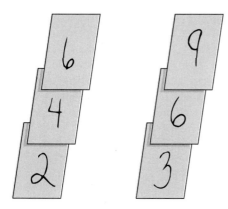

The object of the game is to play the cards from 2 on up. The first player to play all of his or her cards is the winner.

Adaptations: This game can be played with decks of threes, fours, sixes, and so on, called "Three Up," "Four Up," etc. A different deck of cards must be made for each multiple.

■ Bingo Clock Reading

Objective: To give the students practice in associating the time on a clock face, to its written form on a game board, to its spoken form.

Grades: Primary

Materials: (1) Cards that show times on a standard clock. (2) Large game boards with sixteen squares and with times written at the bottom of each square. (3) Sixteen "clock" chips (made by placing gummed labels on gameboard chips and drawing a clock on the face of the label). (4) Markers.

Teaching Procedures: A caller holds up a clock face. The players must decide if the time shown by that clock is on their gameboard. If it is, the player places a marker in the square that contains the written form. The winner is the first person who completes a row in any direction and reads the time in each winning square.

three o'clock	seven o'clock	fifteen minutes after four	twenty minutes after twelve
fifteen minutes after six	twenty minutes after twelve	twenty minutes to eleven	twenty minutes after eleven
five minutes after five	fifteen minutes after ten	twenty-five minutes after one	twenty-five minutes to eleven
nine thirty	five minutes to seven	twenty-five minutes after twelve	ten o'clock

■ Coin Concentration

Objective: To practice reading money amounts in four different notations and to reinforce coin recognition.

Grades: Primary, intermediate to high school (see adaptation for older students)

Prerequisite Behaviors: Coin value, value placement, coin recognition of dollars and cents

Materials: (1) Money picture card. (2) Money-word card. (3) Money-decimal card. (4) Money-cents card.

Teaching Procedures: The game of coin concentration can be played at several levels of difficulty, with varying skill emphasis depending on specific classroom needs. At the simplest level, use only one kind of money card (make two copies of the card and cut apart on solid lines so students play with a total of twenty cards). Decide on the number and type of cards to be used, and place them face down on the table.

The first player turns over two cards, one at a time, trying to match values. If the cards match, the player keeps them. If not, he or she simply turns them back over on the table in their same location. Then the next player tries to make a match by turning over two more cards, and so on, until all the cards are matched with their pair.

The winner is the one with the most matched cards. For variety, ask the students to add the total value of their cards and the player with the highest value wins. To add variety and increase difficulty, put different type cards down and players can match 4¢ to $.04 or to *four cents.*

Adaptations: This activity can be used with older students by increasing the difficulty of the coin values represented and by adding a fifth card. On the fifth card is the name of an object that costs the corresponding amount. For example, if the money value is $329.00 the fifth card may have "Video Cassette Recorder" written on it.

■ Shopping Spree

Objective: To give students practice using money and understanding the concept of addition and subtraction with money.

Grades: Elementary-age students who are having difficulty with the money concepts. (See adaptations for use with older students.)

Materials: (1) Coins and dollar bills (when teaching the more advanced concepts). (2) Pictures of items.

Teaching Procedures: Cut out magazine pictures of things children would like to buy and put a price on the pictures. Start with easy amounts, such as 5¢, 10¢, 25¢, and then in further lessons, increase the complexity of the amounts, to such things as 63¢, 51¢, etc. For higher grades, use of dollar bills can be implemented. Have the students divide into two groups and have half the groups be storeclerks, and have the other half be shoppers. The shoppers buy picture items from the clerk. The shoppers are responsible for giving the correct amount of money. The clerks are responsible for giving the correct change. Then the children trade places.

At a later date, specific amounts of money can be distributed and the children are to select several items without going over their designated amount. Also with a specific amount of money, show two or three different items and ask which item they can afford.

Adaptations: For older students, "pretend" checkbooks can be made and distributed. Each student is given a specified amount in his or her checkbook and must make appropriate deductions as he or she makes purchases.

■ I Have . . .

Objective: To provide practice in auditory memory and application of math skills.

Grades: 3–6

Materials: (1) 3 × 5 cards. (2) Paper and pencils. (3) Pen to write word problems on each card, such as:

> I have 8. Who knows that times 5?

> Sally has 12 dogs. She gave 4 puppies away. How many are left?

Teaching Procedures: Shuffle the cards and take the top card and read it to the students. Then model writing the problem and answering it on the board. Next, choose another card and read it to the class. This time, the students write down the problem and answer it. You then should assist immediately any students who are making errors.

Discuss the answers with the class, and then repeat the steps until a winner obtains a predetermined number of points.

■ "99"

Objective: To generalize and practice adding numbers in one's head or on paper.

Grades: Intermediate to senior high

Materials: (1) Playing cards. (2) Paper and pencils.

Teaching Procedures: Explain that the objective of this game is to add cards up to a score of 99. Establish the following rules:

Jacks and Queens = 10
Kings = 99
Nines = "free turn" pass; to be used anytime
Fours = pass
Aces = 1
Other cards = face value

Each player is dealt three cards. The rest of the cards go face down on a draw pile. The players take turns discarding one card from their hand face up on a discard pile and drawing one card from the draw pile to put back in their hand. As a player discards his or her card, he or she must add the number from the card to any previous score acquired up to that point in the game and give the new score out loud. Note the exception: If a player plays a nine, he or she receives a free-turn pass. If a player plays a four, he or she has to pass a turn with no score. The first player to score higher than 99 loses the game.

■ Shopping

Objective: To provide practice in addition, subtraction, and comparing prices (problem solving).

Grades: Junior high

Materials: (1) Newspaper from which to cut out various supermarket sale ads that include price per item. Mount individual items on cardboard and cover them with clear plastic or just bring the ads. (2) Made-up shopping lists to hand out to the class. (3) Pencil and paper.

Teaching Procedures: Divide the class into small groups. Tell the students that their shopping list contains the items that they will need this week. Assign each group a designated amount for groceries (e.g., $30.00). The object is to buy everything on the list and spend the least. Place on each desk the supermarket sale ads each with the name of its store. After students buy their item they record the price and the store where they bought it. (It's easier if one student in each group buys the meats, one buys the dairy products, and so on.) When the students have bought all the items on the list, tell them to total their bills and be ready to present the results.

■ Cake for Four—No, Make that Six!

By: Sandra Stroud

Objective: Developing students' *concept of fraction* by having them partition an object into equal parts.

Grades: Second through fourth grade (possibly higher)

Materials: For each student: (1) a 6" paper circle; (2) 5 strips construction paper—1/4" wide by 8" long, in a contrasting color to the paper circle; and (3) 8 Teddy Grahams (or other small cookies), placed in a small sandwich bag.

Teaching Procedure: Students move desks together so that each has a partner with whom to compare his or her work. Materials are distributed. The teacher introduces the lesson by telling the students that they are going to take part in a *Let's Pretend* activity that will help them learn that when they eat a piece of cake that has been divided into equal parts they are actually eating a *fraction* of that cake.

The students are asked to imagine that they have just helped their mother (or other grown-up) bake a cake for their supper. It is their favorite kind of cake and, because there are four people in their pretend family, they are planning to divide it into four equal pieces. They are asked to think of the paper circle on their desk as the top of the cake, and to show the teacher—and their partners—how they would use the strips of paper to divide the cake into four equal parts. When each child has successfully demonstrated this first partitioning task, they are asked what fraction of the whole cake each piece is, and how that fraction is written.

Next, they are asked to imagine that their grandmother and grandfather have arrived unexpectedly and that the grandparents have accepted the family's invitation to stay for supper. The family certainly wants to share the cake with their grandparents, so into how many pieces will they now divide their cake? The teacher makes sure that each student shows six equal portions and that they understand that each piece of cake is now 1/6 of the whole—just enough for the six people at the dinner table. However, before that cake is served, Uncle Bob and Aunt Doris arrive! Now the cake will be divided into how many equal pieces? Finally, the time comes to decorate the cake with the Teddy Grahams and to cut and serve the cake. (As a reward for all their good thinking, the students now get to eat the decorations—1/8 at a time!)

Students enjoy the story associated with this activity, and they enjoy comparing their partitioned cakes with those of their peers. (This is a good example of cooperative learning.) They especially enjoy eating their cookies at the end of this activity.

■ Fractions for Breakfast

By: Sandra Stroud

Objective: To help students strengthen their understanding that fractions are subdivisions of whole numbers; also, to build students' conceptualization of fractions being added together.

Grades: Fourth–Sixth

Materials: For each student: (1) a paper towel; (2) a plastic sandwich bag containing one whole graham cracker and two graham cracker halves. (The graham crackers should have indentions which make it easy to snap them into four approximately equal pieces.)

Teaching Procedures: Students move desks together so that each has a partner with whom to compare his or her work. Materials are distributed. The teacher asks the students to place the whole graham cracker at the top of their paper towel in a horizontal position; the two halves are to be placed beneath it. The whole graham cracker is left whole throughout the activity for comparative purposes. Next, the teacher demonstrates and has the students manipulate their graham cracker pieces to reach the following understandings:

1/2 + 1/2 = 1 whole
1/2 + 1/2 = 2/2 = 1 whole
1/4 + 1/4 + 1/4 + 1/4 = 4/4 = 1 whole
1/4 + 1/4 = 2/4 = 1/2
2/4 + 2/4 = 4/4 = 1 whole
2/4 + 1/4 = 3/4
1/8 + 1/8 + 1/8 + 1/8 + 2/8 + 2/8 = 1
1/8 + 1/8 = 2/8 = 1/4
2/8 + 1/8 + 1/8 = 4/8 = 1/2
4/8 + 3/8 = 7/8 (still less than 1 whole)

Next, the teacher encourages the students to manipulate their graham cracker pieces to discover the following concepts:

1. A fractional number that has the same numerator and denominator is always equal to one whole.
2. A fractional number is always less than one whole.
3. As the denominator increases, the size of each fractional piece of "cracker" decreases.

Finally, the teacher and students eat their fractions for breakfast!

This activity helps students understand the concept of fractional parts of whole numbers because they always have a whole graham cracker in front of them with which to form a comparison. As they break the second graham cracker into smaller and smaller equal parts, they can "push" these smaller parts together to re-form a whole cracker. This activity is an excellent one to use to teach students to add and subtract fractions, because the students are actually handling the fractional units of the whole graham cracker.

This activity helps students form a positive association between their learning and the pleasure of eating their graham crackers.

SUMMARY

Developing appropriate mathematics instruction for students with learning and behavior problems involves comprehensive programming with an emphasis on its application to daily living skills. Special attention is given to factors that might influence the math learning abilities of special students. Psychological factors, educational factors, neuropsychological factors, perceptual skills, language skills, and reasoning need to be considered when developing a student's instructional program.

When developing comprehensive programming it is necessary to consider all facets of math instruction including: numeration, place value, facts, computation, time, money, fractions, and verbal problem solving. Success in teaching math is directly related to the student's ability to apply the concepts to math problems that occur in daily living.

Traditional math curricula have provided problems for students with learning and behavior problems. Often the reading level is difficult, the material is not sequenced, and there are not enough problems covering each concept so mastery can be assured before the next concept is introduced. These students need math problems to be directly linked to their real-world application.

Teaching math to students with learning and behavior problems is a challenge—potentially, a very rewarding challenge. Students with learning difficulties have evidenced greater gains through appropriate instruction in math than in most other content areas. Although students have access to computers and calculators which can assist them in solving math problems they understand, they must know what problems they want to solve, the operation needed, and the procedures for computing the answers before they can fully use these instruments to assist in solving problems. Because of the increased need to use mathematics at the workplace, students need to understand mathematics now more than ever before.

THINK AND APPLY

— What factors and learning difficulties might interfere with mathematics learning for students with learning and behavior problems?

— What are five important teaching perspectives that should be considered when designing a math intervention program for students with learning and behavior disorders?

— What are the mathematical skills that need to be taught so that students will have an adequate knowledge of numeration and place value?

— What are the strategies that can be taught to students who are having difficulty with basic math facts?

— How would you convince a fellow teacher that the use of calculators can be helpful when learning mathematics?

— What factors affect successful problem solving and what problem-solving strategy might be effective to assist students in becoming better math problem solvers?

— Why is it so important that learning disability teachers make use of concrete materials and stress the real-life application of math problems?

— Why are traditional math curricula and materials often inadequate for meeting the needs of students with learning disabilities?

Chapter 9

Socialization and Classroom Management

OUTLINE

KEY TOPICS FOR MASTERY

— *Social characteristics of students who have learning and behavior problems*
— *Externalizing behaviors and internalizing behaviors: two dimensions of the social interaction style of students with behavior disorders*
— *How the inactive learning style of students with learning disabilities translates to an inactive style of communication*
— *Low self-concept: an unfortunate trait of many students with learning and behavior problems*
— *Internal locus of control, external locus of control, and learned helplessness: how these concepts relate to student behavior*
— *Appropriate responses to adolescent suicide threats and attempts*
— *Nonverbal learning disability: why a student with this type of learning disability is particularly at-risk for suicide*
— *Symptoms of substance abuse in students*
— *Intervention programs that assist students with learning disabilities and behavior disorders in developing more positive and rewarding social skills*

 BRIGHT IDEA

Turn to page 413 and read Think and Apply.

As Donna Douglas listened to her son, Jeff, playing with a classmate in his room, she closed her eyes and flinched as she heard him say, "That's not how you do it. I know how to do it, give it to me." She hoped the classmate would understand Jeff and not find her son's difficulty interacting with others so disagreeable that he would not return. Donna knew her son was not mean or cruel, but he had a difficult time communicating interpersonally with others. He had trouble making and maintaining friends. He didn't seem to know how to listen and respond to others, and often he expressed himself harshly and inconsiderately.

Mark's special education teacher's first comment to the school counselor was, "I feel let down. Mark and I had an agreement that I would give him free time at the end of the day if he brought a signed note from his regular classroom teachers that indicated his behavior was appropriate in class. After

three days of signed notes and free time, I checked with his regular classroom teachers only to find out that Mark had his friends forge the teachers' initials. The teachers had not seen the note. Though this experience is discouraging, I comfort myself with the thought that two years ago Mark was incapable of spending even thirty minutes in a regular classroom without creating havoc. He has improved and he even has a friend in the regular classroom. It is comforting to know that despite periodic setbacks his social skills have gradually improved."

Jeff and Mark both have social skills deficits. Many students with learning and behavior problems have difficulties in school, at home, and work because of their interaction with others. This chapter will help you understand the social characteristics of students who have learning and behavior problems. How these students are perceived by others and how they respond to others will be discussed. In addition, interventions you might use to improve the social behaviors of your students will be presented, along with programs and activities that may assist in teaching interpersonal social skills. The first issue to be discussed is social competence.

SOCIAL COMPETENCE AND SOCIAL DIFFICULTIES

Social difficulties often characterize students with behavior problems, but what about students with learning disabilities? Since many students with learning disabilities demonstrate difficulties with social skills, a definition of learning disabilities has been proposed that includes social skills deficits. The Interagency Committee on Learning Disabilities offers the following changes to the definition by the National Joint Committee for Learning Disabilities (NJCLD). Changes made to the NJCLD definition are italicized.

> Learning disabilities is a generic term that refers to a heterogeneous group of disorders manifested by significant difficulties in the acquisition and use of listening, speaking, reading, writing, reasoning, or mathematical abilities, *or of social skills.* These disorders are intrinsic to the individual and presumed to be due to central nervous *system* dysfunction. Even though a learning disability may occur concomitantly with other handicapping conditions (e.g., sensory impairment, mental retardation, social and emotional disturbance), *with socio*environmental influences (e.g., cultural differences, insufficient or inappropriate instruction, psychogenic factors), *and especially with attention deficit disorder, all of which may cause a learning problem, a learning disability* is not the direct result of those conditions or influences. (Kavanagh and Truss, 1988, 550–551)

This definition of learning disabilities has not been adopted by the U.S. Department of Education and is presently not used by school districts to identify youngsters. It does indicate, however, that many professionals feel that the social disabilities of youngsters with learning disabilities should be considered as a manifestation of their disabling condition.

Understanding the social difficulties of students with learning and behavior problems begins with an understanding of social competence and the characteristics associated with it. This section discusses the social characteristics of students with learning disabilities along with a description of the social problems associated with adolescents.

Definitions of Social Competence

We have all met people who seem to know what to say and what to do no matter who they are with or what situation they are in. Sometimes we watch with envy as they move from person to person, group to group, sometimes listening, sometimes talking, but always seemingly at ease. We often refer to these people as *socially competent.*

According to Foster and Ritchey (1979), *social competence* is defined as "...those responses, which within a given situation, prove effective, or in other words, maximize the probability of producing, maintaining, or enhancing positive effects for the interactor" (p. 626), and, it should be added, without harm to the other. Social skills are not a specific skill to be acquired, but rather a set of skills that allow one to adapt and respond to the expectations of society. Social competence is a process that begins at birth and continues throughout the life span. The process of social competence begins within the confines of our immediate family and expands to include extended family, friends, neighbors, and social institutions.

Vaughn and Hogan (1990) have described a model of social competence that is analogous to intelligence in that it describes social competence as a higher-order, global construct that is made up of many components. Their model of social competence includes the following four components:

1. *Positive relations with others.* This includes the ability to make and maintain positive relations with a range of people including classmates, teachers, parents, and at later ages, intimate relations.

With students the focus is usually on peer, parent, and teacher relations.

2. *Accurate/age-appropriate social cognition.* This component includes how the child thinks about self and others, as well as the extent to which the child understands and interprets social situations. This component includes self-perceptions, social problem solving, attributions, locus of control, empathy and social judgment.

3. *Absence of maladaptive behaviors.* This component focuses on the absence of behavior problems that interfere with social functioning such as disruptive behaviors, anxiety, attention problems, and lack of self-control.

4. *Effective social behaviors.* This includes the range of social behaviors that are often included in social skills intervention programs. These social behaviors include initiating contact with others, responding cooperatively to requests, and giving and receiving feedback.

The most discriminating characteristic of students with behavior problems is their lack of social competence. These students are referred for special education because of severe difficulty in adapting to society and interacting successfully with others. Whereas the common characteristic of students with learning disabilities is problems in learning, many students with learning disabilities are perceived by their peers and others as having social difficulties. Thus most students with behavior problems and many students with learning disabilities have difficulties with social skills.

Figure 9.1 provides suggestions for teachers in dealing effectively with minority students with behavior problems.

Perceptions of Students with Social Difficulties

The social interaction of students with behavior disorders is often described as having two dimensions: externalizing and internalizing (Achenback, 1991; Achenback and Edelbrock, 1978). Externalizing behaviors are those behaviors that are extremely dis-

turbing or intolerable to *others* (e.g., aggression, hyperactivity, delinquency). Conversely, internalizing behaviors are behaviors that are more likely to adversely affect the student displaying them rather than other people (e.g., depression, immaturity, obsessive-compulsive behavior, shyness).

Students with behavior disorders who exhibit externalizing behaviors appear to be experts at identifying and performing behaviors that are most disturbing to others. Donald, in the following example, is a student who exhibits externalizing behaviors.

When Mr. Kline discovered Donald was to be placed in his fourth-grade class next year, his stomach did a flip flop. "Any student but Donald," thought Mr. Kline, "he's the terror of the school." Every teacher who had Donald in class had come to the teachers' lounge at the end of the day exhausted and discouraged. The real catastrophe was the effect he seemed to have on the rest of the class. Students who were only mild behavior problems seemed to blossom with Donald's encouragement. Donald's hot temper and foul language left him continually fighting with other students. This year he had socked his teacher in the chest when she tried to prevent him from running out of the classroom. While escaping, he shouted, "I'll sue you if you touch me." As he was thinking of next year's plight, Mr. Kline saw Donald running full speed down the hall, knocking over students along the way, screeching as though he were putting on brakes as he turned into his classroom. Mr. Kline knew it was going to be a difficult year.

Students like Donald are frequently avoided by more socially competent students in class and are disliked and feared by other members. They are either loners, who move from one group to the next after alienating its members, or they develop friendships with other students whose behavior is also disturbing to others. These students are extremely difficult classroom management problems.

Students with behavior disorders who exhibit internalizing behaviors are often less disturbing to others but frequently concern others because of their bizarre behavior. Elisa, in the following example, is a student who exhibits internalizing behaviors.

Elisa, a fifth grader, was brought to the school office by her mother. Elisa's parents had just moved

■ **FIGURE 9.1**   *Minority Students and Behavior Problems*

The behavior of minority students is often misunderstood by teachers and responded to inappropriately (Irvine, 1991; Morgan, 1980). Discipline problems and ultimately discouragement on the part of the minority student can result from frequent misunderstanding between teachers and students. Grossman (1995) has identified several considerations for teachers in dealing effectively with the behavior of minority students.

- The home and community often accept and encourage behaviors that may be incompatible with the behaviors in the school setting. Thus, students may receive conflicting messages between home and school about their behavior and may be forced to chose between loyalty to home and community or school. When teachers learn as much as they can about the behaviors that the home and community accept, the teacher may distinguish for the student what behaviors are acceptable in what settings. For example, aggressive and highly emotionally charged behavior may be expected of African American males at home and in their community, but unacceptable in the class setting. Many Hispanic students are viewed by teachers as dependent, passive, and reticent to participate and respond to the teacher. Yet, these behaviors are expected and nurtured in their home and community.
- The same behaviors that reflect problems with some students may not with students from other cultural groups. For example, African American students with internalizing problems may go unnoticed because it is expressed differently. Hispanic students may need help from the teacher, but may not ask for it, therefore, it may be necessary to check frequently with these students to determine if they need assistance, knowing they are unlikely to request assistance when needed. Fitting into the group for some African Americans may mean displaying aggressive and acting-out behavior.
- Some behaviors exhibited by students from different cultural groups may be wrongly attributed and interpreted by teachers. For example, some students who are English language learners may fail to respond, make limited eye contact with the teacher, or appear defiant because of their lack of confidence in using English. Also, some students from other cultures (e.g., Asian groups) are accustomed to clearly defined rules and regulations and may have difficulty interpreting rules that are more implicit.

to the area and her mother brought Elisa to register for school but refused to speak with the school secretary. She demanded to register Elisa with the school principal. In meeting with the school principal, Elisa's mother told him Elisa would sometimes act "funny." She told the principal Elisa only acted that way to get attention and she should be told to "stop" as soon as she tried it. The principal noted that Elisa had not said one word. In fact, she had sat in a chair next to her mother looking down and rocking gently. Elisa's mother said she had been receiving special education services during part of the day and was in a regular classroom most of the day. In the regular classroom, Elisa was a loner. She spoke to no one. When another student approached her, she reared back and scratched into the air with her long nails, imitating a cat. If other children said something to her, she would "hiss" at them. She would sit in the room, usually completing her assignments and, whenever possible, practicing scrolling cursive letters with her multicolored pen. She spent most of the day rocking. She even rocked while she worked.

Problems like Elisa's are usually thought of as being internal and related to their own pathology. Other classmates, recognizing that these children are very different, may make attempts to be compatible, but they are usually rebuked. Students with internalizing behaviors are easy victims for students whose behaviors are more externalizing.

It is important to note that not all youngsters with behavior problems demonstrate either externalizing or internalizing problems. Many youngsters with behavior disorders display *both* externalizing and internalizing problems. Is this difficult to understand? Well, imagine a child who is oftentimes shy and withdrawn who, when frustrated or forced to interact with others, acts out and is aggressive.

Externalizing and internalizing behaviors are more frequently characteristics of students with behavior problems rather than students with learning disabilities. Students with learning disabilities typically display less severe emotional and behavior difficulties. However, many students with learning disabilities have difficulties making and maintaining positive interpersonal relationships with others.

When compared with their nonlearning-disabled peers, students with learning disabilities are:

1. Identified as being more poorly accepted by their peers (Bryan, 1974; Bryan 1976; Vaughn, Elbaum, and Schumm, 1996; Vaughn, McIntosh, and Spencer-Rowe, 1991; Wiener, Harris, and Shirer, 1990)
2. At greater risk for social alienation from teachers and classmates (Seidel and Vaughn, 1991)
3. Less frequently selected to play (Hutton and Palo, 1976)
4. Perceived as having lower social status (Stone and LaGreca, 1990)
5. Less accepted by peers even prior to being identified as learning-disabled (Vaughn, Hogan, Kouzekanani, and Shapiro, 1990)
6. More willing to conform to peer pressure to engage in antisocial activities (Bryan, Pearl, and Fallon, 1989)
7. Less likely than other students to interact with teachers and classmates (McIntosh, Vaughn, Schumm, Haager, and Lee, 1993)

Unfortunately, the lowered social status of students with learning disabilities reflects not only the perceptions of peers but of teachers as well. Teachers perceive students with learning disabilities as less desirable to have in the classroom (Garrett and Crump, 1980; Keogh, Tchir, and Windeguth-Behn, 1974; Vaughn, Schumm, Jallad, Slusher, and Saumell, 1996). One possible interpretation of the lowered social status of students with learning disabilities is that it is a reflection of how the teacher feels about them. The teacher's negative perception of a student with learning disabilities is conveyed to other students in the classroom, thus lowering the child's social status and how the child is perceived and responded to by peers. Some research suggests this may not completely explain the lowered social status of students with learning disabilities, since strangers, after viewing a few minutes of students' social interaction on videotapes, perceive students with learning disabilities more negatively than their nonlearning-disabled peers (Bryan, Bryan, and Sonnefeld, 1982; Bryan and Perlmutter, 1979; Bryan and Sherman, 1980). Additionally, students who are later identified as learning-disabled, as early as two months into their kindergarten year are already more often rejected and less frequently chosen as best friends than other students in the kindergarten class (Vaughn, Hogan, Kouzekanani, and Shapiro, 1990). Whereas teachers view students with learning disabilities more negatively than their nonlearning-disabled peers, they are more favorably disposed toward having students with learning disabilities in their classroom than they are students identified as emotionally disabled or mentally retarded (Abroms and Kodera, 1979; Moore and Fine, 1978). Teachers regard students with emotional disabilities as the most disruptive and the most difficult students to work effectively within the regular classroom.

In general education classrooms where youngsters with learning disabilities are accepted by their teachers, they are also accepted by their peers (Vaughn, McIntosh, Schumm, Haager, and Callwood, 1993). In these classrooms students with learning disabilities were as well accepted and had as many mutual friends as other students.

When discussing the social skills of students with learning disabilities and how they are perceived by others, it is important to realize we are talking about students with learning disabilities as a group.

Not all students with learning disabilities have social difficulties. Whereas students with behavior disorders are characterized by deficits in social skills, many students with learning disabilities are socially competent, making and maintaining friends and struggling to please their teachers and parents. Many adults with learning disabilities who are participating in postsecondary education programs identify their social skills as their strengths.

An additional point to consider is that the findings on the social and behavioral functioning of youngsters with learning disabilities mostly reflect how they compare with their nondisabled peers. Recent studies that compare students with learning disabilities to their low-achieving classmates find few differences in their social or behavioral functioning (Vaughn, Haager, Hogan, and Kouzekanani, 1992; Vaughn, Zaragoza, Hogan, and Walker, 1993).

Characteristics of Students with Social Disabilities

We expect students with behavior disorders to have difficulty in successfully interacting with others. Students with behavior disorders are identified and placed in special programs because their social problems are so interfering that they are unable to function adequately with only the services provided by the regular classroom. Why is it that many students with learning disabilities have difficulty developing and maintaining relationships with others? Research is just at the beginning stages of identifying how students with learning disabilities interact differently from their nonlearning-disabled peers. Figure 9.2 provides suggestions for creating a learning community that celebrates student differences.

Social Interaction
The type and quality of interactions that students with disabilities engage in are different from those of their nonlearning-disabled peers. Students with learning disabilities are more likely to approach the teacher and ask questions (Dorval, McKinney, and Feagans, 1982; McKinney, McClure, and Feagans, 1982). Teachers interact almost four times as often

with students with learning disabilities as with their peers; however, 63 percent of teachers' initiations towards students with learning disabilities involve managing their behavior (Dorval, McKinney, and Feagans, 1982). The interactions students with learning disabilities have with their teachers are often not appropriate to the situation. They impulsively attempt to display their knowledge, request more time to complete assignments, and request time to speak individually with the teacher to ask questions. Teachers report that questions from students with learning disabilities are inappropriate, as they often ask questions when the answer to the question was just stated. Although classroom teachers spend more time with students with learning disabilities, the nature of the involvement during that time is not viewed positively by the teachers (Siperstein and Goding, 1985). One teacher describes it this way: "When Carlos raises his hand, I dread it. He usually asks me what he is supposed to do. I find myself trying to reexplain a thirty-minute lesson in five minutes. I'm sure he can tell I'm frustrated."

In one of the few studies conducted to examine general education teachers' behavior toward middle and high school students with learning disabilities (McIntosh, Vaughn, Schumm, Haager, and Lee, 1993), the findings indicated that middle- and high-school teachers do not treat students with learning disabilities differently from other students in the classroom. There is, of course, a positive and negative side to this finding. From a positive perspective teachers treated all students fairly and impartially, and although praise was infrequently given, it was given at the same rate both to students with learning disabilities and students without learning disabilities. From a negative perspective, youngsters with learning disabilities interacted infrequently with the teacher, other students, and classroom activities, and teachers made few, if any adaptations, to increase the involvement or assure the learning of students with learning disabilities. This study confirms the passive role many youngsters with learning disabilities play in the classroom and speaks to the importance of providing support for general education teachers to encourage and involve students with learning disabilities in the classroom.

■ **FIGURE 9.2**   *Create a Learning Community That Celebrates Diversity*

- Students are children or adolescents first. Look beyond the ways students differ and respect their common needs and goals to be accepted, recognized, and valued members of the community. The classroom community is a primary source of students' perceptions of acceptance. Teachers' attitudes need to celebrate the diversity of students and at the same time recognize that students are more alike than different.
- Focus on abilities. Establish an environment where teachers and students seek and use knowledge about the abilities and expertise of all class members. Myrna Rathkin, a sixth-grade teacher, framed a picture of each student in a decorated star and hung them from the classroom ceiling. Attached to each star were lists of self- and teacher-identified strengths or abilities. All students were encouraged to recognize the knowledge and skills of their fellow students and to discover new ways their fellow students were special. When they did so, they would add them to the list of attributes under the individual's star.
- Celebrate diversity. Teachers can view students' differences as something to be tolerated, mildly accepted, or celebrated. Celebrating diversity means conveying to students the values added by having students as part of their learning community who have different learning styles, behavior profiles, physical abilities, languages, and cultural backgrounds. Sharon Andreaci, a sixth-grade teacher, was thrilled that many students she taught spoke Spanish and represented the cultural backgrounds of several Hispanic groups (e.g., Cuban, Nicaraguan, Columbian, Mexican). She often asked children about their backgrounds and encouraged them to share their knowledge and practices with others. She looked for ways to learn from others by asking such questions as, "Juan, how would you say that in Spanish? Anna, do you agree with Juan? Is there another way to say it in Spanish?"
- Demonstrate high regard for all students. Demonstrating high regard for all students means treating each one of them as special and extraordinary in their own way. It means not having "favorites" even if you think you disguise it. Listen carefully to each student and find something meaningful in what each student says.

Source: Adapted from: S. Vaughn, C. S. Bos and J. S. Schumm (1997). *Teaching Mainstreamed, Diverse, and At-Risk Students in the General Education Classroom.* Boston: Allyn and Bacon.

Communication Difficulties

Being able to express our ideas and feelings and to understand the ideas and feelings of others is an integral part of socialization. Adults and children with good social skills are able to communicate effectively with others, whereas students with learning and behavior problems frequently have trouble in this area. Torgeson (1982) describes the learning style of students with learning disabilities as inactive. An inactive learner is one who is passively involved in the learning process, does not attempt to integrate new information with previously learned information, and does not self-question or rehearse. It appears students with learning disabilities also demonstrate an inac-tive style during the communication process. While communicating with others, students with learning disabilities are less likely to make adaptations in their communication to accommodate the listener. When most of us speak with a young child, we make modifications in how we speak to them, such as using simpler words and asking questions to be sure they understand us. Many students with learning disabilities fail to make these modifications (Bryan and Pflaum, 1978; Soenksen, Flagg, and Schmits, 1981). When discussing the reading difficulties of students with learning disabilities, we talked about their difficulty in responding to ambiguous information in print. In much the same way, students with learning disabilities do not request more information when given ambiguous information through oral communication (Donahue, Pearl, and Bryan, 1980). The student with learning disabilities is often a difficult communication partner who makes few adaptations to his or her audience, does not question inappropriate verbal statements, and does not "code switch," that is, pick up on what was said by the other. For example, boys with learning disabilities and normal-achieving boys were involved in a task in which they were asked to give essential information about a game of checkers (Knight-Arest, 1984). The adult they were supposed to give the information to claimed not to know how to play the game. As found in other studies, the communication skills of students with learning disabilities were less effective than those of normal-achieving students. Students with learning disabilities:

1. Talked more
2. Provided less information
3. Were more likely to use gestures and demonstrations
4. Were less able to respond to the needs of the listener

If the listener appeared confused, they were more likely to repeat the message without reformulating it. It is interesting to note that familiarity with one's partner positively affects the performance on communication tasks of students with learning disabilities, but has no impact for children without learning disabilities (Mathinos, 1987). Perhaps knowledge of one's partners serves as a motivator for students with learning disabilities to use the communication skills they have.

The communication style of students with learning disabilities appears to be egocentric. That is, they do not appear to be interested in the responses of their partner and they demonstrate less shared responsibility for maintaining a social conversation (LaGreca, 1982; Mathinos, 1987). In a study of the friendship-making and conversation skills of boys with and without learning disabilities, LaGreca (1982) reports that the boys with and without learning disabilities did not differ in how to handle social situations (positive and negative), nor did they differ in their knowledge of how to make friends. Naive observers identified the boys with learning disabilities as less adept in social situations, as more egocentric and lacking in reciprocity in their conversations. The impression is that many students with learning disabilities display communication styles that suggest they are just waiting for the speaker to stop rather than being interested in what the speaker is saying.

Individuals with learning disabilities are less able to display interpersonal decentering (Horowitz, 1981) and less able to take on an alternative viewpoint (Wong and Wong, 1980). We know from the communication skills of populations with learning disabilities that they are less likely to make adjustments in their communication with others. It could be that their difficulty taking on the role of the "other" influences both their social relationships with others and their ability to communicate successfully with others.

Since students with learning disabilities are frequently rejected by peers, it could be that this communication pattern is sufficiently frustrating to others that they find the student with learning disabilities an undesirable social partner.

Stone and LaGreca (1984) compared students with and without learning disabilities on their ability to comprehend nonverbal communication. Their findings indicated that when attention is controlled for with students with learning disabilities by reinforcing their attendance to the social cues given, they perform as well as their nonlearning-disabled peers. These authors suggest that the attention problems of students with learning disabilities often appear as poor social skills.

Aggression

Many children with severe behavior disorders are characterized by aggressive behavior. *Aggressive behaviors* include assaultiveness, fighting, temper tantrums, quarrelsomeness, ignoring the rights of others, negative tone of voice, threatening, and demands for immediate compliance. Apply the Concept 9.1 describes five types of aggressive behavior. Aggression does not go away without treatment and is related to such negative outcomes as alcoholism,

APPLY THE CONCEPT 9.1

AGGRESSION AND PEER ACCEPTANCE

In a study conducted by Lancelotta and Vaughn (1989) five types of aggressive behavior and their relation to peer social acceptance were examined. The five types of aggression were:

Provoked Physical Aggression—A youngster who attacks or fights back following provocation from another. An example is a student who hits someone back after being hit by that person.

Outburst Aggression—A youngster who responds in an uncontrollable, outburst manner without apparent provocation. Outburst aggression may or may not be directed at another person. An example is a student who gets angry and throws a fit.

Unprovoked Physical Aggression—A youngster who attacks or acts aggressively toward another person without provocation. An example is a student who starts a fight for no reason.

Verbal Aggression—A youngster who says verbally aggressive things to another person in order to attack or intimidate them. An example is a student who threatens to beat up another.

Indirect Aggression—A person who attacks or attempts to hurt another indirectly so that it is not likely to be obvious who did it. An example is a student who tells the teacher that another student does bad things.

The study demonstrated that girls are less tolerant of all types of aggression than are boys. Also, there was a negative relationship between peer acceptance and subtypes of aggression, with the exception of provoked aggression for boys. This means that boys who fight back when they are attacked first by other boys are not any more likely to be poorly accepted. This, however, is not true for girls who fight back when they are attacked. All of the other subtypes of aggression are related to poor peer acceptance.

---

unpopularity, aggressive responses from others, academic failure, and adult antisocial behaviors. Specific skills for teaching students to deal more effectively with their aggressive responses is an important component of social skills programs for students with behavior disorders.

Appearance

Appearance may be a more important factor influencing the social status of students with learning difficulties than was previously thought. In a study evaluating the social status, academic ability, athletic ability, and appearance of students with learning disabilities (Siperstein, Bopp, and Bak, 1978), researchers found that whereas academic and athletic ability were significantly related to peer popularity, the correlation between physical appearance and peer popularity was twice as great as the other two.

Two children from a study (Vaughn, Lancelotta, and Minnis, 1988) illustrate this point. Chris was a fourth-grade student with learning disabilities who worked as a model for children's clothing in a large department store. Her position gave her access to the latest children's fashions and she was well recognized by both girls and boys in her class as attractive. She ranked first when sociometric data asking peers to rate the extent to which they liked others in the classroom were analyzed. Her best friend, Carmen, who was also identified as learning-disabled, ranked second from the bottom by her classmates on the same sociometric test. In looking at the tests of social skills administered to these students, there was little difference between the scores of Chris and Carmen.

In another study, 35 percent of junior high students with learning disabilities exhibit some problem in grooming, neatness of clothing, posture, and general attractiveness, as compared with 6 percent of the junior high students without learning disabilities. (Schumaker, Wildgen, and Sherman, 1982). Bickett and Milich (1987) found boys with learning disabilities were rated as less attractive than boys without learning disabilities. Since appearance is highly related to popularity, it could be helpful to give feedback and pointers to students who display problems with appearance. Many students with behavior disorders display atypical appearance as a means of demonstrating identification with a group or gang. These students may wear their hair or clothing in nonconforming ways in order to let others know their allegiance. This style may be highly accepted by a particular group and highly rejected by others. These nonconforming appearances often become stylish, as did styles of the punk-rock movement in the late seventies and early eighties.

Attention Problems/Hyperactivity

Attention deficits and hyperactivity are characteristics often observed in students with learning and behavior disorders. In fact, according to one study, 25 to 68 percent of students with Attention Deficit Disorder are also identified as learning disabled (McKinney, Montague, and Hocutt, 1993). Students with attention deficits frequently display a pattern of inattention, while students with hyperactivity often exhibit patterns of impulsivity; these patterns are evident in a variety of contexts including home and school.

In the classroom, inattention is manifested in a failure to pay attention to details, careless mistakes, messy work, and difficulty in persisting with a task until completion (American Psychiatric Association, 1994). Hyperactivity may be exhibited through fidgetiness, inability to engage in quiet activities, blurting out answers, and excessive talking (American Psychiatric Association, 1994).

Students with attention deficits and/or hyperactivity may be treated with medication. Several stimulant medications (e.g., Dexedrine, Ritalin) are available to help students to focus by adjusting those parts of the brain that regulate attention, impulse control, and mood (Hallowell and Ratey, 1995). As with any medication, unwanted side effects may occur. Some of the side effects of stimulant medica-

tions include facial tics, loss of appetite, and difficulty sleeping (Swanson et al., 1993). Some children respond with unpleasant physical symptoms, and are affected by the drugs in some settings but not others. Most children receiving medication for hyperactivity are under the care of a physician whom they see infrequently. Thus the monitoring of the effectiveness of the drug is often the responsibility of parents and teachers. Perhaps the most effective technique for monitoring the effects of the drug is through behavior management. The teacher identifies and defines specific behaviors that are indicative of hyperactivity and then charts the occurrence of these behaviors. Whereas medication may be necessary for some children, attempts to treat the student's learning disability through changing his or her hyperactivity have not been very successful (Routh, 1979).

A learning characteristic frequently associated with hyperactivity is *selective attention,* which is the ability to attend to relevant information and ignore irrelevant information (Hallahan, Tarver, Kauffman, and Graybeal, 1978; Pinel, 1993). This characteristic occurs in children with learning disabilities about two years later than in normal children (Tarver, Hallahan, Kauffman, and Ball, 1976; Tarver, Hallahan, Cohen, and Kauffman, 1977). The delayed development of selective attention with populations with learning disabilities may be related to the conceptual tempo of students with learning disabilities, which is more impulsive than reflective. A more reflective conceptual tempo is associated with success in academic subjects such as reading and math, whereas a more impulsive tempo is associated with learning difficulties. One characteristic of impulsive responders is that they do not stop and think before responding.

Recent interest has focused on the overlap between learning disabilities and attention deficit disorder. Students with learning disabilities displayed significantly more attention problems, but not conduct problems or anxiety, than average achievers (LaGreca and Stone, 1990). In a study conducted by Lambert and Sandoval (1980), 40 percent of the elementary children with attention problems also met stringent criteria for the presence of a learning disability. Since students with attention problems are at high risk for also demonstrating difficulties with their peers, it is important to evaluate the presence (or absence) of attention problems with children with learning disabilities prior to initiating social interventions.

Self-Concept

What we think of ourselves and how we view ourselves is highly related to our comparison group. Thus, it is not surprising that students with learning and behavior difficulties often have poor self-concepts. When, however, students perceive their disability in more positive terms, they also tend to report more positive global self-concepts (e.g., Rothman and Cosden, 1995). These students are aware of how their learning performance compares with others. There is some evidence that students with learning difficulties make higher gains in self-esteem and perception of their abilities when they are placed in special education classes (Battle and Blowers, 1982; Beltempo and Achille, 1990; Vaughn, Elbaum, and Schumm, 1996), whereas other research suggests the special education placement has not significantly affected either self-concept or peer acceptance (Whinnery, 1995). Students with learning disabilities who also experience reading difficulties view themselves more negatively than do students with learning disabilities and normal reading scores (Black, 1974) and older students with learning disabilities view themselves more negatively than do younger students with learning disabilities. In an attempt to interpret the sometimes conflicting results of studies, Morrison (1985) demonstrated that two factors significantly influence self-perception with students with learning disabilities: type of classroom placement (e.g., self-contained, regular classroom) and what aspect of self-perception is being evaluated (e.g., academic, social, behavioral, or anxiety-laden). When achievement is controlled, for example, there are no differences in self-perception measures between students with learning disabilities in resource rooms and self-contained settings (Yauman, 1980).

The self-concept of youngsters with learning disabilities was evaluated prior to and following identification as learning disabled. When compared with classmates without learning disabilities, the self-concept of students with learning disabilities was not significantly lower either before or after identification (Vaughn, Haager, Hogan, and Kouzekanani, 1992). This suggests that placement in a special education resource room had no negative effects on their self-concept.

The self-perceptions of students with learning disabilities have been surprisingly accurate. In general they rate themselves as low on academic ability (Chapman and Boersman, 1980) and like other children on overall feelings of self-worth (Bear, Clever, and Proctor, 1991; Bryan, 1986). They identify reading and spelling as the academic areas in which they are lower than other children and yet perceive themselves as being relatively intelligent (Renik, 1987). A longitudinal study of students with learning disabilities suggests that they may differ from low-achieving students in that they do not become more negative about themselves as they grow older (Kistner and Osborne, 1987).

Teachers and parents need to be aware of the effects of learning and behavior difficulties on self-concept and provide opportunities for students to demonstrate and recognize their abilities. Teachers and parents can provide opportunities for students to demonstrate what they do well and provide encouragement in the areas of difficulty. One parent described it this way: "The best thing that happened to my son is swimming. We knew from the time Kevin was an infant that he was different from our other two children. We were not surprised when he had difficulties in school and was later identified as learning-disabled. His visual motor problems made it difficult for him to play ball sports so we encouraged his interest in swimming. He joined a swim team when he was six and all his friends know he has won many swimming awards. No matter how discouraged he feels about school, he has one area in which he is successful."

Teachers may want to discuss with students the nature of their learning and behavior difficulty and how it affects their performance in specific situations. Assisting students in identifying and predicting how they might respond in situations allows them to prepare for the situation and develop strategies for more successfully dealing with it.

Locus of Control and
Learned Helplessness

Persons with an *internal locus of control* view events as controlled largely by their own efforts, whereas persons with an *external locus of control* interpret the outcome of events as due largely to luck, chance, fate, or other events outside of their own influence. Locus of control proceeds along a continuum, with learning- and behavior-disordered children frequently having a high external locus of control, unable to view the cause of events as related to their own behavior. For this reason, they are not motivated to change events that are undesirable to them because they feel there is little they can do to improve the situation.

Mrs. Mulkowsky, a junior high learning disabilities teacher, said, "My students act as though there is nothing they can do to improve their grades in their regular classes. They feel they are unable to succeed in most of these classes and they give up. They come to my class, sit down, and expect me to tutor them in their regular classes. They act as though it is *my* responsibility. These students are actually the ones who are still working; others have given up entirely and expect little from themselves and little from me."

When students with learning disabilities were compared with two other groups of students without learning disabilities, students with learning disabilities were more likely to interpret positive results as luck than were either of the other two groups (Sobol, Earn, Bennett, and Humphries, 1983). This suggests that when students with learning disabilities perform well, they are less likely to attribute it to their own effort and therefore may be less likely to maintain the effort that produced the positive outcome. In contrast, students with learning disabilities do attribute their failures to being within their own control and not to external factors outside of their control (Dudley-Marling, Snider, and Tarver, 1982). When students with learning disabilities are compared with behavior-disordered students and students who are both learning-disabled and behavior-disordered on three dimensions of locus of control: intellectual, social, and physical (Morgan, 1986), students with learning disabilities had higher internal locus of control on all three dimensions than did the other two groups. The students with learning disabilities and behavior disorders had the most external scores on all three dimensions of locus of control.

It could be that students with learning disabilities have difficulties in social situations because they fail to realize that successful interaction with others can be influenced by their behavior. To assist students in developing an internal locus of control, teachers need to show students the relationships between what they do and its effect on others and reciprocally on themselves. Giving students ownership of their tasks and behavior and teaching them to set their own goals are first steps toward increasing their internal locus of control (Cohen, 1986). Also, teachers may want to interview children to learn more about their locus of orientation (Lewis and Lawrence-Patterson, 1989). Borkowski and colleagues (Borkowski, Weyhing, and Carr, 1988; Borkowski, Weyhing, and Turner, 1986) have used attributional training paired with specific strategy training (for example, in the area of reading) to influence students' use and generalization of strategies. Attributional training helps the student see the role of effort in academic success or strategy use. Reasons for not doing well that do not relate to controllable factors are discouraged. Students are encouraged to see the relationship between strategy use and success, "I tried hard, used the strategy, and did well" (Borkowski, Weyhing, and Carr, 1988, p. 49).

The concept of *learned helplessness* was introduced by Seligman (1975) to explain the response animals and humans have when exposed to a number of trials in which they are unable to influence the outcome. When subjects learn there is no relationship between what they do and their ability to impact the environment or reach their goal, they give up and respond passively. Although learned helplessness, or the perceived inability to influence a situation, may be situation-specific, it often generalizes to other learning situations. For example, when a student with learning disabilities and severe reading problems approaches a reading task, the student is frequently unable to reach his or her goal—being able to read the passage successfully. Whereas the student may initially be very persistent in attempting to read, the student who meets with continued failure learns his or her attempts are useless and there is nothing he or she can do to impact the situation, thus the individual responds as though he or she is "helpless."

Many students with learning problems act is if they have learned helplessness (Thomas, 1979). Learned helplessness leads to lowered self-concept, lethargy, reduction in persistence, and reduced levels of performance. There is a remarkable resemblance between the descriptions of learned helplessness and the observations of special education teachers about students with learning disabilities and behavior disorders. "Learning-disabled children have been portrayed as no longer able to believe that they can learn" (Thomas, 1979, p. 209).

The concepts *learned helplessness* and *locus of control* are highly related. Students who have a feeling of learned helplessness toward a particular academic task perceive there is nothing they can do to impact their ability to perform the task successfully. It is also likely they view results from their "work" on that task as "external" and not related to what they do. Thus there is a high correlation between learned helplessness and external locus of control. Apply the Concept 9.2 describes what teachers might be able to do to affect learned helplessness and locus of control.

Social Difficulties Prevalent During Adolescence

In addition to the characteristics of students with learning and behavior disorders discussed above, several difficulties are prevalent during adolescence that may affect students with special needs. These are social alienation, suicide, anorexia nervosa, and drug and alcohol abuse.

Social Alienation

Social alienation is the extent to which youngsters feel they are part of or have an affinity for the school or the people in the school. Social alienation has been interpreted to refer to alienation from teachers or peers (Seidel and Vaughn, 1991). The notion of alienation has been linked with school dropouts in that youngsters who are socially alienated from their teachers or peers are more at risk for leaving school than are those

who are not (Finn, 1989). Not surprising, social alienation begins early in the youngsters' school career but is most obvious during adolescence. According to Seidel and Vaughn (1991) students with learning disabilities who dropped out of school differed from those who did not on such items as: "I thought of my teachers as friends," "The thing I hated most about school was my teachers," and "Most of my teachers liked me." Students with learning disabilities who dropped out also felt that their classmates "would not have missed them if they moved away," and they did not look forward to seeing their friends at school. Interestingly, these students did not differ on their academic achievement scores but did differ on the extent to which they felt they were socially accepted and liked by their teachers and classmates.

What can teachers do so students feel less socially alienated?

- Try for a small class size that encourages all students to participate.
- Set the tone in the class that all students are valuable and have something important to contribute.
- Take a moment between classes to ask about students and demonstrate you care.
- Allow students to participate in decision making regarding class rules and management.
- Identify youngsters who demonstrate uninvolvement and/or detachment and refer them to the counselor.
- Encourage students to participate in school-related extracurricular activities.

Suicide

Two Leominster, Massachusetts, teenagers died in a shotgun suicide pact next to an empty bottle of champagne, after writing farewell notes that included "I love to die I'd be happier I know it! So please let me go. No hard feelings" (*The Boston Herald*, November 10, 1984, p. 1). Although the autopsy showed high levels of alcohol in the girls' bloodstreams, there were no indications that either girl was involved with drugs or was pregnant. It appeared as though both girls willingly participated in the suicide act. In another note left by one of the girls, she wrote, "I know

APPLY THE CONCEPT 9.2

HOW TEACHERS MIGHT AFFECT LEARNED HELPLESSNESS AND LOCUS OF CONTROL

In order to reduce the impact of learned helplessness and external locus of control on students' behavior, teachers may want to:

1. Reduce the amount of external reinforcement and focus on reinforcing student performance. Rather than saying, "Good work" or "Excellent job," focus on the behaviors, such as, "You really concentrated and finished this biology assignment. You needed to ask for help but you got it done. How do you feel about it?"

2. Link students' behaviors to outcomes. "You spent ten minutes working hard on this worksheet and you finished it."

3. Provide encouragement. Because they experience continued failure, many students are discouraged from attempting tasks they are capable of performing.

4. Discuss academic tasks and social activities in which the student experiences success.

5. Discuss your own failures or difficulties and express what you do to cope with these. Be sure to provide examples of when you persist and examples of when you give up.

6. Encourage students to take responsibility for their successes. "You received a 'B' on your biology test. How do you think you got such a good grade?" Encourage students to describe what they did (e.g., how they studied). Discourage students from saying, "I was lucky," or "It was an easy test."

7. Encourage students to take responsibility for their failures. For example, in response to the question, "Why do you think you are staying after school?" encourage students to take responsibility for what got them there. "Yes, I am sure Billy's behavior was hard to ignore. I am aware that you did some things to get you here. What did you do?"

8. Structure learning and social activities to reduce failure.

9. Teach students how to learn information and how to demonstrate their control of their learning task.

10. Teach students to use procedures and techniques to monitor their own gains in academic areas.

---

it was for the best. I can't handle this sucky world any longer" (*The Boston Herald,* November 10, 1984, p. 7). The cause of the suicide pact is unknown.

After being forbidden to see each other, a 14-year-old-boy and a 13-year-old-girl ran away. Shortly thereafter, the two leaped into a river and drowned (*Miami Herald,* November 9, 1995, p. 10).

Suicide of a child or adolescent is a shocking event. Childhood suicide occurs between the ages of birth and fifteen, and adolescent suicide between the ages of fifteen and nineteen. Many deaths of adolescents are viewed as accidents and not reported as suicide; therefore, the statistics on adolescent suicide are meaningless (Toolan, 1981). However, suicide is one of the top three causes of death for persons under twenty-four years of age. There is agreement, however, that the rate of adolescent suicide is on the rise (Cimbolic and Jobes, 1990; Henry, Stephenson, Hanson, and Hargett, 1993), and female attempts at suicide greatly outnumber male (Hawton, 1982); however, male attempts are more frequently successful.

The suicide attempts of adolescents can frequently be explained by one or more of the following factors:

1. Relief from stress or from stressful situations
2. A demonstration to others of how desperate they are
3. An attempt to hurt or get back at others

4. An attempt to get others to change (Wicks-Nelson and Israel, 1984)

Suicide attempts most frequently occur following interpersonal problems with boy- or girlfriends, parents, or teachers. Often these relationships have had prolonged difficulties. Disturbed peer relationships are a large contributing factor to suicide attempts. Adolescents feel unique, as if there are no solutions to their problems. In addition, adolescents often feel responsible for their problems and are unlikely to seek assistance, thus, leaving them isolated (Culp, Clyman, and Culp, 1995). "Life is a chronic problem. There appears no way out. Solutions previously tried have failed. To end the chronic problem, death appears to be the only way left" (Teicher, 1973, p. 137 in Sheras, 1983).

"Suicidal patients are often very difficult because they so frequently deny the seriousness of their attempts" (Toolan, 1981, p. 320). They often make comments such as, "It was all a mistake. I am much better now." Even though they may attempt to discount the attempt, it should be treated with extreme seriousness.

Hopelessness may be the best indicator of risk for suicide (Beck, Brown, and Steer, 1989). Other variables that are related to suicide include: depression, flat affect, an emotion-laden event, and isolation. Sheras (1983) discusses the following general considerations when dealing with adolescent suicide attempts.

1. All suicide attempts must be taken seriously. Do not interpret the behavior as merely a plea for "attention." Do not try to decide whether the attempt is real or not.
2. Develop or reestablish communication with the person. Suicide is a form of communication from a person who feels he or she has no other way to communicate.
3. Reestablish emotional or interpersonal support. Suicide is an expression of alienation and the person needs to be reconnected with significant others.
4. Involve the adolescent in individual and/or family therapy. Often the adolescent feels unable to establish communication with a significant person (e.g., a parent) and needs assistance from another to do so.
5. Work with the youngster to identify the problem or problems and provide realistic practical solutions to the problems.

Rourke and colleagues (Rourke, Young and Leenaars, 1989) identify a specific subtype of learning disabilities as being at risk for depression and suicide. This subtype is referred to as nonverbal learning disability and includes such characteristics as: bilateral tactile-perceptual deficits, bilateral psychomotor coordination problems, severe difficulties in visual-spatial-organizational abilities, difficulty with nonverbal problem solving, good rote verbal capacities, and difficulty adapting to novel and complex situations. Fletcher (1989) urges that students with nonverbal learning disabilities be identified early and treated. Since verbal skills are highly valued, particularly in school settings, it is likely that many students with nonverbal learning disabilities go unnoticed.

Eating Disorders
Eating disorders may take a variety of forms, and different definitions exist (Button, 1993). Central to each definition, however, is the presence of abnormal patterns of behavior and thought related to eating (American Psychiatric Association, 1994). Levine (1987) indicates that these patterns include:

1. A person's health and vigor reduced or threatened by his or her eating habits
2. Obligations to self and others affected by isolation and secretiveness related to eating problems
3. Emotional instability and self-absorption associated with food and weight control
4. Persistence of dysfunctional eating habits despite warnings that they are affecting the person's health and functioning

Interestingly, eating disorders are not fundamentally about eating, but are multidetermined and multidimensional reflections of the person's disturbance.

Eating disorders are much less prevalent among males, with over 90 percent of cases of bulimia or anorexia nervosa occurring in females (American Psychiatric Association, 1994).

The highest incidence is in females between the ages of fifteen to twenty-four, and it occurs most frequently in higher socioeconomic levels (Jones, Fox, Haroutun-Babigian, and Hutton, 1980). Characteristics associated with anorexia include:

1. Loss of menstrual cycle
2. Sensitivity to cold
3. Sleep disturbance
4. Depression

Characteristics associated with bulimia include:

1. Loss of dental enamel
2. Low self-esteem
3. Anxiety
4. Depression

Because our society places a premium on thinness, exercise, and dieting, the symptoms of eating disorders are often overlooked or not recognized soon enough. The target person insists on remaining thin and does not perceive that she or he has a problem.

Why someone would deliberately starve herself or himself is puzzling. In attempting to unravel the mystery of eating disorders, researchers have examined several factors that may contribute to the disease, including biological factors, such as malfunctioning of the hypothalamus; and psychodynamic factors, such as an enmeshed family which makes it difficult for the adolescent to express individual identity; thus, the adolescent's refusal to eat becomes a form of rebellion. There is little doubt that a combination of these biological and psychological factors contributes to anorexia and bulimia.

Drug and Alcohol Abuse

Parents probably fear nothing more than the possibility their child will abuse drugs. With the increase in drug availability and use in the early to mid-1960s, parents became aware of the numbers of adolescents using drugs. There is a great deal of media attention focusing on the consequences of drug use. Stories of youngsters from stereotypically "normal" families becoming addicted to drugs and committing crimes to maintain their habits are featured in magazines and newspapers across the country.

Parental concerns about the availability and use of drugs among adolescents seem to have strong support. According to a summary by Wicks-Nelson and Israel (1984) of reports from the Department of Justice (1980) and the FBI (1980), 90 percent of a sample of high-school seniors reported that marijuana was very easy or fairly easy to get. Some 59 percent said the same thing about amphetamines and 49.8 about barbiturates. Availability of drugs is not the only concern. According to the 1990 National Household Survey on Drug Abuse, 48 percent of adolescents (aged 12–17 years) had used alcohol at least once; 40 percent had used cigarettes; 15 percent had used marijuana and hashish, and 8 percent had used inhalants.

The pattern of drug and alcohol consumption is the most important issue. Typically the pattern is conceptualized along five points: nonusers, experimenters, recreational users, problem users, and addicts (Krug, 1983).

Since daily marijuana use is second only to cigarette use, teachers need to be familiar with some of the outcomes of marijuana use so they can identify and counsel users. Users may have these adverse psychological effects:

1. Occasional anxiety and suspiciousness
2. Impairment of immediate memory recall
3. Long-term memory disorders
4. Loss of goal-related drive
5. Inability to think and speak clearly
6. Lung damage
7. Increased risk for certain types of cancer
8. Flashbacks
9. Possible suppression of the immune system

It is quite difficult to use characteristics from checklists to identify drug users. Many drug users are aware of the behavioral and physiological consequences of drug use and use disguises such as eyedrops and sun glasses to hide the "red eyes." They have also learned to control their behavior to avoid calling undue attention to themselves. Teachers most often rely on identifying drug abusers through the abusers' self-disclosures or disclosures by concerned others.

Understanding the difference between drug and alcohol use and abuse is difficult. As Zinberg (1984) explains, what would be drug abuse for one person is manageable use for another. Zinberg interviewed many drug users who were functioning well in society and used drugs on a daily basis. This pattern is unusual, however; the majority of daily users have a difficult time functioning in society.

Elementary, junior high, and high school programs are preparing materials and disseminating information about drug and alcohol use. Teachers, particularly at the junior high and high school levels, should be aware of drug and alcohol terminology, characteristics of users, and consequences. Familiarity with local referral agencies providing guidance and assistance to students involved with drugs and alcohol is important for all teachers.

Now that we understand social competence and how students with behavior and learning difficulties feel about themselves, are perceived by others, and interact socially with others, let us focus on intervention theory and specific programs and activities for teaching social skills.

INTERVENTION STRATEGIES

Understanding and using different interventions when attempting to affect the social skills of students with learning disabilities and behavior disorders is extremely important. The variety of social difficulties exhibited by students with learning and behavior disorders is great; using a particular intervention may be effective with one student, yet considerably less effective with another student or another problem. By understanding many approaches, we increase the likelihood of success with all students. The real challenge to teachers is knowing when to use which approach with which child under which condition.

Whereas there is a range of intervention strategies to assist in teaching appropriate social skills to students with learning disabilities and behavior disorders, effective social skills training programs share the same goals (McIntosh, Vaughn, and Zaragoza, 1991). The purpose of social skills training is to teach the students a complex response set that allows them to adapt to the numerous problems that occur in social situations. Common goals of social skills training programs include the ability to do the following:

1. Solve problems and make decisions quickly
2. Adapt to situations that are new or unexpected
3. Use coping strategies for responding to emotional upsets
4. Communicate effectively with others
5. Make and maintain friends

Interpersonal Problem Solving

We spend an extraordinary amount of time preventing and solving interpersonal problems. Whether we are concerned about what to say to our neighbor whose dog barks long and loud in the middle of the night, how to handle the irate customer at work, or our relationships with our parents and siblings, interpersonal problems are an ongoing part of life. Some people seem to acquire the skills necessary for interpersonal problem solving easily and with little or no direct instructions; others, particularly students with learning and behavior disorders, need more direct instruction in how to prevent and resolve difficulties with others.

The goal of interpersonal problem-solving training is to teach students how to employ a wide range of strategies that allow them to develop and maintain positive relationships with others, cope effectively with others, solve their own problems, and resolve conflict with others. The problem-solving approach attempts to provide the student with a process for solving conflicts.

Interpersonal problem solving has been used successfully with a wide range of populations, including adult psychiatric patients (Platt and Spivack, 1972), preschoolers (Ridley and Vaughn, 1982), kindergartners (Shure and Spivack, 1978), students identified as mentally retarded (Vaughn, Ridley, and Cox, 1983), students with learning disabilities (Vaughn, Levine, and Ridley, 1986), and aggressive children (Vaughn, Ridley, and Bullock, 1984). Spivack, Platt and Shure (1976), along with their colleagues at the Hahnemann Medical College, have conducted the most comprehensive examination of the relationship between interpersonal problem solving and adjustment. Their research has led them to explore the effects of interpersonal problem-solving training programs with emotionally disturbed adolescents, disadvantaged preschoolers, and impulsive kindergartners (Spivack, Platt, and Shure, 1976; Shure and Spivack, 1978, 1979, 1980). Based on their work, adaptations and extensions of techniques for teaching interpersonal problem solving to special populations have evolved.

Components of Interpersonal Problem-Solving Programs

Four skills appear to be particularly important for successful problem resolution (Spivack, Platt, and Shure, 1976). First, the student must be able to identify and define the problem. Second, the student must be able to generate a variety of alternative solutions to any given problem. Third, the student must be able to identify and evaluate the possible consequences of each alternative. Finally, the student must be able to implement the solution. This may require rehearsal and modeling. Whereas these four components are characteristic of most interpersonal problem-solving programs, many programs include additional components and procedures.

For example, a social problem-solving intervention was conducted with fifty students with serious emotional disturbances (Amish, Gesten, Smith, Clark, and Stark, 1988). The intervention consisted of fifteen structured lessons which occurred for forty minutes once each week. The following problem-solving steps were taught:

1. Say what the problem is and how you feel.
2. Decide on a goal.
3. Stop and think before you decide what to do.
4. Think of many possible solutions to the problem.
5. Think about what will happen next after each possible solution.
6. When you find a good solution, try it.

The results of the intervention indicated that students with serious emotional disturbances who participated in the intervention improved their social problem-solving skills and were able to generate more alternatives to interviewing and role-playing measures.

Following are descriptions of several interpersonal problem-solving (IPS) programs that have been developed, implemented, and evaluated with students who have learning and behavior disorders.

FAST and SLAM

FAST is a strategy taught as part of an IPS program to second-, third-, and fourth-grade students with learning disabilities identified as having social skills problems (Vaughn and Lancelotta, 1990; Vaughn, Lancelotta, and Minnis, 1988; Vaughn, McIntosh, and Spencer-Rowe, 1991). The purpose of FAST is to teach students to consider problems carefully before responding to them and to consider alternatives and their consequences. Figure 9.3 presents the FAST strategy. In step one, Freeze and Think, students are taught to identify the problem. In step two,

■ **FIGURE 9.3** *FAST: An Interpersonal Problem-Solving Strategy*

FAST

FREEZE AND THINK!
What is the problem?

ALTERNATIVES?
What are my possible solutions?

SOLUTION EVALUATION
Choose the best solution:
  safe?
  fair?

TRY IT!
Slowly and carefully
Does it work?

Alternatives, students are taught to consider possible ways of solving the problem. In step three, Solution Evaluation, students are asked to prepare a solution or course of action for solving the problem that is both safe and fair. The idea is to get students to consider solutions that will be effective in the long run. The fourth step, Try It, asks students to rehearse and implement the solution. If they are unsuccessful at implementing the solution, students are taught to go back to alternatives. Students with learning disabilities practiced this strategy by using real problems generated by themselves and their peers.

- **PROCEDURES:**

1. In each classroom ask peers to rate all same-sex classmates on the extent to which they would like to be friends with them. Students who receive few friendship votes and many "no friendship" votes are identified as rejected. Students who receive many friendship votes and few "no friendship" votes are identified as popular. See Coie, Dodge, and Coppotelli (1982) for exact procedures in assessing popular and rejected students.

2. Rejected students with learning disabilities are paired with same-sex popular classmates and the pair becomes the social skills trainers for the class and school. The school principal announces to the school and to parents through a newsletter who the social skills trainers are for the school.

3. Children selected as social skills trainers are involved in learning social skills strategies and are removed from the classroom two to three times a week for approximately thirty minutes each session.

4. Social skills training includes learning the FAST strategy as well as other social skills such as accepting negative feedback, receiving positive feedback, and making friendship overtures.

5. At the same time period that social skills trainers are learning social skills strategies, their classmates are recording problems they have at home and at school and placing their lists in the classroom problem-solving box (a decorated shoe box). The purpose of the problem-solving box is for students to ask questions about problems they have. Problems from the problem-solving box are used by trainers as they learn the strategies outside of class, as well as for in-class discussion which occurs later and is led by the social skills trainers.

6. After the social skills trainers have learned a strategy, for example, FAST, they teach the strategy to the entire class with backup and support from the researcher and classroom teacher.

7. During subsequent weeks, social skills trainers leave the room for only one session per week and practice the FAST strategy as well as other strategies with classmates at least one time per week. These reviews include large group explanations and small-group problem-solving exercises.

8. Social skills trainers are recognized by their teacher and administrator for their special skills. Other students are asked to consult the social skills trainer when they have difficulties.

- **COMMENTS:** The above approach to teaching social skills and increasing peer acceptance has been successfully applied in two studies with youngsters with learning disabilities (Vaughn, Lancelotta, and Minnis, 1988; Vaughn, McIntosh, and Spencer-Rowe, 1991) but has not been evaluated for behavior-disordered students or adolescents.

Apply the Concept 9.3 shows an activity sheet used as part of a homework assignment for students participating in the training.

Based on principles similar to those of the FAST strategy, SLAM is a technique that can be used to assist students in accepting and assimilating negative feedback and comments from other people (McIntosh, Vaughn, and Bennerson, 1995). The SLAM is practiced in small groups, and presented to the class. The four components of the SLAM strategy are:

1. *STOP*—Stop whatever you are doing.
2. *LOOK*—Look the person in the eye.
3. *ASK*—Ask the person a question to clarify what he or she means.
4. *MAKE*—Make an appropriate response to the person.

APPLY THE CONCEPT 9.3

ACTIVITY SHEET

This activity sheet can be used to give children written practice in using the FAST strategy.

You are in the cafeteria. Another student keeps bugging you. He hits you, pokes you, tries to steal your food, and will not stop bullying you. You start to get angry. What would you do? Use FAST to help you solve the problem.

1. *Freeze and think.* What is the problem?

    _____

    _____

2. *Alternatives.* What are your possible solutions?

    _____

    _____

    _____

3. *Solution evaluation.* Choose the best one. Remember: safe and fair; works in the long run.

    _____

    _____

4. *Try it.* Do you think this will work?

    _____

    _____

A friend of yours is upset. She is teased a lot, especially by a boy named Kenny. She told you that she wants to run away from school. What could you tell your friend to help her solve the problem? Use FAST to help you.

1. _____

    _____

    _____

    _____

2. _____

    _____

    _____

    _____

3. _____

    _____

    _____

    _____

4. _____

    _____

    _____

Figure 9.4 presents the lyrics to the SLAM Strategy Song.

TLC: Teaching, Learning and Caring

Teaching, Learning and Caring (Vaughn, 1987; Vaughn, Cohen, Fournier, Gervasi, Levasseur, and Newton, 1984) is an interpersonal problem-solving skills training program based on the work of Vaughn and Ridley (e.g., Vaughn, Ridley, and Bullock, 1984).

Teaching, Learning and Caring (TLC) is a program developed to teach specific social problem-solving strategies to students with severe emotional disorders and learning disabilities. The program was developed and initiated within a self-contained

■ **FIGURE 9.4**   *Lyrics to the SLAM Strategy Song*

Accepting negative feedback, feedback, feedback.
Accepting negative feedback, feedback, feedback.
Stop what you're doing. Look them in the eye.
Fix your face. We'll tell you why.
Accepting negative feedback, feedback, feedback.
Accepting negative feedback, feedback, feedback.
Listen with your ears to what they say.
This is no time for you to play.
Accepting negative feedback, feedback, feedback.
Accepting negative feedback, feedback, feedback.
Ask a question if you don't understand.
Don't stand there in wonderland.
Accepting negative feedback, feedback, feedback.
Accepting negative feedback, feedback, feedback.
Make a response to their concerns.
Accepting negative feedback is the way to learn.

---

classroom for severely learning- and behavior-disordered students.

The TLC curriculum includes six major components: goal identification, cue sensitivity, empathy, alternative thinking, consequential thinking, and skills implementation. In addition to these core components, a communication mode was identified as a process for listening, responding, and addressing the needs of others, which would facilitate the acquisition of all program components. Figure 9.5 provides a list of the core components of the program.

Social Decision-Making Skills (Elias and Clabby, 1989) is a curriculum based on cognitive interpersonal problem solving and designed for both regular and special education elementary-age students. The curriculum provides for readiness areas and steps for social decision making and problem solving. The teacher's guide is very complete and includes sample worksheets, tips for teaching the skills, and directions for how to structure role plays.

Behavior Therapy

Behavior Therapy, or Applied Behavior Analysis (ABA), is based primarily on operant learning principles. The application of these principles to change maladaptive behaviors is referred to as behavioral therapy.

The major components of ABA include:

1. *Target behaviors are defined operationally.* For example, a teacher described the behaviorally disturbed child in her classroom as "emotional." Although most of us know what *emotional* means, it is likely that each of us imagines a somewhat different behavioral repertoire when we think of a student as behaving in an emotional way. In the same way, if we were asked to chart the emotional behavior of a student, it is unlikely that any two observers would get the same results. For this reason, the teacher is asked to describe the behaviors she observes when the student is acting emotional. "*When I ask her to turn in her work she puts her head down on her desk, sighs, and then crumples her paper.*" Identifying the specific behaviors the student exhibits assists the teacher in clarifying what is disturbing to her, and it also assists in the second step, measurement.

2. *Target behaviors are measured.* To determine the student's present level of functioning and to determine if the selected intervention is effective, target behaviors must be measured before and during intervention. Some behaviors are easy to identify and measure. For example, the number of times John completes his arithmetic assignment is relatively easy to tabulate. However, behaviors such as "out of seat" and "off task" require more elaborate measurement procedures.

The three types of measurement procedures most frequently used are event, duration, and interval time sampling. *Event sampling* measures the number of times a behavior occurs in a designated amount of time. Sample behaviors include the number of times the bus driver reports misconduct regarding a student, the number of times a student is late for class, or the number of times a student does not turn in a homework assignment. *Duration sampling* measures the length of time a behavior occurs. Sample behaviors include the amount of time a student is "out of seat," how long a student cries, or the amount of time a student is "on task." You can see that it is possible to use event and duration samplings for the same behavior. You may want to measure the

■ FIGURE 9.5   *Teaching, Learning, and Caring Skills*

Communication Mode
1. Repeat the content of another's message.
2. Identify the main idea of the content of another's message.
3. Identify the stated feelings in another's message.
4. Identify the underlying feelings in another's message.
5. Identify the main idea of the content of one's message.
6. Identify the underlying feeling in one's message.
7. Use self-disclosure appropriately.
8. Use open and closed questions appropriately.
9. Listen to the problems of another without discounting.
10. Listen to the problems of another and hypothetical situations which influence behavior.

Goal Identification
1. Define own goal(s) when in a problem situation.
2. Define the goal(s) of another when in a problem situation.
3. Identify immediate and long term goals.
4. Share identified goals with the student group and accept feedback.
5. List the steps to reaching identified goals.
6. Chart progress towards reaching goals.
7. Identify and describe the needs and goals of others.

Empathy
1. Identify words which convey emotions, e.g. jealous, hurt, angry, hostile, shy, afraid, furious.
2. Match past situations and the feelings associated with the situation.
3. Discuss the relationship between identifying emotional states as the first step in responding appropriately to them.
4. Identify how you would feel in hypothetical situations.
5. Identify the feelings of others in pictures, films, and hypothetical situations.

Cue Sensitivity
1. Identify environmental cues in pictures and respond by asking questions and summarizing content and feelings.
2. Identify environmental cues in real situations which influence behavior.
3. Identify the personal cues people use and what they mean in role plays and films.
4. Identify the personal cues used by others in real situations.
5. Identify own cues when interacting with others and what they mean.
6. Identify several cues you want to include in your repertoire.
7. Identify cues of others, your typical response to them, and possible alternative responses.

Alternative Thinking
1. Identify likely alternatives to solving hypothetical problems.
2. Identify likely alternatives to solving real problems.
3. Identify nonaggressive alternatives to solving hypothetical problems.
4. Identify nonaggressive alternatives to solving real problems.

(continued)

FIGURE 9.5   *Continued*

Consequential Thinking

1. Predict the likely consequences to a series of events not involving them.
2. Predict the likely consequences to hypothetical stories and role play situations.
3. Predict the likely consequences to interpersonal interactions of others.
4. Identify short run and long run solutions to solving hypothetical problems.
5. Identify problems in the long run when implementing short run solutions to hypothetical situations.
6. Identify the consequences of selected behaviors in interpersonal situations involving others.
7. Identify the consequences of selected behaviors in interpersonal situations involving self.
8. Implement a "stop and think" approach to solving interpersonal difficulties.

Skills Implementation

1. Identify the best procedure for implementing the selected alternative.
2. Identify a person who implements the alternative well and describe what he or she does.
3. Describe the step-by-step process for implementing the selected alternative.
4. Role play, practice, and rehearse the selected alternative.
5. Use feedback from self and others to make changes in the procedure.
6. Implement selected alternative.
7. Evaluate the outcome and the procedure.

Integration

1. Observe models (counselors, teachers, and peers) integrate the problem solving process in solving hypothetical problems.
2. Observe models (counselors, teachers, and peers) integrate the problem solving process in solving real problems.
3. Integrate the problem solving process in solving group problems.
4. Integrate the problem solving process in solving hypothetical problems.
5. Integrate the problem solving process in solving real problems.

Source: S. Vaughn, "TLC-Teaching, Learning, and Caring: Teaching Interpersonal Problem-Solving Skills to Behaviorally Disordered Adolescents," *The Pointer, 31*(2) (1987): 25–30. Reprinted with permission of the Helen Dwight Reid Educational Foundation. Published by Heldref Publications, 1319 18th Street, N.W., Washington, D.C. 20036-1802. Copyright 1987.

behavior both ways or select the measurement procedure that will give you the most information about the behavior. *Interval sampling* designates whether or not a behavior occurs during a specific interval of time. For example, a teacher may record whether a student is reported for fighting during recess periods. Interval sampling is used when it is difficult to tell when a behavior begins or ends and also when a behavior occurs very frequently.

In addition to the measurement of the target behavior, it is helpful to identify the antecedents and consequences of the target behavior. A listing of what occurs before the behavior and what occurs immediately after gives important information that assists in developing an intervention procedure. If every time the student cries, the teacher talks to the student for a few minutes, it could be the teacher's attention is maintaining the behavior. The listing of antecedents may provide information about the environment, events, or people who trigger the target behavior. An analysis of antecedents and consequences facilitates the establishment of a successful intervention procedure.

3. *Goals and treatment intervention are established.* Based on observation and measurement data and an analysis of antecedents and consequences, goals for changing behavior and intervention strategies are established. The purpose of establishing goals is to determine the desired frequency or duration of the behavior. Goal setting is most effective when the person exhibiting the target behavior is involved in establishing the goals. For example, Dukas is aware he gets into too many fights and wants to reduce his fighting behavior. After the target behavior is identified and measured, the teacher and student examine the data and identify that the only time he gets into fights is during the lunch-time recess. They set up a contract in which the teacher agrees to give Dukas ten minutes of free time at the end of each day in which he does not get into a fight. The student agrees with the contract. The teacher continues to measure the student's behavior to determine if the suggested treatment plan is effective.

There are many treatment strategies in behavior therapy that can be used by the teacher to effect change. For example, the teacher may use reinforcers to shape new behaviors, reinforce incompatible behaviors, or maintain or increase desired behavior. The teacher may use extinction, punishment, or time-out to eliminate undesired behaviors. Guidelines for using time-out are presented in Figure 9.6. The teacher may use contracts or token economies to change behavior. These strategies are discussed in Chapter Two, in the section on operant learning theory. With these intervention strategies, consequences are controlled by another (e.g., the teacher). Self-management is a procedure in which the consequences are controlled by the target person. These procedures are particularly effective with older children, adolescents, and adults because the control and responsibility for change is placed in their hands. With assistance from a teacher, counselor, or other

■ FIGURE 9.6 *Time-Out: Guidelines for Effective Implementation*

- Use time-out as a last resort.
- Discuss time-out procedures with school administrators and parents before implementation.
- Put time-out procedures in writing and file with school rules.
- Provide students with information in advance about what behaviors will result in time-out.
- Place students in time-out only for brief time periods (15 to 20 minutes).
- Specify the amount of time the student will be in time-out prior to placement.
- Tell the student to go to time-out. If the student does not comply, the teacher should unemotionally place the student in time-out.
- Use time-out *immediately* following the inappropriate behavior.
- Establish contingencies in advance for the student who fails to comply with time-out rules.
- Always monitor the time-out area.
- When the time specified for time-out is over, the student should join his or her classmates.
- Provide reinforcement for appropriate behavior after time-out.

influential adult, the adolescent implements a self-management program by following three processes.

1. Identify the behavior he or she wants to change (e.g., being late for school).

2. Identify the antecedents and consequences associated with the behavior (e.g., Doreen says, "When the alarm rings I continue to lie in bed. I also wait until the last minute to run to the bus stop and I frequently miss the bus").

3. Develop a plan that alters the antecedents and provides consequences that will maintain the desired behavior. Doreen decides to get up as soon as the alarm rings and to leave for the bus stop without waiting until the last minute. Doreen arranges with her parents to have the car on Friday nights if she has arrived at school on time every day that week. An obvious disadvantage of a self-control model of behavior change is that it relies on the motivation of the student for success. Students who are not interested in changing behaviors and who are not willing to analyze antecedents and consequences and develop potentially successful intervention strategies will be unsuccessful with self-determined behavior change plans.

ASSET: A Social Skills Program for Adolescents

The purpose of ASSET is to teach adolescents the social skills they need to interact successfully with peers and adults (Hazel, Schumaker, Sherman, and Sheldon-Wildgen, 1981). The eight social skills considered fundamental to successful relationships are listed below.

1. *Giving positive feedback.* This skill teaches students how to thank someone and how to give a compliment.
2. *Giving negative feedback.* This skill teaches students to give correction and feedback in a way that is not threatening.
3. *Accepting negative feedback.* This skill teaches students the all-important ability to receive negative feedback without walking away, showing hostility, or other inappropriate emotional reactions.
4. *Resisting peer pressure.* This teaches students to refuse their friends who are trying to seduce them into some form of delinquent behavior.
5. *Problem solving.* This teaches students a process for solving their own interpersonal difficulties.
6. *Negotiation.* This teaches students to use their problem-solving skills with another person to come to a mutually acceptable resolution.
7. *Following instructions.* This teaches students to listen and respond to instructions.
8. *Conversation.* This teaches students to initiate and maintain a conversation.

The Leader's Guide (Hazel, Schumaker, Sherman, and Sheldon-Wildgen, 1981) that comes with the ASSET program provides instructions for running the groups and teaching the skills. Eight teaching sessions are provided on videotapes that demonstrate the skills. Program materials include skill sheets, home notes, and criterion checklists.

━ PROCEDURES: Each lesson is taught to a small group of adolescents. There are nine basic steps to each lesson: (1) review homework and previously learned social skills; (2) explain the new skill for the day's lesson; (3) explain why the skill is important and should be learned and practiced; (4) give a realistic and specific example to illustrate the use of the skill; (5) examine each of the skill steps that are necessary to carry out the new social skill; (6) model the skill and provide opportunities for students and others to demonstrate correct and incorrect use of the skills; (7) use verbal rehearsal to familiarize the students with the sequence of steps in each social skill and provide a procedure for students to be automatic with their knowledge of the skill steps; (8) use behavioral rehearsal to allow each student to practice and demonstrate the skill steps until they reach criterion; (9) assign homework that provides opportunities for the students to practice the skills in other settings. These nine steps are followed for each of the eight specific social skills listed above.

━ COMMENTS: The ASSET program has been evaluated with eight students with learning disabilities (Hazel, Schumaker, Sherman, and Sheldon, 1982). It demonstrated that the students with learning disabilities involved in the intervention increased in the use of social skills in role-play settings. The curriculum guide provides specific teaching procedures and is particularly relevant to teachers working with adolescents.

Mutual Interest Discovery

Rather than specifically teaching social skills, *Mutual Interest Discovery* is an approach to increasing peer acceptance which has been used with students with learning disabilities (Fox, 1989). The rationale is that people are attracted to persons with whom they share similar attitudes. The more we know about someone the more likely it is that we will like them. Structured activities are provided for students with and without learning disabilities to get to know each other with greater acceptance being the outcome.

— **PROCEDURES:** The overall goal of mutual interest discovery is to participate in structured activities with a partner (one partner with learning disabilities and the other without) to identify things you have in common and to get to know your partner better.

1. All students in the class are paired; students with learning disabilities are paired with nonlearning-disabled classmates.

2. Students interact on preassigned topics for approximately forty minutes once each week for several weeks. Preassigned topics include interviewing each other on such things as sports, entertainment preferences, hobbies, and other topics appropriate for the specific age group with which you are working.

3. After the structured activity each member of the pair writes three things he or she has in common or three things he or she learned about the other person.

4. Partners complete a brief art activity related to what they learned about their partner and place it in a mutual art book to which they contribute each week.

5. At the bottom of the art exercise each partner writes two sentences about something new he or she learned about his or her partner. If there is time, art activities and sentences are shared with members of the class.

— **COMMENTS:** Partners who participated in the mutual interest discovery intervention demonstrated higher ratings of their partners over time than did a control group of students. This intervention is not designed to teach specific social skills but to increase the acceptance and likability of students with learning disabilities in the regular classroom. It is likely that this intervention, paired with social skills training, has promise for success with students with learning disabilities.

Structured Learning

Structured learning is a psychoeducational and behavioral approach to teaching prosocial skills to students both with and without disabilities (Goldstein, Sprafkin, Gerhsaw, and Klein, 1980). The procedure has four components and can be implemented by teachers, social workers, psychologists, or school counselors.

The first component is *modeling* and involves a verbal and behavioral description of the target skill as well as the steps that comprise the target skill. At this point the teacher might role play the steps in the skill and other models may also role play, exhibiting the target skill itself. During the second step, students are encouraged to enact role plays based on actual life experiences. These role plays are facilitated by coaching and cues from the teacher. Next, the teacher and other observers provide feedback. Specific attention is paid to elements of each role play that were effective and appropriate. Skills that were not role-played effectively are modeled by the teacher. In the final step, students are provided with opportunities to practice the steps and skills in the real world (e.g., outside the classroom).

The structured learning program for elementary students offers sixty prosocial skills and their constituent steps, arranged into five groups: classroom survival skills, friendship-making skills, skills for dealing with feelings, skill alternatives to aggression, and skills for dealing with stress. The structured learning program for adolescents also has 60 prosocial skills. It differs from the program for elementary students by including skills related to planning and decision making.

Principles for Teaching Social Skills

There are several points teachers need to consider, no matter what social skills program they utilize. These include:

1. *Develop cooperative learning.* Classrooms can be structured so there is a win-lose atmosphere in which children compete with each other for grades and teacher attention, or classrooms can be structured so children work on their own with little interaction between classmates, or classrooms can be structured for cooperative learning so children work alone, with pairs, and with groups, helping each other master the assigned material. Cooperative learning techniques in the classroom result in increases in self-esteem, social skills, and learning

(Johnson and Johnson, 1986). Teachers can structure learning activities so they involve cooperative learning and teach students techniques for working with pairs or in a group. The following four elements need to be present for cooperative learning to occur in small groups (Johnson and Johnson, 1986):

    a. Students must perceive they cannot succeed at the required task unless all members of the group succeed. This may require appropriate division of labor and giving a single grade for the entire group's performance.

    b. Assure individual accountability so each member of the group is assessed and realizes his or her performance is critical for group success.

    c. Teach students the necessary collaborative skills so they are able to function effectively in a group. This may include managing conflicts, active listening, leadership skill, and problem solving.

    d. Allow time for group process. This may include discussing how well the group is performing, developing a plan of action, and identifying what needs to happen.

2. *Involve peers in the training program for low-social-status students.* An important function of social skills training is to alter the way peers perceive students identified as low in social status. Including popular peers in the social skills training program increases the likelihood that they will have opportunities to observe the changes in target students and to cue and reinforce appropriate behavior in the classroom. For example, a study conducted by Vaughn, McIntosh, and Spencer-Rowe (1988), found that popular students involved in the social skills training with low-social-status students were more likely to increase the social-status ratings of the low-social-status students than were popular students not involved in the training.

Even when a social skills program is effective in producing the desired change in target students, it does not always alter the way these students are perceived by their peers (Bierman and Furman, 1984). Involving students with high social status with those with lower social status will improve the way the low-social-status students are perceived by others.

3. *Use principles of effective instruction.* Many teachers claim they do not know how to teach social skills. Considering the social skills difficulties of special education students, methods of teaching social skills to students may need to become part of our teacher training programs (Vaughn, 1985).

Teaching social skills requires implementing principles of effective instruction. These have been used and explained throughout this text and include: obtain student commitment, identify target behavior, pretest, teach, model, rehearse, role play, provide feedback, practice in controlled settings, practice in other settings, posttest and follow-up. A list of social skills that learning- and behavior-disordered students frequently need to be taught follows:

    a. *Body language.* This includes how the student walks, where he or she stands during a conversation, what his or her body "says," gestures, eye contact, and appropriate facial reactions.

    b. *Greetings.* This may include expanding the student's repertoire of greetings, selecting appropriate greetings for different people, and interpreting and responding to the greetings of others.

    c. *Initiating and maintaining a conversation.* This includes a wide range of behaviors such as knowing when to approach someone; knowing how to ask inviting, open questions; knowing how to respond to comments made by others; and maintaining a conversation with a range of persons, including those who are too talkative and those who volunteer little conversation.

    d. *Giving positive feedback.* Knowing how and when to give sincere, genuine, positive feedback and comments.

    e. *Accepting positive feedback.* Knowing how to accept positive feedback from others.

    f. *Giving negative feedback.* Knowing how and when to give specific negative feedback.

    g. *Accepting negative feedback.* Knowing how to accept negative feedback from others.

    h. *Identifying feelings in self and others.* Being able to recognize feelings both in self and others is how the student is able to predict how he or she will feel in a given situation and prepare appropriately for it. Responding appropriately to one's own and others' feelings.

i. *Problem solving and conflict resolution.* Knowing and using problem-solving skills to prevent and solve difficulties.

4. *Teach needed skills.* According to Perlmutter (1986), many social skills training programs fail because youngsters are trained to do things they already know how to do. For example, in a social skills training group with students with learning disabilities, the trainer was teaching the students to initiate conversations with others. Through role playing, the trainer soon learned that the students already knew how to initiate conversations but they did not know how to sustain them. In addition to being taught appropriate skills, students need to learn when and with whom to use the skills. One student put it this way: "I would never try problem solving like this with my father, but I know it would work with my mom."

5. *Teach for transfer of learning.* Many programs for teaching social skills effectively increase students' performance in social areas during the skills training or within a particular context, but the skills do not generalize to other settings (Berler, Gross, and Drabman, 1982). In order for social skills to generalize to other settings, the program must require the rehearsal and implementation of target skills across settings. Social skills training programs need to assure learned skills are systematically demonstrated in the classroom, on the playground, and at home.

6. *Empower students.* Many students with learning difficulties feel discouraged and unable to influence their learning. They turn the responsibility for learning over to the teacher and become "passive" learners. How can we empower students?

a. *Choice.* Students need to feel they are actively involved in their learning.

b. *Consequences.* Students will learn from the natural and logical consequences of their choices.

c. *Document progress.* In addition to teacher documentation of progress made, students need to learn procedures for monitoring and assessing their progress.

d. *Control.* Students need to feel as though they can exercise control over what happens to them. Some students feel as though their learning is in someone else's hands and therefore is someone else's responsibility.

7. *Identify strengths.* When developing social skills interventions for students with special needs, be sure to consider their strengths as well as their needs. Since appearance and athletic ability relate to social acceptance, these areas need to be considered when determining the type of social intervention needed. For example, if a youngster's physical appearance is a strength, the teacher can compliment him or her on hair appearance, what they are wearing, or how "neat" and "sharp" they look. Also, knowing something about the students' areas of strength might be helpful in identifying social contexts that may be promising for promoting positive peer interactions (Vaughn and LaGreca, 1992). For example, it is possible that a student with learning disabilities who is a particularly good swimmer and a member of a swim team would find friendship-making on the swim team an easier task than friendship-making in the academic setting. Students with learning disabilities may benefit from acquiring strengths in appearance and athletic activities so they can have areas of strength from which to build their social skills. While athletic skills are associated with peer success, particularly for boys, many children with learning disabilities do not have the motor ability or eye-hand coordination to succeed in the athletic area. Other areas such as hobbies or special interests can be presented in the classroom so that the student with learning disabilities has an opportunity to be perceived as one who is knowledgeable.

When developing social skills interventions, it may be important to consider the nature of children's friendships or social support outside of the school setting (Vaughn and LaGreca, 1992). It is possible that students with learning and behavior disorders who are not well accepted by their classmates have friends in the neighborhood or within their families (e.g., cousins). Perhaps the most important point to remember is that because a child is not well accepted by peers at school does not necessarily mean that the child does not have effective social relationships outside of the school setting.

8. *Reciprocal friendships.* Reciprocal friendship is the mutual identification as "best friend" by two students. Thus, a student who identifies a youngster as his or her best friend is also identified by that same youngster as a best friend. It has been hypothesized that reciprocal friendships could play an important role in reducing the negative effects of low peer acceptance (Vaughn, McIntosh, Schumm, Haager, and Callwood, 1993). From this perspective, it may be less important to increase the overall acceptance of a student in the classroom and more effective to concentrate on the development of a mutual best friend. Since it is quite unlikely that all youngsters in the classroom are going to like all of the other youngsters equally, the notion of developing a reciprocal friendship is a more realistic goal for most youngsters with learning and behavior problems.

Classroom Management

When someone mentions classroom management, most teachers think of discipline and classroom management rules. Duke and Meckel (1980) refer to classroom management as the procedures needed to establish and maintain an environment in which instruction and learning can occur. Classroom rules, routines, and order play an important part in classroom management (Doyle, 1986). Students need to have expectations for the behaviors and routines of the classroom.

Early in the year it is important to establish processes and procedures that sustain order (Doyle, 1979; Emmer, Evertson, and Anderson, 1980). One way to inform students of the classroom rules is to discuss the rules with them. As new children enter the class during the year, assigning a "veteran" student as a guide or mentor can help the new student understand the rule system of the classroom.

The purpose of some classroom rules is to regulate student behaviors that are likely to disrupt learning and teacher activities or cause damage or injury to property or others. In addition to explicit conduct rules, most classrooms also have a set of im-

plicit rules under which they function (Erickson and Shultz, 1981). Sharing the explicit conduct rules and demonstrating the rewards of working within the rule system is particularly important for students with behavior problems. Making rewards contingent on full class participation can also assist a teacher, because students will encourage each other to work within the rule system.

Ms. Schiller works with junior high students with emotional disorders in a self-contained setting. Establishing conduct rules early in the year and setting up a reward system for "good behavior" is an important part of her program. Ms. Schiller comments:

> As far as I know, all of the students in this class are here primarily because they cannot cope with the rule systems in regular classrooms. This is due to a variety of reasons, and as a part of our social skills program we discuss some of the reasons and how to cope with them. But the majority of the day is focused on academic learning. To accomplish effective learning, we have a set of written and unwritten rules that the students and I are willing to operate under. We establish these rules at the beginning of the year during class meetings. In these meetings we talk about how the school operates and the rules it operates under, and then we decide what rules we want the classroom to function under. Usually it takes several days to establish these rules. The rules we generally decide on are:
>
> During discussions, one person talks at a time.
> When a person is talking, it is the responsibility of the rest of us to listen.
> Work quietly so you won't bother others.
> No hitting, shoving, kicking, etc.
> No screaming.
> Do not take other people's possessions without asking.
> Treat classmates and teachers with respect and consideration.
> When outside the classroom, follow the rules of the school or those established by the supervisor.

Each day when we have a class meeting, we discuss the rules, our success with using these rules, and how the rules have operated. Sometimes we add new rules based on our discussions. I involve the students in this evaluation and decision making. Eventually we begin to decide when the rules can be made more flexible. In this way I hope that I am helping the students assume more responsibility for their own behavior, while at the same time maintaining a learning environment that is conducive to academic as well as social growth.

I think there are three main reasons this rule system works in my classroom. First, the students feel like they own the system and have a responsibility to make it work. We have opportunities to discuss the system and to make changes. Second, we also establish a token system [see Chapter Two] for appropriate behavior and learning. Third, I communicate regularly with the parents, letting them know how their child is performing.

The classroom rules a teacher establishes are dependent on the social context of the school and the classroom, and the teaching-learning process as described in Chapter One. Some guidelines to use in developing and implementing classroom rules and management systems follow.

— Have the students help in selecting rules for the classroom.
— Select the fewest number of rules possible.
— Check with the principal or appropriate administrative personnel to determine if the rules are within the guidelines of the school.
— Select rules that are enforceable.
— Select rules that are reasonable.
— Determine consistent consequences for rule infractions.
— Have students evaluate their behavior in relation to the rules.
— Modify rules only when necessary.
— Have frequent group meetings in which students provide self-feedback as well as feedback to others about their behavior.
— Allow students to provide solutions to nagging class or school issues through problem solving.

Classroom Management and Student Behavior

Lisa Rosario is a first-year, middle school resource room teacher in a suburban school district. She is not happy with the behavior of the students who come to the resource room. She was telling an experienced special education teacher in the same middle school, "I feel like I know what to teach and how to teach, but I just can't seem to get the students to behave so that they can learn. What can I do to make the students change?" The experienced teacher responded by suggesting that Lisa Rosario first look at her own behavior in order to change the behavior of the students in her classroom. Figure 9.7 provides a checklist for teachers to evaluate the effectiveness of their interventions.

Lisa is not alone. Classroom management is identified by teachers as a cause of stress and is

■ **FIGURE 9.7**　*Implementation Checklist*

If your intervention is not working, consider the following:

• Have you adequately identified and defined the target behavior?
• Have you selected the right kind of reinforcer? (What you decided on may not be reinforcing to the student.)
• Are you providing reinforcement soon enough?
• Are you providing too much reinforcement?
• Are you giving too little reinforcement?
• Are you being consistent in your implementation of the intervention program?
• Have you made the intervention program more complicated than it needs to be?
• Are others involved following through (e.g., principal, parent, "buddy")?
• Is the social reinforcement by peers outweighing your contracted reinforcement?
• Did you fail to give reinforcers promised or earned?

Source: From B. Larrivee (1992). *Strategies for Effective Classroom Management: Creating a Collaborative Climate* (p. 259). Boston: Allyn and Bacon. Reprinted with permission.

frequently cited as the reason they leave the teaching profession (Elam and Gallup, 1989; Fettler and Tokar, 1982). Following are some guidelines for Lisa to consider to assist in facilitating more appropriate behavior on the part of her students.

1. *Look for the Positive Behavior and Let Students Know You Recognize It.* Most teachers indicate that they provide a lot of positive reinforcement to their students. However, observations in special and general education teachers' classes indicate relatively low levels of positive reinforcement (McIntosh, Vaughn, Schumm, Haager, and Lee, 1993). Teachers need to provide a lot more positive feedback than they think is necessary.

One of the fundamental rules about positive feedback is that it needs to be both specific and immediate. "Carla's homework is completed exactly the way I asked for it to be done. She has numbered the problems, left space between answers so that they are easy to read, and written the appropriate heading at the top of the paper." A second fundamental rule about positive feedback is that students need to be clear about what behaviors are desirable and undesirable.

A clear list of class rules and consequences is an important step in making classroom management rules clear. Rules and procedures form the structure for classroom management (Brophy, 1988). Procedures that are part of the classroom routines need to be taught to students. Rules provide the structure for the behaviors that are acceptable and unacceptable. Teacher's criteria for what constitutes a behavior problem is the basis for the rules (Emmer, Evertson, Sanford, Clements, and Worsham, 1989). Think back to Lisa Rosario who indicated she had difficulty with classroom management. What became clear after further discussion was that she had difficulty establishing and enforcing classroom procedures. Once the experienced teacher observed in her classroom and assisted her in establishing routines, Lisa experienced significantly fewer difficulties with classroom management.

Positive reinforcement is more effective at the elementary level than in middle school, and least effective with high school students (Forness, 1973; Stallings, 1975). This does not suggest that positive reinforcement should be avoided with older students, but merely that it should be handled in a different way. Elementary students find public recognition in front of the entire class more rewarding than do older students, who prefer to receive individual feedback.

2. *Reinforcers Can Be Used to Encourage Positive Behavior.* As explained in Chapter One, both positive and negative reinforcement increases behavior. Most people think negative reinforcement means something harmful or "negative." As described in Chapter One, positive reinforcement is the presentation of a stimulus (verbal response, physical response such as touching, or a tangible response such as a reward) following the target behavior, intended to maintain or increase a target behavior. A list of reinforcers that teachers may want to consider for use in their classrooms is provided in Figure 9.8.

3. *Token Economy.* A token economy is a structured plan for delivering reinforcers (tokens) following the display of target students behaviors and/or the absence of undesirable student behaviors. Token economies can be adapted for use in a variety of settings, and have been used extensively in special education (Kazdin, 1989). For example, teachers can post in the classroom a list of desirable behaviors (e.g., raising a hand and waiting to be called on by the teacher before talking) as well as undesirable behaviors (e.g., hitting classmates). Posted along with the behaviors are the corresponding number of tokens (e.g., points, chips, tickets) that students may earn for exhibiting target behaviors and eliminating noxious behaviors. Teachers can award tokens as target behaviors occur and/or may deliver tokens after a specific period of time has elapsed (e.g., Johnny receives one token at the start of each hour providing he has not hit a peer during the previous sixty minutes). Teachers can award tokens to individuals as in the previous example, or award the entire class. Either way, the underlying principle is that students will be motivated to earn tokens that are collected and exchanged for previously determined privileges (e.g., a class pizza party, or first choice of equipment at recess).

4. *Changing Inappropriate Behavior.* Behaviors that are interfering are the ones that teachers can

■ **FIGURE 9.8**   *Reinforcers Teachers Can Use to Increase Appropriate Behavior*

Student Provides Self-Reinforcers

- Student gives points to self for behaving well.
- Student says positive things to himself or herself, "I'm working hard and doing well."
- Student monitors his or her own behavior.

Adult Approval

- Verbal recognition from the teacher that the student is behaving appropriately, "John you are following directions on this assignment."
- Physical recognition from the teacher that the student is behaving appropriately. Teacher moves around the classroom and touches students on the shoulder who are behaving appropriately.
- Teacher informs parents or other professionals of the appropriate behavior of the student. This can be accomplished with "good news notes" or verbally.

Peer Recognition

- Teacher informs other students of the appropriate behavior of a student. "The award for Student of the Day goes to the outstanding improvement in behavior demonstrated by (student's name)."
- A box is established in the class where peers can write the names of students who have demonstrated appropriate behavior. These names can be read at the end of the week.
- A designated period of time is allocated at the end of the class period (high school) or day (elementary school) to ask students to recognize their fellow classmates who have demonstrated outstanding behavior.

Privileges

- Students are awarded free time after displaying appropriate behavior.
- Students are allowed to serve in key classroom roles after demonstrating outstanding behavior.
- Students are awarded passes that they can trade in for a night without homework.

Activities

- Students can perform an activity they like (e.g., drawing) after they complete the desired activity (e.g., the activity during that class period).
- Students can perform their tasks on the computer.
- Students can perform their tasks with a partner they select.

Tokens

- Tokens are items (e.g., chips, play money, points) that can be exchanged for something of value.
- Use tokens to reward groups or teams who are behaving appropriately.
- Allow groups of individuals to accumulate tokens that they can "spend" on privileges such as no homework, or free time.

Tangibles

- Tangibles refer to rewards that are desirable objects to students, but usually not objects they can consume (e.g., toys, pencils, erasers, paper, crayons).
- Tokens can be exchanged for tangible reinforcers.
- Tangible reinforcers can be used to reward the class for meeting a class goal.
- Tangible reinforcers may be needed to maintain the behavior of a student with severe behavior problems.

Consumables

- Consumables refer to rewards that are desirable objects to students that they consume (e.g., raisins, pieces of cereal, candy).
- Tokens can be exchanged for consumable reinforcers.
- Consumable reinforcers can be used to reward the class for meeting a class goal.
- Consumable reinforcers may be needed to maintain the behavior of a student with severe behavior problems.

Source: Adapted from: S. Vaughn, C. S. Bos and J. S. Schumm (1997). *Teaching Mainstreamed, Diverse, and At-Risk Students in the General Education Classroom.* Boston: Allyn and Bacon.

most easily identify. It is much easier for teachers to list the behaviors they would like to see reduced than to identify behaviors they would like to have increased. Morgan and Reinhart (1991) identify the following guiding principles to assist in changing inappropriate behavior of students.

- Do not use threats. Consider carefully the consequences you intend to use. Do not threaten students with a consequence you are actually unwilling to use or that will force you to back down.
- Follow through consistently on the rules you make, with the consequences you have pre-determined.
- Do not establish so many rules that you spend too much time applying consequences. You will find yourself continually at war with the students.
- Do not establish consequences that are punishing to you. If you are stressed or inconvenienced by the consequence you may eventually begin to resent the student, which would interfere with your relationship.
- Listen and talk to the student but avoid disagreements or arguments. If you are tempted to argue, set another time to continue the discussion.
- Use logic, principles, and effective guidelines to make decisions. Avoid using your power to make students do something without connecting it to a logical principle.
- Do not focus on minor or personal peeves. Focus on the problems that are the most interfering.
- Treat each student as an individual with his or her own problems and abilities. Avoid comparing students' behaviors or abilities, as this does not assist students in self-understanding or in better understanding the problems and abilities of others.
- Remember that students' problems belong to them and are not your problems. Although their problems may interfere with your work, they are not your problems. Students with behavior or emotional problems are often successful at transferring their prob-

lems to others. Students need to learn to resolve their own conflicts.
- Students often say or do things that are upsetting to teachers. Recognize your feelings and do not let them control your behavior. Do not respond to the upsetting behavior of a student by "striking back," humiliating, embarrassing, or berating the student.
- Solicit the assistance of parents and students in putting the problem in writing to assure that all of you agree on what needs to be changed.
- Get student and parent input on the behavior problem and suggestions for what might reduce it.
- Set up a plan that identifies the problem, consequence, and/or rewards for changes in behavior. See Figure 9.9 and Figure 9.10 for a sample behavioral contract and a self-management plan.

INSTRUCTIONAL ACTIVITIES

This section provides instructional activities related to developing socialization skills. Some of the activities teach new skills; others are best suited for practice and reinforcement of already acquired skills. For each activity, the objective, materials, and teaching procedures are described.

■ Please Help

Objective: To teach students a process for asking for help when needed and yet continuing to work until assistance is given. To have a record-keeping system that allows the teacher to monitor how many times each day he or she assists each student.

Grades: Primary and intermediate

Materials: A 6 × 8 inch card that states "Please Help _____ (student's name)" and then a place to list the date and comments.

■ **FIGURE 9.9** *Sample Behavior Contract*

DATE: _____

Mr. Reynolds will give one point to Joleen when she exhibits any of the following in his classroom:

1. Raises her hand appropriately and waits for the teacher to call on her before responding to a question or seeking information.
2. She sits appropriately (in chair with all four legs on the ground).
3. When annoyed by other students, she ignores them or informs the teacher instead of yelling at and/or hitting others.

After Joleen has earned 10 points, she may select one of the following:

1. She may obtain a twenty-minute coupon to be used at any time to work on the computer.
2. She may serve as the teacher's assistant for a day.
3. She may obtain a fifteen-minute coupon for free time.
4. She may have lunch with the teacher and brought by the teacher.

Joleen may continue to select awards for every 10 points earned. New awards may be decided upon by the teacher and Joleen, and added to the list. I, Joleen Moore, agree to the conditions stated above, and understand that I will not be allowed any of the rewards until I have earned 10 points following the above stated guidelines.

_____
(student's signature)

I, Mr. Reynolds, agree to the conditions stated above. I will give Joleen one of the aforementioned rewards only after she has earned 10 points.

_____
(teacher's signature)

Teaching Procedures: Construct the "Please Help" card for each student, including a place to mark the date and comments. Give all the students a card and inform them that they are to place the card on their desks when they need help. They are to continue working until you or someone else is able to provide assistance.

When you or your assistant is able to provide help, mark the date and time on the card and any appropriate comments such as, "We needed to review the rules for long division," or "She could not remember the difference between long and short vowels," or "He solved the problem himself before I arrived."

PLEASE HELP JENNIFER		
DATE	TIME	COMMENTS

■ **FIGURE 9.10**   *Self-Management Plan*

Name: Kiernen Smathers

Target Behavior: Submit completed homework to the teacher on time or meet with teacher prior to when the assignment is due to agree on an alternative date and time.

Where Behavior Occurs: Mathematics and Science

Goals:

1. Kiernen will use an assignment book and write down the assignments, guidelines, and due dates. The teacher will initial these to assure he understands them and has written them correctly.
2. Kiernen will interpret what he needs to do for each assignment and ask questions as needed.
3. Kiernen will discuss any assignments with the teacher ahead of time if he anticipates not having them ready on time.

Time Line: Meet each Friday to review progress and assignments. Revise plan as needed.

Reinforcer: Kiernen will receive fifteen minutes of extra time to work on the computer each day his assignments are completed.

Evaluation: Kiernen will write a brief description of the program's success.

■ **Problem Box**

Objective: To give students an opportunity to identify problems they are having with others and to feel their problems will be heard and attended to.

Grades: All grades

Materials: Shoe box decorated and identified as "Problem Box."

Teaching Procedures: Show the students the box that is decorated and identified as the "Problem Box." Place the box in a prominent location in the classroom. Tell the students that when they have problems with other students, teachers, or even at home they can write the problems down and put them in the box. At the end of every day, you and the students will spend a designated amount of time (e.g., fifteen minutes) reading problems and trying to solve them as a class. Be sure to tell students they do not need to identify themselves or their notes.

During the designated time, open the problem box and read a selected note. Solicit assistance from the class in solving the note. Direct students' attention to identifying the problem, suggesting solutions, evaluating the consequences of the solutions, and identifying a solution and describing how it might be implemented.

■ **A Date by Telephone**

Objective: To give students structured skills for obtaining a date by telephone.

Grades: Secondary

Materials: Two nonworking telephones.

Teaching Procedures: Discuss with the students why preplanning a telephone call with a prospective date might be advantageous. Tell them that you are going to teach them some points to remember when calling to ask for a date. After you describe each of the following points, role play them so the students can observe their appropriate use:

1. Telephone at an *appropriate time.*
2. Utilize an *icebreaker,* such as recalling a mutually shared experience or a recent event in school.

3. *State what you would like to do and ask him or her to do it.* Ask the person what kinds of things he or she likes to do on the weekend. After there is an initial lull in the conversation, state you would like to take her or him to the movies, state when, and to see what. Then ask the person if he or she would like to go with you.

4. If yes, *make appropriate arrangements* for day, time, and transportation. If no, ask if you can call again.

Be sure that each student has an opportunity to role play.

■ Making and Keeping Friends

Objective: To have students identify the characteristics of students who are successful at making and keeping friends and, after identifying these characteristics, to evaluate themselves in how well they perform.

How Good Are You at Making and Keeping Friends

Next to each item, circle the face that best describes how well you do.

1. I tell friends the truth.

2. I call friends on the phone.

3. I share my favorite toys and games with friends.

Grades: Intermediate and secondary

Materials: Writing materials

Teaching Procedures: Ask the students to think of children they know who are good at making and keeping friends. Brainstorm what these children do that makes them successful at making and keeping friends. On an overhead projector or chalkboard, write the student-generated responses to the characteristics of children good at making and keeping friends. Then select the most agreed on characteristics and write them on a sheet of paper with smiley faces, neutral faces, and frowny faces so students can circle the face that is most like them in response to that characteristic. Finally, ask students to identify one characteristic they would like to target to increase their skills at making and maintaining friends.

■ Identifying Feelings

Objective: To identify the feelings of others and self, and to respond better to those feelings.

Grades: Primary and intermediate

Materials: Cards with pictures of persons in situations where their feelings can be observed or - deduced.

Teaching Procedures: Select pictures that elicit feeling words such as *happy, angry, jealous, hurt, sad, mad,* and so on. Show the pictures to the students and ask them to identify the feelings of the people in the pictures. Discuss what information in the picture cued them to the emotional states of the people. Then ask the students to draw a picture of a time when they felt as the person in the picture feels. Conclude by asking students to discuss their pictures.

■ **I'm New Here (and Scared)**

By Sandra Stroud

Objective: To help students who are new to your community and school make a positive adjustment. For many students, moving to a new school can be an especially traumatic experience.

Grades: K–12

Materials: The *good will* of a group of socially competent student volunteers, and their adult leader—a teacher, guidance counselor, or school administrator.

Teaching Procedures: The adult in charge organizes a school service club whose purpose it is to take new students under its wing and help them feel welcome at their school. Students in this organization can be given sensitivity training to help them understand how new students feel when they move to a new area of the country and enter a new school. The group can discuss and decide upon the many strategies they can use to help new students feel "at home." One of their functions could be to speak to whole classes about how it feels to be a new student at a school, and to suggest how each student at this school can help new students when they arrive.

For a new student, nothing is quite as traumatic when they enter a new school as having no friend or group with whom to sit when they go to the cafeteria for lunch. Therefore, one of a new student's greatest needs is for someone to invite him or her to have lunch with them. This should be the number-one priority of the members of the welcoming club. New students may eventually become members of this club, joining in the effort of welcoming and helping the new students who follow them.

Note: This instructional activity was written by a mother who would have been so grateful if her son's middle school had had such a program when he entered the eighth grade there. As it was, things were pretty rough for him until his band teacher realized that he was skipping lunch. She paved the way for him to begin eating lunch with a group of boys who became his best friends!

■ **I'm in My Own Little House**

By Sandra Stroud

Objective: To help young children acquire a sense of personal "space" as well as an understanding of "other people's space". Many young children have not acquired an inner sense of space—of their own space and of space that belongs to others. As a result, the more active of these youngsters—usually little boys—tend to intrude on other children's space and, in the process, annoy the other children. As a result, they may not be well liked by their classmates. The problem is made worse by the fact that many primary children sit at long tables where the space of one student often overlaps the space of others.

Grades: Primary

Materials: Individual student desks, and colored masking tape.

Teaching Procedure: The teacher arranges the room so that each student desk sits in an area that is three-feet-square. The desks are barely close enough to each other to make it possible for students to pass materials from one student to another without leaving their seats. On the floor around each desk, the teacher outlines the 3-ft.-sq. block with colored masking tape.

The teacher explains the taped areas, or blocks, by telling a story about a child who wanted a little house that was all his own where no one would bother him or his belongings. This was "his" house. Just as his house was his, he knew that the other chil-dren needed their houses and that he shouldn't bother them or their houses either. (Teacher makes up the story according to his or her imagination, or to fit the situation in his or her classroom.)

SUMMARY

This chapter described the social behaviors of students with learning and behavior disorders. Students identified as behavior-disordered display behaviors that are inappropriate and/or harmful to self or others. Many behavior-disordered students have appropriate social skills but do not use them or do not know when and with whom to use them. Other students do not have the skills and need to be taught them.

Students with learning disabilities are frequently identified as having social difficulties. As a group, they are more frequently rejected by their peers and teachers. They have been characterized as having social interaction difficulties, communication difficulties, low role-taking skills, and low self-concepts.

Four interventions to increase appropriate social behavior and decrease inappropriate social behavior were presented: intervention by prescription, interpersonal problem solving, behavior therapy, and ASSET. Intervention by prescription is a model that focuses on the student's impulse management. Appropriate intervention procedures are applied according to the student's need for external control or ability to utilize internal control. Behavioral approaches are utilized when the student has low impulse control and needs external controls; more cognitively oriented interventions are used as the student demonstrates more internal impulse control. Interpersonal problem solving teaches students strategies for communicating effectively with others and solving and preventing interpersonal conflicts with others. Behavioral therapy is based on the principles of applied behavior analysis for increasing and decreasing behaviors.

A number of intervention approaches have been effectively implemented to increase appropriate social behaviors. Four of these approaches were discussed in this chapter and provide effective techniques for developing appropriate social behaviors.

THINK AND APPLY

- What is social competence?
- What are the characteristics of students with social disabilities?
- What are two types of social interventions used with students with learning and behavior problems? What are the procedures for implementing these social interventions?
- What are several principles for teaching social skills to students with learning and behavior problems?
- Why can the communication style of students with learning disabilities be termed egocentric?
- How are student appearance and popularity related?
- Why do students whose behavior is aggressive require professional help?

Chapter 10

Educational Technology

by Arlene Brett, Ph.D.

University of Miami

OUTLINE

KEY TOPICS FOR MASTERY

— *Components of computers and their functions*
— *Role of technology in education*
— *Types and functions of tool software*
— *Functions of word processing and other writing software*
— *Factors to consider when selecting instructional software*
— *Characteristics of multimedia software*
— *Applications of telecommunications in the classroom*

 BRIGHT IDEA

> *Turn to page 443 and read Think and Apply.*

Ms. Kobey's resource room has certainly changed in the last fifteen years. An integral part of the instruction she provides each week to her students with learning and behavior problems includes the use of technology. For example, the students are using word processing as an important tool in their writer's workshop. It is not unusual to find two of her fifth-grade students peer editing at a computer, talking about how to make a report clearer, revising on the screen, and then running a spell check. Ms. Kobey also uses the computer to provide intensive practice of basic math facts and operations, as well as having her early readers read and listen to stories using multimedia programs that read aloud to students. Some of her students exchange letters with students in other parts of the country via electronic mail. Other students are using the Internet to access the home page of the White House to find information for a report on presidents. Mrs. Kobey also uses her computer to write to parents, manage students' records, and to assist in generating IEP's.

This chapter overviews the use of technology, particularly computers, by special education teachers. It provides not only the technology basics but information on tool applications, instructional software, multimedia, and telecommunications and the Internet.

COMPUTER BASICS

Computers and related technology are widely used throughout society and have become increasingly common in educational settings. The student-to-computer ratio in schools has improved to approximately nine to one. However, over half of the computers in schools are outdated and not capable of supporting programs such as multimedia and Internet access (Salvador, 1996). It is important to have adequate and appropriate computer systems so that students can participate in the valuable technological applications currently available.

Selecting computers requires consideration of several factors, including operating system, size, processor speed, memory/storage capabilities, and peripherals. The common brands of computer systems are either IBM and IBM compatible, which use the Windows (Microsoft) operating system, or Macintosh (Apple Computers, Inc.), which use System 7 Operating Software. In general, Macintosh software will not run on Windows computers and vice versa, although some Macintosh computers have a chip which enables them to run IBM software. Macintosh and Windows operating systems are similar in their ease of use. Both have a graphical user interface

(GUI), which provides pull-down menus, windows, and icons that are activated by pointing and clicking, rather than by typing commands. Most software is produced in both Macintosh and Windows versions, but more educational software is currently available for Macintosh than for Windows.

In addition to choosing between Macintosh and Windows environments, consideration should be given to the size (and therefore portability) of the computer. While most special education classrooms have desktop computers, some students with significant learning difficulties are using portable computers (laptops and notebooks) for their personal use as they participate in general education classrooms. For these students, for example those who need a computer for all their writing activities, portability is important (Price, 1994).

All computers, whatever brand or size, are similar in their basic functions: accepting information,

processing information, storing information, and producing output. To accomplish these tasks computer systems are made up of input devices, output devices, a central processing unit, and memory (Figure 10.1).

Input Devices

There are several types of devices used to input data into the computer, but the most common are the keyboard and mouse. A standard computer keyboard has alphanumeric keys, as well as function keys that perform specialized tasks, such as moving a cursor around on the screen, deleting characters, or exiting a program. The functions of these special keys vary according to the software being used.

Students who lack the skills needed to manipulate a standard keyboard or those for whom the keyboard is too cluttered and confusing, may benefit from an alternative keyboard. These keyboards are

■ **FIGURE 10.1** *Elements of a Computer System*

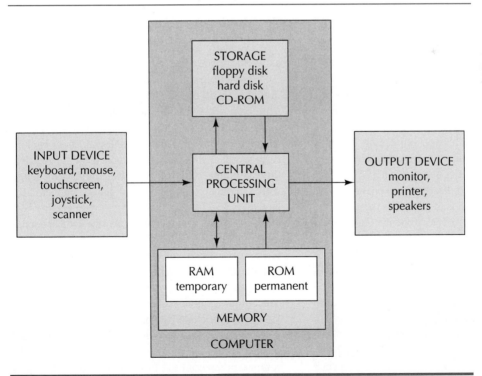

usually larger than standard keyboards and feature fewer keys with more space between each key. *Muppet Learning Keys* (Sunburst), for example, is an alternative keyboard which has large colorful letter and number keys arranged in alphabetical and numerical order. The special function keys are marked with pictures to make them easier to identify. *IntelliKeys* (IntelliTools) and *Concept Keyboard* (Hach Associates) are touch-sensitive keyboards that come with software for creating custom overlays. They can be programmed to have only a few very large keys, represented by pictures or other symbols, as well as letters, numbers, and words.

The mouse is an input device that controls a cursor or pointer on the screen. For most students, mouse input is less demanding than a keyboard. Variations of the mouse include a trackball and trackpad, both of which emulate mouse functions.

Another input device is a touch-sensitive screen such as the *TouchWindow* (Edmark). Students make selections and control the computer by touching different points on the screen. They are able to focus their attention on the screen for both input and output instead of having to shift their attention between the keyboard and the screen.

For students with reading problems, an input device that can be particularly useful is the scanner, which converts pages of printed text or graphics into digital computer input. Once this digital information is entered into the computer, it can be incorporated into word processing, desktop publishing, or other documents or into multimedia presentations. A scanner with optical character recognition (OCR) software and a speech synthesizer can be used as a reading machine. All kinds of text can be scanned into the computer and read back to students. Once text is in the computer it can be enlarged and highlighted to make it easier for students to read on screen. The text can also be printed out in this modified format to create more readable learning materials.

A very promising input technology is speech recognition, which is the ability of the computer to understand and execute spoken commands. This technology is incorporated into the standard operating system of many new computers. The speech recognition software of the Apple Macintosh, for ex-

ample, accepts and executes any computer command spoken aloud, so students can operate the computer by speaking to it.

Output Devices

Information is sent from the computer to one or more output devices, such as monitors or other screen displays, printers, or speakers. Monitors are available in monochrome or color and in various sizes and levels of resolution. The size of text and graphics on the screen can be enlarged for students with learning or visual problems. Large visual display and large printed hard copy can be helpful for students who have problems reading small cluttered pages of print. A large monitor or a liquid crystal display (LCD) panel with an overhead projector is useful for collaborative writing, cooperative learning projects, or large group instruction.

A printer is necessary to produce hard copies of students' work. The most common printers are dot matrix, inkjet, and laser. Dot matrix and inkjet are less expensive than laser printers and are useful for many classroom applications. Laser printers are more versatile and can produce high quality images as well as a wide variety of text.

Computer speech output, either synthesized or digitized, can help support learning (Hebert and Murdock, 1994; Lundberg, 1995; Wise and Olson, 1994). Synthesized speech is produced by storing the sounds of phonemes and then playing them back to form words. This method of speech output requires little computer memory and can output any letter, word, or other combination of letters phonetically. However, synthesized speech varies in quality and may be difficult to understand. Synthesized speech is used in text-to-speech software such as talking word processors, which can read aloud any text entered into the computer. Talking word processors let students hear what they have written, which can enhance the accuracy of their writing (MacArthur, 1996; Raskind and Higgins, 1995).

Digitized speech is made by recording actual speech and converting it into digital format. The computer then converts this digital information back into the original sound. Digitizing produces an accurate replication of language and other sounds, but requires a lot of memory and can only output what has been recorded. This technology is used to produce the high quality speech, music, and other sound found in multimedia CD-ROM software.

Speech-to-text technology is a combination of input and output in which students are able to create text by speaking into the computer. The computer converts their oral language into written text, giving students whose oral language exceeds their written language an alternative means to generate written language. It can also be useful for students who have difficulty typing words because of problems with fine motor skills or spelling (Higgins and Raskind, 1995). IBM's OS/2 Warp operating system includes Voice-Type, which provides voice recognition dictation capabilities. *Dragon Dictate for Windows/DOS* (Dragon Systems, Inc.) and *Power Secretary* (Articulate Systems, Inc.) for Macintosh are also voice recognition dictation systems. Although this technology holds promise for students with learning disabilities, it should still be considered experimental until it is refined to make it easier to use and more accurate in recognizing students' spoken words (Wetzel, 1996).

Central Processing Unit

The actual processing of information is done by the central processing unit (CPU), also called the processor. The CPU carries out instructions and controls the flow of information to other computer components. It determines the overall power of the computer, including how fast it executes commands, how much memory it is able to access, and the amount of information it can process at one time. Software packages usually specify the minimum processor requirements. For example, The Learning Company's *Read, Write, & Type!* program requires at least a 68030/25 megahertz or better processor for Macintosh computers, and 486/25 megahertz or better for Windows.

Memory/Storage

There are two types of computer memory; internal, which is also called primary memory, and external or secondary memory, which is also referred to as storage. Internal memory includes random access memory (RAM) and read only memory (ROM). RAM is the amount of space available to the user for temporarily storing programs and data. Information in RAM is erased when power is turned off. RAM is typically measured in megabytes (approximately 1,000,000 bytes). The computer must have enough RAM to load and run software. RAM requirements are indicated on software packages; for example, *KidWorks Deluxe* requires 8 megabytes of RAM, and *Sammy's Science House* needs 2 megabytes. The other portion of internal memory, read only memory (ROM), contains start-up instructions and is activated when the computer is turned on.

External or secondary memory is typically on magnetic disks or optical discs. Magnetic disks are either floppy or hard disks. Hard disks hold many times more information than floppy disks. Their storage capacity is measured in either megabytes or gigabytes (approximately 1,000,000,000 bytes). Software is usually sold on CD-ROM or on floppy disks and then copied or installed on the user's hard disk.

Optical discs, also known as laser discs, include CD-ROMs and videodiscs. These discs are read with a laser or light beam. They are capable of storing thousands of times more information than magnetic disks. Theoretically, optical discs will not deteriorate in quality since there is no physical contact between the reading device and the disc. CD-ROMs and videodiscs, with their ability to store large amounts of animation and sound, have greatly increased the capabilities of computer software.

THE COMPUTER AS A TOOL

Computers and related technology are utilized in a variety of ways in educational settings. Taylor (1980) categorized these uses as follows:

- As a tool, the computer is used to enhance students' capabilities and help increase the efficiency and quality of their work.
- As a tutor, the computer performs the traditional functions of a teacher, using drill and practice,

tutorial, simulation, problem solving, and exploratory software.

— As a tutee, the computer is programmed or taught by students.

Using the computer as a tool is the most versatile and productive use of computers in schools. Unlike instructional software, which addresses a narrower range of educational goals, tool software can be used across the curriculum to help meet a variety of objectives. Tools not only increase students' productivity, they also help students become more active learners and acquire knowledge in meaningful ways (Grabe and Grabe, 1996). There are many types of tool software, including word processing, desktop publishing, database management, spreadsheet, graphics, and drawing and painting programs (Figure 10.2).

■ **FIGURE 10.2** *Types and Examples of Tool Software*

Type	Examples
Word Processing	*Bank Street Writer* (Scholastic) *Magic Slate* (Sunburst) *WordPerfect* (Novell) *Microsoft Word* (Microsoft) *ClarisWorks* (Claris Corporation) *Microsoft Works* (Microsoft)
Desktop Publishing	*Student Writing Center* (The Learning Company)
Keyboarding	*PAWS in Typing Town* (Thomson Learning Tools) *KidKeys* (Davidson & Associates) *Mavis Bacon Teaches Typing for Kids* (Mindscape) *Read, Write & Type!* (The Learning Company)
Databases	*Field Trip to the Rainforest* (Wings for Learning) *Maps 'n Facts* (Broderbund) *500 Nations* (Microsoft) *Compton's Interactive Encyclopedia* (Compton's New Media) *Grolier Multimedia Encyclopedia* (Grolier Publishing) *Children's World Atlas* (Rand McNally) *TIME Magazine Reference Collection* (SoftKey International, Inc.) *ClarisWorks* (Claris Corporation) *Microsoft Works* (Microsoft)
Spreadsheets	*ClarisWorks* (Claris Corporation) *Microsoft Works* (Microsoft)
Graphics	*Print Shop* (Broderbund) *SuperPrint* (Scholastic) *Award Maker* (Baudville) *Creative Writer* (Microsoft)
Drawing/Painting	*Illustrator* (Adobe) *corelDRAW* (Corel) *KidPix 2* (Broderbund) *Fine Artist* (Microsoft) *ClarisWorks* (Claris Corporation)

Word Processing and Desktop Publishing

Word processing software converts the computer into an electronic tool to enter and edit text, save and load text, and print what has been written. Many word processors include spelling and grammar checkers, thesauruses, and outlining capabilities. Desktop publishing software is similar to word processing, with additional features for formatting text in columns, creating headings, and using different typefaces and fonts to produce a variety of documents. Pictures can be added to the text and edited in different ways. Using desktop publishing software, students can combine pictures and text to produce professional-looking documents.

There are many word processing and desktop publishing programs for students of varying abilities. Student-oriented programs such as *Bank Street Writer* (Scholastic) for grades 3 to 12, and *Magic Slate* (Sunburst) for grades 2 and up, let students begin writing without having to focus on learning the software. *Student Writing Center* (The Learning Company) is a simple desktop publishing program for elementary students. Sophisticated programs such as *WordPerfect* (Novell) and *Microsoft Word* (Microsoft) provide advanced features and are more complicated to learn. Integrated tool software such as *ClarisWorks* (Claris Corporation) and *Microsoft Works* (Microsoft) are easy for students to use. These tools include database, spreadsheet, and other applications as well as word processing. See Apply the Concept 10.1 for a description of integrated software.

Word processing and desktop publishing can be useful in the writing process and writing activities in all areas of the curriculum. They can be powerful tools for helping students with learning and behavior problems who have difficulty with writing tasks. These students typically have problems with the physical process of writing, the conventions of writing, generating content, organizing material, and evaluating and revising their writing. Word processing software can support production of legible text with correct mechanics. It can also help with planning, writing, and revising, as well as with collabo-ration and communication with an audience (Bahr, Nelson, and Van Meter, 1996; MacArthur, 1994; MacArthur, 1996; MacArthur, Graham, Schwartz, and Schafer, 1995; Montague and Fonseca, 1993).

In the *prewriting phase* when students brainstorm, generate ideas, do research, and make a tentative outline, word processing allows them to create lists of ideas in no particular order and then move the ideas around. They can also use outlining software to help them rearrange, categorize, and organize their ideas (Raskind, 1993). Using word processing software, students are relieved of the physical demands of handwriting and the problem of messy erasures.

During the *composing phase* of the writing process, word processors help students concentrate on organizing and connecting their ideas. They can change the order of sentences, insert new ideas, and tie concepts together to produce a first draft. They can think about the meaning of what they are writing instead of focusing on mechanics, knowing that their work can be easily revised. They can save work in progress and go back to it later.

Word processing makes the physical process of revising easier because text can be edited without rewriting the entire paper. However, use of a word processor alone does not teach students how to evaluate and revise. They need strategy instruction and support in order to learn how to improve their writing (Bahr, Nelson, and Van Meter, 1996; MacArthur, 1994).

Word processing can facilitate collaborative writing. Having a legible printed hard copy or text on the screen allows peers to work together on writing projects (MacArthur, 1996). Along with desktop publishing, word processing activities facilitate writing to communicate and writing for an audience. In creating a newsletter for example, students have to modify their writing to meet the needs of a particular audience, which gives them a reason to edit and revise their work.

Software that checks spelling provides significant assistance for poor spellers. It gives them a nonthreatening way to experiment with using words they don't know how to spell. They use longer and more appropriate words knowing the spelling checker can

TECH TALK 10.1

USING MICROCOMPUTERS FOR WORD PROCESSING

Word processing on microcomputers holds great promise not only for students with writing disabilities, but also for students who have problems composing, spelling, or with handwriting. Using word processing software, students can revise and edit text more easily and can publish a neat, legible final product. Reviewing research on the use of microcomputers with students with writing disabilities, Majsterek (1990) observed that research in this area is in its infancy and has yielded mixed findings. Nonetheless, based on the current research, Majsterek made the following initial recommendations about using microcomputers with students with writing disabilities:

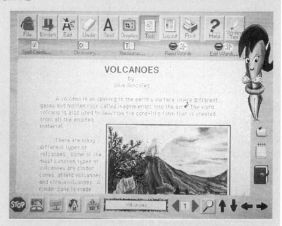

Courtesy of The Learning Company.

- Select computer software that emphasizes a process approach to writing (i.e., prewriting, composing, revising, editing, publishing). Examples are *The Ultimate Writing and Creativity Center* and *Student Writing and Research Center* (The Learning Company, 800-852-2255) *The Writing Workshop* (Milliken Publishing, 1-800-643-0008), and *Kidsworks,* by Davidson & Associates (800-545-7677).
- Select computer software that uses a sequence of menus rather than complicated Control keys or multistep commands.
- Make certain that students are familiar with the writing process before you introduce them to computer software.
- Review the software manual and either adapt for students with reading problems or develop cue sheets to simplify procedures.
- Keep in mind that, for many students, concurrently learning keyboarding, machine skills, and writing software commands can be a demanding task. Teach basic keyboarding and machine skills before you introduce writing-process software.

Courtesy of Davidson & Associates, Inc.

- Keep a balance between writing with and without a word processor so that students will work on handwriting, spelling, and composition skills in both modes.

Source: From S. Vaughn, C. S. Bos and J. S. Schumm (1997). *Teaching Mainstreamed, Diverse, and At-Risk Students in the General Education Classroom* (p. 409). Boston: Allyn and Bacon. Reprinted with permission.

APPLY THE CONCEPT 10.1

INTEGRATED SOFTWARE

Integrated software is a single software package that incorporates several tool functions including word processing, database, spreadsheet, drawing, painting, and communications. Integrated software can be used for many different tasks. It is inexpensive and is often included in the purchase of a computer. In this type of software commands are similar across all applications, so it is easy for students to move from one program to another. Data created using different applications can be combined into one integrated product. Graphs made from a spreadsheet can be imported into a letter, for example, or pictures created in draw or paint applications can be added to a database document.

---

help them. Spelling checkers are limited, however, for the following reasons:

— They flag the words that are not in their dictionary as incorrect (for example, proper nouns).
— They fail to flag errors that are correct spellings of another word (for example, bad for bed).
— They do not supply correct spelling for every misspelled word.

Therefore students should not rely completely on spelling checkers (MacArthur, Graham, Haynes, and DeLaPaz, 1996).

Grammar checkers detect grammar, style, and punctuation errors and provide suggestions on how to correct them. The current versions of this type of software have not been shown to be useful for students with learning disabilities (MacArthur, 1996). Apply the Concept 10.2 describes software that supports writing and helps students complete assignments independently.

Students can use word processing and desktop publishing software in all areas of the curriculum to keep journals and to write letters, stories and reports. They can write and illustrate math story problems for other students to solve, or keep track of and illustrate science experiments. In social studies they can create questionnaires to gather information or create a newspaper about some historic or current event. The list is virtually endless. If writing tools are readily available, students will find many ways to use them.

Keyboarding

While keyboarding is not necessary for using the computer, learning to use the keyboard is an important part of the writing process (Anderson-Inman, Knox-Quinn, and Horney, 1996; MacArthur, Graham, and Schwartz, 1993). When students are able to look at the screen instead of the keyboard, they can focus on what they are writing. Several good keyboarding programs provide basic keyboarding skills:

— *PAWS in Typing Town* (Thomson Learning Tools)
— *KidKeys* (Davidson & Associates)
— *Mavis Bacon Teaches Typing! for Kids* (Mindscape)
— *Read, Write & Type!* (The Learning Company) is an integrated reading, writing, and keyboarding program. It teaches keyboarding by associating sounds with specific fingers. As students learn sounds associated with reading and writing they are also learning their position on the keyboard. This program combines phonemic awareness and keyboarding in a whole language context.

Databases

A database is a collection of information or data stored in digital form on a computer. Database management software provides the ability to enter, store, update, organize, and retrieve information. Although

APPLY THE CONCEPT 10.2

SOFTWARE THAT SUPPORTS INDEPENDENT WRITING

Several types of software are available to help students write independently. Talking word processors help students detect errors in their writing. Examples of talking word processors include:

- *Write:Outloud* (Don Johnston Incorporated), which includes a spelling checker.
- *Write This Way* (Hartley), which highlights spelling and grammatical errors and provides help to correct them.
- *Dr. Peet's Talk/Writer* (Hartley), which is especially for early exploration and discovery of written word. It prints hard copy in standard or large text.
- *KidWorks Deluxe* (Davidson) lets students write and illustrate stories and reads back what they have written.

Word prediction software, such as *Co:Writer* (Don Johnston Incorporated), uses principles of artificial intelligence to predict words from the first one or two letters typed. It provides grammatically correct word choices and correct spelling and automatically capitalizes the first word of each sentence. It provides word choices based on rules of grammar, word relationships, frequency, recency and redundancy of words.

American-Heritage Talking Dictionary (Softkey International) is a dictionary and thesaurus that pronounces words. It has a wildcard feature that lets students put a question mark for letters they are not sure of, making it possible to locate words they don't know how to spell.

not as common in classrooms as word processors, databases are versatile and can be used by students in many ways to meet curricular objectives. There are many instructional applications in which students use existing databases as well as create their own databases about topics in the curriculum.

The number and variety of databases available to students is almost limitless. Software such as *Field Trip to the Rainforest* (Wings for Learning) provides information about plants and animals of the rainforest. *Maps 'n Facts* (Broderbund) is a database of maps and statistical facts about the world. *500 Nations* (Microsoft) provides a rich source of information about Native American tribes, including speech and animation, maps, pictures, videos, and interviews. Multimedia encyclopedias, such as *Compton's Interactive Encyclopedia,* (Compton's New Media) for grades kindergarten through 8 and *Grolier Multimedia Encyclopedia* (Grolier Publishing) for grades 5 through 12, provide information on a wide variety of subjects in the form of text, sound, graphics, and motion. *Children's World Atlas* (Rand McNally) is a database about the world that uses

video clips, photographs, graphs, and fully-narrated descriptions. Other CD-ROM references include *TIME Magazine Reference Collection* (SoftKey International, Inc.) which has in-depth information about the major events of the 20th century.

A wide variety of online databases are available on computer networks such as the Internet and commercial online services. Students use databases to retrieve from a large volume of information what is relevant to a problem, organize and share information, make comparisons, discover commonalities and differences, look for trends, and think critically using data to generate and test hypotheses.

In addition to learning how to find and use information in existing databases, students can create databases of information of interest to them. They determine what information to include, collect the data, and enter it in the database they have created. Once the information has been entered, students can update, organize, retrieve and analyze it.

For example, at the beginning of the year Mrs. Thomas uses *ClarisWorks* software to help her students with behavior and emotional problems create a class database to learn more about each other. After the students decide what information they want to include, Mrs. Thomas helps them designate fields for this information, and students enter the appropriate information about themselves. Figure 10.3 represents a portion of the database created by the students.

Once students have entered their data, Mrs. Thomas helps them organize and search the database in different ways. They sort the information according to students' birth order or favorite subject or to find all the students who were born in August and like math. They form groups to discuss the advantages and disadvantages of being the oldest, middle, youngest, or only child in the family and report to the class. They have a debate as to which is the best subject in school and make graphs to represent the number of students who were born in each of the months. A similar class database could be particularly helpful in an inclusion class to help students focus on their similarities.

Students can also develop databases on presidents, parks, inventions, historic events, famous mathematicians, books, science experiments, and many other topics related to the curriculum. Creating databases gets students actively involved with the subject matter and helps them learn to ask questions and form conclusions. This type of activity involves organizational skills and higher order thinking.

Databases provide students a way to see information organized in a logical format to help them better conceptualize it. Database activities help students categorize, connect, and relate information and use it to draw conclusions (Walker and Williamson, 1995). Specific instruction in information retrieval skills, either from the software itself or through teacher guidance, is necessary to help students with disabilities benefit from database activities (Okolo, Barh, and Rieth, 1993).

Spreadsheets

A spreadsheet, like a database, is a tool for gathering information, manipulating it, and presenting it. A spreadsheet is primarily for numerical data, while databases focus on text. A spreadsheet is a grid of rows and columns. The intersections of rows and columns are cells, which contain text, numbers, or formulas. Formulas are used to calculate new numbers and can be simple mathematical relationships like addition and subtraction or more complex mathematical or statistical relationships such as standard deviation and variance.

Spreadsheet software does accurate calculations of numbers, and enables the user to make quick and easy changes to existing data, then automatically update the calculations. It provides for temporary changing of numbers to see the effect on other numbers for budgetary or other types of forecasting. A powerful feature of many spreadsheet programs is the ability to display data in graphs and charts. By

■ **FIGURE 10.3**   *Class Database*

First Name	Last Name	Birth Month	Birth Order	Best Subject	Favorite Food	How Many Pets
Michael	Paramore	April	Oldest	Science	Chili	1
Joey	Mycek	Feb.	Only	Reading	Cheese	3
Maria	Lopez	Jan.	Middle	Science	Hot dogs	0
Russell	Edwards	April	Youngest	Math	Pizza	2
Manny	Suarez	July	Oldest	Science	Salad	4
Ashley	Northcut	Nov.	Oldest	Reading	Pizza	4
Deanna	Thomas	April	Youngest	Music	Pretzels	0

creating different types of graphs, students are able to visualize numerical relationships that may otherwise be difficult to understand.

In the classroom the use of spreadsheets to perform routine calculations allows students to concentrate on the application and theory instead of getting bogged down in computation. Spreadsheets are helpful in drawing conclusions about how changes affect the bottom line. Spreadsheets are used for budgets, grade books, or any other tasks involving manipulation of numbers. In Ms. Reyes resource science class, students use information from food labels to analyze their own diets. Spreadsheets compute their current caloric and nutrient intake and let students experiment with changes in number and sizes of servings to see the effect on their total number of calories or percentages of the recommended daily allowance (RDA) of nutrients. In Mr. Belido's mathematics class, students have set up a spreadsheet to figure the area and perimeter of rectangles. They use it to experiment with different lengths and widths to make generalizations about how the changes affect perimeter and area. This activity provides a concrete way to see the relationship between the shape of a rectangle and its area. They also use a spreadsheet to solve numeric problems, such as determining how long it will take to save enough money for a bicycle or how much money must be saved each week to have enough in a given amount of time. Students experiment with numbers and draw conclusions based on how the changes affect other values.

In Mr. Leskanic's classroom students use spreadsheet software to record, summarize, and monitor their academic performance and classroom behavior. They keep track of daily points, running totals, and how far they are from their individual goals. The software creates charts and graphs of this information. Figure 10.4 is a portion of the class spreadsheet.

Other Tool Software

In addition to word processing, desktop publishing, database management, and spreadsheet programs, several other tools can prove useful for students and teachers. *Print Shop* (Broderbund), for example, was one of the first graphics utility programs. It is still a popular all purpose program for making banners, signs, stationery, greeting cards, calendars, and other documents combining text and graphics. Programs such as *SuperPrint* (Scholastic) and *Award Maker* (Baudville) also give students and teachers tools for producing bulletin boards, illustrations, awards, letterheads, and a host of other materials. *Creative Writer* (Microsoft) is a multimedia environment with characters and other features to encourage creativity. Students get inspiration, tools, and help needed to explore a variety of writing activities, including stories, poems, banners, newsletters, and greeting cards. Story starters and clip art are available, as well as special letter effects such as color, size, shadows, shaping, sparkle, and fade.

Drawing and painting programs give students and teachers the ability to generate their own pictures. Drawing programs facilitate the production of straight lines, curves, circles, ovals, polygons, and freehand drawings, while paint programs allow for creation of expressive paintings with electronic brushes, pencils, and paints. Highly sophisticated programs such as *Illustrator* (Adobe) and *corelDRAW* (Corel) provide skilled artists the ability to create high-quality art. *KidPix 2* (Broderbund), for children in kindergarten through eighth grade, includes a variety of drawing and painting tools, along with text and picture stamps. Students make pictures and record about 30 seconds of audio to accompany each drawing. *Fine Artist* (Microsoft) is for children eight years of age and older. It includes full-featured painting and drawing tools, along with multimedia projects and provides interactive lessons on basic drawing and perspective. Integrated software such as *ClarisWorks* also includes drawing and painting capabilities.

Other tools that might be particularly helpful for students with learning problems include *Big:Calc* (Don Johnston, Inc.), a calculator program that vocalizes each symbol or operation key as it is pressed, as well as reading the answer. *Graphers* (Sunburst) for kindergarten through fourth grade is a program that constructs graphs from data selected by students. This program does the mechanical and time consuming construction of graphs so students can focus on the meaning.

■ **FIGURE 10.4**   *Class Spreadsheet*

	A	B	C	D	E	F	G	H	I
1	NAME	Mon	Tues	Wed	Thurs	Fri	Cumulative	Target	Points Still
2							Total	Points	Needed
3									
4	Alex	0	2	1			3	20	17
5	Carlos	5	4	4			13	20	7
6	Doyle	3	3	2			8	20	12
7	James	1	2	3			6	20	14
8	Louis	2	4	3			9	20	11
9	Magaly	4	4	3			11	20	9
10	Sharza	2	1	2			5	20	15
11	Taisha	4	3	4			11	20	9

Students enter the number of points they earn each day, and the cumulative total for the week is automatically calculated. At the same time, the number of points still needed is also shown. This spreadsheet shows the number of points through Wednesday.

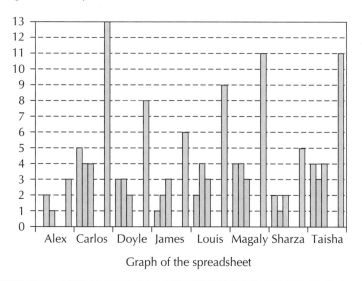

Graph of the spreadsheet

Tool software for teachers includes grade keeping, test making, calendar making, statistical analysis, presentation programs, report generating, and creating teaching aids such as puzzles and worksheets. *Friday Afternoon* (Hartley) for example, produces word-find puzzles, crossword puzzles, bingo cards, flash cards, and worksheets from word banks developed by the teacher. Features such as number of words, level of difficulty, and size of font are determined by the teacher. Teachers can use this software to create products for students with a variety of abilities in any area of the curriculum. Students can also create puzzles, flash cards, and worksheets for each other.

INSTRUCTIONAL SOFTWARE

Computer assisted instruction (CAI), *computer based instruction* (CBI), and *computer as tutor* are all terms that refer to using the computer in an instructional role. The computer in this traditional teacher role provides some type of instructional interaction with students. A variety of good software is necessary in order to use the computer in an instructional capacity.

Types of Instructional Software

Instructional software is traditionally categorized as drill and practice, tutorial, simulation, problem solving, and exploratory. Many instructional programs are a combination of elements from two or more software types.

Drill and Practice
The purpose of drill and practice software is to help students master facts and develop skill fluency, not to understand new material (Grabe and Grabe, 1996). This type of software is intended to supplement instruction already received and provide review and practice of skills. For example *Math Blaster* (Davidson), which provides addition, subtraction, multiplication, and division practice, assumes that students already understand the concept of operations on numbers. *Word Attack 3* (Davidson) is an arcade type program which reinforces vocabulary words. Activities in this program include unscrambling words, matching words with their synonyms, word mazes, and crossword puzzles, all of which give students vocabulary practice.

Tutorial
Tutorial software provides instruction for teaching a new concept or skill. The objectives of this type of software are knowledge acquisition and comprehension. Tutorial software in multimedia format provides a rich learning environment because a variety of media is used to explain ideas and illustrate concepts (MacArthur and Haynes, 1995).

Some tutorials use student responses to determine whether to repeat information or branch to another part of the program. *Mavis Beacon Teaches Typing* (Mindscape), for example, is a keyboarding tutorial that incorporates artificial intelligence to analyze and interpret students' performance and adjust instruction accordingly. Although computer-based tutorials help students learn new material, they are not able to evaluate student responses and respond to students' needs in the same way as teachers do.

Integrated Learning System
Both drill and practice and tutorial software are based on the behavioral approach to learning, in which the goal is to produce a correct response. Some type of feedback or reinforcement is also part of this approach. Another common application of the behavioral approach to instructional software is the *integrated learning system* (ILS), which is a combination of drill and practice and tutorial type software. An ILS assesses students' skills, provides programmed instruction over a network of computers, continuously monitors student progress, adjusts instruction accordingly, and keeps records (Willis, Stephens, and Matthew, 1996). The format of an ILS may be problematic for students with learning problems. Their deficiency in basic skills may prevent them from progressing to activities involving higher level thinking. The progress of these students using an ILS needs to be carefully monitored (Wissick, 1996). Apply the Concept 10.3 provides a description of an integrated learning system.

Problem Solving
Problem solving software presents heuristic problems for which students must figure out or invent solutions. The purpose of this type of software is to

TECH TALK 10.2

COMPUTER-ASSISTED INSTRUCTION

Computer-assisted instruction (CAI) involves learning through the use of computers and multimedia systems. In contrast, computer-managed assessment and instruction uses computers and multimedia systems to obtain and manage information about the learner and learning resources so as to prescribe and better individualize instruction for the students.

What does the research have to say about the effectiveness of computer-assisted instruction? Word processing, paired with writing instruction, consistently produces a positive though relatively small impact on students' writing and their attitude toward writing (Bangert-Drowns, 1993: Cochran-Smith, 1991). Critical to the success of word processing for students with learning disabilities, however, is that it be coupled with systematic instruction in writing (MacArthur, 1993).

The research in reading is also encouraging, although at this point most of the research conducted has been on drill and practice word-recognition programs rather than on multimedia computer systems and CD-ROM books (Higgins & Boone, 1993). Computer-assisted instruction in math has also shown promise (for reviews see Mastroprieri et al., 1991; Woodward & Carnine, 1993).

In *Where in the World is Carmen Sandiego?*® by Broderbund, students explore and learn about dozens of the world's great cities and diverse cultures. School Editions include teacher guides and classroom activities to help teachers provide follow-up activities for the game in which students practice their writing and research skills. Courtesy of Broderbund.

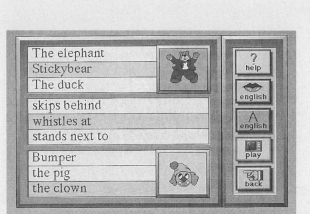

From *Stickybear Reading.* Courtesy of Optimum Resource, Inc.

Source: From S. Vaughn, C. S. Bos and J. S. Schumm (1997). *Teaching Mainstreamed, Diverse, and At-Risk Students in the General Education Classroom* (p. 147). Boston: Allyn and Bacon. Reprinted with permission.

TECH TALK 10.3

VIDEO DISCS AND CD-ROMS HELP TEACH FRACTIONS

Kelly, Carnine, Gersten, and Grossen (1987) compared interactive video disk programs with traditional basal mathematics programs for teaching fractions to students and found that the interactive video programs outscored basal programs on both the post-test and the maintenance checks. The researchers ascribed the success of interactive video disks to the following attributes:

Interactive computer applications also help students visualize information, which fosters problem solving. Shiah, Mastropieri, Scruggs, and Fulk (1994) taught students with learning disabilities to do mathematical word-problem solving on the computer. Students made substantial gains and reported that the pictorial information helped them with word problems.

1. They systematically reviewed previously taught skills.
2. There were discrimination practices among the different strategies.
3. Numerous examples were provided.
4. The terms *numerator* and *denominator* were taught separately.
5. The programs explicitly taught different strategies for problem solving.

© Will Faller

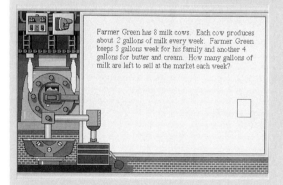

From Stickeybear's Mathtown. Courtesy of Optimum Resource, Inc.

From Math Blaster by Davidson & Associates, Inc.

Source: From S. Vaughn, C. S. Bos and J. S. Schumm (1997). *Teaching Mainstreamed, Diverse, and At-Risk Students in the General Education Classroom* (p. 438). Boston: Allyn and Bacon. Reprinted with permission.

APPLY THE CONCEPT 10.3

INTEGRATED LEARNING SYSTEMS

An integrated learning system (ILS) is a large networked instructional, management, and assessment system which provides an alternative to purchasing individual instructional software. It is composed of *courseware* (lessons, tutorials, skill practice, etc.) that is integrated with existing curriculum and textbooks. It covers one or more curriculum areas (typically math, reading, language arts, science, life skills, and ESL) across a range of grades or levels. The courseware is on a main server, which is connected to several computer stations in a classroom or lab.

The instructional management system of an ILS allows teachers to keep track of student progress and customize the curriculum for particular students or objectives. Each student can be working at a different level or on a different activity, and is assigned to the appropriate activity at the beginning of each session.

An integrated learning system requires a considerable financial investment. Schools need to define what educational problem they want to address with an ILS and work with vendors to customize the ILS environment. Questions to consider when selecting an ILS include:

- Do lessons address important content?
- Is the instructional approach appropriate for the students?
- Is application (rather than memorization) emphasized?
- Will the ILS function as remediation, supplemental instruction, or the principal method of instruction?
- Is an ILS the best use of financial resources?

develop skills in critical thinking. Problem solving software provides an environment for sharing, cooperation, social interaction, and social learning. Programs such as *Strategy Games of the World* (Edmark) help students build and master a set of strategies they can use when they have a problem to solve. Students identify and analyze problems, look for patterns and sequences, break problems into smaller pieces, predict outcomes, eliminate incorrect options, test hypotheses, and synthesize information. This type of program challenges students to think strategically.

Simulation

Simulation software imitates a situation or models the underlying characteristics of a real phenomenon without the limitations of time, distance, cost, or danger associated with the actual situation. Actions that students take in the simulation produce results similar to those in the situation being modeled. This type of software involves application and analysis level of cognition. *Oregon Trail II* (MECC) is an upgraded version of a popular simulation of the journey to the western United States during the mid-1800s. Students make decisions as they face challenges on the trip across the frontier. *Operation Frog* is a science simulation for grades four through ten. Students use this software to participate in a frog dissection, including selection of instruments, removal of body organs, and investigation of body systems.

Problem solving and simulation programs are designed to help students explore possible solutions to problems and discover the consequences of these options. Students with learning problems often lack the strategies for this type of activity. They think the goal of these programs is to win a game, not solve a problem. These students need modeling and guidance in order to benefit from problem solving and simulation software (Okolo, Bahr, and Rieth, 1993).

Exploratory Environment

Exploratory environment software presents material in multimedia format for students to explore and manipulate. This type of software provides information with a high degree of learner control and many options as to how it will be experienced. In *Sammy's Science House* (Edmark), preschool to second-grade students explore science concepts. They build machines and toys, explore weather conditions, sequence pictures to create films, sort pictures of plants, animals, and minerals, and discover how nature and wildlife change from season to season. *Interactive Math Journey* (The Learning Company) provides exploration activities to develop math skills for elementary school students.

Simulation, problem solving, and exploratory programs are based on the constructivist perspective. Learning is viewed as an active process in which students construct new knowledge through exploration and discovery. Knowledge and understanding is pro-duced by students, rather than received from external sources. The teacher's role is one of facilitator and support person rather than dispenser of information. Table 10.1 summarizes the strengths and weaknesses of various types of instructional software.

Students with learning and behavior problems spend more of their time working on drill and practice and tutorial than on constructivist types of software, because these students generally have more need for practice and review than typical learners. Students with reading disabilities, for example, need many opportunities for practice of word reading skills. The computer is an effective vehicle for delivering practice in basic skills (Edwards, Blackhurst, and Koorland, 1995; Okolo, Bahr, and Rieth, 1993;

■ TABLE 10.1   *Advantages and Disadvantages of Instructional Software*

	Advantages	Disadvantages
Drill and Practice	Provides review and practice of skills Motivating Provides feedback Keeps record of responses	Underutilization of computer capabilities Doesn't promote complex thinking May be monotonous
Tutorial	Provides acquisition of new knowledge Provides ability to learn independently Multimedia format presents a rich learning environment	May not accurately evaluate student learning May not meet students' instructional needs
Problem solving	Promotes sharing, cooperation, social interaction, and social learning Promotes critical thinking skills	Students may fail to attend to all the variables Students may interpret the purpose as winning a game, not solving a problem
Simulation	Presents situations otherwise not available Promotes higher-order thinking	Students may fail to discover basic principles Students may draw incorrect conclusions
Exploratory	Gives students a high degree of control over their learning Promotes discovery learning Sound and graphics bypass reading barrier	Students may make poor choices and not get full benefit of the program Students may be overwhelmed or get lost in the program

Wilson, Majsterek, and Simmons, 1996), but teachers need to make sure their students have an opportunity to work with all types of software.

Evaluating Instructional Software

The first step in evaluating software is to establish the purpose for which it will be used. Although many forms for evaluating software are available through organizations, textbooks, journals, and other sources, teachers should develop their own checklists or modify existing instruments according to their particular needs. Figure 10.5 is a checklist of basic characteristics to look for in evaluating software.

Additional considerations in evaluating software for students with special needs include the following:

- The amount and kind of learner control should be related to the nature and degree of student's disability. Students with minor disabilities benefit from a high degree of control over the program.
- Directional feedback is more efficient than motivational feedback.
- Graphics should contribute to the instructional function.
- Screen design should be functional and clear and contribute to the learning process (Larsen, 1995).

Students report that they prefer programs that are challenging, provide clear and concise directions, are visually appealing, and allow them to control the program (Mauldin, 1996).

A number of sources provide software reviews. See Table 10.2 for sources of these reviews.

Multimedia

Multimedia refers to the use of computers to present information in the form of text, images, graphics, sound, animation, and motion video linked together in a nonlinear format. Multimedia is an extension of hypertext, a term coined by Ted Nelson in 1965 to describe using computers to present textual information in nonlinear ways. In hypertext, information contains many juncture points, called *links,* where students can jump to another place in the same text or in different texts. The term hypertext was expanded to hypermedia, which is now more commonly referred to as multimedia. Multimedia computer programs control the presentation of text, graphics, and sound information from CD-ROM, as well as video information from videodiscs or videotape.

Multimedia Software

Multimedia technology has changed the nature of software. Multimedia software is interactive and exploratory. Information is connected by links, so students are not locked into a linear or sequential presentation. Instead, they navigate through programs, choosing from among many options. They can browse or look for specific information. They are free to explore multiple pathways, and, to some extent, control the content of the software.

Electronic books incorporate multimedia technology to expand on the text of a story with animated characters, music, sound effects, and colorful graphics. Stories are read aloud, and words are highlighted as they are spoken. Students can select words for pronunciation and, in some programs, have them defined and illustrated. *Just Grandma and Me* (Broderbund) is an interactive story which can be read in English, Spanish, or Japanese.

Electronic books have been expanded to include activities that target skills in phonics, word recognition, and comprehension. In *Franklin's Reading World* (Sanctuary Woods), students explore Franklin's favorite haunts and play word, sentence, and memory games. Activities are designed to develop phonemic awareness, word recognition, sentence comprehension, and spelling. *The Adventures of Ricky Raccoon* (Thomson Learning Tools) includes graphics and animation to illustrate and support the text. The interactive dictionary lets children hear the pronunciation and definition of a word, along with its use in context in a sentence. These programs provide highly supported reading practice for at-risk readers and make the experience of

■ **FIGURE 10.5** *Basic Characteristics to Consider in Evaluating Software*

Hardware Compatibility

- Compatible operating system
- Sufficient RAM
- Sufficient hard disk space
- Necessary peripherals such as CD-ROM drive, printer, alternative input device, or videodisc player

Content

- Program fits the educational goals and supports the curriculum and the individual educational programs of the students.
- Goals and objectives are clearly stated.
- Stated objectives are met.
- Content is accurate and of sufficient depth.
- Program is free of bias and stereotypes.
- Content is at a level appropriate to students.
- Logical learning sequence is evident, with a low entry and high ceiling.
- Content is suitable for multiple purposes for integration into different curriculum areas and classroom situations.

Methodology

- Instructional approach is appropriate and active discovery learning is emphasized.
- High degree of student involvement is evident.
- Students are agents of change; consistent cause and effect is evident.
- Feedback is appropriate, varied, and able to be understood by students.
- Prompts and other strategies for getting the correct answer are provided.
- Students are led through the information in a logical way.
- Branching depends on students' responses.

Utilization

- Students can control the interaction and the rate of presentation and stop at any point in the program.
- Teachers can change parameters, such as speed of presentation and level of difficulty.
- Students can use the software independently after initial help. Picture menus, simple and precise directions, and onscreen help are available.
- Program can be used by individuals, pairs, small groups or the whole class.
- Program encourages cooperation and interaction.
- Documentation includes objectives, lesson plans, resources and clear directions for the user.
- Management or record keeping component is easy to use.

independent reading available to all students (Torgesen and Barker, 1995).

Some multimedia programs incorporate videodiscs, which provide high quality motion video. In *Animal Pathfinders* (Scholastic), students explore relationships between animals, their habitats, and their behaviors. Students view information on the computer screen and the related video segment on the

■ **TABLE 10.2**   *Sources of Software Reviews*

Software Reviews	Description

Children's Software Review
Publisher:
    Children's Software Review
    Flemington, NJ.
	Previews new software for children 3 to 14 years of age; maintains a cumulative listing of the best titles.

Educational Software and Preview Guide
Publisher:
    International Society for Technology in Education
    Eugene, OR.
	Describes software which has been reviewed for kindergarten through 12th grade classrooms.

High/Scope Buyer's Guide to Children's Software
Publisher:
    High Scope Educational Research Foundation
    Ypsilanti, MI.
	Provides criteria and a rating scale for reviewing software, as well as reviews of programs for children 3 to 7 years of age.

Multimedia Home Companion for Parents and Kids
Publisher:
    Warner Books
    666 Fifth Avenue
    New York, NY.
	Reviews multimedia software for children.

Only the Best
Publisher:
    Association for Supervision and Curriculum
    Development
    Alexandria, VA.
	Includes descriptions of software that received good to excellent ratings from multiple reviewers.

Technology and Learning
    online World Wide Web site at
    http://www.techlearning.com
	Provides searchable software reviews.

color monitor simultaneously. This type of software requires a videodisc player in addition to a multimedia computer system.

Multimedia software, like instructional software in general, should support the goals of the curriculum and the students' IEPs. The content of the software should be coherent, accurate, and appropriate for the students using it. Criteria unique to multimedia software include:

— Clear organization
— Easy navigation
— Ability to print text and images

— High level of interaction between students and the program
— Interactive options with a clear purpose that does not detract from the learning process
— Level of thinking and type of interaction that are appropriate for the students (Phillips, 1996)

The multisensory input and output of multimedia can be especially helpful for students with processing and attentional problems. Many students who are unable to read and write are skilled at getting information from nontextual sources. Students who are impulsive, have spatial difficulties, or are

TECH TALK 10.4

INTERACTIVE MULTIMEDIA

Today teachers and students can design and create multimedia programs of their own to address instructional goals. Interactive multimedia combines on a CD-ROM or videodisc different kinds of information (such as graphics, photos, sound, video, and text) that can be accessed in any order through hypermedia. Hypermedia refers to links in a program that give the "hyperlearner" random access to the contents by clicking on words or images.

Courtesy of Video Discovery.

Authoring tools such as HyperCard, The Digital Chisel, and PowerPoint permit teachers to create their own interactive multimedia lessons. As an alternative to starting from scratch, teachers can also select, reorder, and customize components from databases called "tool kits." For example, the *Bio-Sci II* videodisc tool kit from VideoDiscovery (800-548-3472) is a large database of images, film clips, and textual data on the natural sciences. Teachers can use key words to locate specific topics and resources. They then select, resequence, and add their own material to incorporate their selections into a lesson. Software manufacturers offer many services for "adaptive software" users. For example, Pierian Spring Software (800-472-8578), which publishes the *Digital Chisel,* offers a monthly subscription to educational "clip media" that teachers can integrate into multimedia lessons.

Students and teachers can both benefit from being involved in a cutting-edge creative process. Teachers can develop unique and effective teaching materials, and involving students in creating interactive multimedia can boost motivation and support active learning, cooperative learning, interdisciplinary learning, and individualized instruction.

For more information, see:

Abrams, Arnie H. (1996). *Multimedia Magic* (Boston: Allyn and Bacon).
Collin, Simon. (1994). *The Way Multimedia Works.* (Redmond, WA: Microsoft Press)
Gertler, Nat. (1994). *Multimedia Illustrated.* (Indianapolis, IN: Que Corporation)
Murie, Michael. (1994). *Multimedia Starter Kit for MacIntosh* (Indianapolis, IN: Hayden Books).

Source: From S. Vaughn, C. S. Bos and J. S. Schumm (1997). *Teaching Mainstreamed, Diverse, and At-Risk Students in the General Education Classroom* (p. 210). Boston: Allyn and Bacon. Reprinted with permission.

easily distracted will not benefit from these programs without a teacher who can facilitate their use (Wise and Olson, 1994; Wissick, 1996).

Creating Multimedia

In addition to exploring and learning from multimedia software, students can design and create their own multimedia material. The creation of multimedia involves students as active participants and provides opportunities to engage in authentic reading and writing experiences. They have to understand the material and think through how to represent and communicate their ideas (Grabe and Grabe, 1996). Students creating multimedia are engaged in decision making, development of research skills, cooperative learning, and problem solving. For students who have difficulty demonstrating their understanding, multimedia tools provide alternatives to typical written and oral presentations. Creating multimedia helps students explore content and represent ideas using their own modes of expression.

Students create multimedia projects using words, images and sound. A report on whales, for example, could include written text from a CD-ROM database, imported clip art, drawings, moving pictures from a videodisc, and recorded sound, all linked together in some logical way. Students could write a story with more than one possible ending, record a sound track by reading the story and adding sound effects, and make a page about the authors including scanning in their own photos.

Criteria for judging student multimedia productions are different from those of linear, text-based reports. Students need to articulate the questions that motivated their research and describe how they planned the project. The variety and appropriateness of their sources of material, along with the organization of information, navigation, and media integration are also important (Brunner, 1996).

Creating multimedia requires some additional hardware and software. Sounds, images, and movies must be digitized, which can be done in a number of ways. Voices or other sounds are recorded using a microphone. Photographs taken with a 35 mm camera can be developed as a photo CD, which is digitized information that can be imported into multimedia. Pictures can also be taken with a digital camera, such as Apple's QuickTake or Kodak Digital Science Camera. These filmless cameras take digitized photographs that are instantly transferred from the camera to the computer. A desktop scanner digitizes existing pictures, maps, charts, diagrams, cartoons, and other visual images so they can be incorporated into computer files. Once a picture is imported into a multimedia project it can be edited in a number of ways, including resizing, rotating, and cropping. Pictures can also be drawn or painted, and clip art can be imported from other software. Motion video can be added by connecting the computer to a videodisc player. Video can also be captured from a camcorder or video cassette player through video

input cards and translated into digital format for storage by the computer. A multimedia computer with appropriate software integrates the components into a single multimedia presentation.

Multimedia authoring software for students includes *Digital Chisel* (Perian Springs), *Kid's Studio* (Storm Software, Inc.), and *HyperStudio* (Roger Wagner Publishing). Using authoring software, students can put their writing together with sound and visual images in one presentation. Students are able to acquire the skills to use authoring software if instruction is structured and sequential (Daiute and Morse, 1994; Ferretti and Okolo 1996, Wissick, 1996). Teachers need to adapt the multimedia authoring process for students with learning disabilities. In addition to providing a variety of supports around concrete guidelines, the learning objectives and activities may have to be adjusted to fit students' abilities (Moeller and Jeffers, 1996). Apply the Concept 10.4 provides suggestions for integrating technology into the classroom.

TELECOMMUNICATIONS AND THE INTERNET

The power and versatility of the computer can be significantly enhanced through communication with other computers. Computers communicate through networks connected by cables, telephone lines, or some type of wireless transmission. A network of computers and peripherals in the same room, building, or general vicinity is a local area network (LAN). This type of network allows sharing of hardware, such as printers and scanners, as well as sharing of software and information. It also provides electronic mail and other forms of communication. Local area networks make possible collaborative writing and editing, data collection, and sharing of information.

Computer networking can be extended beyond classrooms and schools to remote sites ranging from other schools in the same district to national and international sites. Individual computers and local area networks are interconnected to form a wide area

APPLY THE CONCEPT 10.4

TIPS FOR INTEGRATING TECHNOLOGY INTO THE CLASSROOM

Recommended practices to make technology a curriculum tool rather than the focus of the curriculum are as follows:

1. Place technology throughout the room so it is available for use by students when they need it.
2. Give students full access to the hardware and software and let them learn how to use it.
3. Encourage a group of students to learn to use a new piece of software and let them teach it to the rest of the students.

4. Use technology to provide new ways of acquiring and representing knowledge.
5. Give students a lot of time to play with and experiment with technology before they use it to accomplish specific tasks.
6. Let students use technology to solve real problems.

Source: Adapted from E. Prickett, K. Higgins and R. Boone (1994). Technology for Learning . . . Not Learning About Technology. *Teaching Exceptional Children, 26*(4), pp. 56–60.

---

network (WAN). These larger connections create greater communication and sharing possibilities.

The Internet

The Internet is a network of computers connected together around the world. It is a global wide area network composed of many individual computers and local area networks. The Internet was created as a nonprofit medium for the government and for universities to conduct research, but in the past few years it has expanded to include a wide spectrum of commercial operations. Unlike commercial online services, the Internet is not privately owned and is not centrally controlled.

Students can use the Internet to send and receive electronic mail, browse databases of information (WWW, Gopher, WAIS), login to remote computers (Telnet), join special interest discussion groups (Usenet) and send and receive programs (FTP). Figure 10.6 summarizes these Internet services.

Electronic mail transmits messages over computer networks and provides a way for people all over the world to communicate with each other instantly. Email delivers messages and generates responses quickly and inexpensively enabling students

■ **FIGURE 10.6**   *Internet Services*

- Electronic mail transmits messages over computer networks.
- Browsers are used to find information in databases on the Internet. Browsers include:
  - The World Wide Web (WWW), which organizes information on the Internet in hypermedia links
  - Gopher, which is a menu system for browsing text information on the Internet
  - Wide Area Information Service (WAIS), which uses keywords to search specific databases such as ERIC
- Telnet provides access to public resources, such as universities and libraries.
- Usenet is an international collection of discussion groups on a wide variety of topics.
- File Transfer Protocol (FTP) provides the ability to transfer files from remote computers.

---

to communicate with people locally or far away. Email can also be used to get information from databases. For example questions can be sent to ERIC via email (askeric@ericir.syr.edu) and will be answered within forty-eight hours. A wide variety of learning projects can be implemented using email.

A form of electronic mail called a listserv is a mailing list about a particular subject. Listservs are user-subscribed services which distribute files and information to their members. Copies of articles submitted by members of the mailing list are sent by email to all other subscribers of that list. Listservs provide a way to get information from specialists or experts in a field and to stay current on topics. The Internet has many listservs on a wide variety of topics, including ALLMUSIC for students interested in all forms of music, ARTIST-L for student artists, and KIDZMAIL, which is a discussion list for children.

Browsing the many databases on the Internet can be accomplished in a number of ways including the World Wide Web, Gopher, and WAIS. The World Wide Web (WWW) is the most popular Internet service. It organizes information on the Internet as a set of hypertext documents connected by hypertext links, as well as hypermedia links to graphics, video, and sound files (Ryder and Hughes, 1997). Web browsers such as *Netscape Navigator* (Netscape Communications Corporation) and *Mosaic* (freeware) provide a graphical user interface in which links and commands are activated by clicking on icons, images, or underlined text. This hypertext format simplifies accessing information so students can focus on what they want instead of how to get it. Apply the Concept 10.5 lists interesting Web sites for students. Yahoo (www.yahoo.com) is a catalog of the Web. It provides thousands of subject-sorted links to Web pages.

Gopher is a huge menu system for browsing text information on the Internet. It is a tool that arranges electronic information into online menu systems organized by subject. Navigation is done through a hierarchy of menus from which data can be viewed, saved, or mailed. Gopher will "go for" files and bring them back automatically. There are gopher sites around the world that contain materials of interest to students. For example, United Nations gopher (gopher://nyork1.undp.org) has U.N. documents along with many databases on political and social topics.

Wide Area Information Service (WAIS) is another tool for searching databases. WAIS allows students to choose a source or database, such as ERIC, for example, and conduct a search using one or more keywords. WAIS contacts the database and returns a list of items that contain the keywords. The items are ranked according to how closely they match the keywords.

Telnet is a program that provides access to resources on remote computers. It can be used to log onto public resources such as universities, the Library of Congress, and the NASA Spacelink information services for educators (telnet://spacelinc.msfc.nasa.gov). Hytelnet is a hypertext interface to locate and work with resources accessible by Telnet.

Usenet is a world-wide collection of computers with "bulletin boards" where messages are posted for everyone to read and respond. It is an international collection of discussion groups, called newsgroups, on a wide variety of topics. Students can subscribe to a newsgroup free of charge and read any articles that have been posted by other subscribers around the world. Most newsgroups post a list of Frequently Asked Questions (FAQ, pronounced "faks") about their particular topic, which is usually very informative and helpful. Education newsgroups include an elementary student chat (news:K12.chat.elementary), teaching language arts (news:K12.lang.arts), and a newsgroup for K-12 teachers (news:k12.chat.teachers). Internet relay chat (IRC) is like a live Usenet. People from around the globe can log into hundreds of chat lines called channels and participate in a live discussion. These discussion groups are widely used by individuals with disabilities, particularly those with hearing impairments.

File Transfer Protocol (FTP) provides easy access to files from remote locations. An FTP site lets students log onto a remote computer and browse through directories and filenames. They can download or transfer copies of files containing text, graphics, audio, or video from other computers networked to the Internet. Project Gutenberg (ftp.deneva.sdd.trw.com), for example, has thousands of out-of-copyright books and historical documents. Using FTP students can download the complete works of William Shakespeare or a movie of Mars taken from the Hubble Space telescope. Archie is an information service that maintains a database of anonymous FTP sites. By connecting to an Archie site, students can search for a filename or keyword.

APPLY THE CONCEPT 10.5

INTERESTING WEB SITES

ExploraNet: The Exploratorium at San Francisco (http://www.exploratorium.edu/) is a science-oriented museum with many interactive learning activities. It has online versions of the museum's exhibits along with instructions on how to build them. Each month there is a list of Ten Cool Sites in science, art, and education.

  Field Museum Online Dinosaurs (http://www. bvis.uic.edu/museum/Dna_To_Dinosaurs.html) has pictures and information on dinosaurs with a lot of sound and animation.

  Megamathematics (http://www.c3.lanl.gov/ mega-math/) explores new ideas in math in ways that are accessible to children. For example, students act out the operation of a finite state machine to help them understand systems that recognize and identify patterns. Activities are connected to NCTM standards.

  Metropolitan Museum of Art (http://www. metmuseum.org/) provides a tour of the collections on display in the galleries. Students view collections along with information about each of them. Paintings and other works can be downloaded into documents or multimedia presentations.

  NASA, the National Air and Space Administration (http://www.nasa/gov/) provides rich sources of information about space exploration. Today at NASA provides links to recent events such as the actual text of the press release about evidence of primitive life on Mars. The Gallery contains video and audio clips as well as still images, which can be downloaded. The Questions and Answers section has the most commonly sought information about the United States space program. Space Science provides information on NASA's planetary exploration, astronomy, and research into the origins of life.

  The White House (http://www.whitehouse.gov/) provides tours and multimedia information about the White House, the executive branch of the government, and the first family. Students can search White House documents and listen to speeches or visit the Help Desk for frequently asked questions. The White House for Kids section has information on White House pets with text and pictures. Caroline Kennedy's pony, Macaroni, and Socks, the Clinton's cat, are among the featured pets.

  Web site addresses or servers may change. If the Uniform Resource Locators (URLS) for these Web sites have changed or the server is not responding, a search engine such as Lycos (http://www.lycos.com/), Webcrawler (http:// webcrawler.com/), or Yahoo (http://www.yahoo.com/) can be used to get an updated URL.

Commercial Online Services

A number of companies including *America Online, CompuServe,* and *Prodigy* provide services such as email, conferencing, databases, and Internet access for a membership fee and additional connect-time charges. *America Online,* for example, provides news, finance, travel, marketplace, entertainment, education, sports, references, kids only, and Internet connection. The education section connects to the Smithsonian and to the Library of Congress. It also has the *Scholastic Network,* in which authors of children's books direct writing workshops and respond to students' questions. Students can send in stories and have an author suggest endings, for example. Commercial online services provide information and assistance for new subscribers, as well as their own telecommunications software.

  A commercial online service of particular interest to classroom teachers is *Kids' Network* (National Geographic), which allows students to participate in science and geography projects. In one such project, students collect information about acid rain in their local area and send it to a central computer. Data from around the country is compiled and sent back to individual schools to be analyzed by students and applied to local problems. Activities such as this give students experience with "real" science research and a sense of contributing to the scientific knowledge base. Having the project on-line also facilitates the sharing of projects with other students and with scientists.

Classroom Applications

Telecommunications can be used in the classroom in many different ways across all curriculum areas. Berenfeld (1996) categorized telecommunications activities into five educational functionalities: tele-access, virtual publishing, tele-presence, tele-mentoring, and tele-sharing.

Tele-access is the use of online resources such as online libraries, databases, and museums to search for real-world information. Students can access remote sources and retrieve all kinds of data, including text, photos, and maps. They can find current information, such as the latest space shuttle photos and pending Congressional legislation. Using online resources, students are able to get information to solve problems and construct their own knowledge. Students who have reading or other learning problems can retrieve information and have it printed out in large print or read aloud by the computer.

Virtual publishing provides a way for students' work to reach audiences beyond the classroom. Classes or individual students can publish poetry, stories, newsletters, or results of science projects, all of which can include graphics and animation along with text. For example, a class study of the local community could result in publication of an online hypermedia documentary about the community. At the most basic level, email can be used to communicate with other classrooms, locally, nationally, or even internationally.

Tele-presence lets students experience events at remote sites. They can journey on real expeditions and look over the shoulder of a scientist. The JASON Project, for example, (http://seawifs.gsfc.nasa.gov/JASON.html) is a live interactive program in which students use the Internet to join scientists investigating the Florida Everglades and Florida Bay. Tele-presence brings the real world into the classroom. Students can learn first hand rather than through symbolic representations.

Tele-mentoring gives students the opportunity to learn from authors, scientists, and other experts. Sites on the Internet, such as professional groups and bulletin boards, are responsive to student inquiries and will answer questions and provide information. The Ask-A-Geologist Program (walrus.wr.usgs.gov/docks/ask-a-) sponsored by US Department of Interior, for example, lets students interact with geologists. Some authors and other professionals publish their email addresses so students can correspond with them. These individuals provide positive role models for students as well as support and mentoring.

Tele-sharing can range from simple email chats between students to elaborate cooperative learning projects involving sharing resources, ideas, experiences, data, and findings. The k12net, for example, provides foreign language discussions where students studying a foreign language can interact with native speakers from other countries. These authentic contacts with native speakers provide practice in a range of skills including reading and writing to develop cultural awareness and communicative competence. Foreign language literacy is promoted in a context for genuine writing. Socially, students develop friendships with computer pen pals, called keypals, using email or leaving messages on bulletin boards.

Students using online activities are able to:

— Work for longer periods of time
— Take on more responsibility for their own learning
— Communicate and produce at a higher level
— Collaborate with peers more effectively
— Take more interest in world events and in understanding the world of adults
— Better understand the ideas they encounter
— Communicate with adults they have never met (Dyrli and Kinnaman, 1996)

These activities help students learn to rely on primary sources of data, develop critical thinking skills, and perceive knowledge as constructed (Ryder and Hughes, 1997). For students with learning problems, telecommunication provides access to people and information that would be less available to them. They

TECH TALK 10.5

TEACHER COLLABORATION AND COMPUTERS

Through the use of computer software, teachers can collaborate with school personnel in other cities, states, and even different countries. Synchronous collaboration occurs when the individuals involved interact at the same time (Collis & Heeren, 1993). *Aspects* is an example of a computer program that enables the user to engage in synchronous collaboration. This computer program allows its users to open and work on the same file(s). Changes made to the file by one user will appear on the screens of all of the current participants. In this manner, users can work together, simultaneously changing text files and drawing files of a shared document. *Aspects* is available from Group Logic (telephone 1-800-476-8781).

Asynchronous collaboration occurs when the participants communicate with each other not only from different places, but also at different times (Collis & Heeren, 1993). For example, *Common Knowledge* allows its users to modify a shared document at any time. Each user then has access to the most recent version of the document, as well as its original version. Commands within the program allow the user to view which specific changes have been made to the document, when these changes were made, and by whom. *Common Knowledge* is available from On Technology (telephone 1-800-548-8871). Technological advancements such as *Aspects* and *Common Knowledge* provide teachers with greater opportunities and increased flexibility in collaboration.

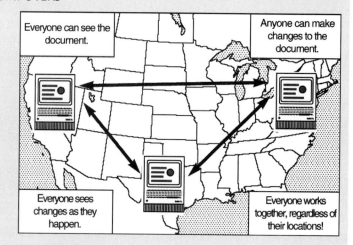

Everyone can see the document.

Anyone can make changes to the document.

Everyone sees changes as they happen.

Everyone works together, regardless of their locations!

Courtesy of Group Logic Inc.

Newsletter Production Schedules

| | | | | Created By: Christine Traulich Tue, 4/25/95 12:31 PM | Modified By: Christine Traulich |

ON Technology

Q2 Newsletter Production Schedules

NEWSLETTER ITEM	SENT TO ART DEPT	WORD COUNT	DUE	DESCRIPTION OF JOB	PERSON RESPONSIBLE
Product Ads		N/A	5/1/95	CK, MMXP, Catalog, DV or I/O?	ckt/pm
Reply Card		N/A	5/1/95		ckt
Title&heading p2&3		N/A	5/1/95		ckt/pm/kd
Table of Contents			5/1/95		ckt/pm
Masthead text		N/A	5/1/95		ckt/pm
Footers p2&3		N/A	5/11/95	FREE trial product name & 800 #	ckt/pm
Article1	4/18/95	770	5/1/95	Common Knowledge main story	ckt
Graphic 1, p.1	4/18/95	N/A	5/1/95	CKMAIN.BMP	ckt
Graphic 1a&1b	4/18/95	N/A	5/11/95	CK.SAM2.BMP and CK Mac screen shot	ckt
Caption 1			5/1/95	For CK screen shots (graphics 1a & 1b)	ckt
Article 2			5/1/95	In or Out? Case Study story	pm
Article 3			5/1/95	In or Out? main story	pm

Courtesy of On Technology Corporation.

Source: From S. Vaughn, C. S. Bos and J. S. Schumm (1997). *Teaching Mainstreamed, Diverse, and At-Risk Students in the General Education Classroom* (p. 125). Boston: Allyn and Bacon. Reprinted with permission.

can expand their interests without being impeded by their disabilities.

The Internet and other online databases provide a way for teachers to access information and share it with each other. Houghton Mifflin's *Education Place* (http://www.eduplace.com), for example, helps teachers integrate the resources of the Internet into the curriculum. Scholastic Network sponsors a series of online discussions on strategies and resources for teaching reading. The Council for Exceptional Children's Web site (http://www.cec.sped.org) has a variety of features including highlights of publications and information on professional development opportunities. *Poor Richard's Publishing* (rwanderman@aol.com) is a forum for questions, answers, access to software, papers, and other resources on learning disabilities.

SUMMARY

Technology is being used in classrooms in productive and exciting ways. Students are gathering information from databases in the classroom and around the world. They are using word processing, desktop publishing, spreadsheet, and graphics software to organize, share, and present this information. Specialized tools, such as talking word processors, spelling checkers, and word prediction are providing support for students who have difficulty with writing.

Students are learning independently from tutorials and exploratory environments and developing mathematics and science reasoning from simulations. They are using instructional software to practice skills and to support construction of knowledge and higher order thinking. Faster and more powerful computers with multimedia capabilities are presenting multisensory experiences, which are particularly helpful for students with learning and behavior problems. High quality speech along with graphics and animation are helping students with reading problems to learn independently.

Technology supports instruction, learning, and inquiry and has the potential to enhance the independence, integration, and well-being of students with learning and behavior problems. While these students will need guidance and structured experiences to benefit from new and more sophisticated technology, it is one of the most promising accommodations we can use with these students to help them reach their potential.

THINK AND APPLY

- Describe the functions of each of the components of a computer system.
- Describe different roles computers might fill in your classroom.
- Describe how tool software can be integrated into the curriculum.
- What factors would you consider when selecting instructional software for your students?
- What are the unique characteristics of multimedia software?
- How can creating multimedia projects benefit students?
- Describe the Internet and give examples of how it can be used in the classroom.
- What is a Logo environment?

Chapter 11

Consultant, Collaborator, and Coteacher

OUTLINE

KEY TOPICS FOR MASTERY

— *Arranging the instructional environment of the special education classroom for large-group instruction, small-group instruction, one-to-one instruction, independent learning, collaborative/cooperative learning, and peer teaching*

— *Arranging the physical environment of the special education classroom*

— *Selecting, developing, and organizing instructional materials and equipment*

— *Scheduling considerations: meeting the needs of special education students and their regular classroom teachers*

— *Classroom management practices that help create an environment in which instruction and learning can occur*

— *Mainstreaming special education students: some of the problems and solutions*

— *Working with regular education teachers to ensure the success of mainstreamed special education students*

— *Three models for consultation and collaboration: Coteaching; Teacher Assistance Teams; Collaboration in the Schools*

 BRIGHT IDEA

Turn to page 481 and read Think and Apply.

When I first decided to be a special education teacher it was because I wanted to help the kids. I felt that I could make a difference in their lives, both educationally and social-emotionally, and I can honestly say I have. Recently, though, I was beginning to feel frustrated as a special education resource room teacher. I was spending 90 percent of my time in my special education classroom working with fairly large, heterogeneous groups of children. While I felt I was still making a difference, I was concerned that there was lots more I should be doing, particularly in the regular education classroom where my students spent more than 50 percent of their day. Another one of my concerns was with the intensity of instruction my students were receiving. I was certain that, as the groups in my resource room were getting larger, the quality of instruction I was able to offer my students was reduced. There were some students who I know would learn to read only if I could work

with them one-to one or in very small groups for 30 minutes a day. I was unable to do it consistently.

I met with my principal and assistant principal and proposed that we redesign the role and function of the special education resource room. I suggested that we have three levels of service delivery. (1) Selected students would be placed in the regular education classroom for the full day. I would work closely with their regular education teacher to monitor their progress. I would work with them in small groups in the classroom several times a week. This level would be for my most independent students who I felt were ready to "phase out" of special education. (2) The second level would be for students who need intensive instruction in one area—reading, for example—but who were functioning relatively well in the regular education classroom in all other areas. These students would be seen by my aide every day for thirty minutes of direct *instruction designed by me. I would work with the student and the aide at least once a week. (3) The third level would be for students who the teacher and I felt worked best when they were able to leave the regular education classroom for a period of time, one to two hours. For the most part, these were students who demonstrated both learning and behavior disorders. Last year was the first year I implemented the new three-level service-delivery model and while there are still some "kinks" I need to work out, overall we (my students and I) had the best year ever.*

The role of the special education teacher is being redefined at the school district, state, and national level. Largely the movement is toward even more involvement with regular education and regular education teachers. The skills special education teachers need to be successful in their new roles go beyond sound instructional practices.

If you ask people in business to list the critical elements for a successful business, they will undoubtedly include *communication* and *sound management.* Although the product, service, and marketing are important, communication and management of the business are the cornerstone. It is the ability of the manager or the management team to make sound decisions regarding product development and research, marketing, service, fiscal policies, and personnel that makes the difference between success and failure. It is also the ability to communicate effectively when making and disseminating decisions that determines how effectively and efficiently the business operates.

In the same way that management and communication are the cornerstone of business, so are they the cornerstone of effective teaching. Whether serving as a consultant, resource, or self-contained teacher, the special education teacher makes thousands of management decisions each day regarding the teaching-learning process and the instructional cycle. It is the ability of the teacher to develop a teaching-learning context that facilitates communication and learning; to set learning and instructional goals and market those goals to others, including the students; and to establish sound classroom and in-

structional policies, routines, and procedures that makes the difference between success and failure. Management and communication are central to the task of teaching (Berliner, 1983; Doyle, 1979, 1986). This chapter deals with the issue of the special education teacher as a manager, communicator, and collaborator.

GETTING STARTED

"I'm really looking forward to next year," commented Ms. Downing as she completed her first year of teaching as a junior high resource teacher. "The first year of teaching has to be the hardest. There is so much to get organized at the beginning of the year, so many decisions to be made, and so many new routines and procedures to learn. You have to figure out what your resources are as well as the students' needs. You also have to decide what type of instructional program you want. Based on this, you need to determine how to arrange the room to facilitate learning, what materials to select or develop, and how to organize the materials so that the students can find them easily. You must decide how to group the students and how to schedule the students into the room. In comparison to this year, next year should be a breeze. I'll be able to spend much more time refining my teaching skills, focusing on the students, and strengthening the program."

In many ways, Ms. Downing is a manager. At the beginning of the year, management decisions are required at a fast and furious pace. We will explore some of the decisions that teachers have to consider in getting started and look at some options they might consider in making those decisions.

Arranging the Environment

In Chapter One, we discussed how the teaching-learning process takes place within a context. Making this context or environment pleasant and conducive to learning can facilitate the teaching-learning process. As teachers, we want to consider both the instructional arrangement and the physical arrangement of that context.

Instructional Arrangement

Instructional arrangement refers to the manner in which the teacher groups the students and selects the format for learning. Generally, there are six instructional arrangements: (1) large-group instruction, (2) small-group instruction, (3) one-to-one instruction, (4) independent learning, (5) collaborative learning, and (6) peer teaching (Mercer and Mercer, 1989). Whether teaching in a resource room where students attend in small- to medium-sized groups for relatively short periods of time each day, or in a self-contained classroom where students spend the majority of their school day, most teachers want to have the flexibility to provide for several different instructional arrangements within their classrooms.

Large-Group Instruction. Large-group instruction usually consists of the teacher lecturing or engaging in discussions with a group of six or more students. It is appropriate to use when the content of instruction is similar for all students. Teachers often employ this type of instructional arrangement when teaching social skills and content area subjects such as social studies, science, health, and career education. This arrangement can be used both for didactic instruction (i.e., instruction where one person, usually the teacher, is providing information) and for interactive instruction (i.e., where the students and teachers are discussing and sharing information). In large-group instruction students usually get less opportunity to receive feedback concerning their performance and less opportunity to receive corrective feedback. Since large-group instruction is the most frequently used arrangement in regular education classrooms, particularly in secondary settings, it is helpful to provide students with experiences in large groups as they make the transition from a self-contained special education classroom to regular education classrooms.

Small-Group Instruction. Small-group instruction usually consists of groups of two to five students and is employed when the teacher wants to be in closer proximity to the students and provide more feedback. This instructional arrangement is often used for teaching specific academic skills, since students are often grouped by skill level when learning basic skills in reading, writing, oral language, and math. When a teacher is using small-group instruction, he or she usually involves one group of students while the remaining students participate in independent learning, cooperative learning, or peer tutoring. Sometimes teachers who work in resource rooms schedule students so that only two to five students come at one time, so that all the students can participate in small-group instruction at once. Many teachers prefer using a horseshoe table for small-group instruction, since it allows them to reach the materials in front of each student in the group easily.

One-to-One Instruction. One-to-one instruction is when the teacher works individually with a student. This instructional arrangement allows the teacher to provide intensive instruction, closely monitoring student progress and modifying and adapting procedures to match the student's learning patterns. The Fernald (VAKT) method of teaching word identification and Reading Recovery, as discussed in Chapter Four, are examples where one-to-one instruction is the recommended instructional arrangement. At least some one-to-one instruction is recommended for students with learning and behavior problems, since it provides the students with some time each day to ask questions and receive assistance from the teacher (Archer and Edgar, 1976). The major drawback of one-to-one instruction is that while one student is working with the teacher, the remaining students need to be actively engaged in learning. To accomplish this, independent learning, collaborative learning, or peer tutoring is frequently used.

Independent Learning. Independent learning is one format for providing students practice with a skill for which they have already received instruction and have acquired some proficiency (Stephens, 1977; Wallace and Kauffman, 1986). We frequently associate independent learning with individual worksheets, but computer activities, various audiovisual assignments such as listening to a taped book, writing a story, reading a library book, or making a map for a social studies unit can also be independent learning activities.

The key to effective use of independent learning activities is selecting activities that the student can complete with minimal assistance. For example, when Samantha selects library books, Ms. Martino asks Samantha to read approximately the first hundred words to her and then she asks Samantha several questions. If Samantha misses five words or less and can answer the questions easily, then Ms. Martino encourages her to read the book on her own. If Samantha misses five to ten words, then Ms. Martino arranges for her to read the book using collaborative learning or peer tutoring. If Samantha misses more than ten words and struggles to answer the questions, then Ms. Martino may encourage her to select another book. In fact, Ms. Martino has even taught Samantha and the rest of the students in her self-contained classroom for students with behavior disorders the "Five-Finger Rule."

> **Five-Finger Rule**   If in reading the first couple of pages of a book, you know the words except for about five and you can ask yourself and answer five questions about what you have read, then this book is probably a good book for you to read.

Cooperative or Collaborative Learning.   Collaborative or cooperative learning is when students work together and use each other as a source for learning. Four basic elements need to be included for small-group learning to be cooperative: interdependence, individual accountability, collaborative skills, and group processing (Johnson and Johnson, 1986; Slavin, 1987, 1991). Interdependence is facilitated by creating a learning environment where the students perceive that the goal of the group is that *all* members learn, that rewards are based on group performance, that materials needed to complete the task are distributed across the members of the group, and that students are given complementary roles that foster the division of labor. Group processing refers to giving the students the opportunity to discuss how well they are achieving their goals and working together (Johnson and Johnson, 1984a).

Two basic formats for cooperative learning are oftentimes used in regular or special education classrooms. With a *group project* students pool their knowledge and skills to create a project or complete an assignment. The students in the group are included in all the decisions and tasks that ensure completion of the project. Using the *jigsaw format,* each student in a group is assigned a task that must be completed for the group to reach its goal. For example, in completing a fact-finding sheet on fossils, each student might be assigned to read a different source to obtain information for the different facts required on the sheet.

Johnson and Johnson (1975) suggest the following guidelines for working cooperatively:

1. Each group produces one product.
2. Group members assist each other.
3. Group members seek assistance from other group members.
4. Group members will change their ideas only when logically persuaded to do so by the other members.
5. Group members take responsibility for the product.

Collaborative learning can be used to complete group projects in content area subjects. In Chapter Six, the process approach to teaching writing employed aspects of collaborative learning. For example, students shared their written pieces with each other to get ideas and feedback about their writing, and in some cases they wrote pieces together. Slavin and his colleagues (Slavin, Stevens, and Madden, 1988) have developed *Cooperative Integrated Reading and Composition* which uses cooperative learning with a process approach for teaching composition and basal-related activities and direct instruction in reading comprehension. They have also designed a mathematics curriculum using cooperative learning, Team Assisted Individualization (Slavin, 1984). Using heterogeneous cooperative learning groups in regular elementary classrooms, the researchers found that these types of programs paired with cooperative learning facilitate the learning of most mainstreamed special education and remedial students.

Providing opportunities to participate in cooperative learning experiences is particularly important for students with behavior and learning problems because it assists these students in developing social skills as well as the targeted academic skill. It assists them in developing positive interactions with peers and in developing strategies for supporting others. These skills are particularly important when students are being mainstreamed into regular classrooms where cooperative learning is employed (Johnson and Johnson, 1984b, 1986).

In orchestrating collaborative learning, it is important to provide the students with enough directions that they know the purpose of the activity and the general rules for working in groups. Initially, the teacher may want to participate as a collaborator, modeling such collaborative behaviors as: (1) asking what the other people think, (2) not ridiculing other collaborators for what they think, and (3) helping other collaborators and accepting help from others. As the students become comfortable in collaborating, they can collaborate independently without the teacher's input.

Peer Teaching.   In this instructional arrangement, one student who has learned the skills assists another student in learning the skills. This teaching takes place under the supervision of the teacher. One advantage of peer teaching is that it increases opportunity for the student learning the skills to respond (Delquadri, Greenwood, Whorton, Carta, and Hall, 1986). Peer teaching achieves this by allowing peers to supervise their classmates' responses. When using peer teaching the teacher needs to plan the instruction and demonstrate the task to the pair. The tutor then works with the learner, providing assistance and feedback.

One important aspect of peer teaching is training the students to serve as peer tutors (Fowler, 1986). They need to learn basic instructional procedures for providing reinforcement and corrective feedback and for knowing when to ask the teacher for assistance. Research focusing on peer tutoring with special education students has most frequently been used to teach or monitor basic skills such as oral reading, answering reading comprehension questions, and practicing spelling words, math facts, and new sight word vocabulary (Gerber and Kauffman, 1981; Scruggs and Richter, 1985).

Another important aspect of peer teaching is cross-age tutoring. In this situation older students instruct younger students. Cross-age tutoring has many advantages including the fact that older students are supposed to know more than younger students; thus there is less of a stigma from being tutored. Also, both the tutor and the tutee enjoy the opportunity to meet someone of a different age. Another aspect of cross-age tutoring that can be effective is the use of students with learning disabilities or behavior disorders to serve as the tutor for younger students who also demonstrate learning or behavior disorders.

Thus peer teaching can serve many roles:

1. Peers teaching peers within the same classroom
2. Peers teaching peers across classrooms but within the same grade level
3. Peers who are older teaching students who are younger
4. Peers with learning and behavior disorders teaching younger nondisabled students
5. Peers with learning and behavior disorders teaching younger students who have learning and behavior disorders

Classwide Peer Tutoring.   Classwide peer tutoring (CWPT) is a structured technique for improving students' reading abilities. Students of different reading levels are paired (e.g., a high or average reader paired with a low reader) and work together on a sequence of organized activities such as oral reading, story retelling, and summarization. The reading material may be a basal reader, trade book or magazine, or other appropriate material. The criterion is that the least able reader in each pair be able to easily read the materials assigned to his/her dyad. The extensive research on CWPT (e.g., Mathes et al., 1994) indicates that when the procedure is implemented consistently (e.g., thirty-minute sessions held three times per week for at least sixteen weeks), students of all ability levels demonstrate improved reading fluency and comprehension.

Physical Arrangement

The physical arrangement of the classroom should provide for the different types of instructional arrangements that will be used in the classroom. In addition, it should reflect a pleasant atmosphere that facilitates efficient learning. Figures 11.1 and 11.2 present two room arrangements. Both rooms contain a teaching area, an individual learning area, an audiovisual/computer area, and a recreational area. The second room arrangement also incorporates learning centers and a time-out area.

As discussed in Chapter Two, a time-out area is an area in which students do not have the opportunity to receive reinforcement. It is usually used as a means for reducing inappropriate behavior. A learning center is an area where instructional materials focus on one curriculum area or topic of study and are arranged in such a manner that students can work in the area individually or cooperatively to accomplish a task. For example, Ms. Marks currently has a social studies learning center in her junior high resource room. In this center she has arranged maps, source books, and trade books on a bookshelf and put a small table with four chairs in the center. Every two to four weeks she introduces the students to a new cooperative learning project for the center (e.g., writing a governing constitution for the classroom, drawing a map of the surrounding neighborhood and locating everyone's homes). The first semester, Ms. Marks used the learning center as a writing skills center, using an individual-learning model, but this semester she switched to a cooperative learning model.

■ **FIGURE 11.1** *Sample Room Arrangement*

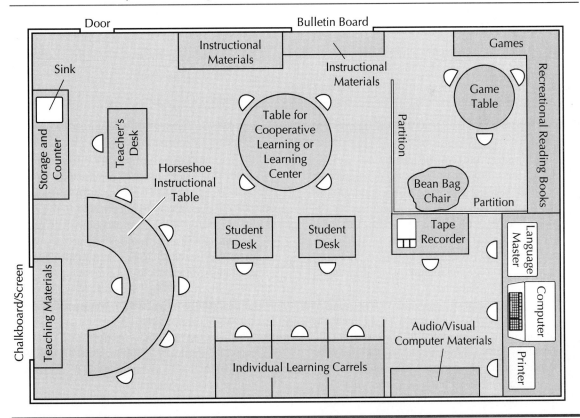

■ **FIGURE 11.2**   *Sample Room Arrangement*

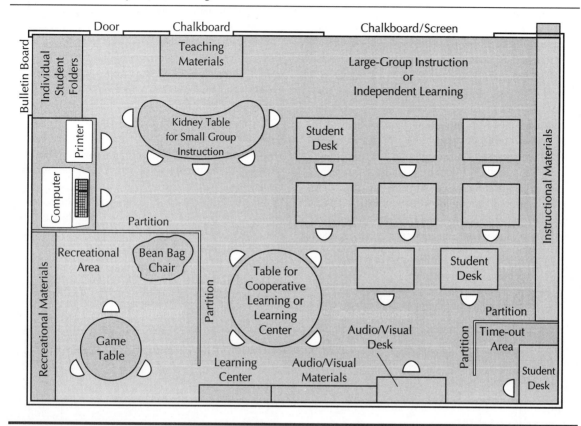

The room arrangement should be flexible enough so that different instructional arrangements can be employed. For example, the individual learning area can be reorganized into a large group instructional area by rearranging the desks. The small group instructional area can also be used for a cooperative learning project.

Several ideas to keep in mind when developing the room arrangement are:

1. To the extent possible, place the recreational and audiovisual/computer areas away from the teaching area. These areas will naturally be somewhat noisier than the other areas.
2. Place student materials in a place where students can easily get to the materials without bothering other students or the teacher.

3. Place your teaching materials directly behind where you teach so that you may reach materials without having to leave the instructional area.
4. If used, place the time-out area out of the direct line of traffic. Also, use partitions that keep a student in the area from having visual contact with other students. (See Chapter Two for principles governing the use of time-out.)
5. Make the recreational area comfortable with a carpet, comfortable reading chairs, and a small game table if possible.
6. Place all the materials needed for a learning center in the learning center area. In this way students will not be moving around the room to collect needed materials.
7. Instruct several students as to where materials and supplies are kept so that when students can-

not find something they do not ask you but ask other students.

8. Establish procedures and settings for students who have completed tasks and/or are waiting for the teacher.

Instructional Materials and Equipment

Selecting, developing, and organizing the instructional materials and equipment is an important aspect of getting a program organized. The instructional materials and the equipment used by the teacher have a major influence on what and how information and skills are taught (Wallace and Kauffman, 1986; Wilson, 1982).

One decision a teacher has to make is whether to purchase materials already available or develop the materials. Some teachers tend to select published materials for their main instructional materials (e.g., sets of literature books based on different themes or units, several reading programs each representing a different approach to reading such as linguistic and phonic approaches). Then they develop instructional aids and games to supplement the program (e.g., flash cards, sentence strips, tape recordings of the stories, board games).

Whether selecting or developing materials, there are several factors to consider:

1. What curricular areas (e.g., reading, English, math, social skills) will I be responsible for teaching?
2. What are the academic levels of the students I will be teaching?
3. In what instructional arrangement(s) do I plan to teach each curricular area?
4. How can the materials be used across the stages of learning (i.e., acquisition, proficiency, maintenance, generalization, and application)?
5. Will the materials provide a means for measuring learning?
6. Are the materials designed for teacher-directed learning, student-to-student learning, or individual learning?

Selecting Published Materials

Besides considering the factors just mentioned, it is also important to think of the cost, durability, consumability, and quality of the published materials. Before purchasing materials it is advantageous to evaluate them. Sample materials can generally be obtained from the publisher or found at educational conferences or district-wide instructional libraries. If possible, talk with other teachers who use the materials to determine when and with whom they are effective. Borrow the materials and have the students try them and evaluate them. Chapter Appendix 11.1 presents a form a teacher can use to evaluate published materials. It focuses not only on general information but on how the material will fit into the teacher's program. Chapter Appendix 11.2 presents a form the students can use to evaluate the materials.

Most teachers have restricted budgets for purchasing instructional materials. Once the instructional materials are selected, it is helpful to prioritize them according to need. Before eliminating materials from that list, determine if they can be obtained through means other than the teaching budget. For example, school districts often have an instructional materials library that allows teachers in the district to check out materials for a relatively long period of time. You may be able to borrow the materials from the library rather than purchase them. Librarians are often interested in additional materials to order; it might be possible to request that they order the materials for the library. Publishers are often interested in how their materials work with low-achieving students and students with learning and behavior problems. They may be willing to provide a set of materials if the teacher is willing to evaluate the materials and provide feedback regarding how they work with the students.

Selecting and Using Instructional Equipment

In addition to selecting instructional materials, the teacher will also want to choose some equipment to facilitate learning. Chapter Ten specifically deals with computers, including the selection of computers, peripherals, and computer software. This equipment, along with various software programs, is becoming an increasingly important part of the tools a teacher has available. In addition to a computer in the classroom and/or the use of a computer lab in the school, there is other equipment that will facilitate learning.

Tape Recorder. Tape recorders are relatively inexpensive and can be used in a variety of ways in the classroom. In selecting a tape recorder, select one of good quality that is easy to operate. Also select a recorder that has a counter. This allows a student to quickly find a particular section in a tape rather than having to hunt for it. Headphones to accompany the tape recorder allow students to listen to the tape recorder without disturbing others. Following are some instructional applications for the tape recorder.

1. Tape record reading books so that students can follow along during recreational reading or for using with repeated reading or the pattern language approach. Apply the Concept 5.1 (page 179) provides guidelines for tape recording books and stories.

2. One way to adapt textbooks is to tape record them. Apply the Concept 7.3 (page 300) presents some suggestions for tape recording textbooks.

3. For some students it is helpful for them to record what they want to write before they write their first drafts. They can tape record their ideas and then listen to them as they write the first drafts.

4. So that the students can hear their progress in reading, have them tape record their reading every two to four weeks. Each student should have his or her own tape that serves as a record of progress. After a student records his or her reading, it is important that the teacher and the student discuss the reading, identifying strengths and areas that need improvement. This tape recording can also be shared with parents to demonstrate progress and continuing needs.

5. Spelling tests can be tape recorded so that students can take them independently. First, record the words to be tested, allowing time for the students to spell the words. After the test is recorded, spell each word so the student can self-check.

6. At the secondary level, class lectures can be taped and then listened to so that the student can review the material and complete unfinished notes.

7. Have students practice taking notes by listening to tape recordings of lectures. By using tape recordings, students can regulate the rate at which the material is presented.

8. Oral directions for independent learning activities can be tape recorded so that students can listen to them. This may prove to be particularly helpful if the teacher is trying to conduct small-group or one-to-one instruction while these students are working on independent learning activities.

9. When working on specific social or pragmatic language skills (e.g., answering the telephone, asking for directions, introducing someone), tape record the students so that they can listen to and evaluate themselves.

10. Many instructional materials contain prerecorded tapes.

Language Master. The language master is an adaptation of a tape recorder. It is a machine that tape records and plays cards that have a piece of recording tape attached along the bottom (see Figure 11.3). The cards are four inches high and range in length from several inches to over a foot. Depending on the length of the card, words, phrases, or sentences can be recorded. The words and sentences are recorded by inserting the card into the card slot on the top of the machine, and gently pushing the card to start it moving over the recording head. As the card moves over the head, the record button is pressed for recording. Listening to the recorded cards is accomplished by the same action, except the record button is not pushed. There are two recording tracks on the tape—one designated for the teacher and one designated for the student. Therefore, the student can listen to the tape to hear what the teacher says, and then pass the card through the machine again to record his or her response. Visual cues (e.g., words, phrases, math problems) can be written directly on the cards. The cards can be made reusable by laminating them or covering them with clear contact paper so that the visual cues can be erased. Teachers can purchase blank cards as well as prerecorded cards. Before purchasing a language master or cards, see if they are available from the district instructional library. The

■ **FIGURE 11.3** *Language Master and Language Master Card*

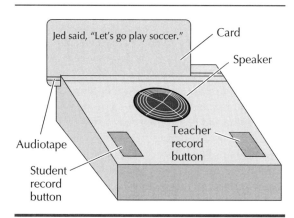

following are suggestions for how a teacher might use the language master in the classroom.

1. Record the word cards, phrase cards, and/or sentence cards for the stories that the students are to read. Students can independently listen to these words prior to reading and/or after reading to provide practice in identifying words. Organize the cards by stories so that students can easily locate the correct words to listen to.

2. Record the math facts, cutting a notch in the tape so that the student hears the fact, the card stops, and when the student is ready he or she engages the card again to hear the answer. Write the fact on the front of the card and the answer on the back.

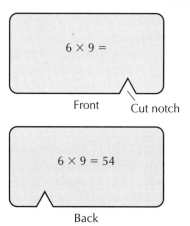

3. Spelling words can be presented orally on the card and the correct spelling written on the back. The student then listens to the word, writes his or her answer, and then turns the card over to check the answer.

4. Record math word problems. The problem can be written on the front and the answer on the back.

5. Record a word family (e.g., *cat, fat, rat, bat*), cutting a notch in the card so that the student hears the words, the card stops, and when the student is ready he or she engages the card again to hear the name of the family. Write the family words on the front of the card and the answer on the back.

6. Record a cloze sentence (e.g., "The little girl is smiling because she is _____."), cutting a notch in the card so that the student hears the sentence, the card stops, and when the student has filled in the blank, he or she engages the card again to hear the answer. Write the sentence on the front of the card and the answer on the back.

7. Have the students write riddles and then put them on language master cards so that the other students can listen. The author may want to sign his or her riddle.

8. Record three to four examples of a specific category (e.g., red, yellow, purple, orange—colors; happy, sad, angry—ways you feel). Cut a notch in the card so that the student hears the examples, the card stops, and when the student has said the category, he or she engages the card again to hear the name of the category. Write the examples on the front and the name of the category on the back.

9. Record vocabulary words and their meanings. Definitions can be provided and students can write in the correct vocabulary words.

10. Select key concepts or facts from social studies or science and record them on the language master.

Overhead Projector. The overhead projector is an excellent teaching tool. It allows the user to display on a screen or blank wall the images from a transparency. Transparencies are generally teacher-made, although some are available with published instructional materials. The overhead projector allows the teacher to model a skill and to highlight, write, color in, and/or point to important information. For example, a teacher may use an overhead projector to demonstrate how to add quotation marks to a story, or a student may use it to demonstrate how he or she worked a long division problem.

In preparing transparencies, write in large, bold writing. Two types of markers are available for making transparencies—permanent markers and nonpermanent markers. Transparencies are also available that can be used in copying machines so that the original is copied onto a transparency rather than a piece of paper.

When using an overhead projector keep the following suggestions in mind:

1. Using an overhead can be easier than a chalkboard for presenting a lecture or leading a discussion since it does not require the teacher to turn around to write.
2. Keep the amount of information presented on the overhead relatively limited.
3. Use a different colored pen to highlight important points.
4. Keep extra markers available when using the overhead.
5. By laying a piece of paper over the transparency, each part of a transparency can be revealed as it is being discussed, thereby helping to focus the students' attention.
6. Use the overhead projector to develop language experience stories.
7. Use the overhead projector to demonstrate editing and revisions in writing.
8. Use the overhead projector along with a "think aloud" procedure to demonstrate math procedures such as how to work long division.
9. Allow students to develop transparencies summarizing individual or group work that they can share with the class as a whole.

Other Small Equipment.   Several other pieces of small equipment should be considered when selecting equipment for either a resource room or a self-contained classroom.

A *stopwatch* can serve as an instructional tool and a motivator. For some tasks it is important that students learn to respond at an automatic level (e.g., sight words, math facts). Students can use a stopwatch to time themselves or their classmates. These times can then be easily recorded on a time chart (see Figure 11.4). Using these charts, students can set goals, record their times, and try to beat previous times.

An *individual writing board* is an excellent tool for obtaining individual written responses during small group and large group discussions. Mr. Howell uses these boards during review sessions in his resource high school history class. During the review sessions he asks students questions and they write their answers on the writing boards. He then asks them to display their boards. In this way each student responds to each question in writing instead of one student orally responding to one question. Mr. Howell and the students feel that this is a better way to review since it requires them to think about and answer every question and to write the answers. Writing is important since it is generally required when the students take tests. Although small chalkboards can be used as individual writing boards, boards with a white erasable writing surface and special felt markers are now available.

A *flannel board* and a *magnetic board* are particularly useful in elementary classrooms. These can be used in teaching and learning centers for such activities as depicting stories, spelling words, and working simple math problems.

As discussed in the math chapter, Chapter Eight, *calculators* are an invaluable tool for students when learning and for teachers when completing many of the routine activities associated with assessment and evaluation.

Ms. Luciani uses spelling masters to reinforce known spelling words and teach new ones. While she does not feel it serves as a substitute for sound spelling instruction, she allows students to use them for practice when they have finished assigned tasks, or when they are waiting for assistance from her.

Developing Instructional Materials
In addition to published materials and equipment, most teachers find the need to develop their own instructional materials. Many of these materials can be

■ **FIGURE 11.4**   *Timing Chart*

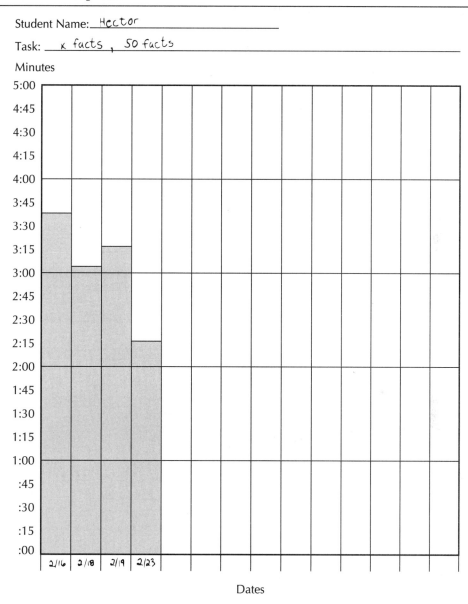

Student Name: Hector

Task: x facts, 50 facts

Minutes

(Dates on x-axis: 2/16, 2/18, 2/19, 2/23)

Dates

used to supplement commercial materials. For example, sentence strips containing the sentences from each story in beginning readers can be made. Many teachers develop materials to provide students with additional practice in skills they are learning. There-

fore, developing self-correcting materials and/or materials in a game format can be advantageous.

Self-Correcting Materials.   Self-correcting materials provide students with immediate feedback.

Students with learning and behavior problems frequently have a history of failure and are reluctant to take risks when others are watching or listening. Self-correcting materials allow them to check themselves without sharing the information with others. Many computer programs and electronic learning games incorporate self-correction into their programs. Several of the suggestions for the language master provide for self-correction (see page 455). Figure 11.5 presents an example of a self-correcting activity that teachers can easily make.

One key to self-correcting materials is immediate feedback (Mercer, Mercer, and Bott, 1984). The materials should be simple enough so that students can learn to use the materials easily and to check their answers quickly. The materials should be varied so that the interest and novelty level remain relatively high.

Another key to developing self-correcting materials is to make them durable so that they can be used and reused. Laminating and covering the materials with clear contact paper are good ways to make materials more durable. Special marking pens or grease pencils can then be used. Using heavy cardboard can also increase the durability of materials.

Instructional Games. Students with learning and behavior problems frequently require numerous op-

■ FIGURE 11.5 *Self-Correcting Activity*

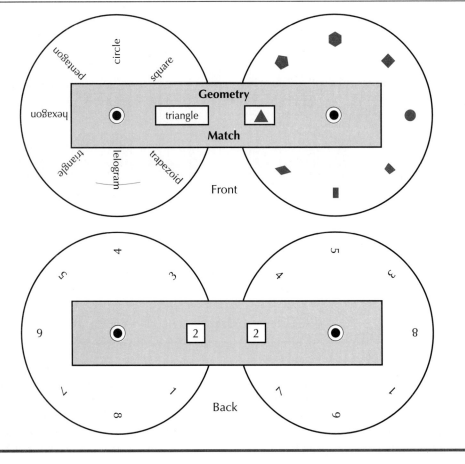

portunities to practice an academic skill. Instructional games can provide this practice in a format that is interesting to the students.

The first step in designing an instructional game is to determine the purpose of the game. For example, the purpose might be to provide practice in:

1. Forming word families (e.g., *-at: fat, sat, cat, rat*)
2. Identifying sight words associated with a specific piece of reading material being used in the classroom
3. Using semantic and syntactic clues by using the cloze procedure (e.g., For dessert Brian wanted an ice _____ cone.)
4. Recalling multiplication facts
5. Reviewing information (e.g., identifying the parts of a flower)

The second step is to select and adapt a game in which to practice a skill or review knowledge. For example, commercial games such as Monopoly, Chutes and Ladders, Candyland, Clue, Sorry, and Parcheesi can be adapted. A generic game board can also be used (see Figure 11.6). Generic game boards can be purchased from some publishing companies. The key in selecting and adapting a game is to require the students to complete the instructional task as part of the turn-taking procedure. For example, when adapting Candyland to practice sight words, students would select a sight word card and a Candyland card. If they can correctly read the sight word then they can use their Candyland card to move as indicated. When adapting Monopoly for math facts, students would have to first select and answer the math fact. If answered correctly, they earn the opportunity to throw the dice and take a turn. When the same skills are practiced by many students in the class, the teacher may want to develop a specific game for the skill. Math Marathon is a specific game in which students move forward on a game board, depicting a marathon race by answering math word problems. Different sets of math word problem game cards can be developed, depending on the math problem-solving levels of the students.

The third step is to write the directions and develop the materials. MacWilliams (1978) recommends making a rough draft of the game and testing it. Posterboard glued to cardboard or manila folders makes a good game board. With manila folders the name of the game can be written on the tab and the board can be stored so that the students can scan the tabs to find the game. The materials for the game can be kept in an envelope inside the folder. The directions for the game and a list of materials that should be found inside may be written on the envelope.

The fourth step is to demonstrate the game to the students so that they can learn to play the games independently.

Organizing and Managing Materials

Selecting and developing materials is only one part of effective materials management. These materials need to be organized in the classroom in such a manner that the teacher and students have easy access to the materials without bothering other students. Let's see what suggestions Ms. Wilcox, an elementary resource teacher, has for developing a materials management system.

It has taken me about three years to really organize the management system for this classroom. One of the most important aspects of this system is that it is color-coded and labeled so that students who can't read well can find and use materials. I have placed all the instructional materials along one wall of my classroom and organized it into sections by academic and content areas. For each academic and content area I have put my teaching materials that I am not currently using on the top shelves. The materials I am currently using I put on a shelf behind the horseshoe table. That way, I can get to them easily. On the middle shelves I put the small group and independent learning activities. The bottom shelves I have reserved for instructional games. One section of the shelf has general instructional materials. This includes generic game boards, different kinds of paper and writing instruments, scissors, glue, and so on. I have

■ **FIGURE 11.6** *Generic Board Game*

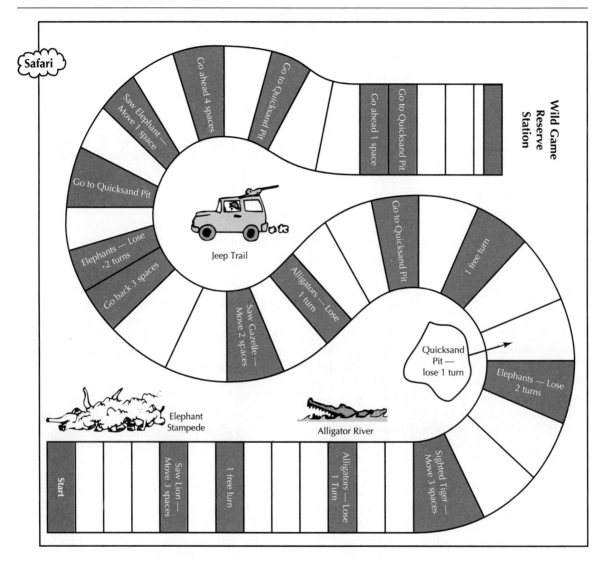

1. You are on a safari, trying to get to the Wild Game Reserve Station.
2. Begin at Start.
3. Each player rolls a die. The player with the highest number goes first.
4. Roll the die and draw a Game Card. If you answer the Game Card correctly, move the number shown on the die. If you do not answer the Game Card correctly, do not take a turn.
5. The first player to get to the Wild Card Reserve Station wins.

color-coded all the textual materials by approximate reading level. I have also color-coded the recreational reading books that are found in the free-time area.

Since I have a limited budget I haven't been able to purchase many practice-type workbooks. One way to make those consumables into nonconsumables is to cover each page with clear contact paper or have the students place an acetate page over them. I staple each page in a file folder and label the tab with the book name and page number, then place all the pages in a box so that the tabs are easily read. I label the box with the name of the skill or workbook. Then the students simply go to the box, pull the assigned page, and complete it. Sometimes I have made answer keys for each page or purchased a copy of the teacher's edition. I place these at the back of the box. The students know that if they are to self-check, they get the answer key or teacher's workbook after finishing the work and then check it.

It took me a while to set up this system but I think it is well worth the time for several reasons. First, it is easy to expand. I keep an inventory list of all my materials on the computer, and I simply add to the list whenever I get new materials and then add the materials to the shelves. [Figure 11.7 contains a sample format for an inventory list.] This way I'm not always redoing the system. Second, I often have six to eight students in my room at once. I want to be able to provide small group and one-to-one instruction. To do this I need a system where students can retrieve the materials they need to use when doing independent and collaborative learning tasks without having to ask me for help. This system does a pretty good job of accomplishing that.

Oh, by the way, there is one other important piece of information. So that the students know how to use the different materials, at the beginning of the year and each time we get new materials the students will be using, we spend

■ **FIGURE 11.7** *Partial Outline for Materials Inventory List*

Reading (R)

R.1   Patterned Language Books
R.2   Language Experience Materials and Activities
R.3   Basal Reading Books and Materials
R.4   Linguistic Readers and Materials
R.5   Phonic Books, Materials, and Activities
R.6   Structural Analysis Materials and Activities
R.7   Cloze Materials and Activities
R.8   Syllabication Materials and Activities
R.9   Comprehension Materials and Activities
R.10 Vocabulary Materials and Activities
R.11 Other Reading Materials and Activities

Mathematics (M)

M.1   Place Value Materials and Manipulatives
M.2   Readiness Materials and Activities
M.3   Addition Materials and Activities
M.4   Subtraction Materials and Activities
M.5   Multiplication Materials and Activities
M.6   Division Materials and Activities
M.7   Fraction Materials and Activities
M.8   Percentages Materials and Activities
M.9   Word Problem Materials and Activities
M.10 Money Materials and Activities
M.11 Measurement Materials and Activities
M.12 Time Materials and Activities
M.13 Geometry Materials and Activities
M.14 Math Series
M.15 Other Math Materials and Activities

(Other curricular areas include: language, writing, social skills, study skills, social studies, science, health, and career/vocation education.)

the first few minutes of the session demonstrating the materials and talking about how to use them. Then I make sure each student has the opportunity to use them within the next several days. In this way, I don't have to explain how to use the same materials to each student individually.

Scheduling

When teachers talk about the most difficult aspects of their jobs, they often mention scheduling. Elementary resource teachers generally work with fifteen or more regular classroom teachers to schedule the students who attend the resource program. Special education teachers also work closely with counselors and teachers at the secondary level to see that students are placed in classes that will help them reach the goals and objectives developed on the individual education program (IEP) as well as meet graduation requirements. Special education teachers working in self-contained classrooms are responsible for their students' entire curriculum. They face decisions regarding how to provide instruction in the various curricular areas (e.g., reading, math, writing, English, social studies, science, art, music), while still providing the students with adequate one-to-one and small group instruction so that the students might reach the educational goals targeted in the academic areas of concern.

Many teachers describe scheduling as the worst aspect of their job. The next section provides some points to consider.

Scheduling within the Classroom

Whether teaching in a resource or self-contained classroom, it is important to use the time students spend in the classroom efficiently. Ms. Wilcox highlighted her concern for scheduling when she discussed the need to provide one-to-one or small group instruction. Mr. Wolf explains his dilemma in scheduling when he discusses his self-contained intermediate-level class for students with learning disabilities.

I am responsible for the educational programs for fourteen learning-disabled fifth- and sixth-grade students. They are in my classroom throughout the day except for twice a week, once when they attend music and once when they attend art. Seven of the students attend regular classes for some subjects: three for social studies, two for science, and two for math. I'm lucky because I have a great teacher aide. My concern in scheduling is that these students have so many needs. All of them are at
least two to three grade levels below in reading and writing. We could easily spend the whole day just on reading, writing, and math. By the time my aide and I work with each student individually or in small groups in reading, most of the morning is over. I could easily spend the rest of the day on writing and math. But that would be unfair to the students. They need to learn social studies, health, science, and career concepts.

There are no easy answers to scheduling. However, the following list presents some guidelines to use when developing a schedule for the classroom, whether it be a resource or self-contained class.

- Schedule time to communicate with regular classroom teachers. The amount of time you schedule will be dependent on the time your students spend in the regular classroom. Generally speaking, consultant teachers should schedule more time than resource teachers, and resource teachers should schedule more time than self-contained teachers. This time will prove invaluable in assisting students to be successful in regular classrooms.
- Schedule time to observe in the regular classrooms in which your students are placed or are going to be placed. This alerts you to the class demands and schedules of the classroom and will help you in planning for your students' learning in that classroom.
- Schedule time to meet with other professionals (e.g., speech/language pathologist, school psychologist).
- Schedule so that you alternate instructional arrangements. For example, do not schedule a student to participate in independent learning activities for more than thirty minutes at a time.
- Plan for time to provide the students with advance organizers, feedback and evaluation. In this way students will know what is going to happen, and they will have the opportunity to think about what they have accomplished.
- Plan time for direct instruction. Sometimes we have students spend the majority of their time in independent learning activities, which results in

little time for them to receive direct instruction from the teacher, aide, or tutor.

— Alternate preferred and less preferred activities or make preferred activities contingent upon less preferred activities.

— Let students know when the time for an activity is just about over. This gives them time to reach closure on the one activity and get ready for the next activity or to ask for a time extension.

— Be consistent in scheduling yet flexible and ready for change.

— Provide a session with each student in which you review his or her schedule in your room and in other teachers' classrooms. Be sure students know what is expected of them.

Figures 11.8 and 11.9 present sample schedules for a resource and self-contained classroom. For the resource room, the schedule for one group of students is presented, whereas the entire day's schedule is presented for the self-contained class.

Developing an Overall Schedule for a Resource Consultant Program

Scheduling students' time while in the special education classroom is one issue, but the overall schedule for a resource room often presents other issues and requires that the teacher work closely with teachers and other professionals in the school. Teachers who assume roles as resource teachers must first clarify and decide what their job responsibilities will

■ **FIGURE 11.8**   *Schedule for Fourth- through Sixth-Grade Students while Attending the Resource Room*

Date: 4/15

Time	José	Amelia	Scott	Todd	Carmen	Frank
10:00	Small-Group Instruction Reading ↓	Language Master Inferential Comprehension Computer Activity	Small-Group Instruction Reading ↓	Social Studies Text Using Request Procedure with Carmen ↓	Social Studies Text Using Request Procedure with Todd ↓	Small-Group Instruction Reading ↓
10:20	Inferential Comprehension Activity on Computer	Small-Group Instruction Reading ↓	Social Studies Text with Self-Questioning	Small-Group Instruction Reading ↓	Small-Group Instruction Reading ↓	Language Master Word Drill Social Studies Text with Self-Questioning
10:40	Writing Process ↓ Spelling	Writing Process ↓ Spelling	Writing Process (Computer) Spelling	Writing Process ↓ Spelling	Writing Process ↓ Spelling	Writing Process Computer Spelling
11:15	Practice Computer	Practice Game	Practice Game	Practice Tape Recorder Test	Practice Game	Practice Game

■ **FIGURE 11.9**   *Sample Schedule for Intermediate Level Self-Contained Class*

Time	Activity			
	Group 1	*Group 2*	*Group 3*	*Group 4*
8:15	Writing Process Students working on reports			
9:15	Reading: Small-group instruction (teacher)	Reading: Independent learning activities	Learning center: Map reading	Reading: Small-group instruction (aide)
9:45	Reading: Independent learning activities	Reading: Small-group Instruction (aide)	Reading: Small-group instruction (teacher)	Learning center: Map reading
10:15	Announcements			
10:20	Recess			
10:45	Math: Group instruction (teacher)		Computer lab for Math practice (aide)	
11:15	Computer lab (aide)		Group instruction (teacher)	
11:50	Lunch			
12:40	Recreational Reading/Writing			
1:00	Social Studies: Large-group instruction			
1:45	Science: Cooperative learning activities			
2:15	Recess			
2:40	Health—Mon./Art—Tues./P.E.—Wed./Special Activity—Thurs., Fri. (Current: Producing a play)			
3:10	Earned "fun time" or time to complete work			
3:30	Dismissal			

be. Generally these responsibilities can be divided into four general areas:

1. directly provide instruction to the students
2. indirectly provide instruction to the students by consulting with regular classroom teachers and parents
3. assess current and referred students
4. serve as an instructional resource for other teachers and professionals within the school

The time a teacher spends in each one of these roles will directly influence the schedule the teacher develops. For example, if the major roles of the teacher are to provide instructional services indirectly to students, to assess current and referred students, and to serve as an instructional resource, then little time will be spent scheduling groups of students into the resource room. Instead, the teacher will serve primar-

ily in the role of a consultant to others. A sample schedule for a consulting teacher is presented in Figure 11.10.

On the other hand, Ms. Wilcox provides direct instruction to most of the students she serves for an average of sixty minutes per day, four days per week. Since she serves twenty-two students, she has developed a schedule that allows her some time to consult with regular classroom teachers, but she has also allocated time to teach and assess current and referred students. To facilitate her scheduling, she grouped students according to grade level for the most part, with the older students attending in the morning and the younger students in the afternoon.

She explains her schedule as follows:

I have arranged for the older students to come in the morning because I feel that I can take over the responsibility for teaching these

■ **FIGURE 11.10** *Consultant Teacher Schedule*

Week of: <u>April 15th</u>

Time	Monday	Tuesday	Wednesday	Thursday	Friday
7:30	IEP meeting	Instructional Review Meeting (2nd grade)	Child Study Team Meeting	IEP Meeting	Instructional Review Meeting (4th grade)
8:15	Work with 5th grade low reading group				→
9:00	Observe and assist LD/EH students in classroom (1st grade)	Assessment	Observe and assist (2nd grade, kindergarten)	3rd grade 4th grade	5th grade 6th grade
11:30	Meet with individual teachers	Planning and material development →		Meet with individual teachers	Planning and material development
12:30	Lunch →				
1:00	Work with 2nd grade low reading group →				
1:30	Conduct study skills classes for selected 4th–6th graders	Conduct social skills class for group of EH students	Conduct study skills class	Conduct social skills class	Conduct study skills class
2:00	Work with Ms. Jones on implementing writing process →			Work with Mr. Peterson on using semantic feature analysis for teaching vocabulary	Assessment
2:30	Provide direct instruction in reading to 5 students with learning disabilities →				
3:30	Dismissal (check with teachers as needed) →				
3:45	End of day				

students reading and writing—the content that is usually taught in the morning in many regular classrooms. I have developed a strong program in teaching reading comprehension, and I am using a process approach to teaching writing [see Figure 11.8]. Currently I am using content area textbooks, trade books, and literature for teaching reading comprehension, and the students are working on writing reports, literature critiques, and short stories on topics of their choice. Since I am responsible for these students' reading and writing, I am accountable for grading these students in these areas. Using this schedule, these students for the most part are in the regular classroom for content area subjects and math. I feel that this is important. When they go to junior high, they will probably be taking regular math, science, social studies, and other content area classes. If they have been missing these classes in the regular classroom during the fourth through sixth grades, they will really have trouble catching up. It's hard enough for these students—we want to give them every advantage possible.

I often provide their reading instruction in content areas such as social studies and science. Thus, while the emphasis is on reading rather than knowledge acquisition, I feel I am extending their background knowledge of concepts they will be taught in social studies and science.

I have the younger students come after lunch, because I feel many of these students need two doses of reading, writing, and math. These students get instruction in these areas in the morning in the regular classroom and then I give them additional instruction in the afternoon. With this arrangement it is important that I communicate with the regular classroom teachers so we each know what the other is doing. We don't want to confuse the students by giving them conflicting information or approaches to reading.

I also have one day a week that I use for assessment, consulting with classroom teachers,

checking on the students in the regular classroom, and meeting and planning with my instructional aide. I feel that this time is very important. All of my students spend most of the school day in the regular classroom. If they are really struggling in those settings, I need to know so that I can provide additional support.

There are always some exceptions to the general guidelines I use for scheduling. I have three students whom I only monitor in the regular classroom. These students see me as a group on my assessment/consulting day. We talk about how it is going and discuss what is working for them and what frustrates them. I feel this time is critical for their successful mainstreaming. I also have two fifth-grade students who have good oral language skills but are reading on the first-grade level. They come for an additional thirty minutes late in the day, and we use the Fernald (VAKT) method to learn sight words.

I also developed a special schedule for my teachers' aide. She works directly with students to supplement and enhance skills they have initiated with me.

Special Considerations for Scheduling in Secondary Settings

Scheduling in resource and consultant programs in secondary settings generally is less flexible than in elementary-level programs. Teachers must work within the confines of the instructional periods and the curricular units that students must complete for high school graduation. One of the major responsibilities for resource/consultant teachers in secondary settings is to determine subject areas in which the students need special classes, and subjects in which they can succeed in regular or special materials classes without instructional support. These decisions about scheduling must be made on an individual basis and should be made with the involvement and commitment of the student as well as the teachers involved.

With the greater use of "learning and study strategies" curriculums in secondary special education programs, secondary special education teachers may want to consider their role as that of learning specialists (Schumaker and Deshler, 1988). For the most part, they teach classes in learning and study strategies that provide students with the necessary skills and strategies to function in regular content classes. These learning specialists may also spend part of their day consulting with the content area teachers/specialists and in some cases may coteach.

CHALLENGES TO SUCCESSFUL MAINSTREAMING AND CONSULTATION

Challenges to Regular Classroom Teachers

There has probably never been a time in history when educators have faced greater challenges than those we face in the United States today. Classroom teachers are required to provide instruction for increasingly diverse student populations and are still held accountable for covering the prescribed curriculum in a manner that ensures that most of the students learn that content. Classroom teachers sometimes feel that they must choose between covering the full content of the curriculum or spending sufficient instructional time on the components of that curriculum to ensure that their slower students learn what they are supposed to learn. Many teachers make the choice to "go on," even when MSE and other low-achieving students have not learned very much. Research has shown, however, that high-achieving students *want* teachers to take extra time and to try differing instructional approaches that help ensure that the lower-achieving students also learn the content (Vaughn et al., 1991). Teachers doubt that their curriculum supervisors, fellow teachers, and the parents of the high-achievers are as flexible about content coverage.

Many special education students need more time to master new concepts and skills, and they master those concepts and skills only if instruction is presented to them in a manner that enables them to "grasp" the new material. Students with learning disabilities, for example, have great difficulty with the learning process. Once they learn a new concept or skill, however, they "have" it and tend not to forget it. Unfortunately, an instructional strategy that works for one student may not work for another. Thus, a teacher must know and use a variety of instructional strategies to ensure that all of the students have an opportunity to learn. This effort takes time and planning, and it may result in less content coverage within a given time frame. Teachers need assurance from their supervisors that when there are several special-needs students in their classroom, they will not be held accountable for covering the full content of the curriculum. The first priority must be to ensure that the students succeed in learning the content that is covered.

Challenges to Teacher Educators

When a regular education teacher is asked to accept a mainstreamed special education student in his or her class, that teacher is, in effect, being asked to become the special education teacher for that student. If regular education teachers are to assume the additional role of special educators, they need to receive the appropriate education for that very important job. The need for special training is accentuated by the fact that for every identified special education student in the classroom, there are usually several other students who have undiagnosed learning or behavior problems. Today's students have many needs and their classroom teachers require very specialized training to help them meet those needs.

In general, the regular education teachers at the middle and high school levels indicate that it is not feasible for them to plan specifically for MSE students (Schumm and Vaughn, 1992). They are willing to make accommodations for MSE students as they teach, and they are willing to help MSE students as their need for help becomes clear, but they generally resist the idea of making special plans for individual students. They cite large classes made up of nonspecial education students with diverse needs of their own. For example, some students in their general education classes presented serious behavior problems, and some were learning English as a second language and had difficulty understanding and communicating in English (McIntosh et al., 1993).

Challenges to Special Education Teachers

If students with learning and behavior problems are to be successful in the mainstream, then special education and regular education teachers must work together so that the students can make both academic and social progress. The strategies that follow may be incorporated into an instructional program whose objective is to assist students in the regular classroom.

— Work closely with the regular classroom teacher.
— Observe in the regular classroom to determine the academic and social demands.
— Simulate the academic and social demands of the regular classroom in the special education classroom.
— Involve the student in the mainstreaming process by setting successful mainstreaming as a shared goal.
— Have the student observe in the regular classroom before being mainstreamed.
— Assist the regular teacher in adapting materials, instruction, and the instructional environment to facilitate the student's needs.
— Monitor the student once he or she is mainstreamed.
— At first, meet regularly with the mainstreamed student to discuss progress and concerns.
— At first, communicate frequently with the regular classroom teacher to discuss progress and concerns.
— Suggest that the regular classroom teacher use a "buddy" system in which the mainstreamed student is paired with a "veteran" to help the mainstreamed student learn the rules, procedures, and routines of the classroom.

Ms. Peress demonstrates many of these strategies as she mainstreams the intermediate-level students with learning disabilities from her self-contained classroom to regular classrooms. Ms. Peress describes her mainstreaming strategy as follows: "I am convinced that these students need to be in regular classrooms if at all possible. However, I've learned that we need to prepare them both socially and academically. Much of what we do in special education classrooms does not prepare them for regular education. They are used to individual and small group instruction, receiving lots of feedback, lots of reinforcement, and being relatively free to ask and receive assistance. This does not reflect what happens in the regular classrooms in this school. Although the teachers are great, they have twenty-eight to thirty-two students in each class. Large-group instruction and cooperative and independent learning are the most frequently used instructional arrangements." Ms. Peress continues:

The first key to making mainstreaming work is to cooperate with the regular classroom teacher and to observe that classroom to determine the learning and social demands.

The second key is to gain a commitment from the student. He or she has to want to work toward the goal. I always describe the classroom demands to the student and sometimes he or she goes to observe. Then we plan how we're going to get ready for "going to Mrs. Fetter's class for math."

The third key is to begin simulating those learning and social demands in my classroom. I start gradually. Usually I start by decreasing the feedback and reinforcement. Next I focus on the academic demands. I get the lessons and textbooks from the classroom teacher and I begin to assign the lessons. At first the rate of learning is matched to the student's learning rate. But once the student is succeeding with the assignments, I begin to increase the rate until it matches that of the regular classroom. As this procedure continues, I continue to reduce the amount of reinforcement and feedback and to work with the student to become a more independent learner.

The fourth key is to wait to begin mainstreaming until the student is working in the same materials and at the same rate as the regular classroom. Then when he or she moves to the classroom the student only has to cope with a new teacher and setting and not with new materials.

The fifth key is to monitor the student and to continue to work with the classroom teacher to modify and adapt materials, methods, and the teaching-learning environment as needed.

I have developed this strategy through experience. Many times I have found that my test scores, informal assessments, and student progress data indicate that the student is reading at grade level. In the past I would jump to the conclusion that the student was ready to return to the regular classroom. Yet too often I would find the student back in my class within three weeks, after failing in the regular classroom. I was really setting the students up for failure. I had only attended to their reading level, not to the social and academic demands.

I've been very successful with this strategy. It's February and already I have all but four of my fourteen students mainstreamed for at least one academic subject (e.g., reading, math, writing, social studies, science).

Ms. Peress's discussion of how she mainstreams her students into the regular classroom demonstrates that she has a philosophy that places importance on communication, collaboration, and consultation with the regular classroom teachers. A number of models for consultation and collaboration between regular educators and special educators have been developed.

What Special Education Students Can Expect in Regular Education Classrooms

Special education teachers need to understand what students with special needs can reasonably expect in regular education classrooms so that they can provide the support and skills necessary for success. While expectations vary considerably between elementary and secondary teachers (Schumm et al., 1992) and obviously from teacher to teacher, there are some common expectations.

— Regular education teachers are willing to make adaptations and accommodations that they can do with little preplanning. These adaptations and accommodations are more likely to occur if they can be done during the instructional process. See Apply the Concept 11.1 for a list of feasible adaptations.

— Mainstreamed special education students are treated by teachers much like other students (McIntosh, Vaughn, Schumm, Haager, and Lee, 1993). This is, of course, both good and bad news. Teachers treat students with special needs with the same respect and consideration provided other students. They provide few accommodations (particularly at the middle and high school level) to meet the individual learning needs of the students.

— Mainstreamed students participate infrequently in class activities, ask fewer questions, and respond rarely to teachers' questions (Baker and Zigmond, 1990; McIntosh et al., 1993). Students with special needs display a passive learning style that does little to increase the likelihood regular education teachers will meet their learning needs.

— Whole-class activities is by far the primary mode of instruction at the middle and high school level and for social studies and science at the elementary level (McIntosh et al., 1993; Schumm et al., 1995). Thus, students with special needs who are accustomed to working in small groups and receiving extensive teacher direction are unlikely to receive these same considerations in the regular education classroom.

— Undifferentiated large-group instruction is representative of what occurs in regular education classrooms (Baker and Zigmond, 1990; McIntosh et al., 1993). Teachers largely follow the sequence of activities provided in the teacher's manual and do not consider the learning needs of groups or individual students.

APPLY THE CONCEPT 11.1

FEASIBLE ADAPTATIONS REGULAR EDUCATION TEACHERS ARE WILLING TO MAKE

Teachers identified the following as HIGHLY feasible to implement:

1. Provide reinforcement and encouragement to assist students with learning.
2. Establish a personal relationship with the mainstreamed student.
3. Involve the mainstreamed student in whole class activities.
4. Establish routines that are appropriate for mainstreamed students.
5. Establish expectations for learning and behavior.

Teachers identified the following as NOT likely to be implemented:

1. Adapt long-range plans to meet the needs of mainstreamed students.
2. Adjust the physical arrangement of the room to meet the needs of mainstreamed students.
3. Use alternative materials or adapt current materials for students with special needs.
4. Adapt scoring and grading criteria for students with special needs.
5. Provide individualizing instruction to meet students' special needs.

Source: Adapted from J. S. Schumm and S. Vaughn (1991). Making adaptations for mainstreamed students: General classroom teachers' perspectives. *Remedial and Special Education,12*(4), pp. 18–27. Used with permission.

Students' Perceptions of Teachers' Adaptations

If students are to be held responsible for their own learning and education, then the perceptions of students should be assessed and considered. A recent series of studies has investigated students' perceptions of regular classroom teachers' adaptations to meet the needs of students with special needs (Vaughn, Schumm, and Kouzekanani, 1993; Vaughn, Schumm, Niarhos, and Daugherty, 1993; Vaughn, Schumm, Niarhos, and Gordon, 1993). The perceptions of students are particularly significant with respect to regular classroom teachers' adaptations because students' perceptions are likely to influence teachers' behavior and teachers are unlikely to make adaptations for students with special needs that they feel would "take away" from nondisabled students. A summary of the findings and their implications for instruction follow.

— Elementary, middle, and high school students overwhelmingly prefer the teacher who makes adaptations to meet the special needs of students. There are three exceptions and these include adaptations in tests, homework, and textbooks. Consistent findings reveal that all students appreciate using the same textbooks and having the same homework. Interviews with students reveal that having the same homework is particularly important because homework serves as the rationale for multiple telephone calls to friends after school. Students who do not have the same homework run the risk of being left out of the social circle.

— Across all grade groupings, high-achieving students are more likely to prefer the teacher who makes adaptations than are low-achieving students. This seems surprising at first because it would seem that high-achieving students would have the least to gain from adaptations the teacher makes to meet the needs of students. The interest in adaptations on the part of high-achieving students seems altruistic.

— Students with special needs placed in the regular education classroom for more than 50 percent of the school day had perceptions of teachers similar to those of the high-achieving students with two exceptions. The students with special needs did not demonstrate significant preferences for no adaptations in tests and textbooks. Since students with special needs are accustomed to having tests and textbooks modified they did not find these procedures unusual on the part of the regular classroom teacher.

— All students want to be taught learning strategies to assist them in acquiring information on their own (Vaughn, Schumm, Klingner, and Saumell, 1995).

CONSULTATION AND COLLABORATION

How to Collaborate

Although both terms, consultation and collaboration, are often used to describe the role of many special education teachers, teachers prefer *collaboration* (Arguelles, Vaughn, and Schumm, 1996; Morrison, Walker, Wakefield, and Solberg, 1994). Why? Teachers indicate that they prefer collaborative modes of working on student problems rather than giving the problem to experts or working on it independently (Morrison et al., 1994). Teachers perceive that collaboration more accurately describes the nature of their relationship. One special education teacher said, "We actually work together to solve problems. It's not like I have all of the answers or she has all of the problems. We really help each other come up with ideas that work." We have found that regular education teachers feel much the same way.

What is collaboration? According to Friend and Cook (1992) "Interpersonal collaboration is a style for direct interaction between at least two coequal parties voluntarily engaged in shared decision making as they work toward a common goal" (p. 5). Collaboration refers to the interaction that occurs between two professionals, often between the special education teacher and the regular education teacher,

and the roles that they play as equal partners in a problem solving endeavor.

As a special education teacher, what are some of the ways you might expect to collaborate with other professionals? As described in the next chapter, a significant part of your role will be to collaborate with parents and any other specialist who is associated with the students with special needs with whom you work. Whether you are working as a resource room teacher, self-contained special education teacher, or coteacher you will also have considerable opportunities to collaborate with regular classroom teachers. You may also work in a program in which most of your work day involves collaboration with other teachers. At the elementary, middle, and secondary school levels, teachers are increasingly working in more collaborative ways with other professionals (Pugach and Johnson, 1995).

One important way you will collaborate with general education professionals is in developing ways to make the curriculum more accessible to students with special needs (Warger and Pugach, 1996). Curriculum planning can address such important issues as identifying changes in curriculum that are forecasted by national boards and professional groups; identify the ways in which these new trends will affect the curriculum and students with special needs; examine the scope and sequence of your present curriculum and determine where changes best fit; identify new goals and discuss the prerequisite skills needed for students with special needs; and identify areas of mismatch or where new curriculum is inappropriate for target students.

Procedures for Collaboration

When you work collaboratively with another professional it is helpful to have a common list of procedures that you follow to resolve the dilemma or solve the problem. Most procedures for peer collaboration include the following five steps:

1. *Initiator and Facilitator.* Usually one member of the team has a problem or issue that needs to be resolved. That person is referred to as the initiator. The person(s) who is assisting with the

problem is referred to as the facilitator. They serve as guides to assist in the resolution of the issue.

2. *Clarifying Questions.* The initiator describes the problem or dilemma. The facilitator attempts to clarify the problem by asking questions.

3. *Summarization.* The problem is summarized by the team. The following format can be used to assist in summarizing the problem: (a) establishing the pattern of behavior, (b) acknowledging the teacher's feelings about the problem, and (c) identifying aspects of classroom and school environments that the teacher can modify (Pugach and Johnson, 1995).

4. *Interventions and Predictions.* The team generates at least three interventions that address the problem. They consider the likely outcomes of each of the interventions identified.

5. *Evaluation.* The team develops an evaluation plan that includes strategies for keeping track of the intervention, recording the student's progress, and meeting again to review progress.

Resources Needed for Collaboration

No resource impedes successful collaboration more than time. Special and general education teachers confirm the difficulties of finding adequate time to effectively collaborate during the work day (Voltz, Elliott, and Cobb, 1994). If time is not built into teachers' schedules, collaboration is simply unlikely to occur on a regular basis. Furthermore, if it is not part of the schedule, then teachers come to resent having to collaborate because it means taking time from their personal schedules. Another critical aspect of time management for special education teachers is finding a mutual time in which they can collaborate with the many teachers with whom they work. This can be especially challenging at the secondary level.

— What are some ways in which collaborative time can be arranged (Vaughn, Bos, and Schumm, 1997)?

— Administrators designate a common time for collaborating professionals to work together (e.g., all fifth-grade team members).

— School boards pay professionals for one extra time period each week that can be used to collaborate or meet with parents.

— School districts provide early dismissal for students one day a week so that team members have a common planning time.

— Teachers schedule brief but focused planning periods with each other on a regularly scheduled basis.

Space for meeting is another needed resource. Often special education teachers feel fortunate if they have an office or a small classroom for their materials. Finding a quiet place to meet is particularly challenging in many schools where overcrowding is the norm.

Additionally, participants in collaborative models need to be familiar with procedures for successful collaboration. An orientation that addresses basic questions about their roles and responsibilities is helpful to all personnel involved in collaboration.

Teacher Assistance Teams

Teacher Assistance Teams (TAT) (Chalfant and Pysh, 1989, 1992; Chalfant, Pysh, and Moultrie, 1979) is a within-building problem-solving model designed to provide a teacher support system for classroom teachers. Chalfant and Pysh identified five reasons schools may struggle with meeting the needs of all students including mainstreamed handicapped students in the regular classroom. First, with more special needs students remaining in the classroom and the general school population growing in terms of the number of at-risk students, the demands on classroom teachers have increased. Second, sufficient funds are not available to provide direct supportive services to all the children who need individualized assistance within our schools. Third, the classroom teacher may lack the time or preparation to plan and individualize instruction for these students. Fourth, because of the necessary assessment and placement safeguards built into the special education support system, this system is oftentimes not responsive to the immediate needs of teachers. Fifth, in some cases the teachers' perceived need for help has led to the overreferral of students for special education assessment and placement (Chalfant, 1987; 1989; Chalfant, Pysh, and Moultrie, 1979).

The Teacher Assistance Team is a school-based problem-solving unit designed to assist teachers in generating intervention strategies. The TAT model provides a forum whereby classroom teachers can meet and engage in a collaborative problem-solving process. The model is based on four assumptions related to teacher empowerment:

1. Considerable knowledge and talent exists among classroom teachers.

2. Classroom teachers can and do help many students with learning and behavior problems. Every effort should be made in the regular classroom before a referral for special education services is made.

3. Teachers can resolve more problems by working together than by working alone.

4. Teachers learn best by doing; the best way to increase teachers' knowledge and skills is by helping them solve immediate classroom problems (Chalfant and Pysh, 1989; Chalfant, Pysh, and Moultrie, 1979).

▬ **PROCEDURES:** The core team is generally composed of three elected members (primarily classroom rather than special education teachers) with the requesting teacher also participating as a team member. The team may ask other teachers, specialists, or the principal to join the team as they deem necessary or to serve as permanent members. One person serves as coordinator and is charged with such responsibilities as alerting the team members to the time and place for the meetings and distributing information prior to the meeting so that the members have read the information prior to the problem-solving meeting.

When teachers refer classroom problems to the team, they complete a request for assistance in which they address four areas:

1. Describe what you would like the student *to be able to do* that he/she does not presently do.

2. Describe what the student *does (assets)* and what he/she *does not do (deficits)*.

3. Describe what you have done to help the student cope with his or her problems.

4. Provide background information and/or previous assessment data relevant to the problem (Chalfant and Pysh, 1981; Chalfant, Pysh and Moultrie, 1979).

Once a request for assistance is received, the person on the team responsible for that case reviews the information obtained from the request for assistance, observes in the classroom if necessary, interviews the teacher to clarify information, and constructs a problem-interaction diagram that visually represents and summarizes the concerns (Chalfant and Pysh, 1992). This information is distributed to the team members prior to the meeting.

At the TAT meeting, the team members complete a thirty-minute problem-solving process for each request consisting of:

1. Reviewing the summary information, providing the opportunity for the teacher to clarify or provide additional information, and reaching consensus on what the problem is

2. Identifying the primary concern and establishing an objective for solving the problem

3. Brainstorming ideas for solving the problem and reaching the objective

4. Having the teacher requesting assistance select intervention strategies, which the teacher and team refine into a classroom intervention plan

5. Developing a means of measuring the success of the intervention plan

6. Establishing a date and time for a fifteen-minute follow-up meeting

Using this type of format, a teacher assistance team generally handles two new requests during a one-hour meeting or one new request and two follow-ups.

▬ **COMMENTS:** The TAT model has been used widely throughout the United States and Canada. This model has been shown to be effective in assisting teachers in coping with the learning and behavior problems of students in the general school population. It is also particularly effective in reducing the number of students inappropriately referred for special education (Chalfant and Pysh, 1989). Its success in reducing the number of inappropriate referrals to special education has resulted in the TAT model being identified in the literature as a prereferral intervention. However, the original intent of the process was to serve as a resource for all students at a school. This process has also been used with students already identified as handicapped with the children's special education and regular education teachers serving as team members and participating in the problem-solving process.

Several factors seem particularly relevant to the success of this model within a school. First, it is important that the school administration support such a program by providing teachers with the time for meetings and some type of support or incentive for serving as team members. Second, school-wide training in effective and efficient problem-solving strategies and the TAT process facilitates the success of the model (Chalfant and Pysh, 1989).

School Collaboration

Collaboration in the Schools (West, Idol, and Cannon, 1989) is one of a number of consultation models that focuses on the special education teacher consulting directly with regular classroom teachers to assist them in the successful mainstreaming of students with learning and behavior problems. This consultation model is based on the concept of collaborative consultation which Idol and West and their colleagues define as "an interactive process that enables people with diverse expertise to generate creative solutions to mutually defined problems. . . . The major outcome of collaborative consultation is to provide comprehensive and effective programs for students with special needs within the most appropriate context, thereby enabling them to achieve maximum constructive interaction with their nonhandicapped peers" (Idol, Paolucci-Whitcomb, and Nevin, 1986, p. 1).

Like TAT, this model grew out of a need to provide more effective and coordinated services for students with special needs. West and Idol (1990) cite three reasons for using consultation models for special-needs students within the schools. One reason is the expense of assessing and placing students with learning and behavior problems in special education. They suggest that collaborative problem solving can serve as a preventative model. The second reason is evidence from research on effective schools (see Purkey and Smith, 1985, for a review), which indicates that collaborative planning and collegial relationships are two key process variables that are present in effective schools. A third reason is based on a professional development needs survey of the members of the Council for Exceptional Children, the major professional organization for special educators. The results indicate that the three top-ranked items focused on collaboration, communication, and consultation between special and regular educators.

The purposes for collaborative consultation are to prevent learning and behavior problems, remediate learning and behavior problems, and coordinate instructional programs (West et al., 1989). The model is based on a set of forty-seven collaborative consultation skills which were validated by experts in the field (West and Cannon, 1988) and are grouped into the following areas:

- Consultation theory/models
- Research on consultation theory, training, and practice
- Personal characteristics
- Interactive communication
- Collaborative problem solving
- Systems change
- Equity issues and value/belief systems
- Evaluation of consultation effectiveness

— **PROCEDURES:** The model is based on a six-stage collaborative consultation process completed by a collaborative team:

> *Stage 1: Goal/Entry.* Roles, objectives, responsibilities, and expectations are negotiated.

APPLY THE CONCEPT 11.2

THE MAINSTREAM ASSISTANCE TEAM

Because consultation is increasingly used in schools and districts throughout the United States, Fuchs and colleagues (Fuchs, Fuchs, and Bahr, 1990) designed a prescriptive approach to problem solving in which the specialist (e.g., the special education teacher or school psychologist) serves in the role of the consultant and the classroom teacher as the consultee. The Mainstream Assistance Team follows four common problem-solving steps:

1. Problem Identification
2. Problem Analysis

3. Plan Implementation, and
4. Problem Evaluation

One of the unique aspects of the Mainstream Assistance Team is that the team uses a list of pre-identified potential interventions to facilitate the process, assist on generating ideas, and saving time. Research indicates that both special and general education teachers were satisfied with the idea, the process, and the outcomes from implementing the program.

Stage 2: Problem Identification. Nature and parameters of the presenting problem are defined.

Stage 3: Intervention of Recommendations. Potential interventions are generated and effects predicted. Recommendations are prioritized and selected. Objectives are developed to specify the intervention details, the procedures, and the means for determining if the problem has been solved.

Stage 4: Implementation of Recommendations. Procedures and plan of action are implemented.

Stage 5: Evaluation. Evaluation of the intervention is completed, including its impact on the child, the consultant and consultee, and the system or context in which the intervention is occurring.

Stage 6: Redesign. Intervention is continued, redesigned, or discontinued based on the evaluation (West and Idol, 1990).

Chapter Appendix 11.3 presents a problem-solving worksheet to use in conjunction with this consultation process. Collaborative consultation may occur at varying levels of teacher and school involvement. For example, a resource and regular English class-

room teacher in a middle school or high school may use collaborative consultation to assist students with learning disabilities who are being mainstreamed into regular English classes. Or an intermediate resource teacher and the speech/language pathologist may work with the intermediate teachers in an elementary school to develop strategies for facilitating concept and language development in the content areas. Or an elementary school may adopt collaborative consultation at the building level with the consultation used in the prereferral process as well as for a means of coordinating the special and regular education programs for special-needs students.

— **COMMENTS:** Like TAT, collaborative consultation has been used in a number of schools and districts throughout the United States and Canada. West and Idol (1990) suggest that a number of factors need to be considered in implementing collaborative consultation. These parallel those relevant to TAT, including systematic and ongoing staff development, administrative support, and scheduling.

Like other educational approaches, consultation and collaboration models have the potential for benefit as well as misuse and misunderstanding. Apply the Concept 11.3 provides a description of potential benefits and misuses.

APPLY THE CONCEPT 11.3

Huefner (1988) has identified several potential benefits and misuses of consultation and collaboration models.

Potential Benefits

1. Reduction of stigma
2. Better understanding across education disciplines
3. On-the-job training for regular education teachers in skills for effectively meeting the needs of special education students
4. Reduced mislabeling of students as disabled
5. The model may be more suitable to meeting the needs of secondary school students
6. Spillover benefits to regular education students from working cooperatively with special education teacher

Potential Misuses

1. Excessive caseload management for special education teacher
2. Unrealistic expectations from viewing the consulting model as a panacea and/or undertraining and overloading the resource teacher
3. Inadequate support and cooperation from regular classroom teachers
4. Converting the model to a tutoring or aide approach
5. Providing inadequate funding
6. Faulty assumptions regarding cost savings
7. Faulty assumptions regarding program effectiveness

Collaboration: Issues and Dilemmas

Since all special education teachers will be working in some collaborative way with regular education teachers and many special education teachers will be working with regular education teachers at least 50 percent of the time, several issues and dilemmas need to be recognized if special education teachers are to perform their job role effectively.

1. *Student "ownership."* One of the issues is the "ownership" of the student with problems. Traditionally, special education students have been the responsibility of the special education teacher, even if they were placed in the regular education classroom for part of the day. This perspective is no longer feasible or desirable. The new perspective is one of shared ownership whereby all educators feel responsible for the success of the mainstreamed special education student.

2. *Individual versus class focus.* In a recent year long case study of the planning and adaptations for mainstreamed special education students of 12 effective regular education teachers (4 elementary,

4 middle school, and 4 high school) (Schumm, Vaughn, Haager, McDowell, Rothlein and Saumell, 1992), the regular education teachers did not plan or make adaptations for individual students but considered the class as a whole. This focus contrasts with that of special education teachers whose planning and instruction is aimed at the needs of the individual student. Neither of these perspectives is inherently better than the other (Glatthorn, 1990), but differing perspectives often promote conflict. Mrs. Vermillion put it this way: "I am a special education teacher and so the direction of my interest is always with the individual students and how the educational setting can be altered to meet his or her needs. During the last few years I realize that I've needed to adjust my perspective if I am to work effectively with regular classroom teachers. When they think about planning for students, they think about the class as a whole."

3. *Content versus accommodation.* When classroom teachers discuss their planning and instruction, one of the most consistent themes is content coverage (Schumm et al., 1992; Vaughn and Schumm, 1994). Classroom teachers feel that many guidelines at the state, local, and school level pressure them to cover more content. Often this need to cover content conflicts with knowledge acquisition. According to Vanessa, a ninth-grade science teacher, "If I waited until the students 'got it' we would never be able to cover all the material" (Vaughn and Schumm, 1994).

This notion of "content coverage" as the horse leading the instructional wagon is a consistent and pervasive problem in regular education and now directly influences the instruction of mainstreamed students with special needs. There is some consensus that "less is more" and that reduced focus on content coverage would enhance the quality of instruction for all learners.

You can imagine the difficulty for regular classroom teachers who feel extreme pressures to cover extensive amounts of content when special education teachers make suggestions that slow down the pace or require them to make adaptations for students' special learning needs. This issue is not insolvable. In a year-long research project designed to increase the planning and adaptations of regular classroom teachers (social studies and science), teachers are willing to make adaptations and accommodations they feel will help students, and do not require extensive amounts of preplanning (Schumm et al., 1992).

4. *Real world versus student's world.* Another dilemma between regular and special education teachers is the purpose of education. Regular classroom teachers feel they are preparing students for the "real world." From their perspective, persons in the real world do not make accommodations for different learning styles. Fundamentally, they view the real world as expecting the same thing from everybody and therefore to best prepare youngsters, their role as teachers is to expect the same thing from every student. This position is more reflective of middle and high school teachers (who feel increased pressures to prepare students for the real world) than elementary teachers (Schumm et al., 1992).

Ms. McDowell, a secondary special education teacher, handles the problem this way: "When regular classroom teachers talk to me about the real world I'm prepared. First, I present them with the idea that students are never going to be successful in the real world if they do not have an opportunity to learn and experience success in their present world. Their present world is that teacher's classroom. Second, I present them with the fact that employers are required by law to make reasonable accommodations for individuals with disabilities. Also, I never ask regular classroom teachers to make adaptations or accommodations that aren't useful to most students in the classroom."

Coteaching

Coteaching or cooperative teaching is when regular and special education teachers work in a coordinated way to jointly teach heterogeneous groups of students in the regular education setting (Bauwens, Hourcade, and Friend, 1989). Cooperative teaching works well within a collaborative consultation program. The key aspects of cooperative teaching follow.

— Special and regular education teachers broadly plan their overall goals and desired outcomes for the class and specific students in the class.
— Both special and regular classroom teachers preside during the same instruction period.
— While one teacher may provide some instruction to the group as a whole, most of the instructional time involves teachers working with small groups or individual students.
— Since students are frequently heterogeneously grouped, the special education teacher works with many students including those identified as benefitting from special education.
— Complementary instruction and supportive learning activities are part of teachers' coplanning and instruction.

Coplanning. As a special education teacher, you will often be coplanning with general education teachers for the students with special needs who are in their classrooms. Sometimes you will also be coteaching in those classrooms, other times you will be assisting the teacher in planning lessons and making adaptations for the students with special needs that will be taught without your assistance.

With long-range coplanning, the special education and general education teachers broadly plan their overall goals and outcomes for the class and the specific students with disabilities who are in the class. This coplanning of broad goals occurs quarterly or more frequently as needed. This planning fits in with the IEP of the student with disabilities.

In coplanning units or lessons, the special education and general education teachers plan specific lessons and outcomes for a unit of study or for a designated period of time (e.g., weekly). The Planning Pyramid (Schumm, Vaughn, and Harris, in press; Schumm, Vaughn, and Leavell, 1994) provides an instructional process for coplanning between special and general education teachers to meet the needs of students with disabilities in general education classrooms. As can be seen in Figure 11.11, a form for unit planning, and in Figure 11.12, a form for lesson planning, forms can be used to facilitate the process. Working together, teachers complete the form to identify their objectives, materials needed, and their roles and responsibilities in delivering the instruction. Essential to the success of the planning pyramid is the identification of core ideas, concepts, vocabulary, and/or principles that the teachers determine as essential for all students to learn. This information is entered at the base of the pyramid. Information that the teacher deems important for most students to learn is written at the middle of the pyramid. Information for a few students to learn is written at the top of the pyramid. Teachers who implement the planning pyramid find that it facilitates not just the organization of the material they intend to teach, but provides guidelines for instruction (Schumm, Vaughn, and Harris, in press).

Coteaching. Joyce Duryea is an elementary special education teacher who has worked as a resource

■ **FIGURE 11.11** *Unit Planning Form*

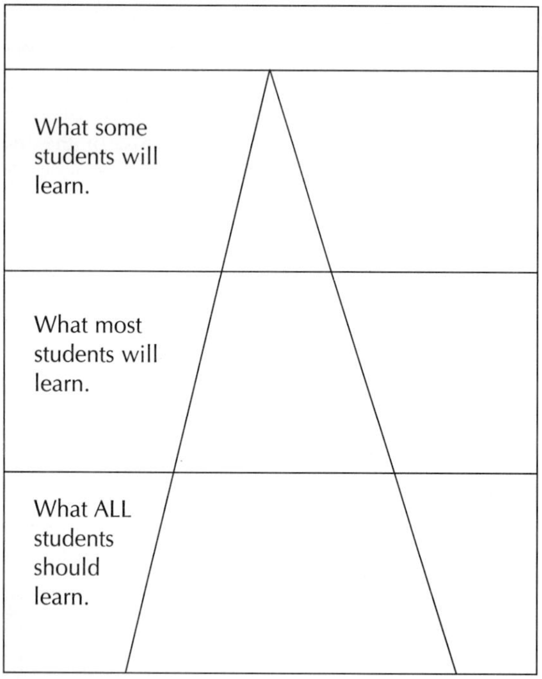

Date: ____________ Class Period: ____________

Unit Title: ______________________________

Materials/Resources:

____

Instructional Strategies/Adaptations:

____

Evaluation/Products:

____

■ **FIGURE 11.12**   *Weekly Coplanning Form*

Time Period: _____   Week Of: _____

Content Area: _____

Goals:	GE	SE

_____   _____

_____   _____

Activities: GE .... SE

Monday _____   _____

Tuesday _____   _____

Wednesday _____   _____

Thursday _____   _____

Friday _____   _____

Material(s): GE .... SE

Monday _____   _____

Tuesday _____   _____

Wednesday _____   _____

Thursday _____   _____

Friday _____   _____

Groups/Students: GE .... SE

Monday _____   _____

Tuesday _____   _____

Wednesday _____   _____

Thursday _____   _____

Friday _____   _____

Evaluation:

_____

_____

Other:

_____

_____

room teacher for nine years. Recently she was asked to work collaboratively with three general education teachers who had approximately five students with disabilities in each of their classrooms. Joyce said, "When I was preparing to be a special education teacher it never occurred to me that I would need to know how to coteach in a regular classroom. I always thought I would have my group of students with special needs and that is the way it would be." However, she has found her new role exciting and challenging. Joyce puts it this way, "I think I'm a better teacher now and I definitely have a much better understanding of what goes on in the regular classroom and what kinds of expectations I need to have for my students."

Based on extended observations and interviews with more than seventy general education/special education teacher teams, we have identified several core issues that must be addressed if coteaching partnerships are likely to be successful (Vaughn and Schumm, 1996).

— Who gives grades and how do we grade? Perhaps the issue that warrants the most discussion prior to coteaching is grading. Special education teachers are accustomed to grading based on the effort, motivation, and abilities of their students. General education teachers consider grades from the perspective of a uniform set of expectations. Communicating about grading procedures for in-class assignments, tests, and homework will reduce the friction frequently associated with grading students with disabilities in the general education classroom.

— Whose classroom management rules do we use and who enforces them? Most general and special education teachers know the types of academic and social behaviors they find acceptable and unacceptable. Rarely is there disagreement between teachers about the more extreme behaviors; however, the subtle classroom management difficulties that are part of the ongoing routines of running a classroom can cause concerns for teachers. It is beneficial for teachers to discuss their classroom management styles and the roles they expect of each other in maintaining a smooth running classroom. Critical to success is determining when and with whom the special education teacher should intervene for discipline purposes.

— What space do I get? When a special education teacher spends part of his/her day instructing in another teacher's classroom, it is extremely useful to have a designated area for him or her to keep materials. Special education teachers who coteach for part of the school day in a teacher's classroom feel more at home and are better accepted by the students when they have a legitimate claim on space including a designated desk and chair.

— What do we tell the students? Teachers often wonder if students should be told they have two teachers or whether they should reveal that one of the teachers is a special teacher? We think it is a good idea to inform the students that they will be having two teachers and to introduce the special teacher as a "learning abilities" specialist. Students both accept and like the idea of having two teachers. In interviews with elementary students who had two teachers (special education and general education) the students revealed that they very much liked having two teachers in the classroom (Klingner et al., in press).

— How can we get time to coplan and coordinate? The most pervasive concern of both general and special education teachers who coteach is obtaining sufficient time during the school day to plan and discuss their instruction and the learning of their students. This is of particular concern for special education teachers who are working with more than one general education teacher. Teachers need a minimum of forty-five minutes of uninterrupted planning time each week if they are likely to have a successful coteaching experience. One suggestion made by several of the teacher teams with whom we have worked is to designate a day or a half-day every six to eight weeks when teachers meet extensively to plan and discuss the progress of students as well as changes in their instructional practices.

SUMMARY

Effective and efficient management and communication are key aspects of "good" teaching, particularly when designing and implementing educational programs for students with learning and behavior problems. This chapter provided information concerning the management and communication responsibilities of special education teachers. Specifically it focused on strategies and ideas for setting up different types of special education programs, utilizing equipment, designing and arranging instructional materials, scheduling, and consulting and collaborating with regular classroom teachers.

This chapter also addressed issues related to collaborating with other professionals. Collaboration involves shared decision making among coequals who have a common interest. Because working collaboratively takes time, issues arise related to planning time and resources, and developing skills. These skills are needed not just by the special education teacher, but by other professionals in the school as well. This chapter provided suggestions and considerations to make coteaching more successful.

Because management and communication vary depending on the setting, we encourage you to arrange to visit several special education programs and speak with the teachers if you are not familiar with different programs and settings for students with learning and behavior problems. This should help you envision how the information presented in this chapter can be used in school settings.

THINK AND APPLY

- Why is effective management and communication important for success as a special education teacher?
- What variables should you keep in mind when making decisions regarding the instruction and physical arrangement of the educational environment?
- What special considerations should a special education teacher keep in mind when planning a schedule for a secondary-level program
- Compare and contrast the models of Teacher Assistance Teams and Collaboration in the Schools.
- What is collaboration and what are some ways professionals can collaborate effectively?
- What are some of the resources professionals need in order to collaborate? How might these be obtained?
- What is the Mainstream Assistance Team and how might it resolve problems?
- What are some of the issues and dilemmas that occur when teachers coteach? How might they be resolved?

APPENDIX 11.1 ━━━━━━━━━━━━━━━━━━━━━━

Materials Evaluation Form

General Information

Name: <u>Schoolhouse: A Word Attack Skills Kit</u>
Author(s): <u>M. Clarke and F. Marsden</u>
Publisher: Science Research Associates

Copyright Date: <u>1973</u>
Cost: <u>$220</u>

Description of the Materials

<u>Purpose of Materials:</u> Provide practice with phonic and structural word analysis skills
<u>Instructional Level(s) of Materials:</u>
  1st–3rd grades
<u>Content of Materials:</u>
  Plastic overlays and markers, 170 exercise cards (2 copies) and answer keys represent
  10 color-coded areas (e.g., initial consonants, vowels), progress sheets
<u>Target Age:</u>
  Could be used with students ages 6–12
<u>Theoretical Approach to Learning:</u>
  Behavior approach in that it assumes skills can be taught in isolation
<u>Type of Instructional Arrangement (Individual, Cooperative Learning, etc.):</u>
  Individual
<u>Teacher Involvement Requirements:</u> Demonstrating mechanics of programs. Checking
  student understanding of directions and pictures. Spot checking of student self-checks.
  Evaluating progress.
<u>Time Requirements:</u>
  10–15 minutes per exercise card.
<u>Space Requirements:</u>
  Materials come in 12" × 12" × 24" box.
<u>Equipment Requirements:</u>
  None

Evaluation	*Poor*	*Fair*	*Good*

1. <u>Materials sequentially organized</u>
  Progress from easy to hard
  Use pictures in early exercises
	1	2	③

2. <u>Materials organized for easy retrieval</u>
  Students should be able to find exercise card
  without assistance
	1	2	③

3. <u>Directions clear</u> Yes and written with a low readability level	1	2	③
4. <u>Provides adequate examples</u> Most of the time	1	②	3

5. <u>Provides for adequate practice</u>
  Would like to see more cards covering each
  phonic or structural element
	①	2	3

Evaluation	*Poor*	*Fair*	*Good*
6. <u>Conducive to providing feedback</u>	1	2	③
Student can self-check and could plot progress			
7. <u>Allows for checking/self-checking</u>	1	2	③
8. <u>Provides suggestions for adapting the materials</u>	①	2	3
No			
9. <u>Provides suggestions for generalization</u>	①	2	3
No, this is a major concern.			
10. <u>Interest Level</u>	1	②	3
Although pictures are fairly easy to interpret, there is a limited number. Format repetitive.			

Description of Role in Instructional Program

How would this material fit into my instructional program?
Only as a reinforcement activity. Need to discuss with students how this practice will help them when they read (generalization).

APPENDIX 11.2

Student Materials Evaluation Form

Student Name: <u>Jason</u>
Date of Evaluation: <u>March 15</u>
Name of Materials: <u>Criminal Justice (textbook)</u>

Evaluation	*Poor*	*Fair*	*Good*
1. <u>Directions are clear.</u>	1	2	③
I understand the activities at the end of the chapter.			
2. <u>Materials are interesting.</u>	1	2	③
Yes. I like the personal stories.			
3. <u>There are enough examples so that I know what to do.</u>	1	②	3
Pretty much			
4. <u>I get enough practice so that I learn the information or the skill.</u>	1	②	3
Only if we discuss it in class			
5. <u>It is easy to determine if I am doing the tasks correctly.</u>	①	2	3
Not really			
6. <u>I like using these materials.</u>	1	2	③
7. <u>I think that these materials teach:</u>			
About how our government works			
8. <u>The thing(s) I like best about these materials is:</u>			
They're interesting			
9. <u>The thing(s) I don't like about these materials is:</u>			
Sometimes it doesn't tell enough and I have to read other places			
10. <u>I would recommend using these materials for:</u>			
Government classes			

APPENDIX 11.3

Problem-Solving Worksheet

Resource Teacher _____

Classroom/Content Teacher _____

Date _____

Problem:

Details: _____

_____

_____

_____

Alternative Solutions	*Possible Consequences*	*Priority*
1. _____	_____	_____
_____	_____	_____
2. _____	_____	_____
_____	_____	_____
3. _____	_____	_____
_____	_____	_____
4. _____	_____	_____
_____	_____	_____
5. _____	_____	_____
_____	_____	_____
6. _____	_____	_____
_____	_____	_____
7. _____	_____	_____
_____	_____	_____
8. _____	_____	_____
_____	_____	_____

Solution to Be Tried First:

_____

Implementation Steps	*When*	*Who*
_____	_____	_____
_____	_____	_____
_____	_____	_____
_____	_____	_____
_____	_____	_____
_____	_____	_____
_____	_____	_____
_____	_____	_____
_____	_____	_____
_____	_____	_____

How Will the Plan Be Monitored?

_____

_____

_____

_____

How Will Progress Be Evaluated?

_____

_____

_____

_____

_____

Date and Time of Next Appointment

_____

_____

Source: Collaboration in the Schools: An Inservice and Preservice Curriculum for Teachers, Support Staff, and Administrators (pp. 187–188) by J. R. West, L. Idol, and G. Cannon, 1989, Austin, Tex.: PRO-ED. Copyright 1989 by PRO-ED, Inc. Reprinted by permission.

Chapter 12

Communicating with Parents and Professionals

OUTLINE

KEY TOPICS FOR MASTERY

— *Principles of good communication: acceptance, effective listening, effective questioning, providing encouragement, keeping the focus of the conversation directed, and developing a working alliance*
— *Effective interviewing skills for special education teachers*
— *Why special education teachers need to be sensitive to parents' concerns and to speak honestly about the child's problems*
— *How special education teachers can work productively with parents and fellow professionals to provide effective help for the special education student*
— *The role of the special education teacher in an effective mainstreaming program.*
— *Guarding against the potential barriers to successful mainstreaming*
— *How to gain the building-principal's interest and involvement in developing a model special education program*

 BRIGHT IDEA

Turn to page 507 and read Think and Apply.

Mrs. Babson works in a hospital emergency room, so she is accustomed to talking to people who are grieving. Mrs. Babson states:

I often speak to parents about the recovery of their children. Fortunately, most of the children have injuries or illnesses in which they will recover completely. I've been trained in the importance of telling the parents as quickly and completely as possible all we know about their child's condition. The only reason I'm telling you this is that I want you to understand that I am accustomed to dealing with difficulties. But I was unprepared for the inconsistent information I would receive about our son.

When our third child, Chad, was born, my husband and I couldn't have been happier. Our first two children were girls, who we enjoy immensely, but both of us were hoping for a boy. Chad walked and talked later than the girls, but I knew boys are often develop-

mentally slower than girls so we were not concerned. Even when he was a preschooler, we knew Chad was different. He often had difficulty thinking of the right word for an object and he was clumsier than other children his age. When we spoke with his pediatrician he informed us that this was not uncommon.

When Chad entered kindergarten he did not know all of his colors and showed little ability to remember the names of the letters in the alphabet. His kindergarten teacher said she had seen a number of students like Chad, often boys, and suggested we keep Chad in kindergarten another year. Our neighbor, who is a teacher, thought this might not be a good idea since Chad was already large for his age. We spoke with the principal, who seemed very busy and thought we should take the advice of the kindergarten teacher. We retained Chad. Spending another year in kindergarten seemed to do little good, however. Chad was still unable to identify letters, though he was very popular because of his size and knowledge of the kindergarten routine.

First grade was worse yet. Chad showed no signs of reading and was confusing letters. His writing resembled that of a much younger child. By now we were very concerned and made several appointments with his first-grade teacher. She was very responsive and suggested that we have Chad tutored during the summer. The tutor said Chad had an attention problem and was having trouble with letter and word reversals. She suggested we have him tested for learning disabilities. The school psychologist agreed to do the testing and it was late in the fall before we were called and given the results.

Though both my husband and I are professionals, we felt somewhat intimidated by the number of school personnel at the meeting. On our way home, as we tried to reconstruct what we heard, we realized that we had misunderstood and missed a lot of information. I heard the school personnel say Chad's intelligence was normal, but my husband thought that it couldn't be normal because his verbal intelligence was low. We decided to make a list of questions to ask at our next meeting. We felt we had made a major stride forward since Chad would now be receiving special instruction one hour each day from a learning disabilities specialist; however, we still felt we understood very little about his problems. I only wish we had been told more completely and quickly about Chad's problem.

Many parents have had similar experiences. They have noticed that their child is different in some areas from other children the child's age. These parents seek advice from friends, medical professionals, and school professionals, and often feel confused and frustrated. When the child is identified as learning-disabled or emotionally handicapped, many parents feel relieved at first, hoping this identification will lead to solutions that will eliminate the child's learning or behavior problem. The difficult adjustments are that the child will probably always have learning

or behavior problems and the special education teacher will be unable to provide any magic cures and certainly no quick solutions.

Learning disabilities and emotional handicaps are complex phenomena and knowledge of all the factors they involve is incomplete. Special education teachers must be sensitive to parental concerns about identification and intervention, and yet speak honestly about what they know and do not know. Teachers must provide parents with encouragement without giving false hopes. Parents need to know what educators' best knowledge of their child's learning and behavior problem is, and also to be informed of what educators are less sure of.

This chapter focuses on the teacher as a communicator. This communication occurs between teacher and parent and between special education teacher and other school-related professionals. The first part of the chapter focuses on principles of communication that can be used with parents and professionals. Effective communication skills are the basic needs in working effectively with parents and other professionals. The second part of the chapter focuses on teachers' roles with parents, on parental needs, and on how to facilitate an interactive relationship between school and home that will allow parents and professionals to exchange information. The third part of the chapter discusses special education teachers' roles with other professionals.

COMMUNICATION SKILLS

In addition to assessment, intervention, curriculum development, and classroom management, a major role for the teacher of students with learning and behavior problems is communication. Effective special education teachers communicate regularly with parents, other special and regular education teachers, school administrators, and other educational and psychological professionals such as the school psychologist, speech and language therapist, and so on. Ability to communicate effectively is a skill that significantly affects an exceptional educator's job success. Despite the importance of this skill, most teachers finish school with no formal training in communication.

Principles of Communication

Some teachers communicate effectively with parents and other teachers with little effort. They seem to be naturals at making other people feel at ease and willing to disclose information. However, most teachers can benefit from specific skills training that teaches them effective communication. The following are some basic principles designed to facilitate the communication process with parents, teachers, and other professionals.

Acceptance

People know if you do not accept them or do not value what they have to say. Parents are aware when teachers do not really want to see them during conferences but are merely fulfilling a responsibility. Lack of acceptance interferes with parental and professional participation in a child's program. Some teachers seem to know how to extend and project their acceptance and interest. Ms. Skruggs has been teaching special education for twelve years. She has worked with a range of parents and professionals during her career—some easier to work with than others. Despite expected frustrations and disappointments, she communicates her care and concern to the parents and professionals with whom she interacts and always manages to find the few minutes necessary to meet with them. Ms. Skruggs claims, "Parents have a great deal to teach me. They have spent a lot of time with their child and have seen patterns of behavior that can assist me in teaching."

Pointers for communicating acceptance include:

1. Demonstrate respect for the parents' knowledge and understanding of their child.
2. Demonstrate respect for the diverse languages and cultures parents and their children represent.
3. Introduce parents to other members of the education team in a way that "sets the tone" for acceptance.

4. Give parents and guardian an opportunity to speak and be heard.
5. Represent the parents to other professionals and assure that a language of acceptance is used by all professionals and parents.

Listening

Effective listening is more than waiting politely for the person to finish. It requires hearing the message the person is sending. Often this requires restating the message to assure understanding. Effective listeners listen for the "real content" of the message as well as listen for the "feelings" in the message. Without using phony or overused statements or parroting what was said, they restate the message and allow the speaker an opportunity to confirm and/or correct. In summary, effective listening involves:

1. Listening for the "real content" in the message
2. Listening for the "feelings" in the message
3. Restating or summarizing content and feelings (but not after every statement!)
4. Allowing the speaker to confirm or correct the perception

Mrs. Garcia, the mother of twelve-year-old Felipe, telephoned his special education resource room teacher, Mr. Sanchez.

Mrs. Garcia: Felipe has been complaining for the past couple of weeks that he has too much work to do in his biology and math classes and that he is falling behind. He says he is flunking biology.

Mr. Sanchez: How much would you say he is studying each night?

Mrs. Garcia: Well it's hard to say. He stays out with his friends until dinner and then after dinner he starts talking about all his homework. Sometimes he sits in front of the TV with his books and sometimes he goes to his room.

Mr. Sanchez: He has mentioned how much work he has to do in my class. I wonder

	if he is feeling a lot of pressure from different teachers, including me?
Mrs. Garcia:	Well, he has said he thinks you are working him too hard. I know sometimes he is lazy but maybe you could talk to him.
Mr. Sanchez:	Felipe works very hard in my class and I expect a great deal from him. I will talk with him after school and arrange a meeting with his other teachers as well.
Mrs. Garcia:	Thank you, and please do not tell Felipe I called. He would be very upset with me.

Questioning

Knowing what type of question to ask will often help individuals in obtaining the information they need. Questions can be *open* or *closed*. An *open question* is a question that allows the respondent a full range of responses and discourages the respondent from short, yes or no answers. Open questions may begin with *How, What, Tell me about,* and so forth. Following are several open questions.

- What do you think might be happening?
- What do you know about _____?
- How do you interpret it?
- What do you suggest?
- How might you describe it?
- How does this relate to his behavior at home?
- Tell me your opinion about _____.

Mrs. Gilmore suspected Matt, one of her students, was staying up very late at night. He was coming to school very tired and seemed to drag all day. He was also resting his head in the afternoon on his desk. She decided to call Matt's father to discuss the problem. She started the conversation by giving Matt's father some information about a meeting of parents that was going to be held in the school district that she thought would be of particular interest to him. She then proceeded to describe Matt's behavior in class. Finally, Mrs. Gilmore asked, "What do you think might be happening?" Matt's father

began to confide that he was not paying much attention to Matt's bedtime and that Matt was staying up late watching movies on the new VCR. Mrs. Gilmore's question gave Matt's father the opportunity to explain what he thought was happening. Rather than posing several possibilities, or telling Matt's father that Matt was staying up too late at night, Mrs. Gilmore asked an open question, which allowed Matt's father to interpret the situation. Matt's father suggested that he would establish a firm bedtime. In this situation, asking an open question both allowed Matt's father to indicate how he felt and to offer a solution.

Involving people in identifying the problem increases the likelihood that they will not feel threatened by you, and they will be willing to make the necessary changes.

Encouragement

Begin and end with something positive but genuine. With every student, even ones who have serious learning and behavior problems, teachers can find something positive to say. Perhaps the child is improving in some area, perhaps he or she contributed some interesting information to a class discussion, perhaps he or she said or did something that was humorous. In addition to hearing positive reports about their children, parents and professionals need encouragement about what they are doing. Since special education teachers often have meetings with parents and professionals to discuss problems, it is important to begin and end these meetings on a positive note. If possible, give genuine, positive feedback to the parents and professionals with whom you work regarding their assistance with a student.

Staying Directed

Follow the lead of parents and professionals whenever they are talking about a student. A skillful consultant is able to respond to others and still keep the discussion focused. It is not uncommon that parents, when speaking about their child, will mention other related home factors that may be influencing their child's progress in school. These may include marital difficulties, financial problems, or other personal problems. When others begin discussing serious problems that are beyond our reach as educators, we need to assist them in finding other resources to help them with their problems.

Listening, summarizing, and responding to the dialogue of parents and professionals often places the teacher in the role of those to whom others divulge confidences. In these situations we need to decide quickly whether the information is within our bounds as educators or we need to refer the parent or professional to someone else. Figure 12.1 provides a list of tips for effective communication with parents and professionals.

Developing a Working Alliance

It is important that, in every way possible, teachers communicate to parents and professionals that all of you share a common goal—developing the best pro-

gram for the child. Whenever possible share information about changes in a child that would be of interest. Let parents know when the student is making exceptional progress. Let other professionals know when their intervention is paying off. Set up a team spirit in which all members feel they are working together to enhance the education and social development of the student.

Developing Interviewing Skills

Special education teachers often work as consultants to regular classroom teachers, to other educational and psychological specialists, and to parents. Consultants need interviewing skills in order to identify problems fully and to implement appropriate interventions. These interviewing skills help meet the

---

■ **FIGURE 12.1** *Facilitating Effective Communication with Parents and Professionals*

1. Indicate respect for parents' knowledge and understanding of their child.
2. Demonstrate respect for the diverse languages and cultures parents and their children represent.
3. Introduce parents to other members of the education team in a way that sets the tone for acceptance.
4. Give parents an opportunity to speak and be heard.
5. Represent the parents to other professionals and ensure that a language of acceptance is used by all professionals and parents.
6. Even when you are busy, take the time to let parents and professionals know that you value them, and that you are just unable to meet with them at *this* time.
7. Avoid giving advice unless it is requested. This does not mean that you can never give suggestions; however, the suggestions should be given with the expectation that the person may or may not choose to implement them.
8. Avoid providing false reassurances to colleagues or parents. Reassurances may make them and

you feel better in the short run but in the long run are harmful. When things do not work out as you predicted, everyone can become disappointed and potentially lose trust.

9. Ask specific questions. Using unfocused questions makes it difficult to conduct a consistent, purposeful conversation.
10. Avoid changing topics too often; this requires that you monitor the topic and direct others to return to the topic.
11. Avoid interrupting others or being interrupted, which disturbs the conversation and makes effective collaboration difficult.
12. Avoid using cliches. A cliche as a response to a problem situation makes the other person feel as though you are trivializing the problem.
13. Respond to colleagues and parents in ways that attend to both the content of their message and their feelings.
14. Avoid jumping too quickly to a solution. Listening carefully and fully to the message will help you get at the root of the problem.

From: S. Vaughn, C. S. Bos and J. S. Schumm (1997). *Teaching Mainstreamed, Diverse, and At-Risk Students in the General Education Classroom.* Boston: Allyn and Bacon. Reprinted with permission.

need to ask questions that inform and to follow up appropriately on information provided. There are five steps to a good interview:

1. *Ask open questions.* As discussed in the previous section, an open question permits respondents a full range of answers, which allows them to bring up a topic or problem they have on their mind. Open questions are generally followed by questions that require more specificity. Mr. Schwab, the special education resource room teacher, began his interview with Mrs. Francosa, the fourth-grade teacher, by asking an open question: "How is John's behavior lately?"

2. *Obtain specificity.* This requires asking questions or making restatements that identify or document the problem. After Mrs. Francosa describes John's behavior in the regular classroom, Mr. Schwab attempts to identify key points and to obtain specificity in describing the behavior: "You said John's behavior is better in the classroom but worse on the playground. Can you identify which behaviors in the classroom are better and which behaviors on the playground are worse?" Without drilling the interviewee, an attempt is made to identify the problem and provide documentation for its occurrence so that an appropriate intervention can be constructed.

3. *Identify the problem.* This is done by the consultant based on information obtained, or it can be done by the person being interviewed, often in the process of answering questions: "It seems like there is good progress in terms of completing classroom work. Let's figure out a way of reinforcing that behavior. There's a problem with his responding to teasing on the playground. His response has been to fight, which is getting him in more trouble. Any thoughts about how we might change that behavior?" After listening to suggestions from the teacher, Mr. Schwab might add, "Let me provide some suggestions that have been effective in the past with other students."

4. *Problem solve.* Suggestions for solving identified problems and implementing the solutions are generated. Both the professional being interviewed as well as the consultant contribute suggestions to solving the problem. Often other professionals are included in the suggestions: "Perhaps we could discuss John's problem with his counselor and ask her to teach him some strategies for coping with teasing. It's also possible to identify the students who are teasing him and reinforce them for not teasing."

The tone for problem solving should be one of flexibility. There are often many possible solutions, few that work with all students. The goal is to find a solution the teacher is willing to implement that is effective for the student.

5. *Summary and feedback.* Summarize the problem and the plan of action. Be sure to indicate who is responsible for what. Whenever possible, establish a timeline for completing the tasks: "You will send home notes to his parents, informing them of his progress in seatwork in the classroom. I will meet with the counselor regarding his problem on the playground, and you will talk with his peers and arrange a system for reinforcing them for not teasing. I'll check back with you during lunch this week to see how things are going. I'm very pleased with this progress and I am sure much of it is due to your hard work and follow-up." Figure 12.2 provides a summary of the interview process.

■ **FIGURE 12.2** *Steps to a Successful Interview*

Step 1: Open Question or Statement:
"Tell me about John's behavior."

Step 2: Obtain Specificity:
"How do the other children respond when John gets angry?"

Step 3: Identify the Problem:
"Sounds like fighting is occurring during noon recess most frequently after John is teased."

Step 4: Problem Solving:
"Let's start by seeing how John perceives the problem and developing an intervention that includes his peers. What might be reinforcing to John and/or his peers?"

Step 5: Summary and Feedback:
"You'll meet with John and his peers tomorrow. I'll speak with the counselor and we'll schedule a team meeting for Wednesday."

Effective consultants listen openly without a defensive posture. They stay focused and remember the needs of the student. They note that solutions effective with previous students and teachers may not be effective in current cases. They look for alternatives that can be implemented and they seek the advice of other professionals. When plans for solving problems are developed, they determine who is responsible for what tasks and provide feedback on performance. Interviews are the key to open communication and effective intervention.

WORKING WITH PARENTS

This section of the chapter will highlight the teacher's role with parents. Family adjustment to a child with learning and behavior problems is discussed first. Within this section, parent adjustment, sibling adjustment, and the problems of constructing an effective summer program will be described. Parents' involvement with the schools and their role in the planning of the child's educational program will be presented.

Family Adjustment

A great deal has been written on parental response to having a child with disabilities. Most of what is written focuses on parents of the mentally retarded and physically handicapped. This literature may provide little insight into the adjustment of parents who have children identified by the schools as learning- or behavior-disordered. Most parents of children with learning and behavior problems do not receive a "diagnosis" until the child is in school. Though they may have identified the child's behavior as different from their other children and peers, most parents are unsure of what the problem is. Often they seek advice from their family physician who either makes referrals to other professionals or suggests they wait until the child enters school. Although many parents are aware their child is different long before diagnosis, they still continue to hope that their observations are incorrect and that the child will outgrow the problem.

From a systems perspective, the family is an important force in the child's learning and development. For this reason, many mental health professionals recommend an integrated approach to working with students with learning disabilities and behavior disorders who are troubled. This integrated approach typically involves all or part of the family in the program. This may include an initial meeting with the entire family, involvement of selected family members, or ongoing clinical help that may involve the family at certain times. Not all families who have children with learning and behavior problems need therapeutic assistance.

Because of concern for their child, mothers of children with learning disabilities often expect less of them than the children expect of themselves (Margalit, Raviv, and Ankonina, 1992). Teachers need to realize when parents are expecting too little of their children and assist them in readjusting their expectations. The misconceptions about children under which many parents and teachers function often tell children that they are unable, and as a result, many children act as though they are unable. Many children with learning disabilities leave school unprepared for work, postsecondary education, and life expectations. Often they leave school with fewer skills than the mentally retarded (Cummings and Maddux, 1985). Teachers can help parents by reminding them to communicate the importance of education to their child; for example, sharing their successes and failures when they were in school, and emphasizing that even when they did not do well they continued to do the best they could.

Simpson (1982) suggests that the needs of parents of exceptional children fall into five general categories:

1. *Information exchange.* Parents need conferences, program and classroom information, progress reports, interpretations of their child's academic and social needs, and informal feedback about their child.

2. *Consumer and advocacy training.* Parents need information about their rights and responsibilities, procedures for interacting during conferences, resources available through the school and community, and assertiveness training.

3. *Home/community program implementation.* Parents need procedures for assisting their child academically and behaviorally at home, including procedures for tutoring and behavior management.

4. *Counseling, therapy, and consultation.* Parents need support groups, consultation, referrals for conflict resolution, problem solving, and therapy.

5. *Parent-coordinated service programs.* Parents need to be in a position to provide services to and receive services from other parents through advisory councils, parent-to-parent participation, advocacy, and other options.

In a study reported by Simpson (1988), the most widely requested services by parents of children with learning and behavior problems were program information and informal feedback.

Adjusting to a child with learning and behavior disorders is difficult; (Simeonsson and Simeonsson, 1993). Understanding how parents are adjusting and interacting with the child based on their interpretation of the child's needs is an important role for the special education teacher.

Siblings

In addition to how parents respond to a child with learning or behavior problems, the response by other siblings is also important. Many parents are concerned because their child with learning disabilities or behavior disorders takes more time and consideration than do their other children. Siblings may feel as though the child with special needs is getting all of the attention and special privileges. It is important for parents to develop schedules so they will have assigned special time for all of their children. A sibling of a child with learning disabilities commented:

> *Everything always seems to center around Scott. He always seems to be the focus of the conversation and whom my parents are concerned about. I do pretty well in school and don't seem to have many problems, so sometimes I feel left out. It really meant a lot to me when my mother and father both scheduled time during the week for me to be alone with*

> *them. Usually my dad and I would go to the park and sometimes we would go on an errand. Often my mom and I would work together in the kitchen, making my favorite dessert, chocolate chip cookies. The best part was that it was just me and them. I really think it helped me be more understanding of Scott. Somehow, I just didn't resent him so much anymore.*

Summers

Summers seem to be particularly difficult for children with learning and behavior problems. They often have too much unstructured time and too many opportunities to discover trouble. The summer is an extended time without exposure to structured learning experiences, and often what was done during the school year is undone during the three months without school. Parents often have a very difficult time with summers because of the additional pressure to find an appropriate educational or social experience. Billy's mother describes it this way:

> *My son, Billy, needs a special summer program so he can learn to play with other kids. . . . My ex-husband, Arthur, thinks I bug Billy too much and that we should leave him alone. That's what happened last summer, and it didn't work. I don't know how to convince him or where to begin to find a good camp. I'm exhausted. I'm doing all I can manage. Last week, the school people reminded me that it was time to plan for the summer. And then they told me how much trouble Billy was having playing with the other children. Maybe I misinterpreted it, but I felt they were saying I should be helping him even more.* (Exceptional Parent, *March, 1984, p. 43*)

Teachers can assist parents during the summer by developing a list of community resources that provide structured programs for children and adolescents. Each community has a range of such programs, some of which include:

1. *Public library.* The public library offers many programs that focus on literacy, including authors reading their books, books on tapes and records, and other special programs.

2. *Children's museums.* Many towns and cities have developed children's museums that offer a range of special programs for children.

3. *Theater groups.* Often local theater groups offer summer programs on acting, cinema, and stage design.

4. *Museums.* Check with local art museums, historic museums, and science museums to determine what types of programs they will be offering during the summer.

5. *Parks and recreation.* Parks offer arts and crafts as well as organized recreational activities during the summer that are often free or very inexpensive.

6. *YMCA, YWCA.* These organizations offer many special summer programs, including day camps, swimming lessons, and arts and crafts.

7. *Universities, colleges, and community colleges.* Often these organizations offer special programs for children in the summer.

Preparing a list of activities available in the community as well as a list of tutors available during the summer helps parents and children with a smooth transition from school to summer, and may help teachers with the transition next fall from summer to school. Perhaps the most important thing is to provide a structured activity each day, without demanding that the entire day be structured.

Parents as Tutors

Parental responsibility is to "insure that the home is a relaxed and pleasant place, a source of strength to the child" (Kronik, 1977, p. 327). Often parents want so much to help that they get overly involved in the child's homework or tutoring. Although spending time with their child in relaxing activities such as reading to the child, going for walks, sitting and talking, going to the zoo, and so on, are recommended by all educational and psychological specialists, few recommend direct instructional tutoring in the home.

Home tutoring by the parent usually creates more problems than it solves. Often children need help with homework assignments; this is not the equivalent of home tutoring. Home tutoring is the supplementing of the child's educational program by the parent in the home. If parents insist on home tutoring, ask them to comply with the following suggestions adapted from Cummings and Maddux (1985).

1. Have specific, realistic goals developed with the special education or classroom teacher.

2. Begin and end each tutoring session with a fun activity in which the child is successful.

3. Keep the tutoring session brief—not more than fifteen minutes for children up to grade six and not more than thirty minutes for older students.

4. Work on small segments of material at a time.

5. Use creative and novel ways of reviewing and teaching new material.

6. Prevent the student from making mistakes. If the student does not know the answer, give it.

7. Keep a tutoring log in which you record a couple of sentences about what you did and how the child performed.

8. Provide encouragement and support.

9. Practice the activities in ways that reduce boredom.

10. Work should be challenging but not too difficult.

11. Tutor at the same time and in the same place so the child has an expectation set for what will happen.

12. If you are getting frustrated or your interactions with your child are strained or stressful during the tutoring, stop. Your relationship with your child is much more important than what you can teach him or her during the tutoring session.

Apply the Concept 12.1 provides an overview of a study that examined parental involvement in literacy development.

APPLY THE CONCEPT 12.1

*PARENT INVOLVEMENT IN READING AND WRITING INSTRUCTION
FOR THEIR CHILDREN*

Hughes (1995) conducted a study of Hispanic parents of children with learning disabilities to determine the type of involvement they value in their child's reading and writing acquisition. Parents were asked to provide information on the types of reading and writing activities that they practiced in the home and the extent to which they thought various reading and writing activities were feasible to implement.

Hispanic parents who participated in the study reported that a wide variety of reading and writing activities were used in the home. Reading to each other was the activity most frequently reported. Parents implemented reading activities more frequently than writing activities. Parents identified the following activities as helpful:

- more communication with teacher about reading and writing activities they could do at home
- further information about how to do the reading and writing activities with their children since the children had difficulties with reading and writing
- more information about appropriate home reading activities in the parents' language (Spanish)

Parent Involvement with Schools

By the time children reach school, parents have already spent five years observing them. Many parents are aware from the day their child enters school that the child is different from other children. Often the child spends two to three difficult years in school before the child is referred for learning disabilities or behavior disorders. During this time, many parents have spent hours communicating with school counselors, psychologists, and teachers. In a study in which parents of students with learning disabilities were interviewed following the initial placement of their child, parents reported having an average of six contacts with the school before their child was identified (Vaughn, Bos, Harrell, and Laskey, 1988). Some of these contacts were initiated by the parent. Often parents feel frustrated and alone. They are unsure what to do and, because of the complexity of their child's condition, professionals are often unable to provide the precise answers parents need. See Apply the Concept 12.2.

Parental Involvement in Planning and Placement Conferences

Turnbull, Turnbull, and Wheat (1982) consider the provisions of PL 94-142 radical because of the extent of parent participation guaranteed. Parents provide consent for evaluation, participate in the program and educational plan, and are kept involved in all decisions regarding the child's educational program.

The rationale for extensive parent involvement is twofold. First, it assures a cooperative role between home and school. Parents can provide information about the child the schools may not have access to, and parents can follow up on educational goals in the home. Second, it assures that parents will have access to information regarding student evaluations and records and can better monitor appropriate placement and programming by the school. One of the greatest potential benefits to the child and family is to involve the parents in the planning and placement conference for the child. The information obtained about the child's learning and behavior problems can increase parental understanding, which leads to changes in

APPLY THE CONCEPT 12.2

WHAT PARENTS OF STUDENTS WITH LEARNING DISABILITIES WANT FROM PROFESSIONALS

In a survey of over 200 parents of children with learning disabilities, parents indicated what they really wanted from professionals (Dembinski and Mauser, 1977). A summary of the findings follows.

1. Parents want professionals to communicate without the use of jargon. When technical terms are necessary, they would like to have them explained so they can understand.
2. Whenever possible, they would like conferences to be held so both parents can attend.

3. They would like to receive written materials that provide information that will assist them in understanding their child's problem.
4. They would like to receive a copy of a written report about their child.
5. Parents would like specific advice on how to manage specific behavior problems of their children or how to teach them needed skills.
6. Parents would like information on their child's social as well as academic behavior.

parent behavior toward the child. In addition, parents learn about the focus of the child's program at school and can follow up on those learning and behavior programs in the home. Unfortunately, this is more often a description of the ideal than the real. Despite the best intentions of school personnel and parents, cooperative and extensive involvement in the placement and planning process is minimal.

There are many explanations for lack of parent involvement in the educational planning. One is that school personnel do not have adequate time to meet with parents and fully explain the child's program, or do not understand how to take advantage of parents' knowledge and preferences (Harry, 1992; Harry, Allen, and McLaughlin, 1995). Often parent meetings must be held early in the morning before parents go to work, or late at night on their way home. These times usually conflict with school personnel schedules and require school personnel to meet with parents outside of their required work time. Because of their dedication and interest in the child, professionals are often willing to meet at these times, but they are not motivated to meet for extended periods of time.

A second explanation is that many parents feel professionals will make the best decisions in their child's interest and do not want to be coparticipants in their child's educational program. This may not indicate a lack of interest in the child's program but

merely less confidence in participating in this way. To assume that all parents want to be actively involved in planning their child's educational program may not be accurate. Winton and Turnbull (1981) found that when they interviewed parents of preschool children with disabilities, 65 percent of the parents identified informal contact with teachers as the activity they most preferred, followed by 13 percent who chose parent training opportunities, and 10 percent identified opportunities to help others understand the child. It is interesting to note that a common theme in studies evaluating parent satisfaction with the placement and IEP conference is that parents state that they feel satisfied with the conference even though data indicate they played relatively passive roles (Lynch and Stein, 1982; Vaughn, Bos, Harrell, and Laskey, 1988). Some 25 percent of the parents of students with learning disabilities who participated in placement and planning conferences did not recall the IEP document itself, and of those who did recall it, few had any knowledge of its content (McKinney and Hocutt, 1982).

It could be that parents would like to be more involved but feel intimidated by the number of professionals and the uncommon terminology.

No matter how well we might know our own children, we are not prepared to talk to teach-

APPLY THE CONCEPT 12.3

CONSIDERATIONS FOR CULTURALLY AND LINGUISTICALLY DIVERSE PARENTS

1. Assume that parents want to help their children.
2. Provide materials in a range of formats including orally, in writing (parents' language), through videotape, and through formal and informal presentations.
3. Provide opportunities for parents to learn the skills and activities the students are learning so they can reinforce them in the home.
4. Provide opportunities for parents to influence their children's educational program.

5. Provide workshops that include role-playing and rehearsing situations between parents and school personnel to increase parents' confidence in working with school personnel.
6. Involve parents from the community who are familiar with the culture of the families and speak the home language of the parents to work at the school.

Adapted from: T. W. Sileo, A. P. Sileo, and M. A. Prater (1996). Parent and Professional Partnerships in Special Education: Multicultural Considerations. *Intervention in School and Clinic, 31*(3), pp. 145–153.

---

ers, principals, psychologists, or counselors, much less participate in the educational decision making process. Although parents do have a lot of information, it is not the "right" kind. When we go to speak to administrators at school we hear about IEP's, MA's, criteria, auditory processing, regulations, and sometimes, due process. At first, there seems to be no correspondence between what we know and what the people in schools are talking about (Exceptional Parent, *March, 1984, p. 41).*

During conferences, special education teachers need to be sensitive to the parents' feelings and needs and serve as advocates for the parents. Often the teacher can "act as if" he or she is the parent and ask questions of the classroom teacher or other professionals that he or she feels the parent may have wanted to ask but did not.

Parent Conferences: Planned and Unplanned

Planned conferences with parents occur frequently and include: multidisciplinary team meetings, annual parent-student meetings, or regularly scheduled meet-

ings to report on academic and behavioral progress. Conferences provide teachers with the opportunity to:

- Review the student's materials, grades, and work progress.
- Meeting with other professionals to provide an overall review and report on student progress.
- Review the student's portfolio, assessment information, and progress reports.
- Provide samples of the student's most recent work.
- Establish and review goals and criteria for academic and behavioral work.

Often conferences with parents are unplanned (Turnbull and Turnbull, 1990). Parents may phone, stop by the school, or schedule a conference with little notice. When this occurs, there are several procedures to remember: listen carefully until the parents have expressed the purpose of their visit, paraphrase what you understand to be their question or issues, and respond to the question and issue as completely as possible. Often parents stop by with a simple question or concern that is a disguise for a larger issue. That is why it's important to listen carefully and wait until parents are finished.

Public Law 99-457 and Parent Involvement

Public Law 99-457, The Education of the Handicapped Act Amendments, passed in 1986, provides guidelines for a free, appropriate public education for all children with disabilities from birth to age three. The law provides for early intervention services that meet the developmental needs of the youngster and his or her family including: physical development, cognition, language, social, and self-help skills. The parents and family play an important role, and an individualized program plan must be designed to meet their needs. This program plan, called the Individualized Family Service Plan (IFSP), should provide a coordinated array of services, including:

— Screening and assessment
— Psychological assessment and intervention
— Occupational and physical therapy
— Speech, language, and audiology
— Family involvement, training, and home visits
— Specialized instruction for parents and the target youngster
— Case management
— Health services that may be needed to allow the child to benefit from the intervention service

What Are the Criteria for Establishing an IFSP?

The IFSP is a family-oriented approach to designing an effective management plan for the youngster with disabilities. The IFSP must be developed by a multidisciplinary team and should include:

— A description of the child's level of functioning across the developmental areas: cognitive, speech and language, social, motor, and self-help
— An assessment of the family, including a description of the family's strengths and needs as

they relate to enhancing the opportunities for the child with disabilities
— A description of the major goals or outcomes expected for the child with disabilities and the family (as they relate to providing opportunities for the child)
— Procedures for measuring progress, including timeline, objectives, and evaluation procedures
— A description of the intervention services needed to provide appropriate help for the child and family
— Specifically when the specialized intervention will begin and how long it will last
— An appointed case manager
— A specific transition plan from the birth-to-three program into the preschool program

Parent Education Programs

In a review of parent involvement programs for parents of children with learning disabilities, the two types of programs most frequently provided for parents were counseling and tutoring (Shapero and Forbes, 1981). Overall findings indicated parent involvement programs can have positive effects on the academic performance of children with learning disabilities. Providing organized parental programs may be helpful to some parents of children with learning and behavior problems. These programs need to be interactive and take advantage of the knowledge and needs of the participants.

One procedure that involves parents in their child's education is described in Apply the Concept 12.4.

A number of variables influence the success of adults with learning disabilities, including parental factors. The educational and economic levels of the parents significantly influence the likelihood that children with learning disabilities will have good jobs that pay well (O'Connor and Spreen, 1988).

Waggoner and Wilgosh (1990) interviewed eight different families regarding their experiences and concerns of having a child with learning disabilities. The results of these interviews elucidated several common themes including: parent involvement in the child's education, parents' relationship with

APPLY THE CONCEPT 12.4

PAIRING TEACHER PRAISE NOTES WITH PARENT PRAISE

Imber, Imber, and Rothstein (1979) found that pairing teacher praise notes with parent praise regarding the note was effective in producing improvement in the academic performance of their children. After praise notes from the teacher were sent home, parents were asked to:

1. Read the note and praise the child as soon as possible.
2. Praise the child in front of others in the family.
3. Place the note where others can see it.
4. Express to the child that they hope the child will receive another one.

the school, support for the parents, social concerns for the child, concerns about the child's future, emotional strains of parenting, and the effects on the family. The interviews indicated that parents needed to be willing to help the child at home with school work and to interact frequently with the school to serve as an advocate for their child. While all of the parents reported at least one positive experience with teachers and the schools, seven out of eight of the parents also reported negative experiences. These negative experiences revolved around teachers feeling not only that the child did not have a "real" problem but also that the child was just not performing as well as he or she could.

WORKING WITH PROFESSIONALS

Consulting and communicating with professionals is an important task for teachers of students with learning and behavior problems. Teachers need to develop and maintain contact with the school psychologist, counselor, speech and language therapist, physical therapist, PE teacher, principal, and other related professionals. Since 90 percent of all students with learning and behavior disorders are mainstreamed for all or part of the day, a positive, cooperative working relationship with the regular classroom teacher may be most important of all.

Communication with Regular Education Teachers

Peters and Austin (1985) describe the characteristics of a leader and a nonleader. Many of these characteristics are important for special education teachers as they often serve as team leaders looking to develop the best programs for students with special needs. Table 12.1 lists these characteristics.

When a student with special needs is placed in the regular classroom, there are several steps the special education teacher can take to communicate effectively with the regular classroom teacher. These steps include:

1. Describe the type of learning or behavior problem the child has and some general guidelines for how to deal with it in the regular classroom.

2. Provide a copy of the child's IEP to the classroom teacher and discuss the goals, objectives, special materials, and procedures needed.

3. Describe the progress reports you will be providing to the home and putting in your files.

4. Develop a schedule for regular meetings and discuss other times that both the classroom teacher and special teacher are available for meetings.

5. Ask the classroom teacher how you can help, and describe the special accommodations that are needed.

In addition to communicating with teachers, there are a number of other services that the special

■ **TABLE 12.1**   *Characteristics of a Leader and a Nonleader*

Leader	Nonleader
Appeals to the best in each person.	Gives orders to staff—expects them to be carried out.
Thinks of ways to make people more successful.	Thinks of personal rewards or how she or he looks to others.
Looks for ways to reinforce them.	
Schedules frequent, short meetings to "touch base."	Meets infrequently with coworkers.
Good listener.	Good talker.
Notices what's going well and improving.	Only notices what's going wrong.
Available.	Hard to reach.
Persistent.	Gives up.
Gives credit to others.	Takes credit.
Consistent and credible.	Unpredictable.
Never divulges a confidence.	Cannot be trusted with confidences.
Makes tough decisions.	Avoids difficult decisions.
Treats teachers and students with respect.	Treats others as if they don't matter.

Source: Adapted from T. Peters and N. Austin, *A Passion for Excellence* (New York: Random House, 1985).

education teacher can provide to facilitate mainstreaming. These services include providing inservice education on special education procedures or methods, bringing in guest speakers to discuss relevant topics, writing newsletters, and developing Teacher Assistance Teams. The special education teacher's role in the Teacher Assistance Team was discussed in Chapter Eleven.

Even when special education teachers develop and maintain an effective communication program with regular education teachers, there are still a number of potential barriers to successful mainstreaming.

1. *The regular classroom teacher may feel unable to meet the needs of the mainstreamed student.* Ms. Clements has been teaching second grade for two years. When she was informed that Samuel, a student

identified as emotionally disturbed, was going to be mainstreamed into her regular classroom for several hours each morning, she panicked. She explained to the principal that she had not taken any coursework in special education and was unable to meet the needs of the new student. The special education teacher met with Ms. Clements. She described Samuel's behavior and explained the progress he was making. She assured Ms. Clements that Samuel would be carefully monitored and that she would check with Samuel and her daily and then less frequently as he adapted to the new setting and schedule. She asked Ms. Clements to explain what types of activities usually occurred during the time Samuel would be in her room, and she identified ways for Ms. Clements to be successful with Samuel. The special education teacher took careful notes and asked many questions about Ms. Clements' expectations so she could prepare Samuel before his transition to the regular classroom. In this situation, communication that provides specific information about the student's learning problems and what the classroom teacher can do to assure a successful learning environment is most helpful. In addition, the special education teacher obtained expectations about the regular classroom so she could best prepare the student for the transition.

2. *The regular classroom teacher may not want to work with the mainstreamed student.* Mr. Caruffe, a seventh-grade science teacher, expected all students to perform the same work at the same time, with no exceptions. He was particularly opposed to having special education students mainstreamed into his classroom because he felt they needed modifications from his core program. His philosophy was, "If students need modifications they don't belong in the regular classroom, they belong in special education." Teachers like Mr. Caruffe can be particularly challenging for the special education teacher. Despite continuous attempts to work out a collaborative effort, educational philosophies can be sufficiently different that the special education teacher feels it is hopeless to attempt mainstreaming in certain classrooms. Problems arise when alternative classrooms are not available without reducing the content areas available to special students. If there are multiple teachers for each content area, students may be mainstreamed into classes where teachers are more accepting. Principals can be helpful by setting school policy that rewards teachers for working appropriately with mainstreamed pupils.

In a survey of elementary, middle, and high school students (Schumm and Vaughn, 1992) the majority of teachers indicated that they felt unprepared to meet the needs of mainstreamed special education students but were willing to have them in their classrooms. This suggests that special education teachers will need to work closely with other teachers to facilitate their knowledge, skills, and confidence.

3. *Finding time to meet regularly with all classroom teachers is difficult.* At the elementary level the special education teacher meets regularly with all classroom teachers who have students mainstreamed for all or part of the day. This consultation includes discussing student progress, planning the student's program, adapting instruction in the regular classroom, and solving immediate academic and social problems with the student. It is better to meet weekly with classroom teachers for a short period of time (ten to fifteen minutes) than to meet less often for longer periods of time. When classroom teachers and their students perceive the special education room as a resource, rather than a closed room for special students, they have positive perceptions of the teacher and the students who attend (Vaughn and Bos, 1987).

At the secondary level, continued involvement with all classroom teachers is a challenge. In large schools the exceptional students' regular classroom teachers vary within content area and by year. It is possible for exceptional education teachers to have over twenty-five teachers with whom they consult. Special education teachers manage this by meeting with teachers in small groups. Sometimes they organize these groups by content area to discuss successful adaptations made within a common content. Sometimes meetings are organized to focus on the needs of a particular student, and all teachers who work with this student meet at the same time. Finding time and maintaining contact with regular education teachers requires creativity and persistence.

4. *Students may not be accepted socially by peers in the regular classroom.* This problem occurs not just with students who have behavior problems but also with students who have learning disabilities. Placing students in classrooms where their peers are displaying appropriate social behaviors does not mean that students with learning and behavior disorders will model these appropriate behaviors (Gresham, 1982). According to both regular and special classroom teachers, the skills most essential to success in the regular classroom are interacting positively with others, following class rules, and exhibiting proper work habits (Salend and Lutz, 1984). Following is a list of behaviors considered important by both regular and special educators for success in the mainstream.

- Follows directions
- Asks for help when it's appropriate
- Begins an assignment after teacher gives assignment to the class
- Demonstrates adequate attention
- Obeys class rules
- Tries to complete task before giving up
- Doesn't speak when others are talking
- Works well with others
- Respects feelings of others
- Refrains from cursing and swearing
- Avoids getting in fights with other students
- Plays cooperatively with others
- Respects property of others
- Shares materials and property with others
- Refrains from stealing property of others
- Tells the truth*

Special education teachers may want to focus on teaching these behaviors before and during mainstreaming.

Working with Paraprofessionals

Many exceptional education specialists work closely with paraprofessionals as teaching assistants. Although teaching assistants never have complete responsibility for planning, implementing, or evaluating a student's program, they often participate in all of these roles. It is important for paraprofessionals not to be assigned to students who the teacher then spends little time seeing. Paraprofessionals need to have their teaching responsibilities rotated among many students so that the teacher spends frequent intervals teaching and evaluating all students. Since paraprofessionals are often responsible for implementing class rules, they need to be completely familiar with class and school rules and their conse-

*Source: From "Mainstreaming or Mainlining: A Competency Based Approach to Mainstreaming" by S. J. Salend and G. Lutz, 1984, *Journal of Learning Disabilities, 17,* pp. 27–29. Copyright 1984 by PRO-ED, Inc. Reprinted by permission.

quences. Many paraprofessionals comment that they are successful in their roles when they have confidence in understanding what is expected of them.

Working with Administrators

The principal is the instructional and administrative leader of the school. The principal's perceptions and interactions with special education will be conveyed to classroom teachers and will be reflected in the procedures established to handle students with special needs. A supportive principal is the key to a supportive staff. When building principals find special education nothing but a headache or more paper work, this message is conveyed to the staff. When principals find special education an opportunity to provide necessary services to students with special needs, this message is also conveyed. An effective relationship between the principal and the special education teacher will promote better programs for students and overall job satisfaction (Cheek and Lindsey, 1986).

Often the principal serves as the leader and coordinator of services between regular and special education. There are five activities principals can perform to facilitate the role of special education in the school (Chalfant and Pysh, 1979, 1986).

1. *Set the tone.* The principal sets a tone that establishes the importance of developing effective and responsive programs for students with learning and behavior problems. Too few teachers view administrators as support personnel. Many special education teachers feel they have to do as much as they can for students with little administrative support. In fact, many teachers state they just wish administrators wouldn't get in the way—they have long since given up on support. Many special education teachers have found that a positive tone about special education can be obtained from building-level principals through informing and involving principals in special education achievements, not just problems; providing feedback about how special education is demonstrating child gains; soliciting parent and community support; and developing good intervention programs that get school and district recognition.

2. *Reinforce teachers for developing programs that respond to the individual needs of students.* Principals can be effective agents for encouraging classroom teachers to develop programs that respond to the individual needs of the special students in their classrooms.

3. *Provide consultation time.* Principals can arrange schedules of their support staff to serve as consultants to regular classroom teachers, providing programs for students with learning and behavior problems. The services of the school psychologist, speech and language therapist, physical therapist, counselor, special education teacher, and other support staff can be made available to regular classroom teachers.

4. *Provide inservice activities to staff.* This includes the provision of workshops, consultants, or lectures, focusing on the needs of staff to provide adequate service to students with learning and behavior disorders.

5. *Organize school-based assistance teams.* School-based assistance teams focus on the development of teams to assist classroom teachers with all students having learning and behavior problems, not just students identified to receive special education services. In fact, the school-based assistance teams (Chalfant and Pysh, 1979, 1983) were originally developed to assist in reducing unnecessary referrals for special education. The next section describes the role of school-based assistance teams.

School-Based Teacher Assistance Teams

The purpose of school-based assistance teams is to develop a team of professionals to work cooperatively with classroom teachers to develop successful programs and strategies in the regular classroom for students with learning and behavior problems. Often these teams are established to eliminate unnecessary testing and referral for special education. Whereas the original purpose was to work with students who have learning and behavior problems who were currently not placed in special education, it is possible to establish teams that focus on students already identified as special-needs students.

Who serves on the team? The membership can include the building principal, two regular classroom teachers, the teacher seeking assistance, and other persons as needed, such as a parent, the student, or a member of the special education staff. Team members can be selected by the staff or appointed by the principal.

How is the team contacted for assistance? When a classroom teacher seeks assistance in solving a student's learning or behavior problems in the classroom, the teacher seeks help from the school-based assistance team. Chalfant and Pysh (1979, 1983) suggest assistance be requested by answering four questions:

1. What do you want the student to do that he or she is not presently doing?
2. What does the student do (assets) and not do (deficits)?
3. What have you done to help the student cope with his or her problem?
4. What other background information and/or test data are relevant to the problem?

What does the team do? The team often responds to a problem identified by the classroom teacher. Frequently the teacher identifies the problem and selects a member of the team to observe the student and/or the teacher. In addition, informal assessment may be conducted. The team generates instructional alternatives and may assist in the implementation of these alternatives. It also establishes policies for monitoring progress and providing feedback.

School-based assistance teams have successfully decreased the number of referrals for special education. They also provide the necessary support needed by classroom teachers to cope effectively with students who have learning and behavior disorders.

SUMMARY

This chapter focuses on an important role for the special education teacher: communicating with parents and professionals. Although most of the chapters in this book discuss strategies for increasing teachers' skills in working directly with students who have learning and behavior disorders, this chapter is about communicating with the key people who interact with the student.

The first part of the chapter discusses the communication skills necessary for interacting with parents and professionals. These skills include acceptance, effective listening, effective questioning, providing encouragement, keeping the focus of the conversation directed, and developing a working alliance. In addition to these communication skills, acquiring interviewing skills such as asking open questions, obtaining specificity, identifying the problem, solving the problem, and providing feedback are discussed.

The second part of the chapter centers on understanding the needs of parents and communicating with them. Parents play a critical role in the successful delivery of services to students with special needs. They are involved in the identification, assessment, and educational planning of their child. Parents who are aware of academic and social goals for the child are more likely to follow up on these goals at home. Unlike other handicapping conditions (e.g., mental retardation and sensory impairment), learning and behavior disorders are often not identified until the student begins school. Although parents may be aware their child is different from peers, they often receive the identification of the learning or behavior disorder only from the school. Special education teachers play a critical role in communicating assessment and educational planning information to parents. They are also the professionals who communicate most frequently with parents regarding the daily progress of their child. This section presents suggestions for facilitating family adjustment as well as procedures for facilitating parent involvement in the placement and programming for their child.

The third part of the chapter presents the special education teacher's role in working with other professionals. Working with professionals is particularly important for teachers of students with learning and behavior problems, as their students are frequently mainstreamed for part of the school day. Often the special education teacher serves as the primary consultant for the regular classroom teacher, who may have few skills in effectively teaching students with special needs. Barriers that may interfere with successful mainstreaming were discussed. Establishing effective working relationships with the school principal is an important role for the special education teacher. The school principal sets the tone in the building for the acceptance of students with special needs.

Although teachers may be effective in providing the academic and social instruction their students require, unless they are equally effective in communicating with parents and professionals, they will be unsuccessful. The special education teacher spends relatively little time with the student, compared to the time the child spends with others. When all persons who interact with the student are working cooperatively to advance educational and social goals, the child's progress is assured.

THINK AND APPLY

- What are the principles of communication that facilitate the communication process with parents, teachers, and other professionals?
- What are the steps for conducting an effective interview?
- What are some of the needs of parents of children with learning disabilities and behavior problems? How might these needs be met?
- How do the parents of children with learning disabilities, particularly mothers, sometimes contribute unwittingly to their child's low self-expectation?
- Why are summers a particularly difficult time for children with learning and behavior problems? What are some possible solutions to the problem of long, unproductive summers?
- What skills are most essential to a student's success in the regular classroom?

APPENDIX A
Educational Publishers

ABC School Supply, Inc.
3312 N. Berkeley Lane Road
P.O. Box 100019
Duluth, GA 30136

Academic Communication
  Associates
Publication Center, Dept. 206
4149 Avenue de la Plata
P.O. Box 586249
Oceanside, CA 92058-6249

Academic Press, Inc.
525 B Street, Suite 1900
San Diego, CA 92101

Academic Therapy Publications
20 Commercial Blvd.
Novato, CA 94949

Adapt Press
691 S. Milpitas Blvd.
Milpitas, CA 95035

A.D.D. Warehouse
300 Northwest 70th Ave., Suite 102
Plantation, FL 33317

Addison-Wesley Publishing
  Company
1 Jacob Way
Reading, MA 01867

Adston Educational Press
P.O. Box 337
Niles, MI 49120

AGS American Guidance Service
4201 Woodland Road
P.O. Box 99
Circle Pines, MN 55014-1796

Allyn & Bacon
160 Gould Street
Needham Heights, MA 02194

American Speech-Language-
  Hearing Association
10801 Rockville Pike
Rockville, MA 20852

Association for Supervision and
  Curriculum Development
1250 N. Pitt Street
Alexandria, VA 22314

Barnell Loft
958 Church Street
Baldwin, NY 11510

Clarence L. Barnhart
P.O. Box 250
Bronxville, NY 10708

Behavioral Research Laboratories
1325 Haward Avenue, No. 319
Burlingame, CA 94010-1310

Bell and Howell
Old Mansfield Road
Wooster, OH 44691-9050

Benefic Press
10300 West Roosevelt Road
Westchester, IL 60153

Bobbs-Merrill Company
Imprint of MacMillan Publishing
  Co., Inc.
200 Old Tappan Road
Old Tappan, NJ 07675

Book-Lab, Inc.
P.O. Box 206
Ansonia Station
New York, NY 10023-0206

Bowmar/Noble Publishers
220 E. Danieldale Drive
De Soto, TX 75115-2490

Boys Town Press
Father Flanagan's Boy's Home
13603 Flanagan Blvd.
Boys Town, NE 68919

Bridges to Reading
P.O. Box 389
Brisbane, CA 94005-0389

Childcraft Education Corp.
20 Kilmer Road
Edison, NJ 08817

Children's Book Press
246 First Street, Suite 101
San Francisco, CA 94105

Communication Skill Builders
3830 E. Bellevue
Tucson, AZ 85716

Continental Press
520 E. Bainbridge Street
Elizabethtown, PA 17022

Council for Exceptional Children
1920 Association Drive
Reston, VA 20191-1589

CPPC
4 Conant Square
Brandan, VT 05733

Creative Publications
5040 W. 111th Street
Oak Lawn, IL 60453

Crestwood Company
Communication Aids for Children
 & Adults
6625 N. Sidney Place
Milwaukee, WI 53209-3259

Critical Thinking Press and
 Software
P.O. Box 448
Pacific Grove, CA 93950

Cuisenaire Company of America,
 Inc.
P.O. Box 5026
White Plains, NY 10602-5026

Curriculum Associates
5 Esquire Road
North Billerica, MA 01862

Dale Seymour Publications
P.O. Box 10888
Palo Alto, CA 94303

Delacorte Press
1540 Broadway
New York, NY 10036-4094

Delmar Publishers
P.O. Box 15015
Albany, NY 12212-5015

Devereux Foundation
P.O. Box 1079
Santa Barbara, CA 93102

Disney Educational Productions
105 Terry Drive, Suite 120
Newtown, PA 18940

Disney Publications
114 Fifth Avenue
New York, NY 10011

Dorling Kindersley Family Library,
 Inc.
7566 Southland Blvd., Suite 107
Orlando, FL 32809

Dominie Press, Inc.
1949 Kellogg Avenue
Carlsbad, CA 92008

Dormac, Inc.
P.O. Box 3903
Bellevue, WA 98009-3903

EBSCO Curriculum Materials
Box 11542
Birmingham, AL 35202

Economy Company
P.O. Box 25308
1901 North Walnut Street
Oklahoma City, OK 73125

ECS Learning Systems
P.O. Box 791437
San Antonio, TX 78279-1437

Edge Enterprises, Inc.
P.O. Box 1304
Lawrence, KS 66044

Edmark Corporation
P.O. Box 3218
Redmond, WA 98073-3218

Educational Activities, Inc.
P.O. Box 392
1937 Grand Avenue,
Baldwin, NY 11510

Educational Productions, Inc.
7412 SW Beaverton Hillsdale
 Highway, Suite 210
Portland, OR 97225

Educators Publishing Service, Inc.
31 Smith Place
Cambridge, MA 02138-1000

Educational Service, Inc.
3915 Plainville Road
Cincinnati, OH 45227

Educational Teaching Aids
620 Lakeview Pkwy.
Vernon Hills, IL 60061

Enrich
Imprint of Price Stern Sloon
11835 Olympic Blvd., 5th Flr.
Los Angeles, CA 90064

Fanlight Productions
47 Halifax Street
Boston, MA 02130

Fearon Publisher
6 Davis Drive
Belmont, CA 94002

Field Educational Publications
609 Mission Street
San Francisco, CA 94105

Flaghouse
150 N. MacQuesten Pkwy.
Mt. Vernon, NY 10550

Fox Reading Research Company
809 E. Timber Ln.
Coeur d'Alene, ID 83814-6541

Frog Publications
P.O. Box 280096
Tampa, FL 33982-0096

Gardner's Book Service
16461 N. 25th Avenue
Phoenix, AZ 85023

Garrard Publishing Company
1607 North Market Street
Champaign, IL 61820

George F. Cram Co., Inc.
P.O. Box 426
Indianapolis, IN 46206

Globe Fearon Educational Publisher
4350 Equity Drive
P.O. Box 2649
Columbus, OH 43216

Greenwillow Books
1350 Avenue of the Americas
New York, NY 10019

Grypon Press
220 Montgomery Street
Highland Park, NJ 18904

Guidance Associates
Communication Park
Box 3000
Mount Kisco, NY 10549

H and H Enterprises
946 Tennessee
Lawrence, KS 66044

D.C. Heath and Company
2700 Richardt Avenue
Indianapolis, IN 46219

Heinemann
361 Hanover Street,
Portsmouth, NH 03801-3959

Holt, Rinehart and Winston
1120 S. Capital of Texas Hwy.
Austin, TX 78746-6487

Houghton Mifflin
222 Berkeley Street
Boston, MA 02116

Hubbard
Drawer 100
Defiance, OH 43512

Human Sciences Press
233 Spring Street
New York, NY 10013-1578

Ideal School Supply Company
11000 South Lavergne Avenue
Oak Lawn, IL 60453

Incentive Publications
3835 Cleghorn Ave.
Nashville, TN 37215

Innovative Learning Concepts, Inc.
6760 Corporate Drive
Colorado Springs, CO 80919-1999

Innovative Learning Publications
Addison-Wesley Publishing
  Company
Route 128
Reading, MA 01867

Instructional Materials Laboratory
University of Missouri Columbia
2316 Industrial Drive
Columbia, MO 65202

Instructor Book Club
Newbridge Book Club
P.O. Box 6009
Delran, NJ 08370-6009

Intellimation
P.O. Box 1922
Santa Barbara, CA 93116-1922

International Reading Association
800 Barksdale Road
P.O. Box 8139
Newark, DE 19714-8139

Jamestown Publishers
2 Prudential Plaza, Suite 1200
Chicago, IL 60601

Janus Books
2501 Industrial Parkway West
Hayward, CA 94545

Jastek Associates
1526 Gilpin Avenue
Wilmington, DE 19800

Lakeshore Learning Materials
2695 E. Dominguez Street
P.O. Box 6261
Carson, CA 90749

Learning Concepts
2501 North Lamar Blvd.
Austin, TX 78705

Learning Skills
2562 Kelton Avenue
Los Angeles, CA 90064

LinguiSystems, Inc.
3100 Fourth Avenue
P.O. Box 747
East Moline, IL 61224

Love Publishing Co.
1777 South Bellaire Street
Denver, CO 80222

Lyons and Carnahan
8255 Central Park Ave.
Chicago, IL 60076

Media Materials
111 Kane Street
Baltimore, MD 21224

Milton Bradley Co.
443 Shaker Road
East Longmeadow, MA 01028

Modern Curriculum Press
4350 Equity Drive
P.O. Box 2649
Columbus, OH 43216

Modern Education Corporation
P.O. Box 721
Tulsa, OK 74101

National Council of Teachers of
  English
1111 Kenyon Road
Urbana, IL 61801

National Education Association
  Publications
1201 16th Street NW
Washington, DC 20036

National Geographic Society
1145 17th Street NW
Washington, DC 20036

New Readers Press
1320 Jamesville Avenue
Box 131
Syracuse, NY 13210

NTC Publishing Group
4255 W. Touhy Avenue
Lincolnwood, IL 60646-1975

Open Court Publishing Co.
332 S. Michigan, Suite 2000
Chicago, IL 60604

Opportunities for Learning
P.O. Box 8130
Mansfield, OH 44901

Orton Dyslexia Society, Inc.
Chester Building, 8600 LaSalle
  Road, Suite 382
Baltimore, MD 21286–2044

P.B.S. Video
1320 Braddock Place
Alexandria, VA 22314-1698

PCI
5221 McCullough Avenue
San Antonio, TX 78212

Penguin USA
375 Hudson Street
New York, NY 10014

Perma-Bound Books
Vandalia Road
Jacksonville, IL 62650

Phonovisual Products, Inc.
P.O. Box 2007
Rockville, MD 20852

Pro-Ed
8700 Shoal Creek Blvd.
Austin, TX 78758

The Psychological Corp.
555 Academic Court
P.O. Box 9954
San Antonio, TX 78204-2498

Psychological and Educational
  Publications, Inc.
1477 Rollins Road
Burlingame, CA 94010-2316

Reader's Digest Services
Educational Division
Readers Digest Road
Pleasantville, NJ 10570

Reading Joy
P.O. Box 2
Wheaton, IL 60189-0002

Recording for the Blind & Dyslexic
20 Roszel Road
Princeton, NJ 08540

Remedia Publications
10135 E. Via Linda, #D124
Scottsdale, AZ 85258-5312

Rigby
P.O. Box 797
Crystal Lake, IL 60039-0797

Riverside Publishing Company
8420 Bryn Mawr Road
Chicago, IL 60631

Scholastic, Inc.
P.O. Box 7502
Jefferson City, MO 65102

Science Research Associates
250 Old Wilson Bridge Road
  Suite 310
Worthington, OH 43085

Scott, Foresman and Company
1900 East Lake Avenue
Glenview, IL 60025

Slosson Educational Publications
140 Pine Street
P.O. Box 280
East Aurora, NY 14052-0280

Sopris West
1140 Boston Avenue
Longmont, CO 80501

Spalding Education Foundation
  News
5930 W. Greenway, Suite 4
Glendale, AZ 85306

Special Child Publications
P.O. Box 33548
Seattle, WA 98133

The Speech Bin, Inc.
1965 25th Avenue
Vero Beach, FL 32960

Steck-Vaughn Company
P.O. Box 26015
Austin, TX 78755

Thinking Publications
424 Galloway Street
P.O. Box 163
Eau Claire, WI 54702

Charles C. Thomas Publisher
2500 E. Fourth Plain Blvd., No. 252
Vancouver, WA 98661

Troll Associates
100 Corporation Drive
Mahwah, NJ 07430

Teacher Created Materials
P.O. Box 1040
Huntington Beach, CA 92647

Therapy Skill Builders
3830 E. Bellevue
P.O. Box 42050-TS5
Tucson, AZ 85733

Tutor Tapes
4327 Sunny Lane
Yorba Linda, CA 92686

VORT Corp.
P.O. Box 60132
Palo Alto, CA 94306

Walker Educational Book Corp.
435 Hudson Street
New York, NY 10014-3941

Western Psychological Services
12031 Wilshire Blvd.
Los Angeles, CA 90025-1251

Webster
A Division of McGraw-Hill
  Book Co.
1221 Avenue of the Americas
New York, NY 10020

The Wright Group
19201 120th Avenue NE
Bothell, WA 98011

Xerox Adaptive Technologies
9 Centennial Drive
Peabody, MA 01960

Zaner-Bloser Company
P.O. Box 16764
Columbus, OH 43216-6764

Zephyr Press Learning Materials
3316 N. Chapel Avenue
P.O. Box 66006-C2
Tucson, AZ 85728

APPENDIX B

Educational Computer Software and Multimedia Publishers

Addison-Wesley Publishing
   Company
1 Jacob Way
Reading, MA 01867

Advanced Ideas, Inc.
591 Redwood Hwy., Suite 2325
Mill Valley, CA 94941

American Educational Computer
(The American Education Corp.)
7506 N. Broadway, Suite 505
Oklahoma City, OK 73116-9016

American Micro Media
19 N. Broadway
P.O. Box 306
Red Hook, NY 12571

AM Technologies, Inc.
831 Beacon Street/B17
Newton, MA 02159

Apple Computer, Inc.
135 E. 57th Street
New York, NY 10022

A-Plus Computing
P.O. Box 26496
Prescott Valley, AZ 86312

Aquarius Productions, Inc.
5 Powderhouse Lane
P.O. Box 1159
Sherborn, MA 01770

Borg-Warner Educational System
600 West University Drive
Arlington, IL 60004

Broderbund
P.O. Box 6125
Novato, CA 94948-6125

Chariot Software Group
3659 India Street, Suite 100c
San Diego, CA 92103

Chatterbox
P.O. Box 7933
F.D.R. Station
New York, NY 10150-2411

Child Development Media, Inc.
5632 Van Nuys Blvd., Suite 286
Van Nuys, CA 91401

Claris Corporation
5201 Patrick Henry Drive
Santa Clara, CA 95052-8168

Classroom Consortia Media
P.O. Box 050228
Staten Island, NY 10305-0004

Closing the Gap
P.O. Box 68
Henderson, MN 56044

Communication Skill Builders
P.O. Box 839954
San Antonio, TX 78283-3954

Computer Curriculum Corporation
1287 Lawrence Station Road
Sunnyvale, CA 94089

Computer Education
P.O. Box 420783
San Diego, CA 92142-0783

Computer Plus
295 Santa Ana Court
Sunnyvale, CA 94086-4512

Critical Thinking Press and
   Software
P.O. Box 448
Pacific Grove, CA 93950

Davidson & Associates, Inc.
19840 Pioneer Avenue
Torrance, CA 90503-1660

Decision Development Corporation
2680 Bishop Drive, Suite 122
San Ramon, CA 94583

Demco Media
Box 14260
Madison, WI 53714-0260

Discis Knowledge Research Inc.
5150 Yonge Street
Toronto, Ontario, Canada M2N 6N2

Dorsett Educational Systems
Box 1226
Norman, OK 73070

EBSCO Curriculum Materials
P.O. Box 1943
Birmingham, AL 35301-1943

Edmark
P.O. Box 97021
Redmond, WA 98073-97021

Educational Micro Systems
P.O. Box 471
Chester, NJ 07930

Educational Teaching Aids
620 Lakeview Pkwy.
Vernon Hills, IL 60061

EduQuest/IBM, Inc. (Cambrix
Publishing)
6269 Variel Avenue, Suite B
Woodland Hills, CA 91367

Edusoft
P.O. Box 2569, Dept. 50
Berkeley, CA 94702

The Electronic Bookshelf, Inc.
R.R. No. 9, Box 64
Frankfort, IN 46041

Encyclopedia Britannica
Educational Corporation
310 S. Michigan Avenue
Chicago, IL 60604-9839

Films for the Humanities &
Sciences
P.O. Box 2053
Princeton, NJ 08534-2053

Follett Library Resources
4506 Northwest Highway Rts. 14
& 31
Crystal Lake, IL 60014

Franklin Learning Resources
One Franklin Plaza
Burlington, NJ 08016-4907

Gamco Industries
Box 1911
Big Spring, TX 79721

Hartley Courseware
9920 Pacific Heights Blvd., No. 500
San Diego, CA 92121-4334

Houghton Mifflin
222 Berkeley Street
Boston, MA 02116

Humanities Software
P.O. Box 950
408 Columbia Street, Suite 222
Hood River, OR 97031

IBM Educational Systems
One Culver Road
Dayton, NJ 08810

IBM Support Center for Persons
with Disabilities
P. O. Box 2150–H06R1
Atlanta, GA 30301

Insight Media
2162 Broadway
New York, NY 10024

Jostens Home Learning
9920 Pacific Heights Blvd., No. 100
San Diego, CA 92121-4430

K–12 Micromedia
172 Broadway
Woodcliff Lake, NJ 07675

Krell Software
P.O. Box 1252
Lake Grove, NY 11755

Laureate Learning Systems
110 East Spring Street
Winooski, VT 05404

The Learning Company
6493 Kaiser Drive
Freemont, CA 94555

Learning Lab Software
20301 Ventura Blvd., No. 214
Woodland Hills, CA 91364-2447

Learning Systems, Ltd. Group
P.O. Box 9046
Fort Collins, CO 80525

Media Materials
111 Kane Street
Baltimore, MD 21224

Micro Learningware
Route 1, Box 162
Amboy, MN 56010-9762

Microsoft Corporation
One Microsoft Way
Redmond, WA 98052-6399

Milliken Publishers
1100 Research Blvd.
St. Louis, MO 63132-5079

Milton Bradley Educational
Division
443 Shaker Road
East Longmeadow, MA 01028

Mindplay
3130 North Dodge
P.O. Box 36491
Tucson, AZ 85740

Mindscape Educational Software
1345 Diversey Parkway
Chicago, IL 60614

Minnesota Educational Computing
Consortium (MECC)
6160 Summit Drive North
Minneapolis, MN 55430-4003

National Geographic Society
Educational Services
1145 17th Street, N.M.
Washington, DC 20036-4688

Opportunities for Learning
P.O. Box 8130
Mansfield, OH 44901

Orange Cherry/Taking Schoolhouse
Software
P.O. Box 309
Westchester Avenue
Pound Ridge, NY 10576

Parrot Software
6505 Pleasant Lake Court
West Bloomfield, MI 48322

Peal Software
P.O. Box 8188
Calabasas, CA 91372

Queue, Inc. (Pelican)
338 Commerce Drive
Fairfield, CT 06430

Quicksoft (Starlite Software Corp.)
P.O. Box 370
Hadlock, WA 98339

Random House School Division
201 East 50th Street, 22nd Floor
New York, NY 10022

Reader's Digest Services
Educational Division
Readers Digest Road
Pleasantville, NJ 10570

Right On Programs, division of
    Computeam
755 New York Avenue
Huntington, NY 11743

Scholastic Software
740 Broadway
New York, NY 10003

Science Research Associates
250 Old Wilson Bridge Road,
    Suite 310
Worthington, OH 43085

Society for Visual Education, Inc.
6677 N. Northwest Hwy.
Chicago, IL 60631-1304

Spinnaker Software
201 Broadway
Cambridge, MA 02139-1901

Springboard Educational Software
338 Commerce Drive
Fairfield, CT 06430

Sunburst Communication
101 Castleton Street
Pleasantville, NY 10570

Teacher Support Software
1035 NW 57th Street
Gainesville, FL 32605

Terrapin Software, Inc.
10 Holworthy Street
Cambridge, MA 02138

Texas Instruments
7800 Banner Drive, MS 3908
Dallas, TX 75265

Tom Snyder Productions, Inc.
80 Coolidge Hill Road
Watertown, MA 02172-2817

Troll Communications L.L.C.
100 Corporate Drive
Mahwah, NJ 07430

Video Discovery, Inc.
1700 Westlake Avenue North,
    Suite 600
Seattle, WA 98109-3012

Universal Learning Technology
39 Cross Street
Peabody, MA 01960

Weekly Reader Software Optimum
    Resources, Inc.
5 Hiltech Lane
Hilton Head, SC 29926

WordPerfect Corporation
1555 N. Technology Way
Orem, UT 84057-2399

Zeitgeist
445 W. Bullard Ave., No. 108
Fresno, CA 93704-1603

References

Aaronson, S. (1975). Notetaking improvement: A combined auditory, functional and psychological approach. *Journal of Reading, 19,* 8–12.

Abroms, K. I., and Kodera, T. L. (1979). Acceptance hierarchy of handicaps: Validation of Kirk's statement, "Special education often begins where medicine stops." *Journal of Learning Disabilities, 12*(1), 15–20.

Abt Associates (1976). *Education as experimentation: A planned variation model* (Vol. 3). Boston: Abt Associates.

Achenbach, T. M. (1991). *Manual for the youth self-report form and 1991 profile.* Burlington, Vt.: University of Vermont Department of Psychiatry.

Achenbach, T. M., and Edelbrock, C. S. (1978). The child behavior profile: II. Boys aged 12–16 and girls aged 6–11 and 12–16. *Journal of Consulting and Clinical Psychology, 41,* 223–233.

Achenbach, T. M., and Edelbrock, C. S. (1991). *Manual for the Children Behavior Checklist.* Burlington, Vt.: Department of Psychiatry, University of Vermont.

Ackerman, P. T., Anhalt, J. M., and Dykman, R. A. (1986). Arithmetic automatization failure in children with attention and reading disorders: Associations and sequela. *Journal of Learning Disabilities, 19*(4), 222–232.

Adams, A., Carnine, D., and Gersten, R. (1982). Instructional strategies for studying context area texts in the intermediate grades. *Reading Research Quarterly, 18*(1), 27–55.

Adams, M. J. (1990). *Beginning to read: Thinking and learning about print.* Cambridge, Mass.: MIT Press.

Adams, M. J., and Brunk, M. (1995). Resolving the 'great debate'. *American Educator, 19*(2), 7, 10–20.

Allen, J., Michalove, B., Shockley, B., and West, M. (1991). "I'm really worried about Joseph": Reducing the risks of literacy learning. *The Reading Teacher, 44,* 458–472.

Allen, R. V. (1976). *Language experiences in communication.* Boston: Houghton Mifflin.

Allen, R. V., and Allen, C. (1966–68). *Language experiences in reading* (Levels I, II, and III). Chicago: Encyclopedia Britannica.

Allen, R. V., and Allen, C. (1982), *Language experience activities* (2nd ed.). Boston: Houghton Mifflin.

Alley, G. R., and Deshler, D. D. (1979). *Teaching the learning disabled adolescent: Strategies and methods.* Denver: Love Publishing.

Allington, R. L. (1983). The reading instruction provided readers of differing reading abilities. *The Elementary School Journal, 83,* 548–559.

Alsup, R. (1982). *WH-questions.* Allen, Tex.: DLM.

Altwerger, B., and Ivener, B. L. (1994). Self-esteem: Access to literacy in multicultural and multilingual classrooms. In K. Spangenberg-Urbschat and R. Pritchard (Eds.), *Kids come in all languages: Reading instruction for ESL students* (pp. 65–81). Newark, Del.: International Reading Association.

Altwerger, B., Edelsky, C., and Flores, B. M. (1987). Whole language: What's new? *The Reading Teacher, 41,* 144–154.

Alvermann, D. E. (1991). The discussion web: A graphic aid for learning across the curriculum. *The Reading Teacher, 45,* 92–99.

Alvermann, D. E., and Moore, D. W. (1991). Secondary school reading. In R. Barr, M. L. Kamil, P. B. Mosenthal, and P. D. Pearson (Eds.), *Handbook of reading research.* New York: Longman, Vol. 2, pp. 951–983.

Alvermann, D. E., and Phelps, S. E. (1994). *Content area reading and literacy: Succeeding in today's diverse classrooms.* Boston: Allyn and Bacon.

Alvermann, D., Bridge, C., Schmidt, R., Seafoss, L., Winograd, P., Paris, S., Priestly, C., and Santeusanio, N. (1989). *Heath reading.* Lexington, Mass.: D.C. Heath.

American Psychiatric Association. (1994). *Diagnostic and statistical manual of mental disorders* (4th ed.). Washington, D.C.

Amish, P. L., Gesten, E. L., Smith, J. K., Clark, H. B., and Stark, C. (1988). Social problem-solving training for severely emotionally and behaviorally disturbed children. *Behavioral Disorders, 13*(3), 175–186.

Anders, P. L., and Bos, C. S. (1984). In the beginning: Vocabulary instruction in content classroom. *Topics in Learning and Learning Disabilities, 3*(4), 53–65.

Anders, P. L., and Bos, C. S. (1986). Semantic feature analysis: An interactive strategy for vocabulary development and text comprehension. *Journal of Reading, 29*(7), 610–616.

Anders, P. L., and Guzzetti, B. J. (1996). *Literacy instruction in the content areas.* Fort Worth: Harcourt Brace College Publishers.

Anders, P. L., and Mitchell, J. N. (May 1980). *Pilgrims, Indians, the Mayflower, and freedom: Interactions among readers, texts, concepts, and questions.* Paper presented at the International Reading Association Convention, St. Louis, Mo.

Anderson, J. R. (1995). *Cognitive psychology and its implications* (4th ed.). San Francisco: W. H. Freeman.

Anderson, L., Brubaker, N., Alleman-Brooks, J., and Duffy, G. (1986). A qualitative study of seatwork in first-grade classrooms. *Elementary School Journal, 86,* 123–140.

Anderson, L. M., Raphael, T. E., Englert, C. S., and Stevens, D. D. (April 1991). *Teaching writing with a new instructional model: Variations in teachers' practices and student performance.* Paper presented at the annual meeting of the American Education Research Association, Chicago.

Anderson, R. C. (1977). The notion of schemata and the educational enterprise. In R. C. Anderson, R. J. Spiro, and W. E. Montague (Eds.), *Schooling and the acquisition of knowledge.* Hillsdale, N.J.: Erlbaum, pp. 415–431.

Anderson, R. C., and Freebody, P. (1981). Vocabulary knowledge. In J. T. Guthrie (Ed.), *Comprehension and reading: Research reviews.* Newark, N.J.: International Reading Association.

Anderson, R. C., Hiebert, E., Scott, J., and Wilkinson, I. (1985). *Becoming a nation of readers: The Report on the Commission on Reading.* Washington, D.C.: National Institute of Education.

Anderson, R. C., Reynolds, R. E., Schallert, D. L., and Goetz, E. T. (1977). Frameworks for comprehending discourse. *American Educational Research Journal, 14,* 367–382.

Anderson, R. C., Wilson, P. T., and Fielding, L. G. (1988). Growth in reading and how children spend their time outside school. *Reading Research Quarterly, 23,* 285–303.

Anderson, T. H., and Armbruster, B. B. (1984). Content area textbooks. In R. C. Anderson, J. Osborn, and R. J. Tierney (Eds.), *Learning to read in American schools: Basal readers and content texts.* Hillsdale, N.J.: Erlbaum, pp. 193–226.

Anderson-Inman, L., Knox-Quinn, C., and Horney, M. (1996). Computer-based study strategies for students with learning disabilities: Individual differences associated with adaption level. *Journal of Learning Disabilities, 29,* 461–484.

Anglin, J. (1970). *The growth of meaning.* Cambridge, Mass.: MIT Press.

Archer, A., and Edgar, E. (1976). Teaching academic skills to mildly handicapped children. In S. Lowenbraun and J. Q. Affleck (Eds.), *Teaching mildly handicapped children in regular classes.* Columbus, Ohio: Merrill.

Arguelles, M. E., Vaughn, S., and Schumm, J. S. (1996). *Executive summaries of 69 schools throughout the state of Florida participating in the ESE/FEFP 1995–1996 pilot program.* Manuscript in preparation.

Armbruster, B. B., and Anderson, T. H. (1988). On selecting "considerate" content area textbooks. *Remedial and Special Education, 9*(1), 47–52.

Ashbaker, M. H., and Swanson, H. L. (1996). Short-term memory and working memory operations and their contribution to reading in adolescents with and without learning disabilities. *Learning Disabilities Research and Practice, 11,* 206–213.

Ashton-Warner, S. (1958). *Spinster.* New York: Simon and Schuster.

Ashton-Warner, S. (1963). *Teacher.* New York: Simon and Schuster.

Ashton-Warner, S. (1972). *Spearpoint.* New York: Alfred A. Knopf.

Atkinson, J. W., and Shiffrin, R. M. (1968). Human memory: A proposed system and its control processes. In K. W. Spence and J. T. Spence (Eds.), *The psychology of learning and motivation: Advances in research and theory* (Vol. 2). New York: Academic Press.

Atwell, N. (1984). Writing and reading literature from the inside out. *Language Arts, 61,* 240–252.

Atwell, N. (1985). Writing and reading from the inside out. In J. Hansen, T. Newkirk, and D. Graves (Eds.), *Breaking ground: Teachers relate reading and writing in the elementary school,* Portsmouth, N.H.: Heinemann, pp. 147–168.

Atwell, N. (1987). *In the middle: Writing, reading, and learning with adolescents.* Portsmouth, N.H.: Heinemann.

Atwell, N. (Ed.) (1991). *Side by side: Essays on teaching to learn.* Portsmouth, N.H.: Heinemann.

Aulls, M. S. (1978). *Developmental and remedial reading in the middle grades.* Boston: Allyn and Bacon.

Ausubel, D. P., and Robinson, F. G. (1969). *School learning: An introduction to education psychology.* New York: Holt, Rinehart and Winston.

Axline, V. (1947). *Play therapy.* Boston: Houghton Mifflin.

Badian, N. A., and Ghublikian, M. (1983). The personal-social characteristics of children with poor mathematical computation skills. *Journal of Learning Disabilities, 16*(3), 154–157.

Bahr, C., Nelson, N., and Van Meter, A. (1996). The effects of text-based and graphics-based software tools on planning and organizing of stories. *Journal of Learning Disabilities, 29*(4), 366–370.

Baker, C. (1993). *Foundations of bilingual education and bilingualism.* Clevedon, England: Multilingual Matters.

Baker, G. A. (1977). *A comparison of traditional spelling with phonemic spelling of fifth and sixth grade students.* Unpublished doctoral dissertation, Wayne State University, Detroit.

Ball, E., and Blachman, B. (1991). Does phoneme segmentation training in kindergarten make a difference in early word recognition and developmental spelling? *Reading Research Quarterly, 26,* 49–86.

Bandura, A. (1977). *Social learning theory.* Englewood Cliffs, N.J.: Prentice-Hall.

Barney, L. (1973). The first and third R's. *Today's Education, 62,* 57–58.

Barrett, T. (1976). Taxonomy of reading comprehension. In R. Smith and T. Barrett (Eds.), *Teaching reading in the middle grades.* Reading, Mass.: Addison-Wesley.

Barron, R. (1969). The use of vocabulary as an advanced organizer. In H. L. Herber and P. L. Sanders (Eds.), *Research in reading in the content areas: First reports.* Syracuse, N.Y.: Syracuse University Reading and Language Arts Center.

Barron, R., and Earle, R. (1973). An approach for vocabulary development. In H. L. Herber and P. L. Sanders (Eds.), *Research in reading in the content areas: Second report.* Syracuse, N.Y.: University of Syracuse, Reading and Language Arts Center.

Bartlett, R. C. (1932). *Remembering.* Cambridge, Eng.: Cambridge University Press.

Bashir, A. S., and Scavuzzo, A. (1992). Children with language disorders: Natural history and academic success. *Journal of Learning Disabilities, 25,* 53–65.

Battle, J., and Blowers, T. (1982). A longitudinal comparative study of the self-esteem of students in regular and special education classes. *Journal of Learning Disabilities, 15*(2), 100–102.

Bauer, R. H. (1987). Control processes as a way of understanding, diagnosing, and remediating learning disabilities. In H. L. Swanson (Ed.), *Advances in learning and behavioral disabilities* (Supplement 2). Greenwich, Conn.: JAI Press, pp. 41–81.

Baumann, J. F., and Bergeron, B. S. (1993). Story map instruction using children's literature: Effects on first graders' comprehension of central narrative elements. *Journal of Reading Behavior, 25,* 407–437.

Baumann, J. F., and Serra, J. K. (1984). The frequency and placement of main ideas in children's social studies textbooks: A modified replication of Braddock's research on topic sentences. *Journal of Reading Behavior, 16,* 27–40.

Bauwens, J., Hourcade, J. J., and Friend, M. (1989). Cooperative teaching: A model for general and special education integration. *Remedial and Special Education, 10*(2), 17–22.

Bear, G. C., Clever, A., and Proctor, W. A. (1991). Self-perceptions of nonhandicapped children and children with learning disabilities in integrated classes. *Journal of Special Education, 24,* 409–426.

Beaumont, C. (1992). Language intervention strategies for Hispanic LLD students. In H. W. Langdon and L. L. Cheng (Eds.), *Hispanic children and adults with communication disorders.* Gaithersburg, Md.: Aspen Publishers, pp. 272–342.

Beck, A. T., Brown, G., and Steer, R. A. (1989). Prediction of eventual suicide in psychiatric inpatients by clinical ratings of hopelessness. *Journal of Consulting and Clinical Psychology, 57,* 309–310.

Beck, J., and McKeown, M. G. (1981). Developing questions that promote comprehension: The story map. *Language Arts, 58,* 913–918.

Becker, W. C. (1977). Teaching reading and language to the disadvantaged—What we have learned from field research. *Harvard Educational Review, 44*(4), 518–543.

Becker, W. C., and Englemann, S. E. (1976). Technical report 1976–1. Eugene: University of Oregon.

Beirne-Smith, M. (1991). Peer tutoring in arithmetic for children with learning disabilities. *Exceptional Children, 57*(4), 330–338.

Beltempo, J., and Achille, P. A. (1990). The effect of special class placement on the self-concept of children with learning disabilities. *Child Study Journal, 20*(2), 81–103.

Berenfeld, B. (1996). Linking students to the infosphere. *Technological Horizons in Education, 23*(9), 76–83.

Bergerund, D., Lovitt, T. C., and Horton, S. (1988). The effectiveness of textbook adaptations in life science for high school students with learning disabilities. *Journal of Learning Disabilities, 21,* 70–76.

Berler, E. S., Gross, A. M., and Drabman, R. S. (1982). Social skills training with children: Proceed with caution. *Journal of Applied Behavioral Analysis, 15,* 41–53.

Berliner, D. C. (1983). The executive who manages classrooms. In B. J. Fraser (Ed.), *Classroom management.* South Bentley: Western Australian Institute of Technology.

Berninger, V. W., Abbott, R. D., Whitaker, D., Sylvester, L., and Nolen, S. B. (1995). Integrating low- and high-level skills in instructional protocols for writing disabilities. *Learning Disability Quarterly, 18,* 293–309.

Berres, F., and Eyer, J. T. (1970). In A. J. Harris (Ed.), *Casebook on reading disability.* New York: David McKay, pp. 25–47.

Betts, E. A. (1946). *Foundations of reading instruction.* New York: American Book.

Bickett, L. G., and Milich, R. (April 1987). *First impressions of learning disabled and attention deficit disordered boys.* Paper presented at the Biennial Meeting of the Society for Research in Child Development, Baltimore, Md.

Bierman, K. L., and Furman, W. (1984). The effects of social skills training and peer involvement on the social adjustment of preadolescents. *Child Development, 55,* 151–162.

Billingsley, B. S., and Wildman, T. M. (1990). Facilitating reading comprehension in learning disabled students: Metacognitive goals and instructional strategies. *Remedial and Special Education, 11*(2), 18–31.

Black, F. (1974). Self-concept as related to achievement and age in learning disabled children. *Child Development, 45,* 1137–1140.

Blackman, S., and Goldman, K. M. (1982). Cognitive styles and learning disabilities. *Journal of Learning Disabilities, 15,* 106–115.

Blair, K. S. (1996). *Context-based functional assessment and intervention for preschool age children with problem behaviors in childcare.* Unpublished dissertation, University of Arizona, Tucson.

Blankenship, C. S. (1984). Curriculum and instruction: An examination of models in special and regular education. In J. F. Cawley (Ed.), *Developmental teaching of mathematics for the learning disabled.* Rockville, Md.: Aspen.

Blankenship, C. S., and Lovitt, T. C. (1976). Story problems: Merely confusing or downright befuddling. *Journal for Research in Mathematics Education, 7,* 290–298.

Blanton, W. E., and Moorman, G. B. (1990). The presentation of reading lessons. *Reading Research and Instruction, 29,* 35–55.

Bley, N. S., and Thornton, C. A. (1981). *Teaching mathematics to the learning disabled.* Rockville, Md.: Aspen.

Bloodgood, J. (1991). A new approach to spelling instruction in language arts programs. *Elementary School Journal, 92,* 203–211.

Bloom, B. S. (1976). *Human characteristics and school learning.* New York: McGraw-Hill.

Bloom, L., and Lahey, M. (1978). *Language development and language disorders.* New York: John Wiley.

Bloom, L., Miller, P., and Hood, L. (1975). Variation and reduction as aspects of competence in language development. In A. Pick (Ed.), *Minnesota symposium on child psychology* (Vol. 9). Minneapolis: University of Minnesota.

Bloomfield, L., and Barnhart, C. L. (1961). *Let's read: A linguistic approach.* Detroit: Wayne State University Press.

Boatner, M. T., Gates, J. E., and Makkai, A. (1975). *A dictionary of American idioms* (rev. ed.). Woodbury, N.J.: Barron's.

Borkowski, J. G., Weyhing, R. S., and Carr, M. (1988). Effects of attributional retraining on strategy-based reading comprehension in learning-disabled students. *Journal of Educational Psychology, 80*(1), 46–53.

Borkowski, J. G., Weyhing, R. S., and Turner, L. A. (1986). Attributional retraining and the teaching of strategies. *Exceptional Children, 53*(2), 130–137.

Bos, C. S. (1979). *Inferential operations in the reading comprehension of educable mentally retarded and average students.* Doctoral dissertation, University of Arizona, Tucson.

Bos, C. S. (1982). Getting past decoding: Using modeled and repeated readings as a remedial method for learning disabled students. *Topics in Learning and Learning Disabilities, 1,* 51–57.

Bos, C. S. (October 1987). *Promoting story comprehension using a story retelling strategy.* Paper presented at the Teachers Applying Whole Language Conference, Tucson, Ariz.

Bos, C. S. (1988). Academic interventions for learning disabilities. In K. A. Kavale (Ed.), *Learning disabilities: State of the art and practice.* Boston: Little, Brown–College Hill, pp. 98–122.

Bos, C. S. (1991). Reading-writing connections: Using literature as a zone of proximal development for writing. *Learning Disabilities Research and Practice, 6,* 251–263.

Bos, C. S., Allen, A. A., and Scanlon, D. J. (1989). Vocabulary instruction and reading comprehension with bilingual learning disabled students. In S. McCormick and J. Zutell (Eds.), *Cognitive and social perspectives for literacy research and instruction* (Thirty-eighth yearbook). Chicago: National Reading Conference, pp. 173–180.

Bos, C. S., and Anders, P. L. (1990a). Effects of interactive vocabulary instruction on the vocabulary learning and reading comprehension of junior-high learning disabled students. *Learning Disability Quarterly, 13,* 31–42.

Bos, C. S., and Anders, P. L. (1990b). Toward an interactive model: Teaching text-based concepts to learning disabled students. In H. L. Swanson and B. Keogh (Eds.), *Learning disabilities: Theoretical and research issues.* Hillsdale, N.J.: Erlbaum, pp. 247–261.

Bos, C. S., and Anders, P. L. (1990c). Interactive teaching and learning: Instructional practices for teaching content and strategic knowledge. In T. E. Scruggs and B. Y. L. Wong (Eds.), *Intervention research in learning disabilities.* New York: Springer-Verlag, pp. 166–185.

Bos, C. S., and Anders, P. L. (1992). A theory-driven interactive instructional model for text comprehension and content learning. In B. Y. L. Wong (Ed.), *Contemporary intervention research in learning disabilities: An international perspective.* New York: Springer-Verlag, pp. 81–95.

Bos, C. S., Anders, P. L., Jaffe, L. E., and Filip, D. (1985). Semantic feature analysis and long-term learning. In J. A. Niles (Ed.), *Issues in literacy: A research perspective* (Thirty-fourth yearbook). Rochester, N.Y.: National Reading Conference, pp. 42–46.

Bos, C. S., and Duffy, M. L. (1991). Facilitating content learning and text comprehension for students with learning disabilities. *Exceptionality Education Canada, 1*(3), 1–13.

Bos, C. S., and Filip, D. (1984). Comprehension monitoring in learning disabled and average students. *Journal of Learning Disabilities, 17*(4), 229–233.

Bos, C. S., and Reyes, E. I. (1996). Conversations with a Latina teacher about education for language-minority students with special needs. *Elementary School Journal, 96,* 343–352.

Bos, C. S., and Van Reusen, A. K. (1986). *Effects of teaching a strategy for facilitating student and parent participation in the IEP process* (Partner Project Final Report G008400643). Tucson: University of Arizona, Department of Special Education.

Boyle, J. R. (1996). The effects of a cognitive mapping strategy on the literal and inferential comprehension of students with mild disabilities. *Learning Disability Quarterly, 19,* 86–98.

Bradley, J. M. (1975). Sight word association procedure. Unpublished manuscript, College of Education, University of Arizona, Tucson.

Bradley, L., and Bryant, P. (1985). *Rhyme and reason in reading and spelling.* Ann Arbor: University of Michigan Press.

Bragstad, B. J., and Stumpf, S. M. (1982). *A guidebook for teaching: Study skills and motivation.* Boston: Allyn and Bacon.

Brainerd, C. J., and Reyna, V. F. (1991). Acquisition and forgetting processes in normal and learning-disabled children: A disintegration/reintegration theory. In J. E. Obrzut and G. W. Hynd (Eds.), *Neuropsychological foundations of learning disabilities.* San Diego: Academic Press, pp. 147–178.

Bransford, J. D., and Johnson, M. D. (1972). Contextual prerequisites for understanding: Some investigations of comprehension and recall. *Journal of Verbal Learning and Verbal Behavior, 11,* 717–726.

Brewer, W. R., and Nakamura, G. V. (1984). *The nature and functions of schemas* (Tech. Rep. 325). Champaign: University of Illinois, Center for the Study of Reading.

Brice, A., and Montgomery, J. (1996). Adolescent pragmatic skills: A comparison of Latino students in English as a second language and speech and language programs. *Language, Speech, and Hearing Services in Schools, 27,* 68–81.

Bridge, C. A., and Burton, B. (1982). Teaching sight vocabulary through patterned language materials. In J. A. Niles and L. A. Harris (Eds.), *New inquiries in reading research and instruction* (Thirty-first yearbook), Washington, D.C.: National Reading Conference, pp. 119–223.

Bridge, C. A., Winograd, P. N., and Haley, D. (1983). Using predictable materials vs. preprimers to teach beginning sight words. *The Reading Teacher, 36*(9), 884–891.

Briggs, D. (1970). Influence of handwriting on assessment. *Educational Research, 13,* 50–55.

Brinckerhoff, L. C., Shaw, S. F., and McGuire, J. M. (1992). Promoting access, accommodations, and independence for college students with learning disabilities. *Journal of Learning Disabilities, 25,* 417–429.

Brophy, J. (1988). Educating teachers about managing classrooms and students. *Teacher and Teacher Education, 4,* 1–18.

Brown, A. L. (1980). Metacognitive development and reading. In R. J. Spiro, B. C. Bruce, and W. F. Brewer (Eds.), *Theoretical issues in reading comprehension,* Hillsdale, N.J.: Erlbaum, pp. 453–482.

Brown, A. L., and Day, J. D. (1983). Macrorules for summarizing texts: The development of expertise. *Journal of Verbal Learning and Verbal Behavior, 22,* 1–14.

Brown, A. L., and Palincsar, A. S. (1982). Including strategic learning from texts by means of informed, self-control training. *Topics in Learning and Learning Disabilities, 2*(1), 1–17.

Brown, A. L., Palincsar, A. S., and Armbruster, B. B. (1984). Instructing comprehension-fostering activities in interactive learning situations. In H. Mandl, N. L. Stein, and T. Trabasso (Eds.), *Learning and comprehension of text.* Hillsdale, N.J.: Erlbaum, pp. 255–286.

Brown, R. (1973). *A first language: The early stages.* Cambridge, Mass.: Harvard University Press.

Bruck, M., and Treiman, R. (1992). Learning to pronounce words: The limitations of analogies. *Reading Research Quarterly, 27,* 375–388.

Brunner, C. (1996). Judging student multimedia. *Electronic Learning, 15*(6), 14–15.

Bryan, J. H., Bryan, T. H., and Sonnefeld, L. J. (1982). Being known by the company we keep! The contagion of first impressions. *Learning Disability Quarterly, 5*(3), 228–293.

Bryan, J. H., and Perlmutter, B. (1979). Immediate impressions of LD children by female adults. *Learning Disability Quarterly, 2,* 80–88.

Bryan, J. H., and Sherman, R. (1980). Immediate impressions of nonverbal ingratiation attempts by learning disabled boys. *Learning Disabilities Quarterly, 3,* 19–29.

Bryan, T., Pearl, R., and Fallon, P. (1989). Conformity to peer pressure by students with learning disabilities: A replication. *Journal of Learning Disabilities, 22*(7), 458–459.

Bryan, T. H. (1986). Self-concept and attributions of the learning disabled. *Learning Disabilities Focus, 1*(2), 82–89.

Bryan, T. H., and Pflaum, S. (1978). Social interactions of learning disability children: A linguistic, social, and cognitive analysis. *Learning Disability Quarterly, 1,* 70–78.

Bryan, T. S. (1974). An observational analysis of classroom behaviors of children with learning disabilities. *Journal of Learning Disabilities, 7*(1), 35–43.

Bryant, N. D., Drabin, I. R., and Gettinger, M. (1981). Effects of varying unit size on spelling achievement in learning disabled children. *Journal of Learning Disabilities, 14*(4), 200–203.

Buchanan, C. O. (1968). *Sullivan Associates programmed reading.* New York: Sullivan Press, Webster Division—McGraw-Hill.

Bulgren J., and Lenz, K. (1996). Strategic instruction in the content areas. In D. D. Deshler, E. S. Ellis, and B. K. Lenz (Authors), *Teaching adolescents with learning disabilities: Strategies and methods* (2nd ed., pp. 409–473). Denver: Love.

Bulgren, J. with Lenz, B. K., Deshler, D. D., and Schumaker, J. B. (1994). *The content enhancement series: The concept comparison routine.* Lawrence, Kans.: Edge Enterprises.

Bulgren, J., Schumaker, J. B., and Deshler, D. D. (1988). Effectiveness of a concept teaching routine in enhancing the performance of LD students in secondary-level mainstream classes. *Learning Disability Quarterly, 11,* 3–17.

Bullock, J. (1991). *Touch math.* Colorado Springs, Colo.: Innovative Learning Concepts.

Bullock, J. (1996). *Touchmath resource center set.* Colorado Springs, Colo.: Innovative Learning Concepts.

Bullock, J., Pierce, S., Strand, L., and Branine, K. (1981). *Touch math teachers manual.* Colorado Springs, Colo.

Bunce, B. H. (1993). Language of the classroom. In A. Gerber (Ed.), *Language related learning disabilities: Their nature and treatment.* Baltimore: Brookes Publishing, pp. 135–159.

Button, E. (1993). *Eating disorders: Personal construct therapy and change.* New York: Wiley & Sons.

Byrnes, J. P. (1996). *Cognitive development and learning in instructional contexts.* Boston: Allyn and Bacon.

Cambourne, B. (1988). *The whole story: Natural learning and the acquisition of literacy in the classroom.* Auckland, N.Z.: Ashton Scholastic.

Cambourne, B. (1995). Toward an educationally relevant theory of literacy learning: Twenty years of inquiry. *The Reading Teacher, 49,* 182–190.

Cambourne, B., and Turnbull, J.(1987). *Coping with chaos.* Portsmouth, N.H.: Heinemann.

Camp, B. W., and Bash, M. A. S. (1981). *The think aloud series: Increasing social and cognitive skills.* Champaign, Ill.: Research Press.

Camp, B. W., Blom, G. E., Herbert, F., and Van Doorninck, W. J. (1977). "Think around": A program for developing self-control in young aggressive boys. *Journal of Abnormal Child Psychology, 5,* 157–169.

Carbo, M. (1978). Teaching reading with talking books. *The Reading Teacher, 32,* 267–273.

Carnine, D. (1989). Teaching complex content to learning disabled students: The role of technology. *Exceptional Children, 55,* 524–533.

Carnine, D. (1991). Curricular interventions for teaching higher order thinking to all students: Introduction to the special series. *Journal of Learning Disabilities, 24,* 261–269.

Carnine, D., Silbert, J., and Kameenui, E. J. (1997). *Direct instruction reading* (3rd ed.). Columbus, Ohio: Merrill.

Carpenter, D., and Miller, L. J. (1982). Spelling ability of reading disabled LD students and able readers. *Learning Disability Quarterly, 5*(1), 65–70.

Carpenter, R. L. (1985). Mathematics instruction in resource rooms: Instruction time and teacher competence. *Learning Disability Quarterly, 8,* 95–100.

Carr, E. G., and Durand, V. M. (1985). Reducing behavior problems through functional communication training. *Journal of Applied Behavior Analysis, 18,* 111–126.

Carr, E., and Ogle, D. (1987). K-W-L plus: A strategy for comprehension and summarization. *Journal of Reading, 30,* 626–631.

Carr, S. C., and Thompson, B. (1996). The effects of prior knowledge and schema activation strategies on the inferential reading comprehension of children with and without learning disabilities. *Learning Disability Quarterly, 19,* 48–61.

Carrier, C. A. (1983). Notetaking research: Implications for the classroom. *Journal of Instructional Development, 6*(3), 19–25.

Carrier, C. A., and Newell, K. (1983). *What dental hygiene under-graduates think about notetaking in lecture classes: Report of a survey.* Unpublished manuscript, University of Minnesota, Minneapolis.

Carroll, J. (1964) *Language and thought.* Englewood Cliffs, N.J.: Prentice-Hall.

Carrow, E. (1973). *Test of auditory comprehension of language.* Austin, Tex.: Urban Research Group.

Casby, M. (1992). An intervention approach for naming problems in children. *American Journal of Speech-Language Pathology, 1*(3), 35–42.

Cawley, J., Fitzmaurice, A. M., Sedlak, R., and Althaus, V. (1976) *Project math.* Tulsa, Okla.: Educational Progress.

Cawley, J. F. (1984). An integrative approach to needs of learning disabled children: Expanded use of mathematics. In J. F. Cawley (Ed.), *Developmental teaching of mathematics for the learning disabled.* Rockville, Md.: Aspen.

Cawley, J. F. and Miller, J. H. (1986). Selected views on metacognition, arithmetic problem solving, and learning disabilities. *Learning Disabilities Focus, 2*(1), 36–48.

Cawley, J. F., and Miller, J. H. (1989). Cross-sectional comparisons of the mathematical performance of children with learning disabilities: Are we on the right track toward comprehensive programming? *Journal of Learning Disabilities, 22,* 250–254, 259.

Ceci, S. (1985). A developmental study of learning disabilities and memory. *Journal of Experimental Child Psychology, 39,* 202–221.

Center, Y., Wheldall, D., Freeman, L., Outhred, L., and Mc-Naught, M. (1994). An evaluation of Reading Recovery. *Reading Research Quarterly (30),* 240–263.

Chalfant, J. C. (1987). Providing services to all students with learning problems: Implications for policy and programs. In S. Vaughn and C. Bos (Eds.), *Research in learning disabilities: Issues and future trends.* Boston: College-Hill, Little Brown, pp. 239–251.

Chalfant, J. C. (1989). Learning disabilities: Policy issues and promising approaches. *American Psychologist, 44,* 392–398.

Chalfant, J. C., and Pysh, M. V. (November 1981). Teacher assistance teams: A model for within-building problem solving. *Counterpoint.*

Chalfant, J. C., and Pysh, J. (1983). Teacher assistance teams. In C. Collin (Ed.), *Keys to success.* Monographs of the Michigan ACLD Conference. Garden City, Mich.: Quality Printers.

Chalfant, J. C., and Pysh, M. V. (1989). Teacher assistance teams: Five descriptive studies on 96 teams. *Remedial and Special Education, 10*(6), 49–58.

Chalfant, J. C., and Pysh, M. V. (1993). Teacher assistance teams: Implications for the gifted. In C. J. Maker (Ed.), *Critical issues in gifted education: Vol III—Gifted students in the regular classroom.* Austin, Tex.: Pro-Ed, pp. 32–48.

Chalfant, J. C., Pysh, M. V., and Moultrie, R. (1979). Teacher assistance teams: A model for within-building problem solving. *Learning Disability Quarterly, 2,* 85–96.

Chall, J. S. (1983). *Learning to read: The great debate* (2nd ed.), New York: McGraw-Hill.

Chall, J. S., and Popp, H. M. (1996). *Teaching and assessing phonics: Why, what, when, how.* Cambridge, Mass.: Educators Publishing Service.

Chamot, A., and O'Malley, J. M. (1994). The CALLA Handbook: How to implement the cognitive academic language learning approach. In K. Spangenberg-Urbschat and R. Pritchard (Eds.), *Kids come in all languages: Reading instruction for ESL students* (pp. 82–103). Newark, Del.: International Reading Association.

Chamot, A., and O'Malley, J. M. (1994). *The CALLA handbook: Implementing the cognitive academic language learning approach.* Reading, Mass.: Addison-Wesley.

Chapman, J. W., and Boersman, F. J. (1980). *Affective correlates of learning disabilities.* Lisse: Swets & Zeitlinger.

Chase, C. H., and Tallal, P. (1991). Cognitive models of developmental reading disorders. In J. E. Obrzut and G. W. Hynd (Eds.), *Neuropsychological foundations of learning disabilities.* San Diego: Academic Press, pp. 199–240.

Cheek, E. H., and Lindsey, J. D. (1986). Principal's roles and teacher conflict: A recapitulation. *Journal of Learning Disabilities, 19*(5), 280–284.

Cherkes-Julkowski, M. (1985). Metacognitive considerations in mathematics for the learning disabled. In J. Cawley (Ed.), *Cognitive strategies and mathematics for the learning disabled.* Rockville, Md.: Aspen.

Chomsky, C. (1969). *The acquisition of syntax in children from 5 to 10.* Cambridge, Mass.: MIT Press.

Chomsky, C. (1976). After decoding: What? *Language Arts, 53,* 288–296.

Christian, B. T. (1983). A practical reinforcement hierarchy for classroom behavior modification. *Psychology in the Schools, 20,* 83–84.

Cimbolic, P., and Jobes, D. A. (1990). *Youth Suicide: Issues, Assessment, and Intervention.* Springfield, Ill.: Charles C. Thomas.

Clark, D. B., and Uhry, J. K. (1995). *Dyslexia: Theory and practice of remedial instruction.* Baltimore, Md.: York Press.

Clark, F. L., Deshler, D. D., Schumaker, J. B., Alley, G. R., and Warner, M. M. (1984). Visual imagery and self-questioning: Strategies to improve comprehension of written materials. *Journal of Learning Disabilities, 17*(3), 145–149.

Clark, J. O. (1990). *Harrup's dictionary of English idioms.* London: Harrup.

Clay, M. M. (1982). *Observing young readers.* Portsmouth, N.H.: Heinemann.

Clay, M. M. (1985). *The early detection of reading difficulties* (3rd ed.). Portsmouth, N.H.: Heinemann.

Clay, M. M. (1991a). *Becoming Literate: The construction of inner control.* Portsmouth, N.H.: Heinemann.

Clay, M. M. (1991b). Introducing a new storybook to young readers. *The Reading Teacher, 45,* 264–273.

Clay, M. M. (1993a). *Observation survey of early literacy achievement.* Portsmouth, N.H.: Heinemann.

Clay, M. M. (1993b). *Reading Recovery: A guidebook for teachers in training.* Portsmouth, N.H.: Heinemann.

Cline, B. V., and Billingsley, B. S. (1991). Teachers' and supervisors' perceptions of secondary learning disabilities programs:

A multi-state survey. *Learning Disabilities Research and Practice, 6,* 158–165.

Coffland, J. A., and Baldwin, R. S. (1985). *Wordmath.* St. Louis: Milliken.

Cohen, M. W. (1986). Intrinsic motivation in the special education classroom. *Journal of Learning Disabilities, 19*(5), 258–261.

Cohen, V. B. (January 1983). Criteria for the evaluation of microcomputer courseware. *Educational Technology,* 9–14.

Coie, J. D., Dodge, K. A., and Coppotelli, H. (1982). Dimensions and types of social status: A cross-age perspective. *Developmental Psychology, 18,* 557–570.

Cole, J. (1989). *Anna Banana: 101 jump rope rhymes.* New York: Morrow Junior Books.

Cole, J., and Calmenson, S. (1990). *Miss Mary Mack and other children's street rhymes.* New York: Morrow Junior Books.

Collis, B., and Heeren, E. (1993). Tele-collaboration and groupware. *The Computing Teacher, 8,* 36–39.

Cooley, E. J., and Ayres, R. R. (1988). Self-concept and success-failure attributions of nonhandicapped students and students with learning disabilities. *Journal of Learning Disabilities, 21*(3), 174–178.

Connolly, A. J. (1985). *Key math teach and practice.* Circle Pines, Minn.: American Guidance Service.

Cornwall, A. (1992). The relationship of phonological awareness, rapid naming, and verbal memory to severe reading and spelling disability. *Journal of Learning Disabilities, 25,* 532–538.

Cosden, M. A., Gerber, M. M., Semmel, D. S., Goldman, S. R., and Semmel, M. I., (1987). Microcomputer use within micro-educational environments. *Exceptional Children, 53,* 399–409.

Coterell, G. (1972). A case of severe learning disability. *Remedial Education, 7,* 5–9.

Council for Children with Behavior Disorders, 1990.

Cousin, P. T., Prentice, L., Aragon, E. Leonard, C., Rose, L. S., and Weekley, T. (1991). Redefining our roles as special educators: Understandings gained from whole language. In S. Stires (Ed.), *With Promise: Redefining reading and writing for "special students."* Portsmouth, N.H.: Heinemann, pp. 165–171.

Cronbach, L., and Snow, R. (1977). *Aptitudes and instructional methods.* New York: Irvington Press.

Cuevas, G., and Driscoll, M. (Eds.). (1993). Reaching all students with mathematics. Reston, Va.: National Council of Teachers of Mathematics.

Cullinan, B. E. (Ed.) (1992). *Invitation to read: More children's literature in the reading program.* Newark, Del.: International Reading Association.

Culp, A. M., Clyman, M. M., and Culp, R. E. (1995). Adolescent depressed mood, reports of suicide attempts, and asking for help. *Adolescence, 30,* 827–837.

Cummings, R. W., and Maddux, C. D. (1985). *Parenting the learning disabled: A realistic approach.* Springfield, Ill.: Charles C. Thomas.

Cummins, J. (1981). *Bilingualism and minority language children.* Ontario: Ontario Institute for Students in Education.

Cummins, J. (1984). *Bilingualism and special education: Issues in assessment and pedagogy.* San Diego, Calif.: College Hill.

Cummins, J. (1989). A theoretical framework for bilingual special education. *Exceptional Children, 56,* 111–119.

Cummins, J. (1991). Interdependence of first- and second-language proficiency in bilingual children. In E. Bialystok (Ed.), *Language processing in bilingual children.* Cambridge, England: Cambridge University Press.

Cummins, J. (1994). The acquisition of English as a second language. In K. Spangenberg-Urbschat and R. Pritchard (Eds.), *Kids come in all languages: Reading instruction for ESL students* (pp.36–62). Newark, Del.: International Reading Association.

Cunningham, P. (1979). Beginning reading without readiness: Structured language experience. *Reading Horizons, 11,* 222–227.

Cunningham, P. M. (1991). *Phonics they use: Words for reading and writing.* New York: Harper Collins.

Cunningham, P. M. (1995). *Phonics they use: Words for reading and writing* (2nd ed.). New York: Harper Collins.

Cunningham, P. M., and Allington, R. L. (1994). *Classrooms that work: They can ALL read and write.* New York: Harper Collins.

Cunningham, P. M., and Cunningham, J. W. (1992). Making words: Enhancing the invented spelling-decoding connection. *The Reading Teacher, 46,* 106–116.

Cunningham, P. M., and Hall, D. P. (1994a). *Making words.* Parsippany, N.J.: Good Apple.

Cunningham, P. M., and Hall, D. P. (1994b). *Making big words.* Parsippany, N.J.: Good Apple.

Daiute, C., and Morse, F. (1994). Access to knowledge and expression: Multimedia writing tools for students with diverse needs and strengths. *Journal of Special Education Technology, 12,* 221–256.

Dale, E. (1966). The art of reading. *The Newsletter, 32,* 1–4.

Dale, E., and Chall, J. (February 1948). A formula for predicting readability. *Educational Research Bulletin, 27,* 37–54.

D'Ambrosio, B., Johnson, H., and Hobbs, L. (1995). Strategies for increasing achievement in mathematics. In R. W. Cole (Ed.), *Educating everybody's children: Diverse teaching strategies for diverse learners* (pp. 121–138). Reston, Va.: Association for Supervision and Curriculum Development.

Darch, C., and Carnine, D. (1986). Teaching content area to learning disabled students. *Exceptional Children, 53,* 240–246.

Davison, A. (1984). Readability formulas and comprehension. In G. G. Duffy, L. R. Roehler, and J. Mason, (Eds.), *Comprehension instruction: Perspective and suggestions.* New York: Longman, pp. 128–143.

DeFord, D. E., Lyons, C. A., and Pinnell, G. S. (Eds.). (1991). *Bridges to literacy: Learning from Reading Recovery.* Portsmouth, N.H.: Heinemann.

Delquadri, J., Greenwood, C. R., Whorton, D., Carta, J. J., and Hall, R. V. (1986). Classwide peer tutoring. *Exceptional Children, 52*(6), 535–542.

DeMaster, V. K., Crossland, C. L., and Hasselbring, T. S. (1986). Consistency of learning disabled students' spelling performance. *Learning Disability Quarterly, 9,* 89–96.

Dembinski, R. J., and Mauser, A. J. (1977). What parents of the learning disabled really want from professionals. *Journal of Learning Disabilities, 10*(9), 49–55.

Deno, S. L. (1985). Curriculum-based measurement: The emerging alternative. *Exceptional Children, 52,* 219–232.

Deshler, D. D., and Schumaker, J. B. (1986). Learning strategies: An instructional alternative for low-achieving adolescents. *Exceptional Children, 52,* 583–590.

Deshler, D. D., Ellis, E. S., and Lenz, B. K. (1996). *Teaching adolescents with learning disabilities: Strategies and methods* (2nd ed.). Denver: Love.

Dettmer, P., Thurston, L. P., and Dyck, N. (1993). *Consultation, collaboration, and teamwork for students with special needs.* Boston: Allyn and Bacon.

de Villiers, J., and de Villiers, P. (1978). *Language acquisition.* Cambridge, Mass.: Harvard University Press.

Devine, T. G. (1978). Listening: What do we know about fifty years of research and theorizing? *Journal of Reading, 21,* 296–304.

Devine, T. G. (1987). *Teaching study skills: A guide for teachers* (2nd ed.). Boston: Allyn and Bacon.

Diaz, S., Moll., L. C., and Mehan, H. (1986). Sociocultural resources in instruction: A context-specific approach. In *Beyond language: Social and cultural factors in schooling language minority students.* Sacramento, Calif.: Bilingual Education Office, California State Department of Education, pp. 187–229.

Díaz-Rico, L. and Weed, K. Z. (1995). *The crosscultural, language, and academic development handbook: A complete K–12 reference Guide.* Boston: Allyn and Bacon.

DiVesta, F. J., and Smith, D. A. (1979). The pausing principle: Increasing the efficiency of memory for ongoing events. *Contemporary Educational Psychology, 4,* 288–296.

Dixon, C. N., and Nessel, D. D. (1992). *Meaning making: Directed reading and thinking activities for second-language students.* Englewood Cliffs, N.J.: Prentice-Hall.

Dixon, R. (1976). *Morphographic spelling.* Chicago: Science Research Associates.

Dixon, R. (1991). The application of sameness analysis to spelling. *Journal of Learning Disabilities, 24,* 285–291, 310.

Dole, J. A., Brown, K. J., and Trathen, W. (1996). The effects of strategy instruction on the comprehension performance of at-risk students. *Reading Research Quarterly, 31,* 62–88.

Dole, J. A., Duffy, G. G., Roehler, L. R., and Pearson, P. D. (1991). Moving from the old to the new: Research on reading comprehension instruction. *Review of Education Research, 61,* 239–264.

Donahue, M., Pearl, R., and Bryan, T. (1980). Learning disabled children's conversational competence: Responses in inadequate messages. *Applied Psycholinguistics, 1,* 387–403.

Dorval, B., McKinney, J. D., and Feagans, L. (1982). Teacher interaction with learning disabled children and average achievers. *Journal of Pediatric Psychology, 7*(3), 317–330.

Doyle, W. (1979). Making managerial decisions in classrooms. In D. L. Duke (Ed.), *Classroom management.* Seventy-eighth yearbook of the National Society for the Study of Education, Part 2. Chicago: University of Chicago Press.

Doyle, W. (1986). Classroom organization and management. In M. C. Wittrock (Ed.), *Handbook of research on teaching* (3rd ed). New York: Macmillan, pp. 392–431.

Dreher, M. J., and Singer, H. (1980). Story grammar instruction is unnecessary for intermediate grade students. *The Reading Teacher, 34,* 261–268.

Dudley-Marling, C. C., Snider, V., and Tarver, S. G. (1982). Locus of control and learning disabilities: A review and discussion. *Perceptual and Motor Skills, 54*(2), 503–514.

Duffy, G. G., and McIntyre, L. D. (1982). A naturalistic study of instructional assistance in primary-grade reading. *Elementary School Journal, 83*(1), 15–23.

Duke, D. L., and Meckel, A. M. (1980). *Managing student behavior problems.* New York: Teachers College Press, Columbia University.

Dunn, L. M., Smith, J. O., Dunn, L. M., Horton, K. B., and Smith, D. D. (1981). *Peabody language development kits* (Rev. ed.). Circle Pines, Minn.: American Guidance Service.

Duran, R. P. (1989). Assessment and instruction of at-risk Hispanic students. *Exceptional Children, 56,* 154–159.

Durkin, D. D. (1978–79). What classroom observations reveal about reading comprehension instruction. *Reading Research Quarterly, 14*(4), 481–533.

Dyrli, O., and Kinnaman, D. (1996). Teaching effectively with telecommunications. *Technology and Learning, 16*(5), 57–62.

D'Zurilla, T., and Goldfired, M. (1971). Problem solving and behavior modification. *Journal of Applied Psychology, 78,* 107–129.

Echevarria, J., and McDonough, R. (1996). An alternative reading approach: Instructional conversations in a bilingual special education setting. *Learning Disabilities Research and Practice, 10,* 108–119.

Eckert, P. (1990). Cooperative competition in adolescent "girl talk." *Discourse Processes, 13,* 91–122.

Edelsky, C., Altwerger, B., and Flores, B. (1991). *Whole language: What's the difference.* Portsmouth, N.H.: Heinemann.

Edwards, B., Blackhurst, A., and Koorland, M. (1995). Computer-assisted constant time delay prompting to teach abbreviation spelling to adolescents with mild learning disabilities. *Journal of Special Education Technology, 12,* 301–311.

Eggen, P. D., and Kauchak, D. (1992). *Educational psychology: Classroom connections.* New York: Macmillan.

Ehri, L. C. (1989). The development of spelling knowledge and its role in reading acquisition and reading disability. *Journal of Learning Disabilities, 22*(6), 356–365.

Ehri, L. C., and Robbins, C. (1992). Beginners need some decoding skill to read words by analogy. *Reading Research Quarterly, 27,* 13–26.

Elam, S. M., and Gallup. A. M. (1989). The 21st annual Gallup poll of the public's attitudes toward the public schools. *Phi Delta Kappan, 71,* 41–54.

Elias, M. J., and Clabby, J. F. (1989). *Social decision-making skills: A curriculum guide for the elementary grades.* Rockville, Md.: Aspen.

Eldredge, J. L. (1995). *Teaching decoding in holistic classrooms.* Boston: Allyn and Bacon.

Ellis, E. (1991). *SLANT: A starter strategy for participation.* Lawrence, Kans.: Edge Enterprises.

Ellis, E. S. (1996). Reading strategy instruction. In D. D. Deshler, E. S. Ellis, and B. K. Lenz (Authors.), *Teaching adolescents with learning disabilities: Strategies and methods* (2nd ed., pp. 61–126). Denver: Love.

Ellis, E. S., Deshler, D. D., Schumaker, J. B., Lenz, B. K., and Clark, R. L. (1991). An instructional model for teaching learning strategies. *Focus on Exceptional Children, 23*(1), 1–22.

Elster, C. (1994). Patterns within preschoolers' emergent readings. *Reading Research Quarterly, 29,* 402–418.

Emery, D. W. (1996). Helping readers comprehend stories from the characters' perspectives. *The Reading Teacher, 49,* 534–541.

Emmer, E., Evertson, C., and Anderson, L. (1980). Effective classroom management at the beginning of the school year. *Elementary School Journal, 80*(5), 219–231.

Emmer, E. T., Evertson, C. M., Sanford, J. P., Clements, B. S., and Worsham, M. E. (1989). *Classroom management for secondary teachers* (2nd ed.). Englewood Cliffs, N.J.: Prentice-Hall.

Engelhardt, Ashlock, and Wiebe (1984). *Helping children understand and use numerals.* Boston: Allyn and Bacon, pp. 89–149.

Engelmann, S., Becker, W. C., Hanner, S., and Johnson, G. (1978). *Corrective reading: Series guide.* Chicago: Science Research Associates.

Engelmann, S., Becker, W. C., Hanner, S., and Johnson, G. (1988; 1989). *Corrective reading.* Chicago: Science Research Associates.

Engelmann, S., and Bruner, E. C. (1988). *Reading mastery.* Chicago: Science Research Associates.

Engelmann, S., and Carnine, D. (1972). *DISTAR arithmetic level I.* Chicago: Science Research Associates.

Engelmann, S., and Carnine, D. (1975). *DISTAR arithmetic level I.* Chicago: Science Research Associates.

Engelmann, S., and Carnine, D. (1976). *DISTAR arithmetic level II.* Chicago: Science Research Associates.

Engelmann, S., and Carnine, D. (1982). *Corrective mathematics program.* Chicago: Science Research Associates.

Engelmann, S., Carnine, D. and Steely, D. G. (1991) Making connections in mathematics. *Journal of Learning Disabilities, 24*(5), 292–303.

Engelmann, S., and Osborn, J. (1987). *DISTAR language I* (2nd ed.). Chicago: Science Research Associates.

Englert, C. S. (1992). Writing instruction from a sociocultural perspective: The holistic, dialogic, and social enterprise of writing. *Journal of Learning Disabilities, 25,* 153–172.

Englert, C. S., Garmon, A., Mariage, T., Rozendal, M., Tarrant, K., and Urba, J. (1995). The early literacy project: Connecting across the literacy curriculum. *Learning Disability Quarterly, 18,* 253–277.

Englert, C. S., and Mariage, T. V. (1991). Making students partners in the comprehension process: Organizing the reading "POSSE." *Learning Disability Quarterly, 14,* 123–138.

Englert, C. S., and Raphael, T. E. (1988). Constructive well-formed prose: Process, structure, and metacognitive knowledge. *Exceptional Children, 54,* 513–520.

Englert, C. S., Raphael, T. E., Anderson, L. M., Anthony, H. M., and Stevens, D. D. (1991). Making strategies and self-talk visible: Writing instruction in regular and special education classrooms. *American Educational Research Journal, 23,* 337–372.

Englert, C. S., Raphael, T. E., Fear, K. L., and Anderson, L. M. (1988). Students' metacognitive knowledge about how to write informational texts. *Learning Disability Quarterly, 11,* 18–46.

Englert, C. S., Rozendal, M. S., and Mariage, M. (1994). Fostering the search for understanding: A teacher's strategies for leading cognitive development in "zones of proximal development." *Learning Disability Quarterly, 17,* 187–204.

Erickson, R., and Schultz, J. (1981). When is a context? Some issues and methods in the analysis of social competence. In J. L. Green and C. Wallat (Eds.), *Ethnography and language in educational settings.* Norwood, N.J.: Ablex.

Estes, T. J., and Vaughn, J. L. (1978). *Reading and learning in the content classroom: Diagnostic and instructional strategies.* Boston: Allyn and Bacon.

Exceptional Parent. (1984, March). *Parent advocacy.* Exceptional Parent, 14(2), 41–45.

Fernald, G. M. (1943). *Remedial techniques in basic school subjects.* New York: McGraw-Hill.

Fernald, G. M. (1988). *Remedial techniques in basic school subjects.* (L. Idol, Ed.). Austin, Tex.: Pro-Ed (original edition 1943).

Ferretti, R., and Okolo, C. (1996). Authenticity in learning: Multimedia design projects in the social studies for students with disabilities. *Journal of Learning Disabilities, 29,* 450–460.

Fettler, F., and Tokar, E. (1982). Getting a handle on teacher stress. *Educational Leadership, 39,* 456–457.

Fielding, L., and Roller, C. (1992). Making difficult books accessible and easy books acceptable. *The Reading Teacher, 45,* 678–682.

Finn, J. D. (1989). Withdrawing from school. *Review of Educational Research, 59,* 117–142.

Fisher, J. L., and Harris, M. B. (1973). Effect of notetaking and review on recall. *Journal of Educational Psychology, 65*(3), 321–325.

Fitzsimmons, R. J., and Loomer, B. M. (1978). *Spelling: Learning and instruction.* (Report No. CS 205 117). Des Moines, Iowa: Iowa State Department of Public Instruction. (ERIC Document Reproduction Service No. ED 176 285).

Flavell, J. H. (1976). Metacognitive aspects of problem solving. In L. B. Resnick (Ed.), *The nature of intelligence.* Hillsdale, N.J.: Erlbaum.

Fleischner, J. E., Nuzum, M. G., and Marzola, E. S. (1987). Devising an instructional program to teach arithmetic problem-solving skills to students with learning disabilities. *Journal of Learning Disabilities, 20*(4), 214–217.

Fletcher, J. M. (1989). Nonverbal learning disabilities and suicide: Classification leads to prevention. *Journal of Learning Disabilities, 22,* 176–179.

Fletcher, R. J., and Rosenberger, N. (1987). Beware of tapping pencils. *Arithmetic Teacher, 34*(5), 6–10. M

Foorman, B. R., Francis, D. J., and Fletcher, J. M. (in press). Early intervention for children with reading disabilities and at risk for developmental reading disabilities. *Scientific studies of reading.*

Forness, S. R. (1973). The reinforcement hierarchy. *Psychology in the Schools, 19,* 168–177.

Foster, S. L., and Ritchey, W. C. (1979). Issues in the assessment of social competence in children. *Journal of Applied Behavior Analysis, 12,* 625–631.

Fowler, G. L., and Davis, M. (1985). The story frame approach: A tool for improving reading comprehension of EMR children. *Teaching Exceptional Children, 17*(4), 296–298.

Fowler, S. A. (1986). Peer-monitoring and self-monitoring: Alternatives to traditional teacher management. *Exceptional Children, 52*(6), 573–582.

Fox, C. (1989). Peer acceptance of learning disabled children in the regular classroom. *Exceptional Children, 56*(1), 50–57.

Frayer, D. A., Frederick, W. C., and Klausmeier, H. J. (1969). *A schema for testing the level of concept mastery* (Working Paper No. 16). Madison: University of Wisconsin, Wisconsin Research and Development Center for Cognitive Learning.

Freeman, E. B., and Person, D. G. (1992). *Using nonfiction trade books in the elementary classroom from ants to zeppelins.* Urbana, Ill.: National Council of Teachers of English.

Freire, P. (1985). Reading the world and reading the word: An interview with Paulo Freire. *Language Arts, 62*(1), 15–21.

Friend, M., and Cook, L. (1992). *Interactions: Collaboration skills for school professionals.* White Plains, N.Y.: Longman.

Fries, C. C. (1963). *Linguistics and reading.* New York: Holt, Rinehart and Winston.

Frith, G. H., and Armstong, W. W. (1986). Self-monitoring for behavior disordered students. *Teaching Exceptional Children, 18*(2), 144–148.

Frith, U. (1980). *Cognitive processes in spelling.* London: Academic Press.

Fromkin, V., and Rodman, R. (1993). *Introduction to language.* New York: Holt, Rinehart.

Fry, E. B. (1977). Fry's readability graph: Clarifications, validity, and extension to level 17. *Journal of Reading, 21,* 242–252.

Fry, E. B., Fountoukidis, D. L., and Polk, J. K. (1985). *The new reading teacher's book of lists.* Englewood Cliffs, N.J.: Prentice-Hall.

Fuchs, D., and Fuchs, L. S. (1994). Inclusive school movement and radicalization of special education reform. *Exceptional Children, 60,* 294–309.

Fuchs, D., Fuchs, L. S., and Bahr, M. W. (1990). Mainstream assistance teams: A scientific basis for the art of consultation. *Exceptional Children, 57,* 128–139.

Fuchs, L., Deno, S., and Mirkin, P. (1984). The effects of frequent, curriculum-based measurement and evaluation on pedagogy, student achievement, and student awareness of learning. *American Educational Research Journal, 21,* 449–460.

Fuchs, L. S., Bahr, C. M., and Rieth, H. J. (1989). Effects of goal structures and performance contingencies on the math performance of adolescents with learning disabilities. *Journal of Learning Disabilities, 22,* 554–560.

Fuchs, L. S., and Deno, S. L. (1991). Pa... tween instructionally relevant measure... *tional Children, 57,* 488–500.

Fuchs, L. S., Fuchs, D., and Hamlett, C. L. (1989). E... structional use of curriculum-based measurement to e... instruction programs. *Remedial and Special education 10*(..., 43–52.

Fuchs, L. S., Fuchs, D., Hamlett, C. L., and Allinder, R. M. (1991). The contribution of skills analysis to curriculum-based measurement in spelling. *Exceptional Children, 57,* 443–452.

Fujiki, M., Brinton, B., and Todd, C. M. (1996). Special skills of children with specific language impairments. *Language, Speech, and Hearing Services in Schools, 27,* 195–201.

Fulk, B. M., and Stormont-Spurgin, M. (1995). Spelling interventions for students with disabilities: A review. *Journal of Special Education, 28,* 488–513.

Gajria, M., and Salend, S. J. (1995). Homework practices of students with and without learning disabilities: A comparison. *Journal of Learning Disabilities, 28,* 291–296.

Gajria, M., and Salvia, J. (1992). The effects of summarization instruction on text comprehension of students with learning disabilities. *Exceptional Children, 58,* 508–516.

Galambos, S., and Goldin-Meadow, S. (1990). The effects of learning two languages on metalinguistic development. *Cognition, 34,* 1–56.

Garcia, E. E. (1991). Effective instruction for language minority students: The teacher. *Journal of Education, 173,* 130–141.

García, G. E., Pearson, P. D., and Jiménez, R. T. (1994). *The at-risk situation: A synthesis of reding research.* Champaign, Ill.: University of Illinois, Center for the Study of Reading.

Garnett, K. (1992). Developing fluency with basic number facts: Intervention for students with learning disabilities. *Learning Disabilities Research & Practice, 7,* 210–216.

Garnett, K., and Fleischner, J. E. (1983). Automatization and basic fact performance of normal and learning disabled children. *Learning Disability Quarterly, 6,* 223–230.

Garret, M. K., and Crump, W. D. (1980). Peer acceptance, teacher preference and self-appraisal of social status among learning disabled students. *Learning Disability Quarterly, 3,* 42–48.

Gast, D., Ault, M., Wolery, M., Doyle, P., and Belanger, S. (1988). Comparison of constant time delay and the system of least prompts in teaching sight word reading to students with moderate retardation. *Education and Training in Mental Retardation, 23,* 117–128.

Gerber, A. (1993). *Language related learning disabilities: Their nature and treatment.* Baltimore: Brookes Publishing.

Gerber, M. M., and Hall, R. J. (1989). Cognitive-behavioral training in spelling for learning handicapped students. *Learning Disabilities Quarterly, 12,* 159–171.

Gerber, M., and Kauffman, J. (1981). Peer tutoring in academic settings. In P. Strain (Ed.), *Utilization of classroom peers as behavior change agents.* New York: Plenum Press, pp. 155–187.

German, D. J. (1987). Spontaneous language profiles of children with word-finding problems. *Language, Speech, and Hearing Services in Schools, 18,* 217–230.

.rman, D. J. (1992). Word-finding intervention for children and adolescents. *Topics in Language Disorders, 13*(1), 33–50.

Gersten, R., Becker, W. C., Heiry, T. J., and White, W. A. T. (1984). Entry IQ and yearly academic growth of children in Direct Instruction programs: A longitudinal study of low SES children. *Education Evaluation and Policy Analysis, 6,* 109–121.

Gersten, R., Carnine, D., and Woodward, J. (1987). Direct Instruction research: The third decade. *Remedial and Special Education, 8*(6), 48–56.

Gettinger, M. (1984). Applying learning principles to remedial spelling instruction. *Academic Therapy, 20*(1), 41–48.

Gettinger, M., Bryant, M. D., and Fayne, H. R. (1982). Designing spelling instruction for learning disabled children: An emphasis on unit size, distributed practice, and training for transfer. *Journal of Special Education, 16*(4), 439–448.

Gibbons, P. (1993). *Learning to learn in a second language.* NSW, Australia: Heinemann.

Gibbs, R. W. (1987). Linguistic factors in children's understanding of idioms. *Journal of Speech and Hearing Research, 54,* 613–620.

Gibson, E. J. (1969). *Principles of perceptual learning and development.* New York: Appleton-Century-Crofts.

Giddan, J. J., Bade, K. M., Rickenberg, C., and Ryley, A. T. (1995). Teaching the language of feelings to students with severe emotional and behavioral handicaps. *Language, Speech, and Hearing Services in Schools, 26,* 3–10.

Gillingham, A., and Stillman, B. W. (1973). *Remedial training for children with specific disability in reading, spelling, and penmanship.* Cambridge, Mass.: Educators Publishing Service.

Glass, G., and Glass, E. (1976). *The Glass-analysis for decoding only.* Garden City, N.Y.: Easier to Learn.

Glatthorn, A. A. (1990). Cooperative professional development: Facilitating the growth of the special education teacher and the classroom teacher. *Remedial and Special Education, 11*(3), 29–35.

Gold, V. (1976). *The effect of an experimental program involving acquisition of phoneme-grapheme relationships incorporating criterion referenced tests with evaluative feedback upon spelling performance of third grade pupils.* Unpublished doctoral dissertation, University of Southern California, Los Angeles.

Goldenberg, C. (1992). Instructional conversations: Promoting comprehension through discussion. *The Reading Teacher, 46,* 316–326.

Goldenberg, C., and Gallimore, R. (1991). Changing teaching takes more than a one-shot workshop. *Educational Leadership, 49*(3), 69–72.

Goldstein, A. P., and Glick, B. (1987). *Aggression replacement training: A comprehensive intervention for aggressive youth.* Champaign, Ill.: Research Press.

Goldstein, A. P., Sprafkin, R. P., Gershaw, N. J., and Klein, P. (1980). *Skillstreaming the adolescent.* Champaign, Ill.: Research Press.

Goodman, K. (1986). *What's whole in whole language?* Portsmouth, N.H.: Heinemann.

Goodman, K. (1993). *Phonics phacts.* Portsmouth, N.H.: Heinemann.

Goodman, K. S. (1967). Reading: A psycholinguistic guessing game. *Journal of the Reading Specialist, 6,* 126–135.

Goodman, K. S. (1984). Unity in reading. In A. C. Purves and O. Niles (Eds.), *Becoming readers in a complex society.* Eighty-third yearbook of the National Society for the Study of Education. Chicago: University of Chicago Press, pp. 79–114.

Goodman, K. S. (1992). I didn't found whole language. *The Reading Teacher, 46,* 188–199.

Goodman, K. S. (1996). *On reading.* Portsmouth, N.H.: Heinemann.

Goodman, K. S., Bird, L. B., and Goodman, Y. M. (1991). *The whole language catalog.* Santa Rosa, Calif.: American School Publishers, Macmillan/McGraw-Hill.

Goodman, K. S., and Goodman, Y. M. (1982). A whole language comprehension centered view of reading development. In L. Reed and S. Ward (Eds.), *Basic skills: Issues and choices* (Vol. 2). St. Louis, Mo.: CEMREL, pp. 125–134.

Goodman, Y. (1980). The roots of literacy. In M. P. Douglass (Ed.), *Claremont Reading Conference forty-fourth yearbook.* Claremont, Calif.: Claremont Reading Conference, pp. 1–32.

Goodman, Y. M. (1996). Revaluing readers while readers revalue themselves: Retrospective miscue analysis. *The Reading Teacher, 49,* 600–609.

Goodman, Y. M., Watson, D. J., and Burke, C. L. (1996). *Reading strategies: Focus on comprehension* (2nd ed.). Katonah, N.Y.: Richard C. Owens.

Goodman, Y. M. and Goodman, K. S. (1990). Vygotsky in the whole-language perspective. In L. C. Moll (Ed.), *Vygotsky and education: Instructional implications and applications of sociohistorical psychology.* Cambridge: Cambridge University Press, pp. 223–250.

Goodstein, H. A. (1981). Are the errors we see the true errors? Error analysis in verbal problem solving. *Topics in Learning and Learning Disabilities, 1*(3), 31–45.

Gordon, J., Vaughn, S., and Schumm, J. S. (1993). Spelling intervention: A review of literature and implications for instruction for students with learning disabilities. *Learning Disabilities Research and Practice, 8,* 175–181.

Gorman-Gard, K. A. (1992). *Figurative language: A comprehensive program.* Eau Claire, Wisc.: Thinking Publications.

Goss, J. L., and Harste, J. C. (1985). *It didn't frighten me!* Worthington, Ohio: Willow Press.

Grabe, M., and Grabe, C. (1996). *Integrating technology for meaningful learning.* Boston: Houghton Mifflin.

Graham, S. (1983). The effect of self-instructional procedures on LD students' handwriting performance. *Learning Disability Quarterly, 6*(2), 231–244.

Graham, S., and Freeman, S. (1986). Strategy training and teacher- vs. student-controlled study conditions: Effects on LD students' spelling performance. *Learning Disability Quarterly, 9,* 15–22.

Graham, S., and Harris, K. R. (1988). Instructional recommendations for teaching writing to exceptional students. *Exceptional Children, 54,* 506–512.

Graham, S., and Harris, K. R. (1989a). Components analysis of cognitive strategy instruction: Effects on learning disabled students' compositions and self-efficacy. *Journal of Educational Psychology, 81,* 353–361.

Graham, S., and Harris, K. R. (1989b). Improving learning disabled students' skills at composing essays: Self-instructional strategy training. *Exceptional Children, 56,* 201–214.

Graham, S., and Harris, K. R. (1993). Teaching writing strategies to students with learning disabilities: Issues and recommendations. In L. Meltzer (Ed.), *Strategy assessment and instruction for students with learning disabilities: From theory to practice* (pp. 271–292). Austin, Tex.: Pro-Ed.

Graham, S., and Harris, K. R. (1994). Implications of constructivism for teaching writing to students with special needs. *Journal of Special Education, 28,* 275–289.

Graham, S., Harris, K. R., and Loynachan, C. (1996). The directed spelling thinking activity: Application with high-frequency words. *Learning Disabilities Research & Practice, 1,* 34–40.

Graham, S., Harris, K. R., and MacArthur, C. A. (1995). Introduction to special issue: Research on writing and literacy. *Learning Disability Quarterly, 18,* 250–252.

Graham, S., MacArthur, C., and Schwartz, S. (1995). Effects of goal setting and procedural facilitation on the revising behavior and writing performance of students with writing and learning problems. *Journal of Educational Psychology, 87,* 230–240.

Graham, S., MacArthur, C., Schwartz, S., and Page-Voth, V. (1992). Improving the compositions of students with learning disabilities using a strategy involving product and process goal setting. *Exceptional Children, 58,* 322–334.

Graham, S., and Miller, L. (1979). Spelling research and practice: A unified approach. *Focus on Exceptional Children, 12*(2), 1–16.

Graham, S., and Miller, L. (1980). Handwriting research and practice: A unified approach. *Focus on Exceptional Children, 13*(2), 1–16.

Graham, S., and Voth, V. (1990). Spelling instruction: Making modifications for students with learning disabilities. *Academic Therapy, 25,* 447–457.

Grasser, A., Golding, J. M., and Long, D. L. (1991). Narrative representation and comprehension. In R. Barr, M. L. Kamil, P. Mosenthal, and P. D. Pearson (Eds.), *Handbook of reading research,* (Vol. II, pp. 171–205). New York: Longman.

Graves, A. W. (1986). Effects of direct instruction and metacomprehension training on finding main ideas. *Learning Disabilities Research, 1*(2), 90–100.

Graves, D. (1985). Personal correspondence.

Graves, D. H. (1983). *Writing: Teachers and children at work.* Portsmouth, N.H.: Heinemann Educational Books.

Graves, D. H. (1985). All children can write. *Learning Disability Focus, 1*(1), 36–43.

Graves, D. H., and Hansen, J. (1983). The author's chair. *Language Arts, 60,* 176–183.

Gresham, F. M. (1982). Misguided mainstreaming: The case for social skills training with handicapped children. *Exceptional Children, 48,* 422–433.

Grimm, J. A., Bijou, S. W., and Parsons, J. A. (1973). A problem solving model for teaching remedial arithmetic to handicapped children. *Journal of Abnormal Child Psychology, 1,* 26–39.

Grossen, B., and Carnine, D. (1992). Phonics instruction: Comparing research and practice. *Teaching Exceptional Children, 25*(2), 22–25.

Grossman, H. (1995). *Special education in a diverse society.* Boston: Allyn and Bacon.

Grottenthaler, J. A. (1970). *A comparison of the effectiveness of three programs of elementary school spelling.* Unpublished doctoral dissertation, University of Pittsburgh.

Gulland, D. M. and Hinds-Howell, D. G. (1986). *The Penguin dictionary of English idioms.* London: Penguin.

Gunning, T. G. (1988b). *Teaching phonics and other word attack skills.* Springfield, Ill.: Charles C. Thomas.

Gunning, T. G. (1995). Word building: A strategic approach to the teaching of phonics. *The Reading Teacher, 48,* 484–488.

Gunning, T. G. (1996). *Creating reading instruction for all children* (2nd ed.). Boston, Mass.: Allyn and Bacon.

Guszak, F. J. (1972). *Diagnostic reading instruction in the elementary school.* New York: Harper & Row.

Hagin, R. A. (1983). Write right or left: A practical approach to handwriting. *Journal of Learning Disabilities, 16*(5), 266–271.

Hall, R. V. (1975). *Behavior modification: Basic principles, managing behavior (Part 2)* (Rev. ed.). Lawrence, Kans.: H & H Enterprises.

Hallahan, D. P., Keller, C. E., McKinney, J. D., Lloyd, J. W., and Bryan, T. (1988). Examining the research base of the regular education initiative: Efficacy studies and the adaptive learning environments model. *Journal of Learning Disabilities, 21,* 29–35, 55.

Hallahan, D. P., Lloyd, J., Kosiewicz, M. M., Kauffman, J. M., and Graves, A. W. (1979). Self-monitoring of attention as a treatment for learning disabled boy's off-task behavior. *Learning Disability Quarterly, 2,* 24–32.

Hallahan, D. P., Tarver, S. G., Kauffman, J. M., and Graybeal, N. L. (1978). A comparison of the effects of reinforcement and response cost on the selective attention of learning disabled children. *Journal of Learning Disabilities, 11*(7), 430–438.

Halliday, M. A. K., and Hassan, R. (1976). *Cohesion in English.* London: Longman.

Hallowell, E. M., and Ratey, J. J. (1995). *Driven to distraction: Recognizing and coping with attention deficit disorder from childhood through adulthood.* New York: Touchstone.

Halpern, N. (1981). Mathematics for the learning disabled. *Journal of Learning Disabilities, 14*(9), 505–506.

Hamayan, E. V., and Damico, J. S. (Eds.), (1991). *Limiting bias in the assessment of bilingual students.* Austin, Tex.: Pro-Ed.

Hamstra-Bletz, L., and Blote, A. W. (1993). A longitudinal study on dysgraphic handwriting in primary school. *Journal of Learning Disabilities, 26,* 689–699.

Hanover, S. (1983). Handwriting comes naturally? *Academic Therapy, 18,* 407–412.

Hansen, J. (1981). The effect of inference training and practice on young children's reading comprehension. *Reading Research Quarterly, 16*(3), 391–417.

Hansen, J. (1985). Skills. In J. Hansen, T. Newkirk, and D. Graves (Eds.), *Breaking ground: Teachers relate reading and writing in the elementary school,* Portsmouth, N.H.: Heinemann, pp. 147–168.

Hansen, J. (1992). Students' evaluations bring reading and writing together. *The Reading Teacher, 46,* 100–105.

Hansen, J., and Hubbard, R. (1984). Poor readers can draw inferences. *The Reading Teacher, 37*(7), 586–590.

Hansen, J., Newkirk, T., and Graves, D. (Eds.). (1985). *Breaking ground: Teachers relate reading and writing in the elementary school.* Portsmouth, N.H.: Heinemann.

Hansen, J., and Pearson, P. D. (1983). An instructional study: Improving the inferential comprehension of good and poor fourth grade readers. *Journal of Educational Psychology, 75*(6), 821–829.

Harper, G. F., Mallete, B. and Moore, J. (1991). Peer-mediated instruction: Teaching spelling to primary school children with mild disabilities. *Reading, Writing, and Learning Disabilities, 7,* 137–151.

Harris, A. J., and Sipay, E. R. (1990). *How to increase reading ability* (9th ed). New York: Longman.

Harris, K. R. (1982). Cognitive-behavior modification: Application with exceptional students. *Focus on Exceptional Children, 15*(2), 1–16.

Harris, K. R., (1985). Conceptual, methodological, and clinical issues in cognitive behavior assessment. *Journal of Abnormal Child Psychology, 13,* 373–390.

Harris, K. R., and Graham, S. (1985). Improving learning disabled students' composition skills: Self-control strategy training. *Learning Disability Quarterly, 8,* 27–36.

Harris, K. R., and Graham, S. (1992). *Helping young writers master the craft.* Cambridge, Mass.: Brookline Press.

Harris, K. R., and Pressley, M. E. (1991). The nature of cognitive strategy instruction: Interactive strategy construction. *Exceptional Children, 57,* 392–404.

Harry, B. (1992). *Cultural diversity, families, and the special education system.* New York: Teachers College Press.

Harry, B., Allen, N., and McLaughlin, M. (1995). Communication versus compliance: African-American parents' involvement in special education. *Exceptional Children, 6*(4), 364–377.

Harste, J. (1990). Jerry Harste speaks on reading and writing. *The Reading Teacher, 43,* 316–318.

Harste, J. C., Short, K. G., with Burke, C. (1988). *Creating classrooms for authors: The reading-writing connection.* Portsmouth, N.H.: Heinemann.

Harste, J., Woodward, V., and Burke, C. (1984). *Language stories and literacy lessons.* Portsmouth, N.H.: Heinemann.

Hasselbring, T. S., and Goin, L. I. (1989). Making knowledge meaningful: Applications of hypermedia. *Journal of Special Education Technology, 10*(2), 61–72.

Hasselbring, T. S., and Goin, L. I. (1993). Integrated technology and media. In E. A. Polloway and J. R. Patton, *Strategies for teaching learners with special needs* (5th ed.). New York: Merrill/Macmillan, pp. 145–162.

Hasselbring, T., Goin, L, and Bransford, J. (1987) Developing automaticity. *Teaching Exceptional Children, 19,* 30–33.

Hazel, J. S., Schumaker, J. B., Sherman, J. A., and Sheldon-Wildgen, J. (1981). *ASSET: A social skills program for adolescents.* Champaign, Ill.: Research Press.

Hazel, J. S., Schumaker, J. B., Sherman, J. A., and Sheldon, J. (1982). Application of a group training program in social skills and problem solving to learning disabled and non–learning disabled youth. *Learning Disability Quarterly, 5,* 398–409.

Heald-Taylor, G. (1987). How to use predictable books for K–2 language arts instruction. *The Reading Teacher, 40*(7), 656–663.

Hebert, B., and Murdock, J. (1994). Comparing three computer-aided instruction output modes to teach vocabulary words to students with learning disabilities. *Learning Disability Quarterly, 9,* 136–141.

Hembree, R. (1986). Research gives calculators a green light. *Arithmetic Teacher, 34*(1), 18–21.

Henderson, E. H. (1990). *Teaching spelling* (2nd ed.). Boston: Houghton Mifflin.

Henry, C. S., Stephenson, A. L., Hanson, M. F., and Hargett, W. (1993). Adolescent suicide and families: An ecological approach. *Adolescence, 28,* 291–308.

Herman, P. A. (1985). The effect of repeated readings on reading rate, speech pauses, and word recognition memory. *Reading Research Quarterly, 20,* 553–574.

Herman, P. A., Anderson, R. C., Pearson, P. D., and Nagy, W. E. (1987). Incidental acquisition of word meaning from expositions with varied text features. *Reading Research Quarterly, 22,* 263–284.

Higgins, E. L., and Raskind, M. H. (1995). Compensatory effectiveness of speech recognition on the written composition performance of postsecondary students with learning disabilities. *Learning Disability Quarterly, 18,* 159–174.

Hirsch, E., and Niedermeyer, F. C. (1973). The effects of tracing prompts and discrimination training on kindergarten handwriting performance. *Journal of Education Research, 67*(2), 81–86.

Holdaway, D. (1979). *The foundations of literacy.* Portsmouth, N.H.: Heinemann.

Holdaway, D. (1979). *Foundations of literacy.* Sydney: Ashton-Scholastic.

Homan, D. R. (1970). The child with a learning disability in arithmetic. *The Arithmetic Teacher, 18,* 199–203.

Horn, E. (1937). *Methods of instruction in the social studies.* New York: Scribners.

Horowitz, E. C. (1981). Popularity decentering ability and role taking skills in learning disabled and normal children. *Learning Disability Quarterly, 4,* 23–30.

Horton, S. V., Lovitt, T. C., and Bergerud, D. (1990). The effectiveness of graphic organizers for three classifications of secondary students in content area classes. *Journal of Learning Disabilities, 23,* 12–22, 29.

Hoskins, B. (1987). *Conversations: Language intervention for adolescents.* Allen, Tex.: Developmental Learning Materials.

Hoskins, B. (1990). Language and literacy: Participating in the conversation. *Topics in Language and Language Disorders, 10*(2), 46–62.

Howe, M. L., Brainerd, C. J., and Kingma, J. (1985). Storage-retrieval process of normal and learning disabled children: A stages-of-learning analysis of picture-word effects. *Child Development, 56,* 1120–1133.

Howe, M. L., O'Sullivan, J. T., Brainerd, C. J., and Kingma, J. (1989). Localizing the development of ability differences in organized memory. *Contemporary Education Psychology, 14,* 336–356.

Hudson, F., Ormsbee, C. K., and Myles, B. S. (1994). Study guides: An instructional tool for equalizing student achievement. *Intervention in School and Clinic, 30*(20), 99–102.

Hudson, P., Lignugaris-Kraft, B., and Miller, T. (1993). Using content enhancements to improve the performance of adolescents with learning disabilities in content classes. *Learning Disabilities Research and Practice, 8,* 106–126.

Hudson, P. J. (1987). *The pause procedure: A technique to help mildly handicapped students learn lecture content.* Unpublished doctoral dissertation, University of Florida, Gainesville.

Huefner, D. S. (1988). The consulting teacher model: Risks and Opportunities. *Exceptional Children, 54,* 403–414.

Hughes, C. A. (1996). Memory and test-taking strategies. In D. D. Deshler, E. S. Ellis, and B. K. Lenz, *Teaching adolescents with learning disabilities: Strategies and methods* (2nd ed., pp. 209–266). Denver: Love.

Hughes, C. A., and Schumaker, J. B. (1991). *Test-taking strategy instruction for adolescents with learning disabilities.* Manuscript submitted for publication.

Hughes, C. A., and Schumaker, J. B. (1991). Test-taking strategy instruction for adolescents with learning disabilities. *Exceptionality, 2,* 205–221.

Hughes, C. A., Schumaker, J. B., Deshler, D. D., and Mercer, C. D. (1988). *The test-taking strategy.* Lawrence, Kans.: Edge Enterprises.

Hughes, C. A., Ruhl, K. L., Deshler, D. D., and Schumaker, J. B. (1995). *The assignment completion strategy.* Lawrence, Kans.: Edge Enterprises.

Hughes, C. A., Schumaker, J. B., and Deshler, D. D. (in preparation). *The essay test-taking strategy.* Lawrence, Kans.: Edge Enterprises.

Hughes, M. E. T. (1995). *Parental involvement in literacy instruction: Perceptions and practices of Hispanic parents of children with learning disabilities.* Unpublished doctoral dissertation, University of Miami, Coral Gables.

Hutchinson, N. L. (1993). Effects of cognitive strategy instruction on algebra problem solving of adolescents with learning disabilities. *Learning Disability Quarterly, 16,* 34–63.

Hutton, J. B., and Palo, L. (1976). A sociometric study of learning disability children and type of teaching strategy. *Group Psychotherapy, Psychodrama and Sociometry, 29,* 113–121.

Hynd, G. W., Obrzut, J. E., and Bowen, S. M. (1987). Neuropsychological basis of attention and memory in learning disabilities. In H. L. Swanson (Ed.), *Advances in learning and behavior disabilities: Memory and learning disabilities.* Greenwich, Conn.: JAI Press, pp. 175–201.

Idol, L., Paolucci-Whitcomb, P., and Nevin, A. (1986). *Collaborative consultation.* Austin, Tex.: Pro-Ed.

Idol, L. (1987a). A critical thinking map to improve content area comprehension of poor readers. *Remedial and Special Education, 8*(4), 28–40.

Idol, L. (1987b). Group story mapping: A comprehension strategy for both skilled and unskilled readers. *Journal of Learning Disabilities, 20*(4), 196–205.

Imber, S. C., Imber, S. C., and Rothstein, C. (1979). Modifying independent work habits: An effective teacher-parent communication program. *Exceptional Children, 46,* 218–221.

Institute for Research in Learning Disabilities (1990a). *Planning for a strategic environment.* Lawrence, Kans.: University of Kansas.

Institute for Research in Learning Disabilities (1990b). *Ensuring strategic instruction.* Lawrence, Kans.: University of Kansas.

Irvine, J. J. (1991). *Black students and school failure: Policies, practice, and prescriptions.* New York: Praeger.

Isaacson, S. (1988). Assessing the writing product: Qualitative and quantitative measures. *Exceptional Children, 54,* 528–534.

Iversen S., and Tunmer, W. E. (1993). Phonological processing skills and the Reading Recovery program. *Journal of Educational Psychology, 85,* 112–126.

Ives, J. P., Bursuk, L. Z., and Ives, S. A. (1979). *Word identification techniques.* Chicago: Rand McNally College Publishing.

Jackson, H. J., and Boag, P. G. (1981). The efficacy of self control procedures as motivational strategies with mentally retarded persons; A review of the literature and guidelines for future research. *Australian Journal of Developmental Disabilities, 7,* 65–79.

Jay, T. B. (January 1983). The cognitive approach to computer courseware design and evaluation. *Educational Technology,* 22–26.

Jayanthi, M., Epstein, M. H., Polloway, E. A., and Bursuck, W. D. (1996). Testing adaptations: A national survey of the testing practices of general education teachers. *Journal of Special Education, 30,* 99–115.

Jiménez, R. T., García, G. E., and Pearson, P. D. (1996). The reading strategies of bilingual Latina/o students who are successful English readers: Opportunities and obstacles. *Reading Research Quarterly, 31,* 90–112.

Johnson, D. D., and Pearson, P. D. (1984). *Teaching reading vocabulary* (2nd ed.). New York: Holt, Rinehart and Winston.

Johnson, D. D., Pittelman, S. D., and Heimlich, J. E. (1986). Semantic mapping. *The Reading Teacher, 39*(8), 778–783.

Johnson, D. J., and Myklebust, H. R. (1967). *Learning disabilities: Educational principles and practices.* New York: Grune and Stratton.

Johnson, D. W., and Johnson, R. T. (1975). *Learning together and alone.* Englewood Cliffs, N.J.: Prentice-Hall.

Johnson, D. W., and Johnson, R. T. (1984a). Classroom learning structure and attitudes toward handicapped students in mainstream settings: a theoretical model and research evidence. In R. Jones (Ed.), *Special education in transition: Attitudes toward the handicapped.* Reston, Va.: ERIC Clearinghouse on Handicapped and Gifted Children, The Council for Exceptional Children.

Johnson, D. W., and Johnson, R. T. (1984b). Building acceptance of differences between handicapped and nonhandicapped students: The effects of cooperative and individualistic problems. *Journal of Social Psychology, 122,* 257–267.

Johnson, D. W., and Johnson, R. T. (1986). Mainstreaming and cooperative learning strategies. *Exceptional Children, 52*(6), 553–561.

Jones, D. J., Fox, M. M., Haroutun-Babigian, H. M., and Hutton, H. E. (1980). Epidemiology of anorexia nervosa in Monroe County, New York: 1960–1976. *Psychosomatic Medicine, 42*(6), 551–558.

Kail, R., and Leonard, L. B. (1986). Word-finding abilities in language-impaired children. *ASHA Monograph Number 25.* Rockville, Md.: American Speech-Language-Hearing Association.

Kameenui, E. J., Simmons, D. C., Baker, S., Chard, D., Dickson, S., Gunn, B., Smith, S., Sprick, M., and Lin, S. (in press). Effective strategies for teaching beginning reading. In E. J. Kameenui and D. W. Carnine (Eds.), *Effective teaching strategies that accommodate diverse learners.* Columbus, Ohio: Merrill.

Kamhi, A. G., and Catts, H. W. (1989). Language and reading: Convergences, divergences, and development. In A. G. Kamhi and H. W. Catts (Eds.), *Reading disabilities: A developmental language perspective* (pp. 1–34). Boston: Allyn and Bacon.

Kaplan, P., Kohfeldt, J., and Sturla, K. (1974). *It's positively fun: Techniques for managing learning environment.* Denver: Love.

Karlin, R. (1980). *Teaching elementary reading* (3rd ed.). New York: Harcourt Brace Jovanovich.

Kauffman, J. M. (1985). *Characteristics of children's behavior disorders* (3rd ed.). Columbus, Ohio: Merrill.

Kauffman, J., Hallahan, D., Haas, K., Brame, T., and Boren, R. (1978). Imitating children's errors to improve spelling performance. *Journal of Learning Disabilities, 11,* 33–38.

Kavanagh, J. F., and Truss, T. J., Jr. (1988). *Learning Disabilities: Proceedings of the National Conference.* Parkton, Md.: York Press.

Kazdin, A. E. (1982). *Single-case research designs.* New York: Oxford University Press.

Kazdin, A. E. (1989). *Behavior modification in applied settings* (4th ed.). Pacific Grove, Calif.: Brooks/Cole.

Kelly, B., Carnine, D., Gersten, R., and Grossen, B. (1987). The effectiveness of videodisc instruction in teaching fractions to learning handicapped and remedial high school students. *Journal of Special Education Technology, 8*(2), 5–17.

Kelly, B., Gersten, R., and Carnine, D. (1990). Student error patterns as a function of curriculum design: Teaching fractions to remedial high school students and high school students with learning disabilities. *Journal of Learning Disabilities, 23*(1), 23–29.

Keogh, B. K., and Donlon, G. McG. (1972). Field dependence, impulsivity, and learning disabilities. *Journal of Learning Disabilities, 5,* 331–336.

Keogh, B. K., Tchir, C., and Windeguth-Behn, A. (1974). Teachers' perceptions of educationally high risk children. *Journal of Learning Disabilities, 7,* 367–374.

Kiewra, K. A. (1985). Investigating notetaking and review: A depth of processing alternative. *Educational Psychologist, 20,* 23–32.

Kimmel, M. M., and Segal, E. (1988). *For reading out loud.* New York: Delacorte.

King-Sears, M. E., Mercer, C. D., and Sindelar, P. T. (1992). Toward independence with key word mnemonics: A strategy for science vocabulary instruction. *Remedial and Special Education, 13*(5), 22–33.

Kinney, G. C., Marsetta, M., and Showman, D. J. (1966). *Studies in display symbol legibility, Part XXI.* The legibility of alphanumeric symbols for digitized television (ESD-TR-66-117). Bedford, Mass.: Mitre Corporation.

Kintsch, W. (1974). *The representation of meaning in memory.* Hillsdale, N.J.: Erlbaum.

Kirk, R. N. (1986). Tape-recording poetry. *The Reading Teacher, 40*(2), 200–202.

Kirk, S. A., and Chalfant, J. C. (1984). *Academic and developmental learning disabilities.* Denver: Love.

Kirk, S. A., Kirk, W. D., and Minskoff, E. H. (1985). *Phonic remedial reading lessons.* Novato, Calif.: Academic Therapy Publications.

Kirkpatrick, E. M., and Schwarz, C. M. (Eds.). (1982). *Chambers idioms.* Edinburgh, Scotland: Chambers.

Kistner, J., and Osborne, M. (1987). A longitudinal study of LD children's self-evaluations. *Learning Disability Quarterly, 10,*(4), 258–266.

Klausmeier, J. H., and Sipple, T. S. (1980). *Learning and teaching process concepts: A strategy for testing applications for theory.* New York: Academic Press.

Klingner, J. K., and Vaughn, S. (1996). Reciprocal teaching of reading comprehension strategies for students with learning disabilities who use English as a second language. *Elementary School Journal, 96,* 275–293.

Klingner, J. K., Vaughn, J. S., and Schumm, J. S. (1996). *Collaborative Strategic Reading.* Miami: University of Miami, School-Based Reseach.

Knight-Arest, I. (1984). Communicative effectiveness of learning disabled and normally achieving 10- to 13-year-old boys. *Learning Disability Quarterly, 7,* 237–245.

Knowlton, E. K. (1982). *Secondary teacher's expectations of learning disabled students* (Research Report No. 75.). Lawrence, Kans.: University of Kansas, Center for Research on Learning.

Korbin, B. (1988). *Eyeopeners! How to choose and use children's books about real people, places, and things.* New York: Penguin.

Kosc, L. (1981). Neuropsychological implications of diagnosis and treatment of mathematical learning disabilities. *Topics in Learning and Learning Disabilities, 1*(3), 19–30.

Kosiewicz, M. M., Hallahan, D. P., Lloyd. J. W., and Graves, A. W. (1982). Effects of self-instruction and self-correction procedures on handwriting performance. *Learning Disability Quarterly, 5*(1), 71–78.

Koziol, S. (1973). The development of noun plural rules during the primary grades. *Research in the Teaching of English, 7,* 30–50.

Krashen, S. (1985). *The input hypothesis: Issues and implications.* London: Longman.

Krauss, R., and Glucksberg, S. (1967). The development of communication competence as a function of age. *Child Development, 40* 255–260.

Kress, R. A., and Johnson, M. S. (1970). Martin. In A. J. Harris (Ed.), *Casebook on reading disability.* New York: David McKay, pp. 1–24.

Kreviski, J., and Linfield, J. L. (1974). *Bad speller's dictionary.* New York: Random House.

Kronik, D. (1977). A parent's thought for parents and teachers. In N. Haring and B. Bateman (Eds.), *Teaching the learning disabled child.* Englewood Cliffs, N.J.: Prentice-Hall.

Krug, R. S. (1983). Substance abuse. In C. E. Walker and McRoberts (Eds.), *Handbook of clinical child psychology.* New York: John Wiley, pp. 853–879.

Kucer, S. B. (1986). Helping writers get the "big picture." *Journal of Reading, 30*(1), 18–25.

LaBerge, D., and Samuels, S. J. (1974). Toward a theory of automatic information processing in reading. *Cognitive Psychology, 6,* 293–323.

Ladas, H. S. (1980). Notetaking on lectures: An information processing approach. *Educational Psychologist, 15*(1), 44–53.

Ladson-Billings, G. (1995). Toward a theory of culturally relevant pedagogy. *American Educational Research Journal, 32,* 465–491.

LaGreca, A. M. (November 1982). Issues in the assessment of social skills with learning disabled children. In *Children's social skills: Future directions,* S. Beck (Chair). Paper presented at the annual meeting of the Association for the Advancement of Behavior Therapy, Los Angeles, Calif.

LaGreca, A. M., and Stone, W. L. (1990). Children with learning disabilities: The role of achievement in their social, personal and behavioral functioning. In H. L. Swanson and B. Keogh (Eds.), *Learning disabilities: Theoretical and research issues.* Hillsdale, N.J.: Erlbaum, pp. 333–352.

Lambert, N. M., and Sandoval, J. (1980). The prevalence of learning disabilities in a sample of children considered hyperactive. *Journal of Abnormal Child Psychology, 8*(1), 33–50.

Lancelotta, G. X., and Vaughn, S. R. (1989). Relation between types of aggression and sociometric status: Peer and teacher perceptions. *Journal of Educational Psychology, 81*(1), 86–90. Reprinted by permission in W. R. Borg, *Applying educational research,* (in press), New York: Longman.

Langan, J. (1982). *Reading and study skills* (2nd ed.). New York: McGraw-Hill.

Langdon, H. W. (1992). Speech and language assessment of LEP/bilingual Hispanic students. In H. W. Langdon and L. L. Cheng (Eds.), *Hispanic children and adults with communication disorders.* Gaithersburg, Md.: Aspen Publishers, pp. 201–271.

Langer, J. A. (1981). From theory to practice: A prereading plan. *Journal of Reading, 25*(2), 152–156.

Langer, J. A., and Nicolich, M. (1981). Prior knowledge and its effects on comprehension. *Journal of Reading Behavior, 13,* 375–378.

Lankford, F. G. (1974). *Some computational strategies in seventh grade pupils.* Unpublished manuscript, University of Virginia.

Larsen, S. C., Parker, R., and Trenholme, B. (1978). The effects of syntactic complexity upon arithmetic performance. *Learning Disability Quarterly, 1*(4), 80–85.

Larsen, S. (1995). What is "quality" in the use of technology for children with learning disabilities? *Learning Disability Quarterly, 18,* 118–130. Lawrence Erlbaum.

Lazar, Warr-Leeper, Nicholson, and Johnson, (1989). Use of figurative language in classrooms.

Leadholm, B., and Miller, J. (1992). *Language sample analysis: The Wisconsin guide.* Madison, Wisc.: Bureau for Exceptional Children, Wisconsin Department of Public Education.

Lee, C. P. (1992). *Taxonomic and frequency associations in memory in learning disabled and non-disabled children.* Unpublished doctoral dissertation, University of Arizona, Tucson.

Legenza, A. (1974). *Questioning behavior of kindergarten children.* Paper presented at the 19th Annual Convention, International Reading Association.

Leinhardt, G., Zigmond, N., and Cooley, W. W. (1981). Reading instruction and its effects. *American Education Research Journal, 18,* 343–366.

Lenz, B. K. (1983). Promoting active learning through effective instruction: Using advance organizers. *Pointer, 27*(2), 11–13.

Lenz, B. K., Alley, G. R., and Schumaker, J. B. (1987). Activating the inactive learner: Advance organizers in the secondary content classroom. *Learning Disability Quarterly, 10*(10), 53–67.

Lenz, B. K., and Bulgren, J. A. (1995). Promoting learning in content classes. In P. A. Cegleka and W. H. Berdine (Eds.), *Effective instruction for students with learning problems* (pp. 385–417). Boston: Allyn and Bacon.

Lenz, K., Bulgren, J., and Hudson, P. (1990). Content enhancement: A model for promoting the acquisition of content by individuals with learning disabilities. In T. E. Scruggs and B. Y. L. Wong (Eds.), *Intervention research in learning disabilities.* New York: Springer-Verlag, pp. 122–165.

Lenz, B. K., Ehren, B. J., and Smiley, L. R. (1991). A goal attainment approach to improve completion of project-type assignments by adolescents with learning disabilities. *Learning Disabilities Research and Practice, 6,* 165–176.

Lenz, B. K., Ellis, E. S., and Scanlon, D. (1996). *Teaching learning strategies to adolescents and adults with learning disabilities.* Austin, Tex.: Pro-Ed.

Lenz, B. K., Schumaker, J. B., Deshler, D. D., and Beals, V. L. (1984). *The word identification strategy* (Learning Strategies Curriculum). Lawrence: University of Kansas.

Leon, J. A., and Pepe, H. J. (1983). Self-instructional training: Cognitive behavior modification for remediating arithmetic deficits. *Exceptional Children, 50*(1), 54–60.

Leong, C. K. (1995). Effects of on-ling reading and simultaneous DECtalk auding in helping below-average and poor readers comprehend and summarize text. *Learning Disability Quarterly, 18,* 101–117.

Lerner, J. W. (1985). *Learning disabilities: Theories, diagnosis, and teaching strategies* (4th ed.). Boston: Houghton Mifflin.

Lerner, J. W. (1997). *Learning disabilities: Theories, diagnosis, and teaching strategies* (7th ed.). Boston: Houghton Mifflin.

Levine, M. P. (1987). *Student eating disorders: Anorexia nervosa and bulimia.* Washington, D.C.: National Education Association.

Lewis, S. K., and Lawrence-Patterson, E. (1989). Locus of control of children with learning disabilities and perceived locus of control by significant others. *Journal of Learning Disabilities, 22,* 255–257.

Liberman, I., and Shankweiler, D. (1979). Speech, the alphabet, and teaching of reading. In L. Resnick and P. Weavers (Eds.), *Theory and practice in early reading* (Vol. 2). Hillsdale, N.J.: Erlbaum, pp. 109–132.

Liberman, I. Y., and Shankweiler, D. (1987). Phonology and the problems of learning to read and write. In H. L. Swanson (Ed.), *Advances in learning and behavioral disabilities* (Supplement 2). Greenwich, Conn.: JAI Press, pp. 203–224.

Licht, B. G. (1983). Cognitive-motivational factors that contribute to the achievement of learning disabled children. *Journal of Learning Disabilities, 16,* 483–489.

Lindamood, P. (1975). *Lindamood Auditory Discrimination in Depth,* Austin, Tex.: Pro-Ed.

Link, D. (1980). *Essential learning skills and the low achieving student at the secondary level: A rating of the importance of 24 academic abilities.* Unpublished master's thesis, University of Kansas, Lawrence.

Lloyd, J. W. (1980). Academic instruction and cognitive behavior modification: The need for attack strategy training. *Exceptional Educational Quarterly, 1*(1), 53–64.

Loban, W. (1976). *Language development: Kindergarten through grade twelve* (Res. Report #18). Urbana, Ill.: National Council of Teachers of English.

Lock, C. (1981). *Study skills.* West Lafayette, Ind.: Kappa Delta Pi.

Loftus, G., and Loftus, E. R. (1976). *Human memory.* Hillsdale, N.J.: Erlbaum.

Lovitt, T. C., and Horton, S. V. (1994). Strategies for adapting science textbooks for youth with learning disabilities. *Remedial and Special Education, 15,* 105–116.

Lucangeli, D., Galderisi, D., and Cornoldi, C. (1995). Specific and general transfer effects following metamemory training. *Learning Disabilities Research and Practice, 10,* 11–21.

Lundberg, I. (1995). The computer as a tool of remediation in the education of students with reading disabilities—A theory-based approach. *Learning Disability Quarterly, 18,* 89–100.

Luria, A. R. (1961). *The role of speech in the regulation of normal and abnormal behavior.* (J. Tizard, Trans.). New York: Liveright.

Lynch, E. W., and Stein, R. (1982). Perspectives on parent participation in special education. *Exceptional Education Quarterly, 3*(2), 56–63.

Lynch, P. (1986). *Big books and predictable books.* New York: Scholastic.

Lyon, G. R. (1985). Identification and remediation of learning disability subtypes: Preliminary findings. *Learning Disabilities Focus, 1,* 21–35.

Lyon, G. R. (1995). Research initiatives in learning disabilities: Contributions from scientists supported by the National Institute of Child Health and Human Development. *Journal of Child Neurology, 10,* S121–S126.

MacArthur, C. A. (1988). The impact of computers on the writing process. *Exceptional Children, 54,* 536–542.

MacArthur, C. (1994). Peers + word processing + strategies: A powerful strategy for revising student writing. *Teaching Exceptional Children, 27*(1), 24–29.

MacArthur, C. (1996). Using technology to enhance the writing processes of students with learning disabilities. *Journal of Learning Disabilities, 29,* 344–354.

MacArthur, C., and Haynes, J. (1995). Student assistant for learning from text (SALT): A hypermedia reading aid. *Journal of Learning Disabilities, 28,* 150–159.

MacArthur, C., Graham, S., and Schwartz, S. (1991). Knowledge of revision and revising behavior among learning disabled students. *Learning Disability Quarterly, 14,* 61–73.

MacArthur, C., Graham, S., and Schwartz, S. (1993). Integrating word processing and strategy instruction into a process approach to writing. *School Psychology Review, 22,* 671–681.

MacArthur, C., Graham, S., Haynes, J., and DeLaPaz, S. (1996). Spelling checkers and students with learning disabilities: Performance comparisons and impact on spelling. *Journal of Special Education, 30,* 35–57.

MacArthur, C., Graham, S., Schwartz, S., and Schafer, W. (1995). Evaluation of a writing instruction model that integrated a process approach, strategy instruction, and word processing. *Learning Disability Quarterly, 18,* 278–291.

MacArthur, C., Graham, S., Schwartz, S., and Schafer, W. D. (1995). Evaluation of a writing instruction model that integrated a process approach, strategy instruction, and word processing. *Learning Disability Quarterly, 18,* 278–291.

MacArthur, C. A., Schwartz, S. S., and Graham, S. (1991). A model for writing instruction: Integrating word processing and strategy instruction into a process approach to writing. *Learning Disabilities Research and Practice, 6,* 230–236.

MacArthur, C. A., Schwartz, S. S., Graham, S., Molloy, D., and Harris, K. (1996). Integration of strategy instruction into a whole-language classroom: A case study. *Learning Disabilities Research and Practice, 11,* 168–176.

MacWilliams, L. J. (1978). Mobility board games: Not only for rainy days. *Teaching Exceptional Children, 11*(1), 22–25.

Mager, R. F. (1975). *Preparing instructional objectives.* Belmont, Calif.: Fearon Publishing.

Maheady, L., Harper, G. F., and Sacca, M. K. (1988). Peer mediated instruction: A promising approach to meeting the needs of learning disabled adolescents. *Learning Disability Quarterly, 11,* 108–113.

Majsterek, D. J. (1990). Writing disabilities: Is word processing the answer? *Intervention in School and Clinic, 26,* 93–97.

Mandler, J. M., and Johnson, N. S. (1977). Rememberance of things passed: Story structure and recall. *Cognitive Psychology, 9,* 111–151.

Mandoli, M., Mandoli, P., and McLaughlin, T. F. (1982). Effects of same-age peer tutoring on the spelling performance of a mainstreamed elementary learning disabled student. *Learning Disability Quarterly, 5*(2), 185–189.

Mann, V. (1991). Language problems: A key to early reading problems. In B. Y. L. Wong (Ed.), *Learning about learning disabilities.* San Diego: Academic Press, pp. 129–162.

Manzo, A. V. (1969). The request procedure. *Journal of Reading, 13,* 123–126.

Manzo, A., and Manzo, U. (1990). *Content area reading: A heuristic approach.* Columbus, Ohio: Merrill.

Manzo, A. V., and Manzo, U. C. (1993). *Literacy Disorders: Holistic diagnosis and remediation.* Fort Worth: Harcourt Brace Jovanovich.

Margalit, M., Raviv, A., and Ankonina, D. B. (1992). Coping and coherence among parents with disabled children. *Journal of Clinical Child Psychology, 21*(3), 202–209.

Markham, L. (1976). Influence of handwriting quality on teacher evaluation of written work. *American Educational Research Journal, 13,* 277–283.

Marsh, L. G., and Cooke, N. L. (1996). The effects of using manipulatives in teaching math problem solving to students with learning disabilities. *Learning Disabilities Research and Practice, 11,* 58–65.

Martin, B., Jr. (1983). *Brown bear, brown bear, what do you see?* New York: Holt.

Martin, B., and Brogan, P. (1971). *Teachers guide to the instant readers.* New York: Holt, Rinehart and Winston.

Martin, J. H., and Friedburg, A. (1986). *Writing to read.* New York: Warner.

Martinez, M., and Teale, W. H. (1988). Reading in a kindergarten classroom library. *The Reading Teacher, 41,* 568–572.

Maria, K. (1989). Developing disadvantaged children's background knowledge interactively. *The Reading Teacher, 42,* 296–300.

Mastropieri, M. A., and Scruggs, T. E. (1989). Reconstructive elaborations: Strategies that facilitate content learning. *Learning Disabilities Focus, 4,* 73–77.

Mastropieri, M. A., Scruggs, T. E., and Shiah, S. (1991). Mathematics instruction for learning disabled students: A review of research. *Learning Disabilities Research and Practice, 6,* 89–98.

Mather, N. (1992). Whole language reading instruction for students with learning disabilities: Caught in the crossfire. *Learning Disabilities Research and Practice, 7,* 87–95.

Mathinos, D. A. (April 1987). Communicative abilities of disabled and nondisabled children. Paper presented at the annual meeting of the Society for Research on Child Development, Baltimore, Md.

Mattingly, J. C., and Bott, D. A. (1990). Teaching multiplication facts to students with learning problems. *Exceptional Children, 56,* 438–449.

Mayer, R. E. (1979). Twenty years of research on advance organizers: Assimilation theory is still the best predictor of results. *Instructional Science, 8,* 133–167.

Mauldin, M. (1996). All you have to do is ask: Middle school students' specifications for software. *Technological Horizons in Education Journal, 24*(2), 90–92.

McCauley, J. K., and McCauley, D. S. (1992). Using choral reading to promote language learning for ESL students. *The Reading Teacher, 45,* 526–533.

McCormick, S., and Cooper, J. O. (1991). Can SQ3R facilitate secondary learning disabled students' literal comprehension of expository text? Three experiments. *Reading Psychology, 12,* 239–271.

McCormick, S. (1992). Disable readers' erroneous responses to inferential comprehension questions: Description and analysis. *Reading Research Quarterly, 27,* 54–77.

McDonough, K. M. (1989). Analysis of the expressive language characteristics of emotionally handicapped students in social interactions. *Behavior Disorders, 14,* 127–139.

McGregor, K. K., and Leonard, L. B. (1989). Facilitating word-finding skills of language-impaired children. *Journal of Speech and Hearing Disorders, 54,* 141–147.

McGuinness, D., McGuinness, C., and Donohue, J. (1995). Phonological training and the alphabetic principle: Evidence for reciprocal causality. *Reading Research Quarterly, 30,* 830–852.

McIntosh, R., Vaughn, S., and Bennerson, D. (1995). FAST social skills training for students with learning disabilities. *Teaching Exceptional Children, 28,* 37–41.

McIntosh, R., Vaughn, S., Schumm, J. S., and Haager, D. (1993). Observations of general education teachers.

McIntosh, R., Vaughn, S., Schumm, J., Haager, D., and Lee, O. (1993). Observations of students with learning disabilities in general education classrooms: You don't bother me and I won't bother you. *Exceptional Children, 60,* 249–261.

McIntosh, R., Vaughn, S., and Zaragoza, N. (1991). A review of social interventions for students with learning disabilities. *Journal of Learning Disabilities, 24*(8), 451–458.

McKenzie, R. G. (1991). Content area instruction delivered by secondary learning disabilities teachers: A national survey. *Learning Disability Quarterly, 14,* 115–122.

McKeown, M. G., and Beck, I. L. (1988). Learning vocabulary: Different ways for different goals. *Remedial and Special Education, 9*(1), 42–52.

McKeown, M. G., Beck, I. S., Sinatra, G. M., and Loxterman, J. A. (1992). The contribution of prior knowledge and coherent text to comprehension. *Reading Research Quarterly, 27,* 78–93.

McKinley, N., and Larson, V. L. (1991, November). *Seven, eighth, and ninth graders' conversations in two experimental conditions.* Paper presented at the annual convention of the American Speech- Language-Hearing Association, Atlanta.

McKinney, J. D., and Hocutt, A. M. (1982). Public school involvement of parents of learning disabled and average achievers. *Exceptional Education Quarterly, 3*(2), 64–73.

McKinney, J. D., and Hocutt, A. M. (1988). Policy issues in the evaluation of the regular education initiative. *Learning Disabilities Focus, 4,* 15–23.

McKinney, J. D., McClure, S., and Feagans, L. (1982). Classroom behavior of learning disabled children. *Learning Disabilities Quarterly, 5,* 45–52.

McKinney, J., Montague, M., and Hocutt, A. (1993). Educational assessment of students with attention deficit disorder. *Exceptional Children, 60,* 125–131.

Meichenbaum, D. (1977). *Cognitive-behavior modification: An integrative approach.* New York: Plenum.

Meichenbaum, D. (1983). Teaching thinking: A cognitive-behavioral approach. In *Interdisciplinary voices in learning disabilities and remedial education.* Austin, Tex.: Pro-Ed.

Meichenbaum, D. (1985). *Stress inoculation training: A clinical guidebook.* Elmsford, N.Y.: Pergamon Press.

Menke, P. J., and Pressley, M. (1994). Elaborative interrogation: Using "why" questions to enhance the learning from text. *Journal of Reading, 37,* 642–645.

Menyuk, P. (1971). *The acquisition and development of language.* Englewood Cliffs, N.J.: Prentice-Hall.

Mercer, C. D., and Mercer, A. R. (1989). *Teaching students with learning problems* (3rd ed.). Columbus, Ohio: Merrill.

Mercer, C. D., and Mercer, A. R. (1993). *Teaching students with learning problems* (4th ed.). New York: Merrill/ Macmillan.

Mercer, C. D., Mercer, A. R., and Bott, D. A. (1984). *Self-correcting learning materials for the classroom.* Columbus, Ohio: Merrill.

Miller, G. A. (1956). The magical number seven, plus or minus two: Some limits on our capacity for processing information. *Psychological Review, 63,* 81–97.

Mills, H., O'Keefe, T., and Stephens, D. (1992). *Looking closely: Exploring the role of phonics in one whole language classroom.* Urbana, Ill.: National Council of Teachers of English.

Misspeller's Dictionary. (1983). New York: Simon and Schuster.

Moats, L. C. (1995). *Spelling: Development, disability, and instruction.* Baltimore, Md.: York Press.

Moeller, B., and Jeffers, L. (1996). Technology for inclusive teaching. *Electronic Learning, 16*(3), 44.

Moll, L. C. (1990). Introduction. In L. C., Moll (Ed.), *Vygotsky and education: Instructional implications and applications of sociohistorical psychology.* Cambridge: Cambridge University Press, pp. 1–27.

Moll, L. C. (1994). Literacy research in community and classrooms: A sociocultural approach. In R. B. Ruddell, M. R. Ruddell, and H. Singer (Eds.), *Theoretical models and processes of reading* (pp. 179–207). Newark, Del.: International Reading Association.

Moll, L. C., and Greenberg, J. B. (1990). Creating zones of possibilities: Combining social contexts for instruction. In L. C. Moll (Ed.), *Vygotsky and education: Instructional implications and applications of sociohistorical psychology.* Cambridge: Cambridge University Press, pp. 319–348.

Montague, M., and Bos, C. S. (1986a). Verbal math problem solving and learning disabilities: A review. *Focus on Learning Problems in Math, 8*(2), 7–21.

Montague, M., and Bos, C. S. (1986b). The effect of cognitive strategy training on verbal math problem solving performance of learning disabled adolescents. *Journal of Learning Disabilities, 19*(1), 26–33.

Montague, M., and Bos, C. S. (1990). Cognitive and metacognitive characteristics of eighth grade students' mathematical problem solving. *Learning and Individual Differences, 2* 371–388.

Montague, M., and Fonseca, F. (1993). Using computers to improve story writing. *Teaching Exceptional Children, 25*(4), 4649.

Montague, M., and Leavell, A. G. (1994). Improving the narrative writing of students with learning disabilities. *Remedial and Special Education, 15,* 21–33.

Moore, J., and Fine, M. J. (1978). Regular and special class teachers' perceptions of normal and exceptional children and their attitudes toward mainstreaming. *Psychology in the Schools, 15*(2), 253–259.

Moran, M. (1980). *An investigation of the demands on oral language skills of learning disabled students in secondary classrooms* (Res. Rep. 1). Lawrence: University of Kansas, Institute for Research in Learning Disabilities.

Morgan, H. (1980). How schools fail black children. *Social Policy, 10*(4), 49–54.

Morgan, S. R. (1986). Locus of control in children labeled learning disabled, behaviorally disordered, and learning disabled/ behaviorally disordered. *Learning Disabilities Research, 2,* 10–13.

Morgan, S. R., and Reinhart, J. A. (1991). *Interventions for students with emotional disorders.* Austin, Tex.: Pro-Ed.

Morocco, C. C., Dalton, B., and Tivnan, T. (1992). The impact of computer-supported writing instruction on 4th grade students with and without learning disabilities. *Reading and Writing Quarterly: Overcoming Learning Disabilities, 8,* 87–113.

Morocco, D. D., and Neuman, S. B. (1986). Word processors and the acquisition of writing strategies. *Journal of Learning Disabilities, 19,* 243–247.

Morrison, G. M. (1985). Differences in teacher perceptions and student self-perceptions for learning disabled and non-handicapped learners in regular and special education settings. *Learning Disabilities Research, 1*(1), 32–41.

Morrison, G. M., Walker, D., Wakefield, P., and Solberg, S. (1994). Teacher preferences for collaborative relationships: Relationship to efficacy for teaching in prevention-related domains. *Psychology in the Schools, 31,* 221–231.

Morrow, L. M. (1992). The impact of a literature-based program on literacy achievement, use of literature, and attitudes of children from minority backgrounds. *Reading Research Quarterly, 25,* 251–275.

Mosberg, L., Johns, D. (1994). Reading and listening comprehension in college students with developmental dyslexia. *Learning Disabilities Research and Practice, 9,* 130–135.

Moss, J. F. (1984). *Focus units in literature: A handbook for elementary school teacher.* Urbana, Ill.: National Council of Teachers of English.

Muma, J. (1986). *Language acquisition: A functional perspective.* Austin, Tex.: Pro-Ed.

Murray, D. (1984). *Write to learn.* New York: Holt, Rinehart and Winston.

Murray, D. (1985). *A writer teaches writing.* Boston: Houghton Mifflin.

Nagel, B. R., Schumaker, J. B., and Deshler, D. D. (1986). *The FIRST-letter mnemonic strategy* (Learning Strategies Curriculum). Lawrence, Kans.: Edge Enterprises.

National Council of Supervisors of Mathematics. (1977). *Position paper on basic mathematical skills*. Minneapolis, Minn.: National Council of Supervisors of Mathematics.

National Research Council (1989). *Everybody counts: A report to the nation on the future of mathematics education*. Washington, D.C.: National Academy Press.

NCTM. (December 1974). NCTM board approves policy statement of the use of minicalculators in the mathematics classroom. *NCTM Newsletter,* p. 3.

Neisser, U. (1967). *Cognitive psychology*. New York: Appleton.

Neisser, U. (1976). *Cognition and reality: Principles and implications of cognitive psychology*. San Francisco: Freeman.

Nelson, A. (1989). *A long hard day on the ranch*. Buffalo, N.Y.: Firefly Books Limited.

Nelson, J. R., Smith, D. J., Young, R. K., and Dodd, J. M. (1991). A review of self-management outcome research conducted with students who exhibit behavioral disorders. *Behavioral Disorders, 16,* 169–179.

Newland, E. (1932). An analytic study of the development of illegibilities in handwriting from the lower grades to adulthood. *Journal of Educational Research, 26,* 249–258.

Nippold, M. A. (1992). The nature of normal and disordered word finding in children and adolescents. *Topics in Language Disorders, 13*(1), 1–14.

Nippold, M. A. (1993). Adolescents language developmental markers in adolescent language: Syntax, semantics, and pragmatics. *Language, Speech, and Hearing Services in Schools, 24,* 21–28.

Nolan, S., Alley, G. R., and Clark, F. L. (1980). *Self-questioning strategy*. Lawrence: University of Kansas, Institute for Research in Learning Disabilities.

Nolet, V., and Tindal, G. (1993). Special education in content area classes: Development of a model and practical procedures. *Remedial and Special Education, 14*(1), 36–48.

Norton, D. E. (1987). *Through the eyes of a child: An introduction to children's literature* (2nd ed.). Columbus, Ohio: Merrill.

Novaco, R. (1975). *Anger control: The development and evaluation of an experimental treatment*. Lexington, Mass.: D. C. Heath.

Nulman, J. H., and Gerber, M. M. (1984). Improving spelling performance by imitating a child's errors. *Journal of Learning Disabilities, 17,* 328–333.

O'Brien, C. A. (1973). *Teaching the language-different child to read*. Columbus, Ohio: Merrill.

O'Brien, D. G., Stewart, R. A., and Moje, E. B. (1995). Why content literacy is difficulty to infuse into the secondary school: Complexities of curriculum, pedagogy, and school culture. *Reading Research Quarterly, 30,* 442–465.

Obrzut, J. E. (1995). Dynamic versus structural processing differences characterize laterality patterns of learning disabled children. *Developmental Neuropsychology, 11,* 467–484.

O'Connor, R. E., and Jenkins, J. R. (1995). Improving the generalization of sound/symbol knowledge: Teaching spelling to kindergarten children with disabilities. *Journal of Special Education, 29,* 255–275.

O'Connor, S. C., and Spreen, O. (1988). The relationship between parents' socioeconomic status and education level, and adult occupational and educational achievement of children with learning disabilities. *Journal of Learning Disabilities 21*(3), 148–153.

Ogle, D. M. (1986). K-W-L: A teaching model that develops active reading of expository text. *The Reading Teacher, 39,* 564–570.

Ogle, D. M. (1989). The know, want to know, learn strategy. In K. D. Muth (Ed.), *Children's comprehension of text: Research into practice* (pp. 205–233). Newark, Del.: International Reading Association.

Okolo, C., Bahr, C., and Rieth, H. (1993). A retrospective view of computer-based instruction. *Journal of Special Education Technology, 12,* 1–27.

Oppenheim, J., Brenner, B., and Doegenhold, B. D. (1986). *Choosing books for kids: Choosing the right book for the right child at the right time*. New York: Ballantine Books.

O'Shea, L. J., Sindelar, P. T., and O'Shea, D. J. (1987). The effects of repeated readings and attentioned cues on the reading fluency and comprehension of learning disabled readers. *Learning Disabilities Research, 2,* 103–109.

Owens, R. E. (1995). *Language disorders: A functional approach to assessment and intervention* (2nd ed.). New York: Merrill/Macmillan.

Palincsar, A. S. (1982). Improving the reading comprehension of junior high students through the reciprocal teaching of comprehension-monitoring. Unpublished doctoral dissertation, University of Illinois, Urbana.

Palincsar, A. S. (1986). The role of dialogue in providing scaffolded instruction. *Educational Psychologist, 21*(1-2), 73–98.

Palincsar, A. S. (1988). *Reciprocal teaching instructional materials packet*. East Lansing, Mich.: Michigan State University.

Palincsar, A. S., and Brown, A. L. (1984). Reciprocal teaching of comprehension fostering and comprehension monitoring activities. *Cognition and Instruction, 1*(2), 117–175.

Palincsar, A. S., and Brown, A. L. (1986). Interactive teaching to promote independent learning from text. *The Reading Teacher, 39*(8), 771–777.

Palincsar, A. S., and Brown, D. A. (1987). Enhancing instructional time through attention to metacognition. *Journal of Learning Disabilities, 20*(2), 66–75.

Palmatier, R. A. (1971). Comparison of four note-taking procedures. *Journal of Reading, 14,* 235–240, 258.

Palmatier, R. A. (1973). A note-taking system for learning. *Journal of Reading, 17,* 36–39.

Palmatier, R. A., and Ray, H. L. (1989). *Sports talk: A dictionary of sports metaphors*. New York: Greenwood.

Parmar, R. S., Cawley, J. F., and Miller, J. H. (1994). Differences in mathematics performance between students with learning disabilities and students with mild retardation. *Exceptional Children, 60,* 549–563.

Parsons, J. A. (1972). The reciprocal modification of arithmetic behavior and program development. In G. Semb (Ed.), *Behavior analysis and education*. Lawrence, Kans.: University of Kansas, Department of Human Development.

Paterson, K. (1978). *The great Gilly Hopkins*. New York: Crowell.

Patterson, J. H., and Smith, M. S. (1986). The role of computers in higher-order thinking. In J. A. Culbertson and L. L. Cunningham (Eds.), *Microcomputers and education*. Eighty-fifth Yearbook of the National Society for the Study of Education. Chicago: University of Chicago Press, pp. 81–108.

Pauk, W. (1974). *How to study in college* (2nd ed.). Boston: Houghton Mifflin.

Paulson, F. L., Paulson, P. R., and Meyer, C. A. (1991). What makes a portfolio a portfolio? *Educational Leadership, 48*(5), 60–63.

Pea, R. D., Kurland, M., and Hawkins, J. (1987). Logo and the development of thinking skills. In Pea, R. D., and Sheingold, K. (Eds.), *Mirrors of minds: Patterns of experience in educational computing.* Norwood, N.J.: Ablex, pp. 178–197.

Pea, R. D., and Sheingold, K. (Eds.). (1987). *Mirrors of minds: Patterns of experience in educational computing.* Norwood, N.J.: Ablex.

Pearson, P. D. (1984). Direct explicit teaching of reading comprehension. In G. G. Duffy, L. R. Roehler, and J. Mason (Eds.), *Comprehension instruction: Perspectives and suggestions.* New York: Longman, pp. 222–233.

Pearson, P. D., and Camperell, K. (1994). Comprehension of text structures. In R. B. Ruddell, M. R. Ruddell, and H. Singer (Eds.), *Theoretical models and process of reading* (4th ed., pp. 448–568). Newark, Del.: International Reading Association.

Pearson, P. D., and Johnson, D. D. (1978). *Teaching reading comprehension.* New York: Holt, Rinehart and Winston.

Pecyna-Rhyner, P., Lehr, D., and Pudlas, K. (1990). An analysis of teacher responsiveness to communicative initiations of children with handicaps. *Language, Speech, and Hearing Services in Schools, 21,* 91–97.

Peetoom, A. (1986). *Shared reading: Safe risks with whole books.* Richmond Hill, Ontario, Calif.: Scholastic-TAB Publications.

Pehrsson, R. S., and Robinson, H. A. (1985). *The semantic organizer approach to writing and reading instruction.* Rockville, Md.: Aspen.

Perez, B., and Torres-Guzman, M. E. (1992). *Learning in two worlds.* New York: Longman.

Perlmutter, B. F. (1986). Personality variables and peer relations of children and adolescents with learning disabilities. In S. J. Ceci (Ed.), *Handbook of cognitive, social, and neuropsychological aspects of learning disabilities.* Hillsdale, N.J.: Erlbaum, pp. 339–359.

Personkee, C., and Yee, A. (1971). *Comprehensive spelling instruction: Theory, research, and application.* Scranton, Pa.: Intext Educational.

Peterson, B. (1991). Selecting books for beginning readers. In D. E. DeFord, C. A. Lyons, and G. S. Pinnell (Eds.), *Bridges to literacy: Learning from Reading Recovery* (pp. 119–138). Portsmouth, N.H.: Heinemann.

Peters, T., and Austin, N. (1985). *A passion for excellence.* New York: Random House.

Phillips, M. (1996). Beyond the best CDs list. *Electronic Learning, 15*(6), 16.

Pinel, J. P. J. (1993). *Biopsychology* (2nd ed.). Boston: Allyn and Bacon.

Pinnell, G. S., DeFord, D. E., Lyons, C. A., and Bryk, A. (1995). Response to Rasinski. *Reading Research Quarterly, 30,* 272–275.

Pinnell, G. S., Fried, M. D., and Estice, R. M. (1990). Reading Recovery: Learning how to make a difference. *The Reading Teacher, 43,* 282–295.

Pinnell, G. S., Lyons, C. A., DeFord, D. E., Bryk, A. S., and Seltzer, M. (1994). Comparing instructional models for the literacy education of high-risk first graders. *Reading Research Quarterly, 29,* 8–39.

Platt, J. J., and Spivack, G. (1972). Social competence and effective problem solving thinking in psychiatric patients. *Journal of Clinical Psychiatry, 28,* 3–5.

Polloway, E., Epstein, M., Polloway, C., Patton, J., and Ball, D. (1986). Corrective reading program: An analysis of effectiveness with learning disabled and mentally retarded students. *Remedial and Special Education, 7,* 41–47.

Premack, D. (1959). Toward empirical behavior laws. *Psychological Review, 66*(4), 219–233.

Pressley, M., Brown, R., El-Dinary, P. B., and Afflerbach, P. (1995). The comprehension instruction that students need: Instruction fostering constructively responsive reading. *Learning Disabilities Research and Practice, 10,* 215–224.

Price, G. (1994). *Effectiveness of use of portable computers with severe specific learning disabilities or dyslexia* (Occasional Papers 26). Southampton, Eng.: Southampton University, Centre for Language Education.

Prickett, E., Higgins, K., and Boone, R. (1994). Technology for learning . . . Not learning about technology. *Teaching Exceptional Children, 26*(4), 56–60.

Prillaman, D. (1981). Acceptance of learning disabled students in the mainstream environment: A failure to replicate. *Journal of Learning Disabilities, 14,* 344–346.

Prutting, C. (1982). Pragmatics as social competence. *Journal of Speech and Hearing Disorders, 47,* 123–124.

Pugach, M. C., and Johnson, L. J. (1995). *Collaborative practitioners, collaborative schools.* Denver, Colo.: Love.

Purkey, S. C., and Smith, M. S. (1985). School reform: The district policy implications of the effective schools literature. *Elementary School Journal, 85,* 353–389.

Putnam, M. L. (1992a). The testing practices of mainstream secondary classroom teachers. *Remedial and Special Education, 13*(5), 11–21.

Putnam, M. L. (1992b). Characteristics of questions on tests administered by mainstream secondary classrooms teachers. *Learning Disabilities Research and Practice, 7,* 129–136.

Putnam, M. L., Deshler, D. D., and Schumaker, J. S. (1993). The investigation of setting demands: A missing link in learning strategy instruction. In L. S. Meltzer (Ed.), *Strategy assessment and instruction for students with learning disabilities* (pp. 325–354). Austin, Tex.: Pro-Ed.

Radencich, M. C., Beers, P. C., and Schumm, J. S. (1993). *A handbook for the K-12 reading resource specialist.* Boston: Allyn and Bacon.

Raines, S. C., and Canady, R. J. (1991). *More story stretchers: More activities to expand children's favorite books.* Mt. Rainier, Md.: Gryphon House.

Raphael, T. E. (1982). Question-answering strategies for children. *The Reading Teacher, 36,* 188.

Raphael, T. E. (1984). Teaching learners about sources of information for answering comprehension questions. *Journal of Reading, 27,* 303–311.

Raphael, T. E. (1986). Teaching question-answer relationships revisited. *The Reading Teacher, 39*(6), 516–523.

Raphael, T. E., and Pearson, P. D. (1982). *The effect of metacognitive awareness training on children's question-answering behavior* (Tech. Rep. No. 238). Urbana: University of Illinois, Center for Study of Reading.

Rashotte, C. A., and Torgesen, J. K. (1985). Repeated reading and reading fluency in learning disabled children. *Reading Research Quarterly, 20*(2), 180–188.

Raskind, M. (1993). Assistive technology and adults with learning disabilities: A blueprint for exploration and advancement. *Learning Disability Quarterly, 16,* 185–196.

Raskind, M., and Higgins, E. (1995). Effects of speech synthesis on the proofreading efficiency of postsecondary students with learning disabilities. *Learning Disability Quarterly, 18,* 141–158.

Rasinski, T. V. (1990). Investigating measures of reading fluency. *Educational Research Quarterly, 14*(3), 37–44.

Readence, J. E., Bean, T. W., and Baldwin, R. S. (1995). *Content area reading: An integrated approach* (5th ed.). Dubuque, Iowa: Kendall/Hunt.

Reed, A. J. S. (1994). *Comics to classics: A parent's guide to books for teens and preteens.* Newark, Del.: International Reading Association.

Reed, V. A. (1994). *An introduction to children with language disorders* (2nd ed.). New York: Macmillan.

Renik, M. J. (April 1987). *Measuring the relationship between academic self-perceptions and global self-worth: The self-perception profile for learning disabled students.* Presented at the Society for Research in Child Development, Baltimore, Md.

Reutzel, D. R., Hollingsworth, P. M., and Eldredge, J. L. (1994). Oral reading instruction: The impact on student reading development. *Reading Research Quarterly, 29,* 40–59.

Reyes, E. I., and Bos, C. S. (in press). Interactive semantic mapping and charting: Enhancing content area learning for language minority students. In R. Gersten and R. Jimenez (Eds.), *Innovative practices for language minority students.* Pacific Grove, Calif.: Brooks/Cole.

Reyes, E. I., Duran, G. Z., and Bos, C. S. (1989). Language as a resource for mediating comprehension. In S. McCormick and J. Zutell (Eds.), *Cognitive and social perspectives for literacy research and instruction* (Thirty-eighth yearbook of the National Reading Conference, pp. 253–260). Chicago, Ill.: National Reading Conference.

Rhodes, L. K. (1979). Comprehension and predictability: An analysis of beginning reading materials. In J. C. Harste and R. Carey (Eds.), *New perspectives on comprehension.* Bloomington: Indiana University, School of Education.

Rhodes, L. K. (1981). I can read! Predictable books as resources for reading and writing instruction. *The Reading Teacher, 34,* 511–518.

Rhodes, L. K., and Dudley-Marling, C. (1996). *Readers and writers with a difference* (2nd ed.). Portsmouth, N.H.: Heinemann.

Richards, G. P., Samuels, S. J., Turnuree, J., and Ysseldyke, J. (1990). Sustained and selective attention in children with learning disabilities. *Journal of Learning Disabilities, 23,* 129–136.

Richardson, J. E. (1971). *The linguistic readers.* New York: Benziger.

Richgels, D. J., Poremba, K. J., and McGee, L. M. (1996). Kindergartners talk about print: Phonemic awareness in meaningful contexts. *The Reading Teacher, 49,* 632–642.

Ridley, C. A., and Vaughn, S. R. (1982). Interpersonal problem solving: An intervention program for preschool children. *Journal of Applied Developmental Psychology, 3,* 177–190.

Rivera, D. P., and Smith, D. D. (1997). *Teaching students with learning and behavior problems* (3rd ed.). Boston: Allyn and Bacon.

Robb, L. (1996). *Reading strategies that work: Teaching your students to become better readers.* New York: Scholastic.

Roberts, G. H. (1968). The failure strategies of third grade arithmetic pupils. *The Arithmetic Teacher, 15,* 442–446.

Roberts, J., and Crais, E. (1989). Assessing communication skills. In D. Bailey and M. Wolery (Eds.), *Assessing infants and preschoolers with handicaps* (pp. 337–389). New York: Macmillan.

Robinett, R. F., Bell, P. W., and Rojas, P. M. (1970). *Miami linguistic readers.* Lexington, Mass.: D. C. Heath.

Robinson, F. P. (1946). *Effective study.* New York: Harper and Brothers.

Rooney, K. J., and Hallahan, D. P. (1985). Future directions for cognitive behavior modification research: The quest for cognitive change. *Remedial and Special Education, 6*(2), 46–51.

Rooney, K. J., and Hallahan, D. P. (1988). The effects of self-monitoring on adult behavior and student independence. *Learning Disabilities Research, 3,* 88–93.

Roser, N. L., Hoffman, J. V., and Farest, C. (1990). Language, literature, and at-risk children. *The Reading Teacher, 43,* 554–559.

Rothman, H. R., and Casden, M. (1995). The relationship between self-perception of a learning disability and achievement, self-concept and social support. *Learning Disability Quarterly, 18,* 203–212.

Rottman, T. R., and Cross, D. R. (1990). Using informed strategies for learning to enhance the reading and thinking skills of children with learning disabilities. *Journal of Learning Disabilities, 23,* 270–278.

Rourke, B. P. (1993). Arithmetic disabilities, specific and otherwise: A neuropsychological perspective. *Journal of Learning Disabilities, 26*(4), 214–226.

Rourke, B. P., Young, G. C., and Leenaars, A. A. (1989). A childhood learning disability that predisposes those afflicted to adolescent and adult depression and suicide risk. *Journal of Learning Disabilities, 22*(3), 169–175.

Routh, D. K. (1979). Activity, attention, and aggression in learning disabled children. *Journal of Clinical Child Psychology, 8,* 183–187.

Rubin, H. (1988). Morphological knowledge and early writing ability. *Language and Speech, 31,* 337–355.

Rubin, H., Patterson, P. A., and Kantor, M. (1991). Morphological development and writing ability in children and adults. *Language, Speech, and Hearing Services in School, 22,* 228–235.

Rude, R. T., and Oehlkers, W. J. (1984). *Helping students with reading problems.* Englewood Cliffs, N.J.: Prentice-hall.

Ruedy, L. R. (1983). Handwriting instruction: It can be part of the high school curriculum. *Academic Therapy, 18*(4), 421–429.

Ruhl, K. L., Hughes, C. A., and Gajar, A. H. (1990). Efficacy of the pause procedure for enhancing learning disabled and nondisabled college students' long- and short-term recall of facts presented through lecture. *Learning Disability Quarterly, 13,* 55–64.

Ruhl, K. L., Hughes, C. A., and Schlos, P. J. (1987). Using the pause procedure to enhance lecture recall. *Teacher Education and Special Education, 10,* 14–18.

Ruiz, N. T. (1989). An optimal learning environment for Rosemary. *Exceptional Children, 56,* 130–144.

Ruiz, N. T., and Figueroa, R. A. (1995). Learning-handicapped classrooms with Latino students: The optimal learning environment (OLE) project. *Education and Urban Society, 27,* 463–483.

Ruiz, N. T, Figueroa, R. A., and Boothroyd, M. (1995). Bilingual special education teacher's shifting paradigms: Complex responses to educational reform. *Journal of Learning Disabilities, 28,* 622–635.

Ruiz, N. T., Garcia, E., and Figueroa, R. A. (1996). *The OLE curriculum guide: Creating optimal learning environments for students from diverse backgrounds in special and general education.* Sacramento, Calif.: Specialized Program Branch, California Department of Education.

Rumelhart, D. E. (1977). *Introduction to human information processing.* New York: John Wiley.

Rumelhart, D. E. (1980). Schemata: The building blocks of cognition. In R. J. Spiro, B. C. Bruce, and W. F. Brewer (Eds.), *Theoretical issues in reading comprehension.* Hillsdale, N.J.: Erlbaum, pp. 33–58.

Rumelhart, D. E. (1985). Toward an interactive model of reading. In H. Singer and R. B. Ruddell (Eds.), *Theoretical models and processes of reading* (3rd ed.). Newark, Del.: International Reading Association.

Ryder, R., and Hughes, T. (1997). *Internet for educators.* Upper Saddle River, N.J.: Prentice Hall.

Salend, S. J. (1994). *Effective mainstreaming: Creating inclusive classrooms* (2nd ed). New York: Macmillan.

Salend, S. J., Jantzen, N. R., and Giek, K. (1992). Using a peer confrontation system in a group setting. *Behavioral Disorders, 17,* 211–218.

Salend, S. J., and Lutz, J. G. (1984). Mainstreaming or mainlining: A competency based approach to mainstreaming. *Journal of Learning Disabilities, 17*(1), 27–29.

Salvador, R. (1996). News and resources. *Electronic Learning, 15*(4), 8–10.

Samuels, S. J. (1979). The method of repeated readings. *The Reading Teacher, 32,* 403–408.

Samuels, S. J. (1987). Information processing abilities and reading. *Journal of Learning Disabilities, 20*(1), 18–22.

Sanger, D., Maag, J. W., and Shapera, N. R. (1994). Language problems among students with emotional and behavioral disorders. *Intervention in School and Clinic, 30,* 103–108.

Saunders, W., Goldenberg, C., and Hamann, J. (1992). Instructional conversation begets instructional conversation. *Teaching and Teacher Education, 8,* 199–218.

Sawyer, V., Nelson, J. S., Jayanthi, M., Bursuck, W., and Epstein, M. H. (1996). Views of students with learning disabilities of their homework in general education classes: Student interviews. *Learning Disability Quarterly, 19,* 70–85.

Scanlon, D. J., and Anders, P. L. (December, 1988). *Conceptual complexity and considerateness of vocation textbooks.* Paper presented at the annual meeting of the National Reading Conference, Tucson, Ariz.

Scanlon, D., Deshler, D. D., and Schumaker, J. B. (1996). Can a strategy be taught and learned in secondary inclusive classrooms? *Learning Disabilities Research and Practice, 11,* 41–57.

Scanlon, D. J., Duran, G. Z., Reyes, E. I., and Gallego, M. A. (1992). Interactive semantic mapping: An interactive approach to enhancing LD students' content area comprehension. *Learning Disabilities Research and Practice, 7,* 142–146.

Schank, R. C., and Abelson, R. (1977). *Scripts, plans, goals, and understanding.* Hillsdale, N.J.: Erlbaum.

Scheuermann, B., Jacobs, W. R., McCall, C., and Knies, W. C. (1994). The personal spelling dictionary: An adaptive approach to reducing the spelling hurdle in written language. *Intervention in School and Clinic, 29,* 292–299.

Schultz, J. B., and Turnbull, A. P. (1984). *Mainstreaming handicapped students: A guide for classroom teachers* (2nd ed.). Boston: Allyn and Bacon.

Schultz, T. (1974). Development of the appreciation of riddles. *Child Development, 45,* 100–105.

Schumaker, J. B., Denton, P. H., and Deshler, D. D. (1984). *The paraphrasing strategy (Learning Strategies Curriculum).* Lawrence: University of Kansas.

Schumaker, J. B., and Deshler, D. D. (1988). Implementing the regular education initiative in secondary schools: A different ball game. *Journal of Learning Disabilities, 21,* 36–42.

Schumaker, J. B., Deshler, D. D., Alley, G. R., and Warner, M. M. (1983). Toward the development of an intervention model for learning disabled adolescents: University of Kansas Institute. *Exceptional Education Quarterly, 4*(1), 45–74.

Schumaker, J. B., Deshler, D. D., Alley, G. R., Warner, M. M., and Denton, P. H. (1982). Multipass: A learning strategy for improving reading comprehension. *Learning Disability Quarterly, 5*(3), 295–304.

Schumaker, J. B., and Lyerla, K. D. (1991). *The paragraph writing strategy.* Lawrence, Kans.: Institute for Research in Learning Disabilities, University of Kansas.

Schumaker, J. B., Nolan, S. M., and Deshler, D. D. (1985). *The error monitoring strategy.* Lawrence, Kans.: Institute for Research in Learning Disabilities, University of Kansas.

Schumaker, J. D., Wildgen, J. S., and Sherman, J. A. (1982). Social interaction of learning disabled junior high school students in their regular classrooms: An observational analysis. *Journal of Learning Disabilities, 11,* 98–102.

Schumm, J. S., and Mangrum, C. T. (1991). FLIP: A framework for textbook thinking. *Journal of Reading, 35,* 120–124.

Schumm, J. S., and Strickler, K. (1991). Guidelines for adapting content area textbooks: Keeping teachers and students content. *Intervention in School and Clinic, 27,* 79–84.

Schumm, J. S. and Vaughn, S. (1991). Making adaptations for mainstreamed students: General classroom teachers' perspectives. *Remedial and Special Education, 12*(4), 18–27.

Schumm, J. S., and Vaughn, S. (1992). Planning for mainstreamed special education students: Perceptions of general classroom teachers. *Exceptionality, 3,* 81–98.

Schumm, J. S., and Vaughn, S. (1992). Reflections on planning for mainstreamed special education students. *Exceptionality, 3,* 121–126.

Schumm, J. S., and Vaughn, S. (1995). *Using Making Words in heterogeneous classrooms.* Miami: School Based Research, University of Miami, unpublished manuscript.

Schumm, J. S., Vaughn, S., Haager, D., McDowell, J., Rothlein, L., and Saumell, L. (1995). Teacher planning for individual student needs: What can mainstreamed special education students expect? *Exceptional Children, 61,* 335–352.

Schumm, J. S., Vaughn, S., and Harris, J. (in press). Collaborative planning for content area instruction. *Teaching Exceptional Children.*

Schumm, J. S., Vaughn, S., and Leavell, A. G. (1994). Planning pyramid: A framework for planning for diverse student needs during content area instruction. *The Reading Teacher, 47,* 608–615.

Schumm, J. S., Vaughn, S., Haager, D., McDowell, J., Rothlein, L., and Saumell, L. (1995). General education teacher planning: What can students with learning disabilities expect? *Exceptional Children, 61,* 335–352.

Schumm, J. S., Vaughn, S., and Saumell, L. (1992). What teachers do when the textbook is tough: Students speak out. *Journal of Reading Behavior, 24,* 481–503.

Schunk, D. H. (1989). Self-efficacy and cognitive achievement: Implications for students with learning problems. *Journal of Learning Disabilities, 22,* 14–22.

Schunk, D. H. (1996). Goal and self-evaluative influences during children's cognitive skill learning. *American Education Research Journal, 33,* 359–382.

Schuster, J. W., Stevens, K. B., and Doak, P. K. (1990). Using constant time delay to teach word definitions. *Journal of Special Education, 24,* 306–318.

Schwartz, S., and Doehring, D. (1977). A developmental study of children's ability to acquire knowledge of spelling patterns. *Developmental Psychology, 13,* 419–420.

Schwartz, S. E., and Budd, D. (1981). Mathematics for handicapped learners: A functional approach for adolescents. *Focus on Exceptional Children, 13*(7), 1–12.

Scott, C. M., and Stokes, S. L. (1995). Measures of syntax in school-age children and adolescents. *Language, Speech, and Hearing Services in Schools, 26,* 309–319.

Scruggs, T. E., and Mastropieri, M. A. (1988). Are learning disabled students "test-wise"?: A review of recent research. *Learning Disabilities Focus, 3,* 87–97.

Scruggs, T. E., and Mastropieri, M. A. (1989a). Mnemonic instruction of LD students: A field-based evaluation. *Learning Disability Quarterly, 12,* 119–125.

Scruggs, T. E., and Mastropieri, M. A. (1989b). Reconstructive elaborations: A model for content area learning. *American Educational Research Journal, 26,* 311–327.

Scruggs, T. E., and Richter, L. (1985). Tutoring learning disabled students: A critical review. *Learning Disability Quarterly, 8*(4), 286–298.

Seidel, J. F., and Vaughn, S. (1991). Social alienation and the LD school dropout. *Learning Disabilities Research and Practice, 6*(3), 152–157.

Seligman, M. E. P. (1975). *Helplessness: On depression, development, and death.* San Francisco: W. H. Freeman.

Shanahan, T., and Barr, R. (1995). Reading Recovery: An independent evaluation of the effects of an early instructional intervention for at-risk learners. *Reading Research Quarterly, 30,* 958–996.

Shannon, P., Kameenui, E., and Baumann, J. (1988). An investigation of children's ability to comprehend character motives. *American Educational Research Journal, 25,* 441–462.

Shany, M. T., and Biemiller, A. (1995). Assisted reading practice: Effects on performance for poor readers in Grades 3 and 4. *Reading Research Quarterly, 30,* 382–395.

Shapero, S., and Forbes, C. R. (1981). A review of involvement programs for parents of learning disabled children. *Journal of Learning Disabilities, 14*(9), 499–504.

Sharma, M. C. (1984). Mathematics in the real world. In J. F. Cawley (Ed.), *Developmental teaching of mathematics for learning disabled.* Rockville, Md.: Aspen.

Shaywitz, S., and Shaywitz, B. (1996, November). *State of the art: Functional MRI of the brain during reading.* Paper presented at the annual meeting of the Orton Dyslexia Society, Boston.

Sheras, P. L. (1983). Suicide in adolescence. In E. Walker and M. Roberts (Eds.), *Handbook of clinical child psychology.* New York: Wiley.

Shiah, R. L., Mastropieri, M. A., Scruggs, T. E., and Fulk, B. J. (1994). The effects of computer-assisted instruction on the mathematical problem solving of students with learning disabilities. *Exceptionality, 5,* 131–161.

Shipley, E., Maddox, M., and Driver, J. (1991). Children's development of irregular past tense verb forms. *Language, Speech, and Hearing Services in Schools, 22,* 115–122.

Shipley, K. B., and Banis, C. J. (1981). *Teaching morphology developmentally.* Tucson, Ariz.: Communication Skill Builders.

Short, K. G., and Burke, C. (1991). *Creating curriculum: Teachers and students as a community of learners.* Portsmouth, N.H.: Heinemann.

Short, K. G., Harste, J. C., with Burke, C. (1995). *Creating classrooms for authors and inquirers.* Portsmouth, N.H.: Heinemann.

Short, K. G., and Pierce, K. M. (Eds.). (1990). *Talking about books.* Portsmouth, N.H.: Heinemann.

Shure, M. B., and Spivack, G. (1978). *Problem solving techniques in child-rearing.* San Francisco: Jossey Bass.

Shure, M. B., and Spivack, G. (1979). Interpersonal cognitive problem solving and primary prevention: Programming for preschool and kindergarten children. *Journal of Clinical Child Psychology, 8,* 89–94.

Shure, M. B., and Spivack, G. (1980). Interpersonal problem solving as a mediator of behavioral adjustment in preschool and kindergarten children. *Journal of Applied Developmental Psychology, 1,* 29–44.

Sileo, T. W., Sileo, A. P., and Prater, M. A. (1996). Parent and professional partnerships in special education: Multicultural considerations. *Intervention in School and Clinic, 31*(3), 145–153.

Simeonsson, R. J., and Simeonsson, N. E. (1993). Children, families and disability: Psychological dimensions. In. J. L. Paul and R. J. Simeonsson (Eds.), *Children with special needs* (pp. 25–50). Orlando, Fla.: Harcourt, Brace, Jovanovich.

Simmonds, E. P. M. (1992). The effects of teacher training and implementation of two methods for improving the comprehension skills of students with learning disabilities. *Learning Disabilities Research and Practice, 7,* 194–198.

Simon, C. S. (Ed.) (1985). *Communication skills and classroom success: Assessment of language-learning disabled students.* San Diego, Calif.: College-Hill.

Simpson, R. L. (1982). *Conferencing parents of exceptional children.* Rockville, Md.: Aspen.

Simpson, R. L. (1988). Needs of parents and families whose children have learning and behavior problems. *Behavioral Disorders, 14*(1), 40–47.

Singer, H., and Donlan, D. (1989). *Reading and learning from text* (2nd ed.). Hillsdale, N.J.: Erlbaum.

Siperstein, G. N., Bopp, M. J., and Bak, J. J. (1978). Social status of learning disabled children. *Journal of Learning Disabilities, 11,* 217–228.

Siperstein, G. N., and Goding, M. J. (1985). Teachers' behavior toward learning disabled and non–learning disabled children: A strategy for change. *Journal of Learning Disabilities, 18,* 139–144.

Skutnabb-Kanagas, T. (1981, February). *Linguistic genocide and bilingual education.* Paper presented at the California Association for Bilingual Education, Anaheim, Calif.

Slavin, R. E. (1984). Team assisted individualization: Cooperative learning and individualized instruction in the mainstreamed classroom. *Remedial and Special Education, 5*(6), 33–42.

Slavin, R. E. (1987). Cooperative learning: Where behavioral and humanistic approaches to classroom motivation meet. *Elementary School Journal, 88,* 29–37.

Slavin, R. E. (1991). Synthesis of research on cooperative learning. *Educational Leadership, 48*(5), 71–82.

Slavin, R. E., Stevens, R. J., and Madden, N. A. (1988). Accommodating student diversity in reading and writing instruction: A cooperative learning approach. *Remedial and Special Education, 9*(1), 60–66.

Slingerland, B. H. (1971). *A multi-sensory approach to language arts for specific language disability children* (Book 1). Cambridge, Mass.: Educators Publishing Service.

Slingerland, B. H. (1976). *A multi-sensory approach to language arts for specific language disability children* (Book 2). Cambridge, Mass.: Educators Publishing Service.

Slingerland, B. H. (1981). *A multi-sensory approach to language arts for specific language disability children* (Book 3). Cambridge, Mass.: Educators Publishing Service.

Sloan, G. D. (1984). *The child as critic* (2nd ed.). New York: Teachers College Press.

Smith, D. D., and Lovitt, T. C. (1982). *The computational arithmetic program.* Austin, Tex.: Pro-Ed.

Smith, E. M., and Alley, G. R. (1981). The effect of teaching sixth graders with learning difficulties a strategy for solving verbal math problems (Research Report No. 39). Institute for Research in Learning Disabilities.

Smith, F. (1978). *Understanding reading* (2nd ed.). New York: Holt, Rinehart and Winston.

Smith, F. (1988). *Understanding reading* (4th ed.). New York: Holt, Rinehart and Winston.

Smith, F., and Goodman, K. S. (1971). On the psycholinguistic method of teaching reading. *Elementary School Journal, 71,* 177–181.

Sobol, M. P., Earn, B. M., Bennett, D., and Humphries, T. (1983). A categorical analysis of the social attributions of learning disabled children. *Journal of Abnormal Child Psychology, 11*(2), 217–228.

Spalding, R. B., and Spalding, W. T. (1990). *The writing road to reading.* New York: William Morrow.

Spangenberg-Urbschat, K., and Pritchard, R. (1994). *Kids come in all languages: Reading instruction for ESL students.* Newark, Del.: International Reading Association.

Spargo, E., Williston, G. R., and Browning, L. (1980). *Time readings: Book one.* Providence, R.I.: Jamestown Publishers.

Spear-Swerling, L., Sternberg, R. J. (1996). *Off Track: When poor readers become "Learning Disabled".* Boulder, Colo.: Westview Press.

Spector, J. E. (1995). Phonemic awareness training: Applications of principles of direct instruction. *Reading and Writing Quarterly: Overcoming Learning Difficulties, 11,* 37–51.

Sperling, G. A. (1960). The information available in brief visual presentation. *Psychological Monographs, 74,* whole no. 498.

Spiegel, D. L. (1995). A comparison of traditional remedial programs and Reading Recovery: Guidelines for success for all programs. *The Reading Teacher, 49,* 86–96.

Spiro, R. J. (1980). Constructive processes in prose comprehension and recall. In R. J. Spiro, B. C. Bruce, and W. F. Brewer (Eds.), *Theoretical issues in reading comprehension.* Hillsdale, N.J.: Erlbaum, pp. 245–276.

Spivack, G., Platt, J. J., and Shure, M. B. (1976). *The problem solving approach to adjustment: A guide to research and intervention.* San Francisco: Jossey Bass.

Stahl, S. A., Hare, V. C., Sinatra, R., and Gregory, J. F. (1991). Defining the role of prior knowledge and vocabulary in reading comprehension: The retiring of number 41. *Journal of Reading Behavior, 23,* 487–508.

Stahl, S. A., Jacobson, M. G., Davis, C. E., and Davis, R. L. (1989). Prior knowledge and difficult vocabulary in the comprehension of unfamiliar text. *Reading Research Quarterly, 24,* 27–43.

Stahl, S. A., and Miller, P. D. (1989). Whole language and language experience approaches for beginning reading: A quantitative research synthesis. *Review of Educational Research, 59,* 87–116.

Stainback, S., and Stainback, W. (1992). *Curriculum consideration in inclusive classrooms: Facilitating learning for all students.* Baltimore: Brooks.

Stallings, J. (1975). Relationships between classroom instructional practices and child development (Rep. No. PLEDE-

C-75). Menlo Park, Calif.: Stanford Research Institute. ERIC Document Reproduction Service No. ED 110 200.

Stallings, J. S., and Kaskowitz, D. H. (1974). *Follow through classroom observation evaluation.* Menlo Park, Calif.: Stanford Research Institute.

Stanovich, K. (1986). Cognitive processes and the reading problems of learning-disabled children: Evaluating the assumption of specificity. In J. K. Torgesen and B. Y. L. Wong (Eds.), *Psychological and educational perspectives on learning disabilities.* Orlando, Fla.: Academic Press, pp. 85–131.

Stauffer, R. G. (1969). *Directing reading maturity as a cognitive process.* New York: Harper and Row.

Stauffer, R. G. (1970). *The language-experience approach to the teaching of reading.* New York: Harper and Row.

Stauffer, R. G. (1976). *Teaching reading as a thinking process.* New York: Harper and Row.

Stein, N. L., and Glenn, C. G. (1979). An analysis of story comprehension in elementary school children. In R. O. Freedle (Ed.), *New directions in discourse processing* (Vol. II). Norwood, N.J.: Ablex, pp. 53–120.

Stephens, T. (1977). *Teaching skills to children with learning and behavior problems.* Columbus, Ohio: Merrill.

Stern, C. (1965). *Structural arithmetic.* Boston: Houghton Mifflin.

Stevens, K. B., and Schuster, J. W. (1987). Effects of a constant time delay procedure on the written spelling performance of a learning disabled student. *Learning Disability Quarterly, 10,* 9–16.

Stevens, K. B., and Schuster, J. W. (1988). Time delay: Systematic instruction for academic tasks. *Remedial and Special Education, 9*(5), 16–21.

Stires, S. (1983). Read audiences and contexts for LD writers. *Academic Therapy, 18*(5), 561–568.

Stires, S. (Ed.) (1991). *With promise: Redefining reading and writing for "special students."* Portsmouth, N.H.: Heinemann.

Stokes, T. F., and Baer, D. M. (1977). An implicit technology of generalization. *Journal of Applied Behavior Analysis, 10,* 349–367.

Stone, W. C., and LaGreca, A. M. (1984). Comprehension of non-verbal communication: A reexamination of the social competencies of learning disabled children. *Journal of Abnormal Child Psychology, 12*(4), 505–518.

Stone, W. L., and LaGreca, A. M. (1990). The social status of children with learning disabilities: A reexamination. *Journal of Learning Disabilities, 23* (1), 32–37.

Stratton, B. D., Grindler, M. C., and Postell, C. M. (1992). Discovering oneself. *Middle School Journal, 24,* 42–43.

Strickland, B. B., and Turnbull, A. P. (1990). *Developing and implementing individual education programs* (3rd ed.). Columbus, Ohio: Merrill.

Sullivan, P., (1992). *ESL in context.* New York: Corwin Press.

Sulzby, E., and Teale, W. H. (1991). Emergent literacy. In R. Barr, M. L. Kamil, P. B. Mosenthal, and P. D. Pearson (Eds.), *Handbook of reading research* (2nd ed, pp. 727–757). New York: Longman.

Sulzer-Azaroff, B., and Mayer, G. R. (1991). *Behavior analysis for lasting change.* Fort Worth, Tex.: Holt, Rinehart and Winston.

Sundbye, N. (1987). Text explicitness and inferential questioning: Effects on story understanding and recall. *Reading Research Quarterly, 22,* 82–98.

Suritsky, S. K., and Hughes, C. A. (1996). Notetaking strategy instruction. In D. D. Deshler, E. S. Ellis, and B. K. Lenz (Authors), *Teaching adolescents with learning disabilities* (2nd ed., p. 267–312). Denver: Love.

Suydam, M. N. (1982). The use of calculators in precollege education: Fifth annual state-of-the-art review. Columbus, Ohio: Calculator Information Center. (ERIC Document Reproduction Service no. ED206454.).

Suydam, M. N., and Weaver, J. F. (1977). Research on problem solving: Implications for elementary-school classrooms. *Arithmetic Teacher, 25,* 40–42.

Swank, L. K., and Catts, H. W. (1994). Phonological awareness and written word decoding. *Language, Speech, and Hearing Services in Schools, 25,* 9–14.

Swafford, K. M., and Reed, V. A. (1986). Language and learning-disabled children. In V. A. Reed (Ed.), *An introduction to children with language disorders.* New York: Macmillan, pp. 105–128.

Swanson, H. L. (1985). Verbal coding deficits in learning disabled readers. In S. J. Ceci (Ed.), *Handbook of cognitive, social and neuropsychological aspects of learning disabilities* (Vol. 1). Hillsdale, N.J.: Erlbaum, pp. 203–228.

Swanson, H. L. (1987). Information processing theory and learning disabilities: An overview. *Journal of Learning Disabilities, 20*(1), 3–7.

Swanson, H. L. (1991). Learning disabilities, distinctive encoding, and hemispheric resources: An information-processing perspective. In J. E. Obrzut and G. W. Hynd (Eds.), *Neuropsychological foundations of learning disabilities.* San Diego: Academic Press, pp. 241–280.

Swanson, H. L. (1996). Information processing: An introduction. In D. K. Reid, W. P. Hresko, and H. L. Swanson (Eds.), *Cognitive approaches to learning disabilities* (3rd ed., pp. 251–286). Austin, Tex.: Pro-Ed.

Swanson, H. L., and Cooney, J. B. (1991). Learning disabilities and memory. In B. Wong (Ed.), *Learning about learning disabilities* (pp. 103–127). San Diego: Academic Press.

Swanson, H. L., and Cooney, J. B. (1996). Learning disabilities and memory. In D. K. Reid, W. P. Hresko, and H. L. Swanson (Eds.), *Cognitive approaches to learning disabilities* (3rd ed., pp. 287–315). Austin, Tex.: Pro-Ed.

Swanson, H. L., and Trahan, M. F. (1992). Learning disabled readers' comprehension of computer mediated text: The influence of working memory, metacognition, and attribution. *Learning Disabilities Research and Practice, 7,* 74–86.

Swanson, M., McBurnett, K., Wigal, T., Pfiffner, L., Lerner, M., Williams, L., Christian, D., Tamm. L., Willcutt, E., Crowley, K., Clevenger, W., Khouzam, N., Woo, C., Crinella, F., and Fisher, T. (1993). Effect of stimulant medication on children with attention deficit disorder: A "review of reviews." *Exceptional Children, 60,* 154–162.

Tancock, S. M. (1994). A literacy lesson framework for children with reading problems. *The Reading Teacher, 48,* 130–140.

Tangel, D. M., and Blachman, B. A. (1992). Effect of phoneme awareness instruction on kindergarten children's invented spelling. *Journal of Reading Behavior, 24,* 233–261.

Tangel, D. M. and Blachman, B. A. (1995). Effect of phoneme awareness instruction on the invented spelling of first-grade children: A one-year follow-up. *Journal of Reading Behavior, 27,* 153–185.

Tarver, S. G., Hallahan, D. P., Kauffman, J. M., and Ball, D. W. (1976). Verbal rehearsal and selective attention in children with learning disabilities: A development lag. *Journal of Experimental Child Psychology, 22,* 375–385.

Taylor, R. (1980). *The computer in the school: Tutor, tool, tutee.* New York: Teachers College Press.

Teicher, J. D. (1973). A solution to the chronic problem of living: Adolescent attempted suicide. In J. C. Schoolar (Ed.), *Current issues in adolescent psychiatry* (pp. 129–147). New York: Brunner/Mazel.

Tharp, R. G., and Gallimore, R. (1988). *Rousing minds to life: Teaching, learning, and schooling in social context.* New York: Cambridge University Press.

Thomas, A. (1979). Learned helplessness and expectancy factors: Implications for research in learning disabilities. *Review of Education Research, 49*(2), 208–221.

Thomas, K. (1978). The directed inquiry activity: An instructional procedure for content reading. *Reading Improvement, 15,* 138–140.

Thompkins, G. E., and Friend, M. (1986). On your mark, get set, write! *Teaching Exceptional Children, 18*(2), 82–89.

Thompson, M. (1977). *The effects of spelling pattern training on the spelling behavior of primary elementary students.* Unpublished doctoral dissertation, University of Pittsburgh.

Thornton, C. A. (1978). Emphasizing thinking strategies in basic fact instruction. *Journal for Research in Mathematics Education,* 215–227.

Thornton, C. A., and Toohey, M. A. (1985). Basic math facts; Guidelines for teaching and learning. *Learning Disabilities Focus, 1*(1), 44–57.

Thornton, C. A., Tucker, B. F., Dossey, J. A., and Bazik, E. F. (1983). *Teaching mathematics to children with special needs.* Menlo Park, Calif.: Addison-Wesley.

Thorpe, H. W., and Borden, K. F. (1985). The effect of multisensory instruction upon the on-task behavior and word reading accuracy of learning disabled students. *Journal of Learning Disabilities, 18,* 279–286.

Tierney, R. J., Carter, M. A., and Desai, L. E. (1991). *Portfolio assessment in the reading-writing classroom.* Norwood, Mass.: Christopher-Gordon.

Tierney, R. J., Readence, J. E., and Dishner, E. K. (1980). *Reading strategies and practices: Guide for improving instruction.* Boston: Allyn and Bacon.

Tierney, R. J., Readence, J. E., and Dishner, E. K. (1995). *Reading strategies and practices: A compendium* (4th ed.). Boston: Allyn and Bacon.

Tikunoff, W. J. (1983). *Compatibility of the SBIF features with other research instruction of LEP students.* San Francisco: Far West Laboratory.

Tindal, G., and Nolet, V. (1996). Serving students in middle school content classes: A heuristic study of critical variables linking instruction and assessment. *Journal of Special Education, 29,* 414–432.

Tindal, G. A., and Marston, D. B. (1990). *Classroom-based assessment: Evaluating instructional outcomes.* New York: Merrill/Macmillan.

Tobias, S. (1978). Achievement treatment interactions. *Review of Educational Research, 46,* 61–74.

Tollefson, N., Tracy, D. B., Johnen, E. P. Buenning, M., and Farmer, A. (1981). *Implementing goal setting activities with LD adolescents* (Res. Rep. No. 48). Lawrence, Kans.: The University of Kansas Institute for Research in Learning Disabilities.

Tompkins, G. E., and McGee, L. M. (1993). *Teaching reading with literature: Case studies to action plans.* New York: Merrill/Macmillan.

Toolan, J. M. (1981). Depression and suicide in children: An overview. *American Journal of Psychotherapy, 35*(3), 311–323.

Torgesen, J. K. (1978). Performance of reading disabled children on serial memory tasks: A review. *Reading Research Quarterly, 19,* 57–87.

Torgesen, J. K. (1982). The learning disabled child as an inactive learner: Educational implications. *Topics in Learning and Learning Disabilities, 2*(1), 45–52.

Torgesen, J. K. (1985). Memory processes in reading disabled children. *Journal of Learning Disabilities, 18*(6), 350–357.

Torgesen, J. K. (in press). The prevention and remediation of reading: Evaluating what we know from research. *Journal of Academic Language Therapy.*

Torgesen, J. K., and Barker, T. A. (1995). Computers as aids in the prevention and remediation of reading disabilities. *Learning Disability Quarterly, 18,* 76–88.

Torgesen, J. K., and Horen, N. M. (1992). Using computers to assist in reading instruction for children with learning disabilities. In S. A. Vogel (Ed.), *Educational alternative for students with learning disabilities.* New York: Springer-Verlag, pp. 159–181.

Torgesen, J. K., and Licht, B. G. (1983). The learning disabled child as an inactive learner: Retrospect and prospects. In J. D. McKinney and L. Feagans (Eds.), *Current topics in learning disabilities.* Norwood, N.J.: Ablex.

Torgesen, J. K., Rashotte, C. A., Greenstein, J., Houck, G., and Portes, P. (1987). Academic difficulties of learning disabled children who perform poorly on memory span tasks. In H. L. Swanson (Ed.), *Advances in learning and behavioral disabilities* (Supplement 2). Greenwich, Conn.: JAI Press, pp. 305–333.

Torgesen, J. K., Wagner, R. K., and Rashotte, C. A. (1994). Longitudinal studies of phonological processing and reading. *Journal of Learning Disabilities 19,* 623–630.

Towell, J., and Wink, J. (1993). *Strategies for monolingual teachers in multilingual classrooms.* Turlock, Calif.: California State University, Stanislaus. (ERIC Document Reproduction Service No. ED 359 797)

Townsend, M. A. R., and Clarihew, A. (1989). Facilitating children's comprehension through the use of advance organizers. *Journal of Reading Behavior, 21,* 15–36.

Trachtenburg, P., and Ferrugia, A. (1989). Big books from little voices: Reaching high risk beginning readers. *The Reading Teacher, 42,* 284–289.

Tralli, R., Colombo, B., Deshler, D., and Schumaker, J. B. (1996) The strategies intervention model: A model for supported inclusion at the secondary level. *Remedial and Special Education, 17,* 204–216.

Traub, N., and Bloom, F. (1970). *Recipe for reading.* Cambridge, Mass.: Educators Publishing Service.

Trelease, J. (1989). Jim Trelease speaks on reading aloud to children. *The Reading Teacher, 43,* 200–206.

Trelease, J. (1995). *The new read-aloud handbook* (4th ed.). New York: Penguin.

Tunnell, M. O., and Jacobs, J. S. (1989). Using "real" books: Research findings on literature based reading instruction. *The Reading Teacher, 42,* 470–477.

Turnbull, A. P., and Turnbull, H. R. (1990). *Families, professionals, and exceptionality: A special partnership* (2nd ed.). Columbus, Ohio: Merrill.

Turnbull, H. R., Turnbull, A. P., and Wheat, M. J. (1982). Assumptions about parental participation: A legislative history. *Exceptional Education Quarterly, 3*(2), 1–8.

Utley, B. L., Zigmond, M., and Strain, P. S. (1987). How various forms of data affect teacher analysis of student performance. *Exceptional Children 53*(5), 411–422.

Vacca, R. T., and Vacca, J. L. (1996). *Content area reading* (4th ed.). Glenview, Ill.: Scott, Foresman and Company.

Vandergrift, K. (1980). *Child and story.* New York: Neal-Schuman.

Van Reusen, A. K., and Bos, C. S. (1990). I PLAN: Helping students communicate in planning conferences. *Teaching Exceptional Children, 22,* 30–32.

Van Reusen, A. K., and Bos, C. S. (in press). *A goal-monitoring strategy.* Lawrence, Kans.: Edge Enterprises.

Van Reusen, A. K., Bos, C. S., Schumaker, J. B., and Deshler, D. D. (1994). *The self-advocacy strategy for education and transition planning.* Lawrence, Kans.: Edge Enterprises.

Vaughn, S. R. (1985). Why teach social skills to learning disabled students? *Journal of Learning Disabilities, 18*(10), 588–591.

Vaughn, S. R. (1987). TLC—Teaching, learning, and caring: Teaching interpersonal problem solving skills to emotionally disturbed adolescents. *Pointer, 31,* 25–30.

Vaughn, S. R., and Bos, C. S. (1987). Knowledge and perception of the resource room. The students' perspective. *Journal of Learning Disabilities, 20,* 218–223.

Vaughn, S. R., Bos, C. S., Harrell, J., and Lasky, B. (1988). Parent participation in the initial placement /IEP conference ten years after mandated involvement. *Journal of Learning Disabilities, 21* 82–89.

Vaughn, S., Bos, C. S., and Lund, K. A. (1986) . . . . But they can do it in my room: Strategies for promoting generalization. *Teaching Exceptional Children, 18,* 176–180.

Vaughn, S., Bos, C. S., and Schumm, J. S. (1997). *Teaching mainstreamed, diverse, and at-risk students in the general education classroom.* Boston: Allyn and Bacon.

Vaughn, S., Cohen, J., Fournier, L., Gervasi, J., Levasseur, T., and Newton, S. (1984). Teaching interpersonal problem solving to behavior disordered adolescents. Paper presented at Council for Exceptional Children, Washington, D.C.

Vaughn, S., Elbaum, B. E., and Schumm, J. S. (in press). New research on inclusion: What are the social outcomes for students with learning Disabilities? *Exceptional Children.*

Vaughn, S., Haager, D., Hogan, A., and Kouzekanani, K. (1992). Self-concept and peer acceptance in students with learning disabilities: A four to five year prospective study. *Journal of Educational Psychology, 84,* 43–50.

Vaughn, S., and Hogan, A. (1990). Social competence and learning disabilities: A prospective study. In H. L. Swanson and B. K. Keogh (Eds.), *Learning Disabilities: Theoretical and research issues.* Hillsdale, N.J.: Erlbaum, pp. 175–191.

Vaughn, S., Hogan, A., Kouzekanani, K., and Shapiro, S. (1990). Peer acceptance, self-perceptions, and social skills of LD students prior to identification. *Journal of Educational Psychology, 82*(1), 1–6.

Vaughn, S., Klingner, J. K., and Schumm, J. S. (1996). *Collaborative strategic reading.* Miami: School Based Research, University of Miami.

Vaughn, S., and LaGreca, A. M. (1992). Beyond greetings and making friends: Social skills from a broader perspective. In B. Y. L. Wong (Ed.), *Contemporary intervention research in learning disabilities: An international perspective.* New York: Springer-Verlag, pp. 96–114.

Vaughn, S., and Lancelotta, G. X. (1990). Teaching interpersonal skills to poorly accepted students: Peer-pairing versus non-peer-pairing. *Journal of School Psychology, 28,* 181–188.

Vaughn, S., Lancelotta, G. X., and Minnis, S. (1988). Social strategy training and peer involvement: Increasing peer acceptance of a female, LD student. *Learning Disabilities Focus, 4*(1), 32–37.

Vaughn, S. R., Levine, L., and Ridley, C. A. (1986). *PALS: Problem solving and affective learning strategies.* Chicago: Science Research Associates.

Vaughn, S., McIntosh, R., Schumm, J. S., Haager, D., and Callwood, D. (1993). Social status and peer acceptance revisited. *Learning Disabilities Research and Practice, 8,* 82–88.

Vaughn, S., McIntosh, R., and Spencer-Rowe, J. (1991). Peer rejection is a stubborn thing: Increasing peer acceptance of rejected students with learning disabilities. *Learning Disabilities Research and Practice, 6*(2), 83–88, 152–157.

Vaughn, S. R., Ridley, C. A., and Bullock, D. D. (1984). Interpersonal problem solving skills training with aggressive young children. *Journal of Applied Developmental Psychology, 5,* 213–223.

Vaughn, S. R., Ridley, C. A., and Cox, J. (1983). Evaluating the efficacy of an interpersonal skills training program with children who are mentally retarded. *Education and Training of the Mentally Retarded, 18*(3), 191–196.

Vaughn, S. and Schumm, J. S. (1994). Middle school teachers' planning for students with learning disabilities. *Remedial and Special Education, 15,* 152–161.

Vaughn, S., and Schumm, J. S. (1995). Responsible inclusion for students with learning disabilities. *Journal of Learning Disabilities, 28,* 264–270, 290.

Vaughn, S., and Schumm, J. S. (1996). Classroom ecologies: Classroom interactions and implications for inclusion of students with learning disabilities. In D. L. Speece and B. Keogh (Eds.), *Research on classroom ecologies: Implications for inclusion of children with learning disabilities* (pp. 107–124). Mahwah, N.J: Lawrence Erlbaum.

Vaughn, S., Schumm, J. S., Jallad, B., Slusher, J., and Saumell, L. (1996). Teachers' views of inclusion. *Learning Disabilities Research and Practice, 11,* 96–106.

Vaughn, S., Schumm, J. S., Klingner, J., and Saumell, L. (1995). Students' views of instructional practices: Implications for inclusion. *Learning Disability Quarterly, 18,* 236–248.

Vaughn, S., Schumm, J. S., and Kouzekanani, K. (1993). What do students with learning disabilities think when their general education teachers make adaptations? *Journal of Learning Disabilities, 26,* 545–555.

Vaughn, S., Schumm, J. S., Niarhos, F. J., and Gordon, J. (1993). Students' perceptions of two hypothetical teachers' instructional adaptations for low achievers. *Elementary School Journal, 94,* 87–102.

Vaughn, S., Schumm, J. S., Niarhos, F., and Daugherty, T. (1993). What do students think when teachers make adaptations? *Teaching and Teacher Education, 9,* 107–118.

Vaughn, S., Schumm, J. S., Niarhos, F., and Gordon, J. (1993). Students' perceptions of two hypothetical teachers' instructional adaptations for low achievers. *Elementary School Journal, 94,* 87–102.

Vaughn, S., Zaragoza, N., Hogan, A., and Walker (1993). A four year longitudinal investigation of the social skills and behavior problems of students with learning disabilities. *Journal of Learning Disabilities, 26,* 353–424.

Veatch, J. (1991). *Whole language and its predecessors: Commentary.* Paper presented at the annual meeting of the College Reading Association. ERIC Document 341–035

Vellutino, F. R., and Scanlon, D. M. (1987). Phonological coding, phonological awareness, and reading ability: Evidence from a longitudinal and experimental study. *Merrill-Palmer Quarterly, 33,* 321–363.

Vogel, S. (1983). A qualitative analysis of morphological ability in learning disabled and achieving children. *Journal of Learning Disabilities, 16,* 416–420.

Voltz, D. L., Elliott, R. N., and Cobb, H. B. (1994). Collaborative teacher roles: Special and general educators. *Journal of Learning Disabilities, 27,* 527–535.

Vygotsky, L. S. (1962). *Thought and language* (E. Hanfmann and G. Vakar, eds. and trans.). Cambridge, Mass.: MIT Press.

Vygotsky, L. S. (1978). *Mind in society: The development of higher psychological processes.* Cambridge, Mass.: Harvard University Press.

Wagner, R. K., Torgesen, J. K., and Rashotte, C. A. (1994). The development of reading-related phonological processing abilities: New evidence of bi-directional causality from a latent variable longitudinal study. *Developmental Psychology, 30,* 73–87.

Walker, D., and Williamson, R. (1995). Computers and adolescents with emotional/behavior disorders. *Closing the Gap, 14*(2), 10–11, 16–17, 29.

Wallace, G., and Kauffman, J. M. (1986). *Teaching students with learning and behavior problems* (3rd ed.). Columbus, Ohio: Merrill.

Wallach, G. P. (1984). Later language learning: Syntactic structures and strategies. In G. P. Wallach and K. G. Butler (Eds.), *Language learning disabilities in school-age children.* Baltimore: Williams and Wilkins, pp. 82–102.

Wallach, G. P., and Miller, L. (1988). *Language intervention and academic success.* Boston: Little, Brown—College-Hill.

Walley, C. (1993). An invitation to reading fluency. *The Reading Teacher, 46,* 526–527.

Warger, C. L., and Pugach, M. C. (1996). Forming partnerships around curriculum. *Educational Leadership, 53*(5), 62–65.

Warren, J. (1970). *Phonetic generalizations to aid spelling instruction at the fifth-grade level.* Unpublished doctoral dissertation, Boston University.

Warren, R. M., and Warren, R. P. (1970). Auditory illusions and confusions. *Scientific American, 223,* 30–36.

Watson, D., and Crowley, P. (1988). How can we implement a whole-language approach? In C. Weaver (Ed.), *Reading process and practice.* Portsmouth, N.H.: Heinemann.

Weaver, C. (1990). *Understanding whole language: Principles and practices.* Portsmouth, N.H.: Heinemann.

Weinstein, G., and Cooke, N. L. (1992). The effects of two repeated reading interventions on generalizations of fluency. *Learning Disability Quarterly, 15,* 21–28.

Welch, M. (November/December 1983). Social skills in the resource room. *ACLD Newsbriefs* (No. 152).

Welch, M. (1992). The PLEASE strategy: A metacognitive learning strategy for improving the paragraph writing of students with mild learning disabilities. *Learning Disability Quarterly, 15,* 119–128.

Wells, G. (1973). *Coding manual of the description of child speech.* Bristol, Eng.: University of Bristol School of Education.

Wepner, S. B., and Feeley, J. T. (1993). *Moving forward with literature: Basals, books, and beyond.* New York: Merrill/Macmillan.

West, G. F. (1978). *Teaching reading skills in content areas: A practical guide to the construction of student exercises.* Oviedo, Fla.: Sandpiper Press.

West, J. F., and Cannon, G. S. (1988). Essential collaborative consultation competencies for regular and special educators. *Journal of Learning Disabilities, 21,* 56–63, 28.

West, J. F., and Idol, L. (1990). Collaborative consultation in the education of mildly handicapped and at-risk students. *Remedial and Special Education, 11*(1), 22–31.

West, J. F., Idol, L., and Cannon, G. (1989). *Collaboration in the schools: An inservice and preservice curriculum for teachers, support staff, and administrators.* Austin, Tex.: Pro-Ed.

Westby, C. E. (1992). Whole language and learners with mild handicaps. *Focus on Exceptional Children, 24*(8), 1–16.

Whinnery, K. W. (1995). Perceptions of students with learning disabilities: Inclusion versus pull-out services. *Preventing School Failure, 40*(1), 5–9.

White, B. (1975). Critical influences in the origins of competence. *Merrill-Palmer Quarterly, 2,* 243–266.

Wicks-Nelson, R., and Israel, A. L. (1984). *Behavior disorders of childhood.* Englewood Cliffs, N.J.: Prentice-Hall.

Wiener, H., Harris, P. J., and Shirer, C. (1990). Achievement and social-behavioral correlates of peer status in learning disabled children. *Learning Disability Quarterly, 13,* 114–127.

Wiig, E. H. (1982a). *Let's talk: Developing prosocial communication skills.* Columbus, Ohio: Merrill.

Wiig, E. H. (1992). Strategy training for people with language-learning disabilities. In L. Meltzer (Ed.), *Strategy assess-*

ment and training for students with learning disabilities: From theory to practice (pp. 167–194). Austin, Tex.: Pro-Ed.

Wiig, E. H., and Bray, C. M. (1983). *Let's talk for children.* Columbus, Ohio: Merrill.

Wiig, E. H., Freedman, E., and Secord, W. A. (1992). Developing words and concepts in the classroom: A holistic-thematic approach. *Intervention in School and Clinic, 27,* 278–285.

Wiig, E. H., and Secord, W. A. (1994). Language disabilities in school-age children and youth. In G. H. Shames, E. H. Wiig, and W. A. Secord (Eds.), *Human communication disorders* (4th ed., pp. 212–247). New York: Merrill.

Wiig, E. H., and Semel, E. M. (1984). *Language assessment and intervention for the learning disabled* (2nd ed.). Columbus, Ohio: Merrill.

Wiig, E. H., and Wilson, C. C. (1994). Is a question a question? Passage understanding by preadolescents with learning disabilities. *Language, Speech, and Hearing Services in Schools, 25,* 241–249.

Williams, F., and Williams, V. (1984). *Microcomputers in elementary education: Perspectives on implementation.* Belmont, Calif.: Wadsworth.

Williams, J. P., Brown, L. G., Silverstein, A. K., and deCani, J. S. (1994). An instructional program in comprehension of narrative themes for adolescents with learning disabilities. *Learning Disability Quarterly, 17,* 205–221.

Williams, P. L., Reese, C. M., Campbell, J. R., Mazzeo, J., and Phillips, G. W. (1995). *1994 NAEP reading: A first look.* Washington, DC: Office of Educational Research and Improvement, U.S. Department of Education.

Williams, S. (1990). *I went walking.* New York: Harcourt.

Willig, A. C., and Ortiz, A. A. (1991). The nonbiased individualized educational program: Linking assessment to instruction. In E. V. Hamayan and J. S. Damico (Eds.), *Limiting bias in the assessment of bilingual students.* Austin, Tex.: Pro-Ed, pp. 281–302.

Willis, J., Stephens, E., and Matthew, K. (1996). *Technoloqy, reading, and language arts.* Boston: Allyn and Bacon.

Wilson, B. A. (1996). *Wilson reading system.* Millbury, Mass.: Wilson Language Training Corporation.

Wilson, C. L., and Sindelar, P. T. (1991). Direct instruction in math word problems: Students with learning disabilities. *Journal of Learning Disabilities, 23*(1), 23–29.

Wilson, D. R., and David, W. J. (1994). Academic intrinsic motivation and attitudes toward school and learning of learning disabled students. *Learning Disabilities Research and Practice, 9,* 148–156.

Wilson, R., Majsterek, D., and Simmons, D. (1996). The effects of computer-assisted versus teacher-directed instruction on the multiplication performance of elementary students with learning disabilities. *Journal of Learning Disabilities, 29,* 382–390.

Winton, P. J., and Turnbull, A. P. (1981). Parent involvement as viewed by parents of preschool handicapped children.

Wise, B., and Olson, R. (1994). Computer speech and the remediation of reading and spelling problems. *Journal of Special Education Technology, 12,* 207–220.

Wissick, C. (1996). Multimedia: Enhancing instruction for students with learning disabilities. *Journal of Learning Disabilities, 29,* 494–503.

Wolery, M., Cybriwsky, C. A., Gast, D. L., and Boyle-Gast, K. (1991). Use of constant time delay and attentional responses with adolescents. *Exceptional Children, 57,* 462–474.

Wong, B. Y. L. (1979). Increasing retention of main ideas through questioning strategies. *Learning Disability Quarterly, 2*(2), 42–47.

Wong, B. Y. L. (1986). A cognitive approach to teaching spelling. *Exceptional Children, 53,* 169–173.

Wong, B. Y. L. (1987). Directions in future research on metacognition in learning disabilities. In H. L. Swanson (Ed.), *Memory and learning disabilities: Advances in learning and behavioral disabilities* (Supplement 2). Greenwich, Conn.: JAI Press, pp. 335–356.

Wong, B. Y. L. (1996). *The ABCs of learning disabilities.* San Diego: Academic Press.

Wong, B. Y. L., and Jones, W. (1982). Increasing metacomprehension in learning disabled and normally achieving students through self-questioning training. *Learning Disability Quarterly, 5,* 228–240.

Wong, B. Y. L., and Wilson, M. (1984). Investigating awareness of and teaching passage organization in learning disabled children. *Journal of Learning Disabilities, 17*(8), 447–482.

Wong, B. Y. L., and Wong, R. (1980). Role taking skills in normal achieving and learning disabled children. *Learning Disability Quarterly, 3,* 11–18.

Wong, B. Y. L., and Wong, R. (1988). Cognitive interventions for learning disabilities. In K. A. Kavale (Ed.), *Learning disabilities: State of the art and practice.* Boston: Little, Brown–College Hill, pp. 141–160.

Wong, B. Y. L., Wong, R., and Blenkinsop, J. (1989). Cognitive and metacognitive aspects of learning disabled adolescents' composing problems. *Learning Disability Quarterly, 12,* 300–322.

Wong, B. Y. L., Wong, R., Perry, N., and Sawatsky, D. (1986). The efficacy of a self-questioning summarization strategy for use by underachievers and learning disabled adolescents in social studies. *Learning Disabilities Focus, 2*(1), 20–35.

Wood, J. W., and Wooley, J. A. (1986). Adapting textbooks. *The Clearing House, 59,* 332–335.

Wood, K. D., Lapp, D., and Flood, J. (1992). *Guiding readers through the text: A review of study guides.* Newark, Del.: International Reading Association.

Woodcock, R. W., Clark, C. R., and Davies, C. O. (1969). *The Peabody rebus reading program.* Circle Pines, Minn.: American Guidance Service.

Woodward, A., and Elliott, D. L. (1990). Textbook use and teacher professionalism. In D. L. Elliott and A. Woodward (Eds.), *Textbooks and schooling in the United States* (Eighty-ninth yearbook of the National Society for the Study of Education, Part I). Chicago, Ill.: University of Chicago Press, pp. 178–193.

Woodward, J. (1995). Technology-based research in mathematics for special education. *Focus on Learning Problems in Mathematics, 17*(2), 3–23.

Woodward, J., and Carnine, D. (1993). Uses of technology for mathematics assessment and instruction: Reflection on a decade of innovations. *Journal of Special Education Technology, 12,* 38–48.

Woodward, J., and Gersten, R. (1992). Innovative technology for secondary students with learning disabilities. *Exceptional Children, 58,* 407–421.

Yauman, B. E. (1980). Special education placement and the self-concepts of elementary school age children. *Learning Disability Quarterly, 3,* 30–35.

Yee, A. (1969). Is the phonetic generalization hypothesis in spelling valid? *Journal of Experimental Education, 37,* 82–91.

Yopp, H. K. (1992). Developing phonemic awareness in young children. *The Reading Teacher, 45,* 696–703.

Zabrucky, K., and Ratner, H. H. (1992). Effects of passage type on comprehension monitoring and recall in good and poor readers. *Journal of Reading Behavior, 24,* 373–391.

Zaragoza, N., and Vaughn, S. (1992). The effects of process instruction on three second-grade students with different achievement profiles. *Learning Disabilities Research and Practice, 7*(4), 184–193.

Zinberg, N. E. (1984). *Drug, set, and setting.* New Haven, Conn.: Yale University Press.

Zorfass, J., Corley, P., and Remz, A. (1994). Helping students with disabilities become writers. *Educational Leadership, 51*(5), 62–66.

Zutell, J. (1993). *Directed spelling thinking activity: A developmental, conceptual approach to advance spelling word knowledge.* Paper presented at the First International and 19th National Conference of the Australian Reading Association, Melbourne, Australia.

Zutell, J., and Rasinski, T. (1989). Reading and spelling connections in third and fifth grade students. *Reading Psychology, 10,* 137–155.

Index